The Dialogue of Constitutional Judges

Tudorel Toader / Marieta Safta

The Dialogue of Constitutional Judges

PL ACADEMIC RESEARCH

Bibliographic Information published by the Deutsche Nationalbibliothek
The Deutsche Nationalbibliothek lists this publication in the Deutsche Nationalbibliografie; detailed bibliographic data is available in the internet at http://dnb.d-nb.de.

Library of Congress Cataloging-in-Publication Data
Names: Toader, Tudorel, author. | Safta, Marieta, author.
Title: The dialogue of constitutional judges / Tudorel Toader, Marieta Safta.
Other titles: Dialogul judecatorilor constitutionali. English
Description: Frankfurt am Main ; New York : Peter Lang GmbH, 2016. | Includes bibliographical references.
Identifiers: LCCN 2016024287 | ISBN 9783631678909
Subjects: LCSH: Constitutional courts–Romania. | Constitutional law–Romania–Foreign influences. | Romania–Politics and government–1989-
Classification: LCC KKR2620 .T6213 2016 | DDC 347.498/035–dc23 LC record available at https://lccn.loc.gov/2016024287

ISBN 978-3-631-67890-9 (Print)
E-ISBN 978-3-653-07031-6 (E-Book)
DOI 10.3726/978-3-653-07031-6

PL Academic Research is an Imprint of Peter Lang GmbH.

Peter Lang – Frankfurt am Main · Bern · Bruxelles · New York · Oxford · Warszawa · Wien

This publication has been peer reviewed.

www.peterlang.com

Table of Contents

Abbreviations

par.	paragraph
apud	quoted after
art.	article
vs.	versus
ch.	chapter
Civ.C.	Civil Code
ECHR	European Court of the Human Rights (Strasbourg)
Jud.C.	Magazine "Curierul Judiciar" (Judicial Courier) – new series
CJEC	Court of Justice of the European Communities (Luxembourg)
CJEU	Court of Justice of the European Union
Convention	Convention for the Protection of Human Rights and Fundamental Freedoms (European Convention on Human Rights)
Crim.C.	Criminal code
Civ. pr. C.	Civil procedure code
Crim. pr. C.	Criminal procedure code
Law	Magazine "Dreptul" (Law) – new series
ed.	edition
Ed.	Publishing House
et alii	and others
etc.	etcetera (and others)
G.D.	Government Decision
ibidem	in the same place
HCCJ	High Court of Cassation and Justice of Romania
OJEU	Official Journal of the European Union
let.	letter
O.M.	Official Gazette of Romania, Part I
a.n.	authors' note
no.	number
G.E.O.	Government's Emergency Ordinance
op. cit.	quoted paper
p.	page
pp.	pages
pt.	point
PR	Pandectele Române – Repertory of jurisprudence, doctrine and legislation – new series
RREL	Romanian Review of European Law
PLR	Public Law Review
RRPL	Romanian Review of the Private Law

abv	above
TFEU	Treaties on the functioning of the European Union
TEU	Treaties on the European Union
EU	European Union
foll.	following
vol.	volume

Foreword

Regardless of the constitutional review model chosen by states, the constitutional courts imposed themselves in the architecture of the rule of law, a development that was also facilitated by the institutional dialogue between them.

Starting from the role of the constitutional courts, their activity must be approached and analysed in the complex system of the relationships determined by this development at national, international and over-national level. Having in view the nature of these relationships, as well as the effects they take, we consider that they can be subsumed to the broad concept of institutional "dialogue". As for the Constitutional Court of Romania, thus there are mechanisms of institutionalised relationship/cooperation both at international level – with other constitutional courts, international or over-national courts, and at national level – with various public authorities and even with the mass-media. Their configuration way determines us to support the idea of a permanent dialogue whose effects are materialised in a process of law constitutionalisation, of "shaping" and adapting the juridical institutions, and eventually, in a process of standardising the law, particularly visible in the matter of regulating the rights and fundamental freedoms and their guarantees.

Even if, after the adoption of the solutions with a constitutional value, certain amendments were made to the legislation, those solutions maintain their validity in the absence of an amendment to the Basic Law; therefore the decisions of the constitutional court refer to the reference norms, on the date of their issuance.

The amplification and the consolidation of the constitutional judges' dialogue, both at national and international level, determine an occurrence phenomenon to common constitutional values. This type of cooperation leads to the constitutionalisation and standardization of the law, as well as to an overall consolidation of the protection of the values of the rule of law in Europe and worldwide.

"The dialogue of constitutional judges" presents the institutional dialogue of the Constitutional Court of Romania on the mentioned coordinates, how it materializes and which are its effects at national and international level.

"Ten dialogues" presents the institutional collaboration mechanisms between the Constitutional Court and the Court of Justice of the European Union, the European Court of the Human Rights, the other constitutional courts, the Venice Commission, the Parliament, the President of Romania, the Government, the Advocate of the People, the courts of law and the mass-media.

Authors

Introduction

The constitutional courts are the courts qualified to achieve the constitutional review, namely the activity to verify the compliance of laws and other normative acts with the provisions of the Basic Law. This type of control on the juridical rules is a consequence of the fact that the legal system is not presented as a not differentiated set of rules, all placed at the same level, but as a hierarchy made up on the criterion of the juridical value of the sources of law, having on top the supremacy of the constitution[1]. Therefore, the pyramidal structure of the legal system is given by the relationship between the law and the normative acts subordinated to the law and also by the upstream position of the constitution whose supremacy, under the institutional aspect, is ensured through the role of the constitutional courts.

The studies in this matter[2] show in this regard that the 20th century in general, but especially its second half, is marked by an emergence phenomenon where "the new constitutionalism"[3] shall be the epicentre, namely a model of democracy, of state organisation which refuses the dogmatism of the legislative sovereignty, gives priority to the fundamental rights and freedoms and imposes the constitutional review achieved through specialised courts. The new constitutionalism has extended itself in "waves" that corresponded to the transformations which took place in the political plan at the level of the states. At present, the formula containing a written constitution, a charter of the fundamental rights and freedoms, an institutionalised constitutional review exists almost all over Europe. Regardless of the constitutional review model chosen by the states, the constitutional courts imposed themselves in the architecture of the rule of law, an evolution facilitated by the closer and closer institutional dialogue among these courts at the European and international level.

Such process was accelerated in Europe by the fall of the communist system whereas the set up of the constitutional courts in the ex-communist countries was perceived as a symbol of the rule of law[4]. Under the circumstances of the post-totalitarian system, the guarantees granted by the constitutional courts had and still have an important role, especially in terms of the issues inherent to the transition towards democracy, issues which are not specific only to Europe. However, it does

---

1 For developments, see M. Troper, D. Chagnollaud, *Traité international de droit constitutionnel – Théorie de la Constitution*, Tome I, Dalloz, Paris, 2012, pp. 756–763.

2 For details, see A.S. Sweet, *Constitutional Courts*, in The Oxford Handbook of Comparative Constitutional Review, Oxford University Press, 2012.

3 M. Shapiro, A. Stone, *The New Constitutional Politics of Europe*, in Comparative Political Studies no. 26/1994, p. 397.

4 L. Solyom, *On the Cooperation of Constitutional Courts*, in *Freedom of expression and separation of powers in the jurisprudence of constitutional courts. General reports of the 10th Conference of the European Constitutional courts*, Budapest, Hungary, 6–9 May 1996, p. 8.

not mean that, in the traditional democracies, their role and the issues approached by them present less importance.

The abovementioned evolution does not constitute only a quantitative phenomenon, but also a qualitative one, as the geographical expansion was accompanied by "an enrichment" of the constitutional review regarding its mission and power, as well as by the acquisition of new competence fields of the constitutional courts subsumed to the large concept of constitutional justice which includes the constitutional review without being reduced to that[5]. The powers of the constitutional courts increased in number and complexity, as it is shown by the doctrine whereas certain authors[6] mentioned mainly the following such powers "common to all constitutional courts and constitutional bodies":

- guarantors for the supremacy of the Constitution, all the powers of the constitutional courts shall be orientated towards the achievement of this purpose; as for the supremacy of the Constitution, it was noted[7] that it is a notion which includes political and legal features and values that express its upstream position not only in the legal system, but also in the entire political system of a state. It is based on the fact that the Basic Law shall be the expression of the Government's will and of the people in the last instance, a will that is strictly connected to the economic, social, political and cultural context of the society where it is expressed. Therefore, the supremacy of the Constitution is not a simple assertion, but it is and it must be a juridical reality in any democratic rule of law, with a series of legal consequences and guarantees, among which the control exercised by the constitutional courts;
- the voice and the guarantor of the Constitution as it was established by the constituent power; it shall be mentioned under this aspect that, according to the classical theory of the democracy, the constituent power of the state, being the expression of the people's sovereignty, creates the Constitution and it shall not be involved in the law-making process, in the effective governing, in the justice administration and in the settlement of cases by courts. The constituent power does not disappear, but it enters into a latent or "sleepy" mood. It shall come back to life and become active when the provisions of the Constitution

5 For this purpose, see I. Deleanu, *Instituţii şi proceduri constituţionale – în dreptul român şi în dreptul comparat (Constitutional institutions and procedures – in the Romanian and comparative law)*, C.H. Beck Publishing House, Bucharest, 2006, pp. 828–832.

6 E. Tanchev, *Implicaţii comparative ale controlului de constituţionalitate (Comparative involvements of the constitutional review)*, in *Curtea Constituţională a României, 20 de ani de existenţă şi 100 de ani de control de constituţionalitate (The Constitutional Court of Romania, 20 Years of existence and 100 Years of Constitutional Review)*, Universul Juridic Publishing House, 2013, pp. 42–59.

7 I. Muraru, *Există un garant al supremaţiei Constituţiei române? (Is there a guarantor for the supremacy of the Constitution of Romania?)* in RRDP no. 1/2011, pp. 130–155.

need to be amended or when the nation or its political elite have taken the political decision to adopt a new Constitution[8]. As long as it is in a latent mood, the Constitutional Court shall be the one that expresses the exact meaning of the constitutional provisions, having the possibility to interpret them provided that they are kept in the limits of the will of the "the founding parents";

- The supreme judicial guarantor of the fundamental human rights as "the foundation in legitimating the judicial control of the constitutionality of laws";
- Guarantors that oblige the state institutions to keep themselves within the constitutional limits of their competences, a power that is achieved through various forms and ways, in the virtue of their constitutional competences;
- Legal and constitutional arbitrage agents in settling conflicts; constitutional courts exercise the constitutional arbitrage whereas the conflicts among the state powers are settled in accordance with the Constitution and within its limits;
- Through the conducted control, the courts forewarn the despotic aspirations of the governing majority; in the context of the liberal democracy, the courts forewarn that the majority annuls the opposition by protecting the minority's rights;
- A safety valve in order to reduce the level of social pressure and restlessness as well as in order to forewarn the destruction and the self-destruction of the constitutional and government system through the illegal, extra-parliamentary or extra-constitutional action;
- Authorities that bring harmony to the national, constitutional and over national values, principles and rules, as well as the settlement of conflicts between the national and over national juridical institutions and systems.

Having in view the complex character and the particular features of the constitutional justice in Europe and in the world, it is difficult to strictly identify models or templates[9]. Nevertheless, while considering certain common specific features, we can identify, in a large meaning, as "models" of constitutional review with the largest extension at present: the American model (a constitutional review exercised within the competences granted to courts of law) and the European model or the Kelsen's model (a control exercised by a unique, particular and specialised constitutional court).

---

8 As for the drafting of the constitution as an act of supreme political decision upon the type and form of political unity, see C. Schmitt, *Constitutional Theory*, Duke Univ. Press, 2008, pp. 75–94.

9 For a presentation of the models of constitutional review, see D. Maus, *Application of the case law of foreign courts and dialogue between constitutional courts*, in Constitutional Law Review no. II, p. 3, on *www.constcourt.ge*.

As a tendency, under the aspect of the option for one or another of these models, it was noticed[10] that between the two World Wars and particularly after the Second World War, several states chose the European model of constitutional review. For example, after 1990, the countries in Central and Eastern Europe, except for Estonia, opted for this model.

In Romania, it was initially consecrated the constitutional review exercised by the power of judges, being institutionalised by the Constitution in 1923[11] and kept by the Constitution in 1938. After the Second World War, there was no longer a constitutional review of laws (the Constitutions in 1948 and in 1952, respectively). Even though the Constitution in 1965 stipulated that the Great National Assembly shall "*exercise the general control of enforcing the Constitution. Solely the Great National Assembly shall decide on the constitutionality of laws*"[12], actually there is no such control. After the fall of the Communist regime, the Constitution in 1991 consecrated the European model of constitutional review of laws and the Constitutional Court was established as an authority independent from any other public authority, having the role of guarantor for the supremacy of the Constitution. Therefore, the option of the constituent legislator fell within the general evolution at the European level, even if the latter aroused many debates in the Constituent Assembly[13].

This tendency to expand the institutionalisation of the constitutional review was explained[14] in various ways: either as a result of the growing awareness of the importance to protect the principles of the rule of law and the fundamental rights and freedoms, or as a result of the governing at several levels, respectively the concern to identify an instrument which could coordinate the states in a federal system, either as a response to the issues involved by the governing alternations, or as a response to the constitutional development of other states and of the

---

10 S. Dürr, *Comparative Overview of European Systems of Constitutional Justice*, one *www.icl-journal.com*, vol. V, no. 2/2011, p. 159.

11 Pursuant to Article 103 (1) of the 1923 Constitution of Romania: *"Only the Court of Cassation in joined sections shall be entitled to judge the constitutionality of the laws and to declare as unable to be enforced the ones which are contrary to the Constitution. The judgement upon the unconstitutionality of the laws is limited only to the case on trial*".

12 Article 43 point 15.

13 F.P. Vasilescu, *Curtea Constituţională a României: un început anevoios (The Constitutional Court of Romania – a difficult beginning)*, in *Curtea Constituţională a României, 20 de ani de existenţă şi 100 de ani de control de constituţionalitate (The Constitutional Court of Romania, 20 Years of existence and 100 Years of Constitutional Review)*, Universul Juridic Publishing House, 2013, pp. 131–136.

14 T. Ginsburg, M. Versteeg, *op. cit.*, pp. 2–3; T. Toader, M. Safta, *Raport sinteză – Controlul de constituţionalitate – tradiţie şi perspective (A synthesis report – The constitutional review – traditions and perspectives)*, in *Curtea Constituţională a României, 20 de ani de existenţă şi 100 de ani de control de constituţionalitate (The Constitutional Court of Romania, 20 Years of existence and 100 Years of Constitutional Review)*, Universul Juridic Publishing House, 2013, pp. 137–150.

transformations that occur at the international level. Regardless of the preferred theory, it is obvious that the institutionalisation of the constitutional review and the creation of specialised courts in order to exercise this control represent one of the most important phenomena of the 20th century and at the beginning of the 21st century[15]. This evolution has certainly some challenges because the issues faced by the constitutional courts are mostly common and aim especially at the relationship with the other state institutions, at ensuring a real independence and authority, materialised eventually in the efficiency of the constitutional justice, respectively in the way in which the decisions of the constitutional courts are complied with and enforced.

Starting from these premises and from the current role of the constitutional courts worldwide, a context which helped with the development of the constitutional review in Romania, this work presents the Constitutional Court of Romania in the complex system of the relations determined by this evolution at the national, international and over-national level. Having in view the nature of these relations as well as the produced effects, we consider that they can be subsumed to the concept with large significations of institutional "dialogue".

Thus, there are mechanisms of institutionalised cooperation among the Constitutional Court and various public authorities, specialists in the legal field as well as in mass-media[16]. Their configuration way determines us to support the idea of a permanent dialogue whose effects are materialised not only in relation to the constitutionalisation of the law, but also into a "shaping" and adaptation of the institutions to this worldwide phenomenon.

By approaching the mentioned institutionalised cooperation mechanisms that we are about to develop below, we are showing that Law no. 47/1992 on the Organisation and Operation of the Constitutional Court[17] stipulates the Court's obligation, within the exercise of its powers, to ask for points of view from the Parliament, Government and the Advocate of the People regarding the constitutionality of the normative acts deferred to its control (in a differentiated way, according to *a priori* or *a posteriori* challenges of unconstitutionality, pursuant to the rules established by its organising and operation law[18]. The Court's request of the viewpoints shall be mandatory but their expression by the mentioned authorities shall be optional.

---

15 *Ibidem.*

16 For details, see T. Toader, M. Safta, in *Justiţia Constituţională – Funcţii şi raporturi cu celelalte autorităţi publice – Drept constituţional comparat* – lucrările celui de-al XV-lea Congres al conferinţei Curţilor Constituţionale Europene (*The Constitutional Justice – Functions and relationships with the other public authorities – The compared constitutional law.* The works of the 25th Congress of the Conference of the European Constitutional Courts, 23–25 May 2011, Universul Juridic Publishing House, Bucharest, 2012.

17 Republished in the Official Gazette of Romania no. 807 of 3 December 2010.

18 In case of the constitutional review of laws, before the promulgation, if the referral is made by the President of Romania, by the Parliament members, by the High

Moreover, the Constitutional Court has the obligation to communicate the ruled decisions, as appropriate, to the President of Romania, to the Parliament, to the Government, respectively to the courts of law, under the conditions provided by its organisation and operation law.

A special discussion is related to the relationship between the Constitutional Court and the courts of law or the commercial arbitrage courts, from the perspective of their role conferred by the Constitution and by the Court's organic law, particularly in the procedure of settling the exceptions of unconstitutionality of laws and ordinances, as well as from the perspective of the effects determined by the decisions delivered by the Constitutional Court upon the practice of the courts especially, and also upon the branches of law in general, in order to achieve their constitutionalisation process.

Court of Cassation and Justice or by the Advocate of the People, the Constitutional Court shall communicate it within 24 hours since the registration, to the presidents of the two Chambers of Parliament and to the Government, mentioning the date when the debates are to take place. If the referral is made by the President of one of the Chambers of Parliament, the Constitutional Court shall communicate it to the president of the other Chamber, to the Government and to the Advocate of the People. If the referral is made by the Government, the Court shall communicate it to the presidents of the two Chambers of Parliament and to the Advocate of the People [Article 16, Law no. 47/1992]. Until the date of the debates, the presidents of the two Chambers of Parliament, the Government and the Advocate of the People may present in written their point of view whereas the Government's point of view may be presented only after it is signed by the Prime Minister (Article 17, Law no. 47/1992);
– in case of constitutional review of treatises or other international agreements, if the referral is raised by the president of one of the two Chambers of Parliament, the Constitutional Court shall communicate it to the President of Romania, to the president of the other Chamber and to the Government. If the referral is made by Parliament members, it shall be communicated to the President of Romania, to the presidents of the two Chambers and to the Government (Article 24, Law no. 47/1992). Until the debate date within the Constitutional Court, the President of Romania, the presidents of the two Chambers and the Government may present in written their points of view (Article 25, Law no. 47/1992);
– in case of constitutional review of the Standing Orders of Parliament, if the referral is made by Parliament members, the Constitutional Court shall communicate it, within 24 hours since the registration, to the presidents of the two Chambers of Parliament, by mentioning the date when the debate is to take place. Until the debate date, the presidents of the two Chambers may communicate the viewpoints of the Standing bureaus (Article 27, Law no. 47/1992);
– in case the Court is notified by the courts of law or by the commercial arbitrage courts about the settlement of an exception of unconstitutionality, after receiving the referral act, the president of the Constitutional Court shall communicate it to the presidents of the two Chambers of Parliament, to the Government and to the Advocate of the People, indicating the date by which they can submit their viewpoints (Article 30, Law no. 47/1992).

As for the reports between the Constitutional Court and other authorities, institutions, legal entities, it is important to mention the provisions of Article 76 of Law no. 47/1992, republished, which establish that "*public authorities, institutions, self-managed public companies, trading companies and all the other organizations shall have to communicate any information, documents, and deeds they hold, and which are requested by the Constitutional Court for the fulfilment of its powers.*" Therefore, the constitutional jurisdiction has the possibility to require such documents and information, and, in correlation, the one who makes the request has the obligation to communicate the required data or information. Also, Article 47 (4) of the Regulations on the Organisation and Functioning of the Constitutional Court[19] stipulates that the Judges-Rapporteur may request specialty advice from certain persons or institutions, with the prior approval from the President of the Court. Pursuant to the provisions of Article 78 of the same Regulations, the Constitutional Court decides upon the cooperation relationships with similar authorities abroad and it may become a member of certain international organisations in the field of constitutional justice.

As for the international level, it is important to notice that the topic of this dialogue was and is frequently approached during national and international meetings and scientific communications, while considering its importance. Thus, for example, the 26th Congress of the Conference of the European Constitutional Courts held between 12 and 14 May in Vienna was dedicated to and showed the cooperation forms among the constitutional courts,among the constitutional courts and the European ones, the consolidation of the institutional position and the dynamics of their development in the past 60 years.

Starting from such reference points presented here, after a short presentation of the Constitutional Court's evolution from its foundation upto the present, under the aspect of the institutional consolidation, we shall analyse the institutional dialogue we have referred to, the way it is materialized and its effects at the national and international level.

19 Approved by Ruling no. 6/2012, published in the Official Gazette of Romania no. 198 of 27 March 2012.

I. The Constitutional Court of Romania Evolution and institutional consolidation[20]

1. The dynamics of regulating the Constitutional Court of Romania

1.1 Constitutional rules of reference

The Constitution approved by the referendum on 8 December 1991 in Romania imposed the European model of constitutional review by entrusting the Constitutional Court, founded as a distinct and independent authority from other public authorities, the mission to guarantee the supremacy of the Constitution[21].

The position given by the constituent legislature to the Constitutional Court of Romania among public authorities was a favourable evolution for it, both in terms of its competence (which was enriched over time by regulating new powers) and in the way by which the Court imposed itself as an essential institution for the rule of law.

The Constitution of Romania enshrines a separate title on the regulation of the Constitutional Court – Title V (Articles 142–147, as revised), containing the following provisions: the role of the Court, its structure, the term of office of its members, the ways regarding the appointment of judges and the election of the President of the Court, the criteria for becoming a judge, the incompatibilities, the independence and the irremovability, the competence of the Constitutional Court and the effects

---

20 T. Toader, M. Safta, *Le rôle de la Cour Constitutionnelle dans la consolidation de l'État de droit*, in East Europa Review no. 2/2012, pp. 116–139.

21 The majority option of the members of the Drafting Commission of the Constitution for a review by a sole, particular and specialized body, has mainly relied on the following arguments, exposed during the works of the Constituent Assembly: by the dispossession of the common law jurisdictions having the competence to review, in disputes between individuals, the constitutionality of laws, to ensure the uniformity of the case-law; the effects resulted from the ascertainment of the compliance of the law with the Constitution or, on the contrary, its rejection, being produced for all and in relation to all, shall constitute undoubtedly a more satisfactory result than the res judicata of a judicial decision; the strict framework in which the review of the constitutionality of laws is achieved reduces considerably the legal uncertainty; the method of appointing the members of the Court shall ensure not only the professionalism of this body, but especially its neutrality; as it is not a body essentially and exclusively judicial and being situated between powers, it can also exercise other prerogative (Minutes of the Session of 14th of May 1991, published in the Official Gazette of Romania, Part II, no. 18 of 16 May 1991, in the *Genesis of the Constitution of Romania – Constituent Assembly working session*, Autonomous Administration – Official Gazette, p. 854 et seq.).

of its decisions. Based on the constitutional texts of reference, Parliament adopted Law no. 47/1992 on the Organization and Operation of the Constitutional Court[22].

Thus, the Constitutional Court of Romania consists of nine Judges appointed for a nine-year term of office that cannot be either extended or renewed. Three Judges shall be appointed by the Chamber of Deputies, three by the Senate, and three by the President of Romania. The following cumulative conditions provided for by Article 143 of the Constitution shall be met in order to be appointed to the Constitutional Court: high legal knowledge, high professional eminence and at least 18 years' experience in the legal field or academic professorial activity. Both the Constitution and the Law on the Organisation and Operation of the Constitutional Court regulates important principles and guarantees on the independence and neutrality of the Constitutional Court's Judges, so as to enable them to objectively exercise judgment, as the Court itself shall be, according to Law no. 47/1992, "*independent from any other public authority*" and obey only to the Constitution and to the provisions of its own law of organization and operation[23].

As adopted in 1991, the Constitution established expressly and within limits the powers of the Constitutional Court, as follows: it adjudicates on the constitutionality of laws before promulgation, upon referral by the President of Romania, the President of either of the Chambers, the Government, the High Court of Cassation and Justice, at least 50 Deputies or at least 25 Senators, as well as ex officio, on any initiative purporting a revision of the Constitution; c) it adjudicates on the constitutionality of the Standing Orders of Parliament upon referral by the President of either of the Chambers, a parliamentary group or at least 50 Deputies or at least 25 Senators; it rules upon objections as to the unconstitutionality of laws and ordinances which are raised before the courts of law; it sees to the observance of the procedure for the election of the President of Romania and confirms the ballot returns; it ascertains any circumstance as may justify the interim in the exercise of office of President of Romania, and it reports its findings to Parliament and to Government; it gives advisory opinion on the proposal to suspend the President of Romania from office; it sees to the observance of the procedure for the organisation and holding of a referendum, and confirms its returns; it verifies whether conditions are met for the citizens' exercise of their legislative initiative; it rules upon challenges as to the unconstitutionality of a political party.

Revision of the Constitution in 2003 was an important moment for the institutional strengthening of the Constitutional Court, as it was achieved the extension of the Court's competence by establishing specific new powers, the extension of subjects entitled to referral, and the effects of decisions rendered as follows :

---

22 Republished in the Official Gazette of Romania no. 807 of 3 December 2010.

23 See T. Toader, M. Safta, *General report prepared for the XVth Congress of the Conference of European Constitutional Courts, Part I – The Constitutional Court's relationship to Parliament and to Government,* available on *www.ccr.ro.*

- it was enshrined the competence to adjudicate on the constitutionality of treaties or other international agreements, upon referral by the President of either of the Chambers, at least 50 Deputies or at least 25 Senators;
- it was enshrined the competence to decide on legal disputes of a constitutional nature between public authorities, at the request of the President of Romania, the President of either of the Chambers, the Prime Minister, or the President of the Superior Council of Magistracy;
- the acknowledgment of a more flexible regulation on the Constitutional Court's competence in terms of a possible regulation of new powers by the organic law of the Constitutional Court[24]. The doctrine underlined the rationale and the importance of introducing this provision, showing that such a legal text, with tradition in the legal system, allows the ordinary legislature to interfere in new situations arising in the life of the institutions without having to amend the Constitution, "it is about the dynamics of law in connection with the dynamics of social life"[25];
- it was enshrined the possibility of the Advocate of the People to raise directly exceptions of unconstitutionality of laws and ordinances and to refer to the Constitutional Court in order to exercise the constitutional review of laws before promulgation;
- it was expressly enshrined the mandatory nature of *erga omnes* of the Constitutional Court's decisions, thus putting an end to all controversies on the matter both in doctrine and in practice;
- Parliament has been deprived of the possibility to negate the effects of the Constitutional Court's decisions delivered in a priori review. This possibility was provided for by the Constitution of 1991 which, prior to the revision in 2003, established in Article 145(1) that: *"In cases of unconstitutionality ascertained in accordance with Article 144 a) and b), the law or regulation shall be submitted for reconsideration. If the law is passed in the same form by a majority of at least two-thirds of the members of each Chamber, the objection of unconstitutionality shall be removed and the promulgation shall be binding".* This provision of the Constitution of 1991, which was duly impugned in the specialised doctrine, allowed Parliament to become a Court of Cassation in a dispute in which it would have been a party. Thus, an unconstitutional law might have become constitutional by a qualified majority of deputies and senators, without the revision of the Constitution, but by the achievement of all stages and the fulfilment of the procedures provided for this. Following the revision of the Constitution in 2003, such possibility of Parliament to invalidate the decisions of the Constitutional

24 Article 146 l) of the Constitution: "*it also fulfils other prerogatives as provided by the Court's organic law*".

25 I. Muraru, A. Muraru, *A century of constitutional review in Romania*, in RRDP no. 2/2012, pp. 171–186.

Court was removed and all the decisions of the Constitutional Court shall be final and generally binding under Article 147(4) of the Constitution.

1.2 Rules of the organic law of reference

The strengthening process of the status and the role of the Constitutional Court were continued through the regulations adopted at the infraconstitutional level. Thus, Law no. 47/1992 on the Organization and Operation of the Constitutional Court[26] was amended by Law no. 232/2004[27], after the revision of the Constitution, when a new power of the Constitutional Court was introduced under Article 146 l) of the Constitution:

- to adjudicate ex officio on the law purporting a revision of the Constitution within five days of its adoption by Parliament.

In 2010, the Court's organic law was amended again by Law no. 177/2010[28], when a new power of the Constitutional Court was regulated:

- to adjudicate on the constitutionality of the Standing Orders of the Plenum of the Chamber of Deputies, of the Standing Orders of the Plenum of the Senate and the Standing Orders of the Plenum of the two joint Chambers of Parliament.

Unlike the power introduced by law in 2004, which was considered to be logical because the bill for revision of the Constitution adopted by Parliament was not subject to constitutional review, which could result in the lack of efficiency for the ex officio control exercised by the Court on the bill or proposal for revision, the expansion of the competence of the Court in 2010 resulted in serious disputes. Inter alia, such amendment was considered to "place the role of a constitutional court at a too low level in the scale of value" and "to allow the Court's control on certain normative Standing Orders of Parliament means to allow that it may decide, instead of Parliament, on certain appointments to offices and public offices, so that the Court could substitute Parliament", reaching the conclusions that "such amendment (supplement) should be considered a serious political and parliamentary error"[29].

The position expressed by the Constitutional Court in this regard was that the establishment of its power to exercise such constitutional review represents the expression of diversification and strengthening of the competence of the Constitutional Court, the sole body of constitutional jurisdiction in Romania, and a gain in the efforts to achieve a democratic rule of law[30]. Upon examination of the case-law of the Constitutional Court and institutional strengthening achieved through it,

---

26 Published in the Official Gazette of Romania no. 101 of 22 May 1992.

27 Published in the Official Gazette of Romania 502 of 3 June 2004.

28 Published in the Official Gazette of Romania no. 672 of 4 October 2010.

29 I. Muraru, A. Muraru, *cited work*, pp. 171–186.

30 Decision no. 727 of 9 July 2012, published in the Official Gazette of Romania no. 477 of 12 July 2012.

we will also refer to the opinion expressed by the Venice Commission, concurring in this respect.

1.3 The competence of the Constitutional Court

According to Article 2(1) of Law no. 47/1992, the Constitutional Court shall ensure the constitutional review of laws, international treaties, Standing Orders of Parliament, and ordinances of the Government, namely the primary regulatory acts.

Thus, the Constitutional Court shall exercise the constitutional review of organic or ordinary laws – before promulgation [Article 146 a) first sentence of the Constitution][31] or after their entry into force [Article 146 d)][32] –, treaties or other

31 Within this type of review, the Court cannot solve the problem of the constitutionality of a law in force. Thus, by Decisions No. 233 of 20 December 1999, published in the Official Gazette of Romania, Part I, No. 638 of 28 December 1999, and No. 89 of 26 January 2010, published in the Official Gazette of Romania, Part I, No. 115 of 19 February 2010, the Court rejected the petitions of unconstitutionality as being inadmissible, because the laws challenged had already been promulgated, and the respective petitions were made after the expiration of the statutory term. Nonetheless, a particular case is reflected in Decision No. 975/2010, where, despite the fact that the petition of unconstitutionality was brought within the statutory two-days deadline prescribed by Law No. 47/1992, the challenged law had already been promulgated by the President of Romania and published in the Official Gazette of Romania, so that it was in force on the date of adjudication by the Court. On that occasion, the Court held that it cannot reject the objection of unconstitutionality as inadmissible strictly on account that the law was promulgated, because the objection of unconstitutionality had been made within the statutory deadline. The Court also held that regardless which form of constitutional review, whether a priori or a posteriori, such may be carried out, in all instances, only in strict compliance, by the public authorities concerned, with Law No. 47/1992, as well as with the provisions of Regulations of the two Chambers of Parliament, that because depriving either form of constitutional review of its substance is inconceivable in a Rule of law. Likewise, bills or legislative proposals, or amendments cannot be subject-matter of this type of review. By its Decision No. 42/1993, the Court stated that Article 146 subparagraph a) the first sentence of the Constitution refers to the "review of constitutionality of laws before their promulgation, which means that the law was passed by Parliament, in the form in which was adopted" and not to "a text of a bill or amendment proposed to Parliament, but not adopted by it, because in the latter case it is not a text of a «law». Consequently, the Constitutional Court has no jurisdiction to review the constitutionality of the text of bills, legislative proposals and amendments submitted to Parliament, but not adopted by it, as is the case of this petition regarding Article 301 of the bill which, following its adoption by Parliament, has become the «Law amending and supplementing the Law No. 35/1992 on foreign investments»".

32 By resolution of exceptions of unconstitutionality raised before the courts of law or commercial arbitration or of exceptions of unconstitutionality made directly by the Advocate of the People.

international agreements before their ratification by Parliament [Article 146 b) of the Constitution and Article 24 of Law no. 47/1992], namely after ratification[33] [Article 146 d) in relation to Article 147(3) of the Constitution and Article 26 (3) of Law no. 47/1992], the Standing Orders of Parliament in force [Article 146 c)], and the ordinances of the Government in force [Article 146 d)].

As for the procedure of revision of the Constitution (thereby constitutional laws), the Constitutional Court adjudicates, ex officio, both on the initiatives for the revision of the Constitution [Article 146 a) second sentence] and on the revision law after its adoption by Parliament (Article 23 of Law no. 47/1992).

Constitutional review can be exercised *a priori* (it refers to the laws adopted by Parliament before promulgation, i.e. as concerns the laws of revision of the Constitution, before being submitted for approval by referendum, as well as the treaties or international agreements before ratification by Parliament) or *a posteriori* [as concerns the international treaties and agreements after ratification (ratification law), the Standing Orders of Parliament, laws and ordinances in force].

Within *a priori* control, the Court examines both the provisions mentioned in the referral and those which necessarily and obviously cannot be separated, being different from that enshrined on the *a posteriori* constitutional review of laws and ordinances in force, where only in case an exception was allowed the Court shall also adjudicate on the constitutionality of other provisions contained in the challenged act, which necessarily and obviously cannot be dissociated from the provisions mentioned in the referral. Therefore, within the *a priori* review, even if the unconstitutionality of the impugned text cannot be found, the Court may also extend ex officio the subject-matter of the referral of unconstitutionality on other legal texts, but the Court shall ascertain the necessary and obvious connection between the challenged legal norm and the one to which it extends the subject-matter of the referral, being a *sine qua non* requirement in order to extend the subject-matter of the control. The reason for this difference between the legal regulations concerning *a priori* and *a posteriori* review consists in the high importance of the

33 Before the revision of the Constitution in 2003, the Constitutional Court could verify only the law ratifying the treaty or international agreement, either through a priori review or through a posterior review. After revision of the Constitution, by virtue of this new task added to the competence of the Constitutional Court, the constitutionality review can be carried out in two stages, on two separate legal acts: pursuant to Article 146 subparagraph b), international treaties or agreements that Romania intends to ratify can be verified before their actual ratification, while according to Article 146 subparagraph a) and subparagraph d), respectively, laws ratifying international agreements and treaties can be reviewed before their entry into force or by incidental proceedings. The norms that govern this specific power should be correlated to the provision contained in Article 11 paragraph (3) of the Constitution, according to which *"Where a treaty to which Romania is to become party comprises provisions contrary to the Constitution, ratification shall only be possible after a constitutional revision"*.

former, meaning that, by its decision, the Constitutional Court can remove certain legal texts (other than those mentioned in the referral, but which are obviously and necessarily connected to the subject-matter of the referral), even before promulgation, publication and entry into force of the law.

Constitutional review may be abstract and its subject-matter relates to the legal norms in the absence of any application, or effectively, meaning the implementation of a verified legal norm to a case. *A priori* review is abstract, while *a posteriori* review can be concrete, when the Court adjudicates on the exceptions of unconstitutionality of laws and ordinances raised before the courts of law or commercial arbitration and on the exceptions of unconstitutionality of laws and ordinances raised directly by the Advocate of the People[34], or abstract, when the Court rules on the constitutionality of the Standing Orders of Parliament.

Within the exercise of such review, the Court shall adjudicate only on the compliance of the impugned provisions with the norms of the Constitution, because, according to Article 2(2) of Law no. 47/1992, the provisions of the abovementioned normative acts "*which violates the provisions and principles of the Constitution*" are unconstitutional. In this context it should be noted that although there is no longer an express text in the Law on the Organization and Operation of the Constitutional

34 Article 146 d) second sentence, introduced upon the revision of the Constitution, is a legal instrument made available to the Advocate of the People as an institutional intervention in order to carry out his task of defending the citizens' rights and fundamental freedoms. The constitutional wording according to which the direct complaint whereby the Advocate of the People may refer to the Constitutional Court for the examination of the constitutionality of laws and ordinances is termed as an "exception" has been criticized as inappropriate, this because it is rather a direct appeal to the constitutional judge, which has been awarded into the exercise of the Advocate of the People alone, with a view to valorising his findings in regard of the incompatibility of certain provisions of the laws and ordinances in force with the constitutional provisions (see Constantin Doldur, *The review of constitutionality in the light of the new provisions of the revised Constitution*, The Constitutional Court Bulletin No. 7/2004, available on www.ccr.ro); in the doctrine it has been stressed that the Advocate of the People can refer to the Court only in regard of matters falling within his sphere of activity, whereas the constitutional text of Article 58 paragraph (1) enshrines a functional specialization of the Advocate of the People, thus limiting his competence to that of defending the rights and freedoms of individuals; consequently, a complaint made by the Advocate of the People which is not subsumed to this purpose oversteps his competence, being inadmissible, and it must be rejected by the Constitutional Court. This notwithstanding, by the Decision No. 1133/2007 rendered on an exception of unconstitutionality directly raised by the Advocate of the People, the Court stated that "Article 146 of the Constitution does not impose conditions [...] as to which cases the Advocate of the People is empowered to refer to the Constitutional Court, respectively, which exceptions of unconstitutionality".

Court[35], any exception of unconstitutionality which does not refer to a law or an ordinance or a provision of a law or of an ordinance, but it refers only to their interpretation or enforcement, such exception is to be rejected as inadmissible, because, according to Article 126 of the Constitution, this power falls within the jurisdiction of the courts of law. Of course, this does not mean that the Court, in exercising its powers, does not interpret the rules on which it adjudicates. As shown[36] even within the constitutional review, in order to determine whether or not a legal provision infringes the Constitution, the content and the specific meaning of that legal provision must be firstly clarified, and that meaning and specific content should to be compared with the Constitution[37]. From this perspective, in a separate chapter, we will examine the issue of the interpretative decisions.

Among the powers concerning the constitutional review of certain normative acts, the weight (reflected by the number of cases) in the activity of the Constitutional Court is given by the settlement of the exceptions of unconstitutionality of laws and ordinances raised before the courts of law or commercial arbitration. Thus, according to Article 146 d) of the Constitution and of Article 29 of Law no. 47/1992, the Court adjudicates[38] on the exceptions raised before the courts of law or commercial

---

35 Prior to amending Law No. 47/1992 by Law No. 232/2004, Article 2 paragraph (3) final sentence of the act expressly provided: *"The Constitutional Court cannot rule on the interpretation and enforcement of the law, but only on its meaning contrary to the Constitution".*

36 G. Koszokar, in *in the "Jurisprudence of the Constitutional Court of Romania and the European Convention on Human Rights" – the works of the National Conference,* Sinaia, 15–16 June 2005, p. 53.

37 In fact, some of the decisions of the Constitutional Court – the so-called interpretative decisions – have found certain legal provisions as being unconstitutional insofar as a certain meaning which is contrary to the Constitution emerged therefrom, which necessarily involved a process of interpretation of the examined norm(s). Thus, for example, by Decision No. 660/2007 (published in the Official Gazette of Romania, Part I, No. 525 of 2 August 2007), the Constitutional Court found unconstitutional the provisions of Article 9 of the Law No. 554/2004 on the Administrative Contentious, "insofar as they allowed proceedings brought before the court of administrative contentious to bear, as their principal subject-matter, on finding the unconstitutionality of an ordinance or a provision in an ordinance". Also by Decision No. 818/2008 (published in the Official Gazette of Romania, Part I, No. 537 of 16 July 2008), the Constitutional Court, accepting the exception of unconstitutionality, found that the provisions of Articles 1, 2 paragraph (3) and Article 27 paragraph (1) of Government Ordinance No. 137/2000 on preventing and sanctioning all forms of discrimination, are unconstitutional "insofar as they can be interpreted in the sense that courts have jurisdiction to annul or refuse the application of normative acts having the force of law, considering such as being discriminatory, and to replace them with judge created norms or with provisions contained in other normative acts".

38 It should be noted in this context that the exception of unconstitutionality is of public order, its author not being entitled to a right of relinquish. In this respect, the

arbitration regarding the unconstitutionality of a law or ordinance or of a provision of a law or ordinance, which is related to the settlement of the case at any stage of the dispute and whatever its subject-matter. The courts of law before which the exception of unconstitutionality is raised are obliged to notify the Constitutional Court, after they verify the conditions of admission provided for by law[39].

The sharp increase in the number of cases over time with the subject-matter of unconstitutionality was not determined only by strengthening the role of the Constitutional Court and the acquisition of the exercise of democratic life by the parties. Frequently, invoking the exceptions of unconstitutionality by the parties was a way to delay the settlement of the cases, whereas, during the settlement of the exception of unconstitutionality by the constitutional court, the judgment of the case in which it was raised was suspended.

In order to avoid such inconveniences, by Law no. 177/2010[40] amending and supplementing Law no. 47/1992 on the Organization and Operation of the Constitutional Court, the Code of Civil Procedure and the Code of Criminal Procedure of Romania, the norms on the *ope legis* suspension were repealed for the cases in which exceptions of unconstitutionality were invoked, namely the provisions set forth in Article 29 (5) of Law no. 47/1992, in Article 303 (6) of the Code of Criminal Procedure and in Article 8 (7) of Law no. 85/2006 on the insolvency procedure[41], which resulted

---

Constitutional Court decided that the exception of unconstitutionality does not rest at the discretion of the party who raised it and is not susceptible of being covered, not even by express waiver or renunciation to its being settled by the court (Decision No. 73/1996, published in the Official Gazette of Romania, Part I, No. 255 of 22 October 1996). Once notified, the Court must proceed to examine the constitutionality of the text criticized, the provisions relative to suspension, discontinuance or extinction of proceedings being not applicable (Decision No. 126/1995, published in the Official Gazette of Romania, Part I, No. 51 of 13 March 1996).

39 Thus, the court of law or the court of commercial arbitration before which the exception is invoked constitutes the first legal screening within the framework of constitutional review, whereas referral to the Constitutional Court shall be made only when the exception of unconstitutionality satisfies the requirements of admissibility (provided also by Article 29 of Law No. 47/1992); the causes of inadmissibility (termed in the doctrine as "legal reasons that prevent the initiation or extension of review proceedings on constitutionality of the law" – I. Muraru, M. Constantinescu, "Causes of inadmissibility in constitutional jurisdiction", Law Review No. 2/1998, p. 3) determine the legal limits of reviewability by way of exception, being related to the Constitutional Court's competence in exercising such review under Article 146 subparagraph d) of the Constitution, they are mandatory and of public order.

40 Published in the Official Gazette of Romania no. 672 of 4 October 2010.

41 Within the *a priori* review of this law, the Court held, by Decision No. 1106/2010, that the intervention of the law-maker whereby it repealed the suspension as of right of proceedings in cases where exceptions of unconstitutionality have been raised actually represents an expression of the State's having undertaken and complied with the obligation to create a legislative framework corresponding to its commitments

in the decrease of the number of cases with the subject-matter of exceptions of unconstitutionality. The abovementioned regulation raised some critical positions, as shown by a part of the doctrine, which held that "it might have been more appropriate if, when invoking the exception of unconstitutionality, the legislature had regulated a case of voluntary suspension"[42]. It was noted that such solution would be preferable given at least two aspects: such a case of voluntary suspension has been regulated in the original wording of Article 23(6) of Law no. 47/1992[43]; the Judge's possibility of raising the exception of unconstitutionality ex officio. It was revealed that, due to the fact that there is no more a case of voluntary or mandatory suspension of judgment, assuming that even the judge invokes the exception of unconstitutionality ex officio, feeling the unconstitutionality of a legal text, such judge will be required to settle the case by applying the law on which he has "doubts" about its constitutionality, therefore, he will be required to justify its decision by a legal text which he impugned himself through the exception of unconstitutionality.

In addition to the powers of constitutional review of the abovementioned acts[44], the following powers also fall within the competence of the Constitutional Court of Romania, as provided for by Article 146 of the Constitution, namely by the organic law of the Constitutional Court:

- it adjudicates on legal disputes of a constitutional nature between public authorities [Article 146 e) of the Constitution];
- it sees to the observance of the procedure for the election of the President of Romania and confirms the ballot returns [Article 146 f)];
- it ascertains any circumstance as may justify the interim in the exercise of office of President of Romania, and it reports its findings to Parliament and to Government [Article 146 g)];

---

under conventions. The new regulation ensures individual access to justice before ordinary courts and also the Constitutional Court, while the parties still enjoy all the means of defence recognized to them by law and, implicitly, the opportunity for the realization in actuality of their rights and interests in the court. The repeal of the ope legis suspension does not impinge on their effective right of access to the courts, as it will not hinder the realization of this right in such manner as to affect its very substance. Moreover, the measure thus adopted strikes a fair balance between individuals with conflicting interests, being intended to guarantee their equality of arms by establishing the legal framework for the exercise of their legitimate rights.

42 C.C. Dinu, *The implications of the adoption of Law no. 177 of 28 September 2010 on the Organisation and functioning of the Constitutional Court, of the Civil Procedure Code and of the Criminal Procedure Code of Romania in the gear of the civil trial*, in RRDP no. 5/2010, pp. 36–46.

43 Published in the Official Gazette of Romania no. 101 of 22 May 1992.

44 For this classification see I. Muraru, op. cit., p. 1394, respectively Ion Deleanu, *Constitutional Institutions and Procedures*, C.H. Beck Publishing House, Bucharest, 2006, p. 832.

- it gives advisory opinion on the proposal to suspend the President of Romania from office [Article 146 h)];
- it sees to the observance of the procedure for the organisation and holding of a referendum, and confirms its returns [Article 146 i)];
- it verifies whether conditions are met for the citizens' exercise of their legislative initiative [Article 146 j)];
- it rules upon challenges as to the unconstitutionality of a political party [Article 146 k)];
- it shall exercise the constitutional review on the resolutions by the Plenum of the Chamber of Deputies, resolutions by the Plenum of the Senate and resolutions by the Plenum of the joint Chambers of Parliament [Article 146 l) of the Constitution in conjunction with Articles 27–28 of Law no. 47/1992 on the Organisation and Operation of the Constitutional Court][45].

Except the powers concerning the procedure for the revision of the Constitution (which shall be exercised ex officio), the Constitutional Court shall pronounce only upon referral by subjects expressly and restrictively provided for by the Constitution or by Law no. 47/1992, and the referrals must be formulated in writing and substantiated. In order to exercise the only powers that the Constitutional Court shall exercise ex officio, Law no. 47/1992 stipulates (as concerns the initiative for the revision of the Constitution) that the initiator of the revision has the obligation to submit the bill or legislative proposal, together with the advisory opinion of the Legislative Council, at the Constitutional Court before the referral to Parliament and the Court shall be entitled to a period of the latest 10 days to rule, in Plenum, with the vote of at least two-thirds of its members. Within 5 days after the adoption of the law for the revision of the Constitution, the Constitutional Court shall pronounce ex officio on such law, with the same majority provided for by law in case of constitutional review of initiatives for the revision of the Constitution[46].

As proposals of *lege ferenda* concerning the powers of the Constitutional Court, it has been also proposed the extension of the competence of the Constitutional Court on the settlement of individual application formulated against judgments delivered in breach of the Constitution or of the Convention[47]. It was noted that this competence of the Constitutional Court must be seen as an "internal level of

---

45 Letter l) of the Constitution shall read as follows: "it *also fulfils other prerogatives as provided by the Court's organic law*".

46 The review of constitutionality on both the initiative of revision and the constitutional laws concerns, on the one hand, the degree and the extent in which that law complies with the revision procedure (*extrinsic* constitutionality), as established by the Basic Law itself (the instituted constituent power can be limited by the originary constituent power); on the other hand, it ensures the observance of substantive limits established for the revision of the Constitution (*intrinsic* constitutionality).

47 I.A. Motoc, *The Constitutional Court of Romania and The European Court of Human Rights – dialogue development*, in the volume The *Constitutional Court of Romania:*

competence", so as the formulation of applications before ECHR should be also conditioned by the exhaustion of such internal procedural remedy. Such an idea is also advanced by the Venice Commission, based on a study on individual access to constitutional justice, which covered various forms of such access in more than 50 countries. As highlighted by one of the representatives of the Venice Commission[48], one of the findings of this study was that free access to the constitutional court, not only against normative acts, but also against individual acts, such as in Spain and in Germany, enables an effective protection of human rights at national level. If such access is available, citizens do not need to bring their issues before the European Court of Human Rights because they will be settled in their country. The same representative pointed out that, in this respect, there is a clear trend of introducing individual access to constitutional justice in Europe.

2. Consolidation of the role of the Constitutional Court by its case-law

2.1 The unconstitutionality of the legal provisions which lead to the limitation of the Constitutional Court's competences

Disputes resulted from the increase of the powers of the Court by introducing within its competence the constitutional review of the resolutions of Parliament were followed by the adoption of Law on amending par. (1) of Article 27 of Law no. 47/1992 on the Organization and Operation of the Constitutional Court, by which this power of the Court was abolished.

Being referred to, within the *a priori* review, the Court upheld the objection of unconstitutionality[49] and found that the legislative solution which excludes from constitutional review the resolutions of Parliament affecting constitutional values and principle is unconstitutional. On that occasion, the Court held that the legislative amendment in order to abolish the power of the Constitutional Court to rule on the constitutionality of resolutions of the Plenum of the Chamber of Deputies, resolutions of the Plenum of the Senate and resolutions of the Plenum of the two joint Chambers of Parliament, without distinction, will only diminish the authority of the Constitutional Court, a fundamental institution of the state, and thus infringe the principle of the rule of law, leading to difficulties in achieving a state policy

20 years of existence and 100 years of constitutional review, Universul Juridic Publishing House, Bucharest, 2013, pp. 30–41.

48 G. Buquicchio, *Individual access to constitutional justice – cornerstone of effective protection of human rights by the Constitutional Court* in the volume The *Constitutional Court of Romania: 20 years of existence and 100 years of constitutional review*, Universul Juridic Publishing House, Bucharest, 2013, pp. 14–16.

49 Decision no. 727 of 9 July 2012, published in the Official Gazette of Romania no. 477 of 12 July 2012.

proper to consolidate and develop a democratic state in which the observance of the Constitution, of its supremacy and of laws shall be binding. The Court underlined that the rule of law, democratic and social, shall not remain a fundamental principle, with purely theoretical valences, with no practical results, but a reality correctly perceived both by public authorities and citizens. However, the exclusion from the constitutional review of all resolutions of the Plenum of the Chamber of Deputies, resolutions of the Plenum of the Senate and resolutions of the Plenum of the two joint Chambers of Parliament is not founded on the rule of law, but, more likely, on reasons of opportunity which, by their nature, involve subjectivity, interpretation and arbitrary and the constitutional justice is based on the rule of law, not on the opportunity. That being so, this power cannot mean an "excessive" competence for the Constitutional Court, but it shall inextricably integrate, once it has been legitimately granted, into a legal mechanism likely to contribute to the achievement of the principle of separation and balance of powers in a rule of law, democratic and social. To assess and to decide on the activity of the Constitutional Court, particularly in terms of quantitative standards, means its incorrect perception and, moreover, the ignorance of the essence of its fundamental role.

On the occasion of the initiative for the revision of the Constitution in 2014, it was implicitly proposed the abolishment of the powers of the Constitutional Court which are enshrined at this moment only by the organic law. By Decision no. 80 of February 16, 2014[50], the Court found the provisions concerned as unconstitutional.

Thus, ruling on the point 120 of the Sole Article of the legislative proposal for the revision of the Constitution, which repealed letter l) of Article 146 of the Constitution – according to which the Constitutional Court *"also fulfils other prerogatives as provided by the organic law (...)"*, the Court noted that, according to the Explanatory Memorandum, this repeal followed a recommendation formulated by Decision no. 799 of 17 June 2011 on the bill for the revision of the Constitution of Romania. The recommendation was justified by the fact that under the constitutional text proposed for repeal, *"the powers of the Constitutional Court can be replicated whenever interests of political forces require amendment or supplement of law on the organization of the Court"*. However, the Court held that, *"by removing the constitutional provision, it is guaranteed the constitutional court's independence and it is preserved the will of the primary constitutional power on the powers of the Court restrictively provided only within the Constitution"*. Noting that the reasons of that decision held the need for the supplement of the provisions of Article 146 a) and c) of the Constitution, in the sense of the constitutionalisation of the norms contained in Article 23 (1) and in Article 27 (1) of Law no. 47/1992, texts governing the powers of the Constitutional Court on the constitutional review of the law for the revision of the Constitution adopted by Parliament and, respectively, the constitutional review of the resolutions of the Plenum of the Chamber of Deputies, resolutions of the Plenum of the Senate and resolutions of the Plenum of the two

50 Published in the Official Gazette of Romania no. 246 of 7 April 2014.

joint Chambers of Parliament, the Court underlined that its recommendation did not concern a simple repeal of Article 146 l) of the Constitution, *"because, in the absence of a contingent amendment of points a) and c) of the same Article, this repeal infringes the provisions of Article 152 of the Constitution – The limits on matters of revision".* Referring to the power consisting in the constitutional review of the revision law of the Constitution adopted by Parliament, the Court held that "it is compelling that the revision law adopted by Parliament, before being subjected to a referendum under Article 151(3) of the Basic Law, be examined by the Constitutional Court in order to establish, on the one hand, whether or not a decision of the Court on the draft law or on the proposal for the revision of the Constitution has been complied with and, on the other hand, whether or not the amendments and supplements to the draft law or to the revision proposal undergoing parliamentary debate and adoption are in compliance with the constitutional principles and provisions related to revision. In the absence of such a review mechanism there is the risk to circumvent the generally binding effect of the decision of the Constitutional Court delivered on the initiative for the revision of the Constitution and to deprive of efficiency the constitutional review exercised, consequences that are incompatible with the principles of the rule of law and the role of the Constitutional Court". Moreover, the need to eliminate such consequences has basically substantiated the regulation of the powers of the Constitutional Court through Law no. 232/2004 amending and supplementing Law no. 47/1992 on the organization and operation of the Constitutional Court[51]. By examining the explanatory memorandum for the adoption of the law, it is found that the legislature has considered the transposition of the new regulations introduced by the revision of the Constitution into the Law no. 47/1992 on the organization and operation of the Constitutional Court, the main coordinates concerned being the regulation of the procedural rules for exercising the powers of the Constitutional Court, the establishment of the necessary correlations and the introduction of a series of guarantees for the express introductions of the *erga omnes* binding nature of the decisions of the Constitutional Court. More precisely, in the wording of the comparative table of the law in force and the amendments proposed, the regulation of the Constitutional Court's power to review the constitutionality of the law for the revision of the Constitution adopted by Parliament is supported by the following argument: *"for a rigorous regulation of the procedure for the review of the initiative for the revision of the Constitution, referred to in Article 151 of the Constitution, republished".*

Strengthening the abovementioned reasons, the Court held, in the same decision, that the legislature has designed this power of the Constitutional Court as being inextricably related to the one concerning the constitutional review of the initiatives for the revision of the Constitution, reason likely to substantiate a joint regulation and the adequate supplementing of Article 146 a) of the Constitution as follows: *"a) to adjudicate on the constitutionality of laws, before promulgation, upon*

51 Published in the Official Gazette of Romania no. 502 of 3 June 2004.

referral by the President of Romania, the President of Parliament, the Government, the High Court of Cassation and Justice, the Advocate of the People, of at least 50 Deputies or at least 25 Senators, as well as ex officio, on the initiatives for the revision of the Constitution and the laws for the revision of the Constitution, prior to their approval through referendum".

As concerns the power of the Constitutional Court to review the resolutions of the Plenum of the Chamber of Deputies, the resolutions of the Plenum of the Senate and the resolutions of the Plenum of the two joint Chambers of Parliament, this represent, according to Decision no. 80/2014, *"an expression of the requirements of the rule of law and a guarantee for the fundamental rights and freedoms"*. The Court held on this occasion and that in this regard, the Venice Commission has retained that "*with its Rules of Procedure and other general rules, Parliament shall, however, adopt normative acts, which are a yardstick for Parliament as a whole and its members individually. Judicial control of the application of such normative acts is an essential element of the rule of law. The absence of judicial control means that the majority in Parliament becomes the judge of its own acts. If only the majority can decide on the observance of parliamentary rules, the minority has nowhere to turn for help if these rules are flouted. Even if the acts concerned are individual ones, this affects not only the rights of the parliamentary minority but, as a consequence, also the right to vote of the citizens who have elected the parliamentary minority*". Therefore, *"judicial control of individual acts of Parliament is therefore not only a rule of law issue but, as the right to vote is affected, even a question of human rights*"[52].

In order to achieve the exercise of such competence in full compliance with the position and the role of Parliament in the rule of law, the Court held that when regulating this power, one should take into consideration that "can be subject to constitutional review only the resolutions of Parliament, adopted after the granting of the new power, resolutions that affect constitutional values, rules and principles or, where appropriate, the organisation and operation of constitutional authorities and institutions"[53].

The conclusion of Decision no. 80/2014 is that the constitutionalisation of the two powers currently regulated at infra-constitutional level is required by the repeal of Article 146 l) of the Constitution. Their removal through a simple repeal of the constitutional text under which they were regulated is likely to violate access to constitutional justice for the safeguarding of constitutional values, rules

---

52 Opinion on the compatibility with Constitutional principles and the Rule of Law of actions taken by the Government and Parliament of Romania in respect of other State institutions and on the Government emergency ordinance on amendment to the Law no. 47/1992 on the Organisation and Operation of the Constitutional Court and on the Government emergency ordinance amending and supplementing Law no. 3/2000 on the organisation of a referendum of Romania, adopted by the Venice Commission at its 93rd Plenary Session, 14–15 December 2012.

53 Decision no. 53 of 25 January 2011, published in the Official Gazette of Romania no. 90 of 3 February 2011.

and principles, i.e. the removal of a guarantee for such values, rules and principles that also include the scope of fundamental rights and freedoms. For the above-mentioned reasons, the Court, unanimously, ascertains the unconstitutionality of the repeal of Article 146 l) of the Constitution, as this is in breach of the limits for the revision provided for by Article 152 (2) of the Constitution, insofar as it is not accompanied by the duly constitutionalisation of the Constitutional Court's powers to review the law for the revision of the Constitution adopted by Parliament and, respectively, to review the constitutionality of the resolutions of the Plenum of the Chamber of Deputies, the resolutions of the Plenum of the Senate and the resolutions of the Plenum of the two joint Chambers of Parliament, resolutions that affect constitutional values, rules and principles or, where appropriate, the organisation and operation of constitutional authorities and institutions.

2.2 The impossibility to resume the regulation of the legislative solutions that are found unconstitutional

Likewise, the Constitutional Court's decision to which we referred to (no. 727/2012) rules on other issues too, introduced with other occasions – that on the Constitutional Court's competence to ascertain the unconstitutionality of certain legislative solutions – which means both from quantitative and quality point of view – more than a simple ascertainment of the unconstitutionality of the legal provision or provisions on which the Court is referred to. Therefore, the constitutional review transcends the strict limits of referrals brought before the Court in order to purify the legal system by those provisions that resume the legislative solutions found as unconstitutional.

Thus, noting that after the referral brought before the Constitutional Court on the unconstitutionality of the Law amending Article 27 (1) of Law no. 47/1992 on the Organization and Operation of the Constitutional Court and before the settlement of this referral, the Government adopted the Emergency Government Ordinance no. 38/2012 amending Law no. 47/1992 on the Organization and Operation of the Constitutional Court[54], containing a sole article enshrining an identical legislative solution[55], the Court ascertained the unconstitutionality of the law on which it was referred, by which the Court's competence to rule upon the constitutionality of Parliament's resolutions is discarded. Moreover, the Court held that – with reference to the subsequent emergency ordinance which was not formally subject to constitutional review – the subsequent primary regulatory acts cannot incorporate the legislative content of an unconstitutional legislative norm and thus extend its

54 Published in the Official Gazette of Romania no. 445 of 4 July 2012.

55 It is noteworthy that the Romanian law system, emergency ordinances shall be applicable forthwith, as they enter into force only after they were submitted to Parliament and published in the Official Gazette of Romania.

existence[56]. The Court outlined the fact that the solution chosen by the Government, to adopt, shortly before the constitutional court could rule upon the constitutionality of the Law amending Article 27 (1) of Law no. 47/1992, an emergency ordinance fully incorporating the legislative content of the impugned law, brings up for debate the Government's unconstitutional and abusive behaviour in relation to the Constitutional Court.

Starting from the ascertainment of the unconstitutionality of the legislative solutions and considering the provisions of Article 147(2) of the Constitution, according to which: "In cases related to laws declared unconstitutional before their promulgation, Parliament must reconsider those provisions concerned in order to bring such into line with the decision rendered by the Constitutional Court" and of paragraph(4) of the same article, according to which: "Decisions of the Constitutional Court shall be published in the Official Gazette of Romania. As from their publication, decisions shall be generally binding and take effect only for the future", by several decisions (no. 728 of 9 July 2012[57], no. 729 of 9 July 2012 and no. 732 of 10 July 2012[58]), the Constitutional Court, pursuant to Article 3 (2) of Law no. 47/1992, decided on its competence to rule upon the constitutionality of the resolutions of the Plenum of the Chamber of Deputies, the resolutions of the Plenum of the Senate and the resolutions of the Plenum of the two joint Chambers of Parliament, taking into consideration, on the one hand, the provisions of the sole article of the Government Emergency Ordinance mentioned above and, on the other hand, the reasons and the operative part of Decision no. 727/2012.

2.3 The Possibility to verify the constitutionality of the repealed Laws and Ordinances

In order to ensure the effective access to constitutional justice, the Constitutional Court of Romania has given a thorough interpretation of the provisions of the Law on the Organization and Operation of the Constitutional Court, provisions which limited the scope of the acts which could be subject to the Court's review through

56 See also Decision no. 1615 of 20 December 2011, published in the Official Gazette of Romania no. 99 of 8 February 2012; the solution was challenged in the doctrine, indicating that, in that case, the Court has ruled ex officio upon the Government Emergency Ordinance no. 38/2012, acting by "an excessive power", as long as the situation when it can rule ex officio concerns the initiative for the revision of the Constitution– see D.A. Tofan, *L'odysee du contrôle de la Cour constitutionelle sur les Resolutions du Parlement et des deux chambres. Il s'agit vraiment de la garantie de la suprematie de la Constitution?*, in *La Cour Constitutionnelle – garant de la suprematie de la Constitution*, European Institute, 2014, pp. 177–193.

57 Published in the Official Gazette of Romania no. 478 of 12 July 2012.

58 Published in the Official Gazette of Romania no. 480 of 12 July 2012.

the exception of unconstitutionality[59] only to those laws and ordinances *in force* when the constitutional review is exercised.

Thus, by Decision no. 766 of 15 June 2011[60], the Court found that the term "*in force*" of the provisions of Article 29 (1) and of Article 31 (1) of Law no. 47/1992 on the Organization and Operation of the Constitutional Court is constitutional insofar as it is interpreted as submitting to the constitutional review the laws or ordinances or provisions therein, whose legal effects continue to produce even when they are no longer in force.

The Court held that, within the Romanian system of concrete review of the constitutionality of laws, the initiation of the *a posteriori* review is only indirect, through the exception of unconstitutionality raised before the courts of law or commercial arbitration, and not through an "*actio popularis*", based on the direct application by any person. The establishment of this review procedure for the constitutionality of the law applicable in the case submitted for settlement before the court of first instance, as a means of access to justice, necessarily involves ensuring the possibility to be used by all those having a right, a legitimate interest and standing. The condition according to which the legal provision challenged for unconstitutionality should be related to the settlement of the case is, obviously, necessary, but also sufficient. Adding a supplementary condition – that the legal provision should also be formally in force, whose failure has the drastic significance of a real dismissal of the referral addressed to the constitutional court concerning the respective exception of unconstitutionality, represents a restriction of the free access to the constitutional court. Thus the repeal or the formal lapsing of a legal standard does not necessarily suppose its inapplicability in all situations. Even if law is alive and, at the same pace as society, it must adapt to the changes, no less normative solutions that they enshrine must comply with the principles of the Basic Law. Once referred to, the

---

59 According to Article 29 of Law no. 47/1992 on the Organisation and Operation of the Constitutional Court: "*(1) The Constitutional Court shall decide upon the exceptions raised before the courts of law or courts of commercial arbitration referring to the unconstitutionality of laws and ordinances which are in force, or any provision thereof, where such is related to adjudication of the case, regardless in which stage of trial proceedings or subject-matter thereof. (2)The exception can be raised at the request of either party or ex officio, by the court of law or of commercial arbitration hearing the case. Likewise, the prosecutor is entitled to raise this exception before the court in cases where he attends trial proceedings. (...) (4) he case shall be referred to the Constitutional Court by the court before which the exception of unconstitutionality was raised, through an interlocutory order which shall include the parties' for and against viewpoints, and the instance's opinion on the exception, together with the evidence provided by the parties. If the exception has been raised ex officio, the interlocutory order shall be motivated, including the parties' arguments, as well as the necessary evidence. Alongside with the interlocutory order, the referring court must also send to the Constitutional Court the full name of the litigant parties and other details comprising necessary data for the accomplishment of the summons proceedings in respect thereof. (...)*".

60 Published in the Official Gazette of Romania no. 549 of 3 August 2011.

Constitutional Court must examine them, without rendering this control conditional upon the discard, under any form, from the active fund of the legislation, of the act challenged for unconstitutionality.

The doctrine[61] retained as the main reasons for reconsidering the case-law of the Constitutional Court on matters of constitutional review concerning legal norms that are no longer in force, as follows: the case-law of European constitutional courts, the introduction of the reasonableness condition for the legal restriction of free access to constitutional justice, the necessity and sufficiency of the admissibility condition of the exception of unconstitutionality in relation to the settlement of the case.

Within the context, we emphasize the landmarks retained in the matter, namely the constitutional courts in Germany, Italy, Hungary, the Czech Republic, Poland, France, where the case-law concerning the legal norms that are no longer in force, but are applicable in the case, is in the sense of the review of the merits of such norms. The need for such review appears as an actual obligation to the constitutional courts, in their capacity as guarantors for the observance of the Constitution, as the amendment or the subsequent repeal of the impugned provision does not automatically remove any infringement of the provisions of the Constitution. In this way, the analysis of the merits of the impugned provisions, in view of discarding those provisions that do not comply with the constitutional requirement, regardless of their current legal existence, represents a much greater importance than the establishment of a purely formal procedural criterion that would stop the proceedings.

By this decision, the Constitutional Court covered practically a gap of competence in the matter of constitutional review of the repealed norms. Then, a step in this regard had already been accomplished with the case-law by which the Court held that the unconstitutionality of an emergency ordinance affects the normative act in its whole, and therefore the repealing of certain provisions laid down in the impugned normative act, after the referral of the constitutional court, has no longer any relevance in the settlement of the exception of unconstitutionality. Thus, although "the provisions of the emergency ordinance have ceased their effects, being norms with immediate temporal applicability, the unconstitutionality found affects the normative act as a whole, so that the effect of this decision also apply to the legal provisions that are no longer in force"[62]. A strong intervention of the Constitutional Court was achieved by Decision no. 838 of 27 May 2009 upon the referral by the President of Romania on the existence of a legal dispute of constitutional nature between the judicial authority, represented by the High Court

61 G. Gîrleşteanu, *The partial reconsideration of the case-law of the Constitutional Court of Romania on the a posteriori constitutional review of laws and ordinances in force – theoretical and practical considerations on Decision no. 766 of 15 June 2011, in Pandectele române* no. 8/2011, pp. 173–188.

62 Decision no. 1221 of 12 November 2008; Decision no. 842 of 2 June 2009; Decision no. 984 of 30 June 2009.

of Cassation and Justice, on the one hand, and the Parliament of Romania and the Government of Romania, on the other hand[63], the Court held that it is "the only authority empowered to exercise the constitutional review of laws or ordinances is the constitutional court. Therefore, not the High Court of Cassation and Justice nor the courts or other public authorities have the competence of constitutional review of laws or ordinances, regardless of whether these are in force or not"[64].

2.4 Sanctions for non-compliance with the decisions of the Constitutional Court

In situations where public authorities have adopted a conduct contrary to the Constitutional Court's decisions, it occurred within its limits of constitutional competence. Thus, for example, the Court challenged the solution chosen by the Government to issue, even the day preceding the one established by the Constitutional Court to rule upon the constitutionality of a law for approval of an emergency ordinance, a new emergency ordinance repealing the emergency ordinance lawfully approved by Parliament, but which fully reiterates the content thereof, stating within the decision pronounced on that occasion that the concerned solution *"questions the constitutional behaviour of legislative nature of the Executive in relation to Parliament and last but least in relation to the Constitutional Court"*[65].

Similarly, within the *a priori* review, having ascertained the unconstitutionality of a normative act that preserved a legislative solution found unconstitutional, the Court held that *"the adoption by the legislature of norms contrary to those ruled in a decision of the Constitutional Court, aiming at preserving the legislative solutions affected by flaws of unconstitutionality, violates the Basic Law"*[66].

Likewise, noting the existence of a legal dispute of constitutional nature between the President of Romania, on the one hand, and the judiciary, represented by the

---

63 Published in the Official Gazette of Romania no. 461 of 3 July 2009.

64 Position defined in relation to that expressed by the High Court of Cassation and Justice, so as the constitutional courts can adjudicate on the constitutionality of the repealed provisions, under the principle of unlimited jurisdiction in the cases which were given for their settlement. Thus, constitutional review and the settlement of the exception of unconstitutionality having as subject-matter the repealed norms, fall within the competence of the courts of law, through *per a contrario* interpretation of Article 147 para. (1), in relation to Article 126 para. (1) of the Constitution, and not within the competence of the Constitutional Court, which, in terms of Article 29 para. (1) of Law no. 47/1992, shall decide only upon the constitutionality of "*laws or ordinances in force, or any provision thereof*", a provisions which shall exclude *de iure* any conflict of competence in this matter.

65 Decision no. 1257 of 7 October 2009, published in the Official Gazette of Romania no. 758 of 6 November 2009.

66 Decision no. 1018 of 19 July 2010, published in the Official Gazette of Romania no. 511 of 22 July 2010.

High Court of Cassation and Justice, on the other hand, resulted from the failure of the High Court of Cassation and Justice of taking into consideration a decision of the Constitutional Court (by which it was found the unconstitutionality of a legal text that imperatively provided the promotion to the rank of colonels and Commanders, thus forcing the President of Romania to grant such ranks, without giving him the opportunity to appreciate whether or not to grant such ranks), the Constitutional Court ruled that, according to Article 94 b) of the Constitution, granting the rank of general is an exclusive power of the President of Romania[67]. Thus, the failure of the court to comply with the Constitutional Court's decisions was sanctioned.

In the same regard, noting the existence of a legal dispute of constitutional nature between the judiciary, on the one hand, and the Parliament of Romania and the Government of Romania, on the other hand (given the two appeals in the interest of the law, the High Court of Cassation and Justice did not limit to clarifying the meaning of certain legal norms or their scope of application, but, by invoking flaws of legislative technique or unconstitutionality flaws, has reinstated the norms that were no longer in force through repeal by normative acts of the legislative authority; but such a legal procedure could only be carried out by the legislative authority), the Constitutional Court held that the High Court of Cassation and Justice has no constitutional competence to carry out the constitutional review of legal provisions[68].

3. Effects of the Constitutional Court's decisions

3.1 Acts of the Constitutional Court

The acts which the Constitutional Court of Romania shall pronounce in the exercise of its powers are: decisions, rulings or advisory opinions, according to the appropriate power in whose implementation they are delivered, under the distinctions made by Article 11 of Law no. 47/1992, namely:

Decisions:

a) on the constitutionality of the laws, before their promulgation, when a case was submitted by the President of Romania, by one of the Presidents of the two Chambers of Parliament, by the Government, by the High Court of Cassation and Justice, by the Advocate of the People, by a number of at least fifty Deputies or of at least twenty-five Senators, as well as ex officio, on initiatives of revision of the Constitution;
b) on the constitutionality of the treaties or other international agreements, before their ratification by Parliament, when a case was submitted by one of the

67 Decision no. 1222 of 12 November 2008, published in the Official Gazette of Romania no. 864 of 22 December 2008.

68 Decision no. 838 of 27 May 2009, published in the Official Gazette of Romania no. 461 of 3 July 2009.

Presidents of the two Chambers, by a number of at least fifty Deputies or of at least twenty-five Senators;

c) on the constitutionality of the standing orders of the Parliament, when a case was submitted by one of the Presidents of the two Chambers, by a parliamentary group or by a number of at least fifty Deputies or of at least twenty-five Senators;
d) it shall decide on the exceptions raised before courts of law or of commercial arbitration regarding the unconstitutionality of the laws and ordinances, as well as on those brought up directly by the Advocate of the People;
e) it shall resolve the legal disputes of a constitutional nature between public authorities, when a case was submitted by the President of Romania, by one of the Presidents of the two Chambers, by the Prime Minister, or by the President of the Superior Council of the Magistracy;
f) it shall decide on the objections regarding the constitutionality of a political party.

Rulings, in cases in which:

a) it shall supervise the observance of the procedure for the election of the President of Romania and it shall confirm the results of the suffrage;
b) it shall ascertain the existence of circumstances which justify the interim in the exercise of the office of President of Romania and it shall report its findings to the Parliament and to the Government;
c) it shall verify the fulfilment of the conditions for the exercising of the legislative initiative by the citizens.

Advisory opinions – on the proposal to suspend from office the President of Romania.

Among these, the Constitution refers only to decisions and advisory opinions, as the rulings are nominated only by Law no. 47/1992, which assigns the same effect as the one enshrined in the Basic Law for decisions[69].

The issue on the effects of the Constitutional Court's decisions is also likely to be considered in the light of developments which were found both at legislative level and at the level of the Constitutional Court's case-law, resulting in reconfigurations including its role and the constitutional review.

---

69 According to expert opinions in doctrine, in this way, Law 47/1992 would add to the Constitution, since it provides that also rulings are acts of the Court, although such are not nominated by constitutional provisions – see I. Muraru, E.S. Tănăsescu (coordinators), *Constitution of Romania – Comments on articles* –,C.H. Beck Publishing House, Bucharest, 2008, p. 1419.

3.2 The erga omnes binding nature of the Constitutional Court's decisions

The Constitution of Romania enshrines the *erga omnes* binding nature of the Constitutional Court's decisions. According to Article 147 (4) of the Constitution: *"Decisions of the Constitutional Court shall be published in the Official Gazette of Romania. As from their publication, decisions shall be generally binding and take effect only for the future"*. Enshrining the generally binding nature of this Court's decisions determines the decisions to be taken into consideration by all subjects of law, just like a normative act, unlike the judgments of the courts of law which take *inter partes litigantes* effects[70].

The current wording of the reference constitutional text, given during the revision of the Constitution in 2003, has caused a series of doctrinal and jurisprudential controversies regarding these effects. In the wording prior to revision, the Constitution stipulated that the Constitutional Court's decisions are binding and take effects only for the future, wording that determined in practice the interpretation according to which the Constitutional Court's decisions would take effects only *inter partes litigantes*. The Constitutional Court had to give an explanation which is in this regard the Decision no. 1/1995 of the Plenum of the Constitutional Court on the binding nature of its decisions delivered within the constitutional review[71], which held the following: *"the idea of supremacy of the Constitution is a conquest of the legal thinking which is connected with the political will in order to effectively guarantee this supremacy through constitutional jurisdiction. Therefore, not incidentally, the Constitution of 1991 established the Constitutional Court in Romania. Its role as guarantor of the supremacy of the Constitution is enshrined in Article 1 para. (3) of Law no. 47/1992, and in order to ensure such role, the Constitutional Court is defined by law as the sole authority of constitutional jurisdiction in Romania, independent of any other public authority and subject only to the Constitution and to its organic law [Article 1 para. (1) and (2)]. (...) The constitutional review shall not be an impediment to democracy, but its necessary instrument, as it shall allow the parliamentary minority and citizens to see to the observance of the provisions of the Constitution, being a necessary counterpart in relation to the parliamentary majority, if it were to depart from the letter and the spirit of the Constitution.*

The democratic legitimacy of such review stems from the election or appointment of constitutional judges solely by constitutional authorities directly elected by the people (the Chamber of Deputies, the Senate, and the President of Romania). That being so,

70 This category does not include the decisions of the High Court of Cassation and Justice, issued following the resolution of appeals in the interest of law, which have a separate legal regime. In Germany, an erga omnes effect is fully established in case of abstract and concrete constitutional review of laws, as well as of individual complaints of unconstitutionality aimed at normative acts. The force of law is attributed to these decisions. Likewise, in Austria, decisions delivered within the constitutional review exercised on normative acts have erga omnes effects.

71 Published in the Official Gazette of Romania no. 16 of 26 January 1995.

it is all the more natural the participation of the Constitutional Court – under the conditions established by the Constitution – in the legislative process. However, in this process, the Constitutional Court is constrained by certain external requirements which aim mainly at the fact that it cannot substitute the legislature, and by certain internal requirements as its solutions should be justified by legal reasoning.

The constitutional review is achieved by decisions which, according to Article 145 para. (2) of the Constitution, are binding and effective only for the future. If the decision ascertains the unconstitutionality, it takes erga omnes effects, i.e. it has a generally binding effect aiming at all public authorities, citizens and legal persons of private law. Due to this fact, a not negligible part of the constitutional doctrine assimilates these decisions with the acts bearing the force of law. This conclusion can be easily drawn by noting the effects of the decisions in various situations of constitutional review:

- *a) the decision that allowed the exception of unconstitutionality makes the law or the ordinance declared unconstitutional or the text within them to no longer apply, as they were repealed by law;*
- *b) the acceptance of the challenge of unconstitutionality in connection with the Regulations of the Parliament makes the texts declared unconstitutional to be inapplicable and requires the Chamber concerned to reconsider these provisions in order to bring them into accord with the stipulations of the Constitution [Article 22 (4) of Law no. 47/1992];*
- *c) the decision that allowed the objection of unconstitutionality of a law before promulgation shall also be generally binding and it shall not be ignored by anyone [...];*
- *d) the decision that ascertains the unconstitutionality of the initiative for the revision of the Constitution shall obstruct the procedure for the revision provided for by Article 147 of the Constitution. Due to the generally binding nature of the decisions of the Constitutional Court, its case-law should be considered by all bodies involved in the drafting and application of laws and orders of the Government, as well as by the Chambers in the drafting or amendment of the Regulations of Parliament".*

Likewise, the current wording of the constitutional text caused a series of interpretations that puts into question the binding nature of certain decisions of the Constitutional Court. In this regard, responding to criticism which claimed that the latter are not also binding, having distinguished between the decisions which ascertain the unconstitutionality or the constitutionality of a law, because such an interpretation would mean that the Court can never think over its own case-law as it is related to its previous findings, the Constitutional Court stated that the text of Article 147 (4) of the Constitution, which enshrines the general binding nature of its decisions, *"does not distinguish based on the types of the decisions pronounced by the Constitutional Court, or on the content of those decisions, which results in the conclusion that all decisions of this Court, as a whole, are generally binding"*[72].

72 Decision no. 2 of 11 January 2012, published in the Official Gazette of Romania no. 131 of 23 February 2012.

Having emphasized these statuaries in a case in which criticism of unconstitutionality concerned the very generally binding nature of the decisions of the Constitutional Court, interpreted by the authors of the exception of unconstitutionality as a limitation of the free access to justice, the Court held as follows: "*The finding, by a decision of the Court, of the unconstitutionality of a legal text has erga omnes legal effects, a consequence deriving from the unique and independent character of the authority of constitutional jurisdiction. Contrary, the Court's decision – of rejection – is still generally binding and effective only for the future, pursuant to Article 147(4) of the Constitution, meaning that public authorities involved in the case in which the exception was raised are bound by the decision, both in terms of the operative part and in terms of considerations that underpinned it, but the legal effect of such a decision falls within the procedural framework of the dispute only where the exception was raised, so it has inter partes nature. Therefore, the same legal text can be brought again for review before the Constitutional Court, considering that new aspects and constitutional grounds may be revealed and that those can justify, in the future, a different solution. The possibility to reiterate the same exception of unconstitutionality, in compliance with legal conditions concerning admissibility, can convert, in the specific constitutional procedures framework, in an appeal, with its own physiognomy, the aim and end of this approach are, in fact, the same as those aiming at promoting a remedy: bringing again before the constitutional court a legal text on which it has previously pronounced rejection solutions, but with the invocation of new issues that are likely to determine the modification of that case-law.*"[73].

It was revealed that the binding nature of the Constitutional Court's decisions is a factor of stability and of development of the Constitution. Thus, "if the multifaceted social pressure exerted on the Constitutional Court by way of objections of unconstitutionality is a disturbing factor for constitutional stability, the act in response is the Constitutional Court decision, aimed at easing the conflict; and it does so by pointing out to the text of law based on which the court hearing the case, whether civil, criminal or any other, must pass judgment. Insofar its decisions have successfully absorbed the changes which occurred at the social level into their own substance, they will give new meanings to the terms of the Constitution, to the concepts which operate its machinery, and thus pave the way to perpetual renewal." Furthermore, it is not irrelevant to mention the observation made by the same author, in the sense that the formal proclamation of the generally binding nature of the Court's decisions cannot be generalized, because, in the absence of their proper substantiation, the obligatory force can become a hostile factor against the stability of the Constitution, especially through the erosion of the Constitutional Court[74].

---

73 Decision no. 302 of 27 March 2012, published in the Official Gazette of Romania no. 361 of 29 May 2012.

74 I. Vida, *The obligatory force of decisions of the Constitutional Court for other courts of law as a stabilising factor of the Constitution and of the judicial practice*, in Pandectele Romane no. 3/2004, p. 202.

3.3 The obligatory force of recitals in the decisions of the Constitutional Court

The statuaries of the Constitutional Court as well as the aspects noted by the doctrine put into question, inter alia, the issue of the obligatory force of recitals into the decisions of the Constitutional Court, as well as the rationale and effects of the interpretative decisions.

In an established case-law, starting with the Decision of the Plenum no. 1/1995[75], the Court held that res judicata which accompanies the jurisdictional acts, and therefore the Constitutional Court's decisions, is attached not only to the operative part, but also to the recitals on which it is based. Accordingly – the Court has noted – Parliament and the Government, respectively public authorities and bodies shall fully comply with both the recitals and the operative part of the decisions pronounced by the Constitutional Court. This particular effect of acts of the Constitutional Court is a consequence of its role, which could not be fully achieved if it would not be accepted the binding nature of the interpretation given by the Court to the texts and the concepts of the Basic Law, the meaning identified by it to the framer's will. It has been indicated[76] that that this process used by the Court is meant to remind public authorities involved in the lawmaking process the issue of effectiveness of constitutional justice[77], in the context of a manifest legislative instability, with profoundly negative effects on the values of the rule of law and legal certainty. Being confronted with situations which, as noted in the Decision no. 1257/2009[78], put into questions the *legislative constitutional behaviour of the Executive in relation to Parliament and not at the latest in relation to the Constitutional Court*", the Court stated in the wording of its decisions, which are the consequences of the ascertainment of unconstitutionality, emphasizing also the binding nature of these recitals. Such practice is necessary because, as noted, it does not only result in the prevention of issuing new unconstitutional normative acts, but also in the discard of those subsequent acts that are based on normative acts which have already been found

75 Published in the Official Gazette of Romania no. 16 of 26 January 1995.

76 M. Safta, K. Benke, *The obligatory force of recitals in the decision of the Constitutional Court, in the Review "Dreptul" no. 9/2010,* pp. 28–55.

77 We mention that the Constitutional Court has also invoked the res judicata attached to the recitals of the decisions of the Constitutional Court, in other decisions, for example, Decision no. 196/2013, published in the Official Gazette of Romania no. 231 of 22 April 2013; Decision no. 163/2013, published in the Official Gazette of Romania no. 190 of 4 April 2013; Decision no. 102/2013, published in the Official Gazette of Romania no. 208 of 12 April 2013; Decision no. 1039/2012, published in the Official Gazette of Romania no. 61 of 29 January 2013; Decision no. 536/2011, published in the Official Gazette of Romania no. 482 of 7 July 2011; Decision no. 414/2010, published in the Official Gazette of Romania no. 291 of 4 May 2010; Decision no. 415/2010, published in the Official Gazette of Romania no. 294 of 5 May 2010.

78 Published in the Official Gazette of Romania no. 758 of 6 November 2009.

unconstitutional and thus preventing the perpetuation of certain circumstances that are incompatible with the rule of law, as provided for by the Basic Law.

As concerns the phrase "res judicata" used by the Court, it was indicated that "the value of the recitals in the economy of the decision represents a significant common matrix applicable with no distinction or difference in relation to all the powers of the Constitutional Court provided for by Article 146 of the Constitution and by Law no. 47/1992", noting that the phrase "res judicata" referred to by the Constitutional Court, attaching it both to the recitals and to the operative part of decisions pronounced by it, is only the expression of *erga omnes* binding nature of the interpretation given by the Court to the Constitution. Such binding nature is based on the constitutional provisions of Article 1 (3) and (5), of Article 142 (1) and of Article 147 (4)[79]. Therefore, it is neither res judicata as a concept of the civil proceedings supplementing the proceedings before the Constitutional Court, nor an "autonomous" concept[80], but the expression of the particular effect of the decisions of the Constitutional Court. Thus, in order to avoid any misunderstanding, it would be necessary to discard the abovementioned phrase which is inappropriate within the context. Furthermore, the recent case-law of the Constitutional Court has ceased to refer to this phrase.

3.4 Interpretative decisions[81]

3.4.1 Conceptual explanations

The complexity of regulations, often accompanied by the lack of qualitative legislation, as well as the need to adjust the constitutional review to certain goals of legal certainty, make the exercise of that review to result not only in the delivery of simple solutions by which the impugned text or texts are found or not in compliance with the Basic Law. Often, the Constitutional Courts can achieve more than a simple ascertainment of compliance of the impugned legal provisions with the Constitution. By their delivered acts, the constitutional courts establish principles and rules, define the powers of public authorities, provide guidance and solutions on how to interpret the Constitution, the infra-constitutional legislation so as to be in compliance with the Basic Law[82], and they even "correct" legislative omissions in relation to the constitutional rules. In turn, these solutions, having a high degree of complexity, influence the legislative assembly and the application of the legal provisions within the general phenomenon of constitutionalisation of law.

---

79 M. Safta, K. Benke, *cited paper,* p. 41.

80 I. Deleanu, S. Deleanu, *Case-law and the jurisprudential upturn*, Universul Juridic Publishing House, Bucharest, 2013. p. 71.

81 T. Toader, M. Safta, *The role of interpretative decisions in the process of constitutionalisation of law*, in the Review "Dreptul" no. 9/2014, pp. 65–88.

82 For example, Constitutional Courts of Austria, Estonia, Lithuania, Romania, and Hungary.

With reference to the Constitutional Court of Romania, it has been noted the abovementioned evolution[83] and the importance of the recitals in decisions, both binding alongside their operative part[84]. It has been also outlined the creative role which resulted in its role of "positive and specific co-legislator"[85] , found by a part of the doctrine. Furthermore, there is an evolution that can be also found in the activity of other constitutional courts and that departs from the traditional role of "negative legislator"[86].

The interpretative decisions delivered by the Constitutional Court give expression to this evolution, so it is helpful to consider the peculiarities, the specific effects and their role within the process of constitutionalisation of law. This typology of decisions may be, to the greatest extent, a base and an evolution of the inter-institutional dialogue.

The achievement of the proposed approach firstly involves the definition of the concept – interpretative decision, which raises the question to categorize the Constitutional Court's decisions, a difficult endeavour, given the diversity in which they can appear. The doctrine achieved such categorization, based on different criteria, of which we will refer here only to the one that interests us in terms of our study, which refers to the concrete "behaviour" of the Constitutional Court, its work creative work – within the limits allowed by the Constitution –, when it comes to settle complex and often unusual issues of constitutionality"[87]. In relation to this criterion, two major categories of decisions have been identified[88]: simple or extreme decisions that find the unconstitutionality or constitutionality of the impugned norm, and intermediate decisions that find the constitutionality or unconstitutionality, but with certain reservations. In turn, such decisions have various classifications[89].

---

83 M. Safta, *Developments in the constitutional review. Constitutional Court between the status of negative legislator and the status of positive co-legislator*, in the Review of the International Conference "Perspectives of business law in the third millennium", volume I, no. 1/2012, pp. 1–21.

84 T. Toader, M. Safta, *The Dialogue between the Constitutional Court of Romania and the European Court of Human Rights, in the Review "Dreptul"* no. 9/2013, pp. 93–121, available on *http://web.ebscohost.com.*

85 I. Deleanu, *The Dialogue of Judges*, in RRDJ no. 1/2012, p. 36; see also I. Deleanu, S. Deleanu, *Case-law and jurisprudential upturn,* Essay, Universul Juridic Publishing House, Bucharest, 2013, p. 71.

86 For a comparative law analysis, see M. Troper, D. Chagnollaud, *Traite international de droit constitutionnel, Tome 3 – Suprematie de la Constitution,* Dalloz, Paris, 2012, p. 150 et seq.

87 I. Deleanu, *Institutions and constitutional procedures,* C.H. Beck Publishing House, Bucharest, 2006, p. 897.

88 *Ibidem.*

89 For example, I. Deleanu classified the intermediate decisions into *interpretative* and *manipulative* decisions. According to the same author, the ones "by which the constitutional court, without ascertaining the unconstitutionality, assigns a specific meaning to the impugned rules, a meaning that would be in compliance with the

Having accepted, of principle, the criterion which led to the abovementioned classification, we will refer to this latter category of decisions, naming them by the concept of interpretative decisions, to which we will assign a broad meaning. Therefore, through interpretative decisions, we refer in broad sense to all decisions of the Constitutional Court who comprise a mere declaration of constitutionality / unconstitutionality of the impugned norms. Within the delimitation between the simple and the interpretative decisions, we consider both the structure and content of the recitals and of the operative part, respectively the circumstantiation of the constitutionality or unconstitutionality, as appropriate, in the operative part of the decision. This is because, in most cases, the interpretations of the Constitutional Court given only in the content of the recitals are inherent to the constitutional review, supporting the construction of reasoning leading to the operative part of the decision. In other words, any decision of the Constitutional Court is based on a legal interpretation, but not any decision of the Constitutional Court is an interpretive decision.

It should be mentioned that neither the Constitution nor the Law no. 47/1992 on the Organization and Operation of the Constitutional Court makes any distinction in terms of the analyzed aspect; they only refer to the constitutionality or unconstitutionality of the normative acts. Of course that the interpretative decisions also find the constitutionality or unconstitutionality, but only in a certain interpretation of the legal text subject to constitutional review. In this way, the legal text is "rescued" in the sense that it can still be applied, but within the binding interpretation established by the Constitutional Court, namely through the repeal of that interpretation that has been found to be unconstitutional.

The delivery of such decisions, which has been existed for a long time in the practice of constitutional courts in Germany, Italy or France, was caused by the desire of legal security in the broad sense, as they are, moreover, characterized as "privileged means used by the constitutional courts to avoid invalidation of legal norms"[90]. The negative effects of such invalidations may be overcome by providing an interpretation of the infra-constitutional rule in compliance with the constitutional norms, in order to achieve their compatibility.

Within the *a priori* review, recourse to the mechanism of the interpretative decisions or delivery of certain decisions according to the law subject to certain interpretations facilitates the enforcement of law, meaning that such law can be

---

Constitution, by way of interpretation of those rules and given the mentioned reasons" are part of the interpretative decisions. It is also noted that the interpretation can be achieved through the operative part by the reference made to the recitals, or even through the recitals of the decision. As concerns the manipulative decisions, it is noted that they are more than outright interpretative decisions, as they aim at transforming the meaning of the law, not to leave a legal void with damaging consequences.

90 G. Drago, *L'execution des decisions du Conseil Constitutionnel*, Economica Publishing House, Paris, 1991, p. 151.

promulgated and will enter into force, taking its effects, but in terms of the mentioned meaning within the constitutional review. Thus, it is avoided the resumption of the legislative process which takes time and resources, sometimes the entry into force of law is vital for the social, political and economic life. With reference to the practice in this regard of the Constitutional Council of France, it was claimed that "*the consistent interpretation is a more subtle and less brutal means of ascertainment of unconstitutionality, which allows the Constitutional Council to order the legislature to comply with the Constitution without resulting in the sanction of a legal norm*"[91].

As concerns the *a posteriori* review, where the subject-matter of the constitutional review is represented by norms in force, the "rescue" of the legal text may be preferable in order to avoid a legislative gap with damaging consequences.

It is no less true that in both situations, the relations between the Constitutional Court and the legislature or the courts of law are called upon to interpret and enforce the law and, as a result of an interpretative decision of the Constitutional Court, such authorities will be required to comply with it as the only correct interpretation for the purposes of compliance with the Constitution, may result in discussions and criticisms concerning the limits of competence of the Court in relation to the competence of these authorities[92].

Further below, we will examine the way of embodiment into practice of the abovementioned decisions, the effects and their role in the process of constitutionalisation of law, the limits of the constitutional review that even the constitutional courts outline them in a necessary "self-restraint" in order to ensure the compliance with the position and the role of each public authority within the rule of law[93].

3.4.2 Modalities to draft the operative parts of the interpretative decisions

Decisions finding the *constitutionality* of the impugned legal norms, to the extent that they are interpreted in a certain meaning

We mention, as an example, the decisions of the Constitutional Court by which it found that:

- The provisions of Article 157(2) of the Standing Order of the Senate, approved by the Resolution of the Romanian Senate no. 28 of 24 October 2005 according to which: "Simple motions adopted by the Senate shall be published in the Official Gazette of Romania, Part I, and shall be binding for the Government and its members, as well as for other persons concerned", are constitutional insofar the adoption of a simple motion by the Senate does not oblige the prime minister

91 *Ibidem*, p. 148.

92 Further, for the situation within the German and Italian law, see G. Drago, *op. cit.*, pp. 151–153.

93 M. Troper, D. Chagnollaud, *cited paper*, p. 150 –"la tentation du self-restraint".

to propose the dismissal from office of a member of the Government whose work was the subject-matter of the motion[94];

- Law on the reorganization of certain public authorities and institutions, rationalization of public spending, support of the business environment and compliance with the framework agreements with the European Commission and the International Monetary Fund is constitutional insofar as the provisions of Chapter IV of the Law does not refer to persons for whom the term of office is expressly set forth in the Constitution[95];
- The term "in force" in the provisions of Article 29(1) and of Article 31 (1) of Law no. 47/1992 on the Organization and Operation of the Constitutional Court, republished, is constitutional insofar as it is interpreted that the laws or ordinances or the provisions therein shall be subject to constitutional review, whose legal effects continue to be taken even when they are no longer in force[96];
- The provisions of Article 259 (2) of Law no. 95/2006 on healthcare reform, according to which: "Contributions payable by pensioners whose retirement incomes exceed 740 lei is 5.5% applied on such incomes and shall be transferred together with the payment of money dues on which is calculated by those in charge with payment of such dues. Application of this rate cannot result in a net pension lower than 740 lei", are constitutional insofar as it is interpreted in the sense that the percentage of 5.5 applies only to retirement incomes exceeding 740 lei[97];
- The provisions of Article V (1) sentence I of the Government Emergency Ordinance no. 15/2012 on the establishment of certain financial measures in the field of social health insurance and of public finance, according to which: "The amounts deducted from the value added tax in order to balance the local budgets of certain local public administration authorities granted in 2012 by Government Decision no. 255/2012 regarding the allocation of an amount from the budget reserve fund at the disposal of Government, stipulated in the state budget for 2012, for certain local public administration authorities, for the payment of arrears in respect of current and capital expenditure, as well as for co-financed projects with non-reimbursable external financing, unused until the entry into force of this ordinance, shall be returned by the principal authorising officers of local budgets into the account of the state budget from which they were collected" are constitutional insofar as such provisions apply only to amounts allocated by Government Decision no. 255/2012 and unused by

94 Decision no. 148 of 21 February 2007, published in the Official Gazette of Romania no. 162 of 7 March 2007.

95 Decision no. 1414 of 4 November 2009, published in the Official Gazette of Romania no. 796 of 23 November 2009.

96 Decision no. 766 of 15 June 2011, published in the Official Gazette of Romania no. 549 of 3 August 2011.

97 Decision no. 223 of 13 March 2012, published in the Official Gazette of Romania no. 256 of 18 April 2012.

local public administration authorities that did not register arrears in respect of current and capital expenditure and did not have ongoing co-financed projects with non-reimbursable external financing until the entry into force of Government Emergency Ordinance no. 15/2012[98];

- Law amending Article 10 of Law no. 3/2000 on the organization and carrying-out of the referendum is constitutional insofar as the referendum is attended by of least half plus one of the number of persons registered on the permanent electoral lists[99];
- The provisions of Article 151 (2) of Law no. 263/2010 on the uniform public pension system are constitutional insofar as interpreted that failure to settle complaints and failure to communicate in due time the decisions of the Central Committee of Appeals, respectively of the Committees of Appeals that operate within the Ministry of National Defence, Ministry of Interior and the Romanian Intelligence Service does not prevent access to justice[100];
- The provisions of Article 124 of the Criminal Code, according to which "Prescription removes criminal liability regardless of how many interruptions may occur, if the term for prescription provided for in Article 122 is exceeded by one more half" are constitutional insofar as they do not prevent the enforcement of the more favourable criminal law for offenses committed under the influence of the old law[101];
- The provisions of Article 118 of Law no. 67/2004 for election of local authorities, according to which "prefects and deputy prefects cannot run and cannot participate in electoral campaigns, under the sanction of dismissal from office, unless they resign at least 50 days before the election" are constitutional insofar as interpreted as meaning that the 50-day period runs from the date of the registration of resignation. In this way it was removed the text interpretation that the 50-day period runs from the date of termination of service by resignation[102];
- The provisions of Article 71 (2) sentence I of Law no. 47/1992 on the Organization and Operation of the Constitutional Court, according to which: "On the date of retirement or recalculation of pensions as have been established up to that time, the Judges of the Constitutional Court shall benefit from a service pension whose amount equals 80% of their monthly gross indemnity(...)" are

98 Decision no. 558 of 24 May 2012, published in the Official Gazette of Romania no. 382 of 7 June 2012.

99 Decision no. 731 of 10 July 2012, published in the Official Gazette of Romania no. 478 of 12 July 2012.

100 Decision no. 956 of 13 November 2012, published in the Official Gazette of Romania no. 838 of 12 December 2012.

101 Decision no. 1092 of 18 December 2012, published in the Official Gazette of Romania no. 67 of 31 January 2013.

102 Decision no. 102 of 28 February 2013, published in the Official Gazette of Romania no. 208 of 12 April 2013.

constitutional insofar as applied to the Judges of the Constitutional Court who exercised this term of office, regardless of the date of retirement[103];

- The provisions of Article 40 (3) of Law no. 41/1994 on the organization and operation of the Romanian Radio Broadcasting Corporation and of the Romanian Television Corporation, according to which "legal entities residing in Romania, including subsidiaries, branches, agencies and their representative offices, as well as the representative offices of foreign legal entities in Romania shall be compelled to pay a fee for public services of radio broadcasting and a fee for public services of television, as beneficiaries of such services" are constitutional insofar as the fee for public services of radio broadcasting and television applies only to legal entities that benefit from such services[104].

The following examples may be given *as exceptions for drafting the operative parts* finding constitutionality or situations in which the Court expressly stated the admission/rejection of the referral of unconstitutionality therein:

- The Court *rejected the objection* of unconstitutionality of the Law amending and supplementing Law no. 3/2000 on the organization and carrying-out of the referendum and found that the provisions of the Law amending and supplementing Law no. 3/2000 on the organization and carrying-out of the referendum are constitutional insofar they do not apply to referendums held within one year since the entry into force of the law[105];
- The Court *upheld the exception* of unconstitutionality and found that the provisions of Article 118^2 (2) a) of the 1969 Criminal Code are constitutional insofar they allow the enforcement of the more favourable criminal law[106];
- The Court *upheld the exception* of unconstitutionality and found that the provisions of Article 4 sentence II of Law no. 165/2013 on measures to complete the process of restitution in kind or by equivalent of property abusively confiscated during the communist regime in Romania are constitutional insofar as the terms of Article 33 of the same Law do not equally apply to cases on restitution of property abusively confiscated, being the case at issue before courts of law on the entry into force courts of the law[107];
- The Court *upheld the exception* of unconstitutionality and found that the provisions of Article 5 of the Criminal Code are constitutional insofar as they do not

103 Decision no. 163 of 12 March 2013, published in the Official Gazette of Romania no. 190 of 4 April 2013.

104 Decision no. 448 of 29 October 2013, published in the Official Gazette of Romania no. 5 of 7 January 2014.

105 Decision no. 334 of 26 June 2013, published in the Official Gazette of Romania no. 407 of 5 July 2013.

106 Decision no. 78 of 11 February 2014, published in the Official Gazette of Romania no. 273 of 14 April 2014.

107 Decision no. 88 of 27 February 2014, published in the Official Gazette of Romania no. 281 of 16 April 2014.

allow the combination of the provisions of successive laws in order to establish and implement the more favourable criminal law[108].

Decisions finding the *unconstitutionality* of the impugned legal norms, insofar as interpreted in a certain sense

Thus, as examples, we mention the decisions by which the Court:

- upheld the exception of unconstitutionality and found that the provisions of Article 50 (2) of Law no. 303/2004 on the statute of magistrates, according to which: "The Superior Council of Magistracy may order ex officio, as the case may be, the dismissal from a management office, based on proposals submitted by the managing colleges of the courts of law or Public Prosecutor's Offices, or as a disciplinary sanction, under the law" are unconstitutional to the extent that their content is understood that the magistrate cannot appeal against a decision by which the Superior Council of Magistracy refuses him/her the exercise of an acquired right[109];
- found that the provisions of Article 362 (1) d) of the Code of Criminal Procedure are unconstitutional to the extent that they do not allow the civil party and the civilly responsible party to exercise the ordinary remedy of the appeal in terms of the criminal nature of the case[110];
- found that the provisions of Article 28 (1) and of Article 36 of the Law on the status of the free movement of Romanian citizens abroad are unconstitutional insofar as related to a minor married woman. The mentioned legal texts were read as follows: Article 28 (1) "The border police personnel shall allow Romanian citizens who have reached the age of 18 and hold a valid travel document to leave the territory of Romania, if they are not in one of the situations that limit the exercise of their right to free movement abroad"; Article 36: "(1) At their request, Romanian citizens who have reached the age of 18 and who have established their residence in Romania shall have the mention on the establishment of their residence abroad cancelled from their ordinary passports and shall be issued Identity Cards, under the law. (2) A Romanian citizen residing abroad and who has been returned to Romania based on a readmission agreement or, as applicable, has been expelled from the territory of his/her state of residence, shall be under the obligation to declare to the Romanian authorities the location where he/she has established his/her residence, under the law, within 15 days of the date of entry into Romania"[111];

108 Decision no. 265 of 6 May 2014, published in the Official Gazette of Romania no. 372 of 20 May 2014.

109 Decision no. 433 of 21 October 2004, published in the Official Gazette of Romania no. 1267 of 29 December 2004.

110 Decision no. 482 of 9 November 2004, published in the Official Gazette of Romania no. 1200 of 15 December 2004.

111 Decision no. 217 of 20 April 2005, published in the Official Gazette of Romania no. 417 of 18 May 2005.

- found that the provisions of Article 12 and of Article 27 of the Law on reproductive health and medically assisted human reproduction, on the right of the physician to decide on the couple's application in terms of the use of techniques of medically assisted human reproduction are unconstitutional to the extent that they do not provide a specialized authority, with control powers, that can be notified by applicants whose application was rejected[112];
- upheld the exception of unconstitutionality of the provisions of Article 1 (2) and of Article 5 (1) of Law no. 61/1993 on state allowance for children and found that these provisions are unconstitutional to the extent that the granting of the state allowance for children is conditioned by the attendance of the compulsory education and the registration with one of the types of education provided by law[113];
- found that Article 5 (2) according to which: "The number of Senators proposed in the Validation Committee by each party, organization of citizens belonging to national minorities, political alliance or electoral alliance shall be based on its members in relation to the total number of Senators and shall be established by negotiations conducted by their representatives" insofar as related to the number of members of parties, organizations of national minorities, political alliances or electoral alliances and not to the political configuration resulting from elections, according to Article 64 (5) of the Constitution, Article 45 (1) according to which: "The number of seats in committees belonging to each parliamentary group, shall be established, within the period decided by the Standing Bureau, by negotiations between the representatives of the parliamentary groups, so as to meet the political configuration of the Senate resulted from the elections. If one of the committee members resigns from the parliamentary group which proposed him, the leader of the group shall propose another representative" to the extent that the group leader and not the parliamentary group is entitled to make proposals concerning the replacement of one member of a parliamentary committee, Article 67 d), Article 76 (1), Article 76 (6), Article 79 (1) and (2), Article 189, Article 190, Article 191 and Article 193 of the Standing Order of the Senate are unconstitutional[114];
- upheld the exception of unconstitutionality and found that the provisions of Article 12 (1) of the Government Ordinance no. 2/2001 on the legal regime of offenses, according to which, "an offense shall no longer be sanctioned if a normative act does not consider it any longer an offense, even if committed before the entry into force of the new normative act", and found the unconstitutionality of

112 Decision no. 418 of 18 July 2005, published in the Official Gazette of Romania no. 664 of 26 July 2005.

113 Decision no. 277 of 21 March 2006, published in the Official Gazette of Romania no. 348 of 18 April 2006.

114 Decision no. 317 of 13 April 2006, published in the Official Gazette of Romania no. 446 of 23 May 2006.

those provisions to the extent that the term "no longer sanctioned" provided for in the text means just the implementation of the sanction, not its execution[115];

- upheld the exception of unconstitutionality and found that the provisions of Article 9 of Law no. 554/2004 on the Administrative Contentious are unconstitutional to the extent that they allow the case before the administrative contentious courts to have as main subject-matter the ascertainment of unconstitutionality of an ordinance or of a provisions of an ordinance[116];
- upheld the exception of unconstitutionality of the provisions of Article 7 (7) of the Law no. 554/2004 on the Administrative Contentious and found that the legal text is unconstitutional to the extent that the period of 6 months from the date of issue of the administrative act shall apply to the prior application brought by the injured party in his/her defence or in his/her legitimate interest, by an individual administrative act, addressed to another subject of law than the addressee of the act[117];
- upheld the exception of unconstitutionality and found that the provisions of Article 10 (5) of Government Emergency Ordinance no. 27/2006 on the Salary and Other Rights of the Judges, Prosecutors and Other Categories of Personnel within the Legal System, according to which: "The elected members of the Superior Council of Magistracy without permanent activity shall also benefit, in addition to the monthly gross indemnity corresponding to the office held within the court or the Prosecutor's Office, from an indemnity of membership equal to 55% of the monthly gross indemnity of the Judge of the High Court of Cassation and Justice" are unconstitutional insofar as it imposes discrimination in terms of salary between the members of the Superior Council of Magistracy with permanent activity and the members of the Superior Council of Magistracy without permanent activity[118];
- upheld the exception of unconstitutionality and found that the provisions of Article 7 of Law no. 85/2006 on insolvency proceedings are contrary to Articles 24 and 53 of the Constitution, insofar as interpreted that the first communication of the procedural documents to persons against whom action is being taken under the provisions of Law no. 85/2006, subsequent to the opening of insolvency proceedings, shall be carried out only through the Insolvency Proceedings Bulletin, and not according to the Code of Civil Procedure[119];

---

115 Decision no. 228 of 13 March 2007, published in the Official Gazette of Romania no. 283 of 27 April 2007.

116 Decision no. 660 of 4 July 2007, published in the Official Gazette of Romania no. 525 of 2 August 2007.

117 Decision no. 797 of 27 September 2007, published in the Official Gazette of Romania no. 707 of 19 October 2007.

118 Decision no. 1059 of 14 November 2007, published in the Official Gazette of Romania no. 860 of 17 December 2007.

119 Decision no. 1137 of 4 December 2007, published in the Official Gazette of Romania no. 31 of 15 January 2008.

- upheld the exception of unconstitutionality of Article 35 (2) i) sentence I and, by extension, the provisions of Article 63 (3) and (4) of Law no. 273/2004 on the legal status of adoption, and found that these provisions are unconstitutional to the extent that they do not stipulate the expression of the consent by natural parents before the court, together with the settlement of declaration of enforceability for the adoption[120];
- upheld the exception of unconstitutionality of the provisions of Article 50 (2) sentence II of Law no. 7/1996 on cadastre and real estate advertising, according to which: "The application against the decision shall be filed with the Local Office and shall be registered in the Land Register ex officio", and found that these provisions are unconstitutional to the extent that they do not also allow the direct access of the applicant to the competent court of law[121];
- upheld the exception of unconstitutionality of the provisions of Article 281 (1) of the Government Emergency Ordinance no. 34/2006 on the award of public procurement contracts, the concession contracts of public works and services, according to which: "The application shall be filed with the Council, under the penalty of nullity thereof, which shall submit the file to the competent court within three days after the deadline for lodging an appeal", and found that the text is unconstitutional to the extent that such text does not also allow that the complaint be directly addressed to the competent court[122];
- upheld the exception of unconstitutionality of the provisions of Article 121 (2) of Law no. 122/2006 on asylum in Romania and found that these provisions are unconstitutional to the extent they do not also stipulate either the possibility that the application be submitted directly to the court of law or the possibility to be also submitted by a representative[123];
- upheld exceptions of unconstitutionality formulated on the provisions of the Government Ordinance no. 137/2000 on the prevention and sanction of all forms of discrimination; the Court ruled that such provisions are unconstitutional to the extent that they result in the meaning that the courts of law have the power to cancel or refuse the enforcement of certain laws, considering that they are discriminatory, and to replace them with rules judicially established or with provisions set forth in normative acts which were not taken into account by the legislature when adopting the normative acts considered discriminatory[124];

---

120 Decision no. 369 of 20 March 2008, published in the Official Gazette of Romania no. 238 of 27 March 2008.

121 Decision no. 467 of 22 April 2008, published in the Official Gazette of Romania no. 422 of 5 June 2008.

122 Decision no. 569 of 15 May 2008, published in the Official Gazette of Romania no. 537 of 16 July 2008.

123 Decision no. 604 of 20 May 2008, published in the Official Gazette of Romania no. 469 of 25 June 2008.

124 Decision no. 818 of 3 July 2008, published in the Official Gazette of Romania no. 537 of 16 July 2008; Decision no. 819 of 3 July 2008, published in the Official Gazette

- upheld the exception of unconstitutionality and found that "the provisions of Article 20 (3) of the Government Ordinance no. 137/2000 on the prevention and sanction of all forms of discrimination are unconstitutional insofar as interpreted as granting competence to the National Council for Combating Discrimination, within its jurisdictional work, in order to cancel or refuse the enforcement of certain laws, considering them discriminatory, and to replace them with rules judicially established or with provisions set forth in other normative acts". The concerned legal provisions shall read as follows: "By the application lodged according to par. (1), the person who feels discriminated shall be entitled to request the removal of the consequences of the discriminatory acts and the restore of the situation before the discrimination"[125];
- upheld the exception of unconstitutionality of the provisions of Chapter I, "General Provisions" (Articles 1–9) of Law no. 144/2007 on the establishment, organization and operation of the National Integrity Agency, exception raised by the same author in the same case, before the same court, and found that these provisions are unconstitutional to the extent that they stipulate the competence of the National Integrity Agency to perform and draw up research and findings papers regarding the verification of assets, conflicts of interests and incompatibilities[126];
- upheld the exception of unconstitutionality and found that provisions of Article 123 (5) of Law no. 128/1997 on the status of teachers, according to which: "For eligible senior managing offices in higher education institutions, the provisions of Article 74 (2) and (3) shall apply without right of appeal", are unconstitutional to the extent that they prevent access to justice for procedural violations[127];
- upheld the exception of unconstitutionality of the provisions of Article 322 point 9 of the Code of Civil Procedure and found that the provisions of Article 322 point 9 of the Code of Civil Procedure are unconstitutional to the extent that these provisions do allow the review of a judgment which, without referring to the merits, infringed upon fundamental rights and freedoms, such violations being found by the European Court of Human Rights. The above mentioned legal text had the following wording: The review of a judgment that remained final before the court of appeal, or by not being appealed, as well as the review

---

of Romania no. 537 of 16 July 2008; Decision no. 820 of 3 July 2008, published in the Official Gazette of Romania no. 537 of 16 July 2008, Decision no. 821 of 3 July 2008, published in the Official Gazette of Romania no. 537 of 16 July 2008; Decision no. 1358 of 11 December 2008, published in the Official Gazette of Romania no. 886 of 29 December 2008.

125 Decision no. 997 of 7 October 2008, published in the Official Gazette of Romania no. 774 of 18 November 2008.

126 Decision no. 415 of 14 April 2010, published in the Official Gazette of Romania no. 294 of 5 May 2010.

127 Decision no. 1614 of 16 December 2010, published in the Official Gazette of Romania no. 118 of 16 February 2011.

of a judgment given by a court of appeal when it refers to the merits, may be required in the following cases: (...) 9. if the European Court of Human Rights found a violation of the fundamental rights or freedoms due to a judgment, and the serious consequences of such violation continues to occur and they can only be remedied by the review of the delivered judgment"[128];

- upheld the exception of unconstitutionality and found that the provisions of Article 257 (2) f) last sentence of Law no. 95/2006 on healthcare reform, as amended by Article I point 4 of the Government Emergency Ordinance no. 107/2010 amending and supplementing Law no. 95/2006 on healthcare reform, are unconstitutional insofar as interpreted that the amount of the minimum contribution to the health insurance fund, owed by people who receive income from the transfer of use of property, income from dividends and interest, income from intellectual property rights achieved individually and/or within a form of association, and other income subject to income tax, cannot be less that the amount of the national gross minimum wage, monthly.[129];
- upheld the exception of unconstitutionality of the provisions of Article 44 (3) of the Government Ordinance no. 92/2003 regarding the Code of Fiscal Procedure and found that these provisions are unconstitutional insofar as interpreted that the issuing fiscal body may proceed to communicate the fiscal administrative act through advertising, thus removing the unjustified order regarding the achievement of the communication methods provided for by Article 44 (2) a) d) of the same Ordinance. According to the impugned legal text: "Communication through advertising shall be achieved by publishing a notice stating that a fiscal administrative act was issued on behalf of the taxpayer, simultaneously on the premises of the issuing fiscal body and on the website of the National Agency for Fiscal Administration. For administrative acts issued by the tax authorities provided for by Article 35, the publication shall be performed simultaneously at their premises and on the website of the concerned local public tax authority; in case of no website, the publication shall be achieved on the website of the county council. In all cases, the fiscal administrative act shall be deemed communicated within 15 days from the date of publishing the notice"[130];
- upheld the exception of unconstitutionality and found that provisions of Article 320^1 of the Code of Criminal Procedure are unconstitutional to the extent that the provisions remove the implementation of the more favourable criminal law[131];

128 Decision no. 233 of 15 February 2011, published in the Official Gazette of Romania no. 340 of 17 May 2011.

129 Decision no. 335 of 10 March 2011, published in the Official Gazette of Romania no. 355 of 23 May 2011.

130 Decision no. 536 of 28 April 2011, published in the Official Gazette of Romania no. 482 of 7 July 2011.

131 Decision no. 1470 of 8 November 2011, published in the Official Gazette of Romania no. 853 of 2 December 2011.

- upheld the exception of unconstitutionality and found that the provisions of Article 1 h) of Law no. 119/2010 on the establishment of certain measures on pensions and of Article 196 j) of Law no. 263/2010 on the unitary public pension system are unconstitutional to the extent that these provisions also apply to audit counsellor[132];
- upheld the exception of unconstitutionality and found that the provisions of Article 21 (2) first sentence of Law no. 554/2004 on Administrative Contentious are unconstitutional insofar as interpreted in the meaning that final and irrevocable judgements delivered by courts of appeal, in violation of the principle of priority of EU law, cannot be subject to revision when they do not evoke the merits of the case[133];
- upheld the exception of unconstitutionality and found that the provisions of Article 257 (2) e) of Law no. 95/2006 on healthcare reform, in their wording since the entry into force and until the amendments made by the Government Emergency Ordinance no. 93/2008 amending and supplementing Law no. 95/2006 on healthcare reform, are unconstitutional to the extent that these provisions oblige the persons who owe the health insurance contribution on pension income to pay this contribution accumulated to the one owed for the income from the transfer of use of property, income from dividends and interest, income from intellectual property rights achieved individually and/or within a form of association, and other income subject to income tax[134].

3.4.3 General characterisation

As a general observation, we note that the interpretative decisions were delivered by the Constitutional Court of Romania especially within the *a posteriori* constitutional review, for the settlement of the exceptions of unconstitutionality.

One possible explanation is given by the fact that the subject-matter of the ***a priori*** constitutional review is the law adopted by Parliament that has not entered into force and has not taken legal effects so as the flaw of unconstitutionality is easy to be remedied and even preferably to be remedied by the legislature's intervention. However, the Court delivered some interpretative solutions, thus allowing the promulgation and enforcement of the law in situations where:

132 Decision no. 297 of 27 March 2012, published in the Official Gazette of Romania no. 309 of 9 May 2012.

133 Decision no. 1039 of 5 December 2012, published in the Official Gazette of Romania no. 61 of 29 January 2013.

134 Decision no. 164 of 12 March 2013, published in the Official Gazette of Romania no. 296 of 23 May 2013.

- it was needed the urgent entry into force of the law[135];
- the unconstitutionality of the law was not determined by substantive or procedural aspects, but by the non-observance of the principle of legal certainty in relation to the date of entry into force so that a new parliamentary debate would have been deprived of its practical utility[136];
- the constitutional issue consisted in an interpretation in conjunction with the legal provisions, in a direction compatible with the Constitution, also under the principle of legal certainty[137].

As concerns the ***a posteriori*** review, as it includes the legal provisions in force, the role and the need for interpretative decisions are much stronger, resulting in their much numerous number. Enshrining the norm an interpretation which would make it consistent with the Constitution, where possible and necessary, is likely to achieve a more subtle constitutionalisation or – as shown – a less aggressive one of the regulatory system, without requiring the intervention of the legislature in order to remedy the flaw of constitutionality.

Likewise, we note that there are both decisions finding the constitutionality under the reserve of interpretation and decisions finding the unconstitutionalality under reserve of interpretation. The interpretations of the Constitutional Court are usually designed to supplement the shortcomings of the law or to lead to an interpretation that is in compliance with the Constitution and the actual methods to accomplish such action are quite different. As for the diversity of such methods, the practice of the Constitutional Court of Romania is similar to the Italian one, which delivers both admission and rejection decisions under the reserve of interpretation.

---

135 Decision no. 1414 of 4 November 2009, published in the Official Gazette of Romania no. 796 of 23 November 2009, where the substance of the impugned law criticized aimed, as shown by its title, at adopting certain measures on the reorganization of public authorities and institutions, rationalization of public expenditure, business support and compliance with the framework agreements with the European Commission and the International Monetary Fund, therefore, urgent measures.

136 Decision no. 334 of 26 June 2013, published in the Official Gazette of Romania no. 407 of 5 July 2013, by which it was rejected the objection of unconstitutionality of the provisions of Law amending and supplementing Law no. 3/2000 on the organisation and holding of the referendum and found that the provisions of Law amending the supplementing Law no. nr. 3/2000 on the organisation and holding of the referendum are constitutional to the extent that they shall not apply to referendums organized within one year since the entry into force of the law.

137 Decision no. 731 of 10 July 2012, published in the Official Gazette of Romania no. 478 of 12 July 2012, by which the Court found that Law amending Article 10 of Law no. 3/2000 on the organisation and holding of the referendum is constitutional, to the extent that it ensures participation in the referendum of at least half plus one of the persons registered on the permanent electoral lists.

Such decisions are classified into two categories: additive and substitute[138]. We refer to decisions by which the Constitutional Court of the Italian Republic[139] introduces a rule that is not included in the examined provision or an interpretation that does not derive from the examined provision.

Equally, examples are also provided by the case-law of the Constitutional Council of France[140], which delivers decisions under the reserve of neutralizing, constructive or directive interpretation. As concerns the first category, such decisions try to eliminate the "poison of unconstitutionality" by discarding the unconstitutional interpretation, usually in criminal matters where are most often used. As for the directive reserve, the interpretation indicates how the law should be applied to its recipients, entailing a limitation for the authorities called upon to apply it. By the reserve of constructive interpretation, the Constitutional Council supplements the lacks in the legal text in order to comply with the Constitution.

In Germany, under the name of "partial qualitative annulment", the constitutional judge also ascertains the nullity – but not of the legal text, but of the possible unconstitutional interpretations. Thus, the norm remains in the active fund of the legislation while the judge finds it unconstitutional to the extent that such norm applies in one way or another, decisively and the reserve of interpretation has a neutralizing role of unconstitutional interpretation.

Having analyzed the mentioned examples in the case-law of the Constitutional Court of Romania, we find that they fall into the typologies presented in the comparative law, as well as into the trends in this respect, a phenomenon that is partly the result of the dialogue between the constitutional courts.

3.4.4 Effects of the interpretative decisions

General characterisation

Constitutional texts do not distinguish, in terms of the effects of Constitutional Court's decisions, in relation to their belonging to one typology: all decisions are generally binding, in their whole given by the operative part and the recitals that support it. However, given the complexity of the effects that the interpretative decisions produce, it is necessary to analyze these effects whose customization was judicially achieved by the Constitutional Court.

In case of finding the constitutionality or unconstitutionality of the law in a particular interpretation, this law does not cease its applicability, but it continues to exist in active fund of the legislation and only the unconstitutional interpretations/interpretations shall be discarded.

---

138 V. Crisafulli, *Le sentenze "interpretative" della Corte Costituzionale*, in Riv.Trim. dir. e proc. civ., 1967, p. 1 s, *apud* M. Troper, *cited paper*, p. 164.

139 For a full examination of the techniques used by the Constitutional Court of Italy, see V.C. Colapietro, *La giurisprudenza costituzionale nella crisi dello Stato sociale*, Padoue, Cedam, 1996, *apud* M. Troper, *cited paper*, p. 164.

140 M. Troper, *cited paper*, p. 165.

As concerns the interpretation found to be constitutional, it is *erga omnes* binding under Article 147 (4) of the Constitution. The Court held in this regard that "irrespective of the interpretations that can be brought to a text, when the Constitutional Court ruled that only one interpretation is consistent with the Constitution, maintaining thus the presumption of constitutionality of the text in this interpretation, both the courts of law and the administrative bodies must comply with the Court's decision and apply it accordingly".

In such a situation where the exception of unconstitutionality is allowed, the provisions of Article 29(3) of Law no. 47/1992, according to which "provisions whose unconstitutionality has been found by prior decision of the Constitutional Court cannot form the subject-matter of an exception"[141]. Therefore, to challenge again the constitutionality of interpretations that have already been excluded from the constitutional framework is tantamount to the infringement of Article 147 (4) of the Constitution in conjunction with Article 29(3) of Law no. 47/1992: "to raise again an exception of unconstitutionality on the same text and on the same grounds tends to infringe the generality binding nature of the Constitutional Court's decision, which is attached including to decisions finding the constitutionality of laws or orders or provisions thereof"; likewise, the following are rejected as inadmissible of such exceptions of unconstitutionality: Decision no. 167 of 26 September 2000[142], Decision no. 145 of 8 May 2001[143] or Decision no. 245 of 18 September 2001[144].

The subject-matter of the constitutional review, including through another exception, may be only the interpretation of the legal norm that has not been discarded from the constitutional framework[145] (either explicitly, by finding the unconstitutionality or implicitly, by finding the constitutionality of another interpretation of the text of reference). The challenge of the latter resulted in the rejection of the referral as inadmissible.

We believe that "saving" the norm in a certain interpretation given by the Constitutional Court should not be followed by the legislature's state of passivity. Even if the norm found constitutional or unconstitutional in a certain interpretation continues to apply within the interpretation established as constitutional, it is desirable that the action of the Constitutional Court to be supplemented by the action of the legislature in order to draft the norm by removing the meaning found unconstitutional or to introduce the necessary supplements within the meaning of the Constitutional Court's decision. Practice proves such interventions of the legislature.

Sometimes such amendments occur shortly after the Constitutional Court's decision is published in the Official Gazette of Romania, an example in this regard is Law

---

141 Decision no. 898 of 30 June 2011, published in the Official Gazette of Romania no. 706 of 6 October 2011.

142 Published in the Official Gazette of Romania no. 642 of 8 December 2000.

143 Published in the Official Gazette of Romania no. 320 of 14 June 2001.

144 Published in the Official Gazette of Romania no. 718 of 12 November 2001.

145 *Ibidem.*

no. 341/2013[146] amending and supplementing Law no. 3/2000 on the organization and carrying out of the referendum, to which Article II was introduced, according to which: "The provisions of this law shall enter into force one year after its publication in the Official Gazette of Romania, Part I". We shall mention that, adjudicating in an *a priori* review on the provisions of this law, the Constitutional Court found[147] that the provisions of the Law amending and supplementing Law no. 3/2000 on the organization and carrying out of the referendum are constitutional insofar as they do not apply to referendums carried out within one year of the entry into force of the law.

Sometimes, the legislative intervention is made at a considerable period of time, on the occasion of essential amendment to the normative acts of reference. For example, following the ascertainment of unconstitutionality of the provisions of the Family Code on the case regarding the denial of paternity, to the extent that these provisions acknowledge the right to file an application regarding the denial of paternity only to the father and not to the mother and the child born in lawful matrimony[148], at the adoption of the new Civil Code the norms of reference have been draw up in compliance with the decision of the Constitutional Court. Currently, Article 414 para. (2) of the Civil Code established that "the paternity can be denied if it is impossible for the mother's husband to be the father" and Article 429 para. (1) of the Code provides that "the application on the denial of paternity can be filed by the mother's husband, the mother, the biological father or the child. Such application can be also filed or, if appropriate, continued by their heirs, under the law". Thus, the interpretative decision resulted in the constitutionalisation effect of the right, on long-term, and determined that, at the adoption of a new legal norm on the same matter, its drafting to be in compliance with the constitutional meaning mentioned by the Court.

Effects of the interpretative decisions on the interpretations given by an appeal in the interest of the law

A distinct situation on the effects of interpretative decisions of the Constitutional Court appears when, upon the text found constitutional/ unconstitutional in a certain interpretation, the High Court of Cassation and Justice had already ruled in order to settle certain legal issues, either through an appeal in the interest of the law or through a prior judgment.

Thus, as concerns the effect of the Constitutional Court's decisions on the judgments pronounced by the High Court of Cassation and Justice within the settlement of the appeal in the interest of the law, Article 474[1] of the Code or Criminal Procedure provides that "the effects of the decision (A/N, the High Court of Cassation and Justice) ceases in case of repeal, of the ascertainment of unconstitutionality or of the

146 Published in the Official Gazette of Romania no. 787 of 16 December 2013.
147 Decision no. 334/2013, aforementioned.
148 Decision no. 349/2001, published in the Official Gazette of Romania no. 240 of 10 April 2002.

amendment of the legal provision that caused the legal issue which is to be settled, unless such legal provisions subsists in the new regulation". The cited text does not distinguish and, therefore, both the pure and simple decisions and the interpretative decisions delivered by the Constitutional Court take the same effect. Whereas, irrespective of the ascertainment of constitutionality or unconstitutionality of the law in a particular interpretation, the Constitutional Court's decisions belonging to this typology determined the removal of the unconstitutional meaning of the norm which is the subject-matter of the constitutional review. All interpretative decisions of the Constitutional Court will result in the cessation of the effects of the decision delivered by the High Court of Cassation and Justice in order to settle appeals in the interest of the law, to the extent that the interpretation given by the high court is found unconstitutional.

Effects of interpretative decisions on the interpretations given through prior judgments in order to settle certain legal issues

Likewise, the same legal reasoning applies when the High Court of Cassation and Justice delivers prior judgments in order to settle certain legal issues. In this case the provisions of Article 4771 of the Code of Criminal Procedure, according to which "the effects of the decision" (A/N, the High Court of Cassation and Justice) ceases in case of repeal, of the ascertainment of unconstitutionality or of the amendment of the legal provision that caused the legal issue which is to be settled, unless such legal provisions subsists in the new regulation". In this regard, for example by Decision no. 265 of 6 May 2014, the Constitutional Court, noting that by Decision no. 2 of 14 April 2014, the High Court of Cassation and Justice, the Panel for the settlement of certain legal issues in criminal matters, ruled that for the application of Article 5 of the Criminal Code, the statute of limitation for criminal liability is an autonomous concept in relation to the concept of penalty, giving unconstitutional meanings to Article 5 of the Criminal Code, within the given interpretation, found that "once this decision is published in the Official Gazette of Romania, the effects of Decision no. 2 of 14 April 2014 of the Supreme Court cease in accordance with the provisions of Article 147 para. (4) of the Constitution and with those of Article 4771 of the Code of Criminal Procedure".

3.4.5 Delimitations of competences

In its case-law, the Court stated that "the unconstitutionality is both an ultimate sanction applied by the constitutional court with repercussions on the normative existence of the law and a part of the normative legal order"[149]. From the perspective of legal certainty, it is sometimes preferable to establish a meaning of the norm in compliance with the Constitution, as the delivery of a simple or extreme decision

149 Decision no. 847 of 8 July 2008, published in the Official Gazette of Romania no. 605 of 14 August 2008; Decision no. 448 of 29 October 2013, published in the Official Gazette of Romania no. 5 of 7 January 2014.

represents a sanction of last resort. This type of intervention raises often criticism towards the Constitutional Court, in terms of the way in which the Court complies with the competence set forth by the Constitution in relation to the competence of other public authorities, especially of the courts of law and of the legislature, a issue which is to be discussed in subsections regarding the dialogue between the Constitutional Court and the legislature, respectively the courts of law.

We believe that the emergence and the increasing number of interpretative decision reveal the diversification of the instruments that the constitutional court can use within the constitutional review. The traditional approach, which conceives the Constitutional Court only as a "negative legislature", has experienced significant reconsiderations, due to the development of the constitutional review which shall be adapted to the increasingly complex legal issues that the constitutional judge shall settle.

In this context, we mention another practice of the constitutional courts, namely "modular" in time of the effects of the decisions delivered by such courts. Thus, for example, in *Germany*, the Federal Constitutional Court finds the non-compliance of the challenged normative act with the Constitution, but it does not declare its nullity, in order to give the legislature discretion and enough time for the adoption of new regulations, if the legislature must have several options in order to remove the unconstitutionality or if it is in the public interest that the transition from an unconstitutional state law to a constitutional one shall occur gradually (particularly where the declaration of nullity would create a situation less compatible with the Constitution than the one at the moment of the delivery of the decision). Among the envisaged measures there may also exist orders by which the application of the unconstitutional law may still be ordered, either with or without amendments. When the perpetuation of the unconstitutional provisions cannot be accepted, not even in an amended form, the Federal Constitutional Court itself shall formulate an order intended to be transitional or of reference. Having stated the non-compliance, the Federal Constitutional Court has also the possibility to refrain from ordering the continuation of the application of the unconstitutional law. But – unlike the declaration of nullity – such a solution is justified only if it simultaneously imposes a term during which the legislature shall enact a new legislation consistent with the Constitution, where the Court considers that a transitional regulation is not essential. Then, the unconstitutional provision shall become unenforceable until the entry into force of the new law and, as such, any proceedings at issue before the courts shall be suspended[150].

In France, Article 62 of the Constitution establishes the effects of the decisions of the Constitutional Council of France, as follows: within the *a priori* review, the provision found unconstitutional cannot be promulgated and implemented; within

---

150 G. Lübbe-Wolff, R. Mellinghoff, R. Gaier, *The Report of the Federal Constitutional Court of Germany at the XVth Congress of the Conference of European Constitutional Courts, Bucharest,* 23–25 May 2011, on *www.ccr.ro.*

the *a posteriori* review, the provision found unconstitutional shall cease its effects for the future, as of the publication date of the decision or at a later date provided therein and the Constitutional Council establishes the conditions and the limits under which the effects of the concerned provision may be challenged; the decisions of the Constitutional Council shall not be subject to appeal as they are binding for the public authorities and for all administrative and judicial authorities. Such provisions results in several legal consequences[151]. In the light of our study, the concern is represented by the possibility of the constitutional judge to "modulate" the effects of its decision both in time and in terms of the application of the challenged norm and to adopt, in the name of the principle of legal certainty, transitional measures regarding the effects of the proivsion which has been found unconstitutional. If the Constitutional Council shall establish such measures, the normative acts for their implementation have just the significance of certain complementary mentions[152].

Similarly, in *Belgium*, the establishment by the Constitutional Court of a term whithin which the legislature shall act, its responsibility to maintain the effects of an unconstitutional normative act until a future date, the ascertainment of the unconstitutionality of a legislative gap are seen as embodiments of the constitutional review, which, far from suppressing the powers of the legislature, gives it the very power of law-making[153].

In Romania there is no possibility for the constitutional court to postpone the effects of the delivered decision, namely to postpone the moment at which the norm found unconstitutional is to cease its effects, given the mandatory provisions of Article 147 para. (4) of the Constitution. However, the interpretative decisions shall be instruments that, in a manner which is not prohibited by constitutional provisions, can practically "modulate" these effects, under the same principle of legal certainty. Thus, such decisions shall allow the maintenance of the challenged norm in the active fund of the law through an interpretation according to the Constitution, until the clarifying intervention of the legislature and even in the absence of such clarification.

Even if the effects of the interpretative decisions within the constitutionalisation process of the law is undoubtedly a positive one, it is not less true that such development of the instrumentation of the constitutional review also requires the achievement of a "self-restraint", and the case-law of the constitutional court prove the search and the establishment of such limits, most often in achieving the legal and political distinction[154], but also in relation to the competence of the courts of

---

151 J.P. Camby, P. Fraisseix, J. Gicquel, *La revision de 2008, une nouvelle Constitution?*, LGDJ, Paris, 2011, p. 334.

152 *Ibidem*, p. 335.

153 M. Bossuyt, R. Leysen, *The Report of the Constitutional Court of Belgium at the XVth Congress of the Conference of European Constitutional Courts, Bucharest*, 23–25 May 2011, on *www.ccr.ro*.

154 See, for example, Decision *Baker v. Carr* of the Supreme Court of the United States of America, where there are mentioned criteria for the identification of a certain

law or of the main or delegated legislature. But since such limits are often difficult to be established, frequently the interpretative decisions are subject to controversies. The identification, on a case by case basis, of the solution meant to meet equally the principles of legal certainty, separation and balance of powers within the state and constitutional loyalty, under the supremacy of the Constitution, falls within the wisdom and balance of the constitutional courts. The development of the cooperation between the constitutional courts and, within such development, the recent concerns[155] for the creation of a common platform where the landmark decisions delivered by all such courts within the exercise of the constitutional review shall be reunited, will also contribute to the achievement of certain common benchmarks and coordinates in this regard at European and global level. Thus, the dialogue between the courts and, through it, the comparative law in constitutional matters gain a great importance.

---

political issue and for its distinction from a legal constitutional issue (L. Fisher, *American Constitutional law*, second edition, New York, McGraw-Hill, Inc., 1995, *apud* E. Zoller, *Droit Constitutionnel*, second edition, PUF, Paris, 1999, pp. 131–137).

155 Proposal discussed within the working session of the XVIth Congress of the Conference of European Constitutional Courts, Vienna, 12–14 May 2014.

II. The Dialogue of the Constitutional Judges at International Level

1. Constitutional framework[156]

It was claimed[157] that the incorporation of international acts on human rights to the constitutions of the states represents one of the current trends at global level[158] and one of the ways – perhaps the most important – by which the constitutions become "international" or "internationalized". To the extent that the rights guaranteed by the constitutions are convergent or even identical to those included in international documents, the constitutions become rather international, with consequences for the entire national legal system.

Falling into these trends, the constitutions of the European states that have recently adopted democratic regimes, as in the case of Romania, contain substantial chapters[159] dedicated to fundamental rights and freedoms with regulations accepted from international documents in the matter. Likewise, some of the new constitutions expressly enshrine the direct applicability and the higher legal status within the legal order of these acts, as well as the obligation of the courts to ensure their direct application[160]. Thus, for example, the Constitution of Bosnia and Herzegovina[161], in Article II – "Fundamental rights and freedoms" – provides in point 1 that it will ensure the highest level of protection of the fundamental rights and freedoms recognized internationally, and in point 2 that the rights and freedoms set out in the Convention for the Protection of Human Rights and in Additional Protocols shall apply directly to Bosnia and Herzegovina and take precedence over all other laws.

---

156 T. Toader, M. Safta, *Report, Part I*, at the works of the XVIth Congress of the Conference of the European Constitutional Courts, Vienna, 12–14 May 2014, *Constitutional Court between national and European law*, available on *http://www.vfgh.gv.at/cms/vfgh-kongress/en/xvi-kongress-2014.html*; T. Toader, M. Safta, *Acceptance of the case-law of the European Court of Human Rights through constitutional review*, in *In Honorem Constantin Bîrsan*, Hamangiu Publishing House, Bucharest, pp. 817–827.

157 W.-C. Chang, J.-R. Yeh, *Internationalization of constitutional law*, in The Oxford Handbook of Comparative Constitutional Law, Oxford University Press, 2012, p. 1167.

158 See, for the relation the recognition of fundamental rights-constitutional review, R. Hirschl, *Towards juristocracy. The origins and consequences of the new constitutionalism*, Harvard University Press, 2007, pp. 17–30.

159 For example, the Constitution of Croatia comprises 55 articles on fundamental rights and freedoms (Title III, "Protection of fundamental rights and freedoms", Articles 14–69), on *http://legislationline.org*.

160 For examples, further, see W.-C. Chang, J.-R. Yeh, *cited paper*, p. 1168.

161 *http://legislationline.org/documents/section/constitutions.*

Point 6 of the same article states that all courts, agencies, governmental bodies in Bosnia and Herzegovina shall observe and enforce the provisions on the protection and guarantee of fundamental rights. The direct applicability, as a result of constitutional provisions, international regulations on human rights, can be also found in European states with a long-standing democratic tradition. Thus, as concerns the Convention for the Protection of Human Rights and Fundamental Freedoms, it has acquired in some states, as a result of the ratification, the status of constitutional law (for example: Austria), in others a high or low position of the Constitution (for example: France[162], Cyprus, Spain, Portugal) or the status of ordinary law (for example: Italy, San Marino)[163].

Another way of incorporating the above-mentioned international regulation in the national legal system is that of legal interpretation. National courts use them in the recitals of the pronounced judgments – with or without a clear constitutional or legal term of reference – or use the interpretations which the supranational courts or the courts in other states give to certain texts of principle relating to fundamental rights and freedoms, resulting in fertilization cross[164], as the doctrine called it, i.e. the accumulation of experiences and judgments of courts in other states, as well as the international ones, with a role of expanding the constitutionalisation process worldwide.

The Constitution of Romania regulates the relationship between legal rules originating from domestic and international law and the harmonization thereof: Article 11, "International law and domestic law", Article 20, "International human rights treaties", and Article 148, "Integration into the European Union".

The provisions of Article 11 of the Constitution read as follows:

Article 11: "*(1) The Romanian State pledges to fulfil as such and in good faith any obligations as may derive from the treaties to which it has become a party.*

(2) Once ratified by Parliament, subject to the law, treaties shall be part of domestic law.

(3) Where a treaty to which Romania is to become party comprises provisions contrary to the Constitution, ratification shall only be possible after a constitutional revision".

---

162 N. Lenoir, *The response of the French Constitutional Court to the Growing Importance of International Law* apud D. Spielmann, *Jurisprudence of the European Court of Human Rights and the constitutional system of Europe*, in The Oxford Handbook of Comparative Constitutional Law, Oxford University Press, 2012, p. 1238.

163 See, further: C. Bîrsan, *European Convention on Human Rights. Comments on articles. Volume I Rights and Freedoms*, All Beck Publishing House, Bucharest, 2005, p. 100; O. Predescu, *The influence of the European Convention for the protection of human rights and fundamental freedoms on the national law of the Member States of the Council of Europe*, in Analele Universităţii Constantin Brâncuşi of Târgu Jiu, Series Legal Sciences, no. 2/2010, on *http://www.utgjiu.ro/revista/jur/pdf/2010-02/3.*

164 C. Saunders, *Judicial engagement with comparative law*; T. Ginsburg, R. Dixon, *Comparative constitutional law*, Elgar Publishing Ltd, 2011, p. 589.

The provisions of 20 of the Constitution read as follows:

Article 20: "*(1) The constitutional provisions relative to the citizens' rights and freedoms shall be interpreted and applied in conformity with the Universal Declaration of Human Rights, with the covenants and other treaties to which Romania is a party.*

(2) Where inconsistency exists between the covenants and treaties on fundamental human rights to which Romania is a party, and national law, the international regulations shall prevail except where the Constitution or domestic laws comprise more favourable provisions".

The provisions of Article 148 of the Constitution, relevant from the viewpoint of this analysis, read as follows:

Article 148: "*(2) Following accession, provisions in the founding Treaties of the European Union, as well as other binding regulations under community law shall prevail over any contrary provisions of domestic law, while observing provisions in the accession instrument.*

((3) Provisions of paragraphs (1) and (2) shall also apply accordingly for the accession to any instrument purporting a revision of the founding Treaties of the European Union.

(4) The Parliament, the President of Romania, the Government, and the judicial authority shall guarantee that any obligations arising from the accession instrument and from provisions under paragraph (2) are put into effect.

(...)".

From reading the three cited texts, we draw the following conclusions:

- treaties ratified by Parliament are part of national law; in the domestic law they have the legal force and position in the hierarchy of normative acts given by the instrument of ratification with the appropriate consequences; the notion of "international treaty" has a broad sense, this includes international acts regardless of their designation (treaty, convention, protocol, charter, statutes, memorandum, etc.);
- human rights treaties to which Romania is a party constitute a separate category: these are integrated in the "constitutional block" and they may have, as appropriate, an infraconstitutional power (a conventional rule in conflict with a constitutional clear rule), strictly constitutional or supra-constitutional (a more favourable conventional rule in conflict with a constitutional generic rule, indefinite and more restrictive), but in any of the assumptions we refer to the supralegislative power[165]; human right treaties to which Romania is a party have priority of application in case of inconsistency with national laws, unless the Constitution or national laws comprise more favourable provisions;
- constituent treaties of the European Union (and other binding community regulations) represent also a category of international acts with a distinct legal

165 C.-L. Popescu, *International protection of human rights– sources, institutions, procedures,* All Beck Publishing House, Bucharest, 2000, pp. 262–269.

status, meaning that they take precedence over the contrary provisions of the national laws; they have a supralegislative but infraconstitutional position.

The provisions of Article 20 and Article 148 of the Constitution require national courts to apply with precedence the provisions of international treaties ("the covenants and other treaties on fundamental human rights to which Romania is a party", respectively "the founding treaties of the European Union, as well as other binding regulations under community law"), if national laws contain contrary provisions [except for the situation envisaged by Article 20 para. (2) final sentence of the Constitution, meant to assure a high protection of fundamental rights and freedoms].

As regards the competence of the Constitutional Court and the constitutional obligations it has to comply with in terms of European law, we distinguish between European human rights treaties and the constituent treaties of the European Union and other binding community regulations.

Concerning the first category mentioned, integration of "the covenants and other treaties to which Romania is a party" in the so-called "constitutional block", means that they constitute, by means of Article 20 of the Constitution, reference standards for the constitutional review. In time, the case-law of the Constitutional Court of Romania has invoked more often Article 20 of the Constitution, in particular by reference to the Convention for the Protection of Human Rights and Fundamental Freedoms and to its interpretation in the case-law of the European Court of Human Rights. The Constitutional Court of Romania has repeatedly held that "following ratification by Romania of the Convention for the Protection of Human Rights and Fundamental Freedoms, through Law no. 30 of 18 May 1994, this Convention became part of the national law, and therefore references to any of its texts is subject to the same regime as that applicable to references to the provisions of the Basic Law"[166].

Referring to European Union law, therefore the interpretation and application of Article 148 of the Constitution, the case-law of the Constitutional Court of Romania has evolved to give rise to essentially the following conclusions:

- The Constitution is the only direct reference standard within the constitutional review;
- European standards can be used within constitutional review only as a rule interposed the direct reference rule (which can only be the Constitution), upon compliance with certain objective conditions (regarding the clarity of the rule) and a subjective condition (relating to the margin of appreciation of the constitutional relevance of the European rule). To this effect, the Constitutional Court of Romania held that "a European legal norm within the constitutional review as replacing the reference one [A/N the Constitution of Romania] involves under Article 148(2) and (4) of the Constitution, a cumulative compliance: on the one

166 Decision no. 146 of 14 July 2000, published in the Official Gazette of Romania no. 566 of 15 November 2000.

hand, this rule must be sufficiently clear, precise and unambiguous in itself or its meaning must have been clearly, precisely and unequivocally established by the Court of Justice of the European Union, on the other hand, that the rule must be circumscribed to a certain level of constitutional relevance so as its legal content might support the possible infringement by the national law of the Constitution – the only direct reference standard in its review of constitutionality. In such a case the Constitutional Court approach is distinct from the simple application and interpretation of the law, jurisdiction belonging to courts and administrative authorities, or from any issues of legislative policy promoted by the Parliament or Government, as appropriate." Constitutional relevance assessment lies with the Constitutional Court of Romania.

A special case is that of the Charter of Fundamental Rights of the European Union, on which the Constitutional Court of Romania established that, in principle, it is applicable within the constitutional review "insofar as it ensures, guarantees and develops the constitutional provisions in the matter of fundamental rights, in other words, to the extent that their level of protection is at least at the level of constitutional rules in the matter of human rights."[167] It is worth specifying that the constitutional basis for invoking the Charter lies in Article 148 of the Constitution, not in Article 20, the Constitutional Court mentioning in this respect[168] the following: "*as concerns the provisions of Article 41 of the Charter of Fundamental Rights of the European Union concerning the right to good administration, the Court notes, first, that they can be invoked in terms of Article 148 and not of Article 20 of the Constitution, as indicated by the author of the exception, because, according to Article 6 (1) of the Treaty on European Union (consolidated version), «The Union recognises the rights, freedoms and principles set out in the Charter of Fundamental Rights of the European Union of 7 December 2000, as adapted at Strasbourg, on 12 December 2007, which shall have the same legal value as the Treaties»*".

Consequently, Article 20 of the Constitution substantiates the constitutional review in relation to European human rights treaties to which Romania is a party. In exercising this review, the Constitutional Court does not make a direct "comparison" between domestic laws and the international treaty / convention, but an analysis mediated by the provisions of the Constitution interpreted in the light of the treaty.

On the grounds of Article 148 of the Constitution, the rules of the European Union law may be a reference tool for constitutional review, with the differentiations established by the constitutional text, within the limits and upon the appreciation of the Constitutional Court of Romania.

---

167 Decision no. 871 of 25 June 2010, published in the Official Gazette of Romania no. 433 of 28 June 2010.

168 Decision no. 12 of 22 January 2013, published in the Official Gazette of Romania no. 114 of 28 February 2013; in the same respect it is also Decision no. 967 of 20 November 2012, published in the Official Gazette of Romania no. 853 of 18 December 2012.

Given the constitutional texts cited above and in particular the provisions of Article 20 of the Constitution, the following are frequently invoked before the Constitutional Court of Romania:

- ✓ The Convention for the Protection of Human Rights and Fundamental Freedoms;
- ✓ the Universal Declaration on Human Rights;
- ✓ the International Covenant on Civil and Political Rights;
- ✓ the International Covenant on Economic, Social and Cultural Rights.

There are also references and other sources of international law, as a rule, those bearing on human rights and fundamental freedoms, most often due to their invocation by the authors of referrals brought before the Court, such as, for example:

- ✓ The Revised European Social Charter, adopted in Strasbourg on 3 May 1996[169];
- ✓ the European Charter for Regional or Minority Languages[170].

In the past years, the Charter of Fundamental Rights of the European Union has been more often invoked. In addressing the issue of reference to sources of European law, we cannot forget the references to the case-law of the European Court of Human Rights, respectively the case-law of the Court of Justice of the European Union.

Starting from the cited constitutional basis and taking into account the role and the position of the Constitutional Court, on the one hand, and of the other mentioned courts, on the other hand, those courts have achieved relationships between them that can be circumscribed to the concept of judicial dialogue.

2. The dialogue between the Constitutional Court of Romania and the European Court of Human Rights

2.1 The position and the role of the European Court of Human Rights in the European constitutional framework

Given the position and the role of the European Court of Human Rights that, furthermore, those of the Court of Justice of the European Union, in terms of the powers that they perform in matters of the protection of fundamental rights and freedoms, it has been expressed the idea according to which they can be considered European constitutional courts[171]. This is because, in matter of fundamental rights, the concerned courts face problems similar to those raised before the national constitutional courts

169 See, for example, Decision no. 5 of 17 January 2013, published in the Official Gazette of Romania no. 109 of 25 February 2013.

170 See, for example, Decision no. 114 of 20 July 1999, published in the Official Gazette of Romania no. 370 of 3 August 1999.

171 A. Voβkuhle, *Multilevel Cooperation of the European Constitutional Courts*, in European Constitutional Law review no. 6/2010, p. 175.

and exercise the judicial review based on a charter of fundamental rights and on procedures comparable to those of constitutional courts.

From this perspective, the relationship between the European Court of Human Rights and the constitutional courts, in a broad sense, are understood as an expression of cooperation on many levels, operating on the basis of systemic concepts such as: unity, difference and diversity, homogeneity and pluralism, separation, interaction and involvement[172].

This view[173], which has the merit of avoiding simplistic approaches such as superiority / subordination and juxtaposition, in favour of autonomy, respect and the ability to act jointly[174], was expressed, in fact, by the European Court of Human Rights. An example in this regard is the work during the XIIth Congress of the Conference of European Constitutional Courts, the President of the European Court of Human Rights has revealed the role of this Court as actor in the field of European constitutional justice, as well as the fact it that works in partnership with national constitutional courts, as a quasiconstitutional court. According to the statements made, what is not in doubt is that the issues which it is called upon to decide are constitutional issues in so far as they concern the fundamental rights of European citizens. These issues are settled at national level, by constitutional courts and national courts. From this perspective, the review exercised by the European Court of Human Rights is a fail-safe device designed to catch the ones that get away from the rigorous scrutiny of the national constitutional bodies[175]. From this perspective, the constitutional court, and in general, the national judge, appears to be the first charged with the task of achieving the protection of fundamental rights and freedoms and, in terms of reference to the European standards concerning these rights, a main "actor" in the process of legislative harmonization and integration of these standards at national level.

This role is supported and facilitated by the existence of legal mechanisms for interconnection between the national level and the international level of protection of human rights, designed for an efficient protection thereof. In Romania, what customizes the dialogue between the Constitutional Court of Romania and the European Court of Human Rights is the substantiation of the cooperation mechanism at the constitutional level.

Given the competence of the European Court of Human Rights, the judicial dialogue analyzed in the present case is circumscribed to the issue on the protection of fundamental rights and freedoms, which constitutes in itself an overall theme of

---

172 A. Voßkuhle, *The protection of human rights within the European cooperation of Courts*, presented at the works of the Venice Commission, 9 March 2013, Venice, Italy, p. 4, on *http://www.venice.coe.int.*

173 *Ibidem.*

174 *Ibidem.*

175 L. Wildhaber, *The place of the European Court of Human Rights in the European Constitutional landscape*, on *http://www.confcoconsteu.org/reports/rep-xii/Report%20 ECHR-EN.pdf.*

dialogue especially under the European system for the protection of fundamental rights where three different types of normative order subsist: national, supranational and international, each with its own laws and institutions for the protection of fundamental rights which overlap and interconnect to provide a comprehensive and enhanced protection of those rights[176]. The Convention for the Protection of Human Rights and Fundamental Freedoms[177], developed within the Council of Europe and signed in Rome on 4 November 1950, is one of the most effective instruments for the protection of fundamental rights, taking into consideration its place in the legal system of the Member States that have ratified the Convention, as well as that fact that it has its own supranational jurisdictional mechanism which shall be taken into account by these Member States[178].

Starting from the constitutional basis which substantiates the relations between the Constitutional Court of Romania and the European Court of Human Rights, we will examine how the mutual acceptance of the case-law of these courts is achieved, equated to the concept of judicial dialogue, as well as the effects of this dialogue.

2.2 Forms of dialogue between the Constitutional Court of Romania and the European Court of Human Rights

2.2.1 General aspects

What customizes the relations between the two Courts is the substantiation of the cooperation mechanism at the constitutional level, by regulating the correlation between national and international legislation in the matter of human rights. The correlation is ensured by the provisions of Article 20 of the Constitution.

Romania became a member of the Council of Europe on 7 October 1993 and on 20 June 1994 ratified the Convention for the Protection of Human Rights and Fundamental Freedoms, thereby this act integrated to the "block of constitutionality". In this respect, the Constitutional Court of Romania held in several decisions that "the ratification by Romania of the Convention for the Protection of Human Rights and Fundamental Freedoms by Law no. 30 of 18 May 1994 published in the Official Gazette of Romania, Part I, no. 135 of 31 May 1994 made this Convention to become part of domestic law, where reporting to any of its texts requires the same regime as the one applicable when reporting to the provisions of the Basic Law"[179]. The same binding nature was established by the Constitutional Court for the interpretation

176 J.S. Bergé, *Legal Application, Global Legal Pluralism and Hierarchies of Norms, European Journal of Legal Studies*, vol. 4, Issue 2 (Autumn/Winter 2011), pp. 241–263.

177 Hereinafter Convention.

178 See Articles 19 and 46 of the Convention; for developments see C. Bîrsan, *European Convention on Human Rights. Comments on articles, volume I, Rights and Freedoms*, All Beck Publishing House, Bucharest, 2005, p. IX.

179 Decision no. 146 of 14 July 2000, published in the Official Gazette of Romania no. 566 of 15 November 2000.

given by the European Court of Human Rights to the texts of the Convention, the constitutional review is often accomplished in light of the constitutional provisions of Articles 11 and 20 and in relation to the practice of this court.

With reference to this concept and particularity, the dialogue between the European Court of Human Rights and the Constitutional Court of Romania can be found by examining the case-law of the two Courts and the cooperation relations established between them, resulting in the orientation to a common language and common standards in order to achieve the protection of human rights and fundamental freedoms, within certain relationships of mutual respect.

The provisions of Article 20 of the Constitution determines that the European Court to be more than just a dialogue partner, its case law provides a mandatory reference framework for the Constitutional Court of Romania, with the specificity determined by the role of the constitutional court and the limits of its jurisdiction. The Romanian constitutional judge assumed his role and authority to ensure the acceptance of the Convention and European court's practice, with effects in the regulation of the issue of fundamental rights and freedoms, as well as in the application of these regulations by national courts. In the practice of the contentious constitutional court there can be identified decisions which, in the interpretation of the constitutional texts on human rights, give priority to the provisions of the Convention, when they are more favourable, as well as decisions which are based, in the determination of the content of the constitutional concepts, on the provisions of the Convention and the interpretation given to them by the European Court of Human Rights. The comparative examination of reference standards in matters of human rights and fundamental freedoms may also reveal situations where the provisions of the Constitution of Romania are more favourable than the regulations of the Convention in the matter; in such case the Constitutional Court held that the constitutional texts take precedence to the detriment of the Convention's texts, less favourable.

The dialogue between the two courts is reflected during official meetings and national and international conferences, as well as judicial ones: respectively the uses/references, as appropriate, to the solutions and interpretations comprised by the acts they pronounce.

2.2.2 The dialogue achieved during official meetings, national and international conferences

Such meetings are held annually on the occasion of the official opening of the judicial year at the European Court of Human Rights, as well as of other activities held within such framework at Strasbourg. These events also approach the relations between the national constitutional courts and the European Court of Human Rights, the case-law, as well as the development of their relations.

Likewise, during the visits of the representatives of the European Court of Human Rights[180] in Romania, important milestones of cooperation and mutual positioning between the two courts have been underlined in order to achieve the common power for the protection of fundamental rights. As concerns the role of the Constitutional Court, it has been noted that it "represents an important factor of the prevalence of law and the protection of citizens' rights and freedoms in this state", and its existence and work "bring to life the principle of subsidiarity underlying the system of the European Convention of Human Rights and of the Court of Strasbourg".

As for the relations between the European Court of Human Rights and the national courts, it was noted that "the constitutional courts and the supreme ones are also High Contracting Parties, so full partners", with whom it is important to maintain permanent relations of exchange and information, especially on the case-law, "as the human rights case is too important so that an international court arrogates to itself any monopoly in this matter"[181]. During such meetings and in the context of the examination of the role of constitutional jurisdiction for the protection of fundamental rights and the importance given by the Constitutional Court of Romania to the Convention and to the interpretation given by the European Court of Human Rights to the Convention, the recent decisions of the European Court of Human Rights regarding Romania were analyzed and, in this context, it was also analyzed the issue of restitution of nationalized property in connection with the Pilot Judgment in Case *Maria Atanasiu and others v. Romania,* where possible solutions in order to avoid future convictions of the Romanian state were discussed[182].

Joint debates were also occasioned by the seminar entitled "Partners for the protection of human rights: Development of the interaction between the European Court of Human Rights and national courts", held by the Council of Europe in Strasbourg, between 9 and 10 September 2002 and, more recently, by the Conference on "Impact of the European Convention on Human Rights and the Case Law on Democratic Changes and Developments Eastern Europe", held at the European Court of Human Rights in Strasbourg, on 18 February 2013.

These actions are accompanied by projects held at national level, an example in this regard is the national conference organized by the Constitutional Court of Romania with the topic "Case-Law of the Constitutional Court of Romania and the European Convention on Human Rights", the results of a larger project initiated and achieved by the Constitutional Court of Romania with the support of the Royal Ministry of Foreign Affairs of Norway. This project consisted in the publication of

180 In 2000, the President of the European Court of Human Rights, Mr. Luzius Wildhaber; in 2003, the Vice President of the European Court of Human Rights, Mr. Jean-Paul Costa, and in 2012, the Vice President of the Court, Mr. Josep Casadevall and the Registrar-in-Chief of Division III, Mr. Santiago Quesada.

181 See *http://193.226.121.81/default.aspx?page=publications/buletin/5/costa (www.ccr.ro).*

182 See *www.ccr.ro*, External relations, March 2012.

a collection of decisions of the Constitutional Court between 1994 and 2003, whose grounds were based on the Convention for the Protection of Human Rights and Fundamental Freedoms and on the case-law of the European Court of Human Rights, in the achievement of a website and the recording of a CD comprising the database included in the above-mentioned collection of decisions, in holding four regional workshops (Bucharest, Timişoara, Cluj-Napoca, Iaşi), attended by 176 judges from courts in 14 counties in Romania, Professors, other specialists in law, as well as in conducting a survey among the Romanian judges who attended these seminars on the basis of a questionnaire concerning the relations between judgments and the case-law of the European Court of Human Rights[183]. On the same line of concern, we should also mention the Protocol on cooperation between the Constitutional Court of Romania and the Ministry of Foreign Affairs, represented by the government co-officer for the European Court of Human Rights signed in 2011, whose purpose is to establish an institutional framework on cooperation and collaboration for mutual support within the scope of the two institutions.

The above-mentioned actions shall reveal the joint effort of the two Courts, within the limits of their own jurisdiction, in order to identify solutions for the full achievement of human rights and fundamental freedoms. This dialogue is also reflected at jurisprudential level.

2.2.3 *Acceptance of the case-law of the European Court of Human Rights through constitutional review*

2.2.3.1 *General aspects and statistical data*

Having examined the data concerning the work of the Constitutional Court of Romania, since its establishment[184], it appears that most of the admission decisions on the referrals addressed to the Constitutional Court (a number of 368 out of 481) were delivered following settlement of the objections of unconstitutionality, settlement of the exceptions of unconstitutionality raised by the parties before the courts of law, by the courts ex officio or by the Advocate of the People, and following the exercise of the constitutional review over the initiatives for the revision of the Constitution.

The circumstantiation of those cases took into account that the challenges therein are usually invoked on the violation of human rights and fundamental freedoms, opportunity for reference to the case-law of the European Court of Human Rights which, in many situations, represented the standard that resulted in the admission solution delivered by the Constitutional Court.

In terms of reliance upon the case-law of the European Court of Human Rights, we note the increased number of cases where the Constitutional Court refers to the

---

183 *www.ccr.ro*, see *The Case-law of the Constitutional Court and the European Convention on Human Rights.*

184 *www.cccr.ro*, Periodical statistics. The reference period taken into account for this statistics is up to 31 October 2014.

judgements of the Strasbourg Court, the increased number of judgements invoked, as well as the increased scope of fundamental rights concerned. Another trend is that of "inclusion" of judgements of the European Court of Human Rights within the a priori constitutional review, given that the decisions delivered by the Constitutional Court in the settlement of the objections of unconstitutionality contain more consistent references to that case-law, especially on issues of legislative technique, with consequences in terms of compliance with the principle of legal certainty.

If, according to a study conducted in 2005[185], between 1994 and 2003 the Constitutional Court invoked the texts of the Convention and the case-law of the European Court of Human Rights as grounds for about 380 decisions (out of the total of almost 3000 issued in that time interval), at present, the Constitutional Court invokes them in such a number in just one year. We consider the situation of 2012, when the Constitutional Court delivered a total of 1098 acts.

It is true that the number of cases decided by the Constitutional Court has experienced a significant increase over time. As it can be noted from examining the statistical data presented, the increase in the number of cases has not been determined, as one might think, by the introduction of new powers of the Constitutional Court during and after the constitutional revision in 2003. With or without the new powers, the substantial activity of the Constitutional Court of Romania consists of settlement of exceptions of unconstitutionality, which reveals the role of this Court in the protection of fundamental rights and freedoms, leading to its strengthening both in terms of volume and substance. And one of the factors behind this development is the reception by the Court, through the mechanism imposed by Article 20 of the Constitution, of the international reference standards, leading, in some cases, to the enrichment of constitutional safeguards of fundamental rights and freedoms, determined by their interpretation and application "in line" with the international regulations.

There were also certain situations, few in number, where the case-law of the Constitutional Court was in contradiction with the case-law of the European Court of Human Rights[186], such as Decision no. 21 of 3 February 2000[187], when the Constitutional Court of Romania established the constitutionality and conventionality of Article 91^1–91^5 of the Code of Criminal Procedure, meaning the acknowledgment of the prosecutor's right to authorise audio / video records. By Judgment of 26 April 2000 delivered in the Case Dumitru Popescu 2 v. Romania, the European Court of Human Rights established that such a conclusion "is certainly in contradiction with the Court's considerations (...) but, as regrettable as this situation may be, we must however recall that, in general, it is not the duty of the Court to analyze the fact or

---

185 See *supra*, section 2.2.2.

186 Further, see I.A. Motoc, *Constitutional Court of Romania and European Court of Human Rights. The development of a dialogue,* in Constitutional Review – tradition and perspectives, pp. 30–41.

187 Published in the Official Gazette of Romania no. 159 of 17 April 2000.

law errors allegedly committed by an internal court. (...) This aspect is also valid in the event it is about an error of application or interpretation of the Court's case-law by the national constitutional judge".

However, the case-law of the European Court of Human Rights represented the exceptions, overall, which had a significant influence on the case-law of the Constitutional Court and the dynamic relations between the two courts developed towards a visible dialogue at present.

2.2.3.2 Areas where the Judgments of the European Court of Human Rights significantly influenced the case-law of the Constitutional Court of Romania. Jurisprudential upturns

Principle of legal certainty. Quality of legislation

Interpreting and applying the constitutional provisions of Article 1 para. (3), stating that "Romania is a state governed by the rule of law (...) ", and of Article 1 para. (5) that "Observance of the Constitution, of its supremacy, and the laws shall be mandatory in Romania", in accordance with the relevant case-law of the European Court of Human Rights, the Constitutional Court of Romania identified four criteria that need to be observed in the law-making activity, subsumed under the principle of legal certainty.

Thus, by Decision no. 61/2007[188], declaring the unconstitutionality of the provisions of Article II para. (1) and (3) of Law no. 249/2006 amending and supplementing Law no. 393/2004 on the status of local elected officials, the Court stated that "the legal provisions under review, due to their improper wording, do not comply with the requirements of legislative technique for legal norms. As concerns these requirements, the European Court of Human Rights constantly stated that "a rule is "foreseeable" if it is formulated with sufficient precision so as to enable any individual – if need be with appropriate advice – to regulate his conduct" (case Rotaru v. Romania, 2000) and « (...)the citizen must be able to have an indication that is adequate in the circumstances of the legal rules applicable to a given case and to foresee, to a degree that is reasonable in the circumstances, the consequences which a given action may entail. In other words, the law must be, in the same time, accessible and foreseeable. » (Case of the Sunday Times v. the United Kingdom, 1979)". The conclusion of the Constitutional Court was that "the legal texts under review do not comply with the four criteria of clarity, precision, foreseeability and predictability as to enable an individual to regulate his conduct and therefore, avoid the consequences of the breach thereof."

Numerous other decisions of the Constitutional Court of Romania, many of admission of objections / exceptions of unconstitutionality, are based on the case law of the European Court of Human Rights in the same matter, respectively Judgements delivered in cases such as: Sunday Times v. The United Kingdom, 1979

188 Published in the Official Gazette of Romania no. 116 of 15 February 2007.

(see: Decision no. 54/2000[189]; Decision no. 189/2006[190]; Decision no. 604/2008[191]; Decision no. 710/2009[192]; Decision no. 838/2009[193]; Decision no. 1258/2009[194];Decision no. 1609/2010[195]; Decision no. 670/2011[196]; Decision no. 799/2011[197]; Decision no. 26/2012[198]; Decision no. 51/2012[199]; Decision no. 681/2012[200]; Decision no. 682/2012[201]), *Rotaru v. Romania, 2000* (see, besides the case-law mentioned above, which comprises, mostly, references to both cases, also: Decision no. 189/2006[202]; Decision no. 604/2008[203]; Decision no. 783/2009[204]; Decision no. 1/2012[205]; Decision no. 494/2012[206]), *Rekvényi v. Hungary, 1999* (Decision no. 799/2011[207]; Decision no. 51/2012[208]; Decision no. 682/2012[209]), *Leempoel & S.A. ED. Cine Revue v. Belgium, 2006*,and *Wingrove v. Great Britain, 1996* (both in Decision no. 1/2012[210]).

It appears that the breach of the requirements of clarity, precision, foreseeability and predictability of legal rules was itself grounds of unconstitutionality [in violation of this Article 1 para. (3) and (5) of the Constitution], or it was associated to violation of specific fundamental rights.

The first situation occurs usually within the a priori constitutional review, also taking into account the abstract nature of this review. For instance, the decisions of admission of the objections of unconstitutionality delivered in 2012, mentioning that within a third thereof the case-law of the European Court is invoked in relation to the violation of Article 1 (5) of the Constitution of Romania (four out of the total of 11 decisions of admission of the objections of unconstitutionality delivered by the Constitutional Court in 2012).

189 Published in the Official Gazette of Romania no. 310 of 5 July 2000.
190 Published in the Official Gazette of Romania no. 307 of 5 April 2006.
191 Published in the Official Gazette of Romania no. 469 of 25 June 2008.
192 Published in the Official Gazette of Romania no. 358 of 28 May 2009.
193 Published in the Official Gazette of Romania no. 461 of 3 July 2009.
194 Published in the Official Gazette of Romania no. 798 of 23 November 2009.
195 Published in the Official Gazette of Romania no. 70 of 27 January 2011.
196 Published in the Official Gazette of Romania no. 421 of 16 June 2011.
197 Published in the Official Gazette of Romania no. 440 of 23 Jun 2011.
198 Published in the Official Gazette of Romania no. 116 of 15 February 2012.
199 Published in the Official Gazette of Romania no. 90 of 3 February 2012.
200 Published in the Official Gazette of Romania no. 477 of 12 July 2012.
201 Published in the Official Gazette of Romania no. 473 of 11 July 2012.
202 Published in the Official Gazette of Romania no. 307 of 5 April 2006.
203 Published in the Official Gazette of Romania no. 469 of 25 June 2008.
204 Published in the Official Gazette of Romania no. 404 of 15 June 2009.
205 Published in the Official Gazette of Romania no. 53 of 23 January 2012.
206 Published in the Official Gazette of Romania no. 407 of 19 June 2012.
207 Published in the Official Gazette of Romania no. 440 of 23 June 2011.
208 Published in the Official Gazette of Romania no. 90 of 3 February 2012.
209 Published in the Official Gazette of Romania no. 473 of 11 July 2012.
210 Published in the Official Gazette of Romania no. 53 of 23 January 2012.

Thus, by Decision no. 1/2012[211], the Constitutional Court held that "in principle, any normative act must meet certain quality requirements, among which foreseeability, which means that it must be sufficiently precise and clear to be applied, so the formulation with sufficient precision of the normative act enables the interested persons – if need be with appropriate advice – to foresee, to a degree that is reasonable in the circumstances, the consequences which a given action may entail. Of course, it may be difficult to draw up laws of a total precision and a certain flexibility may even prove to be desirable, but a flexibility which does not affect the foreseeability of the law (see, in this respect, (...) the case-law of the European Court of Human Rights (...) for example, Judgement of 15 November 1996 in the Case of Cantoni v. France, paragraph 29, Judgement of 25 November 1996 in the Case of Wingrove v. the United Kingdom, paragraph 40, Judgement of 4 May 2000 in the Case of Rotaru v. Romania, paragraph 55, Judgement of 9 November 2006 in the Case of Leempoel & SA ED. Cine Revue v. Belgium, paragraph 59)".

By Decision no. 26/2012[212], the Court stated that "existence of conflicting legislative solutions and cancellation of provisions of law by other provisions contained in the same law are in breach of the principle of legal certainty, due to the lack of clarity and foreseeability of the rule. (...) On the same principle, the Strasbourg Court held that «one of the pillars of the rule of law is the principle of legal certainty». (Judgement of 6 June 2005 in the Case of Androne v. Romania; Judgement of 7 October 2009 in the Case of Stanca Popescu v. Romania). Likewise, the European Court of Human Rights stated that, «where States decide to enact legislation, it must be implemented with reasonable clarity and coherence in order to avoid, in so far as possible, legal uncertainty and ambiguity for the legal persons concerned *(...)*» (Judgement of 1 December 2005 in the Case of Paduraru v. Romania; Judgement of 6 December 2007 in the Case of Beian v. Romania)".

By Decision no. 51/2012[213], the Constitutional Court recalled that the Strasbourg Court "stressed the importance of ensuring accessibility and foreseeability of the law, including in terms of its stability, establishing a set of benchmarks that the legislator must take into consideration to ensure these requirements (cases such as Sunday Times v. the United Kingdom, 1979, Rekvényi v. Hungary, 1999, Rotaru v. Romania, 2000, Damman v. Switzerland, 2005)".

By Decision no. 681/2012[214] the Court referred again to the requirements of accessibility and foreseeability of the law, invoking Judgement of 24 May 2007, in the Case of Dragotoniu and Militaru-Pidhorni v. Romania, Judgement of 29 March 2000, in the Case of Rotaru v. Romania, Judgement of 23 September 1998, in the Case Petra v. Romania, Judgement of 23 November 2000, in the Case of Former King of Greece and Others v. Greece, Judgement of 8 July 2008, in the Case of Fener Rum

211 *Ibidem.*

212 Published in the Official Gazette of Romania no. 116 of 15 February 2012.

213 Published in the Official Gazette of Romania no. 90 of 3 February 2012.

214 Published in the Official Gazette of Romania no. 477 of 12 July 2012.

Patrikligi v. Turkey, Judgement of 26 April 1979, in the Case of Sunday Times v. the United Kingdom.

As to the second situation evoked, respectively both violation of requirements of clarity, precision, foreseeability and predictability of legal rules and violation of specific fundamental rights, it is usually found in the a posteriori constitutional review, by means of the exceptions of unconstitutionality, a concrete review, an instrument that can be used by persons whose rights and legitimate freedoms at achieving these rights have been infringed upon.

As an example, we shall refer to this combination where the Court ascertained the infringement of the free access to justice. Thus pursuant to the consistent case-law of the Constitutional Court of Romania, "the principle of free access to justice (...) involves, inter alia, the adoption by the legislator of clear procedural rules, prescribing with precision the terms and the conditions in which individuals can exercise their procedural rights, including those for review appeals against the decisions of the courts." The lack of such rules has led, for example, to declaring the unconstitutionality of Article 20 (1) of the Contentious Administrative Law no. 554/2004 according to which: "(1) The decision rendered by the court in the first instance can be challenged by means of appeal, within 15 days from pronunciation or from communication", on the grounds that "the parties do not have a certain mark on the period of time in which they can challenge by appeal the decision rendered by the court of contentious administrative in the first instance, which renders their access to justice, by means of the avenue of appeal provided by the law, uncertain and random, therefore limited" (Decision no. 189/2006[215]). For the same reasons, by Decision no. 647/2006[216] the court ascertained the unconstitutionality of the provisions of Article 4 (3) of the Contentious Administrative Law no. 554/2004, according to which: "The solution of the court of contentious administrative is subject to appeal, which is to be declared within 48 hours as from pronunciation or as from communication and which is to be tried within 3 days from registration, by informing the parties of summons by publication."

Likewise, by Decision no. 1609/2010[217], it was ascertained the unconstitutionality of Article 21 para. (2) second sentence of the Law no. 554/2004 on Administrative Contentious, according to which: *"The final and irrevocable judgments in violation of the principle of precedence of Community law, governed by Article 148 para. (2) in conjunction with Article 20 para. (2) of the Constitution of Romania represent a ground for the revision, behind added to those provided by the Code of Civil Procedure. The request for the revision must be filed within 15 days of the communication, which is made, by derogation from the rule enshrined in Article 17 para. (3), to the duly substantiated request of an interested party, within 15 days after delivery. The application must be settled urgently and especially in a maximum period of 60 days from*

215 Published in the Official Gazette of Romania no. 307 of 5 April 2006.
216 Published in the Official Gazette of Romania no. 921 of 14 November 2006.
217 Published in the Official Gazette of Romania no. 70 of 27 January 2011.

registration." The Court held that the impugned text "*has a poor wording, likely to generate confusions and uncertainties that may constitute real obstacles to the exercise of the right of access to justice. (...) The vice of drafting affects, from this perspective also, the right of free access to justice by the interested party's impossibility to know to which court he/she must address the application for the communication of the judgment. Similarly, the phrase «fully reasoned» is a misleading phrase for both the party and the judge. The merits becomes a feature that can be relativized, being no criteria regarding its assessment".*

In terms of the analysis performed on the decisions of admission of the objections of unconstitutionality delivered in 2012, we shall note that the repetition, within more than a third thereof delivered last year, of the same type of argument based on the case-law of the European Court of Human Rights draws attention to a systemic issue of Romanian legislation (lack of coherence, clarity and accuracy), the strong use of the case-law of European Court of Human Rights and the importance of interpreting the texts of Constitution of Romania in accordance with the provisions of the Convention, as interpreted by the Court of Strasbourg, which allowed on such basis the development of certain principles as guarantees for the entire field of fundamental rights and freedoms (principle of legal certainty).

Principle of non-retroactivity of the law

On this principle, we mention, by way of example, the case law in which, based on the practice of the European Court of Human Rights, the Constitutional Court held that the principle of retroactivity of the more favourable criminal law applies also in case of minor offences law. The Court rules as such although the constitutional provisions at that time did not provide for such a rule.

Thus, by Decision no. 318/2003[218], the Court stated that "the constitutional provisions of Article 15 (2), stating that «The law shall only take effect for the future, except the more favourable criminal law», must be interpreted in light of Article 20 (1) of the Constitution, in accordance with the Convention for the Protection of Human Rights and Fundamental Freedoms. (...) From the conventional perspective, the Constitutional Court notes that, in its case-law, the European Court of Human Rights held that nothing prevents states to fulfil their role as guardians of the public interest by establishing and maintaining a distinction between different types of crime. In principle, the Convention does not preclude the trend of «decriminalization» in the Member States of the Council of Europe. However, as noted in its Judgement of 21 February 1994, in the Case Öztürk v. Germany, these fall under Article 6 of the Convention for the Protection of Human Rights and Fundamental Freedoms. (...), the provisions of this Article shall guarantee the right of every «accused person» to a fair trial, regardless of the classification of the offence in the domestic law".

---

218 Published in the Official Gazette of Romania no. 697 of 6 October 2003.

In light of this decision and, therefore, of the case-law of the European Court of Human Rights incorporated therein, Article 15 received a new wording upon the revision of the Constitution in 2003, and currently it enshrines the principle of non-retroactivity of the law, except from the more favourable criminal or contravention law.

The principle of equal rights

Interpreting the provisions of Article 16 (1) of the Constitution, according to which "Citizens are equal before the law and public authorities, without any privilege or discrimination" in conjunction with the provisions of Article 4 on criteria of non-discrimination, and, based on Article 20 of the Constitution, in conjunction with the provisions of Article 14 of the Convention for the Protection of Human Rights and Fundamental Freedoms prohibiting discrimination, the Constitutional Court established that "the principle of equality before the law implies an equal legal treatment for situations which, according to the aim sought, are no different; and the different treatment cannot only be the expression of the exclusive appreciation of the legislator, but it must be justified rationally and objectively"[219]. The Court also held that "the principle of equality, on the one hand, means uniform regulation and non-discriminatory treatment for identical situations and, on the other hand, implies a right to differentiation"[220].In other words, "the principle of equality shall not prevent specific rules, in case of a difference in situations. Formal equality would lead to the same rule, despite the difference in situations. That is why real inequality arising from this differentiation may justify different rules depending on the purpose of the law containing them. Therefore the principle of equality underscores a fundamental right, the right to differentiation, and to the extent that the equality is not natural, to impose it would be tantamount to creating discrimination"[221]. Numerous decisions of admission of the exceptions of unconstitutionality invoke in this regard the Judgement delivered by the European Court of Human Rights in Case Marckx v. Belgium, *1979* (Decision no. 81/1998[222]; Decision no. 148/2001[223]; Decision no. 86/2003[224]; Decision no. 89/2003[225]; Decision no. 217/2003[226];

219 For example, Decision no. 513 of 20 June 2006, published in the Official Gazette of Romania no. 598 of 11 July 2006.

220 For example, Decision no. 1092 of 15 October 2008, published in the Official Gazette of Romania no. 712 of 20 October 2008.

221 Decision no. 107/1995, published in the Official Gazette of Romania no. 85 of 26 April 1996.

222 Published in the Official Gazette of Romania no. 220 of 16 June 1998.

223 Published in the Official Gazette of Romania no. 592 of 20 September 2001.

224 Published in the Official Gazette of Romania no. 207 of 31 March 2003.

225 Published in the Official Gazette of Romania no. 200 of 27 March 2003.

226 Published in the Official Gazette of Romania no. 425 of 17 June 2003.

Decision no. 342/2003[227]; Decision no. 100/2004[228]; Decision no. 969/2007[229];Decision no. 599/2009[230]; Decision no. 1354/2010[231]; Decision no. 573/2011[232]; Decision no. 1470/2011[233]; Decision no. 1483/2011[234]; Decision no. 1615/2011[235]).

Referring to the rights that have constituted subject-matter of examination by the Constitutional Court from the perspective of the principle of equal rights, and without leaving aside the rich-case, for example, on free access to justice[236], right to property[237] or social rights[238], we shall evoke as landmark decision one case where the Constitutional Court has specifically stated that it reconsiders its practice given the provisions of the Convention and the case-law of the European Court of Human Rights.

Thus, by Decision no. 349/2001[239], where, adjudicating on Article 53 and Article 54 of the Family Code, the Constitutional Court held the following: "Whereas, following ratification by Romania of the Convention for the Protection of Human Rights and Fundamental Freedoms, in accordance with Articles 11 and 20 of the Constitution, the Convention has become part of domestic law, in the examination of the exception it is necessary to take into consideration its provisions and the judicial practice of the European Court of Human Rights in the application and interpretation of that Convention. Ruling on whether the interdiction imposed by national law for married women to challenge the presumption of paternity of her

227 Published in the Official Gazette of Romania no. 755 of 28 October 2003.
228 Published in the Official Gazette of Romania no. 261 of 24 March 2004.
229 Published in the Official Gazette of Romania no. 816 of 29 November 2007.
230 Published in the Official Gazette of Romania no. 329 of 18 May 2009.
231 Published in the Official Gazette of Romania no. 761 of 15 November 2010.
232 Published in the Official Gazette of Romania no. 363 of 25 May 2011.
233 Published in the Official Gazette of Romania no. 853 of 2 December 2011.
234 Published in the Official Gazette of Romania no. 853 of 2 December 2011.
235 Published in the Official Gazette of Romania no. 99 of 8 February 2012.
236 For example, Decision of the Plenum of the Constitutional Court no. 1/1994, published in the Official Gazette of Romania no. 69 of 16 March 1994; Decision no. 100/2004, published in the Official Gazette of Romania no. 261 of 24 March 2004; Decision no. 610/2007, published in the Official Gazette of Romania no. 474 of 16 July 2007; Decision no. 67/2003, published in the Official Gazette of Romania no. 178 of 21 March 2003.
237 Decision no. 177 of 15 October 1998, published in the Official Gazette of Romania no. 77 of 24 February 1999; Decision no. 165 of 21 October 1999, published in the Official Gazette of Romania no. 624 of 21 December 1999.
238 Decision no. 104 of 31 October 1995, published in the Official Gazette of Romania no. 40 of 26 February 1996, of Decision no. 1414 of 4 November 2009, published in the Official Gazette of Romania no. 796 of 23 November 2009; Decision no. 277 of 21 March 2006, published in the Official Gazette of Romania no. 348 of 18 April 2006; Decision no. 217 of 15 May 2003, published in the Official Gazette of Romania no. 425 of 17 June 2003.
239 Published in the Official Gazette of Romania no. 240 of 10 April 2002.

husband in relation to the child conceived during the marriage is contrary to the aforementioned Article 8 of the Convention, the European Court of Human Rights decided affirmatively in the case Kroon and Others v. the Netherlands. In this regard, by Judgement of 27 October 1994, it stated that «respect for family life requires that biological and social reality prevail over a legal presumption which, as in the present case, flies in the face of both established fact and the wishes of those concerned without actually benefiting anyone. Accordingly, even having regard to the margin of appreciation left to the State, the Netherlands has failed to secure to the applicants the respect for their family life. There has accordingly been a violation of Article 8». Given this interpretation and application of the Convention for the Protection of Human Rights and Fundamental Freedoms by the European Court of Human Rights, the Constitutional Court considers it necessary to reconsider[240] *its jurisprudence on the settlement of the exception of unconstitutionality of Article 54 (2) of the Family Code (...), and it is to ascertain that the text in question contravenes the provisions of Article 16 (1), Article 26,Article 44 (1) and Article 45 (1) of the Constitution, issues in relation to which it is to declare the exception of unconstitutionality of Article 54 (2) of the Family Code as well founded".*

Free access to justice and right to a fair trial

Among the many decisions by which the Constitutional Court ruled in relation to compliance / non-compliance, as the case may be, with free access to justice, we mention some of the issues raised and decisions rendered, which we consider as relevant for reconsideration of the case law precedents following issuance of certain judgements by the European Court of Human Rights.

Thus, in terms of "reasonable time" of proceedings, the case-law of the European Court of Human Rights determined principle conclusions of the Constitutional Court before the consecration of this requirement in the Basic Law. The Court held that the reasonable time concerns the celerity of proceedings, and not the need to establish for all remedies – including the extraordinary ones – time limits for the exercise thereof (Decision no. 73/1996[241]; Decision no. 96/1996[242]; Decision no. 208/1997[243]), as well as that "the invoked requirement of reasonable time is not analysed conceptually, but individually, specifically taking into account a number of factors specific to each case – the procedure, the nature of the claims, the complexity of the procedure"[244]. In this regard, pronouncing the solution finding unconstitutional the provisions of Articles 2–7 of the Law no. 105/1997 on the resolution of objections, appeals and complaints against acts of control or of taxation

240 Decision no. 78 of 13 September 1995, published in the Official Gazette of Romania no. 294 of 20 December 1995.

241 Published in the Official Gazette of Romania no. 255 of 22 October 1996.

242 Published in the Official Gazette of Romania no. 251 of 17 October 1996.

243 Published in the Official Gazette of Romania no. 302 of 5 November 1997.

244 Decision no. 13/1997, published in the Official Gazette of Romania no. 37 of 6 March 1997.

compiled by bodies of the Ministry of Finance, the Constitutional Court of Romania reversed its jurisprudence on the constitutionality of these provisions, noting that the among the grounds of unconstitutionality of this law it had never been invoked its contrariety to Article 6 par.1 first sentence of the Convention relating to the requirement of "reasonable time". It was considered that the requirement that the dispute be resolved "within a reasonable time" is interesting not only from the purely "temporal" aspect of the judicial administrative procedure established by Articles 2–7 of Law no. 105/1997 but in the context of the provisions of Article 6 of the Convention, on the right to a "fair trial", the purpose of this phrases attracts also the connotation "in a reasonable way". Therefore, the administrative and judicial procedure laid down in Articles 2–7 of Law no. 105/1997 was estimated to be inconsistent with that purpose.[245] In deciding this, the Court acted "in the light of the constitutional provisions of Article 11 [...] and in the light of Article 20 (2) of the Constitution (...)", referring to the case-law of the European Court of Human Rights, where, in relation to the application of Article 6 para. 1 of the Convention, it was established "the requirement consisting of settlement of the case «in a reasonable time» includes dies a quo also the duration of such procedures preceding the referral to the court of law (for example, cases «Golder v. the United Kingdom», 1975 and «Vallee v. France», 1994), and that the «reasonable time» is calculated by the dies ad quem final resolution of the case (for example, cases «Ecklev. the Federal Republic of Germany», 1982 and «Bricmont v. Belgium», 1986)»". The Constitutional Court also held that "In the meaning of the case-law of the European Court of Human Rights it shall not be considered as final settlement of the case the pronunciation of a judgement acknowledging the existence of the right (for example, the existence of the right to compensation under tort) without having determined also the actual amount of the money (e.g., amount of compensation), which would require separate proceedings (in this regard, see the cases «Guincho v. Portugal», 1984 and «Silva Pontes v. Portugal», 1994). Secondly, the same case law says that the procedures for the enforcement of the judgement is not covered by guarantee of «reasonable time» (Cases «X v. the United Kingdom», 1981 and «Alsterlund v. Sweden», 1988)".

We also wish to mention the situation where the issue of access to constitutional justice, from the perspective of the relevant judgements of the European Court of Human Rights, led to an essential reconsideration of the case law of the Constitutional Court, insofar it was related to its competence itself and the purpose was to facilitate access to constitutional justice. Thus, examining the provisions of Article 29 (1) of Law no. 47/1992 on the organisation and operation of the Constitutional Court, according to which "The Constitutional Court shall decide upon the exceptions raised before the courts of law or courts of commercial arbitration referring to the unconstitutionality of laws and ordinances which are in force, or any provision thereof, where such is related to adjudication of the case, regardless in which

245 Decision no. 208 of 25 October 2000, published in the Official Gazette of Romania no. 695 of 27 December 2000.

stage of trial proceedings or subject-matter thereof", it found that the expression "in force" within the cited provisions is constitutional "to the extent it is interpreted as submitting to the constitutionality review the laws or ordinances or provisions therein, whose legal effects continue to produce even when they are no longer in force"[246]. As grounds for that decision the Court referred also to the Judgement of 23 June 1993, delivered by the European Court of Human Rights in the Case Ruiz-Mateos v. Spain, concluding that "Article 6 of the Convention shall apply to constitutional jurisdictions only when they carry out the constitutional review upon referrals from individuals, for the protection of their fundamental rights, either through direct applications, or through exception". For the reasons set forth above, the Constitutional Court of Romania held that "the expression «in force» – condition for the admissibility of the exception of unconstitutionality, therefore a procedural requirement preventing the examination on the merits of the referral of the author of the exception of unconstitutionality –falls under the scope of the protection of the right to a fair trial enshrined by Article 6 in the Convention for the Protection of Human Rights and Fundamental Freedoms, restricting access to constitutional justice".

Right to defence

By Decision no. 145/2000, based on the Convention and the case-law of the European Court of Human Rights, the Constitutional Court of Romania reconsidered its consistent practice on criminal procedural provisions prohibiting representation in court of the defendant in case of offences for which the penalty provided by law was imprisonment exceeding one year. The Constitutional Court held the following: "given that the exception of unconstitutionality of the provisions of Article 174 (1) a) of the Code of Criminal Procedure, concerns the constitutional right to defence, and it has its correspondent in the Convention for the Protection of Human Rights and Fundamental Freedoms, which in light of the constitutional provisions of Articles 11 and 20 is part of the domestic law, it is necessary to examine the exception of unconstitutionality also in light of the judicial practice of the European Court of Human Rights whilst applying the Convention. Thus, concerning the representation of the defendant in criminal proceedings, the European Court of Human Rights ruled in several judgements, including in the following cases: «Poitrimol v. France» (1993), «Lala v. the Netherlands» (1994) and «Pelladoah v. the Netherlands» (1994). In all these cases, the European Court of Human Rights ruled that the interdiction on the defendant's right to be represented by counsel to have his case tried in appeal is a violation of the provisions of Article 6 (1) and (3) c) of the Convention for the Protection of Human Rights and Fundamental Freedoms (...). The Court finds that the solution adopted by the European Court of Human Rights (...) is valid also in case of the provisions of Article 174 (1) a) of the Criminal Procedure Code, which do not allow representation of the defendant in the first instance or during

246 Decision no. 766 of 15 June 2011, published in the Official Gazette of Romania no. 549 of 3 August 2011.

retrial after the dissolution of the judgement upon appeal, in case of offences for which the penalty provided by law is imprisonment exceeding one year". The Court accepted the exception of unconstitutionality and found that the provision "only if the penalty provided by law for the respective offence is fine or imprisonment not exceeding one year" referred to in Article 174 (1) a) of the Code of Criminal Procedure is unconstitutional.

Right to property

The period after 1991 was characterized by the adoption of many regulations with the purpose to repair the injustices committed during the Communist period, the issue of legislation on restitution of property abusively taken is well known, still raising problems in the Romanian legal system, as demonstrated by the very practice of the Court in Strasbourg. The Constitutional Court of Romania had to settle many exceptions of unconstitutionality on these regulations, the issue relating to property giving raise to mutual references in the documents that the two Courts have issued on the matter.

From among the numerous decisions of the Constitutional Court, we mention those that "introduced" into domestic law the case-law of the European Court of Human Rights for to the extensive interpretation of the concepts "good" and "property", giving them a specific meaning related to international human rights Thus, for example, by decision no. 70/2001[247], the Court held that "having regard to the provisions of Article 20 (1) of the Constitution, (...) the provisions of Article 41 (1) and (2) of the Constitution should be interpreted and applied in accordance with the provisions of Article 1 (1) of the First Protocol to the Convention for the Protection of Human Rights and Fundamental Freedoms: (...) In this interpretation the Court finds that the constitutional principle of equal protection of private property must be observed with respect to any property rights, any «possessions». In this respect, the European Court of Human Rights, through its case law, has broadly construed the notion of «possessions» and «property», giving them a specific sense for international law on human rights. Thus, the European Court stated that «the concept of "possessions" (in English, "possessions", in French, "biens") in the first part of Article 1 has an autonomous meaning and is independent from the formal classification in domestic law» (case of "Former King and Others v. Greece", 2000). This meaning «is not limited to ownership of physical goods. [...] certain other rights and interests constituting assets can also be regarded as "property rights", and thus as "possessions" for the purposes of this provision» (case of "Beyeler v. Italy", 2000). Likewise, in the case of "*Gasus Dosier und FΦrdertechnik GmbH* v. The Netherlands", 1996, to determine the scope of the provisions of Article 1, it was decided that «it is therefore immaterial whether Gasus's right [...] is to be considered as a right of ownership or as a security right in rem». The European Court of Human Rights also noted in the Case of "Van Marle and Others v. the Netherlands", 1986, that: « [...]

247 Published in the Official Gazette of Romania no. 236 of 10 May 2001.

clientèle [...] constituted an asset and, hence, a possession within the meaning of the first sentence of Article 1 (P1–1). This provision was accordingly applicable in the present case». Also in the case of "Iatridis v. Greece", 1999 [...] since the applicant holds only a lease of his business premises, this interference neither amounts to an expropriation nor is an instance of controlling the use of property but comes under the first sentence of the first paragraph of Article 1». Furthermore, in the Case of "Pressos Compania Naviera S.A. and Others v. Belgium", 1995, it was decided that «claims for compensation come into existence as soon as the damage occurs. A claim of this nature constituted an "asset" and therefore amounted to "a possession" within the meaning of the first sentence of Article 1 (P1–1). [...] »". Based on the reasons set forth above, the Constitutional Court found that the provisions of Article 19 (3) final sentence of Law no. 85/1992 concerning the refusal to grant interests, as well as to update the price refunded after ascertaining the nullity of the contract of sale of the dwelling, are contrary to the constitutional provisions which enshrine the right to property.

It is worth mentioning also the decisions whereby the Constitutional Court established the conditions for limiting the exercise of the right to property or for allowing deprivation of property in accordance with the Constitution. Thus, substantiating again its solution on the case-law of the European Court of Human Rights, the Court held that "the legislature is competent to establish the legal framework for the exercise of the attributes of the right to property in the sense conferred by the Constitution, so as not to come into collision with the general interest or other legitimate private interests of other legal subjects, thus establishing reasonable limitations on its use, as guaranteed individual right". Deprivation of property must have a legitimate purpose and, for achievement thereof, the respective measure must keep a fair balance between the general interest of the community and the protection of individual fundamental rights[248]. The Court also held that the deprivation of property imposes an obligation on the State to indemnify the owner: "in the absence of a remedy, Article 1 of Protocol No. 1 would provide only illusory and ineffective protection of the right to property". In this regard, it is worth mentioning, for example, decision no. 870/2007[249], where the Court found that the challenged provisions "settle a forced transfer of ownership, which do not observe the provisions concerning the expropriation enshrined by Article 44 (1) and (3) of the Constitution and by Article 1 of the First Protocol to the Convention for the Protection of Human Rights and Fundamental Freedoms In this respect, the European Court of Human Rights stated in its case-law that the ownership deprivation must be provided by the law, it must be in the public interest, it must observe the domestic legal norms and it must observe the relationship of proportionality between the means employed and the aim sought to be realised. As concerns the compensations for the owner of the

248 Decision no. 72 of 26 February 2004, published in the Official Gazette of Romania no. 249 of 22 March 2004.

249 Published in the Official Gazette of Romania no. 701 of 17 October 2007.

ownership right for deprivation of his right, the European Court of Human Rights held that, in absence of a reparatory compensation, Article 1 of Protocol no. 1 would only assure an illusory and ineffective protection of the ownership right, totally in disagreement with the provisions of the Convention (case "James and others v. the United Kingdom", 1986). The deprivation involves therefore the State's obligation to the payment of compensation to the owner, as without payment of an amount reasonably related to its value, the measure represents a disproportionate interference with the right of observance of their assets. The impossibility to obtain even a partial compensation, but adequate in case of deprivation represents a breach of the balance between the requirements on the protection of the ownership right and the exigencies of general type. » For these reasons, and finding that, in this case, the provisions of Articles 8 and 14 of the Government Emergency Ordinance no. 110/2005, which established the maximum sale price of certain medical premises, in a differentiated way, based on categories of settlements, and for the afferent land a fix price of 1 euro/sqm (within the limit of 250 sqm), the Constitutional Court held that "the prices determined as such do not observe the market value of the asset. The visible disproportion between the two values qualifies the price as unreasonable, and thus the requirements imposed by the constitutional and international norms are not fulfilled".

Right to salary and pension rights

Social rights[250] have been increasingly more often invoked in recent years before the Constitutional Court of Romania, a situation in direct connection with the phenomenon of financial crisis that affected the states and their citizens. We shall refer in this context to the reductions of salaries and pensions, caused by this phenomenon, which led to the formulation of many actions and challenges regarding the constitutionality of acts which required such measures.

We approach this issue not so much regarding the influence of the case-law of the European Court of Human Rights over the decisions of the Constitutional Court, as in terms of the intention to present the moving way of the reference standards on fundamental rights, within the meaning of Article 20 of the Constitution, reflected in the decisions of the Constitutional Court. We take in account Decision no. 874/2010[251], whereby the Constitutional Court declared unconstitutional a normative act which established the decrease by 15% of the gross amount of the pensions due or in payment. On that occasion, the Court held that "*in the Case Stec*

---

250 The Constitution of Romania, adopted in 1991 and reviewed in 2003, may be qualified as a fundamental law where social rights know a thorough regulation [*right to education* (Article 32), *right to health protection* (Article 34), *labour and social protection of labour* (Article 41), *prohibition of forced labour* (Article 42), *right to strike* (Article 43), *standard of living* (Article 47), *protection of children and young persons* (Article 49), *protection of disabled persons* (Article 50)].

251 Decision no. 874 of 25 June 2010, published in the Official Gazette of Romania no. 433 of 28 June 2010.

and Others v. United Kingdom, 2006, the European Court of Human Rights established that Article 1 of the Additional Protocol to the Convention does not aim at a right to acquire property in the social security scheme system. It is at the discretion of the state to decide on the application of any social security scheme or to choose the type or amount of benefits it grants in any of these schemes. The only condition imposed on the State is to comply with Article 14 of the Convention on non-discrimination. If, however, the state has adopted a law governing the rights resulted from the social insurance system – regardless of the fact that they may or not result from the payment of contributions –, that law must be regarded as generating a patrimony interest within the meaning of Article 1 of the Additional Protocol to the Convention. In other words, the Court abandoned the distinction between contributory benefits and non-contributory ones in terms of incidence of Article 1 of the Additional Protocol to the Convention [see, in the same regard, Case Andrejeva v. Latvia, 2009 (and not Akdeejeva v. Latvia, 2007, as erroneously indicated in the objection of unconstitutionality)]". However, the Constitutional Court underlined that *"different from the requirements of the Convention for the Protection of Human Rights and Fundamental Freedoms, the Constitution of Romania provides expressly in Article 47 para. (2) the right to pension as a fundamental right. The constitutional text does not qualify the pension only from the perspective of a patrimony interest of the person, but expressly enshrining the pension right as a fundamental right, it requires the state additional constitutional requirements so as to ensure a level of protection of this right superior to that set forth in the Convention and in its additional* protocols. *Under these conditions, Article 60 of the Convention becomes applicable, according to which «no provision of this Convention shall be interpreted as restricting or affecting human rights and fundamental freedoms which may be recognised according to the laws of any contracting party or any other convention to which it is a Party»".* Allowing the exception of unconstitutionality, the Court has therefore given priority to the more favourable constitutional norm, according to the provisions of the Convention and their interpretation given by the European Court of Human Rights.

2.2.4 Reflecting the case-law of the Constitutional Court of Romania in the case-law of the European Court of Human Rights

Although, in principle, the European Court of Human Rights held that the constitutional case-law has no authority over it, as the ascertainment of constitutionality within the national law does not entail automatically the compliance with the provisions of the Convention, this Court it refers to national law and uses comparative law for interpretive purposes and for the definition of autonomous concepts[252]. In this regard, the doctrine[253] distinguishes, well founded, between the positions of

252 B. Selejan-Guţan, *European Court of Human Rights and the national jurisdictions: brief comparative view*, in *In Honorem Constantin Bîrsan…, cited paper*, pp. 633–646.

253 *Ibidem.*

national jurisdictions in the Western democracies and those in post-communist states regarding the supranational jurisdictions and the international law of human rights. Thus, constitutional courts in post-communist countries were not set up as bearers of a tradition of post-war European legal culture and were required to build immediately, their own Europeanised judicial culture, being a difficult requirement, especially in the context of inheritance related to the mentality of the regime last. However, the constitutional courts developed rapidly in this regard and currently they invoke reasons which are appreciated as reference even for the decisions delivered by the European Court of Human Rights.

As concerns the Constitutional Court of Romania, the European Court of Human Rights referred to its case-law, in its judgments, by taking into account relevant considerations for the referred cases.

Thus, for example, in the Judgment of 28 October 1999 in Case Brumărescu v. Romania, invokes Decision no. 73/1995 on the constitutionality of certain provisions of the Law on the settlement of the legal conditions of some buildings designed for dwelling purposes passed into State property[254] (para. 39), respectively the considerations that based the admission of the objection of unconstitutionality of that part of Article 1 (1) of the law, which refers to the buildings passed into State property or of other legal persons, without title. There are also quoted the considerations by which the Court refers to the Parliament's power to appreciate, on the occasion of the law review, regarding the possibility to adopt some measures for the completion of its provisions concerning the right of the persons whose dwellings have been taken by the State, without title, and of their heirs – dwellings for which the State did not acquire the property right – to choose the law enforcement benefit, assuming that they will wish to abandon the uncertain, slow and costly action for recovery of possession.

Judgment of 3 June 2003 delivered in the Case Pantea v. Romania invokes Decision no. 45 of 10 March 1998 on the objection of unconstitutionality of the provisions of Article 504 (1) of the Criminal Procedure Code, whose considerations are quoted, in excerpt (para.147). By this decision, holding that the principle of the State's responsibility for the persons who suffered because of a judicial error committed in the criminal trials must be applied to all the victims of such errors, as well as the fact that the legislator did not agree to the provisions of Article 504 of the Criminal Procedure Code with those of Article 48 (3) of the Constitution, and taking into account that Article 504 of the Criminal Procedure Code established only two possible cases of holding the State responsible for the judicial errors committed in the criminal trials, the Constitutional Court decided that this restriction is unconstitutional regarding the provisions of Article 48 (3) of the Constitution, which do not allow such an abridgement. By Law no. 281/2003[255] the provisions of the Criminal Procedure Code on taking the preventive measure have been amended. Article 504

254 Published in the Official Gazette of Romania no. 177 of 8 August 1995.
255 Published in the Official Gazette of Romania no. 468 of 1 July 2003.

of the Criminal Procedure Code has been amended, leaving open the possibility of the persons illegally deprived of liberty to address the court for obtaining the repair of the damage that was caused to them by this measure[256].

The same decision of the Constitutional Court is mentioned (par. 18) in Decision of 24 April 2008, pronounced in the case Visan v. Romania[257], by which the effects of the Constitutional Court's decision are raised, in relation to the date on which the applicant formulated the action for compensation (6 March 1998), as well as the role of the objection of unconstitutionality in the protection of human rights and freedoms. As indicated above[258], one of the possibly responsible authorities in this case belongs to the legislative power, "due to the lack of concern for the unconstitutional regulation and for the delays in the regulation of the right to compensation in case of judicial error". As stated above, the intervention of the Romanian legislator for the purposes of Decision no. 45/1998 of the Constitutional Court took place only in 2003. The decision of 10 June 2008, pronounced in the case Tase v. Romania, also refers to Decision no. 45/1998 of the Constitutional Court of Romania, actually disclosing the same problems under the aspects of the legislative authority's responsibility, meaning that "the Romanian law did not provide for a procedure available to the applicant for the attainment of the right to compensation for illegal arrest, asked by Article 5 (5) of the Convention"[259].

Judgment of 22 June 2004 delivered in Case Pini and Bertani and Manera and Atripaldi v. Romania mentions (para. 104) the Constitutional Court's decision no. 308/2002[260] on the objection of unconstitutionality of the provisions of Article 7(1) (a) and (2) of the Government Emergency Ordinance no. 25/1997 on the legal status of adoption, approved with amendments by Law no. 87/1998, by which, admitting the objection of unconstitutionality raised in the case, the Court found that the impugned critics are unconstitutional as far as they do not provide for taking the consent of any person or of any authority which would be empowered to exercise parental rights, according to Article 5 § 1 (a) of the European Convention on the Adoption of Children, concluded at Strasbourg on a 24 PRIL 1967, to which Romania adhered by Law no. 15/1993. Then, Law no. 272/2004 on the protection and promotion of the rights of the child[261] and Law no. 273/2004 on the procedure

---

256 *Judgments of ECHR in cases against Romania, 1994–1999, Analysis, consequences, possible responsible authorities,* volume IV, Universitară Publishing House, Bucharest, p. 1353.

257 Published in the Official Gazette of Romania no. 876 of 24 December 2008.

258 *Judgment of ECHR..., op. cit.*, vol. IV, p. 1490.

259 *Ibidem*, p. 1508.

260 Published in the Official Gazette of Romania no. 78 of 6 February 2003.

261 Published in the Official Gazette of Romania no. 557 of 23 June 2004 and republished in the Official Gazette of Romania no. 159 of 5 March 2014.

of adoption[262], there being introduced new rules for the protection of minors and collaterals in the adoption procedures[263].

Judgment of 27 September 2007 delivered in Case Cobzaru v. Romania invokes a reference of the Constitutional Court of Romania – Decision no. 486/1997[264] – which established that Article 278 of the Criminal Procedure Code is constitutional only if it does not hinder the person unsatisfied by the settlement of the complaint against the measures or acts performed by the prosecutor or performed based on the provisions given this one and which do not reach in front of courts to refer a matter to court according to Article 21 of the Constitution, which is to directly apply. It is a reference case regarding the insurance and guarantee of the free access to justice and which determined, otherwise, the amendment of the criminal legislation for the attainment of this right.

Judgment of 24 November 2009 delivered in the Case Ieremeiov v. Romania mentions (para. 19) Decision no. 62/2007 on the objection unconstitutionality of the provisions under Article I paragraph 56 of the Law no. 278/2006 for the amendment and supplementation of the Criminal Code, as well as for the amendment and supplementations of other laws, by which the Constitutional Court found as unconstitutional the repeal of the provisions of the Criminal Code on insult and defamation.

Judgment of 24 March 2009 delivered in the Case Tudor Tudor v. Romania also invokes Decision no. 1.055/2008 on the objection of unconstitutionality of the provisions under Article 2 paragraph (1) subparagraph i), Article 45 paragraph (2) and Article 47 of Law no. 10/2001 regulating the legal status of certain immovable property taken by duress between 6 March 1945 and 22 December 1989[265], by which the Constitutional Court held that "Article 47 of Law no. 10/2001 is unconstitutional, being contrary to the principle of guaranteeing and protecting property as enshrined in Article 44 of the Constitution, being breached the right to property of the bona fides purchaser under the Law no. 112/1995. Thus, natural and legal persons whose ownership over a property under Law no. 10/2001 has been recognized and enforced by irrevocable court order cannot be asked to return the same, as long as such measure is not seriously justified, based on the case of public utility, in the meaning of Article 44 (3) of the Constitution". Similarly, Judgment of 12 October 2010 delivered in the Case Maria Atanasiu and Others v. Romania[266], refers (para. 68–70) to a series of decisions of the Constitutional Court regarding Law no. 112/1995, Law no. 1/2000, Law no. 10/2001 and Law no. 247/2005, with the express mention of Decision no. 830/2008[267], which upheld the objection of unconstitutionality of the provisions of Article I point 60 of Title I of Law no. 247/2005 on reform in property

262 Republished in the Official Gazette of Romania no. 259 of 19 April 2012.
263 *Judgments of ECHR…, op. cit.*, vol. I, p. 158.
264 Published in the Official Gazette of Romania no. 105 of 6 March 1998.
265 Published in the Official Gazette of Romania no. 737 of 30 October 2008.
266 Published in the Official Gazette of Romania no. 778 of 22 November 2010.
267 Published in the Official Gazette of Romania no. 559 of 24 July 2008.

and justice, as well as some additional measures, being found that, by repealing the phrase "immovable property taken with valid title" from the content of Article 29 (1) of Law no. 10/2001, the provisions of Article 15 (2) and of Article 16 (1) of the Constitution are violated.

If the earlier case-law of the European Court of Human Rights – from which only some examples are provided – the mention of the Romanian contentious constitutional court's practice appears more like an establishment of the legal framework of the case referred to court, in the more recent jurisprudence there being found a foundation of the European Court considerations on considerations contained in decisions of the Constitutional Court of Romania.

Thus, for example, by Judgment of 7 February 2012 delivered in the Case Ana Maria Frimu v. Romania and 4 other applications[268], the European Court of Human Rights considered that the reduction of the applicants' pensions, although substantial, constituted a modality to integrate these pensions in the general pension system stipulated by Law no. 19/2000 in order to obtain the budgetary balance and to correct the disparities between the different systems, expressly mentioning at § 44 from the considerations that "like the Constitutional Court, the Court estimates that these reasons could not be considered unreasonable or disproportionate." The reference made is to Decision no. 871/2010[269], by which the Constitutional Court of Romania found the constitutionality of the measure for the transformation of the service pensions (called special) into contributory pensions. The removed financial supplement was not a contributory-based one, but it was granted from the State budget for the consideration of the status of the respective socio-professional categories (servicemen, policemen, specialized support staff).

Also, by Judgment of 20 March 2012 delivered in the Case Ionel Panfile v. Romania[270], the European Court held, expressis verbis, at § 21, the following: "Within the evaluation of the public interests of the contested measures, the Court [A/N the European Court of Human Rights) takes into account the reasoning of the Constitutional Court[271], *which confirmed that the Romanian legislature has imposed new rules regarding the salaries in the public sector aiming to rationalize public spending, as imposed the exceptional context of the global economic and financial crisis (see supra, paragraph 11). Taking also into account that this problem falls under the competence of national authorities, which have direct democratic legitimacy and are situated better than an international court to evaluate the needs and local conditions, the Court did found no reason to wander from the finding of the Constitutional Court, according to which the contested measures pursued a legitimate purpose of public interest (see,*

268 Published in the Official Gazette of Romania no. 870 of 20 December 2012.
269 Published in the Official Gazette of Romania no. 433 of 28 June 2010.
270 Published in the Official Gazette of Romania no. 315 of 11 May 2012.
271 Decision no. 1414/2009, published in the Official Gazette of Romania no. 796 of 23 November 2009.

mutatis mutandis, Valkov and others v. Bulgaria, no. 2.033/04, 19.125/04, 19.475/04, 19.490/04, 19.495/04, 19.497/04, 24.729/04, 171/05 and 2.041/05, 92, 25 October 2011)".

Thus, in Judgment of 4 September 2012 delivered in the Case Nastaca Dolca and others v. Romania, the European Court of Human Rights has remarked that the removal of Article 5 (1) (a) I thesis of Law no. 221/2009, the legal basis of the applicants' request, took place following a constitutional review[272] which is usual in a democratic State and does not represent the result of an extraordinary ad-hoc mechanism (mutatis mutandis, Slavov and others v. Bulgaria, Decision of 2 December 2008, paragraph 99); "the invalidation of the that provision by the Constitutional Court pursued an objective of common interest, related to the proper administration of justice, as results from the motivation of the Constitutional Court, which criticized the vague wording of the legal provisions in the case and underlined the need to avoid the coexistence of several normative acts on compensation for the damages suffered by the politically persecuted persons during the Communist period"[273]. The Court also considered that the development of the national courts' jurisprudence to apply the decision of the Constitutional Court on the unconstitutionality of the provisions which has been the legal base of the applicants' action is not contrary to a proper administration of justice (mutatis mutandis, Atanasovski v. Former Yugoslav Republic of Macedonia, 14 January 2010, para. 38)[274]. It was also reiterated that the interpretation of national legislation is the obligation of national authorities, especially of the courts, and if the applicants perceive as an injustice the fact that the courts responded to the mentioned decisions of the Constitutional Court, such an injustice is inherent to any change in the legal solution that would appear, following the exercise of a normal control mechanism in a democratic State. The Court also recalled, to that effect, that the requirements of the legal security and protection of the legitimate expectation of individuals do not consecrate a legitimate right to a constant jurisprudence (Unédic v. France, paragraph 71). The application in this case of the solution given in the decision of the Constitutional Court of 21 October 2010 did not question the rights finally acquired by the applicant (Unédic

272 Decision no. 1358 of 21 October 2010 and Decision no. 1360 of 21 October 2010, published in the Official Gazette of Romania no. 761 of 15 November 2010, by which the Constitutional Court of Romania has admitted the objection of unconstitutionality of the provisions of Article 5 (1) (a) I thesis of Law no. 221/2009 regarding political convictions and the assimilated administrative measures, pronounced between 6 March 1945 and 22 December 1989, finding, essentially, that the impugned rule creates situations of incoherence and instability, that in the field of granting compensation for the non pecuniary damages there are parallel regulations and that the legal text, as it is written, is too vague, violating the rules referring to the accuracy and clarity of legal standard, "leading to its incoherent implementation, the courts granting compensation of up to 600.000 Euro, which represents an excessive and unreasonable implementation".

273 *http://www.codexnews.com.*

274 *http://www.hotararicedo.ro.*

v. France, paragraph 75 in fine). Moreover, the new legal situation resulted from the decision of the Constitutional Court of 21 October 2010 was perfectly known by the applicants and completely predictable, when the courts adjudicated on their action for damages.

It must be also underlined the convergent jurisprudence of both courts regarding the legislative measure for the reduction of the budgetary employees' salaries. Thus, the Constitutional Court of Romania held within the meaning of the constitutionality of the reduction by 25% of these salaries[275]. Referred to on the same issue, the Court of Strasbourg, by Judgment of 6 December 2011 delivered in the cases *Felicia Mihăieş* v. Romania (application no. 44232/11) and *Adrian Gavril Senteş* v. Romania (application no. 44605/11), found that the Romanian State did not violate the provisions of Article 1 of the Protocol no. 1 to the Convention, in terms of reducing by 25% the salaries, following the implementation of Law no. 118/2010 on certain measures necessary for the restoration of budgetary balance. The European Court of Human Rights recalled that the provisions of the Convention do not confer a right to receive a salary of a certain amount (see Judgment of 19 April 2007 delivered in the case Vilho Eskelinen and others v. Finland, and mutatis mutandis, Judgment of 12 October 2004 delivered in the case Kjartan Ásmundsson v. Island). Further on, the Court held that it is not sufficient for an applicant to invoke the existence of a "real dispute" or a "credible complaint". A claim can be considered as "patrimonial value", within the meaning of Article 1 of the Fist additional Protocol to the Convention, only when it has sufficient banes in the internal law, for example when it is confirmed by a well-established case-law of courts (Judgment of 28 September 2004, delivered in the case Kopecky v. Slovakia). It is the State's obligation to establish what benefits must be paid to its employees from the State budget. The State can order the introduction, suspension or termination of the payment of such benefits through adequate legislative amendments (Judgment of 8 November 2005, delivered in the case Ketchko v. Ukraine). However, when a legal provision is in force and provides for the payment of certain benefits, and the stipulated conditions are observed, the authorities cannot deliberately their payment as long as the legal provisions are in force. Similarly, an applicant can invoke interference into the right to respect for his property, regarding the salaries, when a court decision has recognized the right to a well enough determined claim against the State to be payable (Judgment of 15 June 2010, delivered in the case Muresanu v. Romania). Or, this is not the situation in this case, as revealed by the considerations that the Court exposed further on.[276].

---

275 Decision no. 874/2010, published in the Official Gazette of Romania no. 433 of 28 June 2010: "*The Court finds that the measure for the reduction of the salary/allowance/pay by 25% is a restriction of the exercise of the constitutional right to work affecting the right to salary, with the observance of the provisions of Article 53 of the Constitution*".

276 See the summary on *www.jurisprudentacedo.ro.*

2.3 Conclusions

The issues presented lead to the general conclusion that the dialogue between the Constitutional Court of Romania and the European Court of Human Rights represents one of the constitutional guarantees for the protection of fundamental rights and freedoms. Equally, the two Courts aim at achieving this objective, within the limits and the peculiarities determined by their competence, in compliance with the principle of subsidiarity and national identity.

As concerns the limits of the competence, the European Court of Human Rights mentioned in its case-law, for example, in Judgment of 3 June 2003 delivered in the Case Pantea v. Romania, that it "does not conduct an examination in abstracto of the relevant national legislation and case-law, but it verifies whether the way they were applied to the applicant resulted in a violation of the Convention (see, mutatis mutandis, Padovani v. Italy, Judgment of February 26, 1993, para. 24) ". On the other hand, the Constitutional Court adjudicates only upon the constitutionality (and, implicitly, on the conventionality of the law) and not on its application to specific cases. Therefore, the mechanisms by which the two Courts sanction, in certain cases, the same violation of a fundamental right are essentially different.

As concerns the principle of subsidiarity, it must be underlined that the jurisdiction of the European Court of Human Rights is complementary and subsidiary and, at national level, the main role within the protection of fundamental rights and freedoms is taken, of course, by the national judge.

As concerns the national identity, the specifics and national traditions, these are factors which the national constitutional judge must always take into consideration in order to prevent the jurisprudential "transfer" of certain concepts and interpretations far from the domestic legal reality. However, referring to a "constitutional identity", it was underlined that it is not included either in the text of the Convention for the Protection of Human Rights or in the case-law of the Court of Strasbourg; the references of the latter regarding the notion of "identity" in terms of national, religious, ethnic or cultural identity of the people. Only in the light of these various "identities" has the case-law contributed to the configuration of the "constitutional identity" of States Parties to the Convention[277]. The same author expresses the idea that, especially in the recent decades, this Court expresses a neutral position in relation to the constitutional structure of the Member States, which shall implement the provisions of the Convention into domestic law and ensure them high legality.

In this complex context, the dialogue of the constitutional judge with the European judge serves to the "development" of common standards for the protection of fundamental rights or to the enrichment of the existing ones, with effects in the law making and enforcement at national level. Upon citing earlier decisions of the

277 M. Duţu, *Constitutional review of laws – an instrument promoting the constitutional identity*, in the volume *Constitutional Court – 20 years of existence and 100 years of constitutional review*, Universul Juridic Publishing House, Bucharest, 2013, pp. 106–114.

Constitutional Court, we pointed out that acceptance of judgments of the European Court of Human Rights by those decisions has led even to the enrichment of the Basic Law, i.e. the 2003 revision took into account the conclusions therein. Perhaps a similar approach would be also justified to a future revision of the Constitution, given the current trends and issues of unconstitutionality found most frequently (we shall recall here the analysed case-law in 2012), for example, within the meaning of expressly constitutional regulation of the principle of legal certainty.

Of course, the existing dialogue is subject to a continuous development, corresponding to the developments which even the concerned courts experienced, determined by social and political factors. Such a development consists in the increase of activism as a way of approaching the issues referred to the two Courts and the effects resulted from their case-law.

Thus, regarding the European Court of Human Rights[278], it has been noted its orientation towards the sanction of systemic issues resulted from legislative deficiencies, through pilot judgments[279], which means that the European Court has begun to go beyond the strict approach, through the settlement of each case, and to indicate the type of measures that states should take in order to end the systemic issues which were found. This trend is properly reflected in a restriction of the national legislature's discretion regarding the appropriate measures to comply with this case-law. This change of approach which occurred following the enlargement of the Council of Europe and the inclusion of former communist countries is attributed to the lack of confidence in their legal systems in terms of the way in which human rights and democracy standards are complied with[280].

Likewise, as for the Constitutional Court of Romania, the case-law in the recent years proves such an active attitude. The Court has increasingly emphasized that compliance with the general binding effect of the decisions of the Constitutional Court does not aim just at giving efficiency to the operative parts thereof, but also, equally, to recitals, respectively to the interpretation given by the Constitutional Court to the texts of the Constitution, especially when these texts are those governing the effects of the Court's decisions. The emphasis on the effectiveness of constitutional justice and the mention, within its decisions, of the consequences following the ascertainment of unconstitutionality interfere in order to support a correction effort – within the competence of the Court – certain deficiencies which may affect the Romanian legal system – instability, inconsistency of laws, and removal of the letter and spirit of the Constitution.

---

278 O. Pollicino, *New Emerging Judicial Dynamics of the Relationship Between National and the European Courts after the Enlargement of Europe*", on *http://centers.law.nyu.edu/jeanmonnet/papers/08/081401.pdf*, p. 37.

279 Judgment of 22 June 2004, delivered in Case *Broniowsky v. Poland*, followed by other similar judgments, see, for Romania, Judgment of 12 October 2010, delivered in Case *Maria Atanasiu and Others v. Romania*.

280 O. Pollicino, *cited paper*, p. 39.

The effectiveness of constitutional justice depends on the loyal behaviour of public authorities. The sanction applied by the European Court of Human Rights for the lack of concern in terms of unconstitutional enactments supports directly the need for full accomplishment of this effectiveness. Indirectly, this sanction itself supports the binding nature of the decisions of the European Court of Human Rights as long as several decisions of the Constitutional Court use the judgments of the European court. Ultimately, the effectiveness of the European Court of Human Rights depends on the effectiveness of national courts (and we shall consider in this context a broad approach that also includes the courts of law which are subject to comply with both the case-law of the constitutional court and of the European one).

We may conclude that the judicial dialogue, analysed in the present case, also reveals an element of solidarity between the two Courts.

3. The dialogue between the Constitutional Court of Romania and the Court of Justice of the European Union[281]

3.1 The position and the role of the Court of Justice of the European Union within the European development

According to Article 19 para. (1) of the Treaty on European Union[282], ECJ includes the Court of Justice, the Court and the specialized courts, serving to ensure the observance of the law within the interpretation and application of the Treaties. According to para. (3) of the same article, the ECJ shall decide in accordance with the Treaties: upon applications brought by a Member State, by an institution or by a natural or legal person; on a preliminary basis, upon the request of national courts of law, it shall decide upon the interpretation of Union law or upon the validity of acts adopted by institutions; in other cases provided for in the Treaties. It was argued that this position and role confer upon the ECJ the force of an authority that represents the power of the EU judges[283].

Analysing the powers and the case-law of the ECJ, it is revealed that it fulfils important powers[284], namely: the power of administrative jurisdiction (exercised in order to protect certain subjects of law concerning possible illegal actions of the EU institutions); the power of constitutional justice (including by influencing the structure and powers of the EU and by establishing the relationship between EU

281 Hereinafter ECJ.

282 Consolidated version published in the Official Journal of European Union, C83 of 30 March 2010.

283 R. Schütze, *Constitutional Law of European Union*, Universitară Publishing House, Bucharest, 2012, p. 127.

284 See also N. Diaconu, *European Union Law, Treaty*, second edition, revised, Lumina Lex Publishing House, Bucharest, 2011, p. 193.

law and the law of Member States); the power of international justice (exercised in the settlement of disputes between two or more subjects of international law), the power of court of appeal (the settlement of appeals against the judgments of the Court). As concerns the constitutional power, supported by judicial activism, challenged in some respects[285], we shall recognize the contribution of the ECJ to the development of constitutional principles as part of EU law, principles which have imposed themselves both to the EU institutions and to Member States, when acting within the scope of EU law.

However, the exercise of these powers does not transform the ECJ into a purely administrative / constitutional / international court, etc., within the meaning given to these terms and authorities in the national legal systems. Trying to identify nationally the corresponding court of the ECJ, it was noted[286] that it is a hybrid court, closer to the profile of a national supreme court than of a constitutional court, exercising powers from the competence of both courts[287].

A feature that distinguishes it from any court of a Member State is its mission to "ensure the observance of the law within the interpretation and application of the Treaties" which shall be exercised at two levels: at EU (through direct action) and at Member States level (through preliminary references). The Court has jurisdiction to interpret the provisions of the Treaties, to exercise the review on the non-compliance with the provisions of the Treaty and to review the legality of acts or the refusal the EU institutions to act. In this way, the case-law of the ECJ takes a double effect – one at the union level and one at internal level – in the legal systems of the Member States.

In this context, the national courts of law play a special role, as they also ensure the application and observance of EU law in Member States, within their competence. According to those ruled even by the ECJ[288], any national court, challenged within its jurisdiction, shall be compelled to fully apply European law and protect the rights it confers upon individuals. In this regard, it was argued[289] that the EU is based on a system of cooperative federalism, while the obligation of national courts of law to apply European law arises from the general obligation of loyal cooperation provided for by Article 4 para. (3) of the Treaty on the Functioning of the EU. This cooperation is voluntary and the national courts of law are not hierarchically subordinated or in an institutional structure in the ECJ. According to the same opinion, the national courts of law may be characterized, functionally,

---

285 H. Rasmussen, *On Law and Policy in the European Court of Justice*, Martinus Nijhoff Publishers, 1986, p. 62.

286 V. Skouris, *The Position of the European Court of Justice in the EU Legal order and its Relationship with National Constitutional Courts*, on *www.us-rs.si.*

287 See also F. Jacobs, *Is the Court of Justice of the European Communities a Constitutional Court?*, extract, in P. Craig, G. de Burca, *EU Law Text, Cases and Materials*, 5th ed., Oxford University Press, 2011, p. 65.

288 In Case no. 106/77, *Amministrazione delle Finanze dello Statoc.SimmenthalSpA.*

289 R. Schütze, *cited paper*, p. 287.

as "decentralized European courts" (only partly – for example, as far as they are not entitled to abolish an act of the EU), while institutionally they remain distinct, without any such connection with the ECJ.

From this perspective, the preliminary reference, governed by Article 267 of the Treaty on EU, supports the dialogue between the national judge and the EU judge, within the uniform application of EU law, as the national courts of law shall address to the ECJ either within the interpretation of European standard, or on validity of European standard (the national judge requires the ECJ to review the validity of an act of European law). The judgment of the ECJ is res judicata and binding not only for the national court which has initiated the procedure of preliminary questions, but also for all national courts of the Member States. However, the ECJ has jurisdiction only for the interpretation of EU law, and not for its application in specific individual cases; the assessment of the merits and the delivery of a judgment to that effect fall into the exclusive competence of the national courts. Thus, preliminary reference procedure constitutes "he keystone of judicial federalism of the Union"[290], a "cooperation" federalism where the initiative is assigned to the national courts. Even the ECJ emphasizes in its reports that the development of the EU legal order was largely the result of the dialogue with national courts, through the reference procedure for the delivery of a preliminary judgment. This cooperation has identified essential features of the legal order of the Community (European Community), in particular, its priority over the laws of the Member States, the direct effect of certain provisions and the right to obtain remedy measures when their rights are violated by an infringement of the Community legislation (European Community), for which a Member State is responsible"[291]. It was considered[292] that in this way, the CJEU achieves actually a process of "constitutionalisation" and the treaties become available to the national courts.

If the mechanism of the relationships between the ECJ and the courts of law of the Member States are operational, the relationships between the ECJ and the constitutional courts envisage multiple peculiarities. We believe that, given the role and the specific position in the national legal order[293], the latter cannot be assigned either functionally or institutionally to the category of "decentralized European courts".

Given that the constitutional review also engages issues concerning the interpretation and application of EU law, as well as relations between national and European law, the constitutional courts are not and cannot remain outside the system of voluntary cooperation to which we referred above. Similarly, the trend

---

290 *Ibidem.*

291 The Report of the Court of Justice regarding certain aspects of the Treaty on European Union, *Annual Report of the Court of Justice 1995*, pp. 19–25, on *http://europa.eu/publications/official-documents/index_ro.htm.*

292 E. Stein, *Lawyers, Judges, and the Making of a Transnational Constitution*, in American Journal of International Law no. 75/1, 1981, pp. 1–27.

293 See, for a characterization, T. Toader, M. Safta, *Forms of judicial dialogue between the Constitutional Courts*, in Dreptul no. 6/2013, pp. 173–193.

towards the integration of European development – whose essential engine is the ECJ[294] –requires the identification of "modus vivendi", of certain positions within the relations between the national constitutional courts and the ECJ. Below, we will approach the issues of these relationships, the judicial dialogue that they involve and its consequences.

3.2 The dialogue between constitutional courts and the Court of Justice of the European Union[295]

3.2.1 General aspects

There were expressed views[296] according to which the position and the relations between national constitutional courts and the ECJ could be approached either in an idealistic way – view likely to emphasize the ideas of partnership and cooperation and having as keywords the dialogue, the common values, the partnership – or in a realistic way – view that should focus on the ideas of control and power.

As for us, we believe that positioning in favour of one or the other approach would result in a distorted perspective on those relations, as long as the examination of the case-law development of the constitutional courts and of the ECJ reveals both the existence of certain attempts to assert the ideas of "power", on the one hand or on the other, and a dialogue, materialized even in the use of preliminary ruling by constitutional courts. Relations between national and international legal order within the EU are marked by a natural dynamic, as reflected in the case-law of the constitutional courts, in general, and of the Constitutional Court of Romania, in particular. We either approach this dynamic from a perspective that emphasizes the hierarchy side between constitutional courts and the ECJ, or we regard it as judicial dialogue, the existing changes are obvious at this level over time, with the features determined by the social and historic context specific to each Member State of the EU.

We believe that both the constitutional courts and the ECJ ensure the connection between two legal systems located on different levels, among which there is no hierarchy, a view that certainly involves the dialogue between them. As noted[297], accession to EU put national constitutional systems to deal with three main challenges:

294 R.D. Kelemen, *The political foundations of judicial independence in the European Union*, in Journal of European Public Policy, January 2012, p. 43.

295 Taken from T. Toader, M. Safta, *The dialogue between the Constitutional Court and the Court of Justice of the European Union*, in Dreptul no. 12/2013, pp. 129–162.

296 M. Bobek, *The consequences of the European mandate of the courts of common law on the statute of the constitutional courts*, in RRDE no. 1/2012, p. 44.

297 B. de Witte, *The Lisbon Treaty and National Constitutions, apud* C. Closa, *The Lisbon Treaty and the National Constitutions. Europeanisation and Democratic Implications*, RECON Report no. 9, Arena Report nr. 3/09, Arena, Oslo, 2009, pp. 26–27, on *http://www.reconproject.eu/.html*.

the transfer of certain legislative powers to EU institutions, the direct and priority / supremacy of EU law in relation to contrary national rules, the rearrangement of institutional relations in each Member State. Due to a transfer of sovereignty from the national to the supranational law, peculiarities arise regarding the sensitive issues on the protection of fundamental rights and the affirmation of national identity. Any differences led to the constructive repositioning on both sides – if we consider only the enshrinement and protection of fundamental rights[298]. Eventually, the concept of "dialogue" is not synonymous with the one of "agreement". It involves an exchange of ideas, even contradictory.

Positions of contradiction between the ECJ and the constitutional courts appeared particularly on the issue of supremacy of EU law and the power to sanction the *ultra vires* acts of the EU institutions, issues to which we will refer to below and then we will approach the cooperation mechanism through preliminary ruling. We believe that both issues may be regarded as falling to the judicial dialogue, even if, as concerns the first of these issues, it sometimes determined the antagonistic position of the ECJ and of the constitutional courts.

3.2.2 The constitutional courts' reserved acceptance of the supremacy of European law – the hierarchy of rules – the issues of fundamental rights – ultra vires *review*

By case-law, the CJEU founded the thesis of the supremacy of EU law which has to be integrated in the legal order of each Member State, with the consequence of impossibility for states to make unilateral legal rules prevail against common legal order. We refer to the historic case-law of the CJEU which has qualified the Community / EU as "a new legal order of international law for the benefit of which the States have limited their sovereign rights, albeit within limited fields, and the subjects of which comprise not only Member States but also their nationals"[299], and it held that "the executive force of Community law cannot vary from one state to another in defence to subsequent domestic laws, without jeopardizing the attainment of the objectives of the Treaty"[300], namely that "the validity of a Community measure or its effect within a Member State cannot be affected by allegations that it runs counter to either fundamental rights as formulated by the Constitution of that state or the principles of its constitutional structure"[301]. In other words, according to the case-law of the CJEU, the entire European law prevails over all national

298 See also R.H. Radu, *The European Court of Justice and the Protection of Fundamental Rights*, 5th Warsaw Seminar on Human Rights, Kontrast, Warsaw, 2012.

299 Case 26-62*NV Algemene Transport – en Expeditie Onderneming van Gend & Loos c. Netherlands Inland Revenue Administration* (Judgment of 5 February 1963).

300 Case 6-64 *Flaminio Costa c. E.N.E.L.* (Judgment of 15 July).

301 Case 11-70 *Internationale Handelsgesellschaft mbH c. Einfuhr – und Vorratsstelle für Getreide und Futtermittel* (Judgment of 17 December 1970).

law (even over national constitutions)[302]. These claims are also mentioned by the Council in the Opinion of the Legal Service of 22 June 2007, in which it was held that "it results from the case-law of the Court of Justice that primacy of EC law is a cornerstone principle of Community law. According to the Court, this principle is inherent to the specific nature of the European Community. At the time of the first judgment of this established case-law (Judgment of 15 July 1964, delivered in the Case 6/64, Costa / ENEL), there was no mention of primacy in the treaty. It is still the case today. The fact that the principle of primacy will not be included in the future treaty shall not in any way change the existence of the principle and the existing case-law of the Court of Justice"[303].

As concerns the competent court to rule whether Community measures are *ultra vires*, the CJEU answered firmly by the delivered judgments. Thus, for example, in the Case Foto-Frost[304], stating that it has exclusive authority to rule upon the validity of acts of the Community institutions, although their validity was challenged before a national court, the CJEU held that this is the only acceptable solution because the Treaties have established a full system of judicial review intended to confer CJEU the power to review the legality of acts of the Community institutions. A different solution would jeopardize the coherence of the system of judicial review laid down in the Treaties.

The perspective of constitutional courts is different; both in terms of the unconditional nature of the supremacy of EU law, the ground of this supremacy / priority, and the competent court entitled to decide upon *ultra vires* actions of EU. Thus, constitutional courts accept the idea of constitutional pluralism and the supremacy of EU law – with some circumstantiation and usually in relation to the infraconstitutional norms – but only as a consequence of transfer of some competences under strict conditions set by national constitutions, the latter being still the primary source of any such authority[305]. Likewise, some constitutional courts ruled on the possibility of censorship the exceeding of competence of the EU institutions, usually in the context and in connection with their mission for the protection of fundamental rights.

The Constitutional Council of France does not recognize the primacy of EU law in relation to the Constitution. The Constitutional Council of France regards the Community legal order to be integrated into the national legal order, and not the other way around, the EU regulations have become effective in France by virtue of the constituent power's will, thus, under national constitution (Articles 55 and

302 R. Kovar, *The Relationship between Community Law and National Law, in Thirty Years of Community law*, edited by European Commission, 1981.

303 *http://eur-lex.europa.eu/ro/treaties/dat/12007L/htm/C2007306RO.01025602.htm.*

304 Case C-314/85 *Foto-Frost c. Hauptzollamt Lübeck-Ost*, Judgment of 22 October 1987.

305 K. Kowalik-Banczyk, *Should we polish it up? The polish constitutional tribunal and the idea of supremacy of EU Law*, in German Law Journal, volume VI, no. 10/2005, pp. 1355–1366.

88-1)[306]. In this regard, by Decision 2004 505 DC of 19 November 2004 on the Treaty establishing a Constitution for Europe, the Constitutional Council of France has established that this act does not change the hierarchy of norms within French law, the top of which is still the Constitution. Some authors[307] argued that as long as constitutional norms do not comprise provisions which recognize the priority of international law over the Constitution, it does not either enshrine the primacy of constitutional norms in relation to the international one. However, the supremacy of the Constitution can results from the interpretation of the provisions of Article 54 of the Constitution of France, which provides that, where an international agreement contains a clause contrary to the Constitution, it can be applied only after the amendment of the Constitution[308]. At the same time, the constant position of the Constitutional Council of France was to refuse to exercise the review of the compatibility of laws with the provisions of a treaty on the grounds that it has nothing in common with the constitutional review of laws. However, the Council has recently addressed a question to the CJEU, an initiative that marks a new stage within the dialogue between the French constitutional court and the CJEU.

The Federal Constitutional Court of Germany has enshrined in its case-law the limits of supremacy of EU law, particularly in relation to the issues on fundamental rights, being known in this respect the *as long as* doctrine, developed in decisions Solange I and II. Thus, in Decision Solange I[309], the Court held, essentially, that as long as European legal order has not developed an adequate standard of fundamental rights, the Constitutional Court of Germany would leave "unenforceable" the European law which violates the fundamental rights guaranteed in the German legal system. As a result of developments of European law in this respect, of the case-law of the CJEU[310], of the adoption of a Charter of fundamental rights [311], the same Constitutional Court, in decision Solange II[312], ruled that, in view of these developments,

306 C. Charpy, *The Status of (Secondary) Community Law in the French International Order*, in P. Craig, G. de Burca, *cited paper*, p. 272.

307 M. Banu, *Acceptance of the supremacy principle of the community law in the historical case-law of the national constitutional courts: France, Germany, Italy and Great Britain*, in Romanian Journal of Community Law no. 4/2009, pp. 42–62.

308 An interpretation which may be found in the reasoning of the decision of the Council of State in Case *Sarran, Levacher and Others* of 30 October 1998, reiterated in subsequent cases, such as *Societe Arcelor Atlantique et Lorraine*, of 8 February 2007.

309 Case 2 BVL 52/71 (Judgment of 29 May 1974).

310 The joint statement of the European Council, Commission and Parliament of 5 April 1977; The statement of the European Council of 7 April 1978; Judgment CJEU starting with Case no. 4/73 *J. Nold, kohlen – und Baustoffgrohandlung v. European Commission* of 14 May 1974.

311 Convention for the Protection of Human Rights and Fundamental Freedoms, even if in another reference system, that of the Council of Europe, to which Member State had already acceded.

312 Case 2 BVL 197/83, Judgment of 22 October 1986.

it should be noted that as long as the EU and in particular the case-law of the CJEU, generally ensure effective protection of fundamental rights as against the sovereign powers of the EU which is to be regarded substantially similar to the protection of fundamental rights required unconditionally by the Basic Law of Germany, and in so far as they generally safeguard the essential content of fundamental rights, the Federal Constitutional Court of Germany will no longer exercise its jurisdiction to decide on the applicability of secondary Community legislation cited as the legal basis for any acts of German courts or authorities, and it will no longer review such legislation by the standard of fundamental rights contained in the Basic Law. Continuing this line in the Case *Banana Market*[313], the Federal Constitutional Court of Germany held that the protection of human rights within the Community system is comparable to that conferred by the German Basic Law. Therefore, the referrals of unconstitutionality which aim at the secondary Community legislation, challenged on the grounds that it infringes the fundamental rights guaranteed by the Constitution, are inadmissible unless it is proved that the general European level of protection of human rights is below that offered by the German constitutional system[314].

Another limit in accepting the supremacy of EU law, developed in the case-law of the same Court, refers to the powers of EU institutions and the *ultra vires* review. In the Case *Maastricht*[315], the Federal Constitutional Court of Germany ruled that it reserves its power to declare the inapplicability in Germany of the Community acts adopted *ultra vires*. Subsequently, in this regard, it rules that it reserves its right to review the actions of the European institutions and agencies, firstly to ensure that they do not exceed their competence, and secondly to ensure that the fundamental constitutional rights of German citizens are not violated. The considerations regarding the limits of EU supremacy are set out in Lisbon Case[316], where the Court reiterated the existence of an *ultra vires* blockage of the actions taken by institutions and which exceeded their competence, an issue which has been recently developed in Case *Honeywell*[317]. In the latter decision, the Federal Constitutional Court of Germany ruled that EU law, as autonomous law, remains dependent on assignment and empowerment in the Treaties. For the expansion of their powers, the EU bodies remain dependent on amendments to the Treaties which are carried out by the Member States in the framework of the respective constitutional provisions which apply to them and for which they take responsibility. The Federal Constitutional Court is hence empowered and obliged to review acts on the part of the European bodies and institutions with regard to whether they take place on the basis of manifest transgressions of competence or on the basis of the exercise of competence in the area of constitutional identity which is not assignable

313 Case 2 BVL1/97, Judgment of 7 June 2002.
314 P. Craig, G. de Burca, *cited paper*, pp. 274–275.
315 Case 2 BvR 2134/92 & 2159/92, Judgment of 12 October 1993.
316 Case 2 BvE 2/08, Judgment of 30 June 2009.
317 Case 2 BvR 2661/06, Judgment of 6 July 2010.

(Article 79.3 in conjunction with Articles 1 and 20 of the Basic Law), and where appropriate to declare the inapplicability of acts for the German legal system which exceed competences. However, the German Court underlined that the obligation incumbent to pursue substantiated complaints of an ultra vires act on the part of the European bodies and institutions is to be coordinated with the task which the Treaties confer on the CJEU, namely to interpret and apply the Treaties, in order to safeguard the unity and coherence of EU law. This means to comply with the rulings of the CJEU, and prior to the review of an ultra vires act, the CJEU is therefore to be afforded the opportunity to interpret the Treaties, as well as to rule on the validity and interpretation of the legal acts in question, in the context of preliminary ruling proceedings. Ultra vires review by the Federal Constitutional Court can moreover only be considered if it is manifest that acts of the European bodies and institutions have taken place outside the transferred competences, the breach of competences is in other words "sufficiently qualified". Therefore ultra vires review can be exercised, as stated in the recitals of the same decision, only in a way that is open to European legislation. In accordance with the legal system of the Federal Republic of Germany, the enforcement primacy of EU law should be recognized and should guarantee that the constitutional review powers that are reserved to the Federal Constitutional Court shall be exercised in a way that is open to European legislation.

The Constitutional Court of Italy, in the Case *Frontini*[318], held that the priority of European law can be manifested in relation to the "ordinary" rules of the Italian Constitution, but it cannot be derogated from the fundamental rights of citizens. These are "against limits" for limitations of sovereignty assigned by states in favour of EU[319]. Subsequently, these principles have been reiterated in decision *Spa Granital*[320] and in decision *Fragd*[321], by which the Constitutional Court of Italy considered that EU measures shall not be applied in Italy if they are contrary to fundamental principles on human rights. As in the case of the Constitutional Council of France and the Federal Constitutional Court of Germany, the Constitutional Court of Italy does not accept that EU law should have primacy over national constitution, and it also identifies the ground of this application supremacy / priority within the Constitution of Italy (Article 11), and not in the recitals of the decisions of the CJEU. This constitutional court has also oriented towards a dialogue with the CJEU through preliminary ruling, opening a new stage within the cooperation with the CJEU.

Constitutional courts in Central and Eastern Europe do not have a uniform approach; their case-law can be characterized as cautious regarding the issue of relations between EU law and the Constitution. Distinguishing between the

---

318 *Frontini c. Ministerio della Finanze* (1974).

319 E.S. Tănăsescu, *About the possible constitutionalisation of the community law*, on *www.ccr.ro.*

320 *Spa Granital v. Amministrazione delle Finanze dello Stato*, Case no. 170/84 of 8 June 1984.

321 *Spa Fragd v. Amminidstrazione delle Finanze*, Case no. 232 of 21 April 1989.

pre-accession stage and the post-accession stage to EU, some studies[322] noted the differences in the attitude of the constitutional courts of the candidate states, respectively those which became EU members. Thus, in the post-accession stage, the attitude of the constitutional courts in Eastern Europe (giving as examples, in this respect, Poland, Czech Republic, Hungary, Estonia) became more reserved, in the sense of supplementing the integration discourse of the previous period with phrase like "as long as", "however", rarely met previously. We can say that it is a natural evolution, because in the post-accession period, the constitutional courts have seen actually confronted with issues regarding the relationship between EU law and national law, as well as its consequences, which resulted in orientation towards the practice of other constitutional courts of the founding states of EU or of the countries that joined the EU earlier.

Some constitutional courts in Central and Eastern Europe took over, in part, the German model, and expressed their reservation about absolute priority / supremacy of EU law.

Polish Constitutional Tribunal does not accept the primacy of EU law over national Constitution. As in the case of other constitutional courts, it considers that this principle finds its foundation in the provisions of the Constitution, and not in the case-law of the CJEU. Likewise, this Tribunal considers itself competent to sanction acts issued within the exercise of the powers of EU institutions beyond their limits. A reference in this respect refers to the Treaty of Accession to EU[323] by which the Polish Constitutional Tribunal has ruled that the constitutional texts which shall authorize the delegation of the state's powers on determined matters shall not authorize such delegation to an international organization in order to issue acts or decisions contrary to the Constitution which shall be the supreme law of Poland. Likewise, these provisions shall not authorize the delegation of powers to such an extent that Poland could be unable to continue to exist and operate as a democratic and sovereign state. In case of inconsistency between the norms of the Constitution and of EU law, the options are either the amendment of the Constitution or the amendment of the provisions of EU regulation and, ultimately, the withdrawal of Poland from the EU.

The Constitutional Court of Estonia ruled that the provisions of the Constitution do not allow, as concerns the state powers, their unlimited delegation to EU. But as it becomes obvious that the amendment of the founding treaties of the EU gives rise to a more extended delegation of competence of Estonia to the EU and to a greater interference, in this respect, with the Constitution, it is necessary to

322 D. Piqani, *Constitutional Courts in Central and Eastern Europe and their Attitude towards European Integration*, EJLS, volume I, no. 2, on *http://www.ejls.eu/2/28UK.pdf.*

323 Accession Treaty K18/04 of 11 May 2005.

seek the approval of the holder of sovereignty, the people, and probably to amend again the Constitution[324].

The Constitutional Court of the Czech Republic, characterized by a pro-European speech, experienced a so-called "ultra vires revolution", by declaring a decision of the CJEU as inapplicable in the Czech Republic[325] (C/399/09 Landtová) as ultra vires[326]. In this case, the Czech Supreme Administrative Court addressed a question to the CJEU regarding the compatibility of the case-law of the Constitutional Court and, indirectly, of Article 30 para. (1) of the Czech Charter of Fundamental Rights and Freedoms (which guarantees the right to material security adequate for old age and during periods of incapacity for work, as the access to benefit from this right is conditioned however by the fact that the applicant must be a Czech citizen), with EU prohibition of discrimination on grounds of citizenship or nationality. The Czech Constitutional Court had interpreted this provision in the sense that only Czech citizens who are also residents shall be entitled to such benefits. Upon the request of the administrative court which did not agree with this interpretation, the CJEU confirmed that EU law precludes a national norm which allows the payment of a supplement only to Czech nationals residing within the territory of the Czech Republic.

The Constitutional Court of Latvia held that the transfer of powers cannot go so far as to violate the very essence of the republic as a state of law, sovereign and democratic, based on the observance of human rights[327].

We also mention the fact that the takeovers of the existing models at the moment of accession to EU and the mutual analysis of experiences and case-law of constitutional courts have determined a substantial judicial dialogue between them, in an effort to establish a common relation, as we have previously indicated[328].

The mentioned examples demonstrate the "two-dimensional" nature of the supremacy of EU law, despite the monistic discourse of the CJEU. Most constitutional courts continue to place the authority of EU law into the national legal order, within Constitutions, assuming, at the same time, its role to ensure that the limits of EU competence are properly observed and to protect the rights that are fundamental

---

324 Decision of the Supreme Court of Estonia EST-2012-2-2005, Venice Commission, in Bulletin on Constitutional Case-Law no. 2/2012, p. 291.

325 B. Smulders and K. Eisele, *Reflections on the Institutional Balance, the Community Method and the Interplay between Jurisdictions after Lisbon*, Department of European Legal Studies, Research Paper in Law no. 4/2012, p. 15, on *www.coleurope.eu.*

326 See J. Komarek, *Playing with Matches: The Czech Constitutional Court s ultra vires revolution*, on *http//verbassungsblog.de.*

327 K. Kruma, *Constitutional Courts and the Lisbon Treaty. The Future Based on Mutual Trust, apud The Area of Freedom, Security and Justice. Ten Years on Successes and Future Challenges under the Stockholm Programme*, published by Centre for European Policy Studies, Bruxelles, 2010, p. 43, on *www.isn.ethz.ch.*

328 T. Toader, M. Safta, *Forms..., cited paper*, pp. 173–193.

within the national legal order[329]. These limits were explained by the role and the specificity of constitutional courts, different from the courts of law, considering that all these reservations regarding the absolute priority / supremacy of EU law results from the fact that the constitutional courts cannot accept that another source of law can take primacy over national constitution, an act which is the very source of their own existence[330]. The role of constitutional courts remains that of ensuring the supremacy of the constitution, by taking into consideration the obligations resulting from the accession to EU, but also from the ratified treaties and conventions.

The mechanism of preliminary questions represents a way of achieving the connection between the two legal orders and the two courts at different levels, which result in an interference of the competences of the CJEU in order to interpret EU law within the constitutional review.

In this regard, we can say that the recent developments begin to shape a trend for constitutional courts in order to either use the mechanism of preliminary question, or to accept the possibility of use such mechanism. We also notice that the opening of dialogue through this method comes from the founding members (Belgium, France, Italy) or, anyway, with a greater "experience" in the EU (Austria, Spain), countries in Eastern Europe, which have recently become members, while still being in an area of expectation, defining the competences relations with the CJEU at jurisprudential level, where the German model is the mainly accepted one.

3.2.3 The mechanism of preliminary ruling

The importance of this mechanism is valued differently by the constitutional courts. The Constitutional Court of Austria ruled that refusal to address a preliminary ruling constitutes an infringement of the right to an impartial judgment[331]. In addition, it stated that if it decides upon the compatibility of a national law with the EU Charter, it shall consult in advance with the CJUE in order to clarify the Community provision in question, unless that provision is sufficiently clear as to leave no scope for interpretation[332].

---

329 See P. Craig, G. de Burca, *cited paper*, p. 300.

330 B. de Witte, *Constitutional Aspects of European Union Membership in the Original Six Member States: Model Solutions for the Applicant Countries?*, *apud* A.E. Kellermann et alii, *EU Enlagement: The Constitutional Impact at EU and National Level*, The Hague, Asser, 2001, p. 77.

331 M. Navrátilová, *The Preliminary Ruling before the Constitutional Courts*, p. 4, on *www.law.muni.cz.*

332 Reference to the criteria CILFIT – see Judgment of CJEU of 6 October 1982, delivered in Case 283/81 *SRL CILFIT and Lanificio di Gavardo SpA*; see also B. Smulders, K. Eisele, *Reflections on the institutional balance, the community method and the interplay between jurisdictions after Lisbon*, Department of European Legal Studies, Research Paper in Law no. 4/2012, p. 17, on *www.coleurope.eu.*

The Czech Constitutional Court has established that the refusal to refer a matter to the Luxembourg Court can constitute, in some cases, the infringement of the right to an impartial judgment and to a fair trial, but only if it concerns fundamental issues[333].

As concerns the matters referred to the CJEU, within the procedure of constitutional review, the position of constitutional courts is not uniform. Certain courts (such as those in Austria, Belgium, Italy, Lithuania, Spain, and France) have already made a preliminary reference or declared their readiness to do so (Portugal, Romania)[334]. Other constitutional courts consider that their role is to guarantee the respect towards the rights provided for in the national constitution and not to investigate a possible violation of EU law. The Federal Constitutional Court of Germany has not referred any matter to the CJEU for settlement. Other constitutional courts have not directly approached this aspect.

The Polish Constitutional Tribunal considers that the application of Article 267 does not jeopardize its powers and if it referred to the European court, it would do so only in cases where the application of community law is necessary[335].

The Slovak Constitutional Court denied a motion aiming at making a preliminary reference on the interpretation of a national law implementing a community directive, on the grounds that the interpretation of a national law cannot be subject to a review by the European court[336].

The cases where constitutional courts have brought preliminary reference before the CJEU present certain common elements, but also certain peculiarities.

Thus, the Constitutional Court of Austria has referred several times to the CJEU, in various matters, as follows: in matters of State aid in energy field (Judgment of the CJEU of 8 November 2001 in Case C-143/99); in a case on discrimination against Turkish workers duly registered as belonging to the labour force (Judgment of the CJEU of 8 May 2003 in Case C-171/01); on the interpretation of Articles 6 para. (1) (c) and 7 (c) and (e) of Directive 95/46 / EC of the European Parliament and of the Council of 24 October 1995 on the protection of individuals with regard to the processing of personal data and on the free movement of such data (Judgment of the CJEU of 20 May 2003 in joined cases C-465/00, C-138/01 and C-139/01). In 2012, the Constitutional Court of Austria referred to the CJEU on the examination of the compatibility of Directive 2006/24/EC of the European Parliament and of the Council of 15 March 2006 on the retention of data generated or processed in connection with the provision of publicly available electronic communications services or of public communications networks and amending Directive 2002/58/EC with the Charter of

333 M. Navrátilová, *cited paper*, p. 6.

334 *Ibidem*, p. 7.

335 *Ibidem*, p. 8.

336 *Ibidem*, p. 9.

Fundamental Rights of the European Union. By the Judgment delivered on 8 April 2014, the Court of Justice declared the invalidity of the Directive[337].

The Constitutional Court of Belgium has the most active dialogue with the CJUE as regards the formulation of preliminary reference, and the issues comprised in the formulated references are also very various: transposing into Belgian law the provisions of the Framework Decision 2002/584/JHA on the European arrest warrant and the surrender procedures between Member States (Judgment delivered in Case C 303/05); the validity of Article 2a point 5 of the Council Directive 91/308 / EEC of 10 June 1991 on the prevention of the use of the financial system for the purpose of money laundering, as amended by Directive 2001/97/EC of the European Parliament and of the Council of 4 December 2001 (Judgment of the CJEU of 26 June 2007 in Case no. C-305/05); European Arrest Warrant (Judgment of the CJEU of 21 October 2010 in Case C-306/09). Upon the request of the Constitutional Court of Belgium, the CJEU has also ruled upon the Case C-212/06 concerning care insurance scheme established by a federated entity of a Member State (Judgment of 1 April 2008), C-236/09 on the assessment of insurance risks (Judgment of 1 March 2011), C-182/10 (Judgment of 16 February 2012) and C-567/10 (Judgment of 22 March 2012) on environmental matters, C-197/11 on land and real estate policy in the context of the right to free movement and residence (Joined Cases C 203/11, Judgment of 8 May 2013), C-375/11 on the authorization of electronic communications networks and services (Judgment of 21 March 2013), C-57/12 on healthcare services, social services – Day-care centres and Night-care centres providing assistance and care to elderly persons (Judgment of 11 July 2013). So far, the CJUE has not answered to certain preliminary references made by the Constitutional Court of Belgium, namely: C-195/12 on the promotion of cogeneration based on a useful heat demand in the internal energy market or C-473/12 on the disclosure of personal data for the protection of rights and freedoms to third parties.

The Constitutional Council of France. After a long period of time during which it constantly avoided to refer preliminary references to the CJUE on the ground that it is not within its competence to review the compatibility of the French legislation with international norms, including with EU law, and that an action based on the incompatibility of the French laws with the international and European agreements cannot be considered an unconstitutional action[338], *the Constitutional Council of France* has recently addressed a preliminary reference to the CJEU, opening the dialogue with the European court[339]. Thus, using the urgent preliminary ruling

---

337 Joint Cases C-293/12 and C-594/12 – *Digital Rights Ireland and Seitlinger and Others.*

338 "For the first time ever, the Court of Justice of the European Union is delivering a preliminary ruling at the request of French Constitutional Court", on *http://www.kramerlevin.com/files/Publication.*

339 According to the doctrine, it was actually an expected and necessary development – see: V.H. Labayle, *Question prioritaire de constitutionnalité et question prejudicielle: ordonner le dialogue des judges?*, art. préc.; L. Duvouis, *Droit administratif et droit*

procedure, *the Constitutional Council of France* asked whether Articles 27 and 28 of the Framework Decision 2002/584/JHA of 13 June 2002 on the European arrest warrant and the surrender procedures between Member States must be interpreted as not precluding Member States from providing for an appeal suspending execution of the decision of the judicial authority which rules, within 30 days from receipt of the request, either to the prosecution, sentencing or detention with a view to the carrying out of a custodial sentence or detention order of a person for an offence committed prior to his surrender pursuant to a European arrest warrant, other than that for which he was surrendered, or to the surrender of a person to a Member State other than the executing Member State, pursuant to a European arrest warrant issued for an offence committed prior to his surrender.[340]. By Judgment of 30 May 2013 delivered in Case C-168/13 PPU, the CJEU held that Articles 27 para. (4) and Article 28 para. (3) (c) of the Framework Decision 2002/584 / JHA of the Council of 13 June 2002 on the European arrest warrant and the surrender procedures between Member States, as amended by the Council Framework Decision 2009/299/ JHA of 26 February 2009 must be interpreted as not precluding Member States from providing for an appeal suspending execution of the decision of the judicial authority which rules, within 30 days from receipt of the request, to consent either to the prosecution, sentencing or detention with a view to the carrying out of a custodial sentence or detention order of a person for an offence committed prior to his surrender pursuant to a European arrest warrant, other than that for which he was surrendered, or to the surrender of a person to a Member State other than the executing Member State, pursuant to a European arrest warrant issued for an offence committed prior to his surrender, provided that the final decision is adopted within the time-limits laid down in Article 17 of the same Framework Decision. Likewise, within the delivered decision, the CJEU has achieved important clarifications on the system for the protection of human rights in the Member States, in relation to the Charter of Fundamental Rights of the European Union, holding, inter alia, that the principle of mutual recognition on which the European arrest warrant system is founded is itself founded on mutual confidence between the Member States regarding the fact that their national legal systems are capable of providing equivalent and effective protection of the fundamental rights recognised at European Union level, particularly in the Charter, so that it is therefore within the legal system of the issuing Member State that persons who are the subject of a European arrest warrant can avail themselves of any remedies that allow the lawfulness of the criminal proceedings for the enforcement of the custodial sentence or detention order, or indeed the substantive criminal proceedings which led to that sentence or order, to be contested.

---

de l' Union Europeenne – La jurisprudence Simmenthal dans la force de l'âge. Vers une complétude des compétences du juge national?, in Revue francaise de droit administratif no. 2, March-April 2011, p. 376.

340 C-168/13 PPU – *Jeremy F./Premier minister.*

The Constitutional Court of Italy, characterized as a "recalcitrant player in the European judicial arena"[341], has gradually approached an open attitude to cooperation with both the CJUE and the ECHR. After a period in which it avoided to address preliminary reference to the CJUE, followed by a hesitant attitude regarding the acceptance of this possibility[342], then the return to this possibility[343], in 2008 the Court addressed to the CJEU for a preliminary ruling in the matter of regional tax established by Sardinia, a region with autonomous powers granted by a statute similar to a constitutional law[344]. By Judgment of 17 November 2009 delivered in Case C 169/08, the CJUE stated that Article 49 EC must be interpreted as precluding tax legislation, adopted by a regional authority, as referred to in Article 4 of Law no. 4 of 11 May 2006 of the Region of Sardinia, which establishes a regional tax on aircraft making stopovers for tourist purposes used for the transport of persons or on recreational crafts, only on individuals and legal entities whose tax domicile is outside the territory of the Region. Article 87 para. (1) EC must be interpreted in the sense that tax legislation, adopted by a regional authority, establishing a tax on stopovers, such as that at issue in the main case, imposed only on individuals and legal entities whose tax domicile is outside the territory of the Region, constitutes a State aid measure in favour of undertakings set up within this territory. It is the competence of the national court to note the appropriate consequences from such finding[345].

The Constitutional Court of Lithuania[346] addressed to the CJEU for a preliminary ruling on Article 20 of Directive 2003/54 of the European Parliament and of the Council of 26 June 2003 concerning common rules for the internal market in electricity and repealing Directive 96/92/EC (Judgment of 9 October 2008 in Case C 239/07[347]).

Likewise, *the Constitutional Court of Spain* addressed to the CJEU for a preliminary ruling on the European arrest warrant[348], which occasioned the adoption of a judgment by which the CJUE reaffirmed the principle of supremacy of EU law in relation to national legislation. By its preliminary reference, the CJUE was required to rule whether Article 4a para. (1) of the Framework Decision 2002/584 /JHA, as

341 M. Dani, *Tracking judicial dialogue – The scope for preliminary rulings from the Italian Constitutional Court*, on *http://centers.law.nyu.edu/jeanmonnet/papers/08/081001.pdf.*

342 Case 168/91 *Industria Dolciaria Giampaoli.*

343 Case 536/95 *Messaggero ServiziSri c. Office of Registrar of Padua.*

344 *http://curia.europa.eu.*

345 For a commentary regarding the effects of this decision, respectively of the decision of the Constitutional Court of Italy, in the light of the relationships between the purely national situations and the intra-community ones, see M. Dani, *cited paper*, on *http://centers.law.nyu.edu/jeanmonnet/papers/08/081001.pdf.*

346 Lietuvos Respublikos Konstitucinis Teismas.

347 *http://eur-lex.europa.eu.*

348 *http://curia.europa.eu.*

inserted by the Framework Decision 2009/299 / JHA, must be interpreted as precluding national judicial authorities in circumstances specified in that provision from making the execution of a European arrest warrant conditional upon the conviction in question being open to review, in order to guarantee the rights of defence of the person concerned. In the event of an affirmative answer, Article 4a para. (1) of the Framework Decision 2002/584/JHA is compatible with the requirements deriving from the right to an effective judicial remedy and to a fair trial provided for in Article 47 of the Charter and from the rights of defence guaranteed under Article 48 para. (2) of the Charter. In the event of the second question being answered in the affirmative, Article 53 of the Charter, interpreted systematically in conjunction with the rights recognized under Articles 47 and 48 of the Charter, allows a Member State to make the surrender of a person convicted in absentia conditional upon the conviction being open to review in the requesting State, thus giving those rights a greater level of protection than that deriving from EU law, in order to avoid an interpretation which restricts or infringes a fundamental right recognized by the constitution of that Member State. Replying to the preliminary references, by Judgment of 26 February 2013 in Case C-399/11, the CJUE held that Article 4a para. (1) of the Framework Decision 2002/584/JHA of 13 June 2002 on the European arrest warrant and the surrender procedures between Member States, as amended by Council Framework Decision 2009/299/JHA of 26 February 2009, must be interpreted as precluding the executing judicial authorities, in the circumstances specified in that provisions, from making the execution of a European arrest warrant issued for the purposes of executing a sentence conditional upon the conviction rendered in absentia being open to review in the issuing Member State. Likewise, Article 4a para. (1) of Framework Decision 2002/584, as amended by Framework Decision 2009/299 is compatible with the requirements under Articles 47 and 48 para. (2) of the Charter of Fundamental Rights of the European Union. Finally, Article 53 of the Charter of Fundamental Rights of the European Union must be interpreted as not allowing a Member State to make the surrender of a person convicted in absentia conditional upon the conviction being open to review in the issuing Member State, in order to avoid an adverse effect on the right to a fair trial and the rights of defence guaranteed by its constitution. On this latter point, the CJEU held, in the grounds of its judgment, that the national court shall consider from the outset the interpretation according to which Article 53 of the Charter would generally allow a Member State to apply a level of protection of fundamental rights guaranteed by its constitution if it is higher than the one resulting from the Charter and to oppose it, if applicable, to the application of certain provisions of European Union law. Such interpretation would particularly allow a Member State to apply the execution of a European arrest warrant issued for the purposes of enforcement of a judgment delivered in the absence of certain conditions, whose subject-matter is the avoidance of certain interpretations that restrict or infringe the fundamental rights recognized by its constitution, although the application of such conditions would not be allowed under Article 4a para. (1) of the Framework Decision 2002/584. However, according to the CJEU, such an interpretation of Article 53 of the Charter cannot be accepted because it would undermine the principle of primacy of the Union law, to the extent that it would allow a Member State to prevent the application of certain legal acts of the Union law which are in full compliance with the Charter, since such acts would not comply with the fundamental rights guaranteed by the constitution of the State concerned. The Court also noted that, according to an enshrined case-law, under the principle of supremacy of EU law, which represents a key feature of the Union legal order, the invocation by a Member State of certain provisions of national law, whether constitutional, cannot affect the effect of EU law within its territory. It is true that Article 53 of the Charter confirms that, if an act of EU law involves national enforcement measures, the authorities and national courts shall be free to apply national standards for the protection of fundamental rights, provided that the enforcement does not compromise either the level of protection provided by the Charter, as interpreted by the Court, or the supremacy, unity and effectiveness nature of EU law. The CJEU concluded that permitting a Member State to rely on Article 53 of the Charter in order to make the surrender of a person convicted in the absence of the condition, which is not provided by the Framework Decision 2009/299, so that the sentence to be reviewed in the issuing Member State in order to avoid the infringement of the right to a fair trial and the right of defence guaranteed by the constitution of the executing Member State in that it would call into question the uniform standard of protection of fundamental rights defined by this framework decision, would lead to the infringement of the principles of trust and mutual recognition, which it seeks to consolidate, and therefore, to a compromise of the effective nature of the mentioned framework decision.

The presentation of the preliminary questions submitted by the Constitutional Court to the CJEU illustrates both the diversity of the approached issues and the commonalities, essentially those relating to fundamental rights and freedoms.

3.3 Constitutional Court of Romania and the CJEU

3.3.1 General aspects

Romania joined the European Union in 2007, with a Constitutional Court established in 1992, a Constitution adopted in 1991 and revised in 2003, in order to ensure the constitutional basis for accession. Even if the Romanian Constitutional Court was able to learn from the experience of other constitutional courts and of other Member States of the European Union, building its own case-law with references to the EU law has been a complex process. Examining the case-law of the Constitutional Court of Romania on the relationship between national regulations and European regulations, respectively between the constitutional court and the CJEU, we find that it reflects a cautious attitude, avoiding possible conflicts of jurisdiction, driven in recent years towards the idea of dialogue through preliminary questions, dialogue that has not yet been opened.

3.3.2 The period prior to Romania's accession to the European Union

During this period, the decisions of the Constitutional Court of Romania comprise a series of basic statuaries on the relations between national and Community law, as well as on the obligations of public authorities in relation to the accession to the European Union.

Such basic statuaries are mainly comprised in Decision No. 148/2003 on the constitutionality of the proposal for the revision of the Constitution of Romania[349], by which the Court ruled on whether the provisions on the accession to Euro-Atlantic structures infringe the limits of the revision, in relation to the concepts of sovereignty and independence. Concluding that the texts in question do not violate the constitutional provisions regarding the limits of the revision, the Court held that "the objective pursued by the authors of the legislative proposal to amend and supplement the Constitution of Romania in order to harmonize its provisions with the provisions of the constituent treaties of the European Union and with the binding regulations derived there from, is a necessary political and legal framework (...)". Moreover, "at present, the introduction of these new regulations in the Constitution of Romania for a future accession to the European Union represents a solution that cannot be removed because the accession to Euro-Atlantic structures cannot be accomplished without a constitutional background". However, the Court held that "through the transfer of certain powers to the European Union structures, they do not acquire, by endowment, a *«high competence»*, its own sovereignty. In a reality, EU member states have decided to exercise in common certain powers which, traditionally, relate to the national sovereignty. It is obvious that in the current era of globalization of mankind issues, of interstate developments and of inter-individual communication at global level, the concept of national sovereignty can no longer be conceived as absolute and indivisible, without the risk of an unacceptable isolation".

The pro-European attitude of the Court was accompanied by underlining the consequences resulted from the accession to the European Union, consisting of: integration into national law of the EU's acquis, as well as the obligation to comply with European law. Thus, together with the revision of the Constitution for the purpose of accession, there are established coordinates for the Europeanization process of the national legal system, coordinates on which the very case-law of the Constitutional Court has developed. Thus, as concerns the first mentioned consequence – the integration of the Community acquis into national law –, it is important to mention that the subsequent decisions of the Court (with implications in this matter) emphasize constantly the need for the harmonization of the national legislation with the European one and the obligations of national authorities under this aspect. As concerns the second consequence – the obligation to comply with European law – with the enshrining of the rule on the priority enforcement of Community law in relation to the opposite provisions in the national laws established by the proposal for the

349 Published in the Official Gazette of Romania no. 317 of 12 May 2003.

revision of the Constitution, the Court noted that "Member States of the European Union agreed to place the Community acquis – Treaties establishing the European Union and the regulations derived from them – on an intermediate position between the Constitution and the other laws when it comes to binding European laws"[350]. The Court implicitly understood the same hierarchy of rules, without developing on that occasion the issue of the relations between European law and the Constitution, a development which was not required in the context.

Such coordinates, as outlined, underline the further jurisprudential development, in comparison with that of other European constitutional courts during the analyzed period (Poland, Czechs, Lithuania, Estonia, Latvia), being able to identify, as a general characteristic, a speech favourable to EU integration, focused on the idea of judicial harmonization[351].

The Polish Constitutional Tribunal underlined in this respect that even if European law has no binding force in Poland (at that time, Poland was not a Member State of the European Union), in view of the assumed commitments, the Polish institutions, including the Constitutional Tribunal, are required to ensure maximum compatibility between national law and European law[352].

Likewise, having examined in 2006 the referral on the unconstitutionality of the Law on healthcare reform, the Constitutional Court of Romania held[353] that the challenge regarding the existence of certain regulations applicable to EU structures is unfounded, as "the takeover of certain regulations adopted by EU bodies does not mean an exceed of powers, but an integration of Community law into national law". In a decision delivered in the same year before the accession[354], the Court held that the impugned emergency ordinance "was adopted in order to harmonize the provisions of the legislation in the matter with the provisions of the Accession Treaty (...). The emergency of the measure that was taken was justified by the fact that Romania is closely monitored by the European Commission under the aspect of *«Competition»*, and the violation of these provisions of the Accession Treaty is likely to lead to the activation of the safeguard clause resulting in the postponement of Romania's accession to the European Union (...)".

---

350 Decision no. 148 of 16 April 2003, published in the Official Gazette of Romania no. 317 of 12 May 2003.

351 A. Albi, *EU enlargement and the Constitutions of the Central and Eastern Europe*, Cambridge University Press, 2005, p. 52.

352 Z. Kuhn, *The application of European Union Law in the new member states: several early predictions*, German Law Journal, 2005, p. 566.

353 Decision no. 298 of 29 March 2006, published in the Official Gazette of Romania no. 372 of 28 April 2006.

354 Decision no. 205 of 7 March 2006, published in the Official Gazette of Romania no. 340 of 14 April 2006.

3.3.3 *Post-accession period*

The main coordinates of this period are:

- The continuation of the harmonization process of the national legislation with the European one;
- The use of certain interpretative tools aiming at the guarantee of the consistency of the harmonization process;
- Clear delimitation of powers and constitutional loyalty in the interpretation and application of European Union law.

The continuation of the harmonization process of the national legislation with the European one. Interpretative tools – the case-law of the Court of Justice of the European Union.

According to Article 148 para. (4) of the Constitution of Romania: "The Parliament, the President of Romania, the Government, and the judicial authority shall guarantee that any obligations arising from the accession instrument and from provisions under paragraph (2) are put into effect". Para. (2) of the same article establishes: "Following accession, provisions in the founding Treaties of the European Union, as well as other binding regulations under community law shall prevail over any contrary provisions of domestic law, while observing provisions in the accession instrument".

In many decisions pronounced after 2007, the Constitutional Court found that the main or delegate legislature achieved the harmonization of the national legislation with the European provisions in various matters: asylum, by Law no. 122/2006 on asylum in Romania, published in the Official Gazette of Romania, no. 428 of 18 May 2006[355]; aliens' regime[356], preventing and combating cross-border crime by Law no. 76/2008 on the organization and operation of the National System of Judicial Genetic Data, published in the Official Gazette of Romania no. 289 of 14 April 2008[357]; trademarks by Law no. 84/1998 on trademarks and geographical indications, published in the Official Gazette of Romania no. 161 of 23 April 1998[358]; mutual

355 Decision no. 1033 of 9 October 2008, published in the Official Gazette of Romania no. 757 of 10 November 2008; Decision no. 631 of 12 May 2011, published in the Official Gazette of Romania no. 536 of 29 July 2011.
356 Decision no. 432 of 15 April 2010, published in the Official Gazette of Romania no. 361 of 2 June 2010.
357 Decision no. 666 of 17 May 2011, published in the Official Gazette of Romania no. 502 of 14 July 2011.
358 Decision no. 688 of 31 May 2011, published in the Official Gazette of Romania no. 537 of 29 July 2011.

recognition of judgments in civil and commercial matter[359], mediation[360], consumer protection[361] and others.

In some cases, the reasoning parts of the decisions contain a development of the argumentation as to underline the obligation and importance of the harmonization process, seen as justifying the adoption of certain laws. Thus, for example, the Court held that "in accordance with the provisions of Article 148 (4) of the Constitution, the authorities of the Romanian State assumed the obligation to guarantee that any obligations arising from the the founding Treaties of the European Union, the binding regulations under community law and the accession instrument are put into effect. In this regard, the Government is constitutionally empowered to guarantee, through the means it has at its disposal, the fulfilment of obligations of Romania to the European Union. Thus, the use of emergency ordinances for bringing into accord the national legislation with the Community legislation, where the initiation of the infringement procedure before the Court of Justice had become imminent, is fully constitutional".[362]. Even if such an infringement procedure was not imminent, specific conditions requiring rapid legislative intervention – such as avoiding the negative consequences that would be produced on competition at EU level, respectively ensuring the immediate protection of consumers – have been also retained as justifying the adoption of emergency ordinances[363].

In the post-accession period, the Constitutional Court has more frequently invoked the case-law of the Court of Justice of the European Union, an approach adopted also by other Constitutional Courts also prior accession for the purpose to guide the legislator's action, to explain or to substantiate its measures. We refer to what the doctrine called "interpretative tools" within the reach of the Constitutional Courts used to determine the consistent interpretation of national legislation with EU law.[364]. For example, adjudicating on a piece of legislation regarding the

359 Decision no. 1289 of 4 October 2011, published in the Official Gazette of Romania no. 830 of 23 November 2011.

360 Decision no. 447 of 7 April 2011, published in the Official Gazette of Romania no. 485 of 8 July 2011.

361 Decision no. 1591 of 13 December 2011, published in the Official Gazette of Romania no. 80 of 1 February 2012.

362 Decision no. 802 of 19 May 2009, published in the Official Gazette of Romania no. 428 of 23 June 2009; Decision no. 1070 of 8 September 2009, published in the Official Gazette of Romania no. 703 of 20 October 2009.

363 Decision no. 450 of 3 May 2012, published in the Official Gazette of Romania no. 507 of 24 July 2012, in the same respect, see: Decision no. 1540 of 6 December 2011, published in the Official Gazette of Romania no. 151 of 7 March 2012; Decision no. 802 of 19 May 2009, published in the Official Gazette of Romania no. 428 of 23 June 2009.

364 D. Piqani, *cited paper,* p. 8.

organisation and operation of gambling[365], the Court held that "it is necessary to take into account also the case-law of the Court of Justice of the European Union in the field of freedom to provide services under Article 49 EC. Thus, by the Judgement of 3 June 2010, delivered in the Case C-258/08, Ladbrokes Betting & Gaming Ltd, Ladbrokes International Ltd v. Stichting de Nationale Sporttotalisator, the Court of Justice of the European Union reiterated its practice in that, in the regulation of gambling, Member States have a very wide margin of action. (...) The Member States are free to set the objectives of their policy on betting and gambling according to their own scale of values and, where appropriate, to define in detail the level of protection sought. The restrictive measures that they impose must, however, satisfy the conditions laid down in the case-law of the Court, in particular as regards their proportionality (see, to that effect, the Judgement of 6 March 2007, delivered in the joined cases C-338/04, C-359/04 and C-360/04, Massimiliano Placanica and Others)".

Explaining the legislature's measure also in relation to the case-law of the Court of Justice of the European Union, the Constitutional Court invoked it as one of the reasons likely to support the change in its own practice, Thus, for example, by Decision no. 1237 of 6 October 2010[366] having to decide on a regulation concerning pensions and, in this context, on the issue of equalization of retirement ages for men and women, the Constitutional Court of Romania noted that "it is worth noting the reasons retained by the Court of Justice of the European Union in relation to certain arguments such as those concerning the role of women in the family [...] Based on the principle of ensuring equal pay between women and men for equal work, the Court in Luxembourg, in the Judgement of 13 November 2008, delivered in the case Commission of the European Communities v. Italian Republic C-46/07, but also by the Judgement of 26 March 2009, delivered in the case Commission of the European Communities v Hellenic Republic C-559/07, held that social measures should contribute to ensuring working lives of women equal to men. Imposing different retirement ages is not likely to compensate for the disadvantages and hardships faced by women in their careers because of their social status. It was also recalled that the concern for child rearing should not to be reported only to women but also to men and that, from this perspective, the situation of the two sexes is comparable." In light of these considerations, the Constitutional Court of Romania held that "it is necessary to bring a change in its practice relating to the issue of equalization of retirement ages for men and women"[367]. *Without being able to trenchantly decide on its opportunity, however, opposition to this solution would mean, at present, opposition to a social trend of international magnitude, whose standards Romania is called to comply with." Since one cannot deny the disparities between actual*

365 Decision no. 1344 of 13 October 2011, published in the Official Gazette of Romania no. 32 of 16 January 2012.

366 Published in the Official Gazette of Romania no. 785 of 24 November 2010.

367 Decision no. 90 of 10 February 2005, published in the Official Gazette of Romania no. 245 of 24 March 2005.

social conditions in Romania and these standards, the Constitutional Court held that "the solution adopted by the legislator through the Law on the unified public pension system in the sense of a gradual increase in the retirement age of women over 15 years is the only way to ensure adequacy of this measure to the social reality and to render constitutional the legal norm."

3.3.4 Delimitations of powers at jurisdictional level

After a short period of differentiated case-law[368], the Constitutional Court of Romania decided on the issue regarding the relations of competence among national courts, constitutional courts and the CJUE, in the matter of priority interpretation and application of EU law, implicitly ruling on the obligations of national courts in this context.

Thus, in an established case-law, the Constitutional Court noted[369] that it does not have the power "to examine whether a provision of national law complies with the text of the Treaty establishing the European Community (A/N now the Treaty on the Functioning of the European Union) in terms of Article 148 of the Constitution. Such power, namely to establish whether there is a contrariety between national law and the EC Treaty, belongs to the court of law, which, in order to reach a fair and lawful conclusion, ex officio or upon request of the party, may submit a preliminary question in the meaning of Article 234[370] *of the Treaty establishing the European Community before the Court of Justice of the European Communities. If the Constitutional Court would be deemed competent to adjudicate on the conformity of national legislation with the European legislation, we would face a possible legal dispute between the two courts, which, at this level, is unacceptable".*

Similarly, the Court also held that[371] "the attribution of priority application of the binding Community rules binding in relation to the provisions of the national legislation belongs to the court of law. It is a matter of the enforcement of law, not of constitutionality"[372], and that "within the relations between the Community and

---

368 Decision no. 59 of 17 January 2007, published in the Official Gazette of Romania no. 98 of 8 February 2007; Decision no. 558/2007 published in the Official Gazette of Romania no. 464 of 10 July 2007; Decision no. 1031/2007, published in the Official Gazette of Romania no. 10 of 7 January 2008.

369 Decision no. 1596 of 26 November 2009 published in the Official Gazette of Romania no. 37 of 18 January 2010 or Decision no. 1289 of 4 October 2011, published in the Official Gazette of Romania no. 830 of 23 November 2011.

370 Article 267 TFUE.

371 Decision no. 137 of 25 February 2010, published in the Official Gazette of Romania no. 182 of 22 March 2010.

372 In the same regard, for example, Constitutional Court of Austria, see, for developments G. Kucsko-Stadlmayer, *Constitutional review in Austria – Traditions and new developments*, communication prepared for the International Conference dedicated to the 20th anniversary of the Constitutional Court of Romania, available on CCR – *www.ccr.ro.*

the national law (except the Constitution), we can only refer to priority application of the former in relation to the latter and such matter falls within the competence of the courts".

Thus, the constitutional review[373] is a review of internal rules in compliance with the Constitution. If national rules transpose a European rule, it may be needed to raise a preliminary question before the ECJ and the reporting to the interpretation given by it in order to conduct the constitutional review.

Having developed the above-mentioned recitals in a series of decisions – by which constitutional review was exercised on a certain regulation on which the ECJ had formulated an answer to a preliminary question raised by a Romanian court – the Court ruled on the relations of power among the ECJ, national courts and the Constitutional Court, referring to the mechanism of preliminary questions[374].

As concerns the competence of the CJUE, the Constitutional Court held that, replying to the preliminary questions, it interprets the applicable provisions of the Treaty on the Functioning of the European Union and does not verify the compatibility of the internal act with the provisions of the Treaty. The European court "has no competence to deliver a judgment aiming at the ascertainment of the validity or invalidity of national law. The consequence of certain interpretations of the Treaty may be that a provision of a national law may be incompatible with European law. The effects of this preliminary question are those indicated in the established case-law of the Court of Justice of the European Union, namely that «the interpretation which, in the exercise of competence conferred by Article 177 [now Article 267 of the Treaty on the Functioning of the European Union], the Court gives to a rule of Community law, clarifies and defines, where necessary, the meaning and scope of such rule as it must or should be understood and applied since its entry into force»"[375].

As concerns the national court and its competence, the preliminary question is seen and promoted as a form of judicial dialogue in order to seek "technical" justification for the settlements delivered by the national judge, without affecting its competence or independence.

---

373 The power set forth in Article 146 b) of the Constitution has a different regime.

374 Decision no. 668 of 18 May 2011, published in the Official Gazette of Romania no. 487 of 8 July 2011; Decision no. 1088 of 14 July 2011, published in the Official Gazette of Romania no. 668 of 20 September 2011; Decision no. 921 of 7 July 2011, published in the Official Gazette of Romania no. 673 of 21 September 2011; Decision no. 903 of 30 June 2011, published in the Official Gazette of Romania no. 673 of 21 September 2011.

375 Judgment of 27 March 1980, delivered in Case 61/79, *Denkavit italiana v. Amministrazione delle finanze dello Stato*; Judgment of 2 February 1988, delivered in Case 24/86, *Blaizot v. University of Liege and Others*; Judgment of 15 December 1995, delivered in Case C-415/93, *Bosman and Others v. Union royale belge des sociétés de football association and Others.*

The dialogue between judges, at the initiative of the national judge, constitutes an indispensable tool for the national judge to achieve its duties in relation to the provisions of Article 148 of the Constitution[376]. This is all the more as compliance with these obligations by the courts of law also involve the responsibility of the national judge, an aspect which is noted by the Constitutional Court when it had to examine regulations regarding the sanctioning of disciplinary offences of judges and prosecutors[377].

The argumentation directed to this type of dialogue is developed by also comprising in its scope the constitutional court. By the same decisions, the Court, stating that "it is neither positive legislature nor a court with jurisdiction to interpret and apply EU law in disputes involving subjective right of citizens", allows that it can use a rule of European law within the constitutional review as a rule interposed to that of reference, subject to meeting certain conditions: "this rule must be sufficiently clear, precise and unambiguous in itself or its meaning must have been clearly, precisely and unequivocally established by the European Court of Justice (..), the rule must be circumscribed to a certain level of constitutional relevance, so that its legal content might support the possible infringement by the national law of the Constitution – the only direct reference standard in its constitutional review. In such a case the approach of the Constitutional Court is distinct from the simple application and interpretation of law, jurisdiction belonging to courts and administrative authorities, or from any issues of legislative policy promoted by Parliament or the Government, as appropriate." The Court explicitly stated that "in the light of cumulative set of conditionality, it is up to the Constitutional Court to apply or not in its constitutional review the judgments of the European Court of Justice or to formulate itself of preliminary questions to establish the content of the European rule". The Constitutional Court of Romania has indirectly referred to the theory of the clear act, mentioned by the CJUE in the Judgment of 6 October 1982, delivered in Case 283/81 SRL CILFIT and Lanificio di Gavardo SpA, in which it held that "a national court against whose decisions there is no judicial remedy under national law is required, where a question of Community law is raised before it, to comply with its obligation to bring the matter before the Court of Justice, unless it has established that the question raised is irrelevant or that Community provision in question has already been interpreted by the Court or that the correct application of Community law so obvious as to leave no scope for any reasonable doubt; the existence of such a possibility must be assessed in the light of the specific characteristics

376 For an analysis of the national judge within the accession process, see I. Maher, *National Courts as European Community Courts*, HeinOnline, 14 Legal Stud.226, 1994.

377 Decision no. 2 of 11 January 2012, published in the Official Gazette of Romania no. 131 of 23 February 2012; for developments regarding the case-law of the CJEU, see R.H. Radu, R.M. Giurescu, *Considerations regarding the magistrates' responsibility in the case-law of the Court of Justice of the European Union*, in Judicial Courier no. 11/2012, p. 702.

of Community law, the particular difficulties to which its interpretation give rise and the risk of divergences in judicial decisions within the Community". At the same time, it mentioned the margin of discretion belonging to the constitutional court in order to determine the constitutional relevance of the European norm.

By the above-mentioned decisions, it is found that the constitutional judge of Romania promotes a pluralistic conception and mutual respect between the courts belonging to legal orders which are parties in a proceeding of interference. According to the Court, such an attitude is related to "cooperation between the domestic constitutional court and the European court and to the judicial dialogue between them without raising issues related to the establishment of hierarchies between these courts".

3.3.5 Observance of the Constitution within the harmonization process of the national law with EU law

Developing the basic statuaries laid down in the period prior to accession to the European Union, referring to the transfer of powers in favour of the EU and the articulation between the national constitutional law and EU law, the Constitutional Court of Romania has proceeded, with reference to the case-law of other constitutional courts, to determine the relations between the two legal systems and, in the context, the constitutional identity. Thus, by Decision no. 683 of 27 June 2012[378], the Constitutional Court of Romania held that "according to Article 1 para. (2) of the Treaty on European Union, published in the Official Journal of the European Union, Series C no. 83 of 30 March 2010, it marks a new stage in the process of creating an ever closer union among the peoples of Europe. The essence of the Union is the grant of powers by Member States – still more in number – to achieve their common objectives, of course, without to infringe, in the end, through this grant of powers, the national constitutional identity –Verfassungsidentitat (see Decision of the German Constitutional Court of 30 June 2009, delivered in Case 2 BvE 2/08, on the constitutionality of the Lisbon Treaty).

Therefore, under this line of thinking, Member States maintain their powers that are inherent to preserve their constitutional identity and the grant of powers, as well as rethinking, emphasis or establishment of new guidelines within the powers which have already been granted, is related to the constitutional margin of discretion of Member states. Therefore, the European Union may only act within the powers conferred upon it, having thus conferred powers. (...) Thus, Article 5 para. (2) of the European Union Treaty expressly stipulates that «under the principle of conferral, the Union shall act only within the limits of the competences conferred upon it by the Member States in the Treaties to attain the objectives set out therein. Competences not conferred upon the Union in the Treaties remain with the Member States», which demonstrates that, at present, the European Union is still a union

378 Published in the Official Gazette of Romania no. 479 of 12 July 2012.

of states. (...) Before the entry into force of the Lisbon Treaty, it was difficult to set out the limits of the powers of the European Union, but at the moment there are categories of competences set out in the Treaty on which the European Union has exclusive competence, common competence or competence to support, coordinate or supplement the action of the Member States. Therefore, the action of the Member States is very important in the architectural structure of the European Union as it varies in intensity according to the matter".

As concerns the fulfilment of the authorities' obligations under Article 148 of the Constitution, it must be achieved in compliance with the Basic Law of the country. The Constitutional Court has sanctioned violations of the Constitution resulted from the defective fulfilment of such obligations, even if the intention declared by the legislature was to comply with EU acts. This is a conclusion that can be drawn, for example, of Decision no. 799 of 17 June 2011 on the bill for the revision of the Constitution, which, noting that the elimination of the second sentence of Article 44 para. (8) of the Constitution, according to which: "Lawfulness of acquirement shall be presumed" is unconstitutional because it is tantamount to suppressing a guarantee of the right to property, thus breaching the limits of the revision provided for by Article 152 para. (2) of the Constitution, the Court emphasized that "the regulation of this presumption does not prevent the delegated or primary legislature to adopt, pursuant to Article 148 of the Constitution – Integration into the European Union, regulations to enable full compliance with EU legislation in the fight against crime" (objective envisaged by the initiator of the proposed revision, particularly with reference to the Council Framework Decision 2005/212 / JHA Council of 24 February 2005 on Confiscation of Crime-Related Proceeds, Instrumentalities and Property[379]).

By another decision, the Constitutional Court of Romania found the unconstitutionality of a law transposing a Directive of the European Parliament and of the Council of the European Union (Law no. 298/2008 on the retention of data generated or processed by the providers of publicly available electronic communications services or public communications networks and amending the Law no. 506/2004 on the processing of personal data and privacy protection in the electronic communications sector[380]), mainly for the lack of clarity and precision, holding that "the restriction on the exercise of the right to private life, secrecy of correspondence and freedom of expression, (...) must occur in a clear, predictable and unequivocal manner as to remove, if possible, the occurrence of arbitrariness or abuse of authorities in this area". In the reasoning part of the Court, the shortcomings of drafting the impugned normative act are thoroughly specified, including in relation to the standards required by the European Court of Human Rights in its case-law[381].

---

379 Published in Official Journal of the European Union no. L 68 of 15 March 2005.

380 Decision no. 1258 of 8 October 2009, published in the Official Gazette of Romania no. 798 of 23 November 2009.

381 *Sunday Times v. the United Kingdom*, 1979; *Rotaru v. Romania*, 2000.

With regard to this decision and to the similar case-law of other constitutional courts[382], it was noted, more or less critical[383], that it was delivered without addressing any preliminary question to the Court of Justice of the European Union. Having examined the recitals of this decision, it shall be noted that the Court held the violation of certain fundamental constitutional principles, as well as certain fundamental rights due to the lack of clarity and precision of the national rules transposing the European Directive, resulting in the ascertainment of the unconstitutionality of the transposing law, without proceeding to the approach of any issues that require a certain interpretation by the Court of Justice of the European Union. In such a context, a preliminary question would not have been useful in any way to the constitutional review, perhaps not more than an expression of the existence of a dialogue, without finality within the constitutional review area.

As noted[384], a constitutional court can review the validity of a national provision for the implementation of EU norms, without reference to any provision of the Union. We refer to different provisions resulted from different normative sets that can be interconnected, but the connection is not required and the grounds for the invalidity of the transposing norms may exclusively aim at the national constitution.

We consider the examined decision as a form of judicial dialogue, as long as the reasons of the Constitutional Court of Romania is in full agreement with the statuaries contained in the case-law of the CJEU, which held that "each Member State is bound to implement the provisions of directives in a manner that fully meets the requirements of clarity and certainty in legal situations imposed by the Community legislature, in the interests of the persons concerned established in the Member States. To that end, the provisions of a directive must be implemented with unquestionable legal certainty and with the requisite specificity, precision and clarity"[385]. Legal certainty "requires that the effects of Community legislation be clear and predictable, the purpose of this requirement is to ensure that legal relationships governed by Community law remain predictable"[386]. "*Member States must provide a precise legal framework in the field in question, by adopting rules of law capable of creating a situation which is sufficiently precise, clear and transparent to allow individuals to know their rights and rely on them before national courts*".

On the other hand, on that occasion, the Constitutional Court of Romania did not exclude, de plano, the possibility of addressing a preliminary question with reference to this matter. The possibility exists, as far as the possible constitutional review of the normative act for the transposition of the same Directive will require

382 Federal Constitutional Court of Germany, Constitutional Court of Belgium, Supreme Court of Cyprus, Constitutional Court of the Czech Republic.

383 M. Bobek, *cited paper*, p. 56; D.A. Efrim, G. Zanfir, M.M. Moraru, *The Hesitating steps of the Romanian Courts towards judicial dialogue on EU Law matters*, on *http://www.academia.edu.*

384 M. Bobek, *cited paper*, p. 55.

385 C-354/99 – *Commission v. Ireland*, Judgment of 18 October 2001.

386 T. Tridimas, *The general principles of EU Law*, Oxford EC LAW Library, p. 244.

it. The conditions of addressing such a preliminary question were mentioned by the Constitutional Court of Romania, starting with Decision no. 668/2011 to which we referred. In other words, the role of the Constitutional Court is that of guarantor of the Constitution. The wording of such preliminary questions would be required only if the answer to the preliminary question were relevant in exercising the constitutional review of internal rules in relation to the provisions of the Constitution.

We note that the subsequent developments of both the case-law of the CJUE and the case-law of the Constitutional Court of Romania, demonstrate the existence of the judicial dialogue on the issues analyzed above. Thus, after the first unsuccessful attempt to challenge the Directive before the Court of Justice of the European Union, raised by Ireland and Slovakia[387], it was vested by the Constitutional Court of Austria and the Supreme Court of Ireland, which raised a series of concerns regarding the compatibility of the Directive with the Charter of Fundamental Rights of the European Union and whether it ensures a proper functioning of the internal market of the European Union[388].

High Court (High Court, Ireland), as well as Verfassungsgerichtshof (Constitutional Court, Austria) required the Court of Justice to examine the validity of the directive, particularly in terms of two fundamental rights guaranteed by the Charter of Fundamental Rights of the European Union, namely the fundamental right to privacy and the fundamental right of personal data protection. Both courts raised the following issues: whether the Directive is necessary and appropriate to attain the objectives pursued by it; the compatibility of several provisions of the Directive with the provisions of the Charter, mainly with Article 7 on the right to privacy, and with Article 8 on the right to personal data protection. This issue on the validity lies undeniably in the middle of the issues raised by these cases; the interpretation of the general provisions of the Charter governs its interpretation and application.

By the Judgment of 8 April 2014, delivered in that case, the Court of Justice declared the invalidity of the Directive. The Court held, in essence, that the data to be retained under the Directive allow, among others: (1) to know the identity of the person with whom a subscriber or registered user has communicated and by what means; (2) to identify the time of the communication as well as the place from which that communication took place; and (3) to know the frequency of the communications of the subscriber or registered user with certain persons during a given period. These data, taken as a whole, may allow very precise conclusions to

387 We refer to the action of Ireland of 10 February 2009, supported by Slovakia, requesting the annulment of Directive 2006/24/CE of the European Parliament and of the Council of 15 March 2006 on the ground that it has not been adopted based on a proper legal reason.

388 Joint Cases C-293/12 and C-594/12 – *Digital Rights Ireland and Seitlinger and Others.*

be drawn concerning the private lives of the persons whose data has been retained, such as the habits of everyday life, permanent or temporary places of residence, daily or other movements, the activities carried out, the social relationships of those persons and the social environments frequented by them. The Court considered that by requiring the retention of such data and by allowing the competent national authorities to access those data, the Directive represents a particularly serious interference with the human rights. The fact that data are retained and subsequently used without the subscriber or registered user being informed is likely to generate in the minds of the persons concerned the feeling that their private lives are the subject of constant surveillance.

Having examined whether such an interference with the fundamental rights at issue is justified, the Court found that by adopting the Data Retention Directive, the European Union legislature has exceeded the limits imposed by compliance with the principle of proportionality. In this regard, the Court observes that, taking into account, on the one hand, the important role played by the protection of personal data in the light of the fundamental right to respect for private life and, on the other hand, the extent and seriousness of the interference with that right caused by the directive, the EU legislature's discretion is reduced, with the result that review of that discretion should be strict. Although the retention of data required by the directive may be considered to be appropriate for attaining the objective pursued by it, the wide-ranging and particularly serious interference of the directive with the fundamental rights at issue is not sufficiently circumscribed to ensure that that interference is actually limited to what is strictly necessary. Firstly, the directive covers, in a generalised manner, all individuals, all means of electronic communication and all traffic data without any differentiation, limitation or exception being made in the light of the objective of fighting against serious crime. Secondly, the directive fails to lay down any objective criterion which would ensure that the competent national authorities have access to the data and can use them only for the purposes of prevention, detection or criminal prosecutions concerning offences that, in view of the extent and seriousness of the interference with the fundamental rights in question, may be considered to be sufficiently serious to justify such an interference. On the contrary, the directive simply refers in a general manner to "serious crime" as defined by each Member State in its national law. In addition, the directive does not lay down substantive and procedural conditions under which the competent national authorities may have access to the data and subsequently use them. In particular, the access to the data is not made dependent on the prior review by a court or by an independent administrative body. Finally, the Directive does not provide for sufficient safeguards to ensure effective protection of the data against the risk of abuse and against any unlawful access and use of the data. It notes, inter alia, that the directive permits service providers to have regard to economic considerations when determining the level of security which they apply (particularly as regards the costs of implementing security measures) and that it does not ensure the irreversible destruction of the data at the end of their retention period[389].

By making a comparison of the recitals that substantiated the decision of the Constitutional Court of Romania, respectively the decision of the Court of Justice of the European Union, we find common reasons, such as the same reveal of the lack of proportionality and clarity of the regulation, as well as the emphasize of the standards required by the protection of the right to privacy and private life. In this regard, we consider that the above-mentioned Judgment of the Court of Justice of the European Union reveals significant meanings within the dialogue between European courts and the protection of fundamental rights and freedoms at European Union level.

Moreover, further, by Decision no. 440 of 8 July 2014[390], the Constitutional Court of Romania found that the provisions of Law no. 82/2012 on the retention of data generated or processed by providers of public electronic communications networks and by providers of publicly available electronic communications services and amending and supplementing Law no. 506/2004 concerning the processing of personal data and the protection of privacy in the electronic communications sector are unconstitutional. The Court noted that the Law no. 82/2012 was adopted by the Parliament following the Decision no. 1258 of 8 October 2009 pronounced by the Constitutional Court[391], by which it found that the provisions of Law no. 298/2008 on the retention of data generated or processed by providers of publicly available electronic communications services or public communications networks and amending Law no. 506/2004 on the processing of personal data and privacy protection in the electronic communications sector are unconstitutional, Law no. 298/2008 represents as the first transposition of the Directive 2006/24/EC into the national law. Having analyzed the provisions of Law no. 82/2012, as well as the considerations of principle contained in the Judgment of the Court of Justice of the European Union of 8 April 2014, by which the Directive 2006/24/EC was declared invalid, and in the Constitutional Court's Decision no. 1258 of 8 October 2009, the Constitutional Court held that these are also applicable, in principle, to Law no. 82/2012.

Still recently and subsequent to the Judgments pronounced by the Court of Justice of the European Union, the Constitutional Court of Slovenia found, indicating similar reasons to those noted by the European Court, the unconstitutionality of Articles 162–169 of the Electronic Communications Act, published in the Official Gazette of the Republic of Slovenia no. 109/12.

This is an effect of the judicial dialogue for the achievement of certain common standards for the protection of fundamental rights and freedoms.

---

389 Taken over from – Court of Justice of the European Union, Press statement no. 54/14, Luxembourg, 8 April 2014.

390 Published in the Official Gazette of Romania no. 653 of 4 September 2014.

391 Published in the Official Gazette of Romania no. 798 of 23 November 2009.

3.4 Conclusions

The development of the dialogue between the constitutional courts and the CJUE demonstrates a trend for the conservation of the position and the role of national courts, respectively, for the claim of the position and the role of the CJUE. At the same time, it demonstrates the effort for identification of a common language and common standards, notably in the field of the protection of human rights. It is true that the plurality of sources in the matter – the national constitutions, the Charter of Fundamental Rights and Freedoms, the Convention for the Protection of Human Rights and Fundamental Freedoms, compulsory themselves – determines a risk of collision between the courts called to apply the rules contained therein. The standards for the protection of these rights tend, however, towards uniformity, also through the contribution of courts called upon to interpret those rules and that invoke each other's case-law. In addition, acceptance of the Charter or of the Convention as systems or reference for the exercise of constitutional review – with the distinctions and peculiarities determined by the legal systems from which they originate – enhances the dialogue between courts, by means of preliminary references, as a way of solving such divergent approaches and of "constitutionalisation" at European level of the matter of fundamental rights and freedoms. Thus, the prejudicial matter referred to the CJEU the contemporary and absolutely original concept of convergence of thought and action between national judges and the EU ones, a concept by which, audacious, tends to conceive a Union citizen's right, irrespective of his nationality and geographical area[392].

Using the instrument of preliminary reference by the constitutional courts, as well as invoking the case-law of the CJEU, instruments which both are circumscribed to the concept of judicial dialogue, represent a factor of "harmony" for the national and supranational legal order, as well as a factor of "survival" for both the CJEU and the constitutional courts. At a transnational level, constitutional disputes can take different forms, but the acceptance of the idea of constitutional pluralism involves, essentially, the concern to minimize disputes without compromising the integrity and coherence of each legal order, an objective which can be achieved only through a sustained judicial dialogue.

Finally, the power of CJEU depends also on the way of reporting to the constitutional courts, which have, on the one hand, a broader competence in terms of national legal systems, and on the other hand, are closer to citizens and, from this perspective, they are perceived as having a stronger substantiation in terms of legitimacy. The very principle of the supremacy/priority of the EU law and the effect that it produces in the sense of removing the enforcement of the contrary national rules, can be achieved mainly through the cooperation between the CJUE and the national courts. Most of the preliminary questions submitted by national

392 I. Deleanu, *Dialogue between judges – forms and implications of the dialogue between judges*, in RRDJ no. 1/2012, pp. 17–44.

courts are designed to identify the compliance of national law with EU law[393]. By achieving the constitutionalisation process, the constitutional courts contribute to the Europeanization of national legal systems, by establishing the coordinates of action for public authorities.

The described phenomenon is also translated by a big responsibility of the ordinary national or constitutional judge, who is not just a judge of the national law, but also of EU law and of the Convention for the Protection of Human Rights and Fundamental Freedoms. In this triple role, he/she has the power to ensure the harmonious and conciliatory enforcement of at least three legal systems, based on common values and benchmarks, but which are different in their normative content. Any waiver of this mission in favour of one or another international jurisdiction is susceptible to be criticized by the other jurisdiction or by the citizens whose rights he/she is required to protect[394].

As for the Constitutional Court of Romania, the examination of the case-law reveals that the national constitutional case-law has crystallized a conception regarding: the relationship between national law and European Union law; the competence of the Constitutional Court; the competence of the courts of law and of the CJEU within this report, including the possibility to address for a preliminary question to the CJEU, the framework of the constitutional review of the transposing rules into the national law of rules adopted at EU level and the reference benchmarks in order to exercise such review. Within these coordinates such established, the constitutional court is one of the main factors for the Europeanization of the national legal system, in compliance with the national constitutional identity, a conclusion which is demonstrated by the many cases in which the Court ruled upon the obligations of the national authorities in the light of Article 148 of the Constitution and of the way in which these obligations are fulfilled.

The general idea that emerges from this case-law is that of promotion of mutual respect, based on the understanding of the phenomenon of multiple constitutional systems existing in the European Union, which must coexist within and relate to the autonomous legal order that it entails. It can be seen the opening of certain constitutional courts to the CJEU, but this is conditional on respect for the national identities[395], an attitude generally shared by the constitutional courts.

In this complex context, the dialogue of the constitutional judge with the European judge serves to the development of common standards for the protection of

---

393 K. Lenaerts, *Form and substance of the preliminary ruling procedure*, in D. Curtin, T. Heukels, *Institutional dynamics of European integration*, Dordrecht, Martinus Nijhoff, 1994, pp. 355–380.

394 E.S. Tănăsescu, *Preliminary ruling procedure and the loyal judicial cooperation*, in RRDE no. 3/2012, pp. 32–41.

395 K. Kruma, *Constitutional Courts and the Lisbon Treaty. The future based on mutual trust*, in the paper *The area of freedom, security and justice. Ten years on successes and future challenges under the Stockholm programme*, published by Centre for European Policy Studies, Bruxelles, 2010, p. 45, on *www.isn.ethz.ch*.

fundamental rights or to the enrichment of the existing ones, with effects in the law making and enforcement at national level.

4. The dialogue between constitutional courts[396]

4.1 General aspects[397]

The exposure of role and development of constitutional review and of the courts that exercise such review demonstrate, partially, the existence of a global judicial dialogue. The phenomenon of extending the constitutional review – in terms of its size both quantitative and qualitative – constitutes, among other things, a response to the constitutional development of other states, known also by way of institutionalized cooperation. Likewise, the practice of using the precedents of the case-law of other constitutional courts could constitute an evidence of the same communication. In matters of the protection of fundamental rights and freedoms, this dialogue is a proof, entitling the conclusions in the doctrine[398] regarding the existence, at least at European level, of a common language of constitutionality.

Analyzing the relationship between constitutional courts at European and global level, it is noted that the dialogue between the constitutional courts which exercise the constitutional review exists and it is objectified in various specific forms.

In light of this peculiarity, we will refer below to the following forms of transnational judicial dialogue between the constitutional courts: within certain international bodies set up for this purpose; within bilateral meetings, symposia, conferences organized on different occasions; as using the precedents of other constitutional courts.

4.2 Forms of dialogue between constitutional courts

4.2.1 Dialogue within certain international bodies

We believe that this way of communication between judges/ constitutional courts, is the most representative, both quantitatively and qualitatively: quantitatively as it creates the most and consistent opportunities for the transfer of experience between constitutional judges on topics which are common points of interest; qualitatively, as this kind of dialogue has, to a greater extent than others, the vocation to produce

396 Taken over from – T. Toader, M. Safta, *Forms..., op. cit.*, pp. 173–193.

397 We will use below the phrase "constitutional courts" with the meaning of courts competent to exercise the constitutional review, irrespective of the law system in which their particular name also functions.

398 For example, O. Pollicino, *New emerging judicial dynamics of the relationship between national and the European Courts after the enlargement of Europe*, in Jean Monnet Working Paper no. 14/08, p. 14, on *http://centers.law.nyu.edu/jeanmonnet/papers/papers08.html*.

substantial changes in the conception regarding the constitutional review and the authorities which achieves it.

Such dialogue is necessary as exchanges taking place between judges in different parts of the world, within certain bodies specially constituted with constitutional courts as its members, promote the exchange of ideas and reflection on the concepts and main principles inherent in national constitutions. Even if the texts of constitutions often differ substantially, the discussion on concepts and constitutional main principles connects the constitutional judges in consideration of the common concern to promote constitutionality in their own country. Likewise, since the judges of these courts can be found sometimes in dispute with the other State powers due to the decisions rendered by them, the bodies to which constitutional courts are parties provide a free exchange of information. This can be very important specifically for the guarantee of the constitutional principles which they are required to protect.

4.2.2 International bodies of reference in the field of constitutional justice

a) Conference of European Constitutional Courts

The Conference of European Constitutional Courts[399], established in 1972, brings together 40 constitutional courts and similar European institutions, competent in the field of constitutional justice. The Constitutional Court of Romania became a member of the Conference of European Constitutional Courts in 1994, thus developing relationships with all the Member Courts.

The Conference encourages its members to exchange information among them, especially on issues relating to the methods and practice of constitutional review and provides a forum for the participants to share opinions on institutional, structural and practical problems in the areas of public law and constitutional jurisdiction. Besides, the Conference takes measures to strengthen the independence of constitutional courts as an essential element of the guarantee and implementation of democracy and a state under the rule of law and pays particular attention to the protection of human rights. It strongly supports the improvement of lasting relations between European constitutional courts and similar institutions.

The Conference holds a Congress every three years and its presidency is also renewed every three years, which may be exercised by a constitutional court which has the status of a full member. Between 2008 and 2011, the presidency of the Conference was held by the Constitutional Court of Romania, which held its fifteenth Congress in 2011, in Bucharest. The Congress was attended by delegations of the Member Constitutional Courts, as well as by representatives of certain bodies, as observers, among which the Commission for Democracy through Law (the Venice Commission), the Association of Asian Constitutional Court, the Association of Constitutional Courts using the French Language (ACCPUF), The Ibero-American

---

399 The presentation and the Regulations of the Conference of the European Constitutional Courts are available on *http://www.confeuconstco.org*.

Conference on Constitutional Justice, the Conference of the Constitutional Courts using the Portuguese Language, the Union of Arab Constitutional Courts and Councils.

We will refer to the issues approached during the above-mentioned Congress as it can be an example for the specific way in which the dialogue between the Member Courts of the Conference is achieved, as well as to the topics that are approached within this dialogue. Thus, the topic of the Congress, representing a wide interest among participants, was Constitutional justice: functions and relationship with the other public authorities. The Congress included three plenary sessions, as follows: Plenary session I, with the topic The Constitutional Court's relationship to Parliament and Government; Plenary session II, with the topic Resolution of organic litigations by the Constitutional Court; Plenary III, with the topic Enforcement of Constitutional Court's decisions. Questionnaires were sent to all the constitutional courts/tribunals/similar courts, members of the Conference, in order to facilitate access for all courts to relevant information from the perspective of these topics and to synthesise this information. Likewise, based on these questionnaires, a general report was prepared within the Constitutional Court of Romania and presented at the Congress. This report was the reference framework for thorough discussions aiming at the importance of collaboration between constitutional courts, their collaboration with the political power for the purposes of ensuring that fundamental rights and freedoms are observed, the importance of political culture, considered as an added value that helps some countries adopt constitutional amendments smoother, the importance of consulting the constitutional court with respect to financial issues. Underlining the meaning of the principle of separation of powers, which involves mutual respect and independent functioning of constitutional courts, it has been concluded that it is necessary to reject both one power's attempts to take over the others, as well as politics' attempts to have influence over the functioning of constitutional courts[400]. The works of the Congress, published in two volumes which have been sent to all participants at the Conference, represent a substantial collection of comparative constitutional law, making possible, by referring to the case-law of the Member Constitutional Courts of the Conference, to know it and potentially use it as a precedent.

The latest Congress of the Conference, the XVIth Congress, was held in Vienna from 12 to 14 May 2014 – Congress of the Conference of European Constitutional Courts. The topics approached during the Congress were the following: *Constitutional Courts between Constitutional Law and European Law; Interaction between Constitutional Courts; Interaction between European Courts.* They have formed the subject of the reports prepared by the constitutional courts, members of the Conference of European Constitutional Courts, on whose basis the general report was prepared

---

400 See M. Safta, K. Benke, I. Chiorean, C. Turcu, *XVth Congress of the Conference of the European Constitutional Courts,* published in the Constitutional Court Bulletin no. 1/2011, pp. 45–48, available on *www.ccr.ro.*

and presented at the Congress by the host Constitutional Court. The Congress has revealed the common desire to strengthen the institutional dialogue, i.e. to know the activity and the case-law of all constitutional courts.

b) The Association of Constitutional Courts using the French Language (ACCPUF)

Association of Constitutional Courts using the French Language (ACCPUF)[401] has been founded in 1997 in order to strengthen the relationships between francophone community members and brings together constitutional courts and similar institutions in Africa, Europe, America and Asia. The goal of the Association is to contribute to fostering the rule of law by developing relationships between these courts. For this purpose, it has been encouraged the exchange of ideas and experience between the members of the Association, accompanied by legal and technical cooperation aiming at a better mutual understanding, at the promotion and strengthening of the authority of each institution.

ACCPUF created a number of legal instruments in order to achieve those objectives, namely: a general bulletin constantly updated, including data regarding the organization and powers of the members, thematic publications, summaries of the meetings and questionnaires to which members answered. The approached issues concern both matters of principle (principle of equality, free access to constitutional courts) and individual matters (communication, the role and functioning of constitutional courts during elections). ACCPUF contributes to the database that brings together the main decisions of the constitutional courts, following the agreements signed with the Venice Commission.

The Constitutional Court of Romania has been a member of ACCPUF since 1998[402], and it held one of its Congresses in 2007.

c) World Conference on Constitutional Justice

This organization[403], bringing together Constitutional Courts, Councils and Supreme Courts in Africa, the Americas, Asia and Europe, has been founded as a result of concern and activity held in particular by the Venice Commission, since 1996, in order to establish cooperation and to bring together a number of regional or language based groups of constitutional courts. In order to achieve these objectives, it was held for the first time a Congress of the World Conference on Constitutional Justice in Cape Town from 22 to 24 January 2009, hosted by the Constitutional Court of South Africa in collaboration with the Venice Commission. On the basis

---

401 The presentation of the Association of the Constitutional Courts using the French Language is available on *www.accpuf.org*.

402 See Law no. 59 of 5 March 1998 regarding the affiliation of the Constitutional Court of Romania to the Association of the Constitutional Courts using the French Language (ACCPUF), published in the Official Gazette of Romania no. 111 of 11 March 1998.

403 Statute of the World Conference on Constitutional Justice is available on *www.venice.coe.int*.

of a declaration adopted at this occasion, it was prepared a draft statute, which was then discussed, as amended at the Second Congress, 16–18 January 2011, in Rio de Janeiro, being hosted by the Federal Supreme Court of Brazil in cooperation with the Venice Commission. This Congress, on "Separation of Powers and Independence of Constitutional Courts and Equivalent bodies", was attended by 88 Constitutional Courts, Constitutional Councils and Supreme Courts – including the Constitutional Court of Romania – as well as the 10 regional and linguistic groups of courts from Africa, the Americas, Asia and Europe. The third Congress was held in Seoul from 28 September to 1 October 2014, and its topic was "Constitutional justice and social integration". The Statute of the World Conference on Constitutional Justice was adopted on 23 May 2011 in Bucharest, on the occasion of the XVth Congress of the Conference of European Constitutional Courts.

The main purpose of this form of meetings and joint activities of the constitutional courts was precisely that to facilitate the judicial dialogue between the constitutional judges on a global scale, in order to promote the constitutional justice as a fundamental factor for democracy, the protection of human rights and the rule of law.

d) Other structures of cooperation between constitutional courts

There are also established other "platforms" of cooperation, especially at regional level, such as the Union of Arab Constitutional Courts and Councils; the Conference of Constitutional Control Organs of Countries of New Democracy (CCCOC-ND); the Conference of Constitutional Jurisdictions of the Portuguese-Speaking Countries(CJCPLP); the Conference of Constitutional Jurisdictions of Africa (CCJA); the Southern African Chief Justices Forum (SACJF).

This demonstrates the need and importance of the exchange of ideas and experience, taking also into account regional peculiarities, which gives a certain particularity to the issues faced by the Constitutional Courts.

e) Venice Commission

The European Commission for Democracy through Law, known as the Venice Commission[404], was founded in 1990 and is the Council of Europe's advisory body on constitutional matters. The Constitutional Court of Romania has a close collaboration with this body and within it with the other constitutional courts of the Council of Europe's Member States, respectively the other affiliated States[405]. This collaboration

404 These data are taken over from the website of the Venice Commission – *www.venice.coe.int.*

405 Kyrgyzstan joined in 2004; Chile, in 2005; Republic of Korea, in 2006; Morocco and Algeria, in 2007; Israel, in 2008; Peru and Brazil, in 2009; Tunisia and Mexico, in 2010; Kazakhstan, in 2011. Thus, the Commission consists of 58 Members, in total. Belarus is an associate member, while Argentina, Canada, Sfântul Scaun, Japan, the United States and Uruguay are observers. South Africa and the Palestinian National Authority have a special cooperation statute similar to the observers' one.

is mainly reflected in the transmission, for the publication in the Bulletin of the Venice Commission, of the relevant case-law of the Constitutional Court of Romania, as well as in the transmission of answers to the questions of other constitutional courts formulated on specific constitutional themes. The same possibility to address questions to other courts through the same mechanism is also open, obviously, to the Constitutional Court of Romania. Both the purpose of the Bulletin and of the question / answer dialogue, mentioned above, aim at encouraging the exchange of information between the constitutional courts and their judges in order to settle sensitive legal issues, which often occur simultaneously in several countries. It is worth emphasizing the complex nature of the questions and issues subject to the dialogue between the Members constitutional courts, through liaison officers, in the sense that they equally cover the legislation, case-law and doctrine concerning the issue raised before the constitutional court which has addressed the question. It is thus facilitated the information of all the constitutional courts involved in this mechanism about various constitutional issues and their settlement. In this way, the delivered solutions have a broad and solid substantiation of comparative constitutional law and, at the same time, a database which can easily be accessed and used by the national constitutional judge is continuously enriched.

The Venice Commission does not only represent a framework for the dialogue with the other constitutional courts, but also a dialogue partner, in itself, so we will provide it a separate treatment.

4.2.3 The dialogue within bilateral meetings, conferences and symposiums

The existing cooperation within the international bodies, as those presented above, is joined by the existing bilateral relationships between the constitutional courts. They create the meetings of constitutional judges, the direct dialogue and the deepen common issues, as well as the initiation of certain forms of cooperation at regional level or based on other criteria which have been identified as relevant.

The Constitutional Court of Romania was concerned with the development of bilateral relations with the constitutional courts of European countries in particular and with other similar courts/courts of law. Over time, there were held meetings and exchanges of experience between the Romanian constitutional judges and their counterparts in South Africa, Albania, Andorra, Armenia, Azerbaijan, Bulgaria, Bosnia and Herzegovina, Czech Republic, China, Korea, Russian Federation, Egypt, France, Georgia, Germany, Iran, Italy, Japan, Lithuania, Macedonia, Morocco, the Republic of Moldova, Poland, Portugal, Serbia, Spain, the United States of America, Tunisia, Turkey, Hungary. The meetings held within this cooperation have revealed the fact that various issues faced by the Constitutional Court of Romania – either institutional or judicial – are also found in the activity of the other constitutional courts, which determined the attempt to identify common solutions or to adapt the already identified solutions to the specifics of each court or jurisdictions.

The Constitutional Court of Romania hosted international conferences, a recent example is the conference held in 2012, with the topic: Constitutional Review – Tradition and Perspectives, an event dedicated to the 20th Anniversary of the Constitutional Court of Romania and celebration of the 100th years since the affirmation of constitutional review of laws in Romania. The meeting was attended by delegations of constitutional courts, namely of the Supreme Courts of Albania, Austria, Azerbaijan, Bulgaria, Cyprus, the People's Republic of China, Korea, Croatia, Georgia, Italy, Latvia, Lithuania, Luxembourg, Republic of Macedonia, the Republic of Moldova, Montenegro, Norway, Poland, Russian Federation, Serbia, Thailand, Turkey, Ukraine and Hungary, the President of the Commission for Democracy through Law (the Venice Commission) and special guests from universities and foundations that carry out cooperation programs in the field of constitutional justice.

This cooperation indicates concerns and debates common for the constitutional judges, irrespective of the type of the court that conducts the constitutional review and of its geographical area, as well as the integration of the Constitutional Court of Romania in what we may globally call the community of the constitutional courts.

4.2.4 Reference to the case-law of other constitutional courts

4.2.4.1 General aspects and examples

The cooperation, the exchange of ideas and experiences among the constitutional judges are reflected in the case-law of the constitutional courts. Therefore, we can refer to a broader meaning of the phrase *judicial dialogue* which aims at the use of the case-law of the foreign precedent by the constitutional courts.

Moreover, we consider that what might qualify the citation or reference to the case-law of the other constitutional courts as *judicial dialogue* is precisely the development of their cooperation at regional and global level. This is because the idea of dialogue in itself does not suppose speakers who shall address in parallel to different audiences, such as the case of the constitutional courts[406]. The courts concerned exercise the constitutional review of internal regulations in relation to the national constitution so that the acts delivered by them may involve a consistent judicial dialogue, but, in themselves, they shall address specifically to "domestic audience", to State authorities which must apply these decisions whose purpose is to guarantee the supremacy of the national constitution. The answer of the other constitutional courts is at most a secondary reason for the solution which is to be delivered in a particular case. The increasingly close cooperation between the constitutional courts and the identification of certain common standards regarding the position and the role of these courts and the constitutional review, determine, however, the non-negligence of such secondary reason. From this perspective, the judicial

406 For developments, see D.S. Law, W. Chen Chang, *The limits of global judicial dialogue*, in Washington Law Review, volume 86, 2011, article available on *http://digital.law.washington.edu/dspace-law/handle/1773.1/1061.*

dialogue between the constitutional courts appears as a reference to a reference system regarding the standards of democracy, of the main constitutional principles and of the protection of fundamental rights and freedoms.

The explicit or implicit reliance on the foreign precedent usually occurs when a national court encounters new issues, without precedent in the domestic case-law – it is in its own interest to do research even by way of direct questions (similar to those to which we referred when examining the cooperation of the constitutional courts within the Venice Commission), and to analyze the reasoning and the solutions adopted in similar situations by the other constitutional courts, in order to develop their own reasoning and conclusions. This mechanism of judicial dialogue can acquire certain features according to their regional and linguistic nature to certain structures and organizations, such as the Council of Europe (the assimilation with the Convention for the Protection of Human Rights and Fundamental Freedoms and the interpretation thereof by the European Court of Human Rights) or to the affiliation of States to the European Union, taking account of the specific issues caused by this affiliation. Sometimes, especially in such specific situations, the invocation of other Court's precedents aims at establishing and supporting a certain common approach for the national constitutional courts.

Thus, the examination of the issues regarding the relations between national and EU regulations caused such a dialogue between national constitutional courts. For example, the Constitutional Court of the Czech Republic has referred on several occasions to the case-law of the Federal Constitutional Court of Germany (see, for example, Judgment of 31 January 2012 – Slovak Pensions, Judgment of 3 November 2009 – Treaty of Lisbon II; Judgment of 26 November 2008 –Treaty of Lisbon I)[407]. Similarly, the Constitutional Tribunal of Poland, ruling by Decision of 24 November 2010[408] upon the Lisbon Treaty, invoked the case-law of the constitutional courts of the Czech Republic, Germany, Hungary, Austria, respectively of the Constitutional Council of France.

Likewise, the transposition into national law of European acts or the adoption of normative acts to give effect to the obligations assumed at the European level resulted in situations where constitutional courts, vested with the constitutional review of national normative acts thus adopted, took into account foreign precedents in the same matter. For example, having examined the transposition into national law of Directive no. 2006/24 / EC of the European Parliament and of the Council of 15 March 2006 on the retention of data generated or processed in connection with the provision of publicly available electronic communications services or of public communications networks and amending Directive 2002/58/EC, the Constitutional

---

407 Available on *http://www.concourt.cz* (2012/01/31 – Pl. ÚS 5/12: Slovak Pensions, 2009/11/03 – Pl. ÚS 29/09: Treaty of Lisbon II: 2008/11/26 – Pl. ÚS 19/08: Treaty of Lisbon I).

408 Available on *http://www.trybunal.gov.pl/eng/summaries/documents.*

Court of the Czech Republic held, in the Decision of 22 March 2011[409], the similar conclusions that "were also been drawn by Constitutional Courts in other European countries when examining the constitutionality of legal regulations implementing the aforementioned Directive on Data Retention", namely: the Federal Constitutional Court of Germany, the Constitutional Court of Romania, the Constitutional Court of Bulgaria, the Supreme Court of Cyprus.

Another reference case is the case-law of constitutional courts in connection with the implementation into national law of the Council Framework Decision no. 2002/584/JAIa on the European arrest warrant and the surrender procedures between Member States[410]. Thus, for example, the Constitutional Court of Belgium, ruling upon the constitutionality of the transposition of the above-mentioned Council Framework Decision by Decision no. 128 of 10 October 2007[411], has taken into consideration both the Decision of 27 April 2005 of the Constitutional Tribunal of Poland[412], and the Decision of 18 July 2005[413] of the Federal Constitutional Court of Germany. The Constitutional Court of Romania mentioned, "by way of comparison", in Decision no. 1127 of 27 November 2007 on the exception of unconstitutionality of the provisions of Title III (Articles 77–108) of Law no. 302/2004 on international judicial cooperation in criminal matters[414], the Polish Constitutional Tribunal's Decision of 27 April 2005, respectively the situation of Germany and the reasons for the ascertainment of the unconstitutionality of the initial law transposing the Council Framework Decision on the European arrest warrant.

An overarching topic of judicial dialogue is the issue regarding the protection of the fundamental rights and freedoms. As long as the Convention for the Protection of Human Rights and Fundamental Freedoms and the European Court of Human Rights created a "common language" on fundamental rights and freedoms, at least for the member states of the Council of Europe, it is understandable the orientation

---

409 Available on *http://www.concourt.cz – 2011/03/22 – Pl. ÚS 24/10.*

410 In essence, the Framework Decision gave expression to the Judgment delivered within the Council of Europe in Tampere, of 15 and 16 October 1999, that the formal extradition procedure between the Member States of the European Union shall be replaced, for persons who avoid the enforcement of a custodial sentence, applied through a final judgment, with a simplified surrender procedure, namely to accelerate the formal extradition procedure for persons who avoid their prosecution and judgment; for the interpretation of the Framework Decision, see also R.H. Radu, A. Voicu, *Court of Justice of the European Union*, Case C-396/11, *Radu*, in Judicial Courier no. 4/2013, p. 234.

411 The summary of the decision is available on *www.venice.coe.int*, CODICES – BEL-2007-3-008; see also *http://www.const-court.be/en/common/home.html.*

412 The summary of the decision is available on *www.venice.coe.int*, CODICES – POL-2005-1-005.

413 The summary of the decision is available on *www.venice.coe.int*, CODICES – GER-2005-2-002.

414 Published in the Official Gazette of Romania no. 2 of 3 January 2008.

of the constitutional judges towards the case-law of other constitutional courts where the judgments of the European Court of Human Rights were and still are used. The Constitutional Court of Romania proceeded in this regard in a number of situations.

4.2.4.2 The foreign precedent within the case-law of the Constitutional Court of Romania

The examination of the case-law of the Constitutional Court of Romania reveals that, in most cases, the reliance on the foreign precedent was achieved within the examination of the issues on fundamental rights and freedoms, a wide open field also in the light of Article 20 of the Constitution.

Thus, by Decision no. 107 of 1 November 1995[415], ruling on certain provisions of Law no. 3/1977 on state social insurance pensions and social assistance, the Court referred to the examples of Austria and Germany, finding, inter alia, that "even in situations such as the one in Austria, where the constitutional jurisdiction stated that the principle of gender equality requires the same retirement age, the legislative authority, taking into account the existing socio-professional relations, did not accepted the respective point of view. In Germany, as it results from the decision of the Constitutional Court in Karlsruhe, taking into account the same socio-professional relations as resulted from a broad social inquiry, it decided that different retirement ages are justified at present time".

Also, by Decision no. 140 of 19 November 1996[416], examining the constitutionality of Article 238 para. (1) of Criminal Code, the Constitutional Court has also invoked the "Decision no. 36/1994 of the Constitutional Court of the Republic of Hungary, decision by which the provisions of Article 232 of Law no. IV/1978 of Criminal Code were declared unconstitutional", holding that it "cannot have the significance of an argument for the solution that is to be pronounced in this case, and the reasons in support of that decision cannot make the subject-matter of the examination by the Constitutional Court of Romania".

By Decision no. 113 of 20 July 1999[417], responding to the authors of the objection of unconstitutionality who invoked the foreign precedent in order to support the reasons of unconstitutionality raised, the Court held that "citation by the authors of the referral of a recent decision by the Constitutional Council of France established that in the content of the European Charter of Regional or Minority Languages there provisions contrary to the Constitution of France has no relevance in the case, given the completely different regulation – at constitutional level –, existing in our country with regard to national minorities".

---

415 Published in the Official Gazette of Romania no. 85 of 26 April 1996.
416 Published in the Official Gazette of Romania no. 324 of 4 December 1996.
417 Published in the Official Gazette of Romania no. 362 of 29 July 1999.

In Decision no. 203 of 29 November 1999[418], adjudicating on the objection of unconstitutionality of the provisions of Article 2 (f) of Law on the access to the personal file and the disclosure of the Securitate as a political police, the Court, at the end of the decision, referred to the Decision no. 10 of 22 September 1997of the Constitutional Court of Bulgaria.

In Decision no. 334 of 3 April 2007[419], the Court also referred, regarding persons' right not to incriminate themselves, to the decision of the Supreme Court of the United States of America, in the case Miranda v. Arizona of 1966, holding that "before the interrogation the accused must be informed that he has the right to silence, that any of his statements can be used against him and that he is entitled to be assisted by a lawyer, and if he has insufficient financial resources an ex officio lawyer will be appointed in order to represent him. These are the procedural safeguards effective to secure the privilege against self-incrimination". The Court also invoked the case Dickerson v. The United States of 2000 of the same court, by which the Supreme Court "upheld this principle – the right to silence – as being one of constitutional nature, even if it is not expressly provided for in the Constitution".

In Decision no. 1127 of 27 November 2007[420], referring to the European arrest warrant, the Constitutional Court of Romania mentioned the decision of the Constitutional Court of Poland of 27 April 2005, "by which it was held that Article 607 (1) of the Criminal Procedure Code allowing the surrender of a Polish citizen to another EU Member State according to an European arrest warrant violates Article 55(1) of the Basic Law of Poland, forbidding the extradition of its citizens without any derogating rule". The Court held further that "subsequently, the Constitution of Poland was revised for the purpose of allowing the extradition of its own citizens whenever there is an international obligation in this regard, so that as of November 2006, precisely in order to meet the obligations resulted from the status of EU Members State, the Polish citizens can be surrendered based on an European arrest warrant". At the same time, the Court also referred to the situation of Germany, indicating that "the initial law for the transposition of the framework-decision on the European arrest warrant was declared unconstitutional not because it does not allow the censoring by the German judicial authority of the validity of the precautionary measure or of the decision pronounced in the requesting State, but because it took into account the need to respect fundamental rights, inclusively the right to benefit from a legal remedy, situation which, as indicated, is not regulated in the Romanian law".

418 Published in the Official Gazette of Romania no. 603 of 9 December 1999.
419 Published in the Official Gazette of Romania no. 308 of 9 May 2007.
420 Published in the Official Gazette of Romania no. 2 of 3 January 2008.

By Decisions no. 872 of 25 June 2010[421] and no. 874 of 25 June 2010[422], ruling upon the provisions of the Law on measures necessary to restore budgetary balance, the Constitutional Court of Romania also mentioned some considerations of principle relating to pension rights in the cases settled by other constitutional courts. "The Constitutional Court of Hungary, by Decision no. 455/B/1995 established that pension calculated under the rules of the social security system may not be affected and by Decision no. 277/B/1997 it held that unilateral modification in the amount of pensions is unconstitutional, referring directly to the inability of the legislator to reduce large pensions to increase small pensions. Furthermore, by Decision no. 39/1999 (XII.21), the same constitutional court ruled that the (contributory) pension is a right earned (...) so that modification of its nominal amount is unconstitutional. Moreover, similar considerations are found in Latvia Constitutional Court Decision no. 2009–43–01 of 21 December 2009".

In Decision no. 1358 of 21 October 2010[423] on the admission of the exception of unconstitutionality of the provisions of Article 5 para. (1) a) sentence I of Law no. 221/2009 on political convictions and their related administrative measures, delivered during the period 6 March 1945 – 22 December 1989, the Constitutional Court of Romania referred to the Decision of the Constitutional Court of Hungary no. 1 of 8 February 1995, indicating that by this decision "it was established that the compensation measure provided for in Act no. XXXII of 1992, regulating the compensation for non-material damages for the benefit of the politically convicted persons during the communist period, is not taken based on the existence of a legal obligation taking rise from the past, but the State equitably granted this compensation, so that no person can have a substantial right to compensations for non-material damages"[424].

In this context, concerning the guarantee of fundamental rights and freedoms, the examination of the issues on the free access to justice has given rise to certain decisions whereby the Constitutional Court invoked the foreign precedent when it adjudicated, for example, upon the regulations on the judges' independence or upon the regulations relating to its own competence and, from this perspective, to the free access to constitutional justice.

Thus, as concerns the first case, we mention Decision No. 873 of 25 June 2010[425] on the objection of unconstitutionality of the provisions of Law regarding the establishment of measures in the pension field, by which the Court held the reasons referring to the need to ensure financial security of judges, as guarantee of their independence, contained in the Decision of the Constitutional Court of Lithuania of

421 Published in the Official Gazette of Romania no. 433 of 28 June 2010.
422 Published in the Official Gazette of Romania no. 433 of 28 June 2010.
423 Published in the Official Gazette of Romania no. 761 of 15 November 2010.
424 The same mention appears also in Decision no. 1360 of 21 October 2010, published in the Official Gazette of Romania no. 761 of 15 November 2010.
425 Published in the Official Gazette of Romania no. 433 of 28 June 2010.

12 July 2001 and in the Decision of the Constitutional Court of the Czech Republic of 14 July 2005.

As concerns the issues regarding the competence of the Constitutional Court, we mention Decision no. 766 of 15 June 2011[426], in which the Court found that the phrase "in force" laid down in the provisions of Article 29(1) and of Article 31(1) of Law no. 47/1992 on the Organization and Operation of the Constitutional Court is constitutional insofar as it is interpreted as submitting to the Constitutionality review the laws or ordinances or provisions therein, whose legal effects continue to produce even when they are no longer in force. The Court held on that occasion that, in the case of the practical review carried out through the exception of unconstitutionality, "the case-law of the European constitutional courts concerning standards that are no longer in force, but are applicable in the case, includes the review of the merits of these standards. Thus, in the case of Germany, Italy, Hungary, Czech Republic, Poland or France, based on certain regulatory provisions or jurisprudential guidelines, the constitutional courts considered the analysis of the merits of the impugned provisions, in view of eliminating those provisions that do not follow the constitutional requirements, more important than establishing a purely formal procedural criterion that would stop the proceedings". In the recitals of the decision it has been mentioned Decision of 10 January of the Constitutional Court of the Czech Republic, which established that that the exception of unconstitutionality of a text that was no longer in force would not be rejected as inadmissible, but examined on the merits, "because ordinary courts have the obligation to implement the law, and not to consider a law as unconstitutional and, consequently, not to apply it. When considering that the law that shall be applied is unconstitutional, the ordinary court must refer to the constitutional court; otherwise, by applying this law, it violates the provisions of the Constitution". It was also mentioned Decision no. 2010–16 of 23 July 2010 of the Constitutional Council of France, which noted that the exception of unconstitutionality could also concern a legal provision no longer in force as long as the subsequent amendment or repeal of the impugned provision does not make the violation of these rights and freedoms guaranteed by the Constitution disappear. Another example is given by the Constitutional Court of Lithuania, who, through its Decision of 27 March 2009, stated that, if the legal provision challenged as unconstitutional was amended in its substance, the constitutional court has the obligation to control the standard that it was addressed with, regardless of whether it is still in force or not. It was also noted the example of the Constitutional Court of Hungary, stating that it controls the constitutionality of the legal standard submitted for analysis in the form it had before its amendment, repeal or expiry or when it no longer applied to the dispute before the a quo court.

However, the reference to the case-law of the other constitutional courts occurs also in situations where the Constitutional Court of Romania had to rule on

426 Published in the Official Gazette of Romania no. 549 of 3 August 2011.

regulations concerning the organization and functioning of certain public authorities (in this case Parliament), respectively concerning their competence and relationships with the Constitutional Court.

Thus, by Decision no. 209 of 7 March 2012[427] on the referral of unconstitutionality of Parliament Resolution no. 1 of 9 February 2012 to grant trust to the Government, the Court, examining the role of the Parliament and, thus, of the parliamentary commissions, held that "Parliament «cannot be represented or replaced by any of its internal bodies and which are established by itself, for the simple reason that it cannot delegate to anyone – and the less to a group of parliamentarians – the national sovereignty with which the electorate empowered it following the parliamentary elections»". The Court noted that "the same is also the conclusion recently reached by the Federal Constitutional Court of Germany, through Decision 2BvE 8/11 of 28 February 2012, unanimously pronounced in the second Chamber".

Likewise, by Decision no. 1533 of 28 November 2011[428], adjudicating on the constitutionality of the Law for the approval of the Government Emergency Ordinance no. 71/2009 regarding the payment of certain amounts provided in enforceable titles having as their subject-matter the granting of salary rights to the personnel in the budgetary sector, the Court held, inter alia, that "Parliament must have control over the fundamental decisions in the field of budgetary policy and that it enjoys a margin of appreciation in this area, as it has to ensure the sustainability of the budget and the State economic performance. The Constitutional Court must comply with this margin of appreciation, its review being limited to the obvious violations of constitutional texts (see also the Decision of the German Federal Constitutional Court 2 BvR 987/10 of 7 September 2011 on the settlement of the complaints of unconstitutionality formulated against the package of measures concerning the financial aid granted to Greece and the Euro rescue fund)".

The given examples refer explicitly to the case-law of the other constitutional courts – in the sense of indicating the precedent in the recitals of the Court's decision/judgment. In some situations, the examination of the case-law of the other constitutional courts was determined by the very parties concerned, who presented it in order to substantiate its reasons – in this respect we mentioned Decision no. 107

427 Published in the Official Gazette of Romania no. 188 of 22 March 2012; see 307/2012, published in the Official Gazette of Romania no. 293 of 4 May 2012 on the referral of unconstitutionality of Parliament's Resolution no. 5 of 28 February 2012 regarding the appointment of certain members of the National Audiovisual Council.

428 Published in the Official Gazette of Romania no. 905 of 20 December 2011; see also Decision no. 897 of 25 October 2012, published in the Official Gazette of Romania no. 35 of 16 January 2013.

of 1 November 1995[429], Decision no. 140 of 19 November 1996[430] and Decision no. 113 of 20 July 1999.

But there are also other situations where the use of the case-law of the constitutional court is implicit, in the sense that it is considered in the examination of the comparative law underlying the solution delivered, without being cited. We consider that the absence of an express reference to the case-law of the other constitutional courts can be explained by the fact that the reasoning of the constitutional courts takes into account, firstly, the constitutional rules, the specifics and the peculiarities of the national legislation. The case-law of the other courts may be an argument, but an *obiter dictum* one, and not a basis for finding or not the constitutionality of a legal text or for requiring a response in the body of the acts delivered by a court at a certain moment.

Thus, the number of the decisions in which the foreign precedent is cited is not in itself relevant for what the dialogue / effects of the judicial dialogue represents between the constitutional courts. It essentially refers to the fact that the effects of this dialogue are materialized by the compliance with the limits given by the position and the role of the constitutional courts.

From this perspective, one must distinguish horizontally between the meaning and the effects of the judicial dialogue – between the constitutional courts – and vertically – between these courts and the supranational ones, such as the Court of Justice of the European Union[431]. Thus, if in the first case we refer mainly to a phenomenon of emergence towards the establishment of certain fundamental constitutional principles generally enshrined in the constitutions of democratic states or for the protection of human rights, in the second case we particularly refer to a phenomenon of coexistence, the judicial dialogue appears as a way of prevention

---

429 Published in the Official Gazette of Romania no. 85 of 26 April 1996: "*at the request of the parties, extracts from the White Paper on the Reform of Social Security and Pensions were submitted in the file, concerning issues raised by the present case. Likewise, Decision no. 1 of 28 January 1987 the Federal Constitutional Court of Germany was attached, in which it has been held that the retirement age for women at 60, different from that of men, at 65, does not violate the principle of equal rights set forth in the Constitution, since it corresponds to the various professional and social conditions that exist between men and women, especially due to the obligations of women as mother and within the household. Similarly, Decision no. 12.568/1990 of the Constitutional Court of Austria was also submitted, noting that «gradually, the legislature can and should equalize the retirement age». However, as it is underlined in the fax of 15 September 1995 of the President of the Constitutional Court of Austria, Parliament declared valid the differentiated retirement age limits for men and women, and decided that the issue should be debated after 2019*".

430 Published in the Official Gazette of Romania no. 324 of 4 December 1996: "*as grounds for the exception of unconstitutionality, the applicants also invoked Decision no. 36/1994 of the Constitutional Court of the Republic of Hungary*".

431 We take account only of the situation of the constitutional courts in the Member States of the European Union.

and conciliation of the disputes occurred between the two levels – national and supranational – and of interconnection between the judicial entities which represent them in order to ensure the consistency of the mixed legal system and the pre-eminence of EU law in relation to national rules[432]. In other words, within the relationships between the constitutional courts, the judicial dialogue appears more as a helpful instrument and not as a purpose in itself. This instrument can be more or less visible, depending on the option of the national constitutional judge and on the view regarding the structure and the content of the acts delivered by the constitutional courts.

4.3 Conclusions

The enhancement of the dialogue between the constitutional courts and strengthening of their connection, as shown above, results in a phenomenon of emergence towards common constitutional values, but also in the expansion of the institutionalization of the constitutional review, reconsiderations regarding the competence and the powers of the constitutional courts[433], reconsiderations and improvements regarding the constitutional courts' acts, both in terms of form and reasons which substantiate it, with the consequence of strengthening democracy, the principles of the rule of law, the protection of fundamental rights and freedoms, but also the strengthening of the position and the role of the constitutional courts which are required to protect these values enshrined in the constitutions of the States.

As concerns the strengthening of the role and position of the constitutional courts, it is no coincidence that not one of the major topic of discussions within the various congresses and conferences to which we have referred is the independence of those courts and, in this context, the way in which their acts are imposed and observed by the other authorities. Such debates lead to the development of certain principles which constitute real benchmarks for what the acquired status or the status to be acquired by the constitutional courts in democratic states means.

For example, such a principle is represented by the impossibility to refute the decisions of the constitutional courts by the authorities of the Member States. In the member states of the Conference of European Constitutional Courts, the constitutions of the states or their infraconstitutional legislation do not confer to either

432 See I. Deleanu, *cited paper*, p. 17.

433 An example would be that of the development of the constitutional courts belonging to the European model, from the status of negative legislator (traditional, Kelsen model) to that of positive and particular co-legislator – see M. Safta, *Developments in the constitutional review. Constitutional Courts between the status of negative legislator and the status of positive co-legislator*, on *www.businesslaw conference.ro*; for the analyzed development we consider particularly relevant the meeting and the papers presented at the XIV Congress of the Conference of European Constitutional Courts held in Vilnius in 2009, which focused on the issue of legislative omissions in the constitutional case-law.

Parliament or to any other public authorities the competence to invalidate decisions of the Constitutional Courts. In Poland, for example, in the period from 1985 (the year of establishing the Constitutional Tribunal) until 1997 (the year of enactment of the present Constitution) the judgments of the Tribunal could be subject to rejection by the Sejm. This was a consequence of the assumption, adopted in the communist doctrine of the constitutional law, that the Sejm was the supreme organ in the area of state authority, superior to all other state bodies (including courts and tribunals). Pursuant to Article 7 of the Act of 29 April 1985 on the Constitutional Tribunal (no longer binding today), the Sejm had the competence to reject a given judgment of the Tribunal on the unconstitutionality of a statute if – in the view of the Sejm – the said statute did not infringe on the Constitution. The resolution of the Sejm on the rejection of the Tribunal's judgment required a majority vote of at least two-thirds in the presence of at least half of the statutory number of Deputies. The Sejm had no competence to reject a judgment of the Tribunal if it stated the unconstitutionality of a legal act of lower rank than a statute (such judgments were final). The situation changed with the entry into force of the Constitution of 1997. The situation changed with the entry into force of the Constitution of 1997. Since then the Sejm has had no power to reject the Tribunal's judgments. In accordance with Article 190(1) of the Constitution of 1997, all judgments of the Tribunal have become final in the sense that they may not be challenged or rejected by any other organ of public authority and shall be generally binding.

Similarly, in Romania, that possibility was provided by the 1991 Constitution which, prior to its revision in 2003, established, in Article 145 paragraph (1), that "In unconstitutionality situations ascertained in compliance with Article 144, letters a) and b), the law or regulation shall be sent for re-examination. If the law is adopted in the same form by a majority of at least two thirds of the number of members of each Chamber, the unconstitutionality objection is eliminated, and promulgation becomes mandatory". This provision of the 1991 Constitution, justifiably much criticized in the legal doctrine, allowed for the Parliament to act as a court of cassation in a dispute where it was a party. It was thus possible that an unconstitutional law could become constitutional by the will of a qualified majority of Deputies and Senators, however without a revision of the Constitution undergoing all stages and fulfilling the procedures provided for this specific purpose. Following the 2003 revision of the Constitution, the possibility for Parliament to invalidate a decision of the Constitutional Court was eliminated. This solution is widely enshrined currently in the constitutions of democratic states, a conclusion which has been supported by the reports presented at the XVth Congress of the Conference of European Constitutional Courts held in Bucharest in 2011[434].

434 The Report of the Congress, as well as the national reports of the participating Courts may be seen on the website of the Constitutional Court of Romania – *www.ccr.ro.*

As for the improvement of the constitutional courts' acts, in terms of form and quality of the reasons, this is a continuous phenomenon, but more difficult to be followed. However, one can claim that the development of the ways in which the courts and the constitutional judges interact has systemic effects on the global development of the constitutional review. By involving themselves in open debates on the common substance or methodology issues, the constitutional courts improve the quality of the decisions adopted by them and equally contribute to the creation of a global case-law, especially in the field of human rights.

5. Dialogue between the Constitutional Court of Romania and the Venice Commission

5.1 Venice Commission. Brief history and activity

As we have indicated, the Venice Commission is not only a framework for the dialogue with the other constitutional courts, but also a dialogue partner for the Constitutional Court of Romania, more visible in the recent years, when this body has polarized, during some events, usually political ones, the public attention in Romania.

Developing several benchmarks set out above regarding the history and functioning of the Venice Commission, the first mention should refer to the fact that its official name is the European Commission for Democracy through Law. It has been claimed that it is probably one of the Council of Europe's most successful achievements[435]. Created in 1990 as an advisory body in the field of constitutional law providing opinions upon request by Member States and the organs of the Council of Europe, the Commission for Democracy through Law has become, over time, a reference in constitutional matters, respected for its independent opinions. The idea to create such a body in the form of a group of experts in the field of constitutional law was conceived by the Minister of European Policy of Italy, Mr. La Pergola, a professor of constitutional law and later President of the Constitutional Court of Italy. His choice of the name was to express his conviction that sustainable democracy can only be built in a constitutional framework based on the rule of law. The Commission generally operates in Venice in the Scuola Grande of San Giovanni Evangelista. The Commission shall be assisted by the Secretariat General of the Council of Europe. Given that the Council of Europe has its seat in Strasbourg, the offices of the Secretariat of the Commission are located there as well.

The Commission for Democracy through Law shall be composed of independent experts who have achieved eminence through their experience in democratic institutions or by their contribution to the enhancement of law and political science. Usually, the Commission adopts its opinions by consensus, voting being rather rare.

---

435 R.S. Durr, *The Venice Commission*, in Intergovernmental Organization – suppl., 39 (July 2010), p. 151.

Objections to specific parts of an opinion are often taken into account in the final version of the adopted text.

According to the Statute of the Commission, the Member States and the bodies of the Council of Europe may request opinions from the Commission. As for the States, usually Parliaments, Governments or Ministers may request such opinions. Likewise, the Commission accepts such requests from the constitutional courts or from the Advocate of the People. In all its activity, the Venice Commission promotes the core values of the Council of Europe, namely human rights, democracy and the pre-eminence of the rule of law, as parts of a common constitutional space for Member States[436].

Presenting thoroughly the activity of the Venice Commission in respect of matters relating to the subject of this paper, it is worth emphasizing its activity dedicated to the establishment and support of the constitutional courts in the new democracies in Central and Eastern Europe, a sustained dialogue with them. As shown[437], since its establishment, the Venice Commission has taken into account that it is not enough just to assist the States in adopting democratic constitutions, but also that their provisions are implemented in society. While the enforcement of the constitutions falls within all the State authorities, the constitutional courts and the equivalent institutions are the key actors in reviewing such enforcement.

5.2 Forms of dialogue with the Venice Commission

5.2.1 Dialogue through conferences, seminars, as well as within certain forms of association of the constitutional courts

We have referred to this method when we analyzed the dialogue between the constitutional courts. In addition to those specified there, we emphasize the presence of the representatives of the Venice Commission at international conferences and events held by the Constitutional Court of Romania, so many occasions to strengthen the existing relationships with and within this body, a promoter for dialogue and cooperation at international level, in order to achieve the same goals of democracy.

Thus, for example, on the occasion of celebrating 20 years of existence and 100 years of constitutional review in Romania, the representative of the Venice Commission, Mr. Gianni Buquicchio, who attended the event, claimed, among other things, that "*a real dialogue of the judges and an international cooperation are currently essential factors for the constitutional justice. The exchange of case-law and the use of the constitutional experience at comparative level have contributed to the creation of a real European common heritage of constitutional justice*". Similarly, it was underlined the importance of "*promoting constitutional justice, which is a key element of democracy, human rights and the rule of law*".

436 For details, see G. Buquicchio, P. Garrone, *Vers un espace constitutionnel commun? Le role de la Commission de Venise*, available on *www.venice.coe.int.*

437 R.S. Durr, *cited paper*, p. 161.

5.2.2 *Dialogue through liaison officers. The Joint Council on Constitutional Justice*

The Joint Council on Constitutional Justice was set up by the Venice Commission in 2002, in continuing certain actions which started in 1992 by setting up a documentation centre to promote a mutual exchange of ideas and relevant case-law of the constitutional courts.

For this purpose, the Commission established a network of correspondents (liaison officers) with the constitutional courts. Three times a year, they contribute to the Bulletin on Constitutional Case-Law, published by the Venice Commission, and to the Commission's database (CODICES), allowing a rapid exchange of information on current constitutional issues. Likewise, whenever various specific issues raised before the constitutional courts require a broad documentation of comparative law, the liaison officers can address to the other liaisons officers, through the Venice Commission, in order to transmit relevant information on the issue concerned – legislation, case-law and doctrine in the matter.

The establishment of the Joint Council on Constitutional Justice in 2002 institutionalized this cooperation between the constitutional courts and the Venice Commission, further underlining the role of their attendance to the activities of the Commission. This body is mixed, consisting of members of the Venice Commission and liaison officers appointed by the constitutional courts in more than 50 countries, as well as representatives of the European Court of Human Rights and the Inter-American Court of Human Rights. The annual meetings of the liaison officers of the Member constitutional courts, those associated, as observers or with a special status within the Venice Commission, facilitate the exchange of information on specific issues of constitutional justice and ensure the dissemination of this case-law, finding the way to settle certain specific issues.

5.2.3 *Dialogue with the Venice Commission reflected within the case-law of the Constitutional Court of Romania*

5.2.3.1 *Documentation through liaison officers*

The recent examples of cases in which the Constitutional Court of Romania addressed to the Venice Commission for achieving documentation through its liaison officers are those settled by Decision no. 530 of 12 December 2013 regarding the exception of unconstitutionality of the provisions of Article 16 para. (3) of the Political Parties Act no. 14/2003[438], and by Decision no. 206 of 29 April 2013 regarding the exception of unconstitutionality of the provisions of Article 414^5 para. (4) of the Criminal Procedure Code[439].

438 Published in the Official Gazette of Romania no. 23 of 13 January 2014.
439 Published in the Official Gazette of Romania no. 350 of 13 June 2013.

Thus, in the first of the above-mentioned cases, the Constitutional Court was vested, under Article 146 d) first sentence of the Constitution, with the exception of unconstitutionality of Article 16 para. (3) of the Political Parties Act no. 14/2003, republished in the Official Gazette no. 550 of 6 August 2012 which states: "Acquiring or losing membership within a political party is subject only to the internal jurisdiction of the respective party, according to the party's statute". As grounds for the exception, it was argued that the impugned legal provisions are contrary to Article 21 of the Constitution, regarding free access to justice, as they exclude the courts of law from carrying out the control on the measures ordered by the jurisdictional bodies of the political party regarding its loss of membership.

Having examined the exception of unconstitutionality, the Court first held that it had already ruled on certain exceptions of unconstitutionality of the same legal provisions, consistently rejecting them as unfounded[440], on the ground that: courts of law are not legitimate to exercise justice with regard to violations of internal rules within political parties, as the responsibility in the matter is not regulated by legal rules of common law, but by own rules of ethics; the courts of law have no power to censor the decisions of the so-called "internal jurisdiction of the parties", decisions which are political acts by their nature; within the examination of the fulfilment of the conditions required for the legal establishment of political parties, the court of law shall determine whether the statutory procedures on sanctions ensure the applicant, who is dissatisfied with a decision of the party, the right to effectively and efficiently support his/her cause. However, in terms of the serious legal consequences that the exclusion from the party may produce (in this case – on the mandate of the local elected officials, consisting its cessation) and of the significant number of such cases referred to the constitutional court, the Court considered it necessary to distinguish between the own rules of ethics of the political parties and the rules which have an obvious legal nature as they establish rights and obligations for the party members and the statutory bodies and penalties for breaching statutory provisions and procedures to be followed in these cases. These rules are legally binding and fall within the notion of "law", as it has been established according to the European Court of Human Rights as an autonomous notion. Likewise, these rules constitute the basis for the adoption of certain legal acts, and not of certain "decisions which are political acts by their nature". At the same time, the intervention of the court of law to verify the fulfilment of the conditions required for the legal establishment of political parties represents a separate issue in order to verify the actual application, in each case, the compliance with the status of parties, with

---

440 In this respect, see, for example: Decision no. 952 of 25 June 2009, published in the Official Gazette of Romania no. 571 of 17 August 2009; Decision no. 1255 of 6 October 2009, published in the Official Gazette of Romania no. 783 of 17 November 2009; Decision no. 649 of 19 June 2012, published in the Official Gazette of Romania no. 560 of 8 August 2012, and Decision no. 65 of 21 February 2013, published in the Official Gazette of Romania no. 176 of 1 April 2013.

the statutory proceedings and with the way of determining and applying sanctions. The fact that such issues are governed by legal rules involves the possible exercise of a judicial control and the adoption of legal decisions, and not of political acts.

In light of this approach, the Court considered necessary to reconsider the relevant case-law in the matter and to uphold the exception of unconstitutionality raised in this case. In this respect, the Court held that the regulation subject to constitutional review infringes the provisions of Article 21, according to which no law may restrict the exercise of the right of any individual to go to court for the protection of its legitimate rights, freedoms and interests because, according to Article 16 para. (3) of Law no. 14/2003, the request of any party member who has been applied the penalty of exclusion from the party can never be effectively examined by an independent and impartial judge. Thus, receiving an application challenging the legality of the expulsion from the party, the court of law can only reject the application as inadmissible due to its lack of material competence to judge it, even if it notes that the statutory procedures have been violated. Therefore, in this matter, free access to justice is not only limited, but it is completely annihilated. Consequently, the impugned legal text violates the very substance of the right of access to justice and it is in an antinomy relation with the provisions of Article 6 of the Convention for the Protection of Human Rights and Fundamental Freedoms and with the case-law of the European Court of Human Rights concerning the right to a fair trial (see, for example: Judgment of 10 February 1983, delivered in *Case Albert and Le Compte v. Belgium*, para. 29; Judgment of 25 May 2005, delivered in Case *Buzescu v. Romania*, para. 60).

The same conclusion results also from the fact that, although the jurisdictional bodies of the party function on the basis of certain statutory provisions which mainly should provide the parties the right to opinion, the right of defence and a fair proceeding, they cannot be considered as meeting the specific requirements of an independent and impartial tribunal within the meaning of Article 6 of the Convention for the Protection of Human Rights and Fundamental Freedoms.

In light of these considerations, the Court held that the full jurisdiction of the courts of law is violated, as it is governed by Article 126 para. (1) of the Constitution. The constitutional provisions of Article 126 para. (2) establish that the jurisdiction of the courts of law is determined under the law, and not that no court has the jurisdiction to rule on a dispute. Even if the material jurisdiction for the settlement of a case is assigned to other bodies (the jurisdictional ones, for example) under the special law, their solutions can be challenged before a court, thus complying with the right of access to justice.

Given the provisions of Article 15 para. (1) and (3) of Law no. 14/2003, in the case of disputes arising from the expulsion from party, the members of a political party shall follow the procedure before the internal jurisdictional bodies of the party, required them the enforcement of the statutory provisions and only if they consider that these bodies have infringed the statuary provisions, they shall have the subsequent possibility to refer to the court of law.

The Court also stated that, in this matter, the judicial control can only be exercised on the status and regularity in the performance of the statutory proceedings before the jurisdictional bodies of the party, and not on the opportunity of the applied penalty. Thus, the court vested with the settlement of an application challenging the penalty of exclusion from a party is to analyze whether the statutory rules on the establishment and application of the penalty have been complied with and to determine whether a party's right of defence and opinion has been effectively ensured.

In conclusion, the regulation on the exclusive competence of the jurisdictional bodies of the political party to decide upon the compliance with the statutory rules by the members of political parties and eliminating in this way the judicial control regarding the observance of their own Statute by these bodies is unconstitutional. Giving expression to free access to justice in this matter, the court vested with the settlement of an application challenging the penalty of exclusion from a party is to analyze whether the statutory rules on the establishment and application of the penalty have been complied with and to determine whether a party's right of defence and opinion has been effectively ensured. The judicial control can only be exercised on the status and regularity in the performance of the statutory proceedings before the jurisdictional bodies of the party, and not on the opportunity of the applied penalty.

As for the second case, by Decision no. 206 of 29 April 2013, the Constitutional Court found that "the interpretation on points of law" by Decision no. 8 of 18 October 2010 of the High Court of Cassation and Justice, United Sections, published in the Official Gazette of Romania no. 416 of 14 June 2011, is unconstitutional, contravening the Constitution and the Constitutional Court's Decision no. 62 of 18 January 2007[441]. By the latter decision, the Court had already ascertained the unconstitutionality of "the provisions of Article I section 56 of Law no. 278/2006 amending the Criminal Law, as well as other laws, the part referring to the repeal of Articles 205, 206 and 207 of the Criminal Code".

In order to illustrate the situation of regulations relating to acts of defamation in the Member States of the Council of Europe, the Court presented an analysis of comparative law to the effect that, in two thirds of them, the protection of dignity, honour and reputation is achieved both by means of criminal law and by means of civil law, while only in one third of them such protection can be achieved only by means of civil law. Likewise, the Court invoked the reference case-law of the European Court of Human Rights, indicated in the summary of Steering Committee on Media and Information Society of the Council of Europe[442], being the basis of the comparative law analysis contained in the decision, from which it results, inter alia, that the Court in Strasbourg has not condemned the criminal penalty of insult

---

441 Published in the Official Gazette of Romania no. 104 of 12 February 2007.

442 *http://www.coe.int/t/dghl/standardsetting/media/CDMSI/CDMSI (2012) Misc 11 Rev2_en.pdf.*

/ libel, but the excessive use of criminal penalties in response to acts considered defamatory. The international documents in the matter refer to the quality of law governing defamatory facts, as well as the way of its application, which must also be achieved with clarity and precision, avoiding any exaggeration, as the criminal penalties are applicable in case that the civil ones do not provide an effective protection of the violated rights. In the recitals of the delivered decision, the Court held, therefore, that: "*According to a study conducted in this respect by the Steering Committee on Media and Information Society of the Council of Europe [Steering Committee on Media and Information Society – CDMS] on the legislation in the matter in the Member States of the Council of Europe and its application in the light of the case-law of the European Court of Human Rights – updated based on the information sent by the liaison officers of the constitutional courts to the Constitutional Court of Romania within the cooperation with the Venice Commission –, the criminal provisions on insult and libel define the legislation of most of the Member States of the Council of Europe*". Thus, the Court found that in 34 Member States of the Council of Europe, the protection of dignity is achieved both by means of criminal law, and by means of civil law, as the acts of insult and libel constitute crimes, under the law and the specific features of each state, [Albania, Andorra, Austria, Azerbaijan, Belgium, Bulgaria, Croatia, Denmark, Finland, France, Germany (where both the libel against private life and the libel against public life are incriminated), Greece, Iceland, Italy, Liechtenstein, Lithuania, Luxembourg, Malta, Monaco, Norway, Poland, Portugal, the Czech Republic, San Marino, Serbia, Slovakia, Slovenia Spain, Sweden, Turkey, the Netherlands, Hungary]. In the Russian Federation, the acts in question were decriminalized in 2011 and 2012. In 12 Member States of the Council of Europe, these acts were totally decriminalized – as the protection of human dignity was achieved only by means of civil law – or partially [Ukraine in 2001; Bosnia and Herzegovina in 2002; Estonia in 2002 (with certain exceptions related to subjects qualified as passive); Cyprus in 2003 (with certain exceptions related to subjects qualified as passive); Georgia in 2004; Moldova in 2004; the United Kingdom in 2009; Latvia in 2009; Armenia in 2010; Ireland in 2010; Montenegro in 2011; the Former Yugoslav Republic of Macedonia in 2012]. The acts of insult and libel also constitute offenses, under the law, in certain states which not members of the Council of Europe, for example, in Belarus, Chile and in certain Mexican states. It is worth mentioning that laws often contain distinct regulations on the acts of defamation committed through the press or on the President of the State and on the officials of the State or against the nation.

It is observed the express reference made by the Constitutional Court regarding a documentary made by the Venice Commission, upon certain questions addressed to the liaison officers. It is also observed that they resorted to this method of documentation in cases concerning a main issue of the rule of law: the limits of freedom of association in political parties, namely the limits of freedom of expression.

5.2.3.2 *The invocation of the Venice Commission recommendations. Fields of reference*

The revision of the Constitution

The recent initiative for the revision of the Constitution, upon which the Constitutional Court ruled by Decision no. 80/2014, illustrates the dialogue between the Constitutional Court of Romania and the Venice Commission, through the mutual referrals and the joint conclusions reached on the key points of the review.

Thus, in the Opinion of 21–22 March 2014, adopted at the 98th Plenary Session, the Venice Commission has ruled upon the initiative for the revision of the Constitution, following the request of the Prime Minister of Romania. The opinion made explicit reference to the decision delivered by the Constitutional Court of Romania on the same draft law, indicating also a separation of powers, in order to comply with that decision and the lack of competence of the Venice Commission to rule upon it: "On 17 February 2014, the Constitutional Court of Romania declared, in the light of article 152, the unconstitutionality of certain provisions of the draft revision law. It is not the role of the Venice Commission to assess the constitutionality of given proposals or the judgment of the Constitutional Court (...), the present analysis aims at assessing the proposed amendments to the Romanian Constitution in the light of existing European standards and experience."

It is noted that, on most of the texts on which the Constitutional Court ascertained the unconstitutionality or formulated recommendations by Decision. 80/2014, the Venice Commission also ruled similarly, as a recommendation, and underlined either imperfections of drafting or substantive issues.

From the perspective of the dialogue reflected in the identical solutions identified on the same examined issue, we consider illustrative the conclusions regarding the way of regulation of the Constitutional Court's powers. In the above-mentioned opinion, the Venice Commission held that "Article 146 of the current Constitution lists in a non-exhaustive manner the powers of the Constitutional Court. Point «l» of article 146, states that the Court will «carry out also other duties stipulated by the organic law of the Court», thereby giving constitutional protection to all powers of the Court, including those which are only mentioned in the Court's law. By abrogating the provision in letter «l» without including in the former list those prerogatives having been added to it by organic law, the Constitutional Court seems to lose two important prerogatives: the review of the constitutionality of the law for the revision of the Constitution after its adoption by the Parliament and of resolutions by the Plenary of the Chamber of Deputies, resolutions by the Plenary of the Senate and resolutions by the Plenary of the joint Chambers of Parliament. The Venice Commission finds worrying that the scope of the constitutional control – one key means for ensuring respect for the balance of powers and the rule of law – is reduced. The Romanian authorities are invited to reconsider this amendment, in line with the comments made by Commission, in its 2012 Opinion, with regard to the judicial control off internal acts of the Parliament". Likewise, the Commission noted that this amendment has been ruled unconstitutional, for breach of the Constitutional provisions on the limits of the constitutional revision.

Ruling upon the same issue, the Constitutional Court had already held, by Decision no. 80/2014, that point 120 of the Sole Article of the legislative proposal for the revision of the Constitution which repeals the provisions of Article 146 l) of the Constitution - according to which the Constitutional Court "also fulfils other prerogatives stipulated by the organic law of the Court" in unconstitutional. We have referred to the considerations which substantiated this solution of the Court when we analyzed the manner in which the Court has consolidated its position through its case-law. In this context, we will emphasize only that the constitutional court founded the considerations of its decision, inter alia, on the same Opinion adopted by the Venice Commission as reference, according to which "with its Rules of Procedure and other general rules, Parliament however adopts normative acts, which are a yardstick for Parliament as a whole and its members individually. Judicial control of the application of normative acts is an essential element of the rule of law. The absence of judicial control means that the majority in Parliament becomes the judge of its own acts. If only the majority can decide on the observance of parliamentary rules, the minority has nowhere to turn for help if these rules are flouted. Even if the acts concerned are individual ones, this affects not only the rights of the parliamentary minority but, as a consequence, also the right to vote of the citizens who have elected the parliamentary minority." Therefore, "judicial control of individual acts of Parliament is therefore not only a rule of law issue but, as the right to vote is affected, even a question of human rights"[443].

We note the similar findings reached by the Court, on the one hand, and by the Venice Commission, on the other hand, on the same issues of principle contained in the proposal for the revision, as well as the similar substantiation of such conclusions.

It is worth mentioning that the assistance of the Venice Commission has been more requested by the authorities in Romania, for example, even during the adoption of the Constitution in 1991. As indicated above[444], Romania has been the first country in the region which requested the support of the Commission since 1990.

---

443 Opinion on the compatibility with constitutional principles and the rule of law of actions taken by the Government and the Parliament of Romania in respect of other state institutions and on the Government Emergency Ordinance amending Law no. 47/1992 on the Organisation and Functioning of the Constitutional Court and on the Government Emergency Ordinance amending and supplementing Law no. 3/2000 on the organisation and holding of a referendum in Romania, adopted by the Venice Commission at its 93rd Plenary Session, 14–15 December 2012.

444 F.B. Vasilescu, *Constitutional Court of Romania: a rocky start*, in *Constitutional Court of Romania – 20 years of existence and 100 years of constitutional review*, Universul Juridic Publishing House, Bucharest, 2013, pp. 131–136.

Constitutional review of electoral legislation

Most frequently, the Constitutional Court of Romania invoked the recommendations of the Venice Commission when examining the constitutionality of legislation in electoral matter. The cited document is the Code of Good Practice in Electoral Matters – Guidelines and Explanatory Report, adopted by the European Commission for Democracy through Law at the 52nd Plenary Session (Venice, 18–19 October 2002)[445], an act that underline the principles which form the basis of the Europe's electoral heritage, namely "universal suffrage, equal, free, secret and direct."

These principles and the provisions of the Code were invoked in the case-law of the Constitutional Court of Romania after 2010, oriented towards the emphasis of certain obligations of the legislature in this matter, determined by the ascertainment of various amendments to the electoral legislation and to the shortcomings of the electoral system challenged during the parliamentary elections in 2008 and the presidential elections in 2009. In this case-law, the Constitutional Court underlined the need for the reconsideration of the entire election legislation, emphasising the issues which must be subject to review and the principles which must be considered by the legislature in this regard, and, at the same time, it pointed out the need for the stability of law in electoral matters, an expression of the principle of legal certainty.

Thus, by Decision no. 61 of 14 January 2010[446], the Court held as follows: "In its activity, the Constitutional Court has settled several cases regarding the constitutionality of certain provisions of Law no. 35/2008 on the election of the Chamber of Deputies and the Senate, noting that the current regulation of the Romanian electoral system has many imperfections and, as such, its reconsideration in the light of parliamentary elections in 2012 is required, in order to ensure, in all aspects, the organization and holding of democratic elections in Romania. In this regard, the Court considers it necessary, firstly begin with the economic, political and social reality of the country, with the role of the political parties in the electoral process, with the need for the rationalization of Parliament and, finally, to regulate a type of elections appropriate to the conclusions and which may have correspondent in the types of elections that are found in most European countries".

At the same time, the Court held that "Law no. 35/2009, as subsequently amended and supplemented, regulates an electoral mechanism that has nothing to do with the elements contained in the majority uninominal type of elections, organized in one round and which is used in other countries. It is noteworthy that no electoral system in which a majority uninominal type of elections in one round is regulated provides any threshold, while Law no. 35/2008 provides two types of alternative electoral thresholds. The results of parliamentary elections in November 2008 showed that the mechanism used to award the term of office resulted in results which were not consistent with those specific to a majority uninominal type of elections, results which were determined by mathematic calculations governed by the rules of the electoral

445 *www.venice.coe.int.*

446 Published in the Official Gazette of Romania no. 76 of 3 February 2010.

procedure of the uninominal ballot stipulated by Law no. 35/2008. This is why the appointment of certain MPs was made on the basis of certain calculations and not on the results obtained in the elections, following the cast of the political options".

By Decision no. 503 of 20 April 2010[447], the Court upheld the exception of unconstitutionality of the provisions of Article 48 para. (17) of Law no. 35/2008, as it results in independent candidates elimination from the election procedure, if partial elections, which infringes Article 37 of the Constitution – "The right to be elected".

By Decision no. 51 of 25 January 2012[448], the unconstitutionality of the Law on the organization and conduct of the elections for the authorities of local public administration and of the elections for the Chamber of Deputies and the Senate in 2012, as well as for the amendment and supplement of Title I of the Law no. 35/2008 for the election of the Chamber of Deputies and the Senate, and for amending and supplementing Law no. 67/2004 for the election of local public administration authorities, Law no. 215/2001 on local public administration, and Law no. 393/2004 on the Statute of local elected officials. On that occasion, the Court held critically the frequent amendments to the electoral legislation, noting that Law no. 35/2008 "*was amended two months after its adoption by Parliament by the Government Emergency Ordinance no. 66/2008 (...) and 5 months after its adoption by the Government Emergency Ordinance no. 97/2008 (...). In the latter ordinance, 92 amendments and supplementations were brought to the law, while the law firstly adopted by Parliament in compliance with Articles 75 and 76 para. (1) of the Constitution comprised 76 articles and an annex on constituencies*". At the same time, stating that "*the right to free elections requires the observance of certain requirements, including that of stability of legal norms in electoral matters*" and that "*the stability of such rules constitutes an expression of the principle of legal certainty established implicitly by Article 1 para. (5) of the Constitution*", and noting that the untimely legislative amendment "*may give rise to additional difficulties to the authorities entitled to its enforcement, in terms of adapting to the newly established procedure and to the technical operations that it entails*", and that "*this regulation is susceptible to cause difficulties in exercising the rights to vote, difficulties that may result, ultimately, in the limitation of this right*", the Court ascertained the unconstitutionality of the impugned law. The recitals of the decision took account of the Code of Good Practice in Electoral Matters adopted by the Venice Commission, a document indicating that the stability of the law is crucial to the credibility of the electoral process, and the frequent amendments to the norms and their complex nature may confuse the voter, namely that what must be avoided is not so much the amendment of the voting systems, as their frequent amendment or within a short period of time (less than one year) before the election. Referring to the recitals of Decision no. 61/2010, the Court stated again that "*the current regulation of the Romanian electoral system has certain flaws, and as such, its reconsideration in the light of parliamentary elections in 2012 is required, in*

447 Published in the Official Gazette of Romania no. 353 of 28 May 2010.
448 Published in the Official Gazette of Romania no. 90 of 3 February 2012.

order to ensure, in all aspects, the organization and holding of democratic elections in Romania", underlining "*the need for the reconsideration of the entire electoral legislation relating to the election of the Chamber of Deputies and the Senate, the President of Romania, the European Parliament elections, as well as the election of local public administrative authorities, which is to be gathered in an election code whose specific and common provisions shall ensure, in accordance with the constitutional principles, the organization of democratic, fair and transparent elections*".

As the Constitutional Court held in the cited case-law, the Code of Good Practice in Electoral Matters – Guidelines and Explanatory Report, adopted by the European Commission for Democracy through Law at the 52nd Plenary Session (Venice, 18–19 October 2002), emphasizes the stability of rules of electoral law, "in particular those regulating the electoral system proper, membership of electoral commissions and the drawing of constituency boundaries". The same document also states that "it is not so much changing voting systems which is a bad thing – they can always be changed for the better – as changing them frequently or just before (within one year of) elections. Even when no manipulation is intended, changes will seem to be dictated by immediate party political interests". Emphasizing the same principles, the Report on the timeline and inventory of political criteria for assessing an election adopted by the Council for Democratic Elections at its 34th Meeting (Venice, 14 October 2010) notes, however, that "any reform of electoral legislation to be applied during an election should occur early enough for it to be really applicable to the election". However, in certain circumstances, "exceptions to the one year rule could be accepted, namely where there is a need to rectify, through legislation, unforeseen problems or to provide redress to violations of internationally recognised rights where they had been built into the electoral law".

All these principles and considerations are mentioned by Decision no. 682/2012, when the Court upheld the objection of unconstitutionality and found that the Law on amending and supplementing Law no. 35/2008 for elections to the Chamber of Deputies and the Senate and amending and supplementing Law no. 67/2004 for the election of local public administration authorities, the Law no. 215/2001 on local public administration and Law no. 393/2004 on the Statute of the local officials is unconstitutional.

On the occasion of the latter decision, the Court has established the already mentioned benchmarks regarding the legal force of the recommendations of the Venice Commission, reiterating that "*indeed, this act is not binding, but its recommendations represent the coordinates of democratic elections in relation to which states – characterized as belonging to this type of regime – may express their free option in electoral matters, while respecting the fundamental human rights, in general, and the right to be elected and to elect, in particular*". Likewise, the Court held that "*otherwise, the Code of Good Practice in Electoral Matters is also mentioned as an international document of reference in the case-law of the European Court of Human Rights (for example, Judgment delivered in Case Petkov and others v. Bulgaria on 11 June 2009 or Judgment delivered in Case Grosaru v. Romania on 2 March 2010)*".

Referendum

In this matter, the Constitutional Court has often made reference to the Code of Good Practice on Referendums in the recitals of its decisions[449], mainly when the stability of legislation in the matter of referendum, the validity of the referendum and its effects were called into question.

Thus, as regards the stability of regulations in the matter of referendum, the Code drafted by the Venice Commission states that the fundamental aspects of referendum law should not be open to amendment less than one year before a referendum, or should be written in the Constitution or at a level superior to ordinary law. The fundamental aspects are in particular those concerning: the composition of electoral commissions or any other body responsible for organising the referendum, the franchise and electoral registers, the procedural and substantive validity of the text put to a referendum, the effects of the referendum (with the exception of rules concerning matters of detail), the participation of the proposal's supporters and opponents to broadcasts of public media, turn-out quorum.

The Constitutional Court has referred to these distinctions by Decision no. 736 of 24 July 2012[450], which held that "Unlike the elections, which take place at fixed intervals of time, and their time is known long before their organisation, it is unlikely that the date of a referendum be known a year or long time before it actually takes place. Therefore, the Code of Good Practice on Referendums adopted by the Council for Democratic Elections at its 19th meeting (Venice, 16 December 2006) and by the Venice Commission at its 70th plenary session (Venice, 16–17 March 2007), makes a distinction – when addressing stability of referendum legislation – in terms of its provisions, stating that the fundamental aspects should not be changed in less than a year before a referendum or they should be governed by Constitution or at a level higher than ordinary law. According to Article II 2 c) of the Code, basic rules are the rules concerning: composition of the election commissions or of other body responsible for organising the referendum, the right to vote and the electoral lists; the procedural and substantive validity of the text submitted to referendum, the referendum effects (subject to detailed rules); participation of supporters and opponents of the proposal in public media broadcasts. Given this specificity and the mentioned differentiation, it results that the elements related to the organisation and holding of the referendum – such as the time interval – may be subject to amendments less of a year before the day of organisation thereof, insofar such does not affect the general interest of proper conduct of the referendum".

However, the Court upheld the objection of unconstitutionality and found that the provisions of the sole article paragraph 2 of the Law amending Law no. 3/2000 on the organisation and holding of the referendum, according to which: "Article 34 shall be amended and shall read as follows: «Article 34 – The time interval for

449 Adopted by the Council for Democratic Elections at its 19th meeting and by the Venice Commission at its 70th Plenary Session, Venice, March 2007.

450 Published in the Official Gazette of Romania no. 516 of 25 July 2012.

holding the national referendum shall be established through Government decision»"is unconstitutional. This is because "the schedule of the referendum is one of the elements of procedure for organizing and holding thereof, and not a technical or detail aspect" so that "its establishment is subject to the rule established by Article 73 (3) d) of the Constitution, respectively that of regulation by organic law. Therefore, regulation by Government decision is contrary to the relevant constitutional text. Moreover, such legislation would be likely to result in a state of uncertainty as to an element of this procedure, in contradiction with the principle of legal certainty implicitly established by Article 1 (5) of the Constitution."

The same principle mentioned by the Code of Good Practice in Electoral Matters, this time with direct consequences on the solution delivered in the case, was also emphasized by Decision no. 334 of 26 June 2013[451], where it was held inter alia that "over time, legislative instability in the matter of referendum, due to changes in this legislation, especially in periods when Parliament was preparing a case for dismissal of the President, and currently at the initiation of the revision of the Constitution, has proved to be not only a factor of legal uncertainty, but also a question of civic challenging of this legislation, criticized upon its application", as well as the fact that "Parliament can (and as is clear from the Court's decisions, even should) intervene in this matter of referendum law, provided that it does not subject it to purely conjectural amendments, based on opportunity or political understanding, that favours one or the other political forces represented in Parliament and forming at one point a parliamentary majority." These considerations were, in fact, the basis of the conclusions found in that decision, i.e. "in order to ensure compliance with the general principle of legal certainty in the matter of referendum, in agreement with the recommendations of the Code of Good Practice on Referendums adopted by the Venice Commission, with the Protocol to the European Convention on Human Rights and Fundamental Freedoms and with the International Covenant on Civil and Political Rights, the provisions of the Law amending and supplementing Law no. 3/2000 on the organisation and holding of the referendum are constitutional, but they may not be applied to referendums organised within one year of the entry into force of the amending law." In agreement with the findings of the Court, Law no. 341/2013, which recently amended Law no. 3/2000 on the organisation and holding of the referendum, provides under Article II that "the provisions of this law shall enter into force one year after publication in the Official Gazette of Romania, Part I".

Therefore, it can be observed the atypical nature of this decision, as well as its strong foundation on the recommendations contained in the Code of Good Practice on Referendums.

As for the validity of the referendum and having to rule upon the legislative solution chosen by the legislature in terms of a quorum of participation in the referendum in relation to the constitutional principles of reference, namely those which enshrine the rule of law, the sovereignty and the manner of its exercise, the

451 Published in the Official Gazette of Romania no. 407 of 5 July 2013.

Constitutional Court held, by Decision no. 334/2013, that "the law subject to review regulates, as regards the conditions of validity of the referendum, besides the decrease of the turn-out quorum to 30%, also the condition according to which "the result of the referendum is validated if at least 25% valid votes of those registered on the permanent electoral lists." Therefore, these two minimum conditions must be fulfilled in order to validate the referendum, "which is a way of securing the representativeness of the vote to referendum which is likely to meet the conditions required by the previous case-law of the Constitutional Court".

Likewise, the Court found that this legislative solution complies with the Recommendations of the Venice Commission. Thus, in the Report adopted at the 64th Plenary Session (Venice, 21–22 October 2005) on "Referendum in Europe – An Analysis of the legal rules in European states", it noted that "most states do not provide for a quorum to validate the result of a referendum. Where a quorum does exist, it can take two forms: quorum of participation or quorum of approval (note – it refers to the majority) (...) The quorum of approval is considerably preferable to a quorum of participation, which poses a serious problem. The opponents of the draft proposal submitted to referendum, as several examples have shown, appeal to people to abstain even if they are very much in the minority among the voters concerned by the issue". Similarly, The Guidelines of the Venice Commission – Code of Good Practice on Referendums – recommended not elaborating provisions on the rules applied to quorums. Thus, in the Explanatory Report of the same document, it was held that: "*The quorum of participation (the minimum threshold) results in the interest of the opposition of the proposal to abstain itself rather than to vote against", and also that «encouraging abstentions or imposing the viewpoint of a minority is not a healthy aspect for a democracy. Moreover, it is very tempting to falsify the participation rate in relation to a weak opposition»*".

Following these findings and given the context created by the repetition of the same critics who have brought into discussion the requirement to establish a certain quorum of participation in the referendum as a condition of legitimacy expressed by the people, the Court held, by Decision no. 471 of 14 November 2013[452], that "*The recommendations of Venice Commission are based on an extensive analysis of the existing regulations in the matter of the referendum in the Member States of the Council of Europe, as well as on the experiences of the States that led to the adoption or amendment of the regulations in question. As a result, even if the acts of the Venice Commission are just a recommendation, they cannot be ignored, since they contain a rich practice in the democratic states. The conclusions based on this practice which demonstrate, in relation to the issue examined in this case, that the establishment of a quorum of participation in the referendum may be sometimes a hindrance in achieving the purpose of this democratic exercise, also constitute benchmarks for the Romanian legislature in drafting the legislative solutions in the matter*".

452 Published in the Official Gazette of Romania no. 754 of 4 December 2013.

Regarding the effects of the referendum, the Code of Good Practice on Referendum provides, under section 8, the following: "a).The effects of legally binding or consultative referendums must be clearly specified in the Constitution or by law. b). Referendums on questions of principle or other generally-worded proposals should preferably not be binding. If they are binding, the subsequent procedure should be laid down in specific rules."

Examining the Romanian legislation in this field, we note that it is also deficient in this respect, since it does not expressly provide the effects of the referendum and the procedure to follow[453].

Thus, when examining the constitutionality of the initiative for the revision of the Constitution in 2013, ruling upon the amendments proposed in terms of Articles 90 of the Constitution, referring to the referendum, and invoking the recommendations of the Venice Commission, the Constitutional Court noted as follows: "the referendum, regardless of its nature – binding or consultative referendum, is a way of exercising national sovereignty, based on Article 2 of the Constitution, which enshrines the will of the Romanian framers in the sense that, within representative democracy, national sovereignty belongs to the Romanian people, but it cannot be exercised in a direct way, at individual level, the form of the exercise being the indirect and intermediated one, through the process of election of representative bodies, by expressing the will of citizens in free, regular and fair elections and by referendum. Whereas there may be circumstances in which the issues on which the people is called upon to express its will may affect the interests of elected representatives (such as reducing the number of MEPs or reduce parliamentarians' allowances), the Venice Commission, in the document entitled Guidelines on the holding of referendums, adopted at the 68th Plenary Session (13-14 October 2007), held that referendums should be clearly specified in the Constitution or by law whether referendums are legally binding or consultative. It is preferable for referendums on questions of principle or generally-worded proposals to be consultative. If they are legally binding, the subsequent procedure should be laid down in specific constitutional or legislative rules. In the case of the consultative referendum, the fact that none such subsequent procedure is established does not imply the lack of effect of this referendum. In this light, what distinguishes a consultative referendum from a binding referendum is not primarily the question relating to respect for the will of the people — that will cannot be ignored by the people's elected representatives, whereas it is an expression of national sovereignty — but the effect (direct or indirect) of the referendum. Unlike the binding referendum, the consultative referendum produces an indirect effect in the sense that it requires the intervention of other bodies, mostly legislative bodies, to enforce the will expressed by the electoral body (see

453 See, in the same regard, Constitutional Court's Decision no. 80/2014 on the legislative proposal for the revision of the Constitution of Romania, para. 287.

Decision no. 682 of 27 June 2012, published in Official Gazette of Romania, Part I, no. 473 of 11 July 2013)"[454].

5.3 Conclusions

We note that the experience gained by the Venice Commission over time, from the collaboration with Member States and their institutions, allowed the identification of common standards applicable throughout Europe. The Constitutional Court of Romania, along with the other constitutional courts of the Member States, contributes to strengthen these standards and their implementation, both through sharing its experience at conferences, seminars, sending documentation and summaries of case-law and by requiring, within the exercise of their powers, the rules of democracy and of the rule of law reflected in the above-mentioned standards. Through this dialogue, perhaps more visible than in other analyzed cases, it is achieved that phenomenon of mutual institutional strengthening presented by us in our analysis.

---

454 Decision no. 80/2014, pre-quoted.

III. The Dialogue Between Constitutional Judges and Authorities at the Internal Level

1. Dialogue partners

According to Article 1 para. (4) of the Constitution of Romania: "*The State shall be organized based on the principle of the separation and balance of powers – legislative, executive, and judicial – within the framework of a constitutional democracy*".

The legislative power shall be exercised by Parliament, which, according to Article 61 para. (1) of the Constitution of Romania, "*is the supreme representative body of the Romanian people and the sole legislative authority of the country.*"

The executive power shall be exercised by the President of Romania, who, according to Article 80 para. (1) of the Constitution, "*shall represent the Romanian State and safeguard the independence of the nation, the unity and territorial integrity of the country*", and by the Government, which, as set forth in Article para. (1) of the Constitution, "in *accordance with its governing programme accepted by Parliament, shall ensure the implementation of domestic and foreign policy, and exercise the general management of public administration*".

The judicial power shall be exercised by the courts of law. Thus, Chapter VI of Title III of the Constitution, entitled *Judicial authority*, regulates, in distinct sections, *the Courts of law, the Public Ministry* and *The Superior Council of Magistracy*. Thus, Article 126 para. (1) of the Constitution establishes that: "*Justice shall be meted out by the High Court of Cassation and Justice and by the other courts set up under the law*"; Article 131 para. (1) stipulates that: "*Within judicial activities, the Public Ministry shall represent the general interests of society and it shall defend the legal order, as well as the citizens' rights and freedoms*", regarding the Superior Council of Magistracy, Article 133 para. (1) rules that it "*shall guarantee the independence of the judiciary*".

The Constitutional Court ruled on the constitutional principles governing the activity of these public authorities, as well as on the relationships between them – the limits of power, control and mutual determination –, in line with the principles of the rule of law, both in situations that have concerned a clear separation of powers, and in situations where the regulation of conjunct competencies required the establishment of certain limits of competence which were insufficiently defined by the Constitution. In this way, the regulation of the Constitutional Court and its powers, as well as its developed case-law have led to important configurations of the role of the authorities mentioned within the rule of law and to the development of a system of relationships that may be partially described as an institutional dialogue, which will be separately approached below.

Even if each of the mentioned institutions represents, in the light of the Constitutional Court's decisions and their effects, a potential dialogue partner, its specificity and consistency, as well as the express regulation set forth in the organic law of the Court lead us to refer, in particular, to the dialogue between the Constitutional Court, respectively, the legislative power, the executive power and the judiciary. This is because they are exponents of the system of separation of powers and the case-law which will be presented on this occasion will also provide an insight into the way in which the Constitutional Court ensures the achievement of this regime, which cannot be either understood or established by the provisions of the Constitution as a rigid one. Legal disputes of a constitutional nature settled by the Constitutional Court represented many opportunities to observe this reality and the fact that the principle of separation and balance of powers is necessarily supplemented by another principle, namely that of loyal cooperation.

While not specifically qualified as a constitutional "principle", enshrining constitutional duty of loyalty has become increasingly common in the case-law of the Romanian Constitutional Court. This case-law has evolved from a simple statement of the concepts of "*loyalty*" and "*loyal behaviour*" to circumstantiation of some "*rules of constitutional loyalty*" derived from a principle expressly enshrined in the Constitution – that of separation and balance of powers.

Thus, for example, by Decision no. 356 of 5 April 2007[455] on the request for settlement of the legal dispute of a constitutional nature between the President of Romania and the Romanian Government, submitted by the Prime Minister, the Constitutional Court held that "*institutional relations between the Prime Minister and Government, on the one hand, and President of Romania, on the other hand, must function within constitutional framework of loyalty and cooperation, for the functions regulated separately for each of the constitutional authorities, as cooperation between authorities is a necessary and essential requirement for the effective operation of State's public authorities*".

Developing this line of cases by Decision 1431/2010[456] on the request for settlement of the legal dispute of a constitutional nature between the Romanian Parliament and the Government, submitted the President of the Senate, the Court held, on loyal behaviour, that it is "*an extension of the principle separation and balance of powers*".

By Decision no. 51/2012[457], delivered within the constitutional review of a law before promulgation[458], the Court emphasized, again, "*the importance for proper*

455 Published in the Official Gazette of Romania no. 322 of 14 May 2007.

456 Published in the Official Gazette of Romania no. 758 of 12 November 2010.

457 Published in the Official Gazette of Romania no. 90 of 3 February 2012.

458 Law on the organisation and holding of elections for local public administrative authorities and on the elections for the Chambers of Deputies and the Senate in 2012, as well as amending and supplementing title I of Law no. 35/2008 on the elections for the Chambers of Deputies and the Senate and for the amendment and supplementation of Law no. 67/2004 for the election of local public administrative authorities, of the Law no. 215/2001 and of the Law no. 393/2004 on the Statute of the local elected officials.

functioning of the rule of law, of cooperation between State powers, which must be in the spirit of constitutional loyalty norm".

Furthermore, a similar principle was enshrined in its case-law by the Federal Constitutional Court of Germany, in a more firm and clearly defined manner. This principle[459] – of faithful co-operation between organs (Organtreue) – was first mentioned in a set of constitutional complaint proceedings in which the complainants referred as reasoning for the unconstitutionality of a statute about which they were complaining to the recognised constitutional principle of federal comity (Bundestreue) (also referred to as the principle of conduct which is well-disposed towards the Federation (bundesfreund-lichesVerhalten)) which obliges the Federation and the Länder to give consideration to one another, and had claimed that, by analogy to this, the principle of faithful co-operation between organs applied in the relationship between the constitutional organs of the Federation. The Federal Constitutional Court initially left it open at that time as to whether such a constitutional principle exists and whether, if so, a complainant[460] in constitutional complaint proceedings can invoke it. The Court however explicitly recognised this principle in later rulings[461].

The case-law of the Constitutional Court of Romania has also evolved from a simple statement of the concepts of "loyalty" and "loyal behaviour" to the circumstantiation of certain "norms of constitutional loyalty", implicit in the texts of the Constitution[462]. Thus, "the observance of the rule of law cannot be limited only to the implementation of explicit and formal provisions of the law and of the Constitution. It also involves constitutional behaviour and practices that facilitate the

459 *www.ccr.ro* – extract from the *National Report for the XVth Congress of the Conference of the European Constitutional Courts*, prepared by the Federal Constitutional Court of Germany, rapporteurs: Professor PhD G. Lübbe-Wolff, Professor PhD H.C. R. Mellinghoff, Professor PhD R. Gaier, judges of the Federal Constitutional Court.

460 Collection of decisions of the Federal Constitutional Court (*Entscheidungen des Bundesverfassungsgerichts* –BVerfGE 29, 221 <233>.

461 According to BVerfGE 89, 155 <191>; 97, 350 <374–375>; 119, 96 <122>.

462 Regarding the meaning of the principle of loyal behaviour of public authorities, see Decision no. 1257 of 7 October 2009, published in the Official Gazette of Romania no. 758 of 6 November 2009; Decision no. 1431 of 3 November 2010, published in the Official Gazette of Romania no. 758 of 12 November 2010; Decision no. 51 of 25 January 2012, published in the Official Gazette of Romania no. 90 of 3 February 2012; Decision no. 727 of 9 July 2012, published in the Official Gazette of Romania no. 477 of 12 July 2012; Decision no. 924 of 1 November 2012, published in the Official Gazette of Romania no. 787 of 22 November 2012; Decision no. 972 of 21 November 2012, published in the Official Gazette of Romania no. 800 of 28 November 2012; Decision no. 449 of 6 November 2013, published in the Official Gazette of Romania no. 784 of 14 December 2013.

observance of the formal rules by all constitutional bodies and the mutual respect between them"[463].

We want to emphasize that the dialogue which the Court implicitly carries with each of the analyzed institution is accompanied by an explicit invitation to the institutional dialogue between them in order to identify solutions and constitutional principles in the spirit of loyalty, of the loyal cooperation. This is, moreover, the "key" or "common denominator" of the inter-institutional dialogue at an internal level.

Taking into consideration its role and importance for the protection of fundamental rights and freedoms, we will refer to the Advocate of the People and to the existing dialogue between this institution and the Constitutional Court.

2. The dialogue between the Constitutional Court and Parliament

2.1 General aspects

The relationships and hence the institutional dialogue between the Constitutional Court and Parliament, as a body representing the legislative power, can be approached from two perspectives, with specific reference to the exercise of the two mentioned authorities. Thus, the organization, operation and structure of the Constitutional Court are mainly determined by Parliament, as the parliamentary activity, being exercised in compliance with the supremacy of the Constitution, is subject to the review exercised by the Constitutional Court, within the limits of its powers established by the Basic Law and its organic law. From this perspective, the examination of the limits of competence of the Constitutional Court also represents an interest, on the one hand, and on the other hand, the limits of competence of Parliament, as well as certain distinctions related to the specific effects produced by their acts.

2.2 The relationship of Parliament with the Constitutional Court

2.2.1 Regulation on the organisation and operation of the Constitutional Court. Financial autonomy of the Constitutional Court

The organisation and operation of the Constitutional Court are regulated by Title V of the Constitution and by Law no. 47/1992.

As concerns the provisions on the organization and functioning of the Constitutional Court regulated in the Constitution, they can be amended only through its revision. As a result, any change in the structure of the Constitutional Court,

463 See Opinion of the Venice Commission, section 72.

the mode of appointment, the length and the guarantees of term of office of judges cannot be achieved through an organic or ordinary law, but only through a law amending the Constitution. The procedure for the revision of the Constitution is special, different from that specified for the adoption of other laws. Thus, the constitutional texts of reference expressly provide the initiators for the revise of the Constitution[464], the procedure[465] and the limits on matters of revision[466]. Therefore, any amendment to the constitutional norms regarding the Constitutional Court must undergo this procedure, in which the Constitutional Court has an important role, exercising, ex officio, the constitutional review of the initiatives for the revision [Article 146 a) of the Constitution] and of the law amending the Constitution, adopted by Parliament [Article 23 of Law no. 47/1992].

In the previous chapters we approached the limits on matters of revision, as well as the considerations that substantiated the solution of unconstitutionality of the provisions which proposed the elimination of certain powers of the Constitutional Court.

As concerns the provisions on the organization and operations of the Constitutional Court which are not contained in the constitutional texts of reference, but only in Law no. 47/1992, they may be amended and supplemented by an organic law adopted by Parliament. No normative act requires the Parliament to consult the Constitutional Court in this situation. However, the Constitutional Court may be notified on the exception of unconstitutionality of such law adopted, either before promulgation [Article 146 a) first sentence of the Constitution], either after the entry into force [Article 146 d) of the Constitution], and the recitals indicated on such occasion guide and limit the legislature in its regulatory approach.

---

464 The President of Romania, at the proposal of the Government, by at least one quarter of all Deputies or Senators, as well as by at least 500,000 citizens having the right to vote; the citizens who initiate a revision of the Constitution must belong to at least half the number of the counties in the country, and in each of these counties or in the Municipality of Bucharest, at least 20,000 signatures must be recorded in support of such initiative (Article 150 of the Constitution).

465 The bill or proposal for revision must have been adopted by the Chamber of Deputies and by the Senate, by a majority of at least two-thirds of the members of each Chamber, and if agreement cannot be reached following the mediation procedure, the Chamber of Deputies and the Senate shall, in a joint session, decide by the vote of at least three-quarters of the number of Deputies and Senators; revision shall be final after approval by a referendum held within 30 days from enactment of the bill or proposal concerning such revision.

466 None of the provisions in this Constitution concerning the national, independent, unitary and indivisible character of the Romanian State, the Republican form of government, or territorial integrity, independence of judiciary, political pluralism, or official language shall be object of revision. Likewise, no revision shall be possible if it leads to the suppression of any of the citizens' fundamental rights and freedoms, or their safeguards. The Constitution may not be revised during a state of siege or a state of emergency, or at wartime.

As we have already mentioned, the regulation of the powers of the Constitutional Court is flexible, existing the possibility that, according to the needs, the Court is vested with new powers under its law on organization and operation, which allows the ordinary legislature to be able to intervene in the new situations arising in the activity of the institutions, without the need of amending the Constitution[467]. This possibility was introduced following the revision of the Constitution in 2003[468], when the article which expressly and restrictively established the powers of the Constitutional Court was amended accordingly [Article 146 lit. l)][469]. In other words, if the powers of the Court may be limited only by the revision of the Constitution, their supplementation is allowed only by the organic law of the Court[470].

Law no. 47/1992 regulates two such powers of the Constitutional Court, namely its powers to exercise, ex officio, the constitutional review of the law on the revision of the Constitution, adopted by Parliament [Article 23 of the Law], and its power to exercise the constitutional review of resolutions by the Plenary of the Chamber of Deputies, resolutions by the Plenary of the Senate and resolutions by the Plenary of the joint Chambers of Parliament, when a case is submitted to the Court by one of the Presidents of the two Chambers, by a parliamentary group or by a number of at least fifty Deputies or at least twenty-five Senators [Article 27 of Law no. 47/1992, as amended by Law no. 177/2010[471]].

Law no. 47/1992 on the Organisation and Operation of the Constitutional Court has been amended and supplemented three times (by Law no. 138/1997[472], Law no. 232/2004[473] and Law no. 177/2010[474]). The most significant amendments were determined by the revision of the Constitution, which resulted in a reconsideration of the powers of the Constitutional Court, as well as the effects of the acts delivered in exercising its powers, in order to strengthen its role as guarantor for the supremacy of the Basic Law, an issues which has been analyzed in the first part of this paper.

---

467 I. Muraru, in I. Muraru, E.S. Tănăsescu (coordinators), *op. cit.*, p. 1418.

468 Law on the revision of the Constitution of Romania no. 429/2003, published in the Official Gazette of Romania no. 758 of 29 October 2003.

469 The Constitutional Court "*also fulfils other prerogatives as provided by the Court's organic law*".

470 Pursuant to Article 76 para. (1) of the Constitution, organic laws shall be passed by a majority vote of the members of each Chamber.

471 Published in the Official Gazette of Romania no. 672 of 4 October 2010.

472 Law no. 47/1992 on the Organisation and Operation of the Constitutional Court, as amended and supplemented by Law no. 138/1997, republished in the Official Gazette of Romania no. 187 of 7 August 1997, and following the amendment and supplementation brought by Law no. 232/2004, was republished in the Official Gazette of Romania no. 643 of 16 July 2004. Currently, Law no. 47/1992 has a republished version in the Official Gazette of Romania no. 807 of 3 December 2010.

473 Published in the Official Gazette of Romania 502 of 3 June 2004.

474 Published in the Official Gazette of Romania 672 of 4 October 2010.

Financial autonomy of the Constitutional Court. A separate issue in the context of analyzing the dialogue between the Constitutional Court and the legislative power is its financial autonomy, its establishment and management of the expenditure budget.

According to Article 74 of Law no. 47/1992, the Constitutional Court shall have its own budget, which shall be an integral part of the State Budget and approved by the legislative power. The draft of the budget, as well as its amendment shall be approved by the Plenum of the Constitutional Court[475] and it shall be forwarded to the Government in order to be distinctively included in the draft of the State Budget subject to law-making, which can be adopted or not as such by Parliament. Within the approved budget, the Constitutional Court independently manages its budget funds. The Secretary General of the Court is an authorizing officer[476], and its activity is supervised by the President of the Constitutional Court[477]. As any public institution, the Constitutional Court is subject to the verification exercised by the Court of Accounts[478], which ensure the control over the formation, management and use of the financial resources belonging to the state and to the public sector.

We approached this issue in the context of the dialogue between the Constitutional Court and Parliament, as the financial autonomy is a fundamental dimension of the independence of the Constitutional Court, observing implicitly the Parliament's role in maintaining and strengthening this autonomy. Therefore, Parliament regulates the organization and operation of the Constitutional Court and ensures the prerequisites for exercising its powers in full independence, in accordance with the principled of the rule of law.

2.2.2 Competences in the procedure to appoint constitutional judges

The structure of the Constitutional Court of Romania is regulated by Article 142 of the Constitution and by Article 5 of Law no. 47/1992. In accordance with the aforementioned provisions, the Constitutional Court of Romania shall consist of nine Judges appointed for a term of office of nine years that cannot be prolonged or renewed. Three Judges shall be appointed by the Chamber of Deputies, three

---

475 Article 4 b) of the Regulations on the Organisation and Functioning of the Constitutional Court, approved by Ruling no. 6/2012 of the Plenum of the Constitutional Court, published in the Official Gazette of Romania no. 198 of 27 March 2012.

476 According to Article 24 l) of the Regulations on the Organisation and Functioning of the Constitutional Court, approved by Ruling no. 6/2012, the Secretary General of the Court "shall commit and use budgetary appropriations within their approved limits and destination for expenditures paid with funds allocated from State Budget and State Social Insurance Budget, subject to the law".

477 Article 9 para. (2) of Law no. 47/1992 on the Organisation and Operation of the Constitutional Court.

478 Law no. 94/1992 on the Organisation and Operation of the Court of Accounts, republished in the Official Gazette of Romania no. 282 of 29 April 2009.

by the Senate[479] and three by the President of Romania [Article 142 para. (3) of the Constitution]. Such appointment of judges of the Constitutional Court of Romania was appreciated to be susceptible to ensure a more representative and democratic structure, as it expresses the options of the highest public authorities of the State with electoral legitimacy[480]. However, the appointment of constitutional judges determined also the expression of certain challenges, indicating that the appointment of judges is at the sole discretion of certain political bodies, their activity being conducted under politics and there is a risk of subordination to certain influences which do not fall within the purpose of the Court[481]. It has been also expressed the view[482] according to which, the appointment of constitutional judges should be also attended by the judiciary. This concerns the powers of the Constitutional Court of Romania, to also settle legal disputes of a constitutional nature that may arise between the three powers of the State – legislative, executive and judicial –, as well as the elements of comparative law.

Conducting an examination of comparative law in this respect, it appears that the legislation of reference – Constitutions or laws of organization and functioning of the Courts / Constitutional Tribunals / Supreme Court – establishes that their judges are appointed / elected the representatives of the highest authorities of the State, usually by political bodies.

Constitutional judges are exclusively appointed by Parliament, for example: *Croatia* – The Constitutional Court of the Republic of Croatia shall consist of thirteen judges. All judges shall be elected by Parliament of Croatia (*Hrvatski Sabor*) for a term of office of eight years that can be renewed.

Germany – The Constitutional Court shall consist of two chambers, whereas each chamber shall consist of eight judges. Half of the judges of a chamber are elected by the Bundestag, whereas the other half – by the Bundesrat, i.e. by the directly elected parliamentary assembly which represents the people and by the Länder representatives, based on the rules of proportional representation[483]. The judges appointed by *Bundesrat* shall be directly elected by it, whereas the judges appointed by *Bundestag* shall be indirectly elected by an election committee which shall consist of twelve members who are in turn elected under proportional representation rules. The election

---

479 According to Article 61 para. (2) of the Constitution of Romania, Parliament shall consist of the Chamber of Deputies and the Senate.

480 By Decision no. 1/1995, published in the Official Gazette of Romania no. 16 of 26 January 1995, the Constitutional Court noted that the democratic legitimacy of the constitutional review "*stems from the election or appointment of the constitutional judges exclusively by the constitutional bodies elected directly by the people*".

481 T. Drăganu, *Introduction into the theory and the practice of the rule of law*, p. 126 et seq., in I. Muraru, E. S. Tănăsescu (coordinators), *cited paper*, p. 1389.

482 T. Toader, *Controversies on the appointment of constitutional judges*, in Judicial Courier no. 4/2011, pp. 183–184.

483 Article 94.1 second sentence of the Constitution of Germany.

of the judges requires a two-thirds majority. The term of office of a judge shall be of twelve years, without exceeding the retirement age – sixty-eight years old.

Switzerland – The judges of the Federal Court shall be elected by the Federal Parliament. The federal judges shall be elected for a six-year term of office [Article 145 of the Swiss Constitution and Article 9.1 of the Federal Court Act] and they cannot be dismissed during this period. They can be re-elected for a new six-year term of office, but not later than the 68th birthday (Article 9 of the Federal Court Act). However, it happened that some federal judges were not re-elected for another term of office on the grounds of old age (over the age of seventy and sixty-eight), even when the age limit had not been established under law.

Estonia – The judges of the Supreme Court[484] shall be appointed to office by Parliament (*Riigikogu*), upon the recommendation of the President of the Supreme Court[485]. The president of the Supreme Court shall be appointed by Parliament, upon the recommendation of the President of the Republic[486], whose candidature shall be first approved by the Supreme Court, in United Sections, and by the Council for Administration of Courts[487]. The president of the Supreme Court presides over the Constitutional Review Section which shall consist of nine members, whereas the other members shall be appointed by the Supreme Court in United Sections[488].

Latvia – Parliament (*Saeima*) validates the judges of the Constitutional Court, based on the recommendations formulated by: at least ten members of the Parliament (three of the judges), the Office of Ministers (two judges), the Supreme Court, reunited in Plenum (two judges).

Lithuania – The Constitutional Court shall consist of nine judges, each of them being appointed for a sole nine-year term of office. In its case-law, the Constitutional Court noted that, according to the Constitution, only the subjects indicated expressis verbis by the Constitution shall have the competence to the judges of the Constitutional Court: 1) state authorities, which propose to Parliament (Seimas) the candidatures for the position of judge of the Constitutional Court; 2) *Seimas*, which decides on the appointment as a judge of the Constitutional Court (Decision of the Constitutional Court of 2 June 2005). According to the Constitution, the Constitutional Court consists of members appointed at the initiative of the representatives of all three powers of the State. The proposals of candidatures for the office of judge of the Constitutional Court are made by the President of the Republic (representing the executive power), the President of the Seimas (representing the legislative power) and the President of the Supreme Court (representing the judiciary). The judges of the Constitutional Court are appointed by the Seimas, by resolution, and

---

484 Within which Section of Constitutional Review operates, consisting of nine judges of the Supreme Court (from the Civil Section, Administrative Contentious Section and Criminal Section), a body corresponding to a Constitutional Court.

485 *www.riigiteataja.ee, www.just.ee/23295.*

486 Article 65 para. (7) of the Constitution of Estonia.

487 Article 55 para. (4) of Law on judicial organization of Estonia.

488 Article 29 of Law on judicial organization of Estonia.

the president of the Constitutional Court is appointed from among the judges of the Seimas, upon the proposal of the President.

Macedonia – Article 68 of the Constitution of Macedonia, regulating the competences of the Assembly of the Republic of Macedonia, also establishes, among the other specific powers, that the judges of the Constitutional Court of Macedonia shall be appointed by the Assembly. Furthermore, Article 109 of Chapter IV, particularly assigned to the Constitutional Court of the Republic of Macedonia, rules that it shall consist of nine judges.

Poland – The fifteen judges of the Constitutional Tribunal[489] shall be appointed by the First Chamber of Parliament – Sejm, by an absolute majority of votes, in the presence of at least half of the total number of deputies, following the advisory opinion given by the Commission on Human Rights and Justice on the candidates. The candidates for the office of judge of the Tribunal should be proposed by a number of at least 50 deputies or the Presidium of the Sejm [Article 5 para. (4) of the Constitutional Tribunal Act]. After the Commission on Human Rights and Justice gives its advisory opinion on the candidates, the judges shall be elected by the Sejm by an absolute majority of votes in the presence of at least half of the total number of deputies.

Portugal – the Constitutional Tribunal shall consist of thirteen members[490]. Parliament (The Assembly of the Republic) has the right to appoint ten judges, who shall be elected by a majority of two thirds of present deputies, provided that this percentage is higher than the absolute majority of the deputies who are actually in the exercise of their office. As regards the other three judges, they are co-opted by their colleagues (cooptation procedure).

Slovenia – The Constitutional Court consists of nine judges, elected by the National Assembly of the Republic of Slovenia, upon the proposal of the President of the Republic, by a majority vote. Within 30 days of the notification by the President of the Constitutional Court regarding the vacancy for the office of judge of the Constitutional Court, the President of the Republic shall publish an announcement in the Official Gazette of the Republic of Slovenia, regarding the possibility of submitting candidatures for the office of judge of the Constitutional Court. The President of the Republic is not obliged to propose candidates from among them, but he can make other proposals or he can submit candidatures in addition to the number of vacancies[491].

Hungary – The Constitutional Court consists of fifteen judges elected by Parliament by a qualified majority of two thirds, for a twelve-year term of office[492].

---

489 Article 194 para. (1) of the Constitution of the Republic of Poland; Article 5 para. (2) and (4) of Law on Constitutional Tribunal of Poland.

490 Article 222-1 of the Constitution of Portugal.

491 Article 163 para. (1) of the Constitution of the Republic of Slovenia, Law on Constitutional Courts – Articles 11–14.

492 *http://www.mkab.hu/constitutional-court/about-the-constitutional-court/history.*

At the appointment of the judges of the Constitutional Court, both Parliament and the President participate in this procedure, for example:

France – The nine members of the Constitutional Council are appointed for a nine-year term of office, whereas three of the members of the Council shall be replaced every three years: each member shall be appointed by the President of the Republic, the president of the National Assembly and the president of the Senate[493].

Romania[494] – The Constitutional Court shall consist of nine judges, three judges are appointed by the Chamber of Deputies, three by the Senate, and three by the President of Romania[495]. The proposals of candidature may be handed in to the Legal Committee of each Chamber by the Parliamentary Groups, by Deputies and by Senators. The candidates shall be heard by the Legal Committee and by the plenary of the Chamber, and the report of the Legal Committee shall be motivated with reference to all candidates. By the vote of the majority of its members, on the proposal of its Standing Bureau and on the recommendation of the Legal Committee, each Chamber of Parliament shall appoint, in the capacity of Judge, that person who has got the majority of votes[496].

The constitutional judges are appointed by the President of the State[497]/**King**[498], upon the proposal or recommendation of the other constitutional bodies, for example:

Albania – The Constitutional Court shall consist of nine members appointed for a nine-year term of office, without the right of being re-elected. The constitutional judges shall be appointed by the President of the Republic, upon the approval of the Assembly. The Constitutional Court shall be renewed by one third of the Judges' number every three years, according to the procedure set forth by law.

Austria– The Constitutional Court consists of a President, Vice President, 12 other members, as well as six alternate members,[499] appointed by the Federal President, who shall, however, take into account[500] the recommendations made by the other constitutional bodies, namely: the proposals for the appointment of the President, Vice President, six of its members and three alternate members are forwarded to the Federal Government; other three members and two alternate members are

---

493 Article 56 of the Constitution of France.

494 See, further, in the National Report of the Constitutional Court of Romania, Part I – *Constitutional Court's relationships to Parliament and Government,* authors: Professor PhD T. Toader, dr. M. Safta, on *www.ccr.ro.*

495 Article 142 para. (3) of the Constitution of Romania.

496 Law no. 47/1992 on the Organisation and Operation of the Constitutional Court of Romania.

497 States governed as a republic.

498 States governed as a monarchy.

499 Article 147 of the Federal Constitution (*Bundes-Verfassungsgesetz,* hereinafter B-VG).

500 Article 67 B-VG.

appointed upon the recommendation of the National Council (the Chamber of Parliament directly elected, in proportional representation); the other three members and one alternate member shall be appointed upon the proposal of the Federal Council (the Chamber of Parliament appointed indirectly and which represents the Austrian Länder).

Belgium – The Constitutional Court consists of twelve judges, appointed for life by the King, from a list of two candidates alternatively proposed by the Chamber of Representative and Senate, by a majority of at least two thirds of the present members. Usually, the King shall appoint the first person on the list of that Chamber.

Czech – The Constitutional Court consists of 15 judges; but, as established by the Constitutional Court itself in order to be able to exercise its full competence, a minimum of 12 judges is required to take the oath (so that the Court should be made up) and only in this composition (quorum) the Court will be able to fulfil all the powers conferred by the Constitution. The judges of the Constitutional Court shall be appointed by the President of the Republic, with the consent of the Senate, pursuant to Article 62 e) of the Constitution of the Czech Republic; the countersignature by the Prime Minister is not required.

Cyprus – The Members of the Supreme Court (which exercise powers of constitutional review in this state) shall be appointed by the President of the Republic, seeking the advisory opinion of the Court, which they usually follow.

Denmark – Judges are appointed by the Queen via the Ministry of Justice, but the Minister acts upon recommendation from the Council for the Appointment of Judges (dommerudnævelsesrådet). The Council – composed of three judges, a lawyer and two members representing the civil society – has competence for all the appointments in the judicial system, except for the President of the Supreme Court, who shall be elected by and from the judges of the Supreme Court. After analyzing the appointment requests, the Council shall submit a motivated recommendation to the Minister of Justice.

Ireland – After having selected a candidate for nomination, the Government recommends the nominee to the President, and the President formally appoints the candidate[501].

Luxembourg – The President, Vice President and seven councillors shall be appointed by the Grand Duke, among which five councillors shall be appointed upon the joint advisory opinion of the Superior Court of Justice and the Administrative Tribunal. The President of the High Court of Justice, the President of the Administrative Tribunal and his two councillors at the Court of Cassation shall be members of the Constitutional Court.

Malta – The President of Malta appoints all members of the Judiciary on the advice of the Prime Minister.[502]

---

501 Ireland does not have a system of career judges; for details, see on *www.ccr.ro.*

502 Article 96 of the Constitution of Malta.

Slovakia – The judges of the Constitutional Court shall be appointed by the President of the Republic of Slovakia, upon the proposal of the National Council[503]. The National Council of the Republic of Slovakia proposes a double number of candidates for the judges who are to be appointed by the President.

Spain – The twelve magistrates of the Constitutional Tribunal of Spain shall be appointed by the King, upon the proposal made by four constitutional bodies, namely: Parliament shall appoint eight judges, out of which four shall be appointed by the Congress of Deputies and four by the Senate; The Government shall appoint two judges and the other two shall be appointed by the General Council of the Judicial Power[504].

Representatives of the three powers of the State, namely Parliament, the President and the courts of law shall participate in the appointment of the constitutional judges.

Italy– The Constitutional Court consists of fifteen judges, out of whom five shall be elected by Parliament, five by the highest courts, and five by the President of the Republic [505]. Those appointed from the judiciary shall be appointed by the Court of Cassation (which is in charge with the appointment of three out of five), by the Council of State and by the Court of Accounts (which may appoint one judge) and, usually, they themselves belong to the judiciary.

Serbia– The 2006 Constitution of the Republic of Serbia introduces a mixed system of determining the composition of the Constitutional Court, which involves the election, respectively the appointment of the judges of the Constitutional Court by all three powers: the National Assembly shall elect five judges from ten candidates nominated by the President of the Republic; the President shall nominate other five constitutional judges of the ten candidates nominated by the National Assembly, and the Supreme Court of Cassation shall appoint five judges of the ten candidates proposed in the joint session of the High Judicial Council and the State Prosecutorial Council. In accordance with Article 172 para. (4) of the Constitution of Serbia, one candidate among those appointed from each list of proposals must come from the territory of the autonomous provinces. The term of office shall be of 9 years.

The short presentation regarding the rules applicable to the appointment of the judges of the Constitutional Courts in various states reveals the concern of the national legislatures to identify mechanisms in order to ensure either the involvement of several constitutional bodies in the appointment procedure of these judges (in this respect various procedures of advisory opinion, proposal, appointment are regulated etc., which often involve reaching an agreement between the representatives of the three powers of the State), or the expression of a broad political majority upon the approval of candidates for the office of judge of the Constitutional Court.

We may conclude that:

---

503 Article 134 para. (2) of the Constitution of the Republic of Slovakia.

504 Article 159 of the Constitution of Spain.

505 Article 135 of the Constitution of Italy.

- There are two main systems establishing the composition of constitutional courts: the direct appointment of judges, and respectively, their election; There is also a hybrid system that combines both and moreover, it is the most common;
- two or even three authorities of the powers of the State shall participate in the appointment/election of the constitutional judges, in the sense that, even if the appointments are made by a single authority, the proposals are formulated by several such authorities;
- one may find the orientation towards the regulations of certain appointment procedures at an infraconstitutional level in order to ensure its transparency, involving certain bodies for the analysis/approval of the proposals; in some cases, such procedures are more complex.

In Romania, both the Constitution and the Law on the Organisation and Operation of the Constitutional Court regulate important principles and guarantees regarding the independence and neutrality of the judges of the Constitutional Court, susceptible to allow them to objectively exercise the powers of constitutional jurisdiction, the Court itself is, according to Law no. 47/1992, "*independent of any other public authority*" and it only obeys the Constitution and the legal provisions of its law on organization and operation[506]. In this regard, we should mention the provisions of the Court's organic law, according to which: the competence of the Constitutional Court cannot be contested by any public authority [Article 3 para. (3)]; the Constitutional Court shall be the only authority entitled to decide upon its competence [Article 3 para. (2)]; the Judges of the Constitutional Court cannot be held legally responsible for their opinions and for the votes cast in rendering the decisions [Article 61 para. (2)]; among other duties, the Judges of the Constitutional Court shall be under the obligation "*to perform their function unbiasedly and in abidance by the Constitution*" [Article 64 para. (1) a)]; the Judges shall impart to the President of the Constitutional Court "*any activity which might entail incompatibility with the mandate exercised*" [Article 64 para. (1) d)]; the Judges shall abstain from any activity or manifestation contrary to the independence or dignity of their office [Article 64 para. (1) f)]; the Plenum of the Constitutional Court shall be exclusively competent to establish the Judges' infringements of discipline, the sanctions, and the mode of their application (Article 65); the Constitutional Court shall have its own budget.

---

506 It has been noted in this regard that the independence of the judge results from the inherent constitutional justice – to be subject only to the Constitution and to its organic law –, the Basic Law is the only and fundamental landmark in the exercise of his/her duties. Any form of dependence on any public authority or normative act issued by such authority, other than the Basic Law, would not only be incompatible with the purpose of the Constitutional Court – to ensure the supremacy of the Constitution – but it would simply make it impossible for the constitutional judge to fulfil his/her duties (I. Deleanu, *Institutions and constitutional procedures – in the Romanian and comparative law*, C.H. Beck Publishing House, Bucharest, 2006, p. 818).

As concerns the procedure regarding the appointment of the judges by the Chamber of Deputies and by the Senate, Law no. 47/1992 stipulates that the proposals of candidature may be handed in to the Legal Committee of each Chamber by the Parliamentary Groups, by Deputies and by Senators. Each candidate shall hand in a *curriculum vitae* and documents proving that he or she meets the requirements stipulated by the Constitution[507]. The candidates shall be heard by the Legal Committee and by the plenary of the Chamber, and the report of the Legal Committee shall be motivated with reference to all candidates. By the vote of the majority of its members, on the proposal of its Standing Bureau and on the recommendation of the Legal Committee, each Chamber of Parliament shall appoint, in the capacity of Judge, that person who has got the majority of votes.

According to Article 7 of Law no. 47/1992, the President of the Constitutional Court shall be elected by secret ballot for a period of three years, by majority of the Judges' votes, within five days from the renewal of the Court. For the election of the President, each group of Judges appointed by the Chamber of Deputies, the Senate, and, respectively, by the President of Romania may propose a single candidature. If at the first ballot no candidate gets a majority of votes, a second ballot shall be taken between the first two candidates qualified or selected by drawing lots, if all candidates have received the same number of votes. Proceedings for the election of the President shall be conducted by the Judge who is the eldest of age. The President's term of office may be renewed.

The term of office of a constitutional judge shall begin at the moment of taking the oath before the President of Romania, and shall cease: expiration of the term of appointment, or in case of resignation, disfranchisement, exclusion de jure, or of demise; in situations of incompatibility, or of impossibility of exercising the office of Judge for a period which is longer than six months; in case of infringement of the provisions of Article 16, para. (3)[508] or of Article 40, para. (3)[509] of the Constitution or of severe infringement of the obligations provided under Article 64 of Law no. 47/1992[510]. According to Article 67 para. (2) of Law no. 47/1992, the

507 Judges of the Constitutional Court must have graduated law, and enjoy high professional eminence and at least 18 years' experience in the legal field or academic professorial activity (Article 143 of the Constitution).

508 According to Article 16 para. (3) of the Constitution: "*Public or dignitary offices, whether civil or military, may be held in accordance with the law by persons who are Romanian citizens and have their domicile within the national territory. The Romanian State guarantees equal opportunities for men and women in order to accede to such functions and dignitary offices*".

509 According to Article 40 para. (3) of the Constitution: "*Judges of the Constitutional Court, the advocates of the people, magistrates, active members of the Armed Forces, policemen and other categories of civil servants as determined by an organic law, are forbidden to join political parties* ".

510 According to Article 64 of Law no. 47/1992: "*The Judges of the Constitutional Court shall be under an obligation:*

establishment of the cessation of the mandate shall be made by the President of the Constitutional Court, upon expiration of the term of appointment, or in case of resignation, disfranchisement, exclusion de jure, or of demise, and in the other cases the cessation of the mandate shall be decided in plenum by the majority of votes of the Court's Judges.

There is no possibility that the judges of the Constitutional Court be dismissed by the authorities that have appointed them, which constitutes a guarantee of their independence in the exercise of their term of office. Furthermore, Article 145 of the Constitution expressly provides that the Judges of the Constitutional Court shall be independent in the exercise of their office and irremovable during their term of office. In the exercise of their office, the Judges shall be suspended in case of indictment for a criminal offence. The suspension shall be in force until conviction or, as appropriate, until a not guilty verdict [Article 66 para. (3) of Law no. 47/1992].

The mandate of the Judges of the Constitutional Court can neither be prolonged nor renewed, which also represents a guarantee of the Judge's independence in relation to the public authority that appointed him/her. However, according to Article 68 para. (2) of Law no. 47/1992, in case the mandate has ceased before the expiration of the duration for which the Judge was appointed, and the remaining period exceeds six months, the competent public authority may appoint a new Judge who shall continue the mandate of the Judge replaced. If the period for which the new Judge has been appointed is shorter than three years, the respective Judge can be appointed for a full mandate of nine years at renewal of the Constitutional Court [Article 68 para. (3) of Law].

In order to ensure permanent operation of the Constitutional Court, constitutional rules [Article 142 para. (5)] provide a periodic renewal system of one third of the Court's Judges: "*The Constitutional Court shall, every 3 years, be renewed with one third of its Judges, according to the Court's organic law*". In this way, in case of delays in the appointment of the three judges who shall replace, every three years, those whose nine-year terms of office have expired, it is avoided the creation of gaps

---

a) to perform their function unbiasedly and in abidance by the Constitution;
b) to keep the secret of the deliberations and of the votes, and not to take a public stand, or to give legal opinion in matters within the competence of the Constitutional Court;
c) to express their affirmative or negative vote in adopting the acts of the Constitutional Court, abstention from voting not being permitted;
d) to impart to the President of the Constitutional Court any activity which might entail incompatibility with the mandate exercised;
e) to preclude the use of the office performed for purposes of trade publicity or propaganda of any kind whatsoever;
f) to abstain from any activity or manifestation contrary to the independence or dignity of their office".

in the functioning of the constitutional justice, as six judges shall be permanent in office, a quorum prerequisite for the activity of the Constitutional Court[511].

2.2.3 Possibility to refer to the Constitutional Court

One way by which Parliament enters into *direct dialogue* with the constitutional court is the possibility of the Presidents of both Chambers, respectively of Deputies and Senators, to refer to the Court.

Thus, the presidents of the two Chambers of Parliament may refer to the Constitutional Court as follows:

a) to adjudicate on the constitutionality of laws before promulgation [Article 146 a) sentence I of the Constitution];
b) to adjudicate on the constitutionality of treaties or other international agreements [Article 146 b) of the Constitution];
c) to adjudicate on the constitutionality of the Standing Orders of Parliament [Article 146 c) of the Constitution];
d) to decide upon legal disputes of a constitutional nature between public authorities [Article 146 e) of the Constitution];
e) to ascertain any circumstance as may justify the interim in the exercise of office of President of Romania [Article 146 g) of the Constitution in conjunction with Article 44 of Law no. 47/1992 on the Organisation and Operation of the Constitutional Court][512];
f) to give advisory opinion on the proposal to suspend the President of Romania from office [Article 146 h) of the Constitution of the Constitution in conjunction with Article 42 of Law no. 47/1992 on the Organisation and Operation of the Constitutional Court];
g) to verify whether conditions are met for the citizens' exercise of their legislative initiative [Article 146 j) of the Constitution in conjunction with Article 7 of Law no. 189/1999 on the citizens' exercise of their legislative initiative];
h) to rule upon challenges as to the unconstitutionality of a political party [Article 146 k) of the Constitution in conjunction with Article 39 of Law no. 47/1992 on the Organisation and Operation of the Constitutional Court];
i) to adjudicate on the constitutionality of resolutions by the Plenary of the Chamber of Deputies, resolutions by the Plenary of the Senate and resolutions by the Plenary of the joint Chambers of Parliament [Article 146 l) of the Constitution in conjunction with Article 27 of Law no. 47/1992 on the Organisation and Operation of the Constitutional Court].

---

511 Pursuant to Article 51 para. (1) of Law no. 47/1992: "*The Constitutional Court shall be authorised to act in the presence of two-thirds of the Judges*".

512 For developments of these situations and the authorities competent to refer to the Constitutional Court, see I. Muraru, E.S. Tănăsescu (coordinators), *cited paper*, p. 1409.

As concerns the Deputies (at least 50) and the Senators (at least 25), they may refer to the Constitutional Court as follows:

a) to adjudicate on the constitutionality of laws before promulgation [Article 146 a) sentence I of the Constitution];
b) to adjudicate on the constitutionality of treaties or other international agreements [Article 146 b) of the Constitution];
c) to adjudicate on the constitutionality of the Standing Orders of Parliament [Article 146 c) of the Constitution];
d) to adjudicate on the constitutionality of resolutions by the Plenary of the Chamber of Deputies, resolutions by the Plenary of the Senate and resolutions by the Plenary of the joint Chambers of Parliament [Article 146 l) of the Constitution in conjunction with Article 27 of Law no. 47/1992 on the Organisation and Operation of the Constitutional Court].

2.2.4 Expressing viewpoints in the cases brought before the Constitutional Court

By formulating these viewpoints, Parliament "*associates*" with the constitutional review, giving the Constitutional Court the landmark regarding, in particular, "*ratio legis*" (in case of constitutional review of laws before promulgation, respectively of laws in force) and, respectively, regarding the way in which the constitutional norms governing its organization and operation are interpreted and enforce.

Given the importance and significance of these points of view, their formulation is advisable in all cases referred to the Constitutional Court. A genuine dialogue between the two institutions involves, from our point of view, greater involvement of Parliament in the sense of using procedural opportunities provided by the.

The situations in which Law no. 47/1992 regulates the obligation of the Constitutional Court in that regard are the following:

Constitutional review of laws before promulgation
Article 16 para. (2) and, respectively Article 17 para. (1) of Law no. 47/1992 on the Organisation and Operation of the Constitutional Court provide that "*If the referral was made by the President of Romania, by the Members of Parliament, by the High Court of Cassation and Justice, or by the Advocate of the People, the Constitutional Court shall communicate such to the Presidents of the two Chambers of Parliament and the Government within twenty-four hours from the registration, also specifying the date when the debates are to take place*"; "*The Presidents of the two Chambers of Parliament (...) may present their point of view in writing, by the date of the debates*".

Constitutional review of treaties or other international agreements
According to Article 25 of Law no. 47/1992, "*The President of Romania, the Presidents of the two Chambers of Parliament and the Government may present their point of view in writing, by the date of the debates in the plenum of the Constitutional Court*".

Constitutional review of the Standing Orders of Parliament, respectively resolutions by the Plenary of the Senate and resolutions by the Plenary of the joint Chambers of Parliament
According to Article 27 para. (3) of Law no. 47/1992: "*The Presidents of the two Chambers of Parliament may notify the viewpoints of the Standing Bureau, by the date of the debates*".

Settlement of the exceptions of unconstitutionality referring to laws and ordinances
According to Article 30 of Law no. 47/1992: "*(1) On receiving the interlocutory order provided under Article 29, paragraph (4), the President of the Constitutional Court shall designate the Judge-Rapporteur and also notify the Presidents of the two Chambers of Parliament of the interlocutory order by which the Constitutional Court was apprised (...), indicating the date by which they can submit their viewpoint*".

Settlement of legal disputes of a constitutional nature
According to Article 35 para. (1) of Law no. 47/1992: "*On receiving the request, the President of the Constitutional Court shall communicate it to the parties in conflict, requesting them to express, in writing, their viewpoint on the subject-matter at dispute and the possible ways for resolution(...)*".

2.2.5 Communication of the decisions/rulings/advisory opinions delivered by the Constitutional Court

Considering, on the one hand, the possibility to refer to the Constitutional Court in order to exercise its duties and, on the other hand, taking account of the provisions of Article 147 of the Constitution on the effects of Constitutional Court's decisions, the law expressly provides the obligation of the Constitutional Court to communicate to Parliament its decisions/ rulings/ advisory opinions.

Thus, according to Article18 para. (2) and (3) of Law no. 47/1992: "*(...) The decision by which the unconstitutionality of the law*[513] *has been established shall also be notified to the Presidents of the two Chambers of Parliament and to the Prime Minister. (3) In cases of unconstitutionality which concern the laws, before their promulgation, the Parliament shall be bound to re-examine the respective provisions in order to bring them into accord with the decision of the Constitutional Court*". The notification of the decision to the Presidents of the two Chambers of Parliament aims at opening the procedure for the re-examination of the law in order to bring such into line with the provisions of Article 147 para. (2) of the Constitution, of Article 18 para. (3) of Law no. 47/1992, republished, as well as with the provisions contained in the Standing Orders of the two Chambers of Parliament.

Article 21 para. (2) of the same law, referring to the power of the Constitutional Court regarding the verification of the initiatives for the revision of the Constitution,

513 Before promulgation.

provides that "*The decision of the Constitutional Court shall be notified to the initiators of the bill or legislative proposal, or to their representative, as the case may be*", and according to Article 22, "*the bill or legislative proposal can be presented to the Parliament only together with the decision of the Constitutional Court, notified according to Article 21, para. (2)*".

Similarly, the decision delivered within the exercise of the constitutional review of international treaties shall be communicated to the Presidents of the two Chambers of Parliament [Article 26 para. (2) of Law no. 47/1992].

The decision delivered on matters of the Standing Orders of the two Chambers shall be brought to the notice of the Chamber whose standing orders were debated [Article 28 para. (2) of Law no. 47/1992].

The decision by which the unconstitutionality of a law or of an ordinance which is in force, or of provisions thereof, is established shall be notified to the two Chambers of Parliament [Article 31 para. (4) of Law no. 47/1992].

As concerns the legal disputes of a constitutional nature, the law provides a general rule, as follows: "*The decision which resolves the legal dispute of a constitutional nature shall be final and it shall be communicated to both the applicant, and to the parties in dispute, before its publication in the Official Gazette of Romania, Part I*" [Article 36 of Law no. 47/1992].

According to Article 43 para. (3) of Law no. 47/1992: "*The advisory opinion of the Constitutional Court shall be notified to the Presidents of the two Chambers of Parliament, and to the President of Romania*".

Before publication in the Official Gazette of Romania, Part I, the ruling of the Constitutional Court which establishes whether the procedure for the organization and carrying out of the referendum has been complied with, and confirms its results shall be presented to the Chamber of Deputies and the Senate, in their common session [Article 47 para. (3) of Law no 47/1992].

2.2.6 Conclusions

As one may note, Parliament is involved, in one way or another, in ensuring the exercise of all the powers of the Constitutional Court: the possibility of referral by the possibility of expressing viewpoints, by the obligation to communicate information or by the obligation of the Court to communicate to Parliament its decisions/rulings.

As concerns the duties for which the Constitution or the Law on the Organization and Operation of the Constitutional Court do not provide the possibility to refer to the Court by the subjects of parliamentary origin, the dialogue between Parliament and the constitutional court is achieved by the possibility to express their viewpoints regarding the files of the Court (we take into account, in this context, the duty to settle the exceptions of unconstitutionality raised before the courts of law or the court of commercial arbitration), the possibility of the Constitutional Court to request information from Parliament, as from any other authority (we consider the duty to see to the observance of the procedure for the organisation and holding of a referendum, and to confirm its returns), obligation to communicate to Parliament its decision (we consider the duty to see to the observance of the procedure for the organisation and holding of a referendum, and to confirm its returns), respectively the validation act regarding the elections for the elected President, compiled in three copies, out of which one shall remain at the Constitutional Court, one shall be communicated to Parliament for the oath set forth in Article 82 para. (2) of the Constitution of Romania, republished, and the third shall be given to the elected candidate (we consider the duty to see to the observance of the procedure for the election of the President of Romania and to confirm the ballot returns).

2.3 The Constitutional Court's relationship to Parliament. Constitutional limits of the legislative power

2.3.1 General aspects

Within the exercise of the powers regarding the constitutional review of laws, Standing Orders on the organisation and operation of Parliament and resolutions by Parliament, the Constitutional Court shall adjudicate upon the constitutional principles governing the parliamentary activity, respectively upon the constitutional framework regarding the organisation and operation of Parliament.

The constitutional review substantiate them by achieving, in certain situations, real "limits" of the legislative power, in the spirit and the letter of the Constitution.

2.3.2 Parliamentary autonomy – constitutional limits

Pursuant to Article 61 of the Constitution of Romania: "*(1) Parliament is the supreme representative body of the Romanian people and the sole legislative authority of the country. (2) Parliament consists of the Chamber of Deputies and the Senate*", and pursuant to Article 64 para. (1): "*Each Chamber is organized and functions as set forth in its own Standing Orders. The Chambers' financial resources are provided for in the budgets approved by them*". These constitutional texts enshrine the principle of parliamentary autonomy, embodied, as the Court held in one of its decisions[514], "*in a triple autonomy: statutory, institutional and financial*", stating, at the same time, that under the above-mentioned constitutional provisions," *each Chamber has the right to establish, in limits and in compliance with constitutional provisions, rules of organisation and operation, which, in their substance, constitute the regulations of each Chamber. From this perspective, no public authority may decide, on the matters referred, for the Parliament, and also neither of the Chambers of Parliament may decide, on the same issues, for the other Chamber. As a result, the organisation and operation of each Chamber of Parliament are established by own regulations,*

514 For example, Decision no. 1009 of 7 July 2009, published in the Official Gazette of Romania no. 542 of 4 August 2009.

adopted by own resolution of each Chamber by majority vote of the members of the respective Chamber".

Ruling on the statutory autonomy of Parliament, the Court also stated its limits, in the absence of which the actions of this authority could become arbitrary and, therefore, contrary to the rule of law. In an established case-law, the Court held that the Standing Orders of the two Chambers of Parliament, being enacted by resolutions which concern the Chamber's internal organization, can only determine rights and obligations in regard to MPs, as well as authorities, officials and civil servants, as the case may be, depending on their constitutional relationship with that Chamber[515]. Likewise, the Court also ruled that such autonomy cannot have the significance of autonomy in relation to law[516].

Thus[517], the statutory autonomy enjoyed by the two Chambers of Parliament, pursuant to the constitutional provisions under Article 64 para. (1) entitles them to decide about their own organization and procedures for conducting parliamentary proceedings. Parliamentary Regulations – Regulations of the Chamber of Deputies, Regulations of the Senate and Regulations of the Joint Meetings of the Chamber of Deputies and the Senate – in terms of their legal nature, are resolutions of Parliament. They are adopted by each Chamber or by the joint Chambers, not based on the legislative authority of Parliament, but as autonomous bodies, entrusted with their own power of organization and operation. Each Chamber adopts its own regulations, a normative act by itself, according to the competence conferred by the Constitution. Therefore, statutory autonomy represents the expression of the rule of law, of democratic principles and can operate only within the limits set by the Basic Law.

However, the Court underlined that "*Statutory autonomy cannot be exercised discretionary, abusively, in breach of the constitutional powers of the Parliament. Thus, between constitutional principle on the autonomy of Parliament to establish internal rules of organization and functioning [Article 64(1)] and the constitutional principle on the role of Parliament, as public authority of the State, exercising, according to the Constitution, constitutional democracy specific tasks, (law-making, granting the trust vote based on which the Government is appointed, the withdrawal of the trust granted to the Government by the adoption of a censure motion, the declaration of a status of war, the approval of the national defence strategy for the country etc.), (...)there is a report as between means/instrument and aim/interest. Thus, parliamentary regulations are a set of legal rules designed to organize and discipline the parliamentary work concerning, inter alia, the legislative procedure, the procedure for the appointment or the*

515 Decisions no. 45 and 46 of 17 May 1994, published in the Official Gazette of Romania no. 131 of 27 May 1994; Decision no. 317 of 13 April 2006, published in the Official Gazette of Romania no. 446 of 23 May 2006.

516 Decision no. 1018 of 19 July 2010, published in the Official Gazette of Romania no. 511 of 22 July 2010.

517 Decision no. 209 of 7 March 2012, published in the Official Gazette of Romania no. 188 of 22 March 2012.

investiture of the most important State institutions or public authorities (Government, part of the Judges of the Constitutional Court, part of the members of the Superior Council of Magistracy, members of the Court of Accounts, the Advocate of the People, the Directors of the Intelligence Services) as well as the rules of organization and functioning of each Chamber. Regulatory standards are legal instruments that allow parliamentary activities in order to meet the constitutional powers of the Parliament, a representative authority by which the Romanian people exercises its national sovereignty, in accordance with Article 2 para. (1) of the Constitution"[518].

The review exercised by the Court also complies with this autonomy, as it relates to the parliamentary Standing Orders, to the resolutions amending or supplementing the Standing Orders of Parliament, respectively to the resolutions of the Chambers of Parliament which are normative acts and contain provisions on the organization and functioning of Parliament as a whole or of each Chamber. However, in this regard, the Constitutional Court held that "*it has no jurisdiction to review the constitutionality of the interpretation or application of Parliament Standing Orders. By virtue of the principle of statutory autonomy enshrined in Article 64 paragraph (1) first sentence of the Constitution, the Chambers of Parliament have exclusive jurisdiction to interpret the normative content of its own regulations and decide on how to apply them, and the failure to comply with regulatory provisions can be ascertained and settled exclusively by means of parliamentary procedures and ways*" [Constitutional Court's Decisions no. 44/1993[519], no. 98/1995[520], no. 17/2000[521], no. 47/2000[522]]. Similarly, the Court, noting that in some cases, the challenges were aimed at the incomplete nature of some provision of the Standing Orders, or their incorrect wording, highlighting the need for supplementation or modification thereof, it found that such challenges were exceeding its jurisdiction[523].

2.3.3 Compliance with the principle of "political spectrum"[524]

The Court, upholding the unconstitutionality of certain provisions in the Standing Orders of the Senate and, respectively, of the Chamber of Deputies, has established the meaning of the phrase "political spectrum" which is, according to Article 64 paragraph (5) of the Constitution, the basis for setting-up the composition of the

518 *Ibidem.*
519 Published in the Official Gazette of Romania no. 190 of 10 August 1993.
520 Published in the Official Gazette of Romania no. 248 of 31 October 1995.
521 Published in the Official Gazette of Romania no. 40 of 31 January 2000.
522 Published in the Official Gazette of Romania no. 153 of 13 April 2000.
523 Decision no. 317/2006, published in the Official Gazette of Romania no. 446 of 23 May 2006.
524 Article 64 para. (5) of the Constitution: "The Standing Bureau and parliamentary Committees shall be made up so as to reflect the political spectrum of each Chamber".

Standing Bureau of each Chamber of Parliament[525]. This means its composition as resulted from the elections, based on the proportion each parliamentary group has in respect of all the members of that Chamber. The President of the Chamber of Deputies and the President of the Senate will be designated by virtue of the same political spectrum, whose source is the electoral body's will. The vote given for the election of the President of that Chamber is a political vote, and it cannot be cancelled unless the group which proposed him has required a political revocation, or in case such revocation is a sanction, when this group or another component of the Chamber has required that the President be replaced for having committed acts which entail legal liability. However, replacement is only possible with another person from the same parliamentary group, as they cannot be deprived of their right to the President's position, once it was acquired by virtue of the election results, and in respect of the principle of political spectrum.

The meaning of this wording, as established in the above-mentioned decisions, has been once more invoked in a recent decision[526] of the Constitutional Court, in which Article 64 paragraph (5) of the Constitution was examined in relationship to provisions of Article 64 paragraph (3), respectively Article 64 paragraph (2), second sentence, of the Constitution, concerning the organization of parliamentary groups and election of the other members of the Standing Bureau; these constitutional texts establish different rules, distinct from those imposed under Article 64 paragraph (2), first sentence, of the Constitution, relative to the election of the President of either of the two Chambers of Parliament. Thence, the Court held that movements affecting the structure of current parliamentary groups, as a result of a split-off that may have occurred from the parties represented by each group, or migration of MPs from one group to another, or departure from a group without affiliation to another, mutations which are possible insofar as the Constitution expressly affirms that any imperative mandate shall be null, all these cannot remain without consequences on the representation of parliamentary groups in the Standing Bureau. That is why, unlike the President of each Chamber, who is elected for the duration of that Chamber's term, the other members in the Standing Bureau are elected according to Article 64 paragraph (2), second sentence, of the Constitution, namely at the beginning of each session, in accord with the composition of parliamentary groups at that particular time. And that specific constitutional text, which is related to Article 69 paragraph (2) of the Constitution, ensures that the composition of the leading structures of each Chamber of Parliament will reflect the political restructuring taking place in Parliament, a phenomenon which, similar to political developments in society, cannot be stopped.

---

525 Decision no. 601 of 14 November 2005, published in the Official Gazette of Romania no. 1022 of 17 November 2005, respectively Decision no. 602 of 14 November 2005, published in the Official Gazette of Romania no. 1027 of 18 November 2005.

526 Decision no. 1490 of 17 November 2010, published in the Official Gazette of Romania no. 861 of 22 December 2010.

By the same decision[527], the Constitutional Court has established that the provisions of Article 12 of the Standing Orders of the Chamber of Deputies, as amended by Resolution No. 26/2010 of the Chamber of Deputies, which expressly provide for the possibility of creation of parliamentary groups made up of independent Deputies or Deputies who became independent, and also another rule subject to which Deputies that had become independent during a parliamentary term can set up just one single parliamentary group, while observing the minimum number of 10 Deputies required for its setting up, are constitutional.

Thus, the Court, while recalling its established case-law[528] regarding the unrestricted possibility of MPs to switch from one parliamentary group to another, to join a parliamentary group or form a group of independent parliamentarians, has always sanctioned in such instances those regulatory provisions placing limitations on this right, essentially considering such norms inconsistent with Article 69 paragraph (2) of the Constitution, which rejects any form of imperative mandate. Furthermore, recalling its Decision no. 47/2000[529], whereby it held that "the lack of legal regulations in respect of the possibilities and conditions for the organization into parliamentary groups of those Deputies who have resigned from other parliamentary groups does not amount to violation of any constitutional provision, but is a regulatory omission which cannot be substituted by the Constitutional Court's decisions", the Constitutional Court found that the provisions of Article 12 of the Standing Order of the Chamber of Deputies, as amended, giving expression to the provisions of Article 69 paragraph (2) of the Constitution, according to which "*any imperative mandate is null*", did nothing more than remove the regulatory omission in regard of which the Court had been appealed prior to rendering the latter decision.

2.3.4 The role of the parliamentary committees

By several decisions[530], the Court held that the provisions of Article 64 para. (4) and (5) of the Constitution underline the position and the role of the standing committees within the parliamentary activity. Thus, they are internal working bodies of the Chambers of Parliament whose activity is preparatory in order to provide the deliberative forum with all necessary information to adopt the decision. Thus, these committees are internal working bodies of the Chambers of Parliament whose

527 *Ibidem.*

528 Decision no. 44 of 8 July 1993, published in the Official Gazette of Romania no. 190 of 10 August 1993; Decision no. 46 of 17 May 1994, published in the Official Gazette of Romania no. 131 of 27 May 1994; Decision no. 196 of 28 April 2004, published in the Official Gazette of Romania no. 417 of 11 May 2004.

529 Published in the Official Gazette of Romania no. 153 of 13 April 2000.

530 Decision no. 48 of 17 May 1994, published in the Official Gazette of Romania no. 125 of 21 May 1994; Decision no. 460 of 13 November 2013, published in the Official Gazette of Romania no. 762 of 9 December 2013.

activity is preparatory to provide the deliberative forum with all the necessary elements in order to adopt a resolution. The committees shall consist of a limited number of deputies or senators, specialised in a particular field, having a composition and structure that comply with the political structure of each Chamber. The specialised debates taking place at committees' meetings shall result in reports or opinions which have the role of preparing and facilitating the work of the Chambers and the debates that will take place in the plenary thereof. The need for the establishment of these bodies was required in order to ensure the efficiency of a large deliberative body.

For this reason, the organization and functioning of parliamentary committees are thoroughly regulated under Article 64 para. (1) of the Constitution, through the Standing Order of each Chamber. The constitutional provisions merely express this subordinate role, preparatory for the activity of the committees, differentiated according to their typology which is thus provided by the provisions of Article 64 para. (4) of the Constitution: "*Each Chamber constitutes its standing Committees and may institute inquiry or other special committees. The Chambers may set up joint committees*".

Given the parliamentary committees' ancillary characterisation, the legal nature of the reports or opinions adopted by them is a preliminary act, adopted as a recommendation, to suggest a particular conduct, in terms of decision-making, to the plenary of each Chamber or to the Joint Chambers. Reports and opinions are binding only in terms of requesting them, and not also in terms of the solutions they propose, as the Senate and the Chamber of Deputies are the only deliberative bodies through which the Parliament performs its constitutional powers.

That being so, the Court also held that, "the movement of a constitutional decision centre (Parliament) to its committees is inconsistent with the purpose of the former, explicitly set forth in Articles 111 and 61 of the Constitution".

The circumstances of the role of the parliamentary committees were also established by the Court during the adjudication upon the most recent legislative proposal for the revision of the Constitution. Point 49 of the Sole Article of the proposal for the revision of the Constitution amends Article 64, by inserting a new paragraph, paragraph (4^1), to read as follows: "*(4^1) Any person of public law, private legal person and individual must appear, directly or through legal representative, before a parliamentary committee, following a written invitation from the latter, except for magistrates. The activity of the parliamentary committee cannot substitute for judicial bodies*". With regard to the duties of such committees, the Court held, as it follows from a combined reading of the constitutional texts that, before the committees, it is necessary to appear only those subjects of law which have a specific constitutional relationship with Parliament under Title III, Chapter IV of the Constitution, entitled Relations between Parliament and Government. Other subjects of law may be invited to take part in the debates of the committees. These committees do not have statutory or constitutional empowerment to establish the guilt or innocence of a person, but are the expression of parliamentary scrutiny. Their aim is to clarify the circumstances and causes of those particular events under investigation. Therefore, these committees investigate/verify the facts or circumstances, and not individuals. They have to establish the existence or inexistence of facts for which the committee was created, without establishing the financial, disciplinary, administrative or criminal liability of any person. These committees do not have the power to give a verdict, but to draw up a report on the facts under investigation, indicating the conclusions reached on the basis of papers and documents which they had consulted and the hearings carried out[531]. Having regard to the aforementioned reasons, the Court finds that establishing the obligation on persons of public law other than those covered by Article 111 of the Constitution, private legal persons and individuals to appear directly or through a legal representative, as appropriate, before parliamentary committees is contrary to the role and purpose of these committees and, implicitly, to the constitutional role of Parliament as legislative authority, in breach of the constitutional principle of separation and balance of powers enshrined in Article 1 (4) of the Constitution. Even though the amending proposal stipulates that "The activity of the parliamentary committee cannot substitute for judicial bodies", in fact, through the establishment of a constitutional obligation incumbent on the listed persons to appear before the parliamentary committee of parliamentary investigation, the legislative proposal for revision infringes personal liberty enshrined in Article 23 of the Constitution, which may be restricted only in the cases expressly and restrictively provided for in the Constitution. Furthermore, the proposed changes confer wide powers to this committee, which creates confusion as to the legal nature of its activity and may be described as a form of special jurisdiction, which, although it does not replace the judicial authority, carries out its activity in parallel with the latter. Consequently, the Court concluded, by a majority vote, that the amendment to constitutional provisions infringes the principle of separation and balance of powers and individual liberty, being contrary to the provisions of Article 152 (2) of the Constitution relating to the revision limits[532].

2.3.5 Resolutions of Parliament

The obligation to observe the Constitution, its supremacy and laws
Parliament is required, in all its activity, to comply with this principle laid down in Article 1 para. (5) of the Constitution, giving rise to a number of consequences which aim at the lawmaking activity.

As concerns this obligation, the Court ruled, for example, within the constitutional review of the resolutions of the Plenum of the Senate and of the two joint Chambers of Deputies, when it proceeded to the circumstantiation of its power regarding the constitutional review of these acts. The Constitutional Court has consistently held that "*only resolutions of Parliament adopted after the court was*

531 In this respect, see Decision no. 924 of 1 November 2012, published in the Official Gazette of Romania no. 787 of 22 November 2012.

532 Decision no. 80 of 16 February 2014, published in the Official Gazette of Romania no. 246 of 7 April 2014.

endowed with this new power, resolutions that affect the values, rules and constitutional principles or, as the case may be, the organisation and functioning of authorities and institutions of constitutional rank can be subject to constitutional review"[533]. The challenged Resolutions of the Parliament may have normative or individual nature, as "*the text of Article 27 of Law no. 47/1992 does not create any differentiation between the resolutions that be subject to review carried out by the Constitutional Court in terms of the area in which they were adopted or in terms of the normative or individual nature, which means that all these resolutions are likely to be subject to constitutional review* – ubi lex non distinguit nec nos distingere debemus. *Consequently, the referrals of unconstitutionality concerning such resolutions are de plano admissible*"[534]. The Constitutional Court specifically established that in order to be admissible the referral of unconstitutionality thus raised, the norm of reference should be of constitutional level, so the Court can analyze whether there is any contradiction between the resolutions mentioned in Article 27 of Law no. 47/1992, on the one hand, and the procedural and substantive requirements established by the provisions of the Constitution, on the other hand.

Therefore, the challenges must have a clear constitutional relevance, not a legal or statutory one. Consequently, all resolutions of the plenum of the Chamber of Deputies, of the plenum of the Senate and of the plenum of the two joint Chambers of Parliament may be subject to constitutional review, whether provisions of the Constitution are invoked in support of the challenge of unconstitutionality. These provisions shall be effectively invoked rather than formally[535]. The Court also noted, as concerns resolutions that by their subject are related to the organisation and operation of authorities and institutions of constitutional level, the Court recalls that the norm of reference, within constitutional review, can be both a provision of constitutional level and an infraconstitutional provision, taking into account Article 1(5) of the Constitution. Such orientation of the Court is given by the field of utmost importance in which such resolutions regulate – the authorities and institutions of constitutional level – so that constitutional protection offered to authorities or fundamental institutions of the State must be one accordingly. Consequently, the resolutions of the plenum of the Chamber of Deputies, of the resolutions of the Senate and of the resolutions of the plenum of the two joint Chambers of Parliament aiming at the organisation and operation of authorities and institutions of

---

533 Decision no. 53 of 25 January 2011, published in the Official Gazette of Romania no. 90 of 3 February 2011; Decision no. 54 of 25 January 2011, published in the Official Gazette of Romania no. 90 of 3 February 2011; Decision no. 307 of 28 March 2012, published in the Official Gazette of Romania no. 293 of 4 May 2012; Decision no. 783 of 26 September 2012, published in the Official Gazette of Romania no. 684 of 3 October 2012.

534 Decision no. 307 of 28 March 2012, published in the Official Gazette of Romania no. 293 of 4 May 2012.

535 *Ibidem*; Decision no. 783 of 26 September 2012, published in the Official Gazette of Romania no. 684 of 3 October 2012.

constitutional level may be subject to constitutional review, even if the normative act allegedly violated has infraconstitutional value.

The recitals of the Court on the admissibility of referrals containing challenges of unconstitutionality by reference to the provisions of Article 1 para. (5) of the Constitution, on the obligation to respect the laws (to the extent that they are not formal, but substantiated by reference to a law governing an objective condition), are emphasized in this regard. As the Court noted, the constitutional court has jurisdiction to rule, in the light of such challenges, upon the fact whether the resolutions of Parliament comply with the constitutional principle concerning the rule of law and the obligation to observe the laws: "*the acceptance of the contrary, with the consequence of the exclusion from the exercise of constitutional review of the Resolutions of Parliament of Romania given in breach of the express provisions of the law, would result in placing the supreme representative body of the Romanian people – Parliament, above the law, and in the acceptance of the idea that precisely the constitutional authority to adopt laws can violate them without being sanctioned in any way. Or, in a rule of law, no one is above the law*"[536].

Parliamentary resolutions cannot establish rules for the other subjects of law

In this regard[537], the Constitutional Court found that Article 170 para. (2) of the Standing Order of the Senate was contrary to the provisions of Article 64 para. (1)[538] of the Constitution, because it "establishes obligations for legal subjects other than those to which the organization and operation of this Chamber of Parliament refers". Therefore, through an established case-law, the Court held that the Standing Orders of the two Chambers of Parliament, being enacted by resolutions which concern the Chamber's internal organization, can only determine rights and obligations in regard to MPs, as well as authorities, officials and civil servants, as the case may be, depending on their constitutional relationship with that Chamber[539].

The role of the President of the Chamber in the event of a tie vote

The Constitutional Court[540] upheld the referral on the unconstitutionality of the provisions of Article 40 para. (1)[541] of the Standing Order of the joint sessions of the

---

536 Decision no. 251 of 30 April 2014, published in the Official Gazette of Romania no. 376 of 21 May 2014.

537 Decision no. 601 of 14 November 2005, published in the Official Gazette of Romania no. 1022 of 17 November 2005.

538 According to which: "Each Chamber is organized and functions as set forth in its own Standing Orders. The Chambers' financial resources are provided for in the budgets approved by them".

539 Decisions no. 45 and 46 of 17 May 1994, published in the Official Gazette of Romania no. 131 of 27 May 1994, and Decision no. 317 of 13 April 2006, published in the Official Gazette of Romania no. 446 of 23 May 2006.

540 Article 76 of the Constitution regarding the *Adoption of laws and resolutions.*

541 *In case of even votes, the vote of the President who chairs the joint meeting shall be decisive.*

Chamber of Deputies and the Senate[542], and found that they are unconstitutional, as such afforded onto the President of the Chamber a decisive role in the event of tie votes, which is contrary to constitutional provisions regarding the majority required for the adoption of acts, as such provisions do not contain any such stipulations.

2.3.6 The Status of Deputies and Senators [543]

Unconstitutionality of the incompatibilities set forth in the Standing Orders of the Parliament

The Constitution of Romania refers to the status of Deputies and Senators in Article 73 para. (3) c), according to which: "*By organic laws it shall be regulated (...) the status of Deputies and Senators (...)*", and in Article 65 para. (2) j) according to which: "Chambers can also meet in a joint session, based on the regulations passed by a majority vote of all Deputies and Senators, in order to*: (...) establish the legal status of Deputies and Senators (...)*". In order to enforce these constitutional texts, Law no. 96/2006 on the Statute of Deputies and Senators[544] has been adopted. By Decision no. 279/2006, the Court found that the provisions of Article 35 para. (3) of the Law on the Statute of Deputies and Senators, according to which: "Other main rights, related or derivative may be provided and regulated in a special organic law or in the regulations of the Chamber or in the regulations of joint meetings", are contrary to the provisions of Article 73 para. (3) c) of the Constitution, as the rights of MPs can be established only by an organic law, and not by parliamentary regulations[545].

---

542 Approved by Resolution of Parliament of Romania no. 4/1992, published in the Official Gazette of Romania no. 34 of 4 March 1992.

543 A. Zegrean, M. Safta, *The Statute of deputies and senators. Summaries of the case-law of the Constitutional Court*, in Judicial Courier no. 4/2013, on *http://www.ceeol.com.*

544 Republished in the Official Gazette of Romania no. 763 of 12 November 2008 and subsequently in the Official Gazette of Romania no. 459 of 25 July 2013.

545 By Decision no. 46 of 17 May 1994, published in the Official Gazette of Romania no. 131 of 27 May 1994, ruling upon the constitutionality of the Standing Order of the Senate, the Constitutional Court held the following: "*The Standing Order of the Senate, by its content and the adoption procedure, does not fall into the category of laws. This is because, unlike the law, the Standing Order can only regulate the internal organization and functioning of the Chamber, it shall be voted only by a Chamber and it is not subject to promulgation. It is true that Article 74 of the Constitution provides that the resolutions on the Standing Orders of the Chambers shall be adopted, as the organic laws, by a majority vote of the members of each Chamber, but this majority is not sufficient as to give the Standing Order a different legal nature than that of resolution. The absolute majority required by the Constitution for the adoption of the Resolution on Standing Order of the Senate aims at ensuring the widest possible expression of the senators' will in the regulatory provisions, an usual requirement in a democratic parliamentary system, which involves, by definition, a parliamentary and an opposition majority. That is why the Standing Order of the*

The same rule also concerns the regulation of parliamentary incompatibilities which cannot be established by another type of normative act. In this respect, Article 71 of the Constitution provides the following: "*(1) No one may be a Deputy and a Senator at one and the same time. (2) The capacity to sit as a Deputy or Senator is incompatible with the exercise of any public office in authority, except that of a Member of the Government. (3) Other incompatibilities are established by an organic law*". Within the meaning 71 para. (2) of the Basic Law, the public dignities are those used within public authorities under the Constitution, offices that can be elected or not. Article 81 para. (2) of Law no. 161/2003 regarding certain measures to ensure transparency in the exercise of public dignities, civil service and business environment, preventing and sanctioning corruption[546] determines the meaning of the term enshrined in the constitutional provision establishing that: "*Public dignities, inconsistent with the capacity of deputy or senator, mean the offices within public administration similar to those of Minister, the offices of the Secretary of State, Under-Secretary of State and offices similar to those of Secretary of State and Under-Secretary of State within the specialised bodies subordinated to the Government or ministries, offices within the Presidential Administration, within the apparatus of Parliament and Government, the management offices of specific to ministries, to the other authorities and to public institutions, the offices of local councillors and county councillors, prefects and sub-prefects and the other management offices within prefectures, the offices of mayor, deputy mayor and secretary of the territorial administrative units, the management and execution offices within the decentralized public services of ministries and the other bodies of the territorial administrative units and within the apparatus and the public services of the county councils and local councils, as well as offices that by law do not allow their holders to stand for election*".

The constitutional provisions on incompatibilities were taken and developed by several organic laws. In this respect, the Court stated that: "Parliament may establish by organic law any other incompatibilities with the parliamentary term of office, and not with the public dignities, but with any other public offices and especially with private offices". We refer to: Law no. 96/2006 on the Statute of Deputies and Senators[547] and Law no. 161/2003 regarding certain measures to ensure transparency in the exercise of public dignities, civil service and business environment, preventing and sanctioning corruption[548]. The Court also held the provisions of Law no. 176/2010 on integrity in the exercising of public functions and offices, amending and supplementing Law no. 144/2007 on the establishment, organisation and functioning of the National Integrity Agency, as well as amending and

---

Senate shall be adopted by a resolution and be subject to the constitutional regime of this category of legal acts".

546 Published in the Official Gazette of Romania no. 279 of 21 April 2003.

547 Republished in the Official Gazette of Romania no. 763 of 12 November 2008.

548 Published in the Official Gazette of Romania no. 279 of 21 April 2003.

supplementing other normative acts[549], governing, in Title II, procedures for ensuring the integrity and transparency in the exercise of public offices and dignities, Section 3 of that title is dedicated to the evaluation procedure of the conflicts of interest and incompatibilities.

Noting that, contrary to the constitutional text of reference [Article 71 para. (3)], the incompatibility cases provided for in Articles 198–200 and Article 202 of the Standing Order of the Chamber of Deputies, as well as in Article 177 of the Standing Order of the Senate, the Court held that "*Having regard to the mentioned constitutional text, which provides that other incompatibilities than those provided by the Basic Law shall be established by organic law, it results that the Standing Orders of the Chambers of Parliament can only establish internal procedural rules of application which may detail in this regard, to the extent necessary, the constitutional and legal rules that define the statute of the MP, and not to supplement or amend it in any way*"[550].

The disciplinary liability of MPs

The Court held[551] that "*the independence of the MP and its possibilities for action in the exercise of its term of office do not exempt him/her from disciplinary liability. The parliamentary activity is governed by principles and rules of behaviour, which the legislature inserted in Chapter III of Law no. 96/2006. Thus, Article 9, as amended by this Law, enshrines «the principle of national interest», Article 10 refers to «the principle of legality and good faith», stating that « (1) Deputies and Senators, in their capacity as elected representatives of the Romanian people, shall fulfil their duties and exercise their rights under the Constitution, the country's laws and the Standing Orders of the Chamber of Deputies and the Senate, throughout their term of office exercised by them. (2) Deputies and senators are forbidden to take financial obligations or otherwise before*

549 Published in the Official Gazette of Romania no. 621 of 2 September 2010.

550 Decision no. 81 of 27 February 2013, published in the Official Gazette of Romania no. 136 of 14 March 2013; by Decision no. 45/1994, published in the Official Gazette of Romania no. 131 of 27 May 1994, ruling upon the constitutionality of the Standing Order of the Chamber of Deputies, the Court held that: "*as concerns the status of deputies, it is to be observed that under the Constitution such statute is regulated separately from the internal organization, resulting for good that the Standing Order cannot exceed the limits of its own organization. There is no doubt that in general, regulations on the organization and operation of a structure, including the state, can also contain rules on the statute of the members who are included in its structure. But where the law provides that this is not possible, the regulation may not contain such rules. We can conclude that such limitations are expressly provided for by the Constitution (...). As such, in relation to those provisions of an undeniable clarity, it results the intention of the Constitution to remove certain provisions from the regulatory scope of the Standing Order*"; in the same regard, see Decision no. 46/1994 on the constitutionality of the Standing Order of the Senate.

551 Decision no. 195 of 3 April 2013, published in the Official Gazette of Romania no. 223 of 18 April 2013.

individuals or legal entities, which aim at influencing the exercise of their term of office in good faith, according to their own conscience », and Article 11 and 12 govern the «principle of transparency» and of «fidelity»".

Regarding the parliamentary discipline regime, the Court held that it is a regime specific to the statute of deputies and senators, which does not impede the exercise of the term of office entrusted by the voters. The Court noted that "the forms of disciplinary liability established for deputies or senators are specific to their statute and needs and they must be adapted to this statue, so that they do not impede the exercise of the term of office entrusted by the voters". This is because "representative parliamentary mandate, as determined by the cited provisions of the Basic Law, has important legal consequences. One of these relates to the duties of Parliament, which are exerted continuously, from the time he/she enters the exercise of office until the date of termination of the capacity as Deputy or Senator, whilst the legislature, by regulations it enacts, must not prevent the fulfilment thereof.

Participation in the sittings of the Chamber, whose member the Deputy or the Senator is, represents a core task of the parliamentary term, as it results from the entire set of constitutional provisions governing Parliament, set forth under Title III, Chapter I of the Basic Law. It is expressly governed by Law no. 96/2006 on the Statute of Deputies and Senators in Article 29 (1) – text that was not amended by the law subject to constitutional review, and it was characterised by the legislature as "a legal, moral and statutory obligation".

Therefore, preventing the Deputy or the Senator from attending the sittings of the Chamber whose member he/she is for a period that represents half a year of the four years of the Chamber's length of office, is a measure likely to prevent him/her from achieving the mandate given by the voters. Taking into account that each MP represents the nation, as a whole, conditions must be ensured for the effective exercise of the mandate, conditions that need to be considered also upon establishing disciplinary sanctions". These considerations substantiated the admission of the objection of unconstitutionality of Article I section 14, regarding Article 191 para. (1) and (2) on "Conflict of interests" of the Law amending and supplementing Law no. 96/2006 on the Statute of Deputies and Senators[552].

Taking into account that in the wording of the law following re-examination for bringing it into accord with the decision of the Constitution Court, Article 19^1 para. (1) introduced by Article I (14) of the Law amending and supplementing Law no. 96/2006 on the status of Deputies and Senators made reference to the provisions of Article 53 para. (1) f) of Law no. 96/2006, thus preserving the legislative solution consisting in prohibiting the Deputy or Senator in conflict of interests to participate in the proceedings of the Chamber whose member he/she is, the Constitutional Court ascertained its unconstitutionality, on the grounds mentioned above[553].

---

552 Decision no. 81 of 27 February 2013, published in the Official Gazette of Romania no. 136 of 14 March 2013.

553 *Ibidem.*

Likewise, the Court held that "*since the ascertainment of the unconstitutionality concerns the very legislative solution to which the impugned legal text refers, Parliament must also bring into accord with the Constitutional Court's decision the regulations in force relating to the disciplinary sanctions of deputies and senators, meaning the repeal of the provisions that establish the disciplinary sanction of forbidding their participation in the works of the Chamber to which they belong*".

Unconstitutionality of parliamentary extended immunity beyond the limits of the office

According to Article 72 of the Constitution, no Deputy or Senator shall be held legally responsible for any vote cast or political opinion expressed in the exercise of his office. Noting that "this immunity, intrinsic for the term of office, protects the MP given the acts committed in the exercise of its term of office, such as votes, amendments, speeches, questions and interpellations, reports and advisory opinions presented by the committee to which he/she belongs etc. In other words, parliamentary term of office is exercised in Parliament and its working bodies, as well as in carrying out the duties set by the Chambers in accordance with the law", the Court found that "Article 22 of the Law on the Statute of Deputies and Senators, pursuant to which deputies and senators shall not be held legally responsible for any vote cast or political opinion expressed in the exercise of his office, is contrary to the provisions of Article 72 of the Constitution of Romania by the phrase «in the exercise of his office»". Thus, contrary to the provisions of Article 72 of the Basic Law, this phrase "extends the parliamentary irresponsibility beyond the limits of exercising his/her office, establishing the exemption from liability of deputies and senators also for opinions expressed outside the parliamentary activity"[554].

Observance of the principle of equal rights

In this regard, the Court held that "*although the constitutional and legal status of MPs, as representatives of the people, is different from that of civil servants and, in general, of other citizens, resulting consequently in particularities on the exercise of certain rights, this status cannot be interpreted as justifying a difference in legal treatment in relation to other categories of persons to whom Law no. 176/2010 applies. This is because, in the light of the object and the purpose of this regulation – aimed at ensuring integrity in the exercise of public offices and at preventing institutional corruption – all persons referred to in Article 1 (1) of the law find themselves in the same legal situation, circumscribed in the title itself, through the phrase "public offices", based on which specific obligations are incumbent on them. In this regard, referring to the compatibility of certain procedural peculiarities, including with regards to the exercise of remedies, with the principle of equality of citizens before the law and public authorities, the Constitutional Court stated in principle that "the establishment of special rules, including with regards to remedies, is not contrary to this principle, insofar as they*

554 Decision no. 279 of 22 March 2006, published in the Official Gazette of Romania no. 323 of 11 April 2006.

ensure the equality of all citizens upon enforcement thereof. The principle of equality before the law requires the establishment of equal treatment for situations that, according to the purpose pursued, are not different. (...)Consequently, a different treatment may not only be an exclusive expression of appreciation of the legislature, but must be justified rationally, in compliance with the principle of equality of citizens before the law and public authorities»"[555]. These considerations substantiated the admission of the objection of unconstitutionality of Article I section 3, regarding Article 7 para. (2) d) of Law no. 96/2006 on the Statute of Deputies and Senators, as amended, in terms of the period of 45 days during which the deputy or senator may appeal to the court of administrative contentious the assessment report of the National Integrity Agency. The Court also held that "*the situation of deputies and senators, in terms of the scope of Law no. 176/2010, is the same as the situation of the other categories of officials and public servants to whom the law applies. Consequently, the establishment of a different procedural treatment in this respect is discriminatory*"[556].

In the same respect, the Constitutional Court stated[557] that the distinct legal statute, privileged in terms of criminal liability, established by Article I section 5 and Article II section 3 of the Law amending and supplementing certain normative acts for deputies and senators, is contrary to the principle of equality enshrined in Article 16 para. (1) of the Constitution, which states that "all citizens are equal before the law and public authorities without privileges and discriminations". Furthermore, "those provisions are also contrary to the provisions of Article 16 para. (2) of the Constitution; to the extent that certain issues of law are excluded by virtue of a legal provision adopted in their consideration and applicable only to them, the incidence of a legal regulation constituting the common law in the matter, the legal provisions in question disregard the constitutional principle according to which «no one is above the law»". The Court also held that the privileged legal statute created for the persons who held the elected offices exempted from the provisions of Article 147 of the old Criminal Code and the provisions of Article 175 of the new Criminal Code, is also contrary to the provisions of Article 11 para. (1) of the Constitution, according to which: "*The Romanian State pledges to fulfil as such and in good faith any obligations as may derive from the treaties to which it has become a party*". Thus, ratifying or accessing to the international conventions previously mentioned, the Romanian State has undertaken to respect and strictly implement the international provisions into the national law, namely the obligation to criminalize the active and passive corruption of the persons who fall within the categories "public agent"/ "Member of the national public assemblies"/ "national officer"/ "public officer", concepts which

555 Decision no. 1 of 8 February 1994, published in the Official Gazette of Romania no. 69 of 16 March 1994; Decision no. 81/2013, published in the Official Gazette of Romania no. 136 of 14 March 2013.

556 Decision no. 81 of 27 February 2013.

557 Decision no. 2 of 15 January 2014, published in the Official Gazette of Romania no. 71 of 29 January 2014.

have correspondence, in the Romanian criminal law, in the concepts of "public servant"/ "officer". *Mutatis mutandis*, the Court also held the same reasons in terms of the case of impunity of persons who hold public offices or dignities, obtained through appointment or election, within public authorities, public institutions, institutions or other legal entities of public interest, regarding the crime of conflict of interests.

2.3.7 Constitutional limits of the law-making activity

2.3.7.1 General aspects

Approaching in this framework the issue regarding the adoption of laws, distinctly from that regarding the adoption of the resolutions of Parliament, we shall mention that, in numerous cases, the Court found the unconstitutionality of certain regulations, relying on the provisions of Article 1 para. (5) of the Constitution, which enshrine the above-mentioned principle. Of course, the Constitution means the observance of all principles and rules which it contains, as the purpose of the constitutional review is to ensure such compliance. Actually, the entire case-law of the Constitutional Court delivered in the exercise of the constitutional review of normative acts circumstantiates the legislature's action within the limits of the Constitution.

2.3.7.2 Compliance with the rules of legislative technique[558]

The constitutional importance of the rules of legislative technique

The constitutional ground as concerns the sanction by the Constitutional Court for the infringement of the rules of legislative technique is set forth in Article 1 para. (3): "*Romania is a state governed by the rule of law (...)*", and by Article 1 para. (5): "*Observance of the Constitution, of its supremacy, and the laws shall be obligatory in Romania*". The cited constitutional texts do not either expressly establish requirements regarding the quality of legislation, or establish any mention on the legislative technique. Fulfilling the enforcement of Article 20 of the Constitution, meaning an interpretation of the constitutional provisions in accordance with the Convention for the Protection of Human Rights and Fundamental Freedoms and the interpretation given to them by European Court of Human Rights, the Constitutional Court of Romania provided a constitutional importance to the rules of legislative technique. Emphasizing the developments achieved in a number of decisions, the Court held that "although the rules of legislative techniques have no constitutional value, (...) by regulating them the legislature imposed a series of binding criteria for the adoption of any normative act, whose observance is required in order to ensure

558 M. Safta, *The unconstitutional legislative solutions due to the non-compliance with the rules of legislative technique*, in the volume *Legislative politics among European, national and international regulation – International Conference of Law, European Studies and International Relations*, 2013, Hamangiu Publishing House, 2013, pp. 622–633.

the systematization, uniformity and coordination of the legislation, as well as the content and the appropriate legal form for each normative act".

Therefore, the Court has referred to the provisions of Law no. 24/2000 on the rules of legislative technique for drafting normative acts[559], an aspect which has been expressly mentioned, for example, in Decision no. 666/2007[560], whereby it noted that "according to Article 1 para. (2) of Law no. 24 / 2000 on the rules of legislative technique for drafting normative acts, (...) «Normative acts shall be initiated, developed, adopted and applied in accordance with the Constitution of Romania, republished, with the provisions of this law, as well as with the principles of the rule of law», and according to Article 3 para. (1) of the same law, «The rules of legislative technique are required to drafting bills by the Government and legislative proposals belonging to Deputies, Senators and citizens in exercise of the right of legislative initiative (...)». (...) The obligation to respect these legal provisions also results from the provisions of Article 1 para. (5) of the Constitution, according to which «Observance of the Constitution, of its supremacy, and the laws shall be obligatory in Romania»".

Approaching the issue of compliance with the rules of legislative technique, the Constitutional Court does not examine the possible contradictions between the impugned rules and the provisions of Law no. 24/2000, but the contradiction between the impugned rules and the constitutional provisions enshrining the rule of law, as the law is an act subject to certain mandatory conditions of substance and form. In other words, not at any time and under any circumstances the infringement of a rule of legislative technique shall be an issue of unconstitutionality of a certain regulation, but only if the breach of that rule becomes constitutional in the sense that, affecting the quality of law, it undermines the principle of legal certainty and the rule of law as a whole. This is a broad interpretation of the constitutional norms of reference imposed by the systemic difficulties encountered by the Romanian legislation and supported by the interpretation consistent with the case-law of the European Court of Human Rights, which held, for example, by Judgment of 8 June 2006 delivered in Case *Lupşa v. Romania*, "according to its established case-law, the expression «*in accordance with the law*» (...) refers to (...) the quality of the law in question: requiring that it be accessible to the persons concerned and formulated with sufficient precision to enable them – if need be, with appropriate advice – to foresee, to a degree that is reasonable in the circumstances, the consequences which a given action may entail. (...) domestic law must afford a measure of legal protection against arbitrary interferences by public authorities with the rights guaranteed by the Convention".

Unconstitutionality of laws having an *intuitu personae* nature

According to Article 4 of Law no. 24/2000: "*(1) Regulatory acts shall be drawn up depending on their hierarchy, their category and the public authority having competence for adopting them.(2) The categories of regulatory acts and the competence-related*

559 Republished in the Official Gazette of Romania no. 260 of 21 April 2010.
560 Published in the Official Gazette of Romania no. 514 of 31 July 2007.

norms on their adoption shall be set forth in the Constitution of Romania, republished, and in the other laws.(3) The regulatory acts passed for the enforcement of laws, Government ordinances or decisions shall be issued within the limits and under the norms ordering them".

Given the principle of legality and the notion of legal system understood as juridical norms hierarchically structured in accordance with the content of the regulations and the scope of its beneficiaries, the Constitutional Court has sanctioned the adoption of certain laws covering individual cases.

Thus, finding the unconstitutionality of the Law regulating the legal status of certain assets that belonged to the former sovereign of Romania[561], Mihai I., the Court held that "*in principle, the law usually has a normative character, the primary nature of its regulations being difficultly harmonized with their application to one case or to individual cases. (...) the legislature is entitled to settle certain domains in a different modality of that used within the general regulation or, in other words, to derogate from ordinary law, procedure which, moreover, was already used in this matter. Subscribing to this reason, the Court wishes to clarify that such derogation from the common law can be achieved only through a normative regulation, as it was the case of special laws with a reparatory finality dealing with communities of people (...). The establishment of such derogatory rules was required and justified by the particular legal situation, essentially different from that of the majority of the persons entitled to remedies under the common law, aiming at the ones who were to benefit from these laws; furthermore and essentially from the point of view which represents an interest here, any person in such a situation was entitled to remedies. In the hypothesis in which, the special regulation, different of the constitutive regulation of common law, has an individual character, being adopted intuitu personae, its legitimacy ceases, because of the discriminatory character and, therefore, unconstitutional*".

Similarly, by decision[562] on the referral on unconstitutionality of Law concerning the allocation of a house to a retired general, finding that this law established an *intuitu personae* legal regime, the Court ascertained its unconstitutionality. The Court also held that "*by its subject-matter – allocation of a house –, the law subject to constitutional review refers to an area of law that is in the competence of the bodies of public administration, and not of the Parliament, which does not make laws concerning rights of individual type*".

Observance of normative powers

Giving expression to the same principle of hierarchy of normative acts, this time under Article 147 par. (1) of the Constitution, according to which "*any provisions of the laws and ordinances in force, as well as any of the regulations which are held as unconstitutional, shall cease their legal effects within 45 days from publication of*

561 Decision no. 600 of 9 November 2005, published in the Official Gazette of Romania no. 1060 of 26 November 2005.

562 Decision no. 970 of 31 October 2007, published in the Official Gazette of Romania no. 796 of 22 November 2007.

the decision rendered by the Constitutional Court where Parliament or Government, as may be applicable, have failed, in the meantime, to bring these unconstitutional provisions into accord with those of the Constitution(...)", the Court has established even in the recitals of its decisions, the level of the regulation and the authority required to intervene in the cases referred to it within the exceptions of unconstitutionality. Having ascertained the unconstitutionality of the provisions of Chapter I "General provisions" (Articles 1–9), of Article 11 e), f) and g), of Article 12 para. (2), of Article 13, of Article 14 c), d), e) and f), of Article 17, of Article 38 para. (2) f), g) and h), of Article 42 para. (2), (3) and (4), of Chapter VI, "Verification of assets, incompatibilities and conflicts of interest" (Articles 45–50) and of Article 57 of Law no. 144/2007 on the establishment, organisation and functioning of the National Integrity Agency[563], the Court held as follows: "*the provisions of Article 147 para. (1) of the Constitution distinguish – in regard of the obligation to bring the unconstitutional provisions in accord with those of the Constitution – between the competence of the Parliament, for provisions of laws, on the one hand, and that of the Government, for provisions of its ordinances, on the other hand. Thus, for a period of 45 days after publication in the Official Gazette of Romania, Part I, of this decision, the Government cannot adopt an emergency ordinance with a view to bringing into accord the provisions of Law No. 144/2007, found as unconstitutional, with the provisions of the Constitution, however it may initiate a draft law in line with those established by this decision*".

We consider that it is an interpretation approach of the Constitution aimed at establishing a distinction in terms of the competence of the authorities required to enforce Article 147 para. (1) of the Constitution according to the field and scope of regulation, as well as to limit the excess of lawmaking by way of emergency ordinances.

Making a difference between the regulation subject of the law in relation to that of parliamentary Standing Orders, with respect to the matter of incompatibilities of deputies and senators, the Constitutional Court held[564] as follows: "*in violation of the constitutional text of reference [Article 71 para. (3)], the incompatibility cases are provided for in Articles 198–200 and Article 202 of the Standing Order of the Chamber of Deputies, as well as in Article 177 of the Standing Order of the Senate. Having regard to the mentioned constitutional text, which provides that other incompatibilities than those provided by the Basic Law shall be established by organic law, it results that the Standing Orders of the Chambers of Parliament can only establish internal procedural rules of application which may detail in this regard, to the extent necessary, the constitutional and legal rules that define the statute of the MP, and not to supplement or amend it in any way*".

563 Decision no. 415 of 14 April 2010, published in the Official Gazette of Romania no. 294 of 5 May 2010.

564 Decision no. 81 of 27 February 2013.

Compliance with the requirements regarding the clarity, precision and foreseeability of normative acts

Article 8 of Law no. 24/2000 stipulates that: "*(1) Draft laws, legislative proposals, and the other draft normative acts shall be drawn up in the prescribed typical form of legal norms. (...) (4) A legislative text shall be phrased in a clear, fluent and intelligible manner, without syntax difficulties or obscure or equivocal paragraphs (...)*".

Referring to these requirements, basing its considerations also on the case-law of the European Court of Human Rights in the matter, the Constitutional Court has established a series of criteria that must be complied with in the lawmaking activity: "*clarity, foreseeability and predictability as to enable the concerned subject of law to regulate his behaviour so that to avoid the consequences resulted from the breach thereof*"[565]. Thus, "*a norm cannot be regarded as «foreseeable» if it is formulated with sufficient precision to enable any individual – if need be with appropriate advice – to regulate his conduct*"(Case Rotaru *v. Romania*, 2000), and "*(...)the citizen must be able to have an indication that is adequate in the circumstances of the legal norms applicable to a given case and to foresee, to a degree that is reasonable in the circumstances, the consequences which a given action may entail. In other words, the law must be, in the same time, accessible and foreseeable*" (Case *Sunday Times v. The United Kingdom*, 1979)". In this regard, the considerations of various decisions may be noted, whereby the Court found that, "by the deficient drafting method", the normative acts/ the impugned provisions do not comply with the requirements of legislative technique specific to the legal rules, as provided by Law no. 24/2000 (with special reference to the above-mentioned criteria).

Moreover, watching the evolving case law of the Constitutional Court, finding that the infringement of these criteria has become one of the frequent reasons of unconstitutionality, at least within a priori constitutional review. Thus, as an example, examining considerations admissions decisions objections of unconstitutionality of the Constitutional Court in 2012, it appears that a third[566] hold the reasoning concerning the breach of Article 1 para. (5) of the Constitution, a text interpreted in the light of this case-law, in the sense that it requires a certain quality of legislation, primarily accessibility and predictability.

Thus, the Constitutional Court held[567] that, "*in principle, any normative act must meet certain quality requirements, among which foreseeability, which means that it must be sufficiently precise and clear to be applied, so the formulation with sufficient precision of the normative act enables the interested persons – if need be with*

565 Decision no. 61 of 18 January 2007, published in the Official Gazette of Romania no. 116 of 15 February 2007.

566 Decision no. 26 of 18 January 2012, published in the Official Gazette of Romania no. 116 of 15 February 2012; Decision no. 51 of 25 January 2012 published in the Official Gazette of Romania no. 90 of 3 February 2012; Decision no. 68 of 2 February 2012, published in the Official Gazette of Romania no. 269 of 24 April 2012.

567 Decision no. 1 of 11 January 2012, published in the Official Gazette of Romania no. 53 of 23 January 2012.

appropriate advice – to foresee, to a degree that is reasonable in the circumstances, the consequences which a given action may entail. Of course, it may be difficult to draw up laws of a total precision and a certain flexibility may even prove to be desirable, but a flexibility which does not affect the foreseeability of the law (see, in this respect, [...] the case-law of the European Court of Human Rights [...] for example, Judgement of 15 November 1996 in the Case of Cantoni v. France, paragraph 29, Judgement of 25 November 1996 in the Case of Wingrove v. the United Kingdom, paragraph 40, Judgement of 4 May 2000 in the Case of Rotaru v. Romania, paragraph 55, Judgement of 9 November 2006 in the Case of Leempoel & SA ED. Cine Revue v. Belgium, paragraph 59)".

The Court held in the same regard[568] that "*the Strasbourg Court held that «one of the pillars of the rule of law is the principle of legal certainty». (Judgement of 6 June 2005 in the Case of Androne v. Romania; Judgement of 7 October 2009 in the Case of Stanca Popescu v. Romania). Likewise, the European Court of Human Rights stated that, «where States decide to enact legislation, it must be implemented with reasonable clarity and coherence in order to avoid, in so far as possible, legal uncertainty and ambiguity for the legal persons concerned (...)» (Judgement of 1 December 2005 in the Case of Păduraru v. Romania; Judgement of 6 December 2007 in the Case of Beian v. Romania).*"

The Constitutional Court recalled[569] that the Strasbourg Court "*stressed the importance of ensuring accessibility and foreseeability of the law, including in terms of its stability, establishing a set of benchmarks that the legislator must take into consideration to ensure these requirements (cases such as Sunday Times v. the United Kingdom, 1979, Rekvényi v. Hungary, 1999, Rotaru v. Romania, 2000, Damman v. Switzerland, 2005)*"

By other decisions[570] the Court referred again to the requirements of accessibility and foreseeability of the law, invoking Judgement of 24 May 2007, in the Case of *Dragotoniu and Militaru-Pidhorni v. Romania*, Judgement of 29 March 2000, in the Case of *Rotaru v. Romania*, Judgement of 23 September 1998, in the Case *Petra v. Romania*, Judgement of 23 November 2000, in the Case of *Former King of Greece and Others v. Greece*, Judgement of 8 July 2008, in the Case of *Fener Rum Patrikligi v. Turkey*, Judgement of 26 April 1979, in the Case of *Sunday Times v. the United Kingdom.*

As concerns the admission decisions of the exceptions of unconstitutionality, it appears that a significant number of them[571] refer to the same constitutional text and to the principle of legal certainty.

---

568 Decision no. 26 of 18 January 2012.

569 Decision no. 51 of 25 January 2012.

570 For example, Decision no. 681 of 27 June 2012, published in the Official Gazette of Romania no. 477 of 12 July 2012.

571 Decision no. 494 of 10 May 2012, published in the Official Gazette of Romania no. 407 of 19 June 2012; Decision no. 615 of 12 June 2012 published in the Official Gazette of Romania no. 454 of 6 July 2012; Decision no. 980 of 22 November 2012, published in the Official Gazette of Romania no. 57 of 25 January 2013; Decision

The same principle substantiated the ascertainment of the constitutionality amending Law no. 3/2000 on referendum. The Court has determined in this respect, through a series of decisions, the limits on matters of lawmaking, circumscribed to legal certainty, notably to the stability of rules in this matter. Thus, the Court held[572] that the amendment of the quorum of participation in the referendum is the legislature's prerogative, but the constitutional court must ensure that this instrument is not used for other purposes than the one taken into account by the constituent legislature when establishing the referendum, as an essential legal institution for the rule of law – a form of direct participation of citizens in decision-making procedure. The Court must ensure the observance of the principles of legal stability of laws in the matter of the referendum, as well as the one regarding the loyal consultation of citizens with voting rights, principles which involve the establishment of all conditions for voters in order to know the issues subject to referendum, the legal consequences of decreasing the threshold of participation in elections and the effects produced by the returns of the referendum on the general interests of the community. The principles stated are corollary to the provisions regarding the free elections enshrined in Article 2 para. (1) and Article 62 para. (1) of the Basic Law, constitutional rules which reveal the international regulations contained in Additional Protocol 1 to the European Convention on Human Rights and Fundamental Freedoms and in the International Covenant on Civil and Political Rights. However, given that the threshold for participation is a prerequisite for the referendum in order to be able to express the real and genuine will of the people, being a prerequisite for a genuine democratic manifestations of sovereignty in accordance with the principle stated in Article 2 of the Basic Law, the Court must balance the need for the protection of the citizens' right to decide the participation in the referendum, as a fundamental right, and the desire of a parliamentary majority to impose its political will in the state at a certain time. The Court found that Parliament can (and, as it results from the Court's decisions, it even must) intervene in the matter of the legislation on referendum, provided that it does not subject it to strictly circumstantial amendments, based on allegations of opportunity or political understanding, which gives advantage to one or another political power represented in Parliament and which constitutes at one point a parliamentary majority. However, if a law which aims at the substance of the referendum law, adopted by a parliamentary majority at a time, succeeds in supporting the parliamentary majority for one year, one may assume that it reflects the real electoral majority and that the democracy could not be affected in any way as, moreover, neither the rule of law and democratic nature of Romania.

---

no. 981 of 22 November 2012, published in the Official Gazette of Romania no. 58 of 27 January 2013.

572 Decision no. 334 of 26 June 2013, published in the Official Gazette of Romania no. 407 of 5 July 2013; Decision no. 471 of 14 November 2013, published in the Official Gazette of Romania no. 754 of 4 December 2013.

The Court also noted that the parliamentary majority determined the procedure for the revision of the Constitution. Or, even if it is undeniable that Parliament is the supreme legislative body, this behaviour should be subject to the principle of constitutional loyalty, which requires the cooperation of all the powers of the State, without the use of any disproportionate or unfair means in order to achieve political goals. Preserving the rule of law and democratic nature obliges the Constitutional Court, as the supreme guarantor of the Constitution, to prevent the consequences of the rapid amendment to the legal provisions on matters of referendum and to comply them with the principles of legal stability (which requires clarity, predictability and accessibility), of loyal consultation of citizens with voting rights, of free elections and of the interpretation of good faith in the word and the spirit of the Constitution, principles which represent structural elements/aspects of the general principle of legal certainty, generally accepted within the constitutional democracy.

Therefore, the new regulations must not result in a state of uncertainty on a defining element of this procedure as the options of the ordinary legislature regarding the establishment of the quorum of participation in the referendum may fluctuate in value according to the will of the political majority in Parliament and to the conjectural interests thereof, a circumstance which is likely to create a general state of uncertainty as to an essential element of the referendum, namely its validity. In relation to those noted, the Court found that, in order to ensure the observance of the general principle of legal stability on matters of referendum, in line with the recommendations of the Code of Good Practice on Referendums adopted by the Venice Commission, by Additional Protocol 1 to the European Convention on Human Rights and Fundamental Freedoms and the International Covenant on Civil and Political Rights, the provisions of the Law amending and supplementing Law no. 3/2000 on the organization and holding of a referendum are constitutional, but they may not be applicable to referendums within one year from the entry into force of the amending law.

However, it is true that both the percentage set by the legislature and the lack of a distinction depending on the type of the referendum reveal the lack of rules or distinctions in the Basic Law. As the Constitutional Court has held in Decision No. 471/2013, analyzing the constitutional texts in force and the international acts in the matter, "the provisions of Article 2 para. (1), of Article 90, of Article 95 para. (3) and of Article 151 para. (3) of the Constitution, do expressly rule on a particular threshold of participation in elections, as it has not been identified any text requiring or recommending a quorum of participation in the referendum, all constitutional provisions refer to the stability of electoral legislation, including on referendum"; "where the constituent legislature deemed necessary the regulation of such quorums/ majorities, it established it, in other cases, it left them to the discretion of the ordinary legislature. Thus, it appears that the exercise of sovereignty by the people's representative bodies, specifically the lawmaking procedure, knows a strict and thorough regulation at the constitutional level. As for the exercise of national sovereignty by referendum, the Constitution provides only the subject of the referendum or the matters of national interest (Article 90 of the Constitution), the dismissal of the President of Romania from office [Article 95 para. (3)] and the approval of the revision of the Constitution [Article 151 para. (3)], as well as that its organization and holding is regulated by an organic law [Article 73 para. (1) d)]. Given the difference of legal regime that even the Constitution itself enshrines, the establishment, by way of analogy, of a principle of absolute majority that would be automatically assumed by the Constitution in respect of any decision, cannot be supported. The type of majority required for the adoption of an act/decision has been established in the Basic Law when it deemed necessary, and the constituent legislature has provided that the majority in relation to the legal regime of the institution to which it refers".

We consider it crucial to emphasize the same decision according to which the lack of regulation at the constitutional level in this regard "is not tantamount to the discretion right of the legislature, in the sense that such a quorum, respectively majority for a making a decision of major importance could be set arbitrary".

Observance of rules regarding the integration of a normative act in the whole body of laws

According to Article 13 of Law no. 24/2000: "*A normative act shall have to be organically integrated in the system of legislation, for which purpose: a) a draft normative act shall be correlated with the provisions of the normative acts of higher or equal level, with which it has connections*".

In an established case-law, the Constitutional Court held the comparison of legal provisions and reporting the conclusion which may arise to the constitutional texts and principal do not fall within its competence. However, the Constitutional Court held[573] the following reasons: "*existence of conflicting legislative solutions and cancellation of provisions of law by other provisions contained in the same law are in breach of the principle of legal certainty, due to the lack of clarity and foreseeability of the rule*".

Proceeding to the examination of the allegations regarding the violation of Article 1 para. (3) and (5) of the Constitution, meaning the lack of predictability of regulation, motivated by the existence of inconsistencies in the body of the law subject to review, the Court held that "it is necessary, using this legislative situation, that the two Chambers of Parliament reconsider the texts of their Standing Orders found unconstitutional and ensure a correlation and a uniform treatment of the same issues. It would be desirable that the basic normative acts relating to parliamentary activity, namely Law no. 96/2006, the Standing Order of the Chamber of Deputies, the Standing Order of the Senate and the Regulation on the joint meetings of the Chamber of Deputies and the Senate to be gathered in a single volume, in order to facilitate the parliamentary activity. In this systematization activity, the Legislative Council has an important role which, pursuant to Article 79 of the Constitution, is « *a specialized consultative organ of Parliament that gives advice on*

573 Decision no. 26 of 18 January 2012, published in the Official Gazette of Romania no. 116 of 15 February 2012.

draft normative acts with a view to the systematic unification and coordination of the whole body of laws»"[574].

We consider that this case-law should be mentioned as marking the orientation of a constitutional review towards the sanction of legislative inconsistencies, in the sense that the Constitutional Court of Slovenia has noted, for example, by Decision no. U-I-278/07 of 22 October 2009, respectively the sense according to which the Constitutional Court is not competent to decide on correlation of two laws, unless the principles of the rule of law are violated by their non-correlation and inconsistency.

Compliance with the rules on the uniqueness of regulations in the matter and avoiding duplications

Having ascertained that, pursuant to Article 1 para. (5) of the Constitution "*observance (...) of laws shall be obligatory in Romania*", that, according to Law no. 24/2000, the legislative technique ensures systematization, uniformity and coordination of the laws, as well as the content and appropriate legal form to every normative act, that Article 13 of this law establishes rules governing the principle of the uniqueness and the fact that, according to Article 15, the establishment of the same regulations in two or more normative acts is prohibited in the lawmaking process, and in case of duplication, they shall be removed either by repealing or by concentrating the matter in a unique regulation, the Constitutional Court held the following: "Within the activity of control on the property acquired in the exercise of terms of office or of certain public offices and of verification of the conflicts of interests, there are parallel regulations, namely, on the one hand, Law no. 115/1996 for the declaration and control of assets of officials, magistrates, of persons holding management and control offices and of civil servants (...), as amended and supplemented by Law no. 161/2003 (...) and, on the other hand, Law no. 144/2007 on the establishment, organization and functioning of the National Integrity Agency*(...)*[575]".

Likewise, the Constitutional Court held that the "Law on the Statute of Deputies and Senators was adopted in 2006, 15 years after the entry into force of the Constitution following its approval by the national referendum of 8 December 1991 and suffered amendments in accordance with the law for the revision of the Constitution in 2003. After being amended and supplemented by several normative acts, Law no. 96/2006 was republished in the Official Gazette of Romania, Part I, no. 763 of 12 November 2008. The new amendment, subject to constitutional review in this case, is not susceptible to ensure rigor in terms of consistency and systematization of rules in matter of the Statute of Deputies and Senators. According to Article 14 para. (1) of Law no. 24 / 2000 on the rules of legislative technique for drafting normative acts (...), «The regulations of the same level and with the same subject are normally comprised in a single act». However, in the present, the

574 Decision no. 81 of 27 February 2013.

575 Decision no. 415 of 14 April 2010, published in the Official Gazette of Romania no. 294 of 5 May 2010.

matter of incompatibilities and conflicts of interests, forming the subject-matter of the challenges of unconstitutionality raised in this case is covered by Chapter IV of Law no. 96/2006 on the Statute of Deputies and Senators, Articles 20–26 of Law no. 176/2010 regarding the integrity in exercising public offices and dignities, amending and supplementing Law no. 144/2007 on the establishment, organization and functioning of the National Integrity Agency and amending and supplementing other laws, Book I, Title IV, Chapter III of Law no. 161/2003 on certain measures to ensure transparency in the exercise of public dignities, public functions and in the business environment, the prevention and sanction of corruption, as well as by the Standing Orders of the two Chambers of Parliament. In relation to the mentioned provisions of Law no. 24/2000, it is necessary to uniformly regulate the incompatibilities and the conflicts of interests in order to achieve a systematization of the matter, with the consequence of increasing the accessibility and predictability of the law, which is likely to eliminate the divergent interpretations[576]".

Thus, the mentioned rules develop the constitutional norm of reference and imposed themselves *erga omnes*, being binding including for the adoption of the law.

Compliance with the principle of bicameralism

The Constitution of Romania does not define the principle of bicameralism; but it establishes in Article 61 paragraph (2), that "*Parliament consists of the Chamber of Deputies and Senate.*" On the grounds of this constitutional text, the Romanian Constitutional Court defined the principle of bicameralism, sanctioning, repeatedly, regulations adopted in violation of the interpretation of this principle established by the Court itself in its case-law.

Thus, the Court held that "*«the parliamentary debate of a bill or of a legislative proposal cannot leave aside the assessment thereof in the plenary of the two Chambers of our bicameral Parliament». Therefore, the amendments and supplementations operated by the decisional Chamber on the bill passed by the first Chamber referred must relate to the matter had in view by the initiator and to the form passed by the first Chamber. Otherwise, only one Chamber, namely the decisional chamber might conduct the law-making process, which contravenes the bicameralism principle*"[577].

In addition to the afore stated, the Court also held that "*as long as the Chamber of Deputies is the decisional Chamber, it can introduce in the text of the law new provisions pertaining to its decisional power and that are directly and inseparably connected with the original text of the bill or legislative proposal. Therefore, it is not imperative that both Chambers rule on a legal provision, it is sufficient in the case above stated that only one Chamber, the decisional one, decides*"[578].

576 Decision no. 81 of 27 February 2013.

577 Decision no. 472 of 22 April 2008, published in the Official Gazette of Romania no. 336 of 30 April 2008; Decision no. 710 of 6 May 2009, published in the Official Gazette of Romania no. 358 of 28 May 2009.

578 Decision no. 1466 of 10 November 2009, published in the Official Gazette of Romania no. 893 of 21 December 2009.

Summarizing those previously established, the Court specified that the main criteria to determine the cases where legislative procedure violates the principle of bicameralism, respectively: "*major differences of legal content between the wordings adopted by the two Chambers of Parliament and the existence of a special configuration, significantly different between the wordings adopted by the two Chambers of Parliament*"[579].

Finally, adjudicating on the observance of the same principle enshrined by means of case-law, the Court held that, "*regarding the function of regulation, legislative initiative belongs in equal measure to Deputies and Senators, which involves both the right of MPs to submit a legislative proposal to Parliament and their right to amend any legislative initiative submitted to Parliament. From the MPs right of legislative initiative stems each Chamber's right to decide on legislative initiatives before it. To debate a legislative initiative participate equally, both Chambers of Parliament, in compliance with the principle concerning the power of referral provided by Article 75 of the Constitution, as the two Chambers are autonomous as concerns the adoption of legislative solutions in terms of initiatives under debate. From these principles of the bicameral system results that legislative initiatives may be amended or supplemented by the primary Chamber referred and that its decision is not limited by the content of legislative initiative in the form filed by the initiator, so as the decisional Chamber has the right to modify, complete or to abandon the initiative in question. (...) during debate of legislative initiatives, the Chambers have a personal right of decision, which was limited by the Constitutional Court, in its case law, to the only obligation that the same texts (the same content and same form of legislative initiative) be debated in both Chambers and not to the obligation of adoption of identical solutions*"[580].

Consequences in terms of law-making process resulting from the accession to the European Union

Adjudicating on the proposal for the revision of the Constitution[581] and having to adjudicate whether the provisions concerning accession to the Euro-Atlantic structures infringe upon the limit of revisions, in relation to the concepts of sovereignty and independence, the Court concluded that the respective texts do not represent a violation of such limits. It was claimed that the amendment and supplement of the Constitution of Romania, for the purpose of accession, "*is a necessary political and legal arrangement (...)*"; "*introduction of these new regulations in the Constitution of Romania, at this moment, in view of a future integration into the European Union, represents a solution that cannot be abandoned, because integration into the Euro-Atlantic structures can only be achieved based on pre-existent constitutional*

579 Decision no. 413 of 14 April 2010, published in the Official Gazette of Romania no. 291 of 4 May 2010.

580 Decision no. 1018 of 19 July 2010, published in the Official Gazette of Romania no. 511 of 22 July 2010.

581 Decision no. 148 of 16 April 2003, published in the Official Gazette of Romania no. 317 of 12 May 2003.

basis." The Court also noted that "*through the acts transferring certain powers to the structures of the European Union, these do not achieve, by endowment, «supreme powers», personal sovereignty. In fact, the Member States of the European Union decided to jointly exercise certain powers, which, traditionally, pertain to national sovereignty. It is obvious that in the present era of globalisation of mankind problems, of the interstates evolutions and of the inter-individuals communication to a planetary scale, the concept of national sovereignty can no longer be conceived as absolute and indivisible, without the risk of an unacceptable isolation*".

On this occasion, the consequences related to the accession to European Union were mentioned: integration into national law of the *acquis* communautaire and the obligation to comply with European law. As concerns the first consequence – the integration of the acquis communautaire into national law, the subsequent decisions of the Court constantly emphasized the need to harmonize national legislation with the European legislation and the obligations incumbent on national authorities in this respect. As concerns the second consequence – the obligation to comply with EU law, while establishing the rule concerning the priority of community law over contrary provisions of national laws in the proposal for revision of the Constitution, the Court noted that "*the Member States of the European Union agreed to place the community acquis – the constituent treaties of the European Union and the regulations derived there from – on an intermediary position between Constitution and the other laws, in case of binding European normative acts.*"[582]. The Court has thus established the same hierarchy of norms, a concept which is also common for the other constitutional courts[583], which accept the idea of constitutional pluralism and the supremacy of EU law – with some circumstantiation and usually in relation to the infraconstitutional rules –, but as a consequence of the transfer of certain powers under the conditions provided for by national constitutions, whereas the latter are still the primary sources of any such authority[584].

Ever since those first statuaries of principle, the Constitutional Court of Romania, pursuant to its role as guarantor for the supremacy of the Constitution, circumstantiated the constitutional obligations of public authorities resulting from the accession act imposed by Article 148 of the revised Constitution, which establish under paragraph (4), that "*The Parliament, the President of Romania, the Government, and the judicial authority shall guarantee that any obligations arising from the accession instrument and from provisions under paragraph (2) are put into effect*", and under paragraph (2): "*Following accession, provisions in the founding Treaties of the European Union, as well as other binding regulations under community law shall prevail over any contrary provisions of domestic law, while observing provisions in the accession instrument*".

582 *Ibidem.*
583 Constitutional Council of France, Federal Constitutional Court of Germany, Constitutional Tribunal of Poland.
584 K. Kowalik-Banczyk, *cited paper*, pp. 1355–1366.

By numerous decisions, the Constitutional Court emphasized the need for the harmonization and compatibility of laws that the accession requires. In fact, such obligation was also established at infraconstitutional level, being expressly covered by Law no. 24/2000 on the rules of legislative technique for drafting normative acts, amended[585], which establishes, under Article 22 para. (1), that "*the legislative solutions considered in the new regulation shall take into consideration the European Union regulations in the matter, making them consistent with the latter*".

In the same respect, the Constitutional Court of Romania, examining in 2006 the referral concerning the unconstitutionality of the Law on healthcare reform, held as[586] unfounded the challenge on the existence within the law of rules applicable to the European Union structures as "*taking certain regulations adopted by European Union bodies does not mean exceeding powers, but implementation of Community law into national law*". In another decision delivered in the same year prior to accession[587], the Court held that the impugned emergency ordinance "*was adopted in order to harmonize the current legislation with the provisions of the Accession Treaty (...) The urgency of the measure was justified by the fact that Romania is closely monitored by the European Commission under the heading «Competition», and violation of the respective provisions of the Accession Treaty is likely to lead to activation of the safeguard clause, with the consequent postponement of Romania's accession to the European Union (...)*".

After 2007, the case-law of the Constitutional Court found, on the one hand, that the legislator – primary or delegated – has harmonized national legislation with the EU legislation in various matters[588], and, on the other hand, the development of the reasoning part as to underline the obligation and importance of the harmonization process. Thus, for example, the Court held that "*in accordance with Article 148 para. (4) of the Constitution, the Romanian State authorities have pledged to guarantee the*

---

585 Law no. 29/2011, published in the Official Gazette of Romania no. 182 of 11 March 2011.

586 Decision no. 298 of 29 March 2006, published in the Official Gazette of Romania no. 372 of 28 April 2006.

587 Decision no. 205 of 7 March 2006, published in the Official Gazette of Romania no. 340 of 14 April 2006.

588 Decision no. 1033 of 9 October 2008, published in the Official Gazette of Romania no. 757 of 10 November 2008; Decision no. 631 of 12 May 2011, published in the Official Gazette of Romania no. 536 of 29 July 2011; Decision no. 432 of 15 April 2010, published in the Official Gazette of Romania no. 361 of 2 June 2010; Decision no. 666 of 17 May 2011, published in the Official Gazette of Romania no. 502 of 14 July 2011; Decision no. 688 of 31 May 2011, published in the Official Gazette of Romania no. 537 of 29 July 2011; Decision no. 1289 of 4 October 2011, published in the Official Gazette of Romania no. 830 of 23 November 2011; Decision no. 447 of 7 April 2011, published in the Official Gazette of Romania no. 485 of 8 July 2011; Decision no. 1591 of 13 December 2011, published in the Official Gazette of Romania no. 80 of 1 February 2012.

fulfilment of the obligations resulting from the Treaties establishing the European Union, the EU binding regulations and the accession instrument. In this regard, the Government is constitutionally empowered in that, by the means it has at hand, to ensure fulfilment by Romania of the obligations undertaken before the European Union. Thus, the use of emergency ordinances to harmonize national legislation with the community legislation, where the initiation of the infringement procedure before the Court of Justice was imminent, is fully constitutional"[589]. Even if such *infringement* procedure was not imminent, specific conditions requiring rapid legislative intervention – such as to avoid negative consequences it would have on competition at EU level, respectively to ensure immediate protection of consumers – were also invoked as justifying the adoption of an emergency ordinance[590].

The Court sanctioned the legislature for the failure to comply with the constitutional rules governing the obligations resulting from the accession act with reference to the obligation of loyal cooperation between the Union and the Member States, noting[591] that "*removal by Law no. 299/2011 of the procedural means allowing the reopening of some cases irrevocably settled, but during which settlement the European Union law had been violated, meaning that ensured uniform application of European legislation, as it should have been interpreted as from its entry into force, is likely to violate the obligation undertaken by the Romanian State by the Act of accession, obligation enshrined in Article 4 para. (3) of the Treaty on the European Union and guaranteed by Article 148 para. (4) of the Constitution*". That decision of the Constitutional Court pronounced at the end of 2012, includes, moreover, a broad "advocacy" in meeting the obligations assumed by the Romanian state as a member of the European Union, these obligations being treated dynamically and with regard to all public authorities that the constitutional text reference mentions – Article 148.

Similarly, adjudicating with the *a priori* review on the provisions of Article 38 para. (1) and Article 42 of the Public-Private Partnership Law, in relation to the provisions of Article 148 of the Constitution, and noting the existence of a dispute between Government and the authors of the objection of unconstitutionality with regard to the directive applicable to the contractual and/or institutionalised public-private partnership, the Court held that "*such uncertainty is given by the fact that the legislature has not fulfilled the obligation to indicate, within the contested law, the European Union acts implemented by this law, which is inadmissible*". Furthermore, the Court noted that "*regardless of the applicable Directive (Directive 2014/23/EU*

---

589 Decision no. 802 of 19 May 2009, published in the Official Gazette of Romania no. 428 of 23 June 2009; Decision no. 1070 of 8 September 2009, published in the Official Gazette of Romania no. 703 of 20 October 2009.

590 Decision no. 450 of 3 May 2012, published in the Official Gazette of Romania no. 507 of 24 July 2012; Decision no. 1540 of 6 December 2011, published in the Official Gazette of Romania no. 151 of 7 March 2012; Decision no. 802 of 19 May 2009, published in the Official Gazette of Romania no. 428 of 23 June 2009.

591 Decision no. 58 of 21 February 2013, published in the Official Gazette of Romania no. 155 of 22 March 2013.

of the European Parliament and of the Council of 26 February 2014 on the award of concession contracts or Directive 2014/24/EU of the European Parliament and of the Council of 26 February 2014 on public procurement and repealing Directive 2004/18/EC, both published in the Official Journal of the European Union, Series L, no. 94 of 28 March 2014), (...)both contained conditions coinciding almost to the slightest detail in relation to the unilateral termination or modification of the contract, while the wording of Article 38 (1) of the law contained a regulatory solution tending to evade those conditions". Consequently, the Court ruled that "*the legal solution contained in the impugned text represents a breach by the Parliament of the provisions of Article 148 (4) of the Constitution, which governs its role as guarantor for the compliance with the obligations resulting from the accession instrument*"[592].

2.3.8 The relationship between Parliament and the other public authorities

Parliamentary control over the representation of Romania in the European Council meetings

Adjudicating, on the occasion of the constitutional review of the provisions of Article 2, 3 and 18 of the Law on Cooperation between the Parliament and Government in European affairs, with regard to drafting, settling and finalizing the content of the mandate of representation to the European Council, the Court held a series of principles regarding the parliamentary control over the representation of Romania (by the President or by Prime Minister, according to distinctions made in the same case-law), in the meetings of this institution.

Thus, the Court held under Article10 para. (2) sentence II of TEU, published in the OJ series C no. 326 of October 26, 2012, that "*Member States are represented in the European Council by their Heads of State or Government and in the Council by their governments, themselves democratically accountable either to their national Parliaments, or to their citizens*", emphasizing, at the same time, that "*this text of principle also provides the responsibility of Member States representatives in the European Council either before their national Parliaments, or before citizens, without considering aspects of constitutional order and traditions of the Member States*". Therefore, the Member States of the European Union must determine, based on the national constitutional texts, the national representative to the European Council (President/Prime Minister) and, eventually, establish a national legal framework regarding the relationship between national authorities likely to ensure democratic and, at the same time, efficient representation. In view of this ultimate purpose, the Romanian Parliament adopted the Law on Cooperation between the Parliament and Government in European affairs, establishing, under Article 1 of Chapter I, "*General provisions*", its scope, as follows: "*This law regulates the cooperation between the*

592 Decision no. 390 of 2 July 2014, published in the Official Gazette of Romania no. 532 of 17 July 2014.

Romanian Parliament or one of its Chambers and the Government of Romania, regarding Romania's participation in decision-making process within the European Union and monitoring the harmonization of the national legislation with EU law". Consequently, the subject-matter of the law is "*the cooperation framework between Parliament of Romania or one of its Chambers and the Government of Romania, regarding Romania's participation in decision-making process within the European Union*".

As concerns the impugned law, the Court held that 18 para. (1)-(3) of the law refers to the situation where the power of the President of Romania to participate in the meetings of the European Council was delegated to the Prime Minister; parliamentary control is exercised only on the content of his mandate, whilst Article 18 (4) of the law refers to the possibility of the President of Romania to inform Parliament about the content of the mandate he prepared himself when he decided not to delegate his power of participation in the meetings of the European Council, resulting in two separate situations:

a) when the President of Romania decides to participate personally in the meetings of the European Council, he may present the mandate to Parliament, the content of the mandate being established exclusively by the President of Romania;
b) when he delegates his power of participation in the meetings of the European Council, the President of Romania cannot establish the content of the mandate, and the Prime Minister must submit to Parliament a "draft mandate/mandate proposal" so that the latter would approve the same.

In relation to the above-mentioned recitals, the Court concluded, as follows: "*the parliamentary control over the representation of Romania in the European Council meetings is simply a form of information, in the first case, whilst in the second case, Parliament acquires decision-making power in determining the content of the mandate given its specific relationship with the Government (Article 111 of the Constitution). Parliamentary control over the representation of Romania in the European Council meetings is a form of debate, information and cooperation among the Government, Parliament and the President*".

Conducting an examination of comparative law in this respect, the Court held that the existence of parliamentary control, in whatever form, regarding the establishment of the content of the mandate of the head of delegation at European Council meetings is already an aspect enshrined in all Member States of the European Union. The absence of any information provided by the President to Parliament would determine Romania to be the only European state where the representation in the European Council accomplished by a single institution. Such a state of law was emphasized in the study "Democratic control in the member states of the European Council and the Euro zone summits", drafted in 2013 by the European Commission – Directorate-General for Internal Policies of the European Union – Directorate for Citizens' Rights and Constitutional Affairs, a study which established the following aspects of comparative law: There are seventeen Member States with formal rules explicitly mentioning the European Council in the Constitution or in the Rules of Procedure of parliamentary assemblies (Belgium, Bulgaria, Czech Republic,

Denmark, Finland, Germany, Hungary, Italy, Latvia, Lithuania, Luxembourg, Malta, Poland, Portugal, Slovakia, Spain, and Sweden). These rules treat the issue of informing the Parliament on European Council procedures and decisions and define either the obligation of Government to provide certain written documents on the European Council (i.e. annotated draft agenda, strategy papers, government position, report on results) or the obligation of explanations by the government in oral form; furthermore, in Estonia, Latvia, Lithuania, Slovenia, Slovakia, and Sweden, formal rules with specific procedures on the control over the activity of national representatives of the European Council also prescribe the option or even necessity of Government to consult Parliament and to seek Parliament's opinion. In the case of Lithuania, this is a binding mandate. Regarding the structure of the debate, debates where the Head of Government participates in many cases look like this: a statement by the Head of Government is followed by a debate of question and answer rounds where all parliamentary party groups may participate. In Germany and Luxembourg parliamentary rules of procedure state that the speaking time allocated to each party group corresponds to the number of seats. In Ireland and Italy, the Head of Government does not reply in a parliamentary debate. Neither in Ireland nor in Malta does a true debate follow the Government declaration; the party groups just express their viewpoints (Ireland). More than half of European Union Member States have explicit rules on the documents and information to be provided on the European Council meetings.

The rules related to the control of the national representatives in the European Council have evolved in many Member States of the European Union, notably during the treaties ratification. Thus, we find two categories of rules based on the criterion of formalizing them, i.e. formal rules, normative (Austria, the Czech Republic, Finland, Germany, Hungary, Luxembourg, Portugal, Sweden), but also informal rules, customary (Spain, Sweden, France Italy, Finland, the Netherlands, Ireland, Estonia), rules that corroborate each other. The general trend identified in the Member States is to involve Prime Ministers directly in the parliamentary process (where the power of representation belongs to the Prime Minister) and to concentrate the parliamentary control over the activity of the representative of the Member States of the European Council prior to the holding of its sessions – an *ex ante* control (France, the Netherlands, Ireland or Portugal). As an example, in France, after the Constitutional Treaty was rejected by referendum in 2005, *ex ante* debates were required in the Plenum of Parliament regarding the ordinary sessions of the European Council. Likewise, one may also note that, between March 2011 and March 2012, these three states had the highest rate of *ex ante* debates in plenary regarding the agenda of the European Council (the Netherlands, Ireland and France). These countries, in turn, in principle, have no debates in the specialised parliamentary committees (we usually refer to the Parliamentary Committees of European Affairs). On the other hand, in Estonia, Finland, Portugal, Sweden, Belgium, Lithuania, Slovakia, Latvia and Italy, debates are held before specialised committees, without the involvement of the plenum. However, it is noted that, among the above-mentioned countries, in Portugal, since May 2012, there has been an *ex ante* involvement of the plenum. In contrast, in Denmark and Germany, the debates in plenary and before committees are frequent, this model belongs to the "full parliamentarization" one. This trend shown above is opposed to the traditional model of parliamentary non-involvement in preparing the European Council meetings (Malta, Greece, Romania and the UK). Among the countries with a high rate of debates in plenary before the sessions of the European Council, only Ireland and Denmark hold *ex post* plenary debates. In France or Germany, *ex post* debates are hold before committees and the Netherlands hold such debates at plenary / committee level only in exceptional cases. In the latter parliaments, the lack of the *ex post* debates is the consequence of the large number of *ex ante* parliamentary debates.

The Court presented below the conclusions of the mentioned study regarding the parliamentary control models, according to the level of involvement of the national parliaments in the issue on the agenda of the European Council, as follows:

a) the traditional model, non-involvement in the *ex ante / ex post* control on the activity of the national representative in the European Council (Luxembourg, Hungary);
b) the general model used by Member States in European business, following the normal parliamentary procedure on EU legislation;
c) the expert model, where the European Affairs Committee is very active, but its involvement on the merits of the debated topics is low;
d) the public forum model, which involves *ex ante* and *ex post* plenary sessions;
e) the government accountability model, where the *ex ante* debates are limited and usually occur after the works of the European Council meeting have ended;
f) the "policy maker" model, where the parliamentary activity aims at influencing the Government before the session of the European Council (Germany);
g) the "full parliamentarization" model which offers a combination of technical examination and public debate both before and after the sessions of the European Council (Denmark).

Likewise, the study also identifies four intermediate models:

a) Austria and Sweden are indeed a mix of the government accountability, public forum and expert model;
b) Cyprus model where the President chairs the national delegation and is fully independent from the Parliament. It is worth mentioning that Cyprus is a presidential republic;
c) Greek and Portuguese model is close to the government accountability one, but the Parliament's particular involvement after a European Council meeting suggests that it is a place for discussing the implementation of the decisions taken;
d) Dutch and French model is a "*policy maker*" pattern with some specificity. For example, in France, among the MPs, it is launched the idea that a debate on the agenda of the European Council will cause difficulty to the President of the Republic to support the position of France at the European Council meetings.

From the above-mentioned study, it results that in Bulgaria, Ireland, Malta and the United Kingdom, the Parliament does not have the possibility to draft a resolution regarding the topics approached in the European Council meetings. Likewise, in the ex ante review of the national representative in the European Council, the Parliament's position is either non-binding, either recommended (France, Greece, Hungary, Italy, Luxembourg, Poland, Portugal, Spain), either politically binding (Denmark, Finland, the Netherlands, Sweden), or legally binding (Estonia, Germany, Slovenia, Slovakia, Austria, Latvia, Lithuania).

Consequently and referring to all these considerations, the Court found that the Romanian semi-presidential system cannot exclude parliamentary control over representation of Romania in the European Council meetings. As concerns the political decision to delegate the power of participation in the meetings of the European Council, it must take into account the criteria established by the Court, criteria that are to be underlined when analyzing the relationships between the President and the Government, in the context of the dialogue between the Constitutional Court and these institutions[593].

Information to Parliament

In accordance with the provisions of Article 111 para. (1) of the Constitution, "*The Government and the other organs of public administration must, in the framework of parliamentary control of their activity, supply any information and document as may have been requested by the Chamber of Deputies, the Senate, or parliamentary Committees through their respective Presidents (...)*".

The Court ruled, by Decision no. 297/2006[594], that "*the indication in the constitutional text itself regarding the way in which Parliament bodies may obtain the necessary acts and information from the Government and from the other public administration bodies excludes the possibility to regulate by other normative acts certain new measures in that respect. In other words, since the Constitution expressly and restrictively provides that acts and information may be obtained from those authorities by the Chamber of Deputies, by the Senate, or by parliamentary committees, through their presidents, as the legislature has no power to regulate also the direct access of Deputies and Senators to the data and acts referred to in Article 35 para. (1) i) of the law under review. The provision set forth in section j) of the law, which, under the name of political right, establishes the MPs' «right of access» in the institutions of public administration, is also unconstitutional, exceeding the provisions of Article 111 of the Constitution regarding the relationships between Parliament, Government and the other authorities of public administration, establishing a possible interference of the deputies and senators in the executive activity, being contrary to the principle of separation of powers enshrined in Article 1 para. (4) of the Constitution*"[595].

---

593 See *infra*.

594 Published in the Official Gazette of Romania no. 323 of 11 April 2006.

595 Thus, by Decision no. 46 of 17 May 1994, published in the Official Gazette of Romania no. 131 of 27 May 1994, the Court noted, regarding the Standing Order

The jurisdiction of the authorities involved in the procedure for the suspension of the President of Romania from office

Ruling on the limits of competence of the Constitutional Court in relation to those of Parliament regarding this procedure, the Court held that, "Even if one considers that only the Constitutional Court, given its role as guarantor for the supremacy of the Constitution, provided for in constitutional rules of Article 142 para. (1), may decide whether the charges brought against the President of Romania are to be considered as serious offences or violations of Constitution, Parliament cannot be prevented to exercise its right to suspend or not the President of Romania from office, regardless of positive or negative opinion expressed by the Constitutional Court, which opinion is purely advisory, as set by Article 146 h) of the Constitution. In the procedure for suspension of the President of Romania, governed by Article 95 of the Constitution, the Constitutional Court's role ends with the issuance of the advisory opinion. The effects of suspension consist of interruption of the presidential term until validation of the results of a referendum by the Constitutional Court."[596]

The jurisdiction of the authorities involved in the procedure regarding the prosecution of members of the Government

Proceeding similarly, by Decision no. 270/2008[597], delivered following the settlement of a legal dispute of a constitutional nature, the Constitutional Court grasped, from the interpretation of Article 109 paragraph (2) of the Constitution, reading as follows "*Solely the Chamber of Deputies, the Senate, and the President of Romania have the right to demand criminal prosecution be taken against Members of the Government for acts committed in the exercise of their office. Where criminal proceedings have been requested, the President of Romania may decree suspension from office. Indictment of a Member of the Government will result in his suspension from office. Jurisdiction for*

---

of the Senate that "*the provisions of Article 142 of the Standing Order, to the extent that it establishes a direct legal relationships between the Senator and the local public administrative authorities, county administration and decentralized public services in counties or county interest, are unconstitutional, taking into account the provisions of Article 110 of the Constitution, according to which Senators shall be informed by the Chamber, by the parliamentary committee or under their control, as provided in Article 141 of the Standing Order regarding the information by the central bodies of public administration. The statutory provision grants the right to information from the Chamber and the parliamentary committees to the Senator although it is an aspect of parliamentary control that cannot be conceived as a personal attribute of the Senator. Such a solution is contrary to the administrative autonomy and to the political pluralism at local level, as it would be exercised with reference to the confidential aspects concerning the drafting process of a decision, as well as to the detriment of the political option at local level, if different from that of the party to which the Senator belongs*".

596 Decision no. 730 of 9 July 2012, published in the Official Gazette of Romania no. 473 of 11 July 2012.

597 Published in the Official Gazette of Romania no. 290 of 15 April 2008.

trial belongs to the High Court of Cassation and Justice", the procedure to be followed and the jurisdiction of each of the authorities involved. The Court held that "*in the meaning of this constitutional provision, the submission of referral to one of the three authorities to require prosecution cannot be preferentially or randomly made by the Public Ministry – the Prosecution Office attached to the High Court of Cassation and Justice (...)* because (A/N) *cumulating the capacity as Deputy or Senator with that of Member of Government naturally draws after itself, according to Article 109 paragraph (2), the competence of the Chamber of Deputies or the Senate to require prosecution, as the case may be*". Consequently, "*the Prosecution Office attached to the High Court of Cassation and Justice must address one of the three authorities, as follows: a) the Chamber of Deputies or the Senate – for members of Government or former members of Government (Prime Minister, Minister of State, Minister, Minister Delegate, as the case may be) who at the time of referral, are also Deputies or Senators; b) the President of Romania – for members of Government or former members of Government (Prime Minister, Minister of State, Minister, Minister Delegate) who at the time of referral, are not also Deputies or Senators*". The Court concluded that the text of Article 109 paragraph (2) of the Constitution enshrines "*the absolute right of each of the three public authorities to demand prosecution and the exercise thereof by one of them cannot be detrimental to the other, the right of one not being subject to the right of the others*".

Unconstitutionality of acts by which Parliament may replace the judiciary
Settling legal disputes of a constitutional nature between the above-mentioned authorities, the Constitutional Court ruled that Parliament (the Chamber of Deputies or the Senate), as the supreme representative body of the Romanian people and the sole legislative authority of the country, cannot replace the judiciary or settle, by its own resolutions, disputes which fall within the competence of the courts of law. Likewise, the legislature cannot amend, suspend or cancel the effects of certain final and irrevocable judgments[598].

In this respect, within the *a priori* review, the Constitutional Court found the unconstitutionality of the legal provisions of the Law on preparatory measures regulating the legal status of certain properties transferred into State property after 23 August 1944, providing the suspension of the trials regarding the assets considered by the new legislation, pending before the courts of law, until the adoption of a new law[599]. The main argument of the solution delivered by the Court was that Parliament has no right to interfere in the exercise of the justice process.

Similarly, adjudicating upon a legal dispute of a constitutional nature between the judiciary, represented by the High Court of Cassation and Justice, and the

598 Article 8 of Law no. 76/2012: "Since the entry into force of the Code of Civil Procedure, references contained in the normative acts to judgments «final and irrevocable» or, as the case may be, «irrevocable» shall be understood as references to the «final» judgment.

599 Decision no. 6 of 11 November 1992, published in the Official Gazette of Romania no. 48 of 4 March 1993.

legislative authority, represented by the Senate of Romania, dispute triggered by the Senate's refusal to acknowledge the termination as of right of the capacity as Senator, as result of the final and irrevocable nature of the judgment establishing his state of incompatibility, the Court noted that "*the Senate does not have the constitutional power to achieve justice, namely to solve, applying the law, disputes between subjects of law as to the existence, extent and exercise of their subjective rights. Any interpretation which leads to the exercise of exclusive constitutional powers belonging to another public authority, as they are set out in Title III of the Basic Law, gives rise to a legal dispute of constitutional nature between those authorities*"[600].

Likewise, having noted the issues regarding the enforcement of judgments, as well as the two phases of the lawsuit: judicial phase and enforcement phase, and thus enforcement is therefore circumscribed to the notion of "lawsuit", and, in agreement with the case-law of the European Court of Human Rights, "*the right to a court would be illusory if a Contracting State's domestic legal system allowed a final, binding judicial decision to remain inoperative to the detriment of one party. It would be inconceivable that Article 6 para. 1 should describe in detail procedural guarantees afforded to litigants – proceedings that are fair, public and expeditious – without protecting the implementation of judicial decisions. [...] Execution of a judgment given by any court must therefore be regarded as an integral part of the trial for the purposes of Article 6" (Judgment of 19 March 1997 in Case Hornsby v. Greece, para. 40)*, the Court concluded that "by *submitting to the debate by the Senate the civil sentence no. 5153 of 16 September 2011 of the Bucharest Court of Appeal, final and irrevocable following rejection of the appeal by Judgment no. 3104 of 19 June 2012 of the High Court of Cassation and Justice, judgment that ascertains the state of incompatibility of Mr. Senator (...) followed by the negative vote in terms of enforcement of the judgment, the Senate has acted as a higher court, which affects the fundamental principle of the rule of law, namely the principle of separation and balance of powers – legislative, executive and judicial – within constitutional democracy, enshrined in Article 1(para 4) of the Basic Law*".

Moreover, the Court held that "*the assumption that a Chamber of Parliament, by virtue of its own standing orders, may censor under any aspect a definitive and irrevocable judgment, which has become res judicata, is tantamount to converting this authority into a judicial power, competing with the courts as regards administration of justice. Legitimacy of such an act would result in accepting the idea that in Romania there are individuals/institutions/authorities that do not have to enforce the judgments of the courts specified in the Constitution and the law, so they are above the law. Such an interpretation in terms of autonomy of standing orders is in obvious conflict with Article 1 para. (4), Article 16 para. (2), Article 61 para. (1), Article 124 and Article126 para. (1) of the Constitution*". From this perspective, the

600 Decision no. 972 of 21 November 2012, published in the Official Gazette of Romania no. 800 of 28 November 2012.

Court noted that by the negative vote on the state of incompatibility irrevocably established by a judgment, the Senate acted *ultra vires*, assuming powers that belonged to the judicial power.

Ruling on the behaviour of the legislative authority, represented by the Senate of Romania, which triggered the legal dispute of a constitutional nature, the Court noted that, in order to be consistent with the Constitution, it must refrain from any action which would have the effect of subrogation in another public authority's duties. Therefore, the Senate is obliged to acknowledge the existence of a state of incompatibility, according to the operative part of the final and irrevocable judgment given by any court.

Parliament's obligation regarding the unique interpretation of the law

In a similar situation, the Court ascertained the existence of a legal dispute of a constitutional nature between the judiciary, represented by the High Court of Cassation, and the legislative authority, represented by the Senate of Romania, by the latter's omission finalize the parliamentary procedure regarding the National Integrity Agency.

Referring to the behaviour to be followed in the given situation, the Court ruled that "*the Senate, in its plenary meeting, and not the Senate Committee for Legal Matters, Discipline, Immunities and Validations, is required to decide, by vote, on whether or not Mr (....) capacity as Senator ceases as result of declaration of his state of incompatibility by the National Integrity Agency, in compliance with the procedural provisions set forth in its own regulation on organization and functioning*". Noting that the decision of the Senate that will settle the matter is based on the provisions of Article 25 para. (2) second sentence of the Law no. 176/2010 regarding the integrity in the exercise of public offices, amending and completing Law no. 144/2007 regarding the organization and functioning of the National Integrity Agency and amending and supplementing other normative acts, legal text which provides that: "*If the person has occupied an elective position, he/she cannot occupy the same position for a period of three years from the cessation of the mandate*", and taking account of the two interpretations of the text in questions, the Constitutional Court has ascertained that the letter of the legislature must be consistent with its will. Consequently, the Court held that "*in order to decide whether the capacity as Senator ceases or not, the Parliament shall legally interpret, in advance, the above-mentioned provisions, in accordance with the provisions of Article 69 of Law no. 24/2000 regarding the rules of legislative technique for drafting normative acts, according to which: «(1) Legislative interventions aimed at clarifying the meaning of lawful norms shall be achieved by means of an interpretative normative act of the same level as the act considered, by means of interpretative provisions comprised in a new normative act, or by amending the provision whose meaning should be clarified. (2) The lawful interpretation made under paragraph (1) may confirm or, as applicable, deny or amend the judicial, arbitral or administrative interpretations adopted by that date, in observance of the rights acquired»*" – "*consequently, the Parliament of Romania shall initiate the legislative procedure for the purpose of adopting a law which interprets the provisions of Article 25 para. (2) of Law no. 176/2010*"[601].

Subsequently, being referred to with a case which brought again into question the interpretation of the same text of law and noting that until that moment, being contrary to Article 147 para. (4) of the Constitution, the Parliament has not adopted a law in order to clarify the meaning of the phrase "*the same office*" contained in Article 25 para. (2) second sentence of Law no. 176/2010, the Court proceeded to the circumstantiation of its meaning in accordance with the Constitution, holding that, although "in this hypothesis an inaction of the legislative authority is put into discussion, the Court, based on its role as guarantor for the supremacy of the Constitution, set forth in Article 142 (1) of the Basic Law, cannot ignore the flaw of unconstitutionality thus determined"; "in the absence of a law to clarify the meaning of the above-mentioned phrase, the Court held that the persistence of a rule, which, through its unclear nature, was likely to be subject to multiple interpretations, which could lead to diametrically different legal solutions in a key area of the rule of law – filling of elective offices –, was contrary to the constitutional principle of the obligation to observe the Constitution, its supremacy and the laws".

Thus, assuming that the intention of the legislature was to sanction the persons found to have violated the legal rules on incompatibilities or in the situation of a conflict of interests, without making any difference between the type of elective functions held, the Court finds that the assignment to the phrase "*the same office*" of the sole meaning of "office having generated the incompatibility or a conflict of interests" is likely to render ineffective the legal standard in question, contrary to the spirit of Law no. 176/2010. Consequently, in order to integrate the provisions of the second sentence of Article 25 (2) in the word and spirit of Law no. 176/2010 so that they should correspond to the real intention of the legislature at the time of their adoption, "their content must be interpreted as meaning that, once the existence of a state of incompatibility or a conflict of interests has been definitively ascertained, the respective person loses the right to hold any other elective office set forth in Article 1 of the law for a period of 3 years after the ending of the respective term of office"; "*in the word and spirit of the law, it can only subsist the interpretation that a person who has held, for example, the office of local or county councillor and on whom the incompatibility status or the breach of the conflict of interest were found, cannot hold, for a period of 3 years as from the cessation of the term office, in any other eligible office (for example, senator, deputy, mayor, local councillor, etc.)*". The Court upheld the exception of unconstitutionality raised in this and found that the provisions of the second sentence of Article 25 para. (2) of Law no. 176/2010 on integrity in the exercising of public offices and functions, amending and supplementing Law no. 144/2007 on the establishment, organisation and functioning of the National Integrity Agency, as well as amending and supplementing other normative acts,

---

601 Decision no. 460 of 13 November 2013, published in the Official Gazette of Romania no. 762 of 9 December 2013.

are constitutional in so far as the phrase "*the same office*" refers to all *elective offices* set forth in Article 1 of the same[602].

Observance of the Constitutional Court's decisions

In terms of the effects of the decisions and the obligations which, appropriately, fall within the legislative authority (be it the main legislature – Parliament – either the delegate one – the Government), Article 147 of the Constitution distinguishes by the nature of the duty in whose exercise it has been delivered the decision finding the unconstitutionality.

Thus, where the Court declares the unconstitutionality of laws, before their promulgation [Article 146 subparagraph a) of the Constitution], the Parliament must re-examine those provisions in order to bring them into accord with the Constitutional Court's decision[603]. In this respect, Law No. 47/1992 determines the Court's obligation to communicate the decision whereby it has found the law unconstitutional to the Presidents of both Chambers of Parliament and to the Prime Minister, in order to open the procedure for re-examination of the law, so as to comply with the provisions of Article 147 para. (2) of the Constitution, of Article 18 para. (3) of Law no. 47/1992, republished[604], as well as with the provisions contained in the Standing Orders of the two Chambers of Parliament[605]. The Constitution does not establish a deadline in which Parliament should proceed in order to eliminate unconstitutionality flaws found by the Constitutional Court, thus it cannot be compelled to legislate[606]. In 2010, however, the Chamber of Deputies amended its Standing Order[607], by incorporating a number of rules and time-limits as regards the procedure to be followed in the event of a finding of unconstitutionality of certain legal provisions by the Court (both within *a priori* and *a posteriori* review). Thus, according to Article 134 of the Chamber of Deputies' Standing Order, in cases of unconstitutionality of laws prior to their promulgation, and where the Chamber of Deputies was the first Chamber notified, the Standing Bureau, in its first meeting held after the publication of the Constitutional Court's decision in the Official Gazette of Romania, shall notify the Committee for Legal Affairs, Discipline, and Immunities and the specialized Standing Committee which was notified in first

---

602 Decision no. 418 of 3 July 2014, published in the Official Gazette of Romania no. 563 of 30 July 2014.

603 Article 147 para. (2) of the Constitution.

604 Republished in the Official Gazette of Romania no. 807 of 3 December 2010.

605 Decision shall be communicated to the President of Romania in order to avoid the promulgation of a law which has been found unconstitutional (and if it has been found the constitutionality of the impugned legal provisions, the President shall be able to promulgate the law within 10 days as from the date the decision of the Court has been communicated to him).

606 T. Drăganu, *Legal effects of the Constitutional Court's decisions in the light of the provisions of the revised Constitution*, in RDP no. 1/2004, p. 78.

607 Resolution no. 14/2010, published in the Official Gazette of Romania no. 397 of 15 June 2010.

instance with the draft law or the legislative proposal, in order to reconsider the provisions declared unconstitutional. The same procedure applies also in the situation where the relevant provisions are remitted by the Senate, having acted as the first Chamber notified. The deadline set by the Standing Bureau for the report drafting by the mentioned committees may not be longer than 15 days, such report shall be included in the agenda on a priority basis, and adopted with the majority required by the ordinary or organic nature of the legislative initiative subject to re-examination. Upon re-examination, the necessary technical-legislative correlations will be done and, after adoption, the re-examined provisions are sent to the Senate, if the latter is the decision-making Chamber.

In the event of a finding of unconstitutionality of a treaty or international agreement, based on Article 146 b) of the Constitution (that is, within an *a priori* review), such cannot be ratified[608]. As for the decision rendered under *a posteriori* review [according to Article 146 subparagraph d) of the Constitution], the Law No. 590/2003 on treaties[609] establishes in Article 40 paragraph (4), second sentence that if the Constitutional Court, in fulfilling its review powers, decides that the provisions of a treaty which is in force are unconstitutional, the Ministry of Foreign Affairs, together with the ministry or institution under whose jurisdiction falls the main area regulated by that treaty, shall take steps, within 30 days, to initiate the necessary procedures for the treaty renegotiation or validity termination as against the Romanian party or, as applicable, for the revision of the Constitution.

In case of an *a posteriori* review, the provisions of laws and ordinances in force, and those of regulations found to be unconstitutional, shall cease their legal effects within 45 days from publication of the Constitutional Court's decision if, during this period, the Parliament or Government, as the case may be, do not bring the unconstitutional provisions in line with the provisions of the Constitution. During this period, the provisions found unconstitutional are suspended de jure. The decision of the Constitutional Court in respect of the Regulations of Parliament shall be notified to the Chamber whose Regulations have been examined so that, where certain provisions thereof have been found unconstitutional, such may take steps to re-examine these provisions within 45 days, in order to bring them into accord with the provisions of the Constitution. Decisions whereby the Court has found laws, ordinances or provisions of laws or ordinances in force as being unconstitutional shall be communicated to the two Chambers of Parliament and to the Government, as well as – for information purposes – to the public authorities concerned. The only sanction for failure to comply with the deadline of 45 days, and with the obligation set forth by the constitutional norm of reference, is that the text found to be unconstitutional shall cease its legal effects upon expiry.

608 Article 147 para. (3) of the Constitution.

609 Published in the Official Gazette of Romania no. 23 of 12 January 2004.

Pursuant to Article 136 of the Chamber of Deputies' Standing Order[610], in cases of unconstitutionality of provisions of the laws and ordinances in force, as well as of those of Regulations which pursuant to Article 147 paragraph (1) of the Constitution cease their legal effects within 45 days from the publication of the Constitutional Court's decision, term during which these are suspended de jure, and in the event that the Chamber of Deputies was the first Chamber notified, the Chamber's Standing Bureau shall notify the Committee for Legal Affairs, Discipline, and Immunities, and also the specialized standing Committee under whose scope of activity the respective legal norm falls, in order to re-examine the provisions, thus harmonizing them with the provisions of the Constitution. The reviewed provisions shall be included in a legislative initiative, which is distributed to the Deputies and, after expiry of the 7-day deadline, inside which amendments may be submitted, the two committees shall, no later than 5 days, draft a report on that legislative initiative, which is taken for debate and adoption by the Plenary of the Chamber of Deputies. Such legislative initiative must be adopted with the majority required by the nature of the legal norm in question and thereafter sent to the Senate.

The Court ruled on the extension and the content of the procedure for the re-examination of the law, for example, by Decision no. 975/2010[611], holding that "*the decision whereby the objection of unconstitutionality was partially upheld led to the initiation as of right of the complementary procedure of re-examination of the law by Parliament in order to bring into line the unconstitutional provisions with the decision of the Constitutional Court, according to Article 147 paragraph (2) of the Basic Law. In this procedure, Parliament can amend also other legal provisions only if they are in inseparable connection with the provisions declared as unconstitutional, to ensure consistency of regulation and, as far as necessary, it will re-correlate other provisions of the law in question (...)However, within the review procedure governed by Article 147 paragraph (2) of the Constitution, Parliament has no constitutional power to change the legal provisions found to be constitutional, but it can only bring into line the unconstitutional provisions with the decisions of the Constitutional Court; certainly, as noted above, Parliament can amend also other legal provisions only if they are in inseparable connection with the provisions declared as unconstitutional. Therefore, «other improvements» that would cover only the impugned law can be operated only by other laws or ordinances for modification and supplementation*".

In practice, one may note that the timely reaction of the primary or delegated law-maker in regard of modification of the law (or of the other act declared unconstitutional) and its harmonization with the Basic Law, in accordance with the Constitutional Court's decision, also depends on the constitutionally loyal conduct

---

610 Republished in the Official Gazette of Romania no. 762 of 13 November 2012, pursuant to Article II of the Resolution no. 7/2011 of the Chamber of Deputies on the amendment and supplementation of the Standing Order of the Chamber of Deputies, published in the Official Gazette of Romania no. 262 of 13 April 2011.

611 Published in the Official Gazette of Romania no. 568 of 11 August 2010.

of these authorities. The Constitutional Court cannot compel them to legislate, neither can it substitute them for purposes of amending or supplementing the norm whose constitutionality has been reviewed. That because, in every instance of adjudication on normative acts being submitted to review, the Court's examination is exclusively related to issues of constitutionality, Article 2 paragraph (2) of Law No. 47/1992 establishing in this respect that the provisions of acts that are being subject to review by the Court, and which infringe the provisions or principles of the Constitution, are unconstitutional. The Court cannot amend or supplement the legal texts impugned, therefore it cannot replace the legislator, it cannot interpret and apply these texts in the instant cases, thus not being able to substitute itself for the ordinary courts or the High Court of Cassation and Justice, which, according to Article 126 paragraph (3) of the Constitution, "*ensures the uniform interpretation and application of the laws by all other courts, according to its competence*"; likewise, it cannot proceed to comparing legal norms to each other or to relating the conclusion that would arise from such comparison, to constitutional texts and principles.

In this context, one should mention a few situations when the Constitutional Court of Romania was requested to look into how the Romanian Parliament brought a law in accord with the decision handed down within its *a priori* review. Thus, by Decision No. 419/2005 [612], upon request by the President of Romania concerning the manner in which the Romanian Parliament brought in line the provisions of the Law on reform in the areas of property and justice as well as certain adjacent measures, with the Decision No. 375/2005[613], the Court found that such harmonization had been accomplished.

In other instances, the Court found that the flaws of unconstitutionality had been perpetuated in the new normative act adopted by Parliament, for which reason it declared also the new text as being unconstitutional. Thus, by Decision no. 1018/2010[614], taking into consideration its previous decision (no. 415/2010) and the Parliament's obligation to adjust the unconstitutional provisions with those of the Basic Law, the Court decided that "*adoption by the legislature of norms contrary to what the Constitutional Court established by its decision, whereby it tends to maintain the legislative solution tainted by unconstitutionality flaws, is contrary to the Basic Law. However, in a State of law, such as Romania has been proclaimed in Article 1 paragraph (3) of the Constitution, public authorities do not enjoy any autonomy in relationship to law, as the Constitution establishes in Article 16 paragraph (2) that nobody is above the law, and in Article 1 paragraph (5) that compliance with the Constitution, its supremacy and the laws shall be obligatory*".

The analysis of these effects raises the question of the effectiveness of constitutional justice, which is reflected in how the acts of the Constitutional Court are observed and enforced. In this respect, it was claimed that "*the effectiveness of decisions has*

612 Official Gazette of Romania no. 653 of 22 July 2005.
613 Official Gazette of Romania no. 591 of 8 July 2005.
614 Official Gazette of Romania no. 511 of 22 July 2010.

been and is closely related to the loyal behaviour of constitutional authorities". Since this behaviour involves a wide discretion and a component of relativity, we consider that legislative intervention is necessary in the sense of expressly enshrining certain mechanisms of enforcement or certain sanctions for the failure to comply with the Constitutional Court's decisions.

Presenting in this regard a brief examination of comparative law, we note that, in some European countries, even the constitutional courts can play a role in designating the competent body to enforce its decision or / and to establish the way in which it shall be enforced[615].

Thus, in *Austria*, enforcement of decisions rendered by the Constitutional Court is implemented by the ordinary courts or by the Federal President, according to the distinctions made in the Federal Constitution. Where the Federal President is the one authorized to enforce such decisions, then the request to the President has to be made by the Constitutional Court. Furthermore, the enforcement shall lie, in accordance with the President's instructions, with the Federal or the Länder authorities, including the Federal Army, appointed at his discretion for the purpose.

In *Croatia*, the Government ensures the enforcement of the Court's decisions and rulings through the bodies of the central administration. The Court itself may determine which body shall be tasked for the enforcement of its decision or its ruling, as well as the manner in which the decision or ruling must be enforced. Consequently, the Court in fact orders the competent bodies to implement general and/ or individual measures which derive of its decisions. At the same time, the Court is authorized to indicate the procedure, the deadlines and the specific means for the enforcement of its decisions (Russia), but it may also place an obligation on the competent state bodies to ensure enforcement of its decision or observance of its opinion (Ukraine).

In *Germany*, usually the Federal Constitutional Court may ensure the enforcement of its decisions by its own means; thus, it may establish, in that decision, by which it is to be enforced and the method of enforcement and it may order the measures required to effectively "enforce" its decisions. The Court is also entitled to task individuals, authorities or organs which are subject to the German State power to carry out concrete enforcement measures. Therefore, the Court knows two forms regarding the assignment of the enforcement tasks: the Court may either task a body in general terms to enforce its decisions and leave it to implement the execution measures at its own discretion, or the Court may entrust a body with a concrete execution measure which is precisely determined, and hence make the tasked party "the executing body" of the Court. Inasmuch as it may be necessary, the Court may also commission other bodies to implement temporary injunctions.

615 Examples can be find on the website *www.ccr.ro* – XVth Congress of the European Constitutional Courts, General Report, Part I – *Constitutional Court's relationship to Parliament and Government*, authors: T. Toader, M. Safta.

In *Serbia*, the Constitution has also vested the Constitutional Court with the power to issue a special ruling regulating the manner in which its decision will be enforced and which is also binding. Enforcement is either made directly or via a competent state administration authority in the manner laid down in the Constitutional Court ruling. The Court may determine which authority should implement the decision and the manner of implementation, if necessary. This practically entails an authorisation for the Constitutional Court to fill the legal gap arising from its finding of unconstitutionality. In terms of their legal nature, such a decision differs from those rendered within the constitutional review.

In the case of the *amparo* constitutional review, the organic Law of the Constitutional Tribunal of Spain provides that it may order "*who shall bear the responsibility to enforce judgment and, as the case may be, resolve the incidents arising in the course of enforcement*." Executory provisions may also be included in the decision passed or in any other subsequent acts. The Tribunal may also declare null any decision that would go against the one being handed down in the exercise of its powers when enforcing such decisions.

2.4 The Constitutional Court – "positive and specific co-legislator"[616]

2.4.1 Introductive considerations

Apart from the examination of the relationships and the implicit dialogue of the Constitutional Court in cases specifically determined, we will analyze in this chapter an issue which concerns the development of the activity of the Constitutional Court of Romania (which reflects similar developments at international level) and which departs it from its traditional status of "negative legislator".

Thus, the acts delivered by constitutional courts/Courts/Tribunals/Councils in exercising their duties have a specific legal regime determined, on the one hand, by the status of these authorities and, on the other hand, by the fact that the effects produced by these acts are enshrined in the Basic Laws of States. In Romania, the generally binding nature of the Constitutional Court's decisions is constitutionally enshrined and these decisions apply to all subjects of law, just as the normative acts, unlike court judgements, which produce *inter partes litigantes*

616 The phrase belongs to Professor Ion Deleanu, see, in this regard, I. Deleanu, *The dialogue of judges*, in RRDJ no. 1/2012, p. 36; see also: I. Deleanu, S. Deleanu, *Case-law and jurisprudential upturn*, Essay, Universul Juridic Publishing House, Bucharest, 2013, p. 71; M. Safta, *Developments in the constitutional review. Constitutional Court between the status of negative legislator and the status of positive co-legislator*, in the review of the International Conference "Perspectives of business law in the third millennium", volume I, no. 1/2012, pp. 1–21.

effects[617]. Similarly, in Poland and Serbia, decisions of Constitutional Courts have generally binding effect. In Germany, an *erga omnes* effect is fully established in case of abstract and concrete constitutional review of laws, as well as of individual complaints of unconstitutionality aimed at normative acts. The force of law is attributed to these decisions. Likewise, in Austria, decisions delivered within the constitutional review exercised on normative acts have *erga omnes* effects[618].

Given the aforementioned, even if the acts of Constitutional Courts are generically described as "*case-law*" a common concept used to describe the totality of judgments delivered by courts at all levels, a distinction must be made in relation to their value as source of law9 [619]. It was stated[620] in that respect, with reference to the role of constitutional jurisdiction bodies and the effects of acts delivered by the same, that, by their case-law, "*have determined a rearrangement of traditional positions occupied by the time of their emergence by other judicial and political agents. In these circumstances, the legislator does no longer hold the monopoly over the formation of national will. The classical concept that the law is the work of Parliament is now obsolete*". This is because, in exercising their powers, Constitutional Courts do more than simply a certification that the disputed legal provisions are or are not in accordance with the Constitution.

In stating the grounds for the acts delivered, the Courts establish principles and rules, delimitate powers of public authorities, give guidance and solution in relation to the interpretation of both the Constitution and the infraconstitutional legislation[621] and even "repair", in accordance with the constitutional norms, legislative omissions.

Thus, Constitutional Courts belonging to the European model depart more and more from their traditional role as "negative legislator" – which refers to the effect of their acts consisting in removal from the legal system of those rules contrary to the Basic Law – as long as, officially interpreting the Constitution, reveal the

617 This category does not include the decisions of the High Court of Cassation and Justice, rendered following the resolution of appeals on points of law, which have a separate legal regime.

618 For details, see *www.ccr.ro* – the XVth Congress of European Constitutional Courts, General Report, V.Z. Puskas, Benke Karoly, *Enforcement of Constitutional Court's Decisions.*

619 in the Romanian law system, courts' case-law is not a creative source of law but it is, as stressed by some authors (I. Deleanu, *cited paper*, p. 25) – "*«normative force», within the meaning of this phrase attributed to «guide», the «model», the «reference», the «benchmark» for legal practice, doctrine and legislature*"– see the reference to C. Thibierge *et alii*, *La force normative. Naissance d'un concept*, LGDJ, Bruylant, 2009.

620 C. Gilia, *The theory of the rule of law*, C.H. Beck Publishing House, Bucharest, 2007, p. 272.

621 For example: The Constitution Court of Austria, Estonia, Lithuania, Romania or Hungary.

content of constitutional and even infraconstitutional rules, whose effects "are nothing but specific forms of «impulse» or «coercion» of the legislator to proceed in a certain sense"[622], guide the development of the entire legal system[623]. 13The powers entrusted to the constitutional jurisdiction bodies through the Constitutions of States and their active position in benefiting of these powers leads to a situation – as noted – where the law is no longer the exclusive product of Parliament and, under certain circumstances, of Government, but, at the same time, of Constitutional Courts, which have become "*actors of the complex law-making process*"[624].

2.4.2 "Correction" of legislative omissions through constitutional case-law

The Court seems to have a more activist behaviour, on the verge of the lawmaking, by the "correction" of legislative omissions. This occurs in those situations where the primary or delegated legislature fails to comply with its positive obligation of enacting rules achieving the constitutional requirements. It is a different situation from that concerning the legislature's negative obligation – to refrain from enacting rules contrary to the constitutional provisions.

Neither the Constitution nor the organic law of the Constitutional Court of Romania enshrine *expressis verbis* a power of the Constitutional Court to correct the legislative omissions or gaps. In fact, the same situation occurs in most States that enshrine the same model of constitutional review[625], except for Portugal, whose Constitution provides, under Article 283.1, the power of the Constitutional Court to review legislative omissions. Nonetheless, some Constitutional Courts established, in their case-law, by means of interpretation of the principles specifically or implicitly provided in the Constitutions, their power to correct such omissions.

The case-law of the Constitutional Court of Romania includes, in relation to the legislative omissions problem, two classes of decisions: the first category, the most representative in terms of number, is that of decisions in which the exceptions of unconstitutionality of alleged legislative omissions are rejected as inadmissible; the second category is that of decisions where legislative omission was the argument for finding the unconstitutionality of certain legal provisions. We will refer only to the latter category, which is particularly interesting from the perspective of this study, and which reflects the existing trends in the case-law of other European

622 I. Deleanu, *cited paper*, p. 36.

623 The XIVth Congress of the Conference of the European Constitutional Courts – *Problems of legislative omission in constitutional jurisdiction*, Vilnius, 2009 – General Report published by the Constitutional Court of the Republic of Lithuania, p. 51; as concerns the Conference of the European Constitutional Courts, Congresses and published reports, see *https://www.vfgh.gv.at/cms/vfgh-kongress/fr/index.html.*

624 C. Gilia, *cited paper*, p. 273.

625 The XIVth Congress of the Conference of the European Constitutional Courts – *Problems of legislative omission in constitutional jurisdiction*, Vilnius, 2009 – General Report published by the Constitutional Court of the Republic of Lithuania.

Constitutional Courts (Italy, Poland, Spain, Czech Republic, Germany, Hungary), respectively that to eliminate legislative omissions, essentially considered as having significance of inadequate execution of the legislature's obligation to establish rules imposed by the Constitution.

In this respect, the Court found that the provisions of Article 54 para. (2) of the Family Code *are unconstitutional to the extent that* they only acknowledge the father's, and not also the mother's and the child's born in wedlock the right to commence an action to disclaim paternity. The Court held that the enshrining "*through the provisions of Article 54 para. (2) under the Family Code, of the right to contest the presumed paternity only in favour of the presumed father, excluding the mother and the child born in wedlock, equally entitled to the legitimate interest to promote such action, represents an infringement of the principle of equal rights provided by Article 16 para. (1) of the Constitution. (...)Likewise, the provisions under Article 54 of the Family Code, to the extent in which they refuse the acknowledgement for the mother of the right to disclaim the presumed paternity, contravene also the provisions under Article 44 para. (1) of the Constitution* (in its wording prior to revision, A/N) *which enshrines the equality between spouses as one of the principles on which the family institution is based on. (...)The Court also holds that the impugned text contravenes also paragraph 2 of Article 26 of the Constitution, to the extent in which it does not acknowledge also the child's right to contest the presumed paternity, circumstance meant to impose him/her a certain legal status established through somebody else's will, which he/she must accept passively, without being able to take action for the modification thereof, which can only represent a denial of the right acknowledged for each and every natural person, through the constitutional article abovementioned, to freely dispose of himself/herself. The Court considers that the acknowledgement, in favour of the child, of the right to contest the presumed paternity, as an expression of the constitutional right of each and every person to freely dispose of himself/herself, does not encroach upon the rights and freedoms of others, on public order, or morals, and, therefore, it finds no justification for the infringement of the constitutional provision. Therefore, the non acknowledgement, as concerns the child, of the right to establish his/her own affiliation towards father, in concordance with the reality, against a fiction, right acknowledged though to the presumed father, represents an obvious breach of the constitutional text*"[626].

2.4.3 The constitutional review of repealing norms

2.4.3.1 General aspects

Another issue concerning the delimitation of powers between Parliament and the Constitutional Court aims at making a distinction between the repeal of the legal norm and the ascertainment of its unconstitutionality.

626 Decision no. 349 of 19 December 2001, published in the Official Gazette of Romania no. 240 of 10 April 2002.

The authorities which may require the repeal, respectively the ascertainment of the unconstitutionality are different, which determines that also the legal effects produced in these situations to be different. The debates on this issue, which we consider useful to approach in the context of the dialogue between Parliament and the Constitutional Court, appeared with reference to the ascertainment of the unconstitutionality of the norms which have repealed the provisions of the Criminal Code on insult and libel. The considerations below are meant to emphasize these effects in a particular case, determined by the non-compliance with a decision of the Constitutional Court and the intervention of the Constitutional Court in the re-establishment of constitutional status, within the alternative examination of the limits of intervention of the legislature in order to bring into accord the provisions found unconstitutional with the provisions of the Constitution.

2.4.3.2 Repeal – concept, regulation, effects

Law no. 24/2000 regarding the rules of legislative technique for drafting normative acts[627] defines repeal as a "*legislative event*", thus providing for in Article 58 para. (1), that "*after a normative act has come into effect, throughout the duration of its existence, various legislative events may take place, such as: amendments, additions, repeals, republishing, suspension, or others similar*".

Repeal is described under Article 64 para. (1) of the same law, according to which: "*The provisions comprised in a normative act that are contrary to a new regulation of the same level or of a higher level, shall be repealed. Repeal may be total or partial*". It results that the repeal is the legislative event which consists in the cessation of the effects of the legal norm determined by the entry into force of a new norm, being the expression of a new manifestation of the legislature's will[628].

As it is a legislative event, the repeal shall be ordered by the legislature through a normative act, thus, in this respect, Article 58 para. (3) of Law no. 24/2000 stipulates that "*legislative events may be ordered by subsequent normative acts of the same or higher level, whose sole subject-matter is that event, but also by other subsequent normative acts which mainly regulate a certain number of topics, and, as a related measure, order such events in order to ensure the correlation of the two interfering normative acts*". This is the situation of an explicit repeal whose form and substantive requirements are provided for in Article 65 of Law no. 24/2000, according to which: "*(1) A repeal may be ordered, as a rule, by means of a distinct provision at the end of a normative act regulating a certain number of topics, if it should affect prior normative provisions, related to the last regulation.(2) Within the operations aimed at systematising and unifying the legislation, distinct normative acts of repeal may*

627 Published in the Official Gazette of Romania no. 260 of 21 April 2010.

628 See: I. Vida, *Formal legistics – Introduction to technical and legislative procedure*, Universul Juridic Publishing House, Bucharest, 2012, pp. 135–143; D.C. Dănişor, I. Dogaru, G. Dănişor, *General theory of law*, C.H. Beck Publishing House, Bucharest, 2006, pp. 329–332.

be drawn up and adopted, whose sole subject-matter is the repeal of several normative acts. (3) In view of the repeal, the normative provisions being contemplated shall be expressly determined, starting with the laws and then continuing with the other normative acts, by mentioning all their identification data". However, the repeal may also be implicit, noting in this respect the provisions of Article 67 of the same normative act – "Implicit legislative event" –, which establishes, in para. (1), that: "*In special cases, where the identification of all contrary norms has not been possible when drawing up and adopting a regulation, one may presume they have made the subject-matter of their implicit amendment, supplementation or repeal*".

As concerns the effects determined by the repeal, Article 64 para. (3) of Law no. 24/2000 provides that: "*The repeal of a provision or normative act shall be final. It shall not be permissible for the repeal of a prior repealing act to reinstate the original normative act. Government ordinances having stipulated repealing norms, which have been rejected by the Parliament, by law, are an exception to this*". It is certainly a solution required by reasons of legal certainty. The beneficiaries of the law should know exactly the norm which they must comply with and not to seek and infer the legislature's will from a possible series of "*repeals of the repeals*". Even in the case of implicit repeal, "The Legislative Council shall have the obligation to identify all the lawful provisions having undergone implicit legislative events and to propose the necessary steps for their express amendment, supplementation or repeal to the Parliament and the Government, respectively" [Article 67 para. (2) of Law no. 24/2000].

The repealing norms may be subject to constitutional review as any other legal norms, the only requirements are related to the level of regulation of the acts concerned [laws and ordinances, according to the distinctions set forth in Article 146 a) and d) of the Constitution, respectively parliamentary Standing Orders, according to Article 146 c) of the Constitution]. In this respect there is also an established case-law of the Constitutional Court, which, being vested with exceptions of unconstitutionality of certain such norms, began their constitutional review, noting that "*Article 146 d) of the Constitution makes no exception for the repealing legal provisions in terms of constitutional review*"[629].

2.4.3.3 Decisions ascertaining the unconstitutionality of the repealing norms

An inventory of all the situations where the repealing provisions were subject to constitutional review would not be useful in terms of this study, so we will refer only to the situations in which there were upheld exceptions of unconstitutionality covering repealing norms and to the effects of those decisions, as they were mentioned even by the Constitutional Court.

Thus, by Decision no. 20 of 2 February 2000[630], the Court ascertained the unconstitutionality of the provisions of Article 198 of Law on public pension system and

---

629 Decision no. 62 of 18 January 2007, published in the Official Gazette of Romania no. 104 of 12 February 2007.

630 Published in the Official Gazette of Romania no. 72 of 18 February 2000.

other social insurance rights, repealing Article 103 of Law no. 92/1992 on the judicial organisation. On that occasion, the Constitutional Court held that "*this repeal of the legal regulation relating to the Service Pension of Magistrates is contrary to the current requirements which important international documents directly expresses on the Rights of magistrates, given the importance of their role in defending the rule of law*".

By Decision no. 62 of 18 January 2007[631], ascertaining the unconstitutionality of the Provisions of Article I section 56 of Law no. 278/2006 amending and supplementing the Criminal Code, as well as amending and supplementing other laws, the part referring to the repeal of Articles 205, 206 and 207 of the Criminal Code, the Court essentially held that, by the decriminalization of the crimes of insult and calumny "*it was created an inadmissible legislative lacuna, contrary to the constitutional provision that guarantees human dignity as a supreme. In absence of the legal protection provided for by Articles 205, 206 and 207 of the Criminal Code, human dignity, honour and reputation do not benefit of any other form of real and adequate legal protection*".

By Decision no. 778 of 12 May 2009[632], the Court ascertained the unconstitutionality of the provisions of Article I section 4 of the Government Ordinance no. 34/2001 amending and supplementing Law no. 146/1997 on judicial stamp duty, text repealing Article 15 f^1) of this law providing the exemption from payment of judicial stamp duty of actions and applications, including those for the exercise of appeals, concerning the ascertainment and granting of indemnities for non-material damage prejudicial to the honour, dignity or reputation of an individual. As grounds for the delivered solutions, it was claimed that the repealing violates the provisions of Article 1 para. (3) and of Article 21 para. (1) and (2) of the Constitution of Romania, as well as of Article 6 of the Convention for the Protection of Human Rights and Fundamental Freedoms, the Court held that the repealed norm represented a particular way of legal protection of those features of the human personality – defined in Article 1 para. (3) of the Constitution of Romania as supreme values in the rule of law.

By Decision no. 783 of 12 May 2009[633], ascertaining the unconstitutionality of the provisions of Article I section 185 of Law no. 356/2006 amending and supplementing the Code of Criminal Procedure, as well as amending other laws, the Court held that "*the repeal of section 17^1 of Article 385^9 para. (1) of the Code of Criminal Procedure, by eliminating the possibility to challenge a judgment, through appeal, on the grounds that it is contrary to the law or that there was a wrongful application of the law, deprives the party concerned of any possibility to effectively exercise its violated right.. (...) the repeal of section 17^1 of Article 385^9 para. (1) of the Code of Criminal Procedure ensures the existence of the legal remedy only for some of the cases of violation of the criminal substantive law, listed in sections 12- 17, 19 and 20 of the same article, and*

631 Published in the Official Gazette of Romania no. 104 of 12 February 2007.
632 Published in the Official Gazette of Romania no. 465 of 6 July 2009.
633 Published in the Official Gazette of Romania no. 404 of 15 June 2009.

on the other hand, it creates a regulatory vacuum in what concerns the dismantling of the illegal judgment when the civil law is violated".

By Decision no. 694 of 20 May 2010[634], the Court found unconstitutional the provisions of Law no. 356/2006 Article I section 184 amending and supplementing the Criminal Procedure Code, as well as amending other laws concerning the amendment of the provisions of Article 385^9 para. (1) section 12 of the Criminal Procedure Code, holding that "*the elimination from the Romanian procedural legislation of the possibility of challenging a judgment by means of appeal when the constitutive elements of a crime are not fulfilled generates inability to repair the consequences which could be caused by a possible erroneous conviction*".

By Decision no. 1039 of 5 December 2012[635], ascertaining the unconstitutionality of Law no. 299/2011 in its whole, was substantiated on the fact that "*the elimination by Law no. 299/2011 of procedural means which allowed the re-opening of certain trials settled through an irrevocable judgment, but during which the European Union law was violated, means which ensured the unitary enforcement of the European law, as it should have been interpreted since its entry into force, is susceptible to infringe the obligation undertaken by the Romanian Stated through the Accession Act, obligation provided for in Article 4 para. (3) of the Treaty on the European Union and guaranteed by Article 148 para. (4) of the Constitution*".

Developing such arguments in Decision no. 206 of 29 April 2013[636], which refers *in extenso* to the issues regarding the effects of the decisions ascertaining the unconstitutionality of the repealing norms, the Court indicated that "*in such cases, it is not about a «repeal of the repeal» in order to deem applicable the provisions of Article 64 para. (3) second sentence of the Law no. 24/2000 according to which «Repeal of a previous repealing act cannot result in reinstatement of the initial normative act»– provisions binding on the legislature in the law-making activity – but about a specific effect of the decision finding unconstitutional a repealing provision, effect based on the constitutional provisions of Article 142 (1) that enshrine the Constitutional Court's role as guarantor of the supremacy of the Constitution and of Article 147 (4) stating that the Court's decisions are generally binding*".

2.4.3.4 The effects of ascertaining the unconstitutionality of the repealing norms

The above-mentioned reasons, especially in the context of Decision no. 62/2007 delivered by the Constitutional Court ascertaining the unconstitutionality of the provisions of Article I section 56 of Law no. 278/2006 amending and supplementing the Criminal Code, as well as amending and supplementing other laws, the part referring to the repeal of Article 25, 206 and 207 of the Criminal Code, were examined in the legal specialized literature, certain viewpoints being in line with

634 Published in the Official Gazette of Romania no. 392 of 14 June 2010.
635 Published in the Official Gazette of Romania no. 61 of 29 January 2013.
636 Published in the Official Gazette of Romania no. 350 of 13 June 2013.

those held by the Constitutional Court, whilst others approached them from a critical point of view.

Thus, certain authors[637] reveal the effects of the decisions finding the unconstitutionality of repealing norms, as they were circumstantiated by the Constitutional Court, indicating that "under the conditions that any new normative act has not been adopted until now by the Parliament of Romania, following the admission of the exception of unconstitutionality, a new normative act regarding the offences against dignity, and given the fact that the period of 45 days provided by the Constitution is exceeded, the provisions of Article I section 56 of Law no. 278/2006 shall no longer take effects. Therefore, Articles 205, 206 and 207 of the Criminal Code remain in force, in the wording prior to the repeal (...). We should note that by this decision the Constitutional Court re-established the constitutional and legal normality".

Similarly, another study[638] found that "*by Decision no. 62/2007 adopted by the Constitutional Court by majority vote, the court ruled that the repeal of Articles 205, 206 and 207 of the Criminal Code is unconstitutional. As a consequence, these criminalizations have automatically re-entered into force*". Further, in a critical approach of the separate opinion formulated in this case, it was noted that "*the constitutional obligativity of a fundamental right cannot be at the legislature's discretion, which would lie outside the Constitution in this case. Alongside with the laws of other democratic states, the case-law of the Constitutional Court and certain authors consider as useful the criminalization of insult and libel*"[639].

The same effects of Constitutional Court's decisions finding the unconstitutionality of the repealing norms are implicitly supported by the authors who have challenged the criminalization of insult and libel and the limitation in this way of the freedom of expression[640].

There were also expressed viewpoints which challenged the solution adopted by the Constitutional Court[641], expressing them in the sense that "*(...) the repeal of Articles 205–206 of the Criminal Code, being declared unconstitutional, Articles I*

---

637 I. Muraru, M.N. Vlădoiu, *Protection of human dignity as a constitutional value*, in RDP nr. 3/2007, p. 7.

638 I. Lascu, *Reflections on the crimes of insult and libel*, in Criminal Law Review no. 2/2008, p. 127.

639 V. Dabu, *Constitutionality of repealing provisions which criminalise insult and libel*, in Dreptul no. 6/2007, pp. 167–197.

640 M.C. Sima, *Limitation of free of expression*, in Criminal Law Review no. 3/2007, p. 182, with a *Note* on behalf of the Editorial Board, signed by G. Antoniu, in which it is argued, inter alia, that "*the criminal sanction of such acts* (A/N, insult and libel) *was more effective than civil and contravention sanctions, given the frequency of these events, the real possibility of turning quickly into more serious offences of physical or mental violence, as well as the danger to recourse to acts of private justice by those dissatisfied, which would seriously disturb law and relationships of social life*".

641 E.S. Tănăsescu, *Commentary on the Constitutional Court's Decision no. 62/2007*, in Judicial Courier no. 4/2007, p. 12.

section 56 of Law no. 278/2006 has become inapplicable. However, this finding does not produce the legal effect of not being into force of the said legal provisions and it does affect in any way other provisions of other normative acts, which ceased their existence before the delivery of the decision by the Constitutional Court. What has been referred to the constitutional review was not the Criminal Code, but Law no. 278/2006, therefore, the Court could not rule upon the Criminal Code, but only upon the law that decriminalized offences of insult and defamation from the Criminal Code". Likewise, it is also noted and that *"following the ascertainment of the unconstitutionality of the repealing normative act, in its capacity of negative legislature, the Constitutional Court cannot establish the re-entry into force of repealed legal norms, because, in this way, the express and imperative provisions of Article 62 para. (3) of Law no. 24/2000 on the rules of legislative technique for drafting normative acts are violated".*

It was also claimed[642] that "*however, the repeal can be done in several ways, and the repealing way chosen by the legislature is reflected on the Constitutional Court's competence. Thus, if the legal norm is repealed by its repeal with another norm, the Court's competence is limited to the constitutional review of the content of the new regulation. In this case, the effect of declaring the repealing norm unconstitutional is that Parliament will have to bring into accord the norm with the provisions of the Constitution, within 45 days, the non-compliance shall lead to the cessation of the legal effects of the norm. However, the situation is different if the repealing norm simply abolishes the previous norm without replacing it with any other norm. Thus, the Court has basically no content of a new norm to report to the constitutional provisions. Consequently, the Court shall have to rule whether or not it may decide upon the omissions of the legislature". The same author considers that "the legal norm cannot be re-entered into force unless it complies with the principle of parallel forms and competences, namely by same body, expressing the same will and in the same form".*

Referring to Decision no. 62/2007 of the Constitutional Court and, from this perspective, as concerns the effects of the Constitutional Court's decisions ascertaining the unconstitutionality of the repealing norms, the courts of law have a non-uniform practice. Thus, some courts of law held that the provisions of Articles 205, 206 and 207 of the Criminal Code are in force as a consequence of this decision, whilst other courts of law considered that the decision does not take such effect[643].

642 G. Gîrleşteanu, *Considerations on Decision no. 1039 of 5 December 2012 on the exception of unconstitutionality of the provisions of Law no. 299/2011 repealing para. (2) of Article 21 of Law no. 554/2004 on administrative contentious and of Article 21 para. (2) first sentence of Law no. 554/2004 on administrative contentious*, in PR no. 3/2013, p. 109, also with reference to D.C. Dănişor, S. Răduleţu, *Commentary on the Constitutional Court's Decision no. 62 of 18 January 2007*, in Judicial Courier no. 3/2007, pp. 14–21, and M. Nica, *Commentary on the Decision of the High Court of Cassation and Justice, Criminal Section, no. 2203 of 4 June 2010*, in PR no. 1/2011, p. 175.

643 Decision no. 1148/2008 of Prahova Tribunal, *apud* D. Rebegea, *Legal effects of the Constitutional Court's Decision no. 62/2007 regarding persons' criminal responsibility*

This non-unitary practice gave rise to the delivery of Decision no. 8 of 18 October 2010 by the High Court of Cassation and Justice, in the United Sections[644], a decision which marks the only inconsistency of the Supreme Court on the recognition of the effects of decisions finding the unconstitutionality of repealing rules as these effects were circumstantiated by the Constitutional Court[645]. It is found that subsequent to Decision No. 8/2010, the High Court of Cassation and Justice returned, for the settlement of appeals on points of law, on its case-law regarding the effects of the Constitutional Court's decisions finding the unconstitutionality of repealing rules with respect to the Constitutional Court's decisions on the whole, given by recitals and the operative part. Thus, by Decision no. 3 of April 4, 2011[646], the High Court of Cassation and Justice held, within an appeal on points of law, that "by Decision no. 62/2007, the Constitutional Court has removed any doubts about the effects of declaring the unconstitutionality of certain repealing provisions, stating that, in case they are found unconstitutional, they shall take no legal effects under the terms set forth in Article 147 para. (1) of the Constitution, and the legal provisions which were the subject-matter of the repeal shall continue to take legal effects. This interpretation

---

for committing acts of insult and libel, in Dreptul no. 11/2009, p. 145 – As grounds for this opinion, it was stated that the Constitutional Court's decision cannot be assimilated to a law which criminalises certain offences as crimes, and the legislature is entitled to adopt such normative acts; in the same regard it is also Decision of the High Court of Cassation and Justice, Criminal Section, no. 2203 of 4 June 2010, in which it was held, with reference to Decision no. 62/2007 of the Constitutional Court that "*by this decision, the Constitutional Court cannot become positive legislature, and the provisions repealed by the legislature do not automatically enter in force once the decision is adopted. So that the legal provisions concerning the offences of insult and libel can enter again in force, the legislature's action shall be needed, as it is the only one entitled to establish the acts which fall under criminal scope and become crimes*".

644 Published in the Official Gazette of Romania no. 416 of 14 June 2011.

645 As an example of decision for this case, we mention Decision no. 2461/2009, rendered by the Criminal Section of the High Court of Cassation and Justice, in which it was noted that "*by the Constitutional Court's Decision no. 783 of 12 May 2009 – published in the Official Gazette on 15 June 2009 – the Court upheld the exception of unconstitutionality of the provisions of Article I section 185 of Law no 356/2006 amending and supplementing the Code of Criminal Procedure. The Constitutional Court motivated that Article 385^9 para. (1) section 17^1 of the Code of Criminal Procedure, by the provisions found unconstitutional, violated the constitutional provisions of Article 21 on the free access to justice and of Article 20 of the Constitution regarding the international treaties on human rights in relation to the provisions of Article 6 on the right to a fair trial and of Article 13 on the right to an effective remedy of the Convention for the Protection of Human Rights and Fundamental Freedoms. That being so, the challenge formulated by the defendants with reference to the cassation case set forth in Article 385^9 para. (1) section 17^1 of the Code of Criminal Procedure becomes present and possible*".

646 Published in the Official Gazette of Romania no. 350 of 19 May 2011.

given by the Constitutional Court itself to the effects of a decision finding the unconstitutionality of a repealing text makes the judgments of the internal courts which rejected the applicant's request on the ground that the Constitutional Court cannot activate a repealed text, to be in total absence of legal grounds. (...) However, according to Article 11 para. (3) of Law no. 47/1992, republished, the Constitutional Court's decisions are binding, which means that they must be enforced as such, not only in terms of the operative part of the Decision, but also in terms of the recitals which justify it". The same decision revealed that the courts of law are "bound to comply with the Constitutional Court's decisions and not to give effectiveness to normative acts declared unconstitutional". Further, the High Court of Cassation and Justice, by Decision no. 11 of October 8, 2012[647], pronounced within an appeal on points of law, resumed the case-law of the Constitutional Court regarding the effects of its decisions on the repealing norms declared unconstitutional.

Concluding on the importance of distinctions between the activity of the legislature (repeal) and that of the Constitutional Court (the ascertainment of the unconstitutionality), we mention that for the particular situation of finding the unconstitutionality of the provisions of laws and ordinances in force, as well as of those of the regulations, Article 147 para. (1) of the Constitution establishes that they "*shall cease their legal effects within 45 days as from the publication of the decision rendered by the Constitutional Court where Parliament or Government, as may be applicable, have failed, in the meantime, to bring these unconstitutional provisions into accord with those of the Constitution. For this limited length of time the provisions declared unconstitutional shall be suspended as of right*".

"*Cessation of legal effects*" of the legal provisions, as an effect of the Constitutional Court's decisions finding the unconstitutionality, was established by the constituent legislature as a concept distinct from the repeal, since it aims at the expressions of the will of different authorities with different competences. Even if, in practice, the consequences produced by the repeal and by the ascertainment of the the unconstitutionality of a legal norm (the latter on the expiry of 45 days from the publication of the decision of the Constitutional Court and if the legislature does not intervene to bring the unconstitutional provisions into accord with the Constitution) are in the sense that the norm no longer applies, the two concept cannot be confused.

Therefore one cannot claim that the constitutional court accomplish the repeal of the law, as no one can claim that the legislature ascertains the unconstitutionality of the law.

Likewise, it also cannot be claimed that the competence of Parliament, as sole legislative authority, would be prejudiced. Contrary to other opinions, which refer to the need for a parallelism of forms and powers to "the re-entry into force" of a legal norm, this principle is not incident in the given situation, a situation which concerns the specific framework of the constitutional review, the purpose and its effects, and not the lawmaking activity. Thus, the legal effect of a repealing norm consists of the

647 Published in the Official Gazette of Romania no. 734 of 31 October 2012.

cessation of the effects of the repealed norm. As a result, the lack of legal effect of the repealing norm by the ascertainment of its unconstitutionality will result in the removal cessation of the legal effects of the repealing norm, with the consequence that the latter will begin to take legal effect. Another legal reasoning would lead the circumvention of the provisions of Article 147 para. (4) of the Constitution. This is because the passivity of the legislature would practically lead to a "revival" of the norm found unconstitutional, as long as the unconstitutionality situation caused by the cessation of the legal effects of the repealed norms would continue to exist, in the absence of a legislative intervention. Such a situation, which deprives the constitutional review and the role of the Constitutional Court of effectiveness, is unacceptable, as it is incompatible with the rule of law.

2.4.4 Interpretative decisions

Another situation which expresses both the role of Constitutional Courts as negative legislature and that as positive legislature is the "confirmation"" of a certain interpretation of the legal norm (interpretative decisions). This is because, eliminating a certain interpretation of the legal norm as being unconstitutional (which gives expression to its traditional role), the Court retains at same time a certain meaning, being thus associated to the legislature in giving a certain meaning to the statutory provision in accordance with the word and spirit of the Constitution (which expresses the role of positive co-legislature). The Court thus does not create a new rule, but provides to a pre-existing rule an unequivocal meaning, one that is consistent with the Basic Law.

Thus, adjudication on the constitutionality of the provisions of Article 29 para. (1) of Law no. 47/1992, according to which: "*The Constitutional Court shall decide upon the exceptions raised before the courts of law or courts of commercial arbitration referring to the unconstitutionality of laws and ordinances which are in force, or any provision thereof, where such is related to adjudication of the case, regardless in which stage of trial proceedings or subject-matter thereof*", the Constitutional Court ruled that "the phrase «in force» of the provisions of Article 29 para. (1) and of Article 31 para. (1) of Law no. 47/1992 on the Organization and Operation of the Constitutional Court is constitutional insofar as it is interpreted as submitting to the constitutional review the laws or ordinances or provisions therein, whose legal effects continue to produce even when they are no longer in force"[648]. By this decision, the Court gave a certain meaning to the will of the legislator, basically emphasizing the moment of application in time of legal norms envisaged by it (or that it had to consider so that norm be consistent with the Basic Law) upon establish the condition that the norm that is subject to constitutional review by way of exception of unconstitutionality to be "in force".

---

648 Decision no. 766 of 15 June 2011, published in the Official Gazette of Romania no. 549 of 3 August 2011.

Thus issues regarding the interpretative decisions were examined in a previous chapter.

2.4.5 Expressing recommendations for the legislature

Another category of decisions of the Constitutional Court where we can notice the departure from the traditional role of "negative legislature" is given by those which formulate "recommendations" for the legislature. We consider relevant in this respect, as concerns the Constitutional Court of Romania, the decisions rendered in exercising its power to rule, *ex officio*, on initiatives for the revision of the Constitution.

Thus, for example, by Decision 799/2011 on the bill concerning the revision of the Constitution, initiated by the President of Romania, at the Government's proposal, ruling on the proposal for amending Article 61 of the Basic Law – Role and structure of (Parliament), the Court held that, "*having examined the contents of the revision bill and the explanatory memorandum thereof, one can note that the largest proposed change concerns the shift to a unicameral Parliament and setting a maximum number of 300 MPs, with the proper re-correlation of the constitutional text referring to the Parliament, Senators and legislative procedure*". Noting that "*the proposed amendment in this regard is consistent with the national referendum of 22 November 2009, initiated by the President of Romania and confirmed by the Constitutional Court* (...)", and that the amendment "*does not affect any of the limits in matter of revision provided by Article 152 of the Constitution, but is only a political choice on which the participants to the procedure for revision of the Constitution will decide*", the Court, further, made a series of observations and recommendations for the derived constituent legislature.

The Court held that "*however, in expressing this option, the tradition of the Romanian State and the advantages offered by a bicameral structure of Parliament in relation to a unicameral structure should not be ignored. (...) Traditionally, the Romanian Parliament had a bicameral structure. This structure of the legislative forum, enshrined in 1864, through the «Developing Statute of the Paris Convention» of the Romanian Ruler Alexandru Ioan Cuza, continued to exist under the rule of the 1866 1923 and 1938 Constitutions, being interrupted only during the communist regime, when national representation was unicameral – Grand National Assembly. After the revolution of 1989, by Decree-Law no. 92/1990 for the election of the Parliament and the President of Romania, published in the Official Gazette of Romania, Part I, no. 35 of 18 March 1990, the act under which elections were held in May 1990, was reintroduced the bicameralism formula. The 1991 Constitution restated, with some modifications, this structure of Parliament, upheld on the occasion of the 2003 revision of the Basic Law. Modification of relevant text, made on the occasion of the revision, aimed only the change to a system of functional bicameralism. The advantages of a bicameral structure of the legislative forum are quite obvious. Thus, it is avoided the concentration of power in Parliament, because its Chambers will prevent each other from becoming a support for an authoritarian regime. At the same time, it provides debates and a framework for successive analysis of laws by two different bodies of the legislative forum, which provides greater guarantee of the quality of the legislative act. Adoption of laws in a unicameral parliament is made after several successive "readings" of a text, as, it is, in fact, proposed in this draft law for revision of the Constitution. Being carried out by the same legislative body, readings can become an artificial formality, or can be removed for emergency reasons. Bicameralism determines that the second reading of the law be always carried out by another assembly, which is likely to cause a sharp critical perception. It is thus provided the opportunity for better critical cooperation, common and collective decision-making debate, being emphasized the formation of the will of the parliamentary state. In addition, the bicameralism minimizes the risk of majority rule, promoting dialogue between majorities of both Chambers, as well as between parliamentary groups. Cooperation and legislative supervision are extended in this way, thus demonstrating that the bicameral system is an important form of separation of powers, which does not function only between the legislative, the executive and the judiciary, but also within the legislative power. Both tradition which, being connected to the being of the Romanian State, defines and represents the same, as well as the mentioned advantages are strong grounds for reflection on the occasion of option for one of two formulas: unicameralism or bicameralism."*

Likewise, Decision no. 80 of 16 February 2014 on the legislative proposal for the revision of the Constitution of Romania[649] comprises various recommendations on both the substantive solutions and on the wording of the draft law for the revision. An example in this respect is the recommendation regarding the effects of the referendum. Thus, the Court held that "*Whereas there may be circumstances in which the issues on which the people is called upon to express its will may affect the interests of elected representatives (such as reducing the number of MEPs or reduce parliamentarians' allowances), the Venice Commission, in the document entitled Guidelines on the holding of referendums, adopted at the 68th Plenary Session (13-14 October 2007), held that referendums should be clearly specified in the Constitution or by law whether referendums are legally binding or consultative. It is preferable for referendums on questions of principle or generally-worded proposals to be consultative. If they are legally binding, the subsequent procedure should be expressly laid down in specific legislative rules. (...)The Court recommends, by unanimous vote, the regulation in Article 90 Para. (1) of the Constitution of the legal effects of the consultative referendum and the subsequent procedure for conducting such scrutiny*".

The role of the Constitutional Court in the rule of law, in terms of the analyzed development, raises, of course, the question whether the Court's association, as shown, in the legislative process, is compatible with the principle of separation and balance of powers enshrined in Article 1 Para. (4) Of the Constitution. We consider that the answer can only be positive: yes, the role of the Constitutional Court is compatible with the principle of separation of powers. We disagree in this respect with the opinion of some experts claiming that the Constitutional Courts are a third

649 Published in the Official Gazette of Romania no. 246 of 7 April 2014.

Chamber of Parliament[650]. This because the activity of the Court is justified by its specific power. In exercising this power, the Constitutional Court has proceeded and shall proceed to the explanation, interpretation (systematic, grammatical, teleological) or reasoned support of rules created by the constitutional or derived, primary or delegated legislator, namely to boost the latter in creating rules to cover situations not covered, but which should be regulated. In other words, the Court supports the development of law, with different instruments and in carrying out different tasks from those of the legislature. Hence, both formulations – "*negative legislature*" and "*positive legislature*" seem objectionable, and that is why we prefer the formulation co-legislator that takes into account both hypotheses, and that does not suggest an institutional substitution. This formulation gives expression to the institutional dialogue which shall exist between the Constitutional Court and Parliament, a dialogue which constitutes the premise of the constitutionalisation process of the law, as a whole.

2.4.6 The decisions of the Constitutional Court – a source of law

Another consequence of the Constitutional Court's acts constitutionally enshrined, as well as of the development analyzed, is the fact that they are acknowledged the role of source of law. This role was emphasized even by the Court, which held – even if initially only on its traditional role – that "*the decision finding the law unconstitutional is part of the normative order and by its effect the unconstitutional provision ceases its future application*"[651]. Developing this idea upon the constitutional review of the regulation that established the misconduct of judges and prosecutors consisting in failure to comply with the Constitutional Court's decision, the Court held that the legislation "gives expression to the provisions of Article 1 paragraph (5) of the Constitution, establishing that «*Observance of the Constitution, of its supremacy, and the laws shall be obligatory in Romania*», in conjunction with Article 142 paragraph (1), establishing that «*The Constitutional Court shall be the guarantor for the supremacy of the Constitution*»"[652]. The issues raised in that case, settled by Decision 2/2012[653] on the objection of unconstitutionality of the Law amending Law 303/2004 on the status of judges and prosecutors and the Law 317/2004 on the Superior Council of Magistracy, strengthen the conclusions of this study, in the sense of development of the Constitutional Court and of its role. These relate mainly to the distinction which is said to exist in terms of the erga omnes obligation, between the decisions of admission rendered by the Constitutional Court, respectively of that of rejection of referrals of unconstitutionality, and the distinction between

650 In the same regard, see C. Gilia, *cited paper*, p. 273.

651 Decision no. 847 of 8 July 2008, published in the Official Gazette of Romania no. 605 of 14 August 2008.

652 Decision no. 2 of 11 January 2012, published in the Official Gazette of Romania no. 131 of 23 February 2012.

653 *Ibidem*.

the binding character of the operative part of the decision and the considerations on which it relies. By Decision 2/2012, answering to the criticism whereby, distinguishing between decisions ascertaining the unconstitutionality, respectively the constitutionality of a piece of legislation, it was argued that the latter are not of binding nature, the Court held that the text of Article 147 paragraph (4) of the Constitution, which enshrines the general binding nature of its decisions, "*does not distinguish between the types of decisions rendered by the Constitutional Court, nor on the content of these decisions, which leads to the conclusion that all decisions this Court, as a whole, are generally binding*".

We believe that the wording used by the Court, i.e. "*as a whole*" does not refer to the decision in its entirety, but to its ratio decidendi, that is the reasons directly influencing the decision – whether its solution is to accept or reject the referral of unconstitutionality – thus the essence of legal reasoning that substantiates it. As in case of precedent in common law[654], "*ratio decidendi* must be distinguished from *obiter dicta*, that is what the judge declares without such being absolutely necessary". It seems indisputable that the court refers to the solution and the motivation that substantiates it, as a unit of legal reasoning. Another interpretation cannot be accepted given the diversity of decisions rendered by the Constitutional Court because their application according to the letter and spirit of the Constitution could not be obtained unless providing efficiency to considerations supporting the decision delivered by the Court. But the legal rigor requires a necessary distinction within these considerations.

It is worth noting that this role of the Constitutional Court involves and requires great responsibility. We do not refer only to the solutions rendered by the Court, but also to their reasoning, as well as to the need for sound arguments for jurisprudential reversal whose frequency may be a disturbance factor for legal certainty. The challenges that the doctrine[655] has brought to some of the acts delivered by the Constitutional Court raise often the issue of competence relationships and the observance of the powers and the role of the Constitutional Court in relation to those of the primary or delegated legislature. Without going into an analysis of such challenges, we should mention, however, the idea of the need for balance and the fall within the norms of the Constitution and within the principles of the rule of law, regarding the activity and acts of the Constitutional Court, on the one hand, respectively of the Parliament (and, incidentally, of any other authority), on the other hand.

2.5 Conclusions

The presented legal provisions and the case-law reveal that the fact that there is a constitutional and legal framework susceptible to support the dialogue between the Constitutional Court and Parliament. It is obvious that the constitutional case-law

---

654 D.C. Dănişor, I. Dogaru, Gh. Dănişor, *cited paper*, p. 145.

655 V.M. Ciobanu, *Constitutional Court – a guarantor for the supremacy of the Constitution, a lawmaking power or a parliamentary expert*, in RRDP no. 3/2009, pp. 72–95.

circumstantiates the activity of Parliament and its relationships with the other public authorities, as the legislature governs the organization and operation of the Constitutional Court, ensuring the premises for the fulfilment of its the constitutional role. Even if not explicitly, it causes an institutional dialogue.

Of course, sometimes the "limitations" imposed by the Court, as its apparent intrusion into the legislative activity, resulted in challenges both in the legal and political aspects, especially in situations where the Court has "imposed" a certain interpretation of the constitutional provisions, such as to determine, for example, a particular type of protection of the constitutional values, such as the criminalization of the acts of insult and libel.

Which would be the length of time of such limits imposed by the Constitutional Court and, in general, by the constitutional courts? Answering this difficult question, which endangers, on the one hand, the binding nature of the decisions of the constitutional courts and the authority of those courts, with the legislature's freedom to adjust the legislation according to the social and economic developments specific to a modern, dynamic and free society, the Federal Constitutional Court of Germany provided the following solution: the decisions of the constitutional court do not aim at imposing an absolutely rigid obligation which the legislature must take into account, but a flexible manner to react. Therefore, in case of a reiteration of a norm, the legislature should not ignore the reasons that substantiated the ascertainment of its unconstitutionality. A new approach of the legislature in this respect is justified only where there are special reasons, first of all as a result of the significant changes in respect of matters of fact or of law, determined for the constitutional review, or from the change of the view that substantiated it. In the absence of such reasons, the Constitutional Court has no basis to reconsider its case-law and, therefore, it shall ascertain again the unconstitutionality of the norm which is to be subject to its review. This reasoning is substantiated by the same Court on an unwritten fundamental principle, of loyal cooperation between the state bodies (Organtreue), which the Federal Constitutional Court of Germany applies in its case-law and which gives expression to the obligation of the constitutional bodies to demonstrate mutual respect and to refrain from any contrary action. Specifically, the legislature shall cease to diminish the authority of the Court, adopting an identical or similar law immediately after the Court censured the initial regulation[656].

We believe that, as guarantor for the supremacy of the Constitution, the Constitutional Court can and should consider these issues underlying the adoption of the normative acts when it is notified on their unconstitutionality, limiting in this

656 See, including for the cases in which the Federal Constitutional Court of Germany ruled in this respect, the Report prepared for the XVth Congress of the Conference of the European Constitutional Courts, held at Bucharest, between 23–25 May 2011, available on the website of the Constitutional Court, *www.ccr.ro.*

respect, the action of the legislature in order to ensure a fair balance between the needs for the protection of fundamental rights and freedoms[657].

Moreover, the idea was emphasized during various meetings between the constitutional courts that have discussed these relationships, noting that "the main role of the institution of the legislature – Parliament – is lawmaking; the most important areas of the social life are regulated by law. The myth of infallibility of Parliament or the law, very popular at the beginning of the last century, was refuted long time ago; it has also collapsed the theory that the law, as an expression of the common will of the people's representatives, cannot cause any prejudice to people. The legislative institution is a political institution of power, whose decisions are based on political agreement and compromise, therefore, the review exercised by the Constitutional Court on the laws adopted by Parliament is an essential factor for the protection of human rights and freedoms. Legitimacy and legality of a law are understood as the compliance with the Constitution – the supreme law of the country – which is the foundation of justice, of human rights and fundamental freedoms and substantiates the relationships between the authorities and the human being. Therefore, one of the main roles of the Constitutional Court is the assessment of the legal acts adopted by the legislative institution regarding their compliance with the Constitution. The legislature's activities are lawful unless they exceed the limits provided for by the Constitution, whose supremacy is guaranteed by the Constitutional Court. A harmonious relationship between the Constitutional Court and the legislature is also important in the sense that it demonstrates the way in which the legal system, the creation of the legislative power, adapts to the supreme law of the country – the Constitution – and whether the effective prevalence of the constitutional norms is guaranteed"[658].

3. The dialogue between the Constitutional Court and the President of Romania

3.1 General aspects

Similarly as concerns the dialogue with the legislative power, the relationships and hence the institutional dialogue between the Constitutional Court and the executive power, represented by the President of Romania and the Government, can be approached from two perspectives.

657 in the case-law of other constitutional courts, in was held in this regard that, in terms of constitutional review, where two fundamental rights collide, it is essential to take account of both and none of fundamental rights shall be excluded from the consideration. The Court shall establish rules on the existence of the two rights, with a possible mention of which of them should be given priority, depending on the specific circumstances of the case (see Decision no. 444/09 of 12 April 2012 of the Constitutional Court Slovenia).

658 See Lithuania – the XVth Congress of the Conference of the European Constitutional Courts, Bucharest, 23–25 May 2011, available on *www.ccr.ro.*

Referring in this chapter to the President of Romania, we should note that it has powers in determining the structure of the Constitutional Court, by appointing three of the Court's judges, he is involved in its activity by the possibility to formulate viewpoints and referrals in the cases expressly and restrictively provided by law, whereas the activity of the President of Romania, being exercised in respect of the supremacy of the Constitution, is subject to the review exercised by the Constitutional Court, within the limits of its powers set forth in the Basic Law and its organic law.

Pursuant to Article 80 para. (2) of the Constitution, the President of Romania shall sees to the observance of the Constitution and the proper functioning of the public authorities and to this effect; he shall act as a mediator between State Powers, as well as between the State and society. However, as underlined[659], watchfulness to the observance of the Constitution does not mean that the President is the guarantor of the Constitution, as this latter role belongs to the Constitutional Court. The observance of the Constitution shall not be watched only by the President, but also by all State authorities, in accordance with their powers, taking account of the provisions of Article 1 para. (5) of the Constitution, according to which "*Observance of the Constitution, of its supremacy, and the laws shall be obligatory in Romania*".

From this perspective, it is worth mentioning the cases where the Constitutional Court ruled upon the powers of the President of Romania and upon the limits of its jurisdiction, as the dialogue between these two institutions aims at the same desire of observing the Basic Law of the State.

3.2 The relationships between the President of Romania and the constitutional court

3.2.1 Competences in the procedure to appoint constitutional judges

Pursuant to Article 142 para. (3) of the Constitution, the President of Romania shall appoint three of the Constitutional Court's judges.

3.2.2 The possibility to refer to the Constitutional Court

A direct way of the President of Romania to access to the constitutional justice is the possibility to challenge it under the circumstances restrictively provided for by law, as follows:

a) to adjudicate upon the constitutionality of laws, before their promulgation [Article 146 a) sentence I of the Constitution]. Thus, out of a number of 267 of referrals founded on the provisions of this article set forth in the Constitution which have been settled so far, a number of 33 referrals were formulated by the

659 I. Muraru, E.S. Tănăsescu (coordinators), *cited paper*, p. 755.

President of Romania. Among them, 17 objections of unconstitutionality were upheld or partially upheld;

b) to settle the legal disputes of a constitutional nature between public authorities [Article 146 e) of the Constitution]. Thus, out of a number of 28 referrals on legal disputes of a constitutional nature which have been settled by the Constitutional Court so far, 16 cases were related to the President of Romania as the author of the referral (6) or as a party, the referral being formulated by another authority (10);
c) to ascertain any circumstance as may justify the interim in the exercise of office of President of Romania [Article 146 g) of the Constitution in conjunction with Article 44 of Law no. 47/1992 on the Organisation and Operation of the Constitutional Court]. Effectively, this concerns the temporary impossibility of the President of Romania to exercise his powers[660]. So far, the Constitutional Court has not been referred by the President of Romania in this respect.

As concerns **the objections of unconstitutionality**, the provisions of Article 146 a) first sentence of the Constitution of Romania, according to which "*The Constitutional Court (...)adjudicates on the constitutionality of laws before promulgation, upon referral by the President of Romania, the President of either of the two Chambers, the Government, the High Court of Cassation and Justice, the Advocate of the People, at least 50 Deputies or at least 25 Senators (...)*" are also set forth in Article15 para. (1) of Law no. 47/1992 on the Organisation and Operation of the Constitutional Court, according to which: "The Constitutional Court shall pronounce on the constitutionality of the laws before their promulgation upon referral by the President of Romania, by one of the Presidents of the two Chambers of Parliament, by the Government, by the High Court of Cassation and Justice, by the Advocate of the People, by a number of at least fifty Deputies or of least twenty-five Senators".

The law, irrespective of its nature – organic or ordinary –, the adoption procedure – normal, emergency or by Government's assumption of responsibility before the two Chambers of Parliament –, may be appealed to the Constitutional Court on grounds of unconstitutionality by the subjects mentioned by the cited constitutional text, without any distinction, before the President of Romania issues the promulgation decree.

The decision whereby the objection of unconstitutionality has been partially upheld results in the initiation as of right of the complementary procedure of re-examination of the law by Parliament in order to bring into line the unconstitutional provisions with the decision of the Constitutional Court, according to Article 147 paragraph (2) of the Basic Law. After Parliament brings the provisions found unconstitutional into accord with the decision of the Constitutional Court, the President of Romania is obliged to promulgate the law within 10 days, according to Article

---

660 For a development of these situations and the competent authorities to refer to the Constitutional Court, see I. Muraru, E.S. Tănăsescu (coordinators), *cited paper*, p. 1409.

77 para. (3) of the Constitution. During this period, the President can promulgate the law in any of the days available to him, by issuing a decree pursuant to Article 100 of the Basic Law, which shall be published in the Official Gazette of Romania, Part I, together with the law.[661]

The Court held that if a law is declared unconstitutional in its entirety such a decision has a final effect on that normative act, resulting in the cessation of the legislative process on the respective regulation. On the other hand, given that the provisions of Article 61para. (1) of the Constitution provide that "*Parliament is the supreme representative body of the Romanian people and the sole legislative authority of the country*", its power to legislate on a particular area cannot be limited if the adopted law meets the requirements of the Basic Law. Therefore, the legislator's option to legislate in the matter in which the Constitutional Court upheld a referral of unconstitutionality on a law in its entirety involves the resumption of the whole legislative process provided by the Constitution and the Standing Orders of the two Chambers of Parliament.[662] It is obvious therefore that, in this situation, the President of Romania is no longer obliged to promulgate the law.

As concerns **the legal disputes of a constitutional nature**, the Court held that it may be referred by the President of Romania, even if such a dispute exists between other public authorities and not between them and the author of the referral. Ruling on the admissibility of such referral, the Court held that, "*in accordance with Article 146 e) of the Constitution, the Constitutional Court «shall solve legal disputes of a constitutional nature between public authorities». In this regard, the public authorities which could be involved in a legal dispute of a constitutional nature are solely those contained in Title III of the Constitution, namely Parliament, consisting of the Chamber of Deputies and the Senate, the President of Romania, as a single-member public authority, the Government, the central public administration bodies and the local public administration bodies, as well as the judicial bodies. In order to exercise the competence provided for by the Constitution, the Court is notified by «the President of Romania, one of the presidents of the two Chambers, the Prime Minister or the President of the Superior Council of Magistracy». The subjects of law vested by the Basic Law to refer to the Court are restrictively provided, the constitutional provision cannot distinguish whether the authorities as they represent are or not parties to the dispute referred to the Court*".

Consequently, the President of Romania is entitled to formulate the referral regarding the settlement of a legal dispute of a constitutional nature between judiciary, on the one hand, and Parliament of Romania and the Government of Romania, on the other hand, even if he was not a party to that dispute[663].

---

661 Decision no. 975 of 7 July 2010, published in the Official Gazette of Romania no. 568 of 11 August 2010.

662 Decision no. 308 of 28 March 2012, published in the Official Gazette of Romania no. 309 of 9 May 2012.

663 Decision no. 838 of 27 May 2009, published in the Official Gazette of Romania no. 461 of 3 July 2009.

As already shown, this dialogue is one of the effective ways whereby the President sees to the observance of the Constitution[664].

3.2.3 The possibility to express viewpoints in the cases brought before the Constitutional Court

In case of constitutional review of treaties or other international agreements. Pursuant to Article 24 para. (2)-(4) of Law no. 47/1992, in case of constitutional review of treaties or other international agreements, if the referral has been brought by one of the Presidents of the two Chambers of Parliament, the Constitutional Court shall notify it to the President of Romania, to the President of the other Chamber, as well as to the Government. If the referral has been brought by a parliamentary group, the Constitutional Court shall notify it to the President of Romania, to the Presidents of the two Chambers of Parliament and to the Government. Pursuant to Article 25 of the same normative act, until the date of debate in the Plenum of the Constitutional Court, the President of Romania, the Presidents of the two Chambers of Parliament and the Government may express, in writing, their viewpoints.

In case of legal disputes of a constitutional nature where it is a party, the President of Romania may communicate his viewpoint on the subject-matter at dispute and the possible ways for resolution [Article 35 para. (1) of Law no. 47/1992].

In case of issuing an advisory opinion on the proposal of suspension from office. Pursuant to Article 43 para. (2) of Law no. 47/1992, within the procedure in order to issue an advisory opinion on the suspension of the President of Romania from office, the latter shall be notified of the date fixed for the debate and he may offer explanations regarding the imputations brought to him.

It is noted that the expression of viewpoints can be made in cases where either the President has the capacity of a party (legal disputes of a constitutional nature) or the constitutional procedures in which he is involved are under discussion (conclusion of international treaties, namely the procedure of suspension from office).

3.2.4 The Constitutional Court shall communicate to the President the referrals, as well as its decisions/rulings/advisory opinions delivered by it, under the conditions provided for by law

To avoid an untimely promulgation of the law that is the subject-matter of the referral of unconstitutionality within the *a priori* review, the Constitutional Court is obliged to communicate the referral raised by one of the presidents of the two Chambers of Parliament, by MPs, by the Government, by the High Court of Cassation and Justice or by the Advocate of the People, on the day of its registration. After settling the referral, the decision shall be communicated to the President of Romania [Article 18 para. (2) of Law no. 47/1992]. Thus, the admission of the referral

664 I. Muraru, *There is a guarantor..., cited paper*, pp. 130–155.

will prevent the promulgation by the President as its rejection will cause the renewal of the obligation of promulgation, insofar as an objection of unconstitutionality is not formulated even by the President on the same normative act or the President does not require Parliament to reconsider the law.

The decision delivered with the constitutional review of treaties or other international agreements shall be communicated to the President of Romania, taking into account that, according to Article 91 para. (1) of the Constitution, "*The President concludes, in the name and on behalf of Romania, international treaties negotiated by the Government, which he then submits to Parliament within a reasonable time (...)*".

According to Article 36 of Law 47/1992, the decision which settles a legal dispute of a constitutional nature shall be final and communicated to the author of the referral, as well as to the parties in dispute, prior to its publication in the Official Gazette of Romania, Part I.

Likewise, according to Article 43 para. (3) of Law no. 47/1992, the advisory opinion of the Constitutional Court for the suspension of the President of Romania from office shall be communicated to the Presidents of both Chambers and to the President of Romania.

Finally, according to Article 53 para. (2) of Law no. 370/2004 for the election of the President of Romania, the validation act regarding the elections shall be compiled in three copies, one of which shall remain at the Constitutional Court; one shall be presented to Parliament for taking the oath set forth in Article 82 para. (2) of the Constitution of Romania, republished, and the third shall be given to the elected candidate.

3.3 The relationship between the Constitutional Court and the President of Romania

3.3.1 Competences in the procedure to appoint constitutional judges

According to Article 146 f) of the Constitution, the Constitutional Court sees to the observance of the procedure for the election of the President of Romania and confirms the ballot returns.

The constitutional provisions are developed at the infraconstitutional level by the provisions of Law no. 47/1992 on the Organization and Operation of the Constitutional Court and of Law. 370/2004 for the election of the President of Romania.

The Constitution and the mentioned infraconstitutional legislation confer upon the Constitutional Court the status of "electoral judge", the phrase "sees to the observance of the procedure" contained in the constitutional text of reference aiming both at fulfilling the technical-material and legal procedures specific to the electoral procedures, and at ensuring the settlement of electoral disputes arising from incidents that may arise in the presidential election, namely to confirm and submit the ballot returns to Parliament.

According to Law no. 370/2004 for the election of the President of Romania, the review exercised by the Constitutional Court may aim at contesting the registration or the refusal to register candidates, at contesting the settlement method of the incidents related to the holding of the electoral campaigns and at contesting the election results.

Settlement of challenges regarding the registration or rejection to register candidatures or election signs

According to Article 31 para. (1) and (2) of Law no. 370/2004, within 24 hours since the expiry term set forth in Article 29 para. (2)[665], respectively in Article 30 para. (6)[666] of the same normative act, candidates, political parties, organizations of national minorities, political alliances, electoral alliances and voters may challenge the registration or the rejection to register candidatures or election signs, as appropriate. Challenges shall be made in writing and filed with the Constitutional Court. The challenges shall be settled within two days of registration. The rulings are final and they shall be immediately communicated to the Central Electoral Bureau and published in the Official Gazette of Romania, Part I.

In the matter of challenging the registration of the candidature proposals, the case-law of the Constitutional Court is very rich; each of the election years is characterized by a large number of such challenges.

The decisions whereby the Constitutional Court rules upon the meaning of the phrase "presidential term of office" are also of reference. Thus, settling the challenges regarding the registration of candidatures for the office of President of Romania, motivated by the fact that the candidate was at his third term of office, in the elections in 1996, as he held the office of President of Romania for the term of office between 1992 and 1996, as well as before it, the Court held that no preconstitutional normative act enshrines the concept of presidential term of office, as this concept was regulated for the first time by the Constitution in 1991. According to the considerations which substantiated the rulings rejecting the challenges, "the presidential term of office has specific and unprecedented constitutional determinations in relation to the previous regulations. These determinations concern mainly the functions deriving from the term of office, the conditions for the acquisition, validation and commencement of the term of office, its duration, the entailed incompatibilities and immunities, the duties deriving from the term of office and, therefore, the relationships between its holder and the other public authorities, the holder's responsibility for the way in which he/she exercises the term of office. No other office, acquired based on certain regulations prior to the Constitution, had such a term of office as substantiation, so that it must be admitted that the provisions of the Constitution of Romania mark a rupture or relocation solution of the concept of head of state

---

665 Article 29 para. (2): "*The registration and rejection of the registration of candidatures by the Central Electoral Bureau shall be made by decision within 48 hours at most of the submission thereof*".

666 Article 30 para. (6): "*The registration and rejection of the registration of electoral signs shall be made by the Central Electoral Bureau, by decision, together with the registration and rejection of the registration of candidatures*".

fundamentally different. Consequently, the presidential term of office governed by the Constitution of Romania cannot be placed in the extension of certain durations of exercising the office of President of Romania, before the fundamental law entries into force". The Court also noted that Article 81 para. (4) of the Constitution provides that "No one may hold the office of President of Romania but two terms of office at the most, and these may also follow one after the other", and that, in order to demonstrate the constitutional illegitimacy of the candidature for the office of President of Romania, constant reference should be made only to this "office", thus ignoring the second component of the regulation contained in Article 81 para. (4), namely the concept of "term of office". However, "the office of President" cannot be abstracted from the wording of the regulation, without taking account of the concept of "term of office". In other words – the Court also stated that – "in order to compare the concept of head of state, in the current regulation, to the previous situations, one should note that the concept of the President of Romania is also defined, among others, by the constitutional term of office. In the absence of such «term of office», before the entry into force of the Constitution, any association with legal situations preceding the Constitution is unfounded"[667].

By Ruling no. 40/2000[668], the Constitutional Court upheld a challenge concerning the registration of a candidate for the office of President of Romania, noting that, although he had his domicile in the country[669], he had dual citizenship, which is contrary to the constitutional provisions of Article 16 para. (3). The admission of the challenge resulted in the elimination of that candidature proposal. After the revision of the Constitution, Article 16 para. (3) no longer forbids Romanian citizens with dual citizenship to have access to elective public dignities.

In 2004, 2009 and 2014, the Court also settled a large number of challenges concerning the registration/ rejection of registration of candidatures for the office of President of Romania, noting, as appropriate, their unfoundedness, inadmissibility or lateness. It is worth mentioning the rulings by which the Constitutional Court argued that the exercise of the a posteriori constitutional review of laws and ordinances can be done only by way of exception of unconstitutionality, within the power provided by Article 146 d) of the Constitution, according to which the Constitutional Court "*rules upon exceptions as to the unconstitutionality of laws and ordinances which are raised before the courts of law or commercial arbitration; an*

667 Ruling no. 1 of 8 September 1996, published in the Official Gazette of Romania no. 213 of 9 September 1996, see also Ruling no. 3/1996. In the same regard, see: Rulings no. 4/1996; no. 5/1996; no. 6/1996; no. 7/1996; no. 10/1996; no. 11/1996; no. 13/1996; no. 16/1996; no. 30/1996; no. 34/1996; no. 35/1996; no. 36/1996; no. 41/1996; no. 45/1996; no. 52/1996; no. 57/1996; no. 62/1996; no. 69/1996; no. 3/2000; no. 5/2000; no. 6/2000; no. 9/2000; no. 21/2000; no. 25/2000; no. 32/2000; no. 46/2000.

668 Published in the Official Gazette of Romania no. 622 of 30 November 2000.

669 The requirement of the residence within the country can be found in the legislation of Macedonia.

exception of unconstitutionality may also be raised directly by the Advocate of the People", in compliance with the procedure laid down by Law no. 47/1992 on the Organization and Operation of the Constitutional Court, and not within the power provided by Article 146 f) of the Constitution, according to which the Constitutional Court "*sees to the observance of the procedure for the election of the President of Romania and confirms the ballot returns*"[670].

Settlement of challenges concerning the hindrance of a party or a political formation, or of a candidate to carry out the electoral campaign

Pursuant to Article 42 para. (7) of Law no. 370/2004, challenges concerning the hindrance of a party or a political formation, or of a candidate to carry out the electoral campaign under the law shall be settled by the Constitutional Court, with the majority vote of judges, within 48 hours at most of their registration.

In 2009, the Court upheld two challenges regarding the non granting and the non-distribution of airtime according to law by the joint Standing Bureaux of the two Chambers of Parliament and by the public broadcaster – the Romanian Television Corporation – and ordered the Standing Bureaux of the two Chambers of Parliament and the representatives of the Romanian Television Corporation to establish the timetable for the election campaign and the distribution of airtime on the national television channel for the candidates for the office of President of Romania[671].

Settlement of challenges regarding the cancellation of election results

Purusant to Article 52 para. (1) of Law no. 370/2004, "*The Constitutional Court shall cancel the elections if the voting and the ascertaining of the results took place fraudulently in such a way as to modify the allotment of the term of office or, as the case may be, the order of the candidates participating in the second round. Under these circumstances, the Court shall order the round to be repeated on the second Sunday since the cancellation of the elections*". The petition for the cancellation of the elections may be filed by the political parties, political alliances, electoral alliances, organizations of citizens belonging to national minorities represented in the Council of National Minorities and by the candidates who participated in the elections within 3 days at most of the closing of voting. The petition must be motivated and accompanied by the evidence it is grounded on. The Constitutional Court shall settle the petition by the date set by law for making public the election result.

Thus, for example, in the presidential elections in 2009, the Plenum of the Constitutional Court ordered the Central Electoral Bureau to reconsider and recount the invalid ballots in order to determine whether there are differences between the data recorded in the statement of the vote and the established reality. Following

670 For example, Ruling no. 3 of 20 October 2009, published in the Official Gazette of Romania no. 722 of 26 October 2009.

671 Rulings no. 25 and no. 27 of 4 November 2009, published in the Official Gazette of Romania no. 760 of 9 November 2009.

this procedure and the identification of a total number of 2.247 votes validly cast (distributed as follows: 1.260 votes validly cast for one candidate, and 987 votes validly cast for the other candidate), the Court found that the number of the valid votes identified is not susceptible, on the one hand, to prove the existence of fraud, but rather errors inherent in a process of such scale and complexity, and, on the other hand, it is not likely to affect in any way the allotment of the term of office[672].

On that occasion, the Court also proceeded to analyze the provisions relating to the cancellation of elections. Thus, in accordance with Article 2 section 30 of Law no. 35/2008 for the election of the Chamber of Deputies and the Senate and amending and supplementing Law no. 67/2004 for the election of local public administration authorities, Law no. 215/2001 on Local Public Administration and Law no. 393/2004 on the Statute of local elected officials[673], *election fraud is "any unlawful action that occurs before, during or after the closing of voting or during vote counting and signing of statements of the vote and which results in the distortion of the voters' will and in creating advantages materialized in additional votes and mandates for a political party, a political alliance, electoral alliance or an independent candidate*"[674]. Under the legal provisions cited, the Court held that "*the cancellation of elections can only intervene if the voting and the ascertaining of the results took place fraudulently; not any fraud in the election process is tantamount to election fraud, but only the fraud which is susceptible to modify the allotment of the term of office (or, as the case may be, the order of the candidates participating in the second round); the petition for the cancellation of elections must be motivated and accompanied by the evidence it is grounded on*".

Confirmation and validation of election result

According to Articles 53–54 of Law no. 370/2004, the Constitutional Court shall validate the result of each round, shall ensure the publication of the election result in the media and in the Official Gazette of Romania, Part I, for each round, and shall validate the election result for the President elect.

The second round shall take place under the conditions provided for in Article 81 (3) of the Constitution of Romania, republished, two weeks after the first round, in the same polling stations and constituencies, the electoral operations being carried out by the same electoral bureaux and based on the same electoral rolls as in the first round. In the second round, only the first 2 candidates who obtained the highest number of votes validly cast for the entire country in the first round shall

672 Ruling no. 39 of 14 December 2009, published in the Official Gazette of Romania no. 924 of 30 December 2009.

673 published in the Official Gazette of Romania no. 196 of 13 March 2008.

674 Article 2 section 30 shall currently be read as follows: "election fraud – any unlawful action that occurs before, during or after the closing of voting or during vote counting and signing of statements of the vote and which results in the distortion of the voters' will and in creating advantages materialized in additional mandates for an election competitor".

participate. The Constitutional Court shall confirm that number within 24 hours of the receipt of the statements of the vote provided for in Article 23 (3) by making public the full names of the two candidates who shall participate in the second round, and the voting day set according to paragraph (1).

The validation document shall be drawn up in 3 copies, out of which one shall stay with the Constitutional Court, one shall be sent to the Parliament for the oath to be taken as provided for in Article 82 (2) of the Constitution of Romania, republished, and the third one shall be handed in to the elected candidate.

3.3.2 The Court's competences within the suspension procedure as well as the referendum for the suspension of the President of Romania from office

Referring to the political responsibility of the President of Romania [675], the Court held that by his position and role, resulted from direct election by the people – which gives him an equivalent level of legitimacy with Parliament, which is also elected directly – the President of Romania cannot be a participant in a parliamentary debate as this would mean that he shall assume political responsibility, which is contrary to his constitutional position, placing him in a position similar to that of the Government which, according to Article 109 para. (1) of the Constitution, shall be politically responsible before Parliament. Within the political responsibility, Article 95 of the Constitution may be applicable to the President of Romania, an article which concerns the suspension from office, in which case the electorate, and not Parliament, can dismiss the President, and the provisions of Article 112 may become applicable to the Prime Minister, regarding the questions, interpellations, and simple motions, or Article 113 of the Constitution, regarding the motion of censure, in which case Parliament may dismiss the Government.

The procedure for the suspension and dismissal of the President of Romania from office suspension is governed by Article 95 para. (3) of the Constitution[676], whose provisions are developed by Law no. 47/1992 on the Organization and Operation of the Constitutional Court [677], Law no. 3/2000 on the organization and holding of the referendum[678] and the Regulations of the joint meetings of the Chamber of Deputies and the Senate (hereinafter called Regulations), approved by Parliament Resolution no. 55/2013[679].

---

675 Decision no. 87 of 30 September 1994, published in the Official Gazette of Romania no. 292 of 14 October 1994.

676 According to which: "*If the proposal of suspension from office has been approved, a referendum shall be held within 30 days for removing the President from office*".

677 Republished in the Official Gazette of Romania no. 807 of 3 December 2010.

678 Published in the Official Gazette of Romania no. 84 of 24 February 2000, as subsequently amended and supplemented.

679 Published in the Official Gazette of Romania no. 394 of 1 July 2013.

According to the above-mentioned normative acts, the procedure for the suspension and dismissal of the President from office undergoes the following steps[680]:

- ✓ initiation of the proposal for suspension from office of the President by at least one third of the Deputies and Senators and immediate notification thereof to the President [Article 95 para. (2) of the Constitution and Article 80 para. (1) of the Regulations];
- ✓ consultation of the Constitutional Court, reason why the proposal for suspension from office of the President of Romania together with the evidence in its support shall be communicated, in copy, to the Constitutional Court, by the president who chaired the joint meeting of the two Chambers [Article 95 para. (1) and Article 146 h) of the Constitution, Article 42 para. (2) of Law no. 47/1992 and Article 81 paragraphs (1) and (2) of the Regulations];
- ✓ issuance by the Constitutional Court of the advisory opinion concerning the suspension from office of the President of Romania and its communication to the Presidents of the two Chambers of Parliament and to the President of Romania [Article 146 h) of the Constitution and Article 43 of Law no. 47/1992];
- ✓ the debate on the proposal for suspension from office of the President in the joint meeting of the Chamber of Deputies and the Senate [Article 95 para. (1) of the Constitution and Article 81 paragraphs (3) and (4) of the Regulations];
- ✓ approval of the proposal for suspension and communication to the Constitutional Court, by the president who chaired the joint meeting of the two Chambers of Parliament, based on the resolution adopted in joint meeting, of the request for establishing the existence of circumstances which justifies the interim in the exercise of office of President of Romania [Article 95 para. (3) and Article 146 g) of the Constitution in conjunction with Article 44 of Law no. 47/1992];
- ✓ ascertainment by the Constitutional Court of the existence of such circumstances and communication of findings to Parliament and Government [Article 146 g) of the Constitution in conjunction with Article 44 of Law no. 47/1992];
- ✓ establishment by Parliament, by resolution, of the object and the date of the national referendum for dismissal of the President, within maximum 30 days of the date of approval of the proposal for suspension from office [Article 95 para. (3) of the Constitution and Article 15 para. (1) b) of Law no. 3/2000];
- ✓ holding of the referendum;
- ✓ the Constitutional Court establishes whether the procedure for the organisation and holding of the referendum was observed and confirms its results [Article 146 i) of the Constitution and Article 46 para. (1) of Law no. 47/1992];
- ✓ before publication in the Official Gazette of Romania, Part I, the decision of the Constitutional Court is submitted to the Chamber of Deputies and the Senate, met in joint session [Article 146 a) of the Constitution and Article 47 para. (3) of Law no. 47/1992];

680 Constitutional Court's Decision no. 734 of 24 July 2012, published in the Official Gazette of Romania no. 516 of 25 July 2012.

- ✓ entry into force of the measure for dismissal from office of the President of Romania on the day of publication in the Official Gazette of Romania, Part I, of the Constitutional Court's ruling for confirmation of the returns of the referendum [Article 45 of Law no. 3/2000].

One may note that within this procedure, the Court intervenes in several phases, the whole process is thus subject to a constitutional review: the issuance of the advisory opinion on the proposal for the suspension from office, the ascertainment of any circumstance as may justify the interim in the exercise of office of President, to see to the observance of the procedure for holding the referendum and to confirm its returns. Given the importance of the President within the state powers, the intervention of the Constitutional Court and its permanent dialogue, especially with Parliament and the President-elect and the interim one, during this procedure, serve his classification into the principles and limits of the rule of law.

By a series of decisions, the Court has limited its competence and that of Parliament within the procedure for the suspension of the President of Romania from office, a procedure about which one can say that we refer to conjunct competences, so more difficult to be circumstantiated.

Thus, rejecting as inadmissible the application for settlement of the legal dispute of a constitutional nature between Parliament of Romania and the President of Romania[681], application in which it was argued that Parliament ordered the suspension of the President of Romania from office, knowingly ignoring one of the essential conditions provided for by Article 95 para. (1), respectively the commitment of serious offences whereby the President of Romania violates the provisions of the Constitution, and that Parliament had no power to rule upon the proposal for suspension without the commitment of serious offences by the President of Romania regarding the violation of the constitutional provisions, the qualification of the facts as serious offences was the argument of the Constitutional Court and it held, in essence, the following: "*even if it were considered that only the Constitutional Court, in terms of its role as guarantor for the supremacy of the Constitution, provided by the constitutional norms of Article142 para. (1), can qualify the facts alleged against the President of Romania as serious offences or not, regarding the violation of the Constitution, Parliament cannot be prevented in exercising the right to suspend or not the President of Romania from office, irrespective of the opinion, positive or negative, of the Constitutional Court, opinion which is purely advisory, as stipulated in Article 146 h) of the Constitution. Within the procedure for the suspension of the President of Romania from office, governed by Article 95 of the Constitution, the role of the Constitutional Court shall end upon the issuance of the advisory opinion*".

Similarly, the Court rejected the challenge against a resolution of Parliament, whereby it was practically required the sanction of a potential breach by Parliament of a ruling of the Constitutional Court, which was to be pronounced within

681 Decision no. 730 of 9 July 2012, published in the Official Gazette of Romania no. 473 of 11 July 2012.

the exercise of its power provided for in Article 146 i) of the Constitution and "*any resolution of Parliament, subsequent to the Constitutional Court's decision, which would establish the organisation and holding of a new referendum within the same proceedings based on Article 95 of the Constitution, proceedings completed at the time of publication in the Official Gazette of Romania of the Constitutional Court's decision rendered on the referendum*". As concerns these challenges, the Court held that "*in the exercise of its powers, as circumstantiated in Decision no. 727/2012, the Constitutional Court decides on Parliament resolutions affecting constitutional values and principles. The Court cannot examine and decide on future and possible actions and acts of Parliament departing from the assumption of ill-faith in the interpretation and application of a text contained in a resolution of this public authority and of any behaviour contrary to the requirement of constitutional loyalty and the principles of the rule of law*"[682].

In light of the institutional dialogue, both with the President of Romania and Parliament, it is worth mentioning the way in which the Constitutional Court has defined a series of concepts which are used by the fundamental law to regulate the procedure for suspension from office of the President of Romania.

Thus, for example, by the Advisory Opinion no. 1/2007[683] on the proposal for suspension from office of the President of Romania, the Court proceeded to the interpretation and enforcement of the provisions of Article 95 para. (1) of the Constitution stipulating that the President of Romania may be suspended from office in case he has committed serious offences in violation of the Constitution, text which does not define the notion "serious offences". Consequently, to rule whether the conditions for the suspension from office of the President of Romania are fulfilled, the Constitutional Court has firstly established the definition of this concept, holding in this respect the following: "*It is obvious that an act, i.e. an action or inaction, in breach of the provisions of the Constitution, is serious in comparison even to the infringement subject. But in the regulation of the procedure of suspension from office of the President of Romania, the Constitution is not limited to this meaning, because, otherwise, the notion «serious offences» would make no sense. Analyzing the distinction contained in the quoted text and taking into account that the Basic Law is a normative legal act, the Constitutional Court finds that not any violation of the Constitution can justify the suspension from office of the President of Romania, but only «serious offences», in the complex meaning of this notion in law science and practice. From a legal perspective, to appreciate the seriousness of an offence against the value that it harms, as well as its harmful consequences, potential or already occurred, the means employed, the individual offender and, not least, his subjective position and the purpose for which he committed the offence. Applying these criteria to the acts of violation of the constitutional legal order referred to in Article 95(1) of the Basic Law, the Court holds that the serious offences in violation of the provisions of the Constitution could*

---

682 Decision no. 734 of 24 July 2012, published in the Official Gazette of Romania no. 516 of 25 July 2012.

683 Published in the Official Gazette of Romania no. 258 of 18 April 2007.

be those act of decision or the failure to comply with mandatory decision acts, whereby the President of Romania would hamper the functioning of public authorities, would suppress or restrict the citizens rights and freedom, would disturb constitutional order or would aim to change the constitutional order or other acts of the same nature that would have or might have similar effects".

Pursuant to the *erga omnes* binding nature of the Constitutional Court's decisions, whenever a constitutional concept is invoked before the Court, whose definition or clarification was conceptually made by it, the Court's analysis will be conducted within the framework established by the Court itself. As concerns an example taken from an opinion of the Court, we consider that, although the solution delivered by the Court is advisory (which is the specific legal nature of the opinion), the interpretation given by the Court to the constitutional text of reference (Articl 95) shall be binding.

Consistent debates and a rich case-law of the Constitutional Court have been developed in relation to the concept of referendum and the referral to the Court aims, most often, at regulations or situations where the main discussions concerned the referendum regarding the dismissal of the President of Romania. We mainly refer to the regulation that conditions the validity of a national referendum by a quorum (minimum percentage) of participation: [Article 5 para. (2) of Law no. 3/2000]. Whereas the text of Article 5 para. (2) of Law no. 3/2000, governing the quorum of participation, does not distinguish between the types of national referendum regulated by the Constitution, it results that it is applicable to all three types of referendum. The Constitutional Court held in this regard, by Decision no. 731/2012[684], that "*the condition to be fulfilled for the validity of the referendum is also the same for all types of referendum, as Article 5 para. (2) of Law no. 3/2000 requires an absolute majority which consists of half plus one of the voters enrolled on the permanent electoral lists*". The legislative amendment, for the purpose of establishing a quorum of participation of 30% of the persons enrolled on the permanent electoral lists (which replaced the quorum of half plus one of the voters enrolled on the permanent electoral lists provided by the old regulation) has been referred to the Constitutional Court. By Decision no. 334 of 26 June 2013[685], the Constitutional Court rejected as unfounded the objection of unconstitutionality and found that "*the provisions of the Law amending and supplementing Law no. 3/2000 on the organization and holding of the referendum is constitutional to the extent that they shall not be applied to referendums organized within one year of the entry into force of the law*". The Court delivered such an interpretative decision on the ground of compliance with the principle of legal certainty.

684 Published in the Official Gazette of Romania no. 478 of 12 July 2012.
685 Published in the Official Gazette of Romania no. 407 of 5 July 2013.

3.3.3 *The Constitutional Court's role on the exercise of the constitutional powers granted to the President of Romania*

Powers of representation of the Romanian State. The obligations of the President of Romania arising from EU accession

The fulfilment by the Romanian authorities of obligations arising from the statute of Romania as a member of the EU has sometimes determined different interpretations of the incident norms, with the consequence of certain legal disputes of a constitutional nature.

Such a case is the conflict between the President of Romania and the Prime Minister on the issue of country representation in the European Council[686]. In this case, the Court had to establish the competence of the authorities concerned in accordance with the provisions of the Constitution, but in relation to the obligations imposed by the European Act of reference, an opportunity to establish certain direct connections between the two levels – national and European – reflected at an institutional level. Of course, the Court's interpretation concerned constitutional provisions, but through this interpretation the Court also imposed a certain conception on the institutional relationships in terms of the incident acts of the European Union, underlining in this way the obligations which fall within the national public authorities under Article 148 para. (4) of the Constitution.

In order to achieve this circumstantiation, the Constitutional Court examined the provisions of the Treaty on European Union, which govern the competence and the role of the European Council, finally reaching the conclusion that "the wording in Article 10(2) second sentence and Article 15(2) of the Treaty, concerning the composition of the European Council – the Heads of State or Government of the Member States – is generic and does not oblige Member States with a two-headed executive to ensure representation by both the Head of State and the Government, but rather by a teleological interpretation of the text, the idea is that its purpose is to provide representation of the Member State at the highest level by the competent public authority".

Based on this conclusion, the Court proceeded on this occasion (as well as later, when it declared unconstitutional certain provisions of the Law on the cooperation between Parliament and Government in European affairs[687]) to a systematic interpretation of the Constitution, noting that "Article 80(1) of the Constitution is a constitutional text of principle. Therefore, it should not be interpreted restrictively, but in the spirit of the Constitution, or in conjunction with Article 91 and Article 148 para. (4) of the Constitution, the latter text providing expressly that the Parliament, the President of Romania, the Government, and the judicial authority

686 Decision no. 683 of 27 June 2012, published in the Official Gazette of Romania no. 479 of 12 July 2012.

687 Decision no. 784 of 26 September 2012, published in the Official Gazette of Romania no. 701 of 12 October 2012.

shall guarantee «any obligations arising from the accession instrument». One of those obligations consists of the highest representation of Romania in the European Council, i.e. by the public authority which has competence to commit Romania at the State level. Otherwise, the provisions of Article 148(4) of the Constitution on the President of Romania would be lacking substance; it is, however, admitted in principle that any norm is created in order to produce legal effects".

Analyzing the constitutional role and the duties of those authorities, the Court ruled that "*in exercising his constitutional powers, the President of Romania participates in the meetings of the European Council in his capacity as Head of State. This task may be delegated by the President of Romania, specifically, to the Prime Minister*"[688].

In order to substantiate this conclusion, the Court found that "*according to Article 80(1) of the Constitution, the President of Romania represents the Romanian state, which means that in the area of foreign policy he leads and commits the State. This constitutional text enables him to draw future lines that the State will follow in its foreign policy, practically to determine its orientation in foreign relations, taking into account, of course, the national interest. Such a conception is legitimized by the representative nature of the function, as the President of Romania is elected by citizens through universal, equal, direct, secret and freely expressed suffrage. In foreign policy, the Prime Minister has the constitutional competence to ensure the implementation of the foreign policy of the country [Article 102 para. (1) of the Constitution], which means that, according to the guidelines established by the State representative externally, which is the President of the State, the Government, through its representative, is to properly implement measures undertaken by the State. Therefore, the Court finds that the Government's role in foreign policy is rather technical, and it must follow and comply with the obligations to which Romania is committed at the State level. Thus, the Government's role is rather derivative and not original, as it is the one of the President of Romania; therefore, since it is not a delegated power, but a power belonging to the President of Romania, representation of the State may be delegated by him through an express act of will when deemed appropriate*".

Subsequently developing these reasons and underlining the competence of the President within its relationships with the Prime Minister and Parliament, the Court emphasized that "*the specific act of will of the President of Romania delegating the representation of the Romanian State must take into account certain objective criteria, such as: (1) the best positioned public authority in relation to the topics addressed within the Council of Europe, (2) the position of the President of Romania or of the Prime Minister on these topics must be legitimised by a viewpoint in accordance with that of Parliament (3) difficulties entailed by the task of implementation of the decisions taken in the European Council.*

Such a political act delegating representation in the European Council meetings must also take into account the above-mentioned criteria in order to achieve a consensus

688 Decision no. 683 of 27 June 2012, published in the Official Gazette of Romania no. 479 of 12 July 2012.

between the public authorities involved: the President of Romania, respectively the Prime Minister, and the decision thus made must also take account of the constitutional principle of loyal cooperation"[689].

Powers on the initiative for the revision of the Constitution
Pursuant to Article 150 para. (1) of the Constitution, "*A revision of the Constitution may be initiated by the President of Romania at the proposal of the Government, by at least one quarter of all Deputies or Senators, as well as by at least 500,000 citizens having the right to vote*".

Adjudicating upon the sole initiative for the revision of the Constitution initiated by the President of Romania, on the proposal submitted by the Government, the Constitutional Court ruled on the exercise of this power. Thus, having to decide whether the intervention of the President, for the purpose of amending and supplementing the bill for revision of the Constitution proposed by the Government, constitutes a violation of the constitutional norms in matter of initiation of revision, rules that circumscribe its limits, the Court held that the provisions of Article 150 of the Constitution, listing the holders of the right to initiate the revision of the Constitution (the President of Romania, the Deputies and Senators, respectively the citizens), establish a number of conditions on the exercise of this right. In case of the President of Romania, the said provisions render conditional the concerned right only on the formulation of a proposal in this regard by the Government. Establishing that the revision "*may be initiated by the President of Romania*", the constitutional text does not distinguish on the powers of the President of Romania as holder of the right of initiative for the revision of the Constitution, nor establish any obligation or prohibition in his respect. Therefore, the President of Romania, once he receives the Government's proposal for the revision of the Constitution, has full freedom to decide whether to initiate or not the revision of the Constitution, and, if he decides to initiate it, he can partially assume as such or he can supplement the Government's proposal. A different interpretation of the constitutional text, for the purpose of assigning a formal role in this procedure to the President of Romania, which is to submit to Parliament a bill on revision of the Constitution as proposed by the Government, would be likely to deprive of content his right of initiative. However, this right was conferred upon him by the constituent legislature precisely taking into account the role and position held by the President of Romania in the political system of society, which allows him to know its progress and prospects of development and to make use of these findings, including by initiating an amendment process of the Basic Law of the State, when, through the Government's proposal in this regard, an agreement is reached between the two representatives of the executive power on the initiation of such a process. For the reasons set forth above, the Court found that the right of legislative initiative for

689 Decision no. 449 of 6 November 2013, published in the Official Gazette of Romania no. 784 of 14 December 2013.

the revision of the Constitution was made in compliance with Article 150 paragraph (1) of the Constitution of Romania [690].

Powers within the appointment procedure of the Government[691]

As for the investiture procedure of the Government, the substance of the matter consists of the provisions of Articles 85, 103 and 104 of the Constitution, developed, and as for the parliamentary procedure, Articles 71–76 of the Regulations on the joint meetings of the Chamber of Deputies and the Senate[692].

From the analysis of the above-mentioned legal provisions, it results that such procedure undergoes the following steps:

- ✓ The President of Romania designates a candidate to the office of Prime Minister, following his consultation with the party which has obtained absolute parliamentary majority, or – where no such majority exists – with the parties represented in Parliament [Article 85 para. (1) and Article 103 para. (1) of the Constitution];
- ✓ The candidate designated to the office of Prime Minister shall, within 10 days from designation, seek the Parliament's vote of confidence on the programme and the complete list of the Government [Article 103 para. (1) of the Constitution];
- ✓ Standing Bureaux of the two Chambers shall immediately reproduce and deliver to the Deputies and Senators the programme and the list of the Government, when these shall be received from the candidate appointed for the office of Prime Minister (Article 85 of the Regulation);
- ✓ The Standing Bureaux set the date of the joint meeting of the Chamber of Deputies and the Senate in maximum 15 days from the receipt of the programme and list of the Government and they also take all actions to convene the Deputies and the Senators [Article 86 para. (1) of the Regulation];
- ✓ Each candidate for the office of Minister shall be heard during the joint meeting by the Standing Committees of the two Chambers which activity object corresponds to the scope of the future Minister; the Committees shall prepare a justified joint advisory opinion which shall be presented to the candidate for the office of Prime Minister [Article 86 para. (2) of the Regulation];
- ✓ The programme and the complete list of the Government shall be taken up for debate in the joint meeting of the Chamber of Deputies and the Senate and

---

690 Decision no. 799 of 17 June 2011, published in the Official Gazette of Romania no. 440 of 23 June 2011.

691 For details, see M. Safta, *The role of the President of Romania in the investiture procedure of Government and the appointment procedure of Ministers. Developments in the case-law of the Constitutional Court of Romania*, in Revista Transilvană de Ştiinţe Administrative, volume 30, no. 1, p. 156.

692 Regulations of 3 March 1992 on the joint activities of the Chamber of Deputies and the Senate, republished in the Official Gazette of Romania no. 461 of 25 July 2013.

Parliament grants (or not) its confidence by a majority vote of Deputies and Senators [Article 103 para. (3) second sentence of the Constitution];

- ✓ The Chair of meeting shall give the floor to the candidate appointed for the office of Prime Minister, after the approval of the agenda, in order for him/her to present the programme and the list of the Government; upon the request of the representatives of the Parliamentary Groups of the Chamber of Deputies and the Senate, the Chair shall give the floor to them to express viewpoints of those Groups on the programme and the list of the Government;
- ✓ After the conclusion of the debates, the proposal for the grant of confidence to the Government shall be submitted for voting (which is a secret vote by balls), and the Chair shall notify the results of the poll, which shall be recorded in the minutes concluded for this purpose (Articles 87–89 of the Regulation);
- ✓ The Resolution of the Parliament on the grant of the vote of confidence, signed by the President of the Chamber of Deputies and by the President of the Senate (Article 90 of the Regulation) shall be immediately submitted to the President of Romania or, as appropriate, the President of Romania shall be informed that the vote of confidence has not been granted to form the Government, in order for him/her to appoint another candidate for the office of Prime Minister (Article 77 of the Regulation);.
- ✓ The President of Romania appoints the Government based on the Parliament's vote of confidence [Article 85 para. (1) of the Constitution];
- ✓ The Prime Minister, the Ministers, and the other Members of the Government shall take an oath [Article 104 para. (1) of the Constitution].

From the examination of the mentioned procedural stages, as they are provided by law, it results that the investiture procedure of the Government shall be initiated and completed by the President of Romania.

Thus, the President has an exclusive right for the appointment of the candidate for the office of Prime Minister[693]. The obligation to consult with the party which

693 As concerns the candidate for the office of Prime Minister, the specialised literature held that "*it can be a politician, possibly the leader of the majority party, but, equally, it may be a person who has not been politically integrated, a specialist, i.e. a technocrat* " (M. Oroveanu, *Administrative Law Treaty*, second edition, revised and supplemented, Cerna Publishing House, Bucharest, 1998, p. 436); "*there is no constitutional obligation regarding the candidate's political or parliamentary affiliation, but only the parliamentary majority requirement to obtain political support* " (I. Santai, *Administrative Law and Administrative science*, volume I, Alma Mater Publishing House, Sibiu, 2009, p. 176); "*the constitutional text was drafted so as to permit as many formulas for the appointment of the candidate for the office of Prime Minister, who may be the leader of a political party, a technocrat from outside parties, a specialist who is actually a deputy or a senator or a specialist who is not a member of the Government*" (M. Constantinescu, A. Iorgovan, I. Muraru, E.S. Tănăsescu, *cited paper*, p. 167) – cited in I. Muraru, E.S. Tănăsescu (coordinators), *cited paper*, p. 960.

has absolute majority in Parliament, or if there is no such majority, with the parties represented in Parliament, provided by Article 103 para. (1) of the Constitution, does not also determine an obligation of the President to appoint the candidate who represents that party's option or meets the option of those parties. The fact that this right is exclusive does not mean that it is also discretionary, as the behaviour of political parties cannot be also discretionary, through their representatives attending the consultations. Thus, the allotment by the President of the mandate to a person other than the one for whom an option was expressed during the mentioned consultations, in order to form the list for the next Government, involved the risk that it may not have parliamentary support and therefore, not to be given the vote of trust by Parliament. On the other hand, a discretionary act – of the President or of the political parties, by their representatives during the consultations prior to the appointment of the candidate for the office of Prime Minister – can be examined from the perspective of a principle underlined by the Constitutional Court in its case-law, namely that of constitutional loyalty.

If the appointment of the candidate for the office of Prime Minister is an exclusive right of the Head of State, the finalization of the investiture procedure of the Government, respectively its appointment, does not involve anymore any right of option on his part. In this respect, by Decision no. 98/2008[694], the Constitutional Court held that "*the legal document under which the President of Romania makes the appointments is the Parliament Resolution, adopted under Article 85 para. (1), Article 103 para. (3) of the Constitution and the relevant provisions of the Regulations on the joint meeting of the Chambers of Parliament. From the text of the Constitution it results that, in the cases set forth in Article 85 para. (1) and (3), the appointment of ministers by the President of Romania is an act of enforcement of the Parliament Resolution and of investiture, on this basis, of ministers, by the Head of State. The resolution of the supreme representative body of the Romanian people [Article 61 para. (1) of the Constitution] is a binding act, which the President could not refuse it than by committing serious offences of violation of the Constitution*".

As concerns the appointment procedure of the Government, the exercise of conjunct powers in order to achieve the same constitutional objective constituted the premise of an institutional blockage when the involved public authorities did not cooperate and failed to agree, repeatedly. This is another aspect which the arbitrary action of the public authorities can meet, especially when the letter of the law is not sufficient to clearly limit their competence.

Powers within the appointment procedure of Ministers

The Constitutional Court of Romania has also settled a legal dispute of a constitutional nature determined by the refusal of the President to act on the proposal submitted by the Prime Minister on an appointment to the office of Minister of

694 Published in the Official Gazette of Romania no. 140 of 22 February 2008.

Justice, while the constitutional text of reference – namely Article 85 – provides no procedure to be followed in the event of such refusal.

In order to identify the procedure to be followed and the limits of competence of the President of Romania and, respectively of the Prime Minister, in the given situation, the Court sought the meaning of the norm of Article 85 para. (2) of the Constitution, "*in the letter of this text, as well as in the basic principles and spirit of the Basic Law*". Having examined the other constitutional provisions establishing rules applicable to the relationships between the two public authorities concerned and applying them, by analogy, to the case at issue, the Court established[695] that: "*while applying Article 85 para. (2) of the Constitution, the President of Romania, not having the right of veto, may ask the Prime Minister only once, upon statement of grounds, to nominate a different person for the office of minister, (...)* and (A/N) *as concerns the Prime Minister's possibility to reiterate his first proposal, the Court finds that such possibility is excluded by fact that the President of Romania declined the proposal. Therefore, the Prime Minister must nominate a different person for the office of minister*"[696].

The same appointment procedure of ministers determined the examination and definition by the Constitutional Court of the relationships between all the public authorities involved, i.e. President – Prime Minister – Parliament, as well as the clarification of the concept of interim office of minister, enshrined in the Constitution.

Thus, in 2009, the Court was notified by the President of the Senate of Romania on legal disputes of a constitutional nature determined, according to the allegations of the author of the referral, by the decrees of the President by which, after taking note of the resignation of ministers belonging to a certain political party and finding their cessation of their office as members of the Government, he appointed as interim ministers a number of members of Government in office, belonging to another political party. As grounds for the referral, the provisions of Article 85 para. (3) of the Constitution were invoked, a text which requires that the appointment

695 Decision no. 98 of 7 February 2008, published in the Official Gazette of Romania no. 140 of 22 February 2008.

696 In deciding so, the Court noted that "*as concerns the number of cases in which the President of Romania may request the Prime Minister to make a different nomination for the office of Minister, the Court finds that, in order to prevent the occurrence of an institutional blockage in the lawmaking process, the constituent legislature provided for in Article 77 para. (2) of the Basic Law the President's right to return a law to Parliament for reconsideration, only once. The Court found that this solution acts as a constitutional principle in the settlement of legal disputes between two or several public authorities which have conjoint duties in the adoption of a measure provided by the Basic Law and that this principle can be generally applied in similar cases. Applied to the government reshuffle and to the appointment of ministers in case of vacancy of offices, this solution is likely to eliminate the blockage that would arise through the possible repeated refusal of the President to appoint a minister upon the proposal of the Prime Minister*".

of ministers shall be based on Parliament's approval, granted upon the proposal of the Prime Minister, where the proposal of "reshuffle" changes the "structure" or the "political composition" of the Government.

The Court found that the President of Romania acted under and within the limits of the Constitution, as Article 85 para. (3) of the Constitution applies to the situation of "*government reshuffle*". However, "*the interim is always carried out by a member of the Government, and not by a person who is not registered on the list approved by Parliament by being conferred the vote of investiture, and the appointment of the interim minister is conferred for a limited period under the constitutional text – not exceeding 45 days. By designation of one or more interim ministers there is no government reshuffle, the essence of which is (...), the replacement of members of the Government with persons who are not on the list approved by the Parliament on investiture. Any changes in the political structure or composition of Government, referred to in the same constitutional text, can be analysed for and about the government reshuffle, and not about a transitional period, in which the Government operation is assured by the ministers remained in office, until appointment of new members holder of the office of minister. Moreover, interpretation in the meaning that also in case of designation of one or more members of the Government as interim ministers they should be subject to verification and approval by Parliament lacks of efficiency the interim and leads to institutional bottlenecks, with negative consequences for the operation of the entire Government and for its program approved by Parliament*". In conclusion, "*the designation of interim ministers, governed by Article 107 of the Constitution, does not involve the exercise of Parliament's power referred to in Article 85 para. (3) of the Basic Law, it cannot be claimed the infringement by the President of Romania of that power or of the "preliminary procedure" imposed by the same constitutional text*"[697]. For these reasons, the Court found no legal dispute of a constitutional nature.

Powers on the organization of advisory referendum

Pursuant to Article 90 of the Constitution, "*The President of Romania may, after consultation with Parliament, ask the people of Romania to express their will as to questions of national interest, by a referendum*".

This constitutional text has given rise to decisions whereby the Court adjudicated upon the role and the relationship between Parliament and the President of Romania in relation to lawmaking, aimed at the procedure of organization and holding of the referendum, regulated by the provisions of Law no. 3/2000[698].

Thus, being notified with the exception of unconstitutionality of the provisions of Article 12 para. (1) of Law no. 3/2000, which expressly and restrictively specified

697 Decision no. 1559 of 18 November 2009, published in the Official Gazette of Romania no. 823 of 30 November 2009; see also Decision no. 1560 of 18 November 2009, published in the Official Gazette of Romania no. 824 of 30 November 2009.

698 Published in the Official Gazette of Romania no. 84 of 24 February 2000.

the "*matters of national interest*"[699] referred to in Article 90 of the Constitution, the Constitutional Court ascertained their unconstitutionality. By the decision delivered on that occasion [700], the Court held that "*Article 90 of the Constitution establishes the exclusive competence of the President in determining the matters of national interest that are subject to referendum, even if the consultation with Parliament is mandatory. Only the President of Romania shall have the right to decide on matters of national interest and, within them, to establish by decree, the specific issue which is subject to referendum and the date of holding it*". Consequently, the restrictive mention set forth in Article 12 para. (1) of Law no. 3/2000 of certain situations regarded as "*matters of national interest*" "*is susceptible to limit the right of the President to consult the people, being known that, in time, the national interest may differ, as new situations may arise at any moment so that the holding of a referendum may be requested*". In conclusion, the "*establishment by law of matters of national interest represents an involvement of the Parliament in the exercise of the exclusive powers conferred by the Constitution upon the President and, as such, a disregard of the principle of separation and balance of powers within the constitutional democracy*".

These considerations have been reiterated in the decisions delivered within the exercise of its power to see to the observance of the procedure for the organisation and holding of a referendum, and to confirm its returns[701], and the Court has also noted that this exclusive right of the President is based on the constitutional provisions of Article 80 on the "Role of the President", of Article 2 para. (1), according to which "*national sovereignty belongs to the Romanian people, who shall exercise it through their representative bodies (...)as well as by means of a referendum*", of Article 81 para. (2) regarding the electoral legitimacy the President of Romania which is equal to the legitimacy of Parliament, and of Article 1 para. (4) according to which "*the State shall be organized based on the principle of the separation and balance of*

---

699 "*A. Adoption of certain measures on the reform and economic strategy of the country;*
B. Adoption of particular political decision regarding:
a) the general regime of public and private property;
b) the organisation of local public administration, of territory, as well as the general regime on the local autonomy;
c) the general organisation of education system;
d) the structure of the national system of defence, the organisation of the army, the participation of armed forces to certain international operations;
e) to enter into, sign or ratify certain international agreements for an indefinite period of time or for more than 10 years;
f) Romania's integration into European and Euro-Atlantic structures;
g) general regime of denominations".

700 Decision no. 567 of 11 July 2006, published in the Official Gazette of Romania no. 613 of 14 July 2006.

701 Ruling no. 7 of 7 November 2007, published in the Official Gazette of Romania no. 759 of 8 November 2007.

powers – legislative, executive, and judicial – within the framework of a constitutional democracy"[702].

The Court has also noted that, although the establishment of the date of holding a national advisory referendum on matters of national interest is specified in the exclusive power of the President of Romania set forth in Article 90 of the Constitution, however, in order to avoid any suspicions regarding the election results, respectively the results of the referendum, it is appropriate that the two election procedures shall not be held on the same day, even if practical reasons, on matters of finance, would justify their simultaneous organization.

Powers on the award of decorations and titles of honour

The Court held a series of statuaries of principle regarding the competence of the President of Romania, presenting it in relation to that of the Prime Minister regarding the countersignature of the decrees issued by the President.

In this respect, the Court found that the exercise by the President of Romania of its power to confer decorations or titles of honour [Article 94 letter a) of the Constitution] requires the concurrent exercise by the Prime Minister of its power referred to in Article 100 para. (2) of the Constitution which expressly provides that such decree – the legal act of the President of Romania – shall be countersigned by the Prime Minister. Consequently, the exercise by the President of Romania of its power to confer decorations or titles of honour by decree is subject to an external requirement, namely the countersignature of the decree, a requirement in the absence of which such decree cannot be issued.

The purpose for which the constituent legislature introduced the obligation of countersignature of presidential decrees laid down in Article 100 para. (2) of the Constitution is given both by the need of review of the legality of the act of the President and by the need for a form of political responsibility in the sense that one of the public authorities involved in the procedure of issuance of the decree awarding decorations must assume responsibility before Parliament.

As the President is not politically accountable to Parliament, this responsibility lies with the Prime Minister for the act of countersignature. Therefore, in view of the countersignature of the decree awarding decorations, the President of Romania and the Prime Minister, prior to the issuance of the decree, have the possibility to have a preliminary consultation, even an informal one. This constitutional mechanism enables, on the one hand, the plenary and direct manifestation of parliamentary control over the activity of the Prime Minister and, ultimately, over the activity of the Government. On the other hand, it also ensures, in this way, a balance between State powers, the executive, represented by the President and the Prime Minister,

702 Ruling no. 33 of 26 November 2009, published in the Official Gazette of Romania no. 918 of 29 December 2009.

on the one hand, and the legislative, represented by Parliament, on the other hand, avoiding the possibility of abuse of power from the executive[703].

Therefore, the Court found that the President of Romania has the power to issue the decree awarding decorations, while the Prime Minister has the power to countersign it; legal acts of the President (decrees), as well as legal acts of the Prime Minister (countersignature) in addition to their legal component have a strong political significance; the political responsibility assumed by the Prime Minister for acts committed during the mandate covers also the countersigning of presidential decrees; none of the two subjects of law can compel the other to perform or to consent to the enforcement of acts that would affect either the political support of the electorate, or that of Parliament; the consensus should characterise the relationship between the two subjects of law when they must work together to issue a decree (signature/ countersignature); and, finally, the lack of countersignature of the Prime Minister leads to the inexistence of the decree awarding decorations.

Under these circumstances, the Court found that the Prime Minister has the power to refuse to countersign a constitutional decree awarding decorations both for reasons of legality and for reasons related to opportunity.

As concerns the issue of expressing a statement of grounds for the refusal to countersign the decree, the Court held that "the issuance of the decree awarding decorations attests the existence of an agreement of will between the President of Romania and the Prime Minister, i.e. between the vertices of the executive power, as result of consultations held between the two public authorities. Usually, their initiation falls within the responsibility of the Government and Parliament, except for the cases provided for in Article 4 para. (3) of Law no. 29/2000, whereby the initiative falls within the responsibility of the President of Romania. However, in all these cases, the award of decorations involves a subjective element on the part of the public authorities competent for this procedure. Thus, both the initiation of the procedure and the award itself of decorations are the result of the subjective assessments of these authorities who, for their conduct, are responsible, politically speaking, directly or indirectly, to the electorate or to Parliament, as the case may be. It follows a subjective assessments contest which ultimately could result in the issuance or non-issuance of the decree awarding the decoration, without the person proposed for decoration be aggrieved in any of his rights since he has only an expectation on the award of the decoration and not a right. Accordingly, the statement of grounds for the refusal to countersign the decree can neither be regarded as part of the refusal or as having a justified or unjustified nature and therefore it cannot be the subject of a judicial review carried out perhaps by the Constitutional Court.

Therefore, what produces legal effect is not the statement of grounds for the refusal or the justified nature of the statement of grounds for the refusal, but the refusal to countersign the decree. The statement of grounds would be nothing else

703 See also A. Iorgovan, *Legal regime of presidential decrees and of the responsibility of the President of Romania on their issuance*, in RDP no. 1/2005, pp. 53–74.

but an indication of the subjective reasons underlying the decision, without a legal purpose of this technical action as to generate a new competence for the President of Romania. The Constitution does not provide either specifically or implicitly that the President of Romania could compel the Prime Minister to countersign a decree awarding a decoration in the event of an initial refusal on the part of the latter. It follows that the statement of grounds for refusal in itself has no legal consequence, so that the hypothesis set forth in paragraph 51 C) becomes irrelevant regarding the eventual possibility of the President of Romania, in case of a reasoned refusal, to take note of it, to not accept the reasons there given and, therefore, in these circumstances, to compel the Prime Minister, directly or indirectly, to countersign the decree awarding the decoration"[704].

Promotions to the ranks of marshal, general and admiral

By way of settlement of an exception of unconstitutionality, the Court held that, under the provisions of Article 94 b) of the Constitution, the President of Romania, in exercising its powers as head of state and commander of the armed forces, "*promotes to the rank of marshal, general and admiral*". This power constitutes a right of the President, and not an obligation, so that the Head of the State may determine whether he promotes or not to these ranks, without being conditioned by law, as it is the case regarding the appointments of public offices.

Noting that the impugned norms, respectively Article 66 para. (3) of Law no. 80/1995 on the Statute of Military Staff[705], provided, in an imperative way, the promotion in rank of Colonels and Commanders in office when they were put on reserve status or when they were directly discharged, whether they met the conditions of seniority in rank and obtained the mark required by law, the Court concluded that "*the power of the President of Romania provided under Article 94 subparagraph b) of the Constitution appears in this case as a formal intervention to meet certain legal provisions ,which deprives this authority of the very substance of the constitutional power*"[706]. Consequently, the Court upheld the exception of unconstitutionality raised and found that the provisions of Article 66 para. (3) of Law no. 80/1995 on the Statute of Military Staff are contrary to Article 94 b) of the Constitution.

This conclusion has also been indicated on the occasion of settling a legal dispute of a constitutional nature when, ascertaining the existence of such a dispute between the President of Romania, on the one hand, and the judiciary, on the other hand, represented by the High Court of Cassation and Justice, on the other hand, pursuant to Article 146 e) of the Constitution and according to the practice of the contentious constitutional court in the matter, resulted due to the fact that the High Court of Cassation and Justice had not taken account of the Constitutional Court's

704 Decision no. 285 of 21 May 2014, published in the Official Gazette of Romania no. 285/2014.

705 Published in the Official Gazette of Romania no. 155 of 20 July 1995.

706 Decision no. 384 of 4 May 2006, published in the Official Gazette of Romania no. 451 of 24 May 2006.

Decision no. 384 of 4 May 2006[707], as well as in the light of the provisions in force, the Constitutional Court found that, under Article 94 b) of the Constitution, the promotion to the rank of general is an exclusive power of the President of Romania.

Appointment of judges/prosecutors to offices

By Decision no. 375 of 6 July 2005[708], the Court held that "*if the President of Romania would have no right of examination and assessment of the proposals submitted by the Superior Council of Magistracy for the appointment of judges and prosecutors or in certain management offices or if he could not refuse the appointment either motivated or even once, the powers of the President of Romania, set forth in Article 94 c) in conjunction with Article 125 para. (1) of the Constitution, would be void in content and importance*". The Court also noted that the current wording of Article 31 para. (3) of Law no. 303/2004 on the Statute of judges and prosecutors[709], stipulates that: "*The President of Romania may refuse once the appointment of judges and prosecutors provided for in paragraph (1). The motivated refusal shall be immediately communicated to the Superior Council of Magistracy*".

Political statement of the President of Romania and its relationships with the political parties

The position of the President among the powers of the State and its role as mediator among them and between the State and the society has often been discussed within the formulation of certain political statements or its politically positioning. Such cases have been brought before the Constitutional Court by way of referrals covering legal disputes of a constitutional nature.

The Court found[710] that "*within the fulfilment of their constitutional terms of office, the representatives of the public authorities, through their positions, are required to avoid creating conflict situations between powers. The constitutional status of the President and of the Prime Minister, as well as their role within the constitutional democracy compels them to choose the appropriate forms of expression, so that (...) they shall not turn into elements that could generate legal disputes of a constitutional nature between them*".

However, the Court noted that "*the constitutional prerogatives as well as the democratic legitimacy conferred by his election by voters throughout the country require the President of Romania to have an active role, and his presence in political life cannot be summarised to a symbolic and formal exercise. The function of safeguard enshrined in Article 80 (1) of the Constitution involves, by definition, careful observation of the existence and functioning of the State, vigilant oversight on how do the actors of public life operate – public authorities, organisations legitimised by the Constitution,*

---

707 Published in the Official Gazette of Romania no. 451 of 24 May 2006.

708 Published in the Official Gazette of Romania no. 591 of 8 July 2005.

709 Republished in the Official Gazette of Romania no. 826 of 13 September 2005.

710 Decision no. 435 of 26 May 2006, published in the Official Gazette of Romania no. 576 of 4 July 2006.

civil society – and observance of the principles and rules established in the Constitution, protection of values enshrined in the Basic Law. Neither the surveillance nor the duty of guarantee shall be passively performed, by contemplation, but by dynamic and concrete activity. Given these considerations, the Court finds that the President of Romania, by virtue of his powers and legitimacy, may express political views and options, make comments and criticism on the functioning of public authorities and their representatives, make proposal for reforms or measures as he deems desirable to national interest. But the opinions, comments, preferences or requests made by the President are not of decisional nature and they do not have legal effects, and public authorities remain solely responsible on whether to accept or ignore them. In any case, the exercise by the President of an active role in political and social life of the country cannot be characterised as behaviour contrary to the Constitution"[711].

According to those ruled by the Court, the prohibitions set forth in Article 84 para. (1) of the Constitution, according to which, during the term of office, the President of Romania cannot be a member of any political party and exercise any other public or private office, "do not exclude the possibility to further express political views, commitments and goals set out in its election program or to advocate and act so as to achieve them, while complying with the constitutional prerogatives". Moreover, "*the role of mediator among the powers of the State and between the State and the society, set forth in Article 80 para. (2) second sentence of the Constitution, requires the impartiality of the President of Romania, but it does not exclude the possibility to express his viewpoint regarding the best way of settling the disputes arisen and it does not confer upon him the status of political competitor*".

On the same occasion, ruling upon the limits of freedom of expression as they are provided for in the Basic Law, the Court held that it stipulates in Article 72 para. (1), with the marginal title "Parliamentary immunity", that "*No Deputy or Senator shall be held legally responsible for the votes cast or the political opinions expressed while exercising their office*". In accordance with Article 84 (2) of the Constitution "*The President of Romania enjoys immunity. The provisions of Article 72 (1) shall apply accordingly*". By analysing the legal significance of the concept of immunity, the Court finds that it is a constitutional guarantee, a measure of legal protection of the mandate, which is aimed at ensuring the independence of the mandate's holder against any outside pressure or abuse. The guarantee provided for in Article 72 (1) of the Constitution encourages the holder of the mandate to adopt an active role in the political life of the society, as it removes his legal responsibility for the political opinions expressed while exercising the public office. However, the holder of the mandate remains responsible under the law for all acts and offences committed during the period when he exercised the public office and which are not related with votes or political opinions.

711 Advisory Opinion no. 1 of 5 April 2007 on the proposal for the suspension from office of the President of Romania, published in the Official Gazette of Romania no. 258 of 18 April 2007.

The immunity of the President of Romania
From the analysis of the legal and constitutional provisions regarding the immunity of the President of Romania, the Court held that, within the exercise of its duties, the President of Romania is entitled to immunity under its two aspects: irresponsibility for the public viewpoints expressed in the exercise of his term of office and inviolability, within the limits set forth in Article 96 of the Constitution – the impeachment for high treason. By virtue of the inviolability to which the presidential term of office is entitled, during its exercise, the President cannot be subject to any criminal proceedings, except that set forth in Article 96 of the Constitution[712].

Similarly, the Court found that the immunity constitutes a constitutional guarantee, a measure of legal protection of the mandate, which is aimed at ensuring the independence of the mandate's holder against any outside pressure or abuse. The immunity is inherent to the office of public dignity, during the exercise thereof, and not to the person who temporarily exercises this office. Immunity is mandatory and it does not constitute a subjective right which the holder may use or waive according to his own interest. The concept of immunity, under its two aspects, protects the President of Romania against the possible pressures or abuses that could be committed against him, being thus ensured independence, freedom and security in the exercise of his rights and obligations conferred upon him by the Constitution and laws. Considering the fulfilment of this term of office, which involves the exercise of the state authority, so certain powers of a constitutional nature, and the special legal status, the person who exercises the office of President of Romania is not in the same legal situation with the other citizens. That being so, the legal regime applicable to certain different situations can only be a different one: the suspension of prosecution, on the ground of a temporarily legal impediment for the initiation of criminal proceedings, can operate regarding the immunity of the President of Romania only on the person who exercises this office of public dignity. During the suspension of the prosecution, the term limitation for criminal liability with respect to the person who temporarily exercises the office of public dignity shall be suspended, according to Article 156 of the Criminal Code and it shall be reinitiated after the cessation of the term of office as President of Romania.

3.4 Conclusions

The legal provisions and the case-law submitted reveal that there is a constitutional and legal framework likely to support the dialogue between the Constitutional Court and the President of Romania. Likewise, it is found that, most often, the intervention of the Constitutional Court was as to clarify certain constitutional

712 Decision no. 678 of 13 November 2014, published in the Official Gazette of Romania no. 886 of 5 December 2014.

concepts, most often in relation to the exercise of conjunct powers of the President and of the other public authorities. The situations that may arise in practice, which obviously cannot be exhaustively provided by the constituent legislature, may create disputes and challenges of powers between the public authorities.

The intervention of the Constitutional Court was usually required by way of invoking certain legal disputes of a constitutional nature. The Court established rules, through the systematic interpretation of the Constitution, since the refusal to judge, on the ground that the law does not stipulate it, means denial of justice.

This situation results in at least two conclusions: on the one hand, the need for a clearer definition of the constitutional framework of reference regarding the powers of the two representatives of the executive and, on the other hand, their activity needs to be circumscribed to the imperative of loyal behaviour.

As concerns the invocation of the constitutional principle of loyal behaviour, referring to the relationships between the President and the Prime Minister – which were often the subject-matter of the legal disputes settled by the Court –, the Court held that the implementation of this principle is a legal bivalent operation, being equally enforceable against both public authorities. Therefore, based on this principle, the President has the opportunity to consult with the Prime Minister to achieve a consensus between the two peaks of the executive power before the Prime Minister's countersignature is required on the decree conferring decorations and honorary titles. On the other hand, although no constitutional text obliges the Prime Minister to state the reasons which led to the refusal for countersigning the decree, however, in the spirit of the same constitutional principle, it would be useful if the Prime Minister also worked openly with the President, including by initiating consultations with him. Likewise, given that neither was any consultation initiated by the President or the Prime Minister, nor was motivated the refusal for countersigning, the Court held that the initiator of the decree may open, in turn, a constitutional dialogue with the Prime Minister in order to clarify the reasons which led to the refusal for countersigning the decree mentioned and the fulfilment of a consensus, so as not to reach the referral of the Constitutional Court, the latter having no power to mediate such a consensus[713].

We believe that such decision strongly illustrates our claim in the introductory chapter dedicated to the dialogue between the Constitutional Court and the authorities at internal level, in the sense that its main feature is given by the permanent invitation to an inter-institutional dialogue between them.

---

713 Decision no. 285 of 21 May 2014, published in the Official Gazette of Romania no. 478 of 28 June 2014.

4. The dialogue between the Constitutional Court and the Government of Romania

4.1 General aspects

Institutional dialogue between the Constitutional Court and the Government is to be analyzed from two perspectives.

Thus, the Government of Romania is involved in the activity of the Constitutional Court, in particular by the possibility to express viewpoints and to refer to it in the cases expressly and restrictively provided by law, as the Government's activity, being exercised in compliance with the supremacy of the Constitution, shall be subject to the review exercised by the Constitutional Court.

4.2 The relationship between the Government and the constitutional court

4.2.1 The possibility to refer to the Constitutional Court

A direct way of the Government to access to the constitutional justice is the possibility to challenge it under the circumstances expressly and restrictively provided for by law, as follows:

- to adjudicate on the constitutionality of laws, before their promulgation [Article 146 a) first sentence of the Constitution].

Thus, out of a number of 267 objections of unconstitutionality brought before the Constitutional Court, ten of them were raised by the Government and concerned: Law approving the Government Ordinance no. 15/2008 on wage increases that are granted in 2008 for teachers[714], Law amending and supplementing Law no. 19/2000 on the public system of pensions and other social insurance rights[715], Law rejecting the Government Emergency Ordinance no. 25/2007 on the establishment of certain measures for reorganisation of the Government working apparatus[716], Law rejecting the Government Emergency Ordinance no. 24/2007 regarding the establishment of certain measures for reorganisation of the central public administration[717], Law amending and supplementing Law no. 128/1997 on the Status of the Teaching

714 Decision no. 1093 of 15 October 2008, published in the Official Gazette of Romania no. 711 of 20 October 2008.

715 Decision no. 1092 of 15 October 2008, published in the Official Gazette of Romania no. 712 of 20 October 2008.

716 Decision no. 972 of 31 October 2007, published in the Official Gazette of Romania no. 828 of 4 December 2007.

717 Decision no. 971 of 31 October 2007, published in the Official Gazette of Romania no. 828 of 4 December 2007.

Staff[718], provisions of Article I points 10 and 14 of Law amending and supplementing certain provisions of the Criminal Code[719], Law approving the Government Ordinance no. 25/1995[720], Law amending and supplementing Law no. 53/1991 on the allowances and other right of the Senators and Deputies, as well as the wages of personnel belonging to the system of the Parliament of Romania, republished[721], Law regarding the support granted by the State to agricultural producers[722], Article 10 para. (3) of Law on the state allowance for children[723].

- to rule upon challenges as to the constitutionality of a political party [Article 146 k) of the Constitution, in conjunction with Articles 39–40 of Law no. 47/1992 on the Organisation and Operation of the Constitutional Court].

So far, this power has not been exercised.

- the Prime Minister may refer to the Constitutional Court as to settle legal disputes of a constitutional nature between public authorities [Article 146 e) of the Constitution].

Out of a number of 28 cases on legal disputes of a constitutional nature brought before the Constitutional Court, the Prime Minister was the author of the referral in 7 of such cases. Thus, in 5 cases, the legal dispute of a constitutional nature on which the Constitutional Court has been challenged aimed at the constitutional relationships with the President of Romania in the procedure for the appointment of ministered in the events of government reshuffle[724], the representation of Romania

718 Decision no. 666 of 16 July 2007, published in the Official Gazette of Romania no. 515 of 31 July 2007.

719 Decision no. 211 of 1 November 2000, published in the Official Gazette of Romania no. 568 of 15 November 2000.

720 Decision no. 36 of 2 April 1996, published in the Official Gazette of Romania no. 75 of 11 April 1996.

721 Decision no. 6 of 24 January 1996, published in the Official Gazette of Romania no. 23 of 31 January 1996.

722 Decision no. 64 of 16 November 1993, published in the Official Gazette of Romania no. 310 of 28 December 1993.

723 Decision no. 47 of 15 September 1993, published in the Official Gazette of Romania no. 233 of 28 September 1993.

724 Decision no. 356 of 5 April 2007 on the request to settle the legal dispute of a constitutional nature between the President of Romania, formulated by the Prime Minister Călin Popescu Tăriceanu, published in the Official Gazette of Romania no. 322 of 14 May 2007; Decision no. 98 of 7 February 2008 on the request to settle the legal dispute of a constitutional nature between the President of Romania and the Government of Romania, formulated by the Prime Minister Călin Popescu Tăriceanu, published in the Official Gazette of Romania no. 140 of 22 February 2008; Decision no. 158 of 19 March 2014 on the request to settle the legal dispute of a constitutional nature between the President of Romania and the Government

to the European Council[725] and, respectively, *certain concrete acts and actions of the President of Romania about which the author of the referral claimed that they affect the duties and the powers of the Government of Romania in relation to the organisation and holding of the elections*[726]. As concerns the other two disputes where the Prime Minister was the author of the referral, the former concerned the relationships to Parliament, on the Government's liability over a bill[727], and the latter concerned the relationships with the legislative power and the judiciary, on grounds of violation of the principle of separation of powers and an abuse of power by the judiciary[728].

4.2.2 The possibility to express viewpoints in the cases brought before the Constitutional Court

According to Articles 16 and 17 of Law no. 47/1992 on the Organization and Operation of the Constitutional Court, if the referral of a law before promulgation has been brought before the Constitutional Court by the President of Romania, by Parliament, by the High Court of Cassation and Justice or by the Advocate of the People, the Constitutional Court shall communicate it within 24 hours from the registration, to the Presidents of the two Chambers of Parliament and to the Government, also specifying the date when the debates are to take place, and if the referral was made by one of the Presidents of the two Chambers of Parliament, the Constitutional Court shall communicate such to the President of the other Chamber and to the Government, as well as to the Advocate of the People. The Government, as well as the other authorities mentioned-above, may present their point of view

---

of Romania, formulated by the Prime Minister Victor-Viorel Ponta, published in the Official Gazette of Romania no. 292 of 22 April 2014.

725 Decision no. 441 of 9 July 2014 on the request to settle the legal dispute of a constitutional nature between the Government, represented by the Prime Minister, on the one hand, and the President of Romania, on the other hand, published in the Official Gazette of Romania no. 657 of 5 September 2014.

726 Decision no. 284 of 21 May 2014, on the request to settle the legal dispute of a constitutional nature between the President of Romania and the Government of Romania, formulated by the Prime Minister Victor-Viorel Ponta, published in the Official Gazette of Romania no. 495 of 3 July 2014.

727 Decision no. 1525 of 24 November 2010 on the request to settle the legal dispute of a constitutional nature between the Government of Romania, on the one hand, and the Parliament of Romania which consists of the Chamber of Deputies and the Senate, on the other hand, published in the Official Gazette of Romania no. 818 of 7 December 2010.

728 Decision no. 988 of 1 October 2008 on the request formulated by Mr. Călin Popescu-Tăriceanu, the Prime Minister of the Government, regarding the existence of a legal dispute of a constitutional nature between the legislative power and the executive one, on the one hand, and the judicial power, on the other hand, published in the Official Gazette of Romania no. 784 of 24 November 2014.

in writing, by the date of the debates. The Government's point of view shall be presented only under the signature of the Prime Minister.

According to Article 24 para. (2)-(4) of Law no. 47/1992, in case of constitutional review of treaties or other international agreements, if the referral was made by one of the Presidents of the two Chambers of Parliament, the Constitutional Court shall communicate it to the President of Romania, to the President of the other Chamber, and to the Government. If the referral is made by Members of Parliament, the Constitutional Court shall communicate it to the President of Romania, to the Presidents of the two Chambers of Parliament and to the Government. According to Article 25 of the same law, the Government, as well as any other authorities mentioned above, may present their point of view in writing, by the date of the debates in the plenum of the Constitutional Court.

According to Article 30 para. (1) of Law no. 47/1992, in case of referring to the Constitutional Court with an exception of unconstitutionality, on receiving the interlocutory order, the President of the Constitutional Court shall designate the Judge-Rapporteur and also communicate it to the Presidents of the two Chambers of Parliament, to the Government and to the Advocate of the People, indicating the date by which they can submit their viewpoint.

In case of legal disputes of a constitutional nature where the Government is a party, it has the possibility to submit its viewpoint on the content of the dispute and the possible ways for resolution [Article 35 para. (1) of Law no. 47/1992].

In case of adjudicating upon challenges regarding the constitutionality of a political party, the Government may be represented by the Ministry of Justice.

The Constitutional Court shall request the viewpoints of all the above-mentioned authorities, but their absence does not prevent the settlement of cases.

4.2.3 Communication of the decisions/rulings adjudicated by the Constitutional Court, under the conditions provided for by law

The decision by which the unconstitutionality of a law before promulgation has been established shall be communicated to the Prime Minister [Article 18 para. (2) second sentence of Law no. 47/1992].

Likewise, the decision rendered within the review of treaties or other international agreements shall be communicates to the Government [Article 26 para. (2) second sentence of Law no. 47/1992], as well as the decision by which the unconstitutionality of a law or of an ordinance which is in force, or of provisions thereof, is established [Article 31 para. (1) of Law no. 47/1992].

The decision establishing the existence of the circumstances justifying the interim in the exercising of the office of President of Romania shall be notified to the Parliament and to the Government [Article 44 para. (1) of Law no. 47/1992].

We should also mention the general text set forth in Article 36 of Law no. 47/1992 according to which the decision which resolves the legal dispute of a constitutional nature shall be final and it shall be communicated to both the author of the referral, and to the parties in dispute, before its publication in the Official Gazette of Romania, Part I.

4.3 The relationship between the Constitutional Court and the Government

4.3.1 General aspects

The Constitutional Court was repeatedly required to adjudicate upon the interpretation and application of the constitutional norms governing the status, role and activity of the authorities belonging to the executive power, both within the exercise of the constitutional review of laws before promulgation, of laws and ordinances in force, and within the exercise of its power to settle legal disputes of a constitutional nature between public authorities.

By its case-law, the Court circumstantiated the constitutional role of the executive in relation to the other two powers, in terms of the requirements of the rule of law. In light of those analyzed in this chapter, we consider as relevant the case-law delivered by the Constitutional Court regarding the interpretation and application of Article 109, "Liability of members of the Government", respectively of Article 114, "Assuming responsibility by the Government", and of Article 115, "Legislative delegation".

4.3.2 Liability of members of the Government

The provisions of Article 109 of the Constitution of Romania govern **the liability of members of the Government**, having two sides: *political liability* [Article 109 para. (1)] and *criminal liability* [Article 109 para. (2)].

Political liability of members of the Government
As concerns this form of liability of the members of the Government, it is worth mentioning the recitals by which the Constitutional Court ruled upon the simple motion and the motion of censure, upon the distinction between them and upon the effects produced by them.

Thus, for example, adjudicating upon the provisions of Article 157 para. (2) of the Standing Order of the Senate[729], according to which "*simple motions adopted by the Senate shall be published in the Official Gazette of Romania, Part I, and shall be binding for the Government and its members, as well as for the other persons concerned*", and establishing that they are constitutional to the extent that the adoption of a simple motion by the Senate does not oblige the Prime Minister to propose the dismissal of a member of the Government whose activity was the subject-matter of

729 Published in the Official Gazette of Romania no. 948 of 25 October 2005.

the motion[730], the Court examined the constitutional norms governing the simple motion, providing a clear presentation of its legal status.

The Court held that, by adopting a simple motion under Article 112 para. (2) of the Constitution, the Chamber of Deputies or the Senate express their position on an issue of domestic or foreign politics or, as the case may be, on an issue that was the subject-matter of an interpellation. The mentioned constitutional text "*does not provide the possibility that, through such a motion, either of the Chambers of Parliament, upon the expression of its position, may also order concrete measures, mandatory for the Government, such as the dismissal from office of a minister, and it does not either empower the Chambers to provide such a possibility in the regulation*". In this regard, the Court held that within the constitutional system of Romania, as in most of the other countries, the parliamentary control does not generally provide any sanction. The only exception when the parliamentary control also provides sanctions is in the situation when such control is exercised by the motion of censure, whose adoption has as results the dismissal of the Government. The notion of "simple motion" was inserted in the Constitution during its revision, when the new wording of Article 112 para. (2) also enlarged the content of the motion. The Chamber which adopts it may express its position not only on an issue that was the subject-matter of an interpellation, but also on other issues of domestic or foreign politics. "*By the simple motion, a more effective instrument was made available for MPs in order to achieve the parliamentary control on the Government, but the adoption of a simple motion does not directly result in the legal dismissal from office of a member thereof. However, the simple motion has political effects, emphasizing a victory of the political forces that have initiated and supported it, with an appropriate echo in the public opinion. Therefore, the lack of such a legal effect of the simple motion does result in the annihilation of its political effects, because, if the executive ignores the simple motion, the two Chambers of Parliament have the possibility to make us, if necessary, of the motion of censure*".

The Constitutional Court also held that, in terms of the effects on the Government and its members, there are substantial differences between the two types of motions. Thus, the investiture of the Government takes place, according to Article 103 para. (3) of the Constitution, by granting trust to the Government by a majority vote of deputies and senators, following the debate, in the joint meeting of the two Chambers, the programme and the list of the Government. The withdrawal of the trust granted to the Government shall be made, according to Article 113 para. (1) of the Constitution, by the adoption of a motion of censure in the joint meeting of the two Chambers, by a majority vote of deputies and senators. Unlike the simple motion, the adoption of a motion of censure results directly in the dismissal of the Government as a whole.

The third type of motion, known in the law and the practice of many countries, namely the individual motion, is not provided for by the Constitution of Romania.

---

730 Decision no. 148 of 21 February 2007, published in the Official Gazette of Romania no. 162 of 7 March 2007.

Individual motion has legal effects similar to those of the motion of censure, but not the whole Government, but only on certain individualized members thereof. As such, the introduction of a request concerning the dismissal of a member of the Government into a simple motion cannot result in legal obligations for the Government, the Prime Minister or for other persons.

However, as concerns the dismissal of a member of the Government, in the event of government reshuffle, the Court held that, pursuant to Article 85 para. (2) of the Constitution, the Government can be revoked or appointed exclusively by the President, upon the proposal of the Prime Minister. Article 106 of the Constitution provides also, among the cases when membership of the Government ceases, "*other cases provided by law*". Neither the Constitution nor any other law provides the cessation of membership of the Government through the mandatory revocation based on a simple motion. The simple motion is a legal act, but it does not produce such an effect. The reasons set out above do not lead to the conclusion that the simple motion has no legal effects and it would not be binding. The simple motion does not take *ipso iure* legal effects, but *ipso facto* legal effects; "*Through such a motion, the Chamber which adopts it expresses its viewpoint on certain important issues of domestic and foreign politics and it may find deficiencies in various areas of the activity of the Government, of the public administration bodies, of their leaders or members. The Government and the public administration bodies are obliged to take into account the content of the motion and to act according to the view expressed by the Chamber, so as to remedy the deficiencies identified. The binding nature does not mean that the Government or any other public administration body would be obliged to apply the provisions of the motion on taking organizational measures , such as the appointment and dismissal from office, which are exclusively conferred upon them by the Constitution or other laws*".

Likewise, ruling on the legal regime of the motion of censure in a case that covered a legal dispute of a constitutional nature in a situation that concerned the Government's assumption of responsibility on a bill[731], the Court held that "*the motion of censure truly constitutes a constitutional instrument which has been made available to Parliament in order to exercise the parliamentary control over activity of the Government. The motion of censure is generally governed by Article 113 of the Constitution, and certain particular aspects of this legal institution are governed by Article 114 para. (2) and (3) of the Constitution. These latter constitutional provisions define the motion of censure filed in the procedure of the Government's assumption of responsibility as a «caused» one, without distinguishing it, in terms of the legal nature and the purpose, from the motion of censure regulated by Article 113 of the Constitution*". The Court also held that the provisions of the Constitution "*do not cover two categories of motions of censure, but, on the contrary, the motion of censure as a legal concept is singular, governed by Article 113 of the Constitution; the specific elements which*

---

731 Decision no. 1525 of 24 November 2010, published in the Official Gazette of Romania no. 818 of 7 December 2010.

concern the motion of censure initiated in the event of the Government's assumption of responsibility reveal only two procedural aspects (the initiation context – after presenting the programme, the general political statement or the bill covering the assumption of responsibility – and the constitutional possibility of initiation – regardless whether its signatories have already initiated in the same parliamentary session a motion of censure according to Article 113 of the Constitution) and a substantial aspect (in case of rejection of the motion of censure, the programme, the general political statement or the bill shall be considered adopted), which cannot qualify the motion of censure set forth in Article 114 of the Constitution as an instrument of parliamentary control different from the motion of censure governed by Article 113 of the Constitution". Hence the conclusion that "*by voting a motion of censure, regardless of the fact that it was submitted under Article 113 or Article 114 of the Constitution, exercising in this way the parliamentary control, the trust conferred upon the Government shall be withdrawn, resulting thus in its dismissal*". Parliament has no power to prevent the Government to decide whether to assume its responsibility; likewise, once this decision has been taken, Parliament cannot prevent Government to continue the procedure, since this would lead to inadmissible situations in which a minority Government might never be able to assume its responsibility, which flagrantly violates Article 114 of the Constitution. Similarly, the Government may not withdraw either its request for the assumption of responsibility, as it is its own irrevocable act. In this constitutional context, "*submitting the motion of censure signifies the onset of parliamentary control over the activity of the Government and constitutes* mutatis mutandis *an irrevocable act for the purposes of initiating such control; this is an instrument made particularly available to the parliamentary opposition and not least an expression of opposition in relation to the measures taken by the Government. Consequently, the prevention of submitting and the refusal to debate a motion of censure which has already been filed are contrary to the Constitution, as this would be tantamount to the elimination of the possibility of the parliamentary opposition to censorship and control the government decisions regarding the assumption of responsibility*".

Criminal liability of members of the Government

Given the consequences resulted from the assumption of criminal liability by the members of the Government, but also the fact that this requires the exercise of the joint powers of the three powers of the State, the constitutional and legal framework that governs it represented the subject-matter of the analysis conducted by the constitutional court on several occasions, the Court established, in relation to this framework, the authorities which can demand the prosecution of the members and the former members of the Government for the acts committed in the exercise of their office and who, at the moment of the applications, were also a Deputy or a Senator, as well as the procedural rules applicable to the prosecution procedure for the members and the former members of the Government for acts committed in the exercise of their office.

Thus, pursuant to Article 109 para. (2) first sentence of the Constitution, "*Solely the Chamber of Deputies, the Senate, and the President of Romania have the right to demand criminal prosecution be taken against Members of the Government for acts committed in the exercise of their office*". Being notified to adjudicate upon the application for the settlement of a legal dispute of a constitutional nature between the Public Ministry – the Public Prosecutor's Office attached to the High Court of Cassation and Justice, on the one hand, and the two Chambers of Parliament – on the other hand, arising from the different way in which these public authorities interpret and apply the provisions of Article 109 para. (2) first sentence of the Constitution in connection with the request for the prosecution of members and former members of the Government, in respect of acts committed in the course of exercising their duties, who, at the time of submission, were also a Deputy or a Senator, the Court held that[732], if the Public Prosecutor's Office attached to the High Court of Cassation and Justice is to notify one of the three authorities set forth in Article 109 para. (2) of the Constitution – *the Chamber of Deputies, the Senate, and the President of Romania* – to demand prosecution of one member of the Government, **the solution is different**, as it depends on the fact whether he is or not also a Deputy or a Senator at the time of the application. Accordingly, "*the Prosecutor's Office attached to the High Court of Cassation and Justice must address to one of the three authorities, as follows: a) to the Chamber of Deputies or the Senate – for the members or the former members of the Government (Prime Minister, Minister of State, Minister, Minister delegate, as applicable) who, at the time of the referral, were also a Deputy or a Senator; b) to the President of Romania – for the members or the former members of the Government (Prime Minister, Minister of State, Minister, Minister Delegate) who, at the time of the referral, were not a Deputy or a Senator*".

Both by the decision rendered in the settlement of the legal dispute of a constitutional nature, and by a series of decisions rendered on the provisions of Law no. 115/1999, the Court also held that, as concerns the offences committed in the exercise of their office, the criminal prosecution of the members of Government must be fulfilled in compliance with the same procedural norms[733]. This is because, as concerns the term of office of a member of the Government, the Constitution did not establish government immunity, but another measure of protection, namely the limitation of the right to request his/her criminal prosecution for acts committed in the exercise of his/her office. The provisions of Article 109 para. (2) of the Basic Law

---

732 Decision no. 270 of 10 March 2008 on the requests formulated by the President of the Chamber of Deputies and the President of the Senate regarding the existence of a legal dispute of a constitutional nature between the President of Romania, the Ministry of Justice and the Prosecutor's Office attached to the High Court of Cassation and Justice, on the one hand, and the Parliament of Romania, on the other hand, as well as the request of the President of the Superior Council of Magistracy on the legal dispute of a constitutional nature between the Public Ministry and the Parliament of Romania – the Chamber of Deputies, published in the Official Gazette of Romania no. 290 of 15 April 2008.

733 Decision no. 93 of 16 June 1999, published in the Official Gazette of Romania no. 300 of 28 June 1999.

establishes a measure of protection for the term of office exercised by the members of the Government, thus having the objective nature of a procedural constitutional guarantee, aiming at the protection of the public interest, namely the accomplishment of the government act by exercise of the term of office, and this measure for the protection of the public interest subsists even after the cessation of the term of office of the members of the Government.

Pursuant to these reasons[734], the Court found unconstitutional the provisions of Law no. 115/1999, according to which the criminal prosecution and trial of former members of the Government for the offences committed in the course of exercising their duties shall be performed under the common law, whilst the special provisions set forth in this law are not applicable, pointing out that the effect of finding the unconstitutionality of this text, with the consequence of its loss of legal effectiveness "*shall involve that the derogatory regime to criminal prosecution and trial of the currently-in-office members of the Government, for criminal offences committed in this capacity, be extended to its former members as well*"[735].

4.3.3 Government's assumption of responsibility on a bill[736]

4.3.3.1 Concept. Constitutional text of reference

Pursuant to Article 61 para. (1) second sentence of the Constitution, "*Parliament is (...) the sole legislative authority of the country*". The Constitution further provides that the Government can avail itself of two instruments which can serve it to enter the sphere of primary regulation or social relations – either by its assumption of responsibility before the Parliament[737], or by enactment of ordinances, respectively

734 Decision no. 665 of 5 July 2007, published in the Official Gazette of Romania no. 547 of 10 August 2007.

735 Moreover, in relation to all this case-law, being notified again on the unconstitutionality of the Law amending Law no. 115/1999 on ministerial responsibility, the Court, allowing the objection and ascertaining the unconstitutionality of this law, this time for extrinsic reasons – the violation of the constitutional principle of bicameralism –, has noted that "*the Court ruled by several decision on the unconstitutionality of Law no. 115/1999 on ministerial responsibility, as well as that challenges regarding some of its provisions were expressed in the doctrine, so that the Court considers it is appropriate to proceed to the re-examination of the law, as a whole, so as to comply with all the formulated observations*".

736 M. Safta, *Government's assumption of responsibility on a bill. Case-law of the Constitutional Court in the matter*, in Constitutional Court Bulletin no. 2/2010, on *www.ccr.ro*.

737 Article 114 of the Constitution; see, for more details, A. Varga, *Government's assumption of responsibility, a special law-making and control parliamentary procedure*, in E.S. Tănăsescu, Şt. Deaconu (coordinators), *About Constitution and Constitutionalism. Liber amicorum Ioan Muraru*, Hamangiu Publishing House, Bucharest, 2006, p. 225.

emergency ordinances[738]. These powers do not represent an interference with "the Parliament's legislative monopoly", as long as those procedures are used under the terms of the Constitutions[739]. Due to the fact that the constitutional texts of reference, namely Article 114, "Assuming responsibility by the Government", and Article 115, "Legislative delegation", do not explain in a very accurate way the two concepts, the Constitutional Court, as guarantor for the supremacy of the Constitution, was entrusted with the role to grasp, from the interpretation of the Basic Law, the rules governing such matters. This is also in the context of a genuine legislative effervescence of the Government, especially as a delegate legislature, determining the legal doctrine to conclude that the exception established by the two constitutional texts turned into a rule[740].

Government's assumption of responsibility on a bill represents an indirect legislative way of adopting, i.e. not by debating it within the ordinary legislative procedure, but by discussing a political issue above all, about the staying or dismissal of the Government. It was proved[741] that, by assuming responsibility, the Government seeks to achieve its will by a tacit and global vote in Parliament, respectively it assumes the risk of being dismissed. The Constitutional Court defined the Government's assumption of responsibility on a bill as "*a joint procedure, or parliamentary control, since it allows initiation of a motion of censure, and a regulatory procedure, since the bill on which the Government assumes responsibility shall be deemed as adopted if such motion was not filed or, if it was filed, it was rejected*"[742], noting, in one of its decisions[743], that the role of the this procedure is "*to coagulate a parliamentary majority, but also to overcome the obstructionist acts of the opposition in the legislative debate*".

The provisions of Article 114 of the Constitution, which are the relevant provisions in this matter, stipulate that the Government's assumption of responsibility shall be taken "*before the Chamber of Deputies and the Senate, in joint session*", and as a result:

- the Government shall be dismissed if a motion of censure, filed within three days after the presentation of the bill, is passed in accordance with Article 113, i.e. by a majority vote of deputies and senators;

---

738 Article 115 of the Constitution.

739 Decision no. 298 of 29 March 2006, published in the Official Gazette of Romania no. 372 of 28 April 2006.

740 D. Apostol Tofan, in I. Muraru, E.S. Tănăsescu (coordinators), *cited paper*, p. 1078.

741 I. Deleanu, *Institutions and constitutional procedures – in Romanian law and comparative law*, Servo-Sat Publishing House, Arad, 2003, pp. 571–572.

742 Decision no. 34 of 17 February 1998, published in the Official Gazette of Romania no. 88 of 25 February 1998.

743 Decision no. 1415 of 4 November 2009, published in the Official Gazette of Romania no. 796 of 23 November 2009.

- if the Government has not been dismissed, the bill presented, amended or supplemented, as the case may be, with amendments accepted by the Government, shall be deemed adopted.

The Constitution does not provide therefore, in Article 114, any conditions on the nature of the bill, its structure, on the number of bill on which the Government may assume responsibility during the same day or during another given period, or on the moment when the Government decides to assume responsibility.

Over time, the Government assumed responsibility in different situations: on a bill for approval of an ordinance[744], on a bill that contained several subjects of regulation[745], on a bill in process of parliamentary debate before the Senate, already adopted with amendments by the Chamber of Deputies[746], on some rules of great complexity and even on several bills on the same day[747].

Since compliance with the generally binding nature of the Constitutional Court's decisions does not mean only to render effectiveness to the operative part of the decisions, but, equally, to their recitals, respectively to the interpretation given by the Court to the texts contained in the Basic Law, the summary of conclusions resulting from the case-law regarding this constitutional institution is of real interest.

4.3.3.2 Statuaries in the case-law of the Constitutional Court

The Government's assumption of responsibility on a bill and the legislative delegation are not governed by the same rules and conditions

On 23 February 2006, the Constitutional Court was referred to with respect to the unconstitutionality of the Law on healthcare reform, adopted in accordance with Article 114 para. (3) of the Constitution, by the Chamber of Deputies and the Senate, in joint session, on 21 February 2006. One of the critiques discussed the relationship between the two constitutional institutions which enable the Government to regulate in an area reserved to the Parliament, as the authors of the referral claimed that: "the restrictive conditions under which emergency ordinance can be adopted, according to Article 115 para. (4) and (6) of the Revised Constitution, the spirit of these regulations should be considered, by analogy, upon examination of the constitutionality of the law-making by assumption of responsibility".

---

744 Decision no. 34 of 17 February 1998, published in the Official Gazette of Romania no. 88 of 25 February 1998.

745 Decision no. 147 of 16 April 2003, published in the Official Gazette of Romania no. 279 of 21 April 2003, of Decision no. 375 of 6 July 2005, published in the Official Gazette of Romania no. 591 of 8 July 2005.

746 Decision no. 233 of 20 December 1999, published in the Official Gazette of Romania no. 638 of 28 December 1999; Decision no. 1431 of 3 November 2010, published in the Official Gazette of Romania no. 758 of 12 November 2010.

747 See also C.-L. Popescu, *Legal uncertainty caused by legislative aberrations*, in Judicial Courier no. 9/2009, p. 484.

In response to this critique, the Court held[748] that the process of assumption of responsibility by the Government and that of legislative delegation are not governed by the same rules and conditions as "*there are significant constitutional differences between approval of a bill by means of Government's assumption of responsibility and the adoption of an emergency ordinance. The restrictive conditions for regulation by emergency ordinance cannot be considered when examining the constitutionality of the law-making by the Government's assumption of responsibility, as upon interpretation and application of constitutional provisions and principles, the analogy method is not allowed. If the constituent legislature wished to impose the same conditions for both legislative procedures, it would have expressly done so*".

The Government can assume responsibility on bills referring to organic or ordinary laws, to the approval of an emergency ordinance[749], but not to constitutional laws

On 4 February 1998, the Constitutional Court was referred to with respect to the constitutionality of the Law approving Government Emergency Ordinance no. 88/1997 on the privatization of companies, adopted in the procedure of the Government's assumption of responsibility on a bill. The authors claimed, among other things, that "it is inadmissible to approve an emergency ordinance by the Government's assumption of responsibility". In that respect, they argued that this emergency ordinance is conditioned on the existence of the exceptional case and cannot consist in normal and customary rules, but in factual circumstances which require maximum emergency for adoption of the measure and implementation thereof, and the fact that the entry into force of such an ordinance depends on its prior submission to Parliament demonstrates the binding nature of the control exercised by Parliament on such exceptional measures taken by the Government. The Government has already assumed responsibility once the emergency ordinance was adopted, so there is no need for another assumption of responsibility, but instead it should be subject to debate by Parliament in the normal legislative procedure.

Rejecting this challenge, the Court held[750] that: "*the constitutional provision does not distinguish on the nature of that bill. It results that it can be an organic or an ordinary law, excluding the constitutional law for the revision of the Constitution, for*

---

748 Decision no. 298 of 29 March 2006, published in the Official Gazette of Romania no. 372 of 28 April 2006.

749 There was also an opinion [A. Varga, *cited paper*, in E.S. Tănăsescu, Şt. Deaconu (coordinators), *cited paper*, p. 229] according to which "*the greatest risk deriving from the procedure of assumption of responsibility by the Government is that it relativizes the provisions of Article 73 of the Constitution concerning the categories of laws. Practically – as concerns the legislative process – it cancels the difference between organic and ordinary laws, whereas this distinction is not reflected in the law adopted in such manner*".

750 Decision no. 34 of 17 February 1998, published in the Official Gazette of Romania no. 88 of 25 February 1998.

which there is a special procedure, (...) under which the Government cannot act as an initiator. To add another restriction (...) concerning the approval of an emergency ordinance would only mean to amend the constitutional text of Article 113[751]*(...)*".

The Court also ruled, on the same occasion, that "*it does not find relevant the distinction pointed out in the referral between a bill comprising only the legislature's intentions and a bill which, referring to the approval of an ordinance, concerns an «act already made». It is true that the ordinance produces effects prior to its approval or rejection by law. But, as a government act, only if it is approved by the legislature, does it become a legislative act. That is why approval of an ordinance does not have the meaning underlined in the referral, namely that of a simple «ratification», and for the legislature the fact that the effects of the ordinance occur prior to its approval does not represent a restriction or a condition that might affect its legislative competence and, implicitly, the applicability of the constitutional procedures established in view of exercise of this competence*".

The Government assumes responsibility on a bill which may have a complex nature, be divided into multiple titles, chapters and sections, and may cover several areas, if there is a link between them, or if there is a single purpose or interest

The Constitutional Court has been referred to, in several occasions, with objections of unconstitutionality concerning laws adopted by the Parliament through the procedure of assumption of responsibility, and these laws comprised different areas of regulation.

Thus, for example, on 3 April 2003, the Court was referred to on the unconstitutionality of the Law on certain measures to ensure transparency in the exercise of public offices, and in the business environment, and to prevent and punish corruption. The first challenge of unconstitutionality was the assertion that "the Government assumed responsibility on no less than 15 laws", which contravenes the constitutional provisions in this matter, which refer to "a bill".

The Court rejected the objections raised, holding[752] that "*the legislature may regulate by a law a complex group of social relationships, in order to achieve a desirable result for the entire society. (...)Such regulations do not depart from the rules governing the drafting of a bill, as established by Law no. 24/2000 on legislative technique rules for drafting normative acts, but due to their complexity they do not have the same composition as a bill regulating a single matter. Taking into account the sole purpose of the new regulation (...), the way in which it is structured is not likely to affect (...) the provisions of Article 113 para. (1)*[753] *of the Constitution*".

Similar considerations also substantiated the decision rendered with respect to the referral of unconstitutionality of the Law on healthcare reform, a decision

751 Currently, Article 114 of the revised Constitution.

752 Decision no. 147 of 16 April 2003, published in the Official Gazette of Romania no. 279 of 21 April 2003.

753 Article 114 para. (1) of the revised Constitution.

in which it was held that the provisions of Article 114 of the Constitution do not provide the requirements that must be met by a bill in terms of its structure and scope of the regulatory field, so that the bill "*may also have a complex nature, may be divided into multiple titles, chapters and sections, and cover several areas, if there is a link between them, or if there is a single purpose or general interest*"[754].

In the same respect, by Decision no. 1557/2009[755] it was held that the assumption of responsibility can concern also two or several bills or a package of such bills, which can be simple or complex, "*the only requirement imposed by the constitutional texts concerns the type or class of acts on the Government may assume responsibility, i.e. a programme, a statement of general policy, or a bill*".

The Government may assume responsibility on several bills in the same parliamentary session, even on the same day

The Court was referred to in late 2009 with three objections of unconstitutionality concerning three laws adopted on the same day by means of Government's assumption of responsibility.

In two of the referrals, respectively that concerning the Framework-Law on the unitary pay of public sector employees[756], as well as that concerning the National Education Law[757], the authors invoked the violation of Article 114 of the Constitution, on the grounds that, as long as the Government benefited from a secure majority in Parliament, it abusively used the procedure consisting in the assumption of

---

754 Decision no. 298/2006, the Official Gazette of Romania, Part I, no. 372 of April 28, 2006; see also Decision no. 375/2005, the Official Gazette of Romania, Part I, no. 591 of July 8, 2005; however, in the dissenting opinion to Decision no. 1414/2009 concerning the objection of unconstitutionality of the Law on the reorganization of public authorities and institutions, rationalization of public expenditure, business community support and compliance with the framework agreements with the European Commission and International Monetary Fund, published in the Official Gazette of Romania, Part I, no. 796 of November 23, 2009, it was emphasized that "*the regulation prescribed as a law is in fact an amount of regulations on various areas with no connection between them whatsoever, containing different matters, such as: public authorities, budgetary payrolls, competence of legal persons, their reorganization, pensions and wages, environmental issues, companies, business community, agricultural community and agricultural activities, ending with Chapter IX – Final provisions, which in 13 articles, with points and sub-points, amends and repeals dozens of legislative acts. That is why we consider that not only this legislative package does not meet the conditions laid down in Article 114 of the Constitution, but this very regulation cannot form a single unitary bill. The regulation is heterogeneous and confusing, and before its adoption by Parliament it did not meet the requirements for a bill [...] on which the Government may assume responsibility*".

755 Published in the Official Gazette of Romania no. 40 of 19 January 2010.

756 Decision no. 1415 of 4 November 2009, published in the Official Gazette of Romania no. 796 of 23 November 2009.

757 Decision no. 1557 of 18 November 2009, published in the Official Gazette of Romania no. 40 of 19 January 2010.

responsibility, which might endanger the entire lawmaking procedure set forth in the Constitution. This happens because, on the one hand, three bills were adopted on the same day under the special procedure and, on the other hand, historical reality proves that the executive uses abusively this procedure (for the fifth time in less than nine calendar months). The authors also claimed that the constitutional text of Article 114 allows the Government, during one term of office, to make use of the assumption of responsibility during a more tough time, when it encounters difficulties in the parliamentary debate on a bill. However, by assuming responsibility on three bills in one day, it substituted the legislative work of Parliament.

Replying to these challenges[758], the Court held that there is no infringement of the provisions set forth in Article 114 of the Constitution, because, on the one hand, the expression "*on a bill*" must be understood broadly, and, on the other hand, "*from a systematic interpretation of Article 114 para. (1) in conjunction with Article 113 para. (4) of the Basic Law, it clearly results that lawmaking by means of Government's assumption of responsibility can theoretically take place more than once, whereas the number of motions of censure occurred as a result of the special lawmaking procedure is not limited to one during the same session*".

The Government may assume its responsibility on a bill, regardless of the stage of the legislative procedure of that bill

Adjudication upon the provisions of the Framework-Law on the unitary pay of public sector employees, the Court held[759] that "*The Government can make use of the procedure of assumption of responsibility, regardless of the stage of the legislative procedure. The role of such procedure is to coagulate a parliamentary majority, but also to overcome the obstructionist actions of the opposition in the legislative debate*".

This conclusion is reinforced by a recent decision of the Court, rendered as a result of a request for settlement of a legal dispute of a constitutional nature between the Parliament and the Government, submitted by the President of the Senate[760], a dispute arisen in the context of the Government's assumption of responsibility on a bill that was in the parliamentary debate, respectively before the Senate, as a decisional Chamber. Basically, the principle previously stated by the Court by Decision no. 1415/2009 has found realization in a particular situation that had never been subjected to the analysis of the Court, even if there were cases in which the Government had assumed responsibility on bills after referral to Parliament for initiation of the legislative procedure on the bills. For example, by Decision no. 34/1998[761], the Court ruled, within the *a priori* review, on the constitutionality of a law for approval of an emergency ordinance, a law adopted by means of Government assumption

758 *Ibidem.*

759 Decision no. 1415 of 4 November 2009, published in the Official Gazette of Romania no. 796 of 23 November 2009.

760 Decision no. 1431 of 3 November 2010, published in the Official Gazette of Romania no. 758 of 12 November 2010.

761 Published in the Official Gazette of Romania no. 88 of 25 February 1998.

of responsibility. However, as shown even in the views expressed in that case, up to the day of Government's assumption of responsibility on the bill approving an emergency ordinance, the parliamentary procedure for adoption of the law for approval had not begun, so there was no question of duplication or interruption of this procedure.

Likewise, in November 1999, the Government assumed responsibility on the bill regarding the Status of civil servants, which became Law no. 188/1999, a bill which had passed the debate in the first Chamber and it was subject to debate before the second Chamber. The Government assumed its responsibility on the initial wording of the law. Being referred to on the unconstitutionality of the law adopted by this procedure, the Court rejected it as inadmissible because, in the meantime, the law had already been promulgated and published in the Official Gazette of Romania.

As concerns the recent Decision no. 1431/2010, although it was rendered in the settlement of a legal dispute of a constitutional nature, the "center of gravity" of the solution pronounced and, consequently, of the reasoning of the Court, is given by the concrete circumstances of Government's assumption of responsibility on the National Education Bill. According to the operative part of the decision, "*assumption of responsibility by the Government before the Chamber of Deputies and the Senate, on the grounds of Article 114 para. (1) of the Constitution, on the National Education Bill, is unconstitutional and gave rise to a legal dispute of a constitutional nature between Government and Parliament, whereas the bill was already in lawmaking process at the Senate, as the decisional Chamber*".

This approach of the issue brought to the Court's attention is consistent with its case-law delivered in exercise of the powers set forth in Article 146 e) of the Constitution. Thus, by Decision no. 53 of 28 January 2005[762], the Court claimed that a legal dispute of a constitutional nature involves "*concrete acts or actions by which an authority or several authorities claim powers, duties or competences which, according to the Constitution belong to other public authorities, or failure of some public authorities, by declining jurisdiction or by refusing to perform certain acts falling within their obligations*". Thus, in exercising these powers, the Court is not invested with performing an abstract analysis of certain rules, but with adjudicating upon certain "*concrete acts or actions*" of one or several public authorities; in this case, it is required to adjudicate upon the Government's assumption of responsibility on a specific bill, in a specific situation. The referral, the submissions of the parties, mentioned in the decision, as well as the evidence, as it results from the same decision, had in view a specific act of the Government, on a certain bill, its concrete condition and situation. Therefore, the Court was not called to rule on whether the Basic Law allows, in principle, the Government's assumption of responsibility on a bill that was under parliamentary debate, but on the question whether, in that specific situation, there was a legal dispute of a constitutional nature occurred as a result of Government's assumption of responsibility on the National Education Bill,

762 Published in the Official Gazette of Romania no. 144 of 17 February 2005.

a bill that was under parliamentary debate. Likewise, the answer to this question led to the examination of the specific situation of this assumption of responsibility, and the results are presented by the Court in the reasoning part of the decision, as, indeed, it presented in the reasoning part of all decisions rendered for the settlement of legal disputes of a constitutional nature when being referred to.

As to the question of principle, namely whether the Government may assume responsibility on a bill under parliamentary debate, it, however, received an implicit answer, since, according to the decision, the Government's assumption of responsibility on the National Education Bill is unconstitutional (for reasons widely presented in the reasoning part), which triggered a legal dispute of a constitutional nature between the Government and Parliament, whereas at the time of the Government's assumption of responsibility, the bill was in the lawmaking process at the Senate, as a decisional Chamber. By way of interpretation, the fact that the Government assumed responsibility on a bill heard in parliamentary debate is not itself unconstitutional, and this is only a legal prerequisite for a potential constitutional dispute, a dispute that can arise if the Government exercised its power under Article 114 of the Constitution, "*in violation of the constitutional framework that circumstantiates it*", infringing thus the jurisdiction of another authority, exercised in parallel and concurrently, as noted in the case. The phrase "*since the bill was in lawmaking process at the Senate, as a decisional Chamber*", contained in the reasoning part of the decision, explains the existence of the dispute caused by the unconstitutional act of the Government, and not by the unconstitutionality of this act. The Government's act violates the provisions of Article 114 of the Constitution for other reasons, as shown below.

The Government may reach this simplified modality of lawmaking, by assumption of responsibility, only *in extremis*

These considerations essentially grounded the only solution of admission of an *a priori* referral of unconstitutionality[763], for violation, by the law subject to review, of Article 114 of the Constitution, "Assuming Responsibility by the Government".

It was indicated that, in September 2009, three objections of unconstitutionality on the unconstitutionality of three laws adopted on the same day by means of the Government's assumption of responsibility were brought before the Court. The Court upheld one of the referrals[764] concerning the National Education Law, noting that, in principle, this simplified lawmaking procedure (assumption of responsibility) must be used only *in extremis*, "*when adoption of the bill in normal or emergency procedure is no longer possible or when the political structure of Parliament does not permit adoption of the bill in normal or emergency procedure*", conditions that do not exist in the case under consideration, insofar the National Education Law, unlike the other two laws on which the Government assumed responsibility on the same day,

763 Decision no. 1557 of 18 November 2009, published in the Official Gazette of Romania no. 40 of 19 January 2010.

764 *Ibidem.*

was due to take effect according to Article 78 of the Constitution, "*whereas nothing required the imminence of such need*". In that respect, the Court stated that "*the procedure of Government's assumption of responsibility on a bill refers to its adoption in conditions of maximum celerity, the content of regulation aiming at establishing certain urgent measures in an area of extreme importance, and their implementation must occur immediately. (...) Therefore, even if at first glance the possibility of assumption of responsibility is not subject to any condition, as the timing and content of the initiative is theoretically at the sole discretion of Parliament, this cannot be something absolute, because Government's exclusivity is opposable only to Parliament, and not to the Constitutional Court as guarantor for the supremacy of the Basic Law*".

Thus, "*the Government's right to establish the content and structure of a bill is not absolute, it must be subject to conditions imposed or detached from reality or the vital nature of law for its government programme. To ignore such restrictions is tantamount to undermining a balance between State powers, denying to annihilation the legislative role as Parliament's main function, by minimizing the concept of representation*".

It is noted that, by this decision, the Court established, by way of systematic and teleological interpretation of the Constitution, the existence of certain limits to the adoption of a bill by the procedure of Government's assumption of responsibility, in the absence of such limits we would face the risk of transforming an exception in a rule which would endanger the rule of law.

By Decision no. 1431 of 3 November 2010[765], rendered following the request for the settlement of a legal dispute of a constitutional nature between the Parliament of Romania and the Government, submitted by the President of the Senate, the Court, allowing the referral, reinforced the interpretation of the provisions of Article 114 of the Constitution, stating that "*accepting the idea that the Government may assume responsibility on a bill at will, anytime and under any circumstances, would be tantamount to transforming this authority in a public legislative authority, competing with the Parliament as regards the power to legislate. However, such an interpretation given to the provisions of Article 114 of the Basic Law is in total contradiction with the ruling of the Constitutional Court in the cited case-law* (A/N, Decision no. 1557/2009) *and therefore would contradict the provisions of Article 147 para. (4) of the Constitution, which enshrine the* erga omnes *obligation of the Constitutional Court's decisions and flagrantly violate the provisions of Article 1 para. (4) and Article 61 para. (1) of the Constitution*".

Analysing the actual situation referred to the Court by the author of the request for the settlement of the legal dispute of a constitutional nature, in terms of principle consideration drawn from the mentioned case-law, "*which definitely circumscribe the conditions under which the Government may assume responsibility on a bill*", the Court found that Government's assumption of responsibility on the National Education Bill, under parliamentary debate, in the Senate, as a decisional Chamber, has no justification. Thus, "*the condition of emergency that might have required such*

765 Published in the Official Gazette of Romania no. 758 of 12 November 2010.

measure by the Government is not met insofar the measures provided in the bill become effective starting with the 2011–2012 school year, and some of them even starting with the 2012–2013 school year". The Court did not agree with the reason stated in the Government's viewpoint in the meaning that "*the bill was in real blockage whereas the referral to the Senate with the bill occurred on 21 May 2010*" or with "*the attempt to impose the idea that the duration of lawmaking in this Chamber is excessive*". In this respect, the Court also noted that Article 75 of the Constitution does not establish either a term for the debate procedure of bills in the decisional Chamber or a criterion to esteem the reasonable period during which the legislative procedure shall be finalized in this Chamber, even in the account of its decisional nature. The Court also found that although according to Article 76 para. (3) of the Constitution, "*upon the request of the Government or upon its own initiative, the Parliament may pass bills or legislative proposals using an emergency procedure, established in accordance with the Standing Orders of each Chamber*", in the filed documents it was not identified any step taken by the Government, addressed to the Senate, to debate the bill using the emergency procedure. It has been concluded, following this examination, that "*there was (...) no evidence of any blockage or parliamentary inactivity, referring to the bill in question*", all the more "*since, in order to assess the duration for debating the law in the Senate (...) it should be considered that this was largely overlapped with the parliamentary recess period, i.e. the period between 30 June and 1 September 2010*". Therefore, "*Government's assumption of responsibility on the National Education Bill violates the provisions of Article 114 of the Constitution, according the case-law of the Constitutional Court. Likewise, in this case, as in the case referred to the Court and settled by Decision no. 1.557 / 2009, the avoidance of the procedure of examination and debate of the bill, both in the specialized committees and in the plenum of each Chamber of Parliament, according to the competencies provided for by Article 75 of the Constitution, and the use of the assumption of responsibility on a bill cannot find grounds either in fact or in law*".

As a conclusion, the Court found that "*Government's assumption of responsibility on the National Education Bill, while the bill was in the lawmaking process in the Senate, as a decisional Chamber, triggered a legal dispute of a constitutional nature between the Government and the Parliament, as the exercise by the Government one of its powers, in breach of the constitutional framework that circumstantiates it, violated the legislative competence of Parliament as sole authority. Legitimation of such an act with the argument that Article 114 of the Constitution makes no distinction about the Government's possibility to assume responsibility, an argument based on the idea that anything which is not prohibited is allowed, could lead eventually to the creation of an institutional blockage, meaning that the Parliament would be unable to legislate, i.e. to exercise its fundamental role, that of a sole legislative authority*".

We consider that the whole issue concerning the limits of Government's assumption of responsibility on a bill – in the absence of express constitutional provisions – must be examined with reference to the principles of the Basic Law, and particularly with reference to the principle of separation and balance of powers covered by Article 1 para. (4) of the Constitution. It is not acceptable that the provisions of

Article 114 of the Constitution, which govern the procedure of the Government's assumption of responsibility on a bill, to be interpreted as permitting the Government to replace the Parliament, and therefore to legislate anytime and under any circumstances, and again, it is not acceptable that the provisions of Article 61 of the Constitution, which enshrine the role of Parliament as supreme representative body and sole legislative authority, be construed to allow the Parliament to abuse of its role through a possible "blockage" of the Government's legislative initiatives. In other words, the Government may assume responsibility on one or more bills on the same day or within the same parliamentary session, regardless of the complexity of the bill in question, and even if it is under parliamentary debate, as long as it uses this procedure *in extremis*, observing the conditions established by the Constitutional Court following the interpretation of Article 114, especially in conjunction with the provisions of Article para. (4) of the Constitution. Accepting an opposite idea would have the significance of a ban beyond both the word and spirit of the Constitution, such as to cause an imbalance between the executive and the legislative power, represented by the two public authorities – Parliament and Government.

But apart from all these considerations, it is clear that, in the current wording, Article 114 of the Basic Law does not expressly establish limits of the procedure of assumption of responsibility by the Government on a bill.

Thus in the context of a future revision of the Constitution, these limits should be established specifically, and not just inferred from the interpretation of Article 1 para. (4) of the Constitution, in conjunction with the provisions that enshrine the role of the respective public authorities. A possible model could be that of France, there the procedure of Government's assumption of responsibility is limited both in terms of the subject and of the number of bills[766], a limitation that occurred following the revision of the Constitution on 23 July 2008. Prior to the revision, the Government was able to use this lawmaking procedure whenever it deemed necessary and regardless of the nature of the text on which it assumed responsibility[767]. The experience that led to this amendment of the Constitution of France, as well as the debates that accompanied in Romania the pronunciation by the Constitutional Court of the mentioned decisions, emphasize the need that the power of Government be subject to some strict and clearly expressed rules. Exacerbation of debates, confrontation of ideas and the difficulty in identifying solutions during the parliamentary debates which accompany the adoption of a bill are not proper

766 A bill in relation to tax or to social security funding, as well as another bill or legislative proposal per session – ordinary or extraordinary.

767 During the ninth legislature, for instance, the French Government used for 39 times such a procedure, based on the provisions of Article 49 para. (3) of the French Constitution – see *http://www.assemblee-nationale.fr/connaissance/responsabilite.asp*.

arguments to support a "transfer" of constitutional powers between the legislative and the executive.

The initiatives for the revisions of the Constitution in 2011, respectively in 2014, tried to supplement these lacks in the current constitutional regulation. On the occasion of adjudication upon these initiatives, the Court found that "*the quantitative limitation of the Government's possibility to use this procedure within one parliamentary session eliminates the premises of abusive exercise by the Government of its constitutional right to assume responsibility before Parliament, and, as concerns the legislative authority, the latter can fully exercise its power, as established by Article 61 para. (1) of the Constitution*"[768]. The Court also recommended the supplementation of the provisions of Article 114 para. (1) of the Constitution, in the sense of limiting the object on which the Government may assume responsibility to a program, a statement of general policy or a bill that would consistently regulate social relations concerning one area. The Court indicated that "*the lack of such conditioning on the scope of regulation of the bill would lead to the circumvention of the constitutional provisions proposed to be amended, namely the possibility to assume responsibility only once in a session, because they entitle the Government to assume responsibility by means of a bill that formally meets the constitutional requirements, but which, by a complex structure and a heterogeneous content, would encompass rules of very different social areas*"[769].

4.3.4 Legislative delegation

4.3.4.1 Concept. Constitutional text of reference

Legislative delegation represents a transfer of legislative powers to the executive authorities through an act of will of Parliament or constitutionally, in exceptional cases.

Article 115 of the Constitution of Romania enshrines two types of acts by which the executive power is entitled to enforce the legislative delegation, as follows:

- *simple ordinances*, which can be issued only by an Act on delegating powers, therefore, under a legislative delegation granted by the legislature [Article 115 para. (1)] and, if the Act on delegating powers so requests, ordinances shall be submitted to Parliament for approval, not later than prescribed by the time-limits of delegation [Article 115 para. (3)];

768 Decision no. 799 of 17 June 2011, published in the Official Gazette of Romania no. 440 of 23 June 2011.

769 *Ibidem*; in the same regard, see Decision no. 80 of 16 February 2014, published in the Official Gazette of Romania no. 246 of 7 April 2014.

- *emergency ordinance* [Article 115 para. (4)], where the legislative delegation shall be granted by the Constitution itself and they shall be submitted to Parliament for approval[770].

The constitutional text of reference enshrines a number of express limitations in terms of legislative delegation. Thus, as concerns the ordinances issued under an Act on delegating powers, pursuant to Article 115 para. (1), they cannot cover areas subject to organic laws. Regarding the emergency ordinances, the constituent legislature has established a number of express limitations by the provisions of Article 115 para. (4) and (6), provided that, in the absence of certain definitions of the terms comprised in the texts to be cited, the Constitutional Court proceeded in its case-law to the interpretation of their meaning, thus making the necessary distinctions between the two categories of normative acts and in terms of the legal regime of each of them.

4.3.4.2 Statuaries in the case-law of the Constitutional Court

As for the regime of the emergency ordinances issued by the Government, the Court ruled on the following constitutional limits, expressly established by the provisions of the Basic Law or resulted from the interpretation of these texts:

a) **Article 115 para. (4) of the Constitution of Romania: "The Government may adopt emergency ordinances solely in exceptional cases which call for regulations without delay, and must set forth the reasons for that emergency in their very content"** (prior to the revision of the Constitution, the constitutional text of reference used the phrase "*exceptional cases*", both were impugned due to "their inconsistent nature, still at the Government's discretion"[771]).

The notion of "exceptional case"

By Decision no. 255 of 11 May 2005[772], adjudicating within the *a priori* review upon the law approving an emergency ordinance, the Court ruled on the mentioned constitutional provisions in order to obtain the meaning of the constituent

770 According to Article 115 para. (5) of the Constitution: "*Emergency ordinances shall only take effects after their tabling for debate in the Chamber which is competent to be referred to, in an emergency procedure, and after publication in the Official Gazette of Romania. If not in session, the Chambers shall be convened within 5 days after tabling or, as the case may be, after forwarding. Where the Chamber thus referred has failed, within 30 days of the tabling date, to decide on that ordinance, such shall be deemed as having been approved and shall be sent to the other Chamber which shall likewise decide in an emergency procedure. An emergency ordinance which comprises norms pertaining to the rank of organic laws must be approved by a majority as it is stipulated under Article 76 paragraph (1)*".

771 D. Apostol Tofan, in I. Muraru, E.S. Tănăsescu (coordinators), *op. cit.*, p. 1096.

772 Published in the Official Gazette of Romania no. 511 of 16 June 2005.

legislature's will and, in relation to the identified meaning, the meaning of the terms used therein, in the wording after the revision, in comparison with the regulation prior to the revision of the Constitution[773].

Thus, referring to the above-mentioned limit, the Court found that "*Apart from the trenchant character of the formula used by the constituent legislature, its intention or purpose, consisting in the restriction of the field in which the Government may substitute the Parliament, adopting primary norms for certain reasons which it is sovereign in determining, are clearly underlined by the difference between the constitutional text in force and the previous one, former Article 114 para. (4) of the Constitution, in its initial form. According to that text, Government's possibility to adopt emergency ordinances was conditioned exclusively by the existence of certain exceptional cases. The term «exceptional cases» used in the former wording was replaced, in the new wording, with that of «exceptional situations». Moreover, although the difference between the two terms, from the point of view of the degree of deviation from ordinary or common which they express, is obvious, the same legislature felt that it is necessary to clarify these aspects and not to leave any interpretation that would minimize such difference, by adding the collocation «which call for regulations without delay», enshrining thus in terminis the imperative of the regulation emergency. Finally, for reasons of legislative rigour, it instituted the exigency on the statement of the reasons for the emergency in the very content of the ordinance adopted outside a law of delegation*".

Referring to the phrase "*exceptional case*", provided by the constitutional text prior to the revision of the Constitution, the Court found that it was defined in relation to "*the necessity and emergency of the regulation of a situation which, due to exceptional circumstances, imposed the adoption of immediate solutions, in order to avoid a serious breach of the public interest*"[774]. For the same purpose, of a better defining of the exceptional case, the Court mentioned this is characterised by its objective nature, "*in the sense that its existence does not depend on the Government's will, which, in such circumstances, is compelled to react promptly in order to defend a public interest by emergency ordinances*"[775]. Finally, the Court found[776] that those previously stated are "*even more pertinent, today* (A/N, after the revision of the Constitution and following the replacement of the phrase «exceptional case» with that of «exceptional situation»), *if we have in view the fact that the mentioned viewpoint*

773 Law no. 429/2003 on the revision of the Constitution of Romania was published in the Official Gazette of Romania no. 758 of 29 October 2003; the Constitution was republished, with updated names and new numbering for texts, in the Official Gazette of Romania no. 767 of 31 October 2003.

774 Decision no. 65 of 20 June 1995, published in the Official Gazette of Romania no. 129 of 28 June 1995.

775 Decision no. 83 of 19 May 1998, published in the Official Gazette of Romania no. 211 of 8 June 1998.

776 Decision no. 255 of 11 May 2005, published in the Official Gazette of Romania no. 511 of 16 June 2005.

has full support precisely in the word of the constitutional regulation of reference, in its present wording".

Thus, for example, the Court held that there was an exceptional situation which justifies the adoption of an emergency ordinance amending the Fiscal Code, given that Article 4 para. (1) of the Fiscal Code establishes the rule of its amendment and supplementation by law within 6 months before the date of entry into force. On the occasion of constitutional review of the Law approving the Government Emergency Ordinance no. 34/2009 regarding the budget rectification for 2009 and the regulation of certain financial-fiscal measures[777], the Court held that when adopting the emergency ordinance in question, "*the Government was and it still is in an exceptional situation that requires emergency measures aimed just at strengthening the country's economic situation and at maintaining the effectiveness of the national public budget*".

Likewise, by Decisions no. 188 of 2 March 2010[778] and no. 190 of 2 March 2010[779], the Court found the constitutionality of the provisions of the Government Emergency Ordinance no. 71/2009 on payment of certain amounts provided in executory titles intended to grant salary rights to the public sector employees, holding that the adoption of the impugned normative act "*was determined by the existence of a substantial number of cases concerning the granting of salary rights, which led to an inability of the state authority to enforce the judgments which have been already delivered in this matter, particularly in the current context of acute economic crisis*", given thus "*the settlement of an exceptional situation by regulating certain temporary measures and derogations from the common law on matters of enforcement of judgments*".

The Court found that "*the motivation of the emergency and the exceptional situation, whose regulation cannot be postponed, as set forth in the preamble of the emergency ordinance, cannot be accepted in the light of the requirements of Article 115 para. (4) of the Constitution, since for the continuation of certain structures of the apparatus of the Government, derived from the duties set by Government Emergency Ordinance no. 3/2009, as well as of the labour relationships with the staff, there is no adequate legislative framework so that the activity, the duties and the obligations may continue. Moreover, the Government would have continued to finalize the bill submitted to Parliament in order to be debated and adopted within the emergency procedure, which would have led to the observance of the Parliament's role of sole legislative authority of the country, as it is set forth in Article 61 of the Basic Law*"[780].

The Court also noted that the transposition and implementation of a Directive into national legislation (to be set up on 11 June 2010) cannot justify itself, meeting the requirements of Article 115 para. (4) on the existence of extraordinary

777 Decision no. 786 of 13 May 2009, published in the Official Gazette of Romania no. 400 of 12 June 2009.

778 Published in the Official Gazette of Romania no. 237 of 14 April 2010.

779 Published in the Official Gazette of Romania no. 224 of 9 April 2010.

780 Decision no. 1555 of 17 November 2009, published in the Official Gazette of Romania no. 916 of 28 December 2009.

circumstances, retaining, however, that "*such a conclusion is supported by the fact that the Government has not taken the necessary steps and has not submitted any bill in Parliament that would follow the implementation of Directive (...) so that the Government could not rely on its own fault for its failure to transpose in good time*". The Court held, however, that the extraordinary situation "*was determined by the context of economic and financial difficulties which required quick and ferm actions, likely to diminish the economic crisis and the austerity measures that it has generated, and the need to take positive steps not to undermine the objective of achieving the internal market of the European Union*"[781]. With reference to the transposition of internal rules into national law, the Court held in principle that "the national measures necessary in order to implement the directive must be in principle adopted by Parliament as an ordinary legislature"[782], stating, in another case, that "according to Article 148 para. (4) of the Constitution, the Romanian authorities have committed to ensure the fulfilment of obligations resulted from the Founding Treaties of the European Union, from the binding Community regulations and from the Accession Act. In this regard, the Government is empowered constitutionally, by the means which are made available, to ensure fulfilment of Romania's obligations in relation to the European Union. Thus, the use of emergency ordinances for bringing the national legislation into line with the Community one where the infringement procedure before the Court of Justice was imminent is fully constitutional"[783]. However, "with reference to the justification of an exceptional situation by the fact that Romania would risk to determine the infringement procedure as long as the European Commission did not notify the Court of Justice of the European Union within this procedure, there is no exceptional situation in the case-law of the constitutional court"[784].

The notion of "emergency"

As concerns the emergency, the Court held that it cannot be accredited or motivated by usefulness of the regulation[785], by its opportunity or its reasoning[786]. The emergency of the measure cannot also be justified also by the need for the harmonization of the Romanian legislation with the European one, since "*the amendment or the unification of the legislation in one field or another does not justify, by itself, the*

781 Decision no. 1059 of 11 December 2012, published in the Official Gazette of Romania no. 73 of 4 February 2013.

782 Decision no. 1599 of 9 December 2010, published in the Official Gazette of Romania no. 67 of 26 January 2011.

783 Decision no. 802 of 19 May 2009, published in the Official Gazette of Romania no. 428 of 23 June 2009.

784 Decision no. 2 of 17 January 2013, published in the Official Gazette of Romania no. 110 of 25 February 2013.

785 Decision no. 255 of 11 May 2005, published in the Official Gazette of Romania no. 511 of 16 June 2005.

786 Decision no. 109 of 9 February 2010, published in the Official Gazette of Romania no. 175 of 18 March 2010.

issuance of an emergency ordinance"[787]. But the use of the emergency ordinances is constitutional in order to bring the national legislation in line with the Community one where the infringement procedure before the Court of Justice of the European Union was imminent[788].

According to those ruled by the Court, "*the lack or the failure to explain the emergency for the regulation of the exceptional situations, such as to justify the adoption of a measure to remove the stability of the legal institution, regulated by the establishment of the duration period regarding the exercise of certain offices, clearly constitutes a constitutional barrier for the adoption by the Government of an emergency ordinance for the purposes indicated. To decide otherwise means to void of content the provisions of Article 115 of the Constitution regarding the legislative delegation and to provide freedom to Government in order to adopt, within the emergency procedure, normative acts which shall be regarded as laws, anytime and – taking into account the fact that the emergency ordinance can also regulate matters covered by organic laws – in any field*"[789].

Likewise, ruling on the meaning of the phrase "*exceptional situation*" and on the notion of "*emergency*", the Court held that they are not equivalent – "*the urgency of the regulation is not tantamount to the existence of an exceptional situation, as the operative regulation could also be achieved by way of the normal procedure of lawmaking*"[790].

b) Article 115 para. (6): "Emergency ordinances cannot be adopted in fields pertaining to constitutional laws, nor may these affect the status of the State fundamental institutions or any of the rights, freedoms and duties set forth in the Constitution, the electoral rights, or envisage any measures for the forcible transfer of assets into public property".

With reference to the meaning of the notion "*affect*" used by the constituent legislature, the Court held that "*the emergency ordinances cannot be adopted if they «affect», if they have negative consequences, but, instead, they can be adopted if they have, by the regulations contained therein, positive consequences in the fields in which they intervene*"[791].

---

787 Decision no. 15 of 25 January 2000, published in the Official Gazette of Romania no. 267 of 14 June 2000.

788 Decision no. 802 of 19 May 2009, published in the Official Gazette of Romania no. 428 of 23 June 2009.

789 Decision no. 258 of 14 March 2006, published in the Official Gazette of Romania no. 341 of 17 April 2006.

790 Decision no. 421 of 9 May 2007, published in the Official Gazette of Romania no. 367 of 30 May 2007.

791 Decision no. 1189 of 6 November 2008, published in the Official Gazette of Romania no. 787 of 25 November 2008.

Under this interpretation of the constitutional text, by Decision no. 82/2009[792], the Court declared unconstitutional the Government Emergency Ordinance no. 230/2008 amending certain normative acts in the field of pensions, which prohibits to cumulate pensions with the income achieved from professional activities carried out within public authorities and institutions and, accordingly, the persons in the situation referred to were obliged to opt either for pension or for the income achieved following professional activities, noting that both the pension rights provided by Article 47 para. (2) of the Constitution and the labour right enshrined in Article 41 of the Basic Law are affected by limitation, ascertaining for these reasons its unconstitutionality[793].

By Decision no. 104/2009[794], the Court established that the amendment of the competence to settle disputes covering the grant of certain salary rights to the staff within the legal system violates the provisions of Article 115 para. (6) of the Constitution as it affects the regime of a fundamental state institution, the High Court of Cassation and Justice, whose constitutional status is provided by Article 126 para. (4) of the Constitution. Thus, "falling with the competence of the supreme court to settle of appeals against judgments delivered by courts of appeal in first instance has the effect to extent its scope of competence and to oversize its activity, given that, according to Law no. 304/2004 on judicial organization, republished, as subsequently amended and supplemented, there is no specialised section for the settlement of labour conflicts and disputes within the High Court of Cassation and Justice".

Likewise, being notified with the objection of unconstitutionality of the Law approving the Government Emergency Ordinance no. 37/2009 on certain measures for the improvement of the activity of the public administration, the Court held that this is unconstitutional because the emergency ordinance approved by Parliament under the law has affected the legal regime of the decentralized public services[795].

In another case[796], the Court found that "*the provisions of the Government Emergency Ordinance no. 3/2009 violate the provisions of Article 115 para. (6) of the Constitution, because it affects the fundamental rights, such as citizens' equal rights, labour rights and the rights of labour social protection, as enshrined in the constitutional provisions of Articles 16 and 41*". That situation concerned the condition introduced by the Government Emergency Ordinance no. 3/2009, which provided employment solely based on the trust granted by the Prime Minister, upon the approval of the Deputy Prime Minister, as appropriate, a condition considered by the Court as "*an essentially subjective one, which is the result of a person's uncensored option*". Such

792 Published in the Official Gazette of Romania no. 33 of 16 January 2009.

793 For a critical point of view regarding this decision, see E.S. Tănăsescu, *Commented case-law*, in Judicial Courier no. 2/2009, p. 89.

794 Published in the Official Gazette of Romania no. 73 of 6 February 2009.

795 Decision no. 1257 of 7 October 2009, published in the Official Gazette of Romania no. 758 of 6 November 2009.

796 Decision no. 1039 of 9 July 2009, published in the Official Gazette of Romania no. 582 of 21 August 2009.

provision *"constitutes the requirement to sign or terminate an individual employment contract on the basis of random criteria, purely subjective, although the professional competence is the one which should govern these relationships, competence that can always be assessed based on objective criteria"*, so that the impugned legal texts also violate, in addition to the provisions of Article 41 of the Constitution, the constitutional principle of citizens' equal rights, *"since they introduce a condition which constitutes an unjustified exemption from the provisions of the Labour Code, placing the persons concerned in a situation of clear legal inequality in relation to the other employees"*.

Distinguishing on the meaning of the concept of "*affection*", the Court has also held in another case, where it ascertained the unconstitutionality the Government Emergency Ordinance no. 91/2013 concerning the procedures to prevent insolvency and the insolvency, that "*Direct affection is achieved by the mere suspension of the broadcasting licence. In this case, due to the restriction on programs broadcasting, the debtor subject to Law no. 504/2002 will witness the termination of advertising contracts, contracts which, in most cases, represent the main source of income. Thus, although the emergency ordinance aims, where possible, to give the debtor the opportunity to redress, the effects are to the contrary, leading to rapid onset of bankruptcy proceedings. The conduct imposed to the debtor by the delegated legislature does not appear to be proportionate to the aim pursued, exceeding the normal conditions for the conduct of its business. In assessing the proportionality of the measure account must be given to the fact that the delegated legislature did not indicate in the preamble to the emergency ordinance or in the substantiation note the reasons why it opted for a different treatment of the debtor that is subject to the provisions of Law no. 504/2002, by establishing an additional penalty, the suspension of the broadcasting license. (...) Indirect affection is achieved by the fact that citizens who benefited from the activity of the debtor subject to Law no. 504/2002 cannot continue to do so insofar the debtor is subject to the Audiovisual Law no. 504/2002, as amended, following the opening of the procedure and until the date of confirmation of the reorganisation plan*"[797].

c) when adopting an emergency ordinance, Government shall comply with the provisions of Article 115 para. (4) and (6), but also with the provisions of Article 61 para. (1) of the Constitution[798].

We refer to a limit set by the Court, by way of case-law. Thus, through a series of decisions[799], the Court established that "*the adoption of emergency ordinances for the sole purpose to counter a measure of legislative policy concerning teaching staff wages*

797 Decision no. 447 of 29 October 2013, published in the Official Gazette of Romania no. 674 of 1 November 2013.

798 See B. Karoly, *Recent developments in the case-law of the Constitutional Court of Romania on the conditions under which the Government adopts emergency ordinances*, in Constitutional Court Bulletin no. 1/2009, p. 26.

799 Decision no. 842 of 2 June 2009, published in the Official Gazette of Romania no. 464 of 6 July 2009.

approved by the Parliament violates Article 1 para. (4), Article 61 para. (1), Article 115 para. (4) of the Basic Law"[800]. Therefore, as the Court noted by Decision no. 27/1998, even if "*the ordinance, being the expression of legislative delegation, necessarily involves the possibility to amend or repeal laws in force, according to the limits of the legislative authority, which, in case of emergency ordinances, is referred to in para. (4) of Article 114 of the Constitution*", is contrary to the constitutional provisions that the Government, by issuing an emergency ordinance, be against a law which has already been adopted by Parliament, as the legislative powers delegated to the Government could not prevent the implementation of a primary regulatory act adopted by the very legislative power in the exercise of its initial powers.

Ruling also explicitly in this respect, the Court held in another case that "*the adoption of the analysed emergency ordinance also violates the provisions of Article 61 para. (1) of the Constitution of Romania, according to which «Parliament is the supreme representative body of the Romanian people and the sole legislative authority of the country», the provisions of Article 73 para. (3) l), as well as the principle of separation of powers enshrined in Article 1 para. (4) of the Constitution. In this respect, the Constitutional Court held that regulation via ordinances and emergency ordinances constitutes, as expressly provided in Article 115 of the Constitution, a task performed by the Government under the legislative delegation, and stepping over the limits of this delegation, established by the very text of the Constitution, is an unacceptable interference in the legislative jurisdiction of Parliament, i.e. a violation of the principle of separation of powers*"[801].

With reference to such principles, the Court ruled in another case that "*the adoption by the Government of Emergency Ordinance no. 91/2013 was not motivated by the need to regulate in an area where the primary legislature has not intervened. On the contrary, there were rules in this matter, even if not encoded in a single normative act, so it was especially necessary to emphasise and explain the urgency of the regulation in this area by the Government. The Court has already encountered similar situations in this case-law when it sanctioned an emergency ordinance issued in an area already covered by Parliament.*

For example, in Decision no. 1.221 of 12 November 2008, published in the Official Gazette of Romania, Part I, no. 804 of 2 December 2008 (...). In other words, as long as the conditions for the adoption of an emergency ordinance are not complied with, the Government cannot intervene in an area already covered by"[802].

---

800 As the Court noted, by the provisions of the emergency ordinance found unconstitutional, "the salary increases to which education staff would have been entitled under Law no. 221/2008" were decreased.

801 Decision no. 544 of 28 June 2006, published in the Official Gazette of Romania no. 568 of 30 June 2006.

802 Decision no. 447 of 29 October 2013, published in the Official Gazette of Romania no. 674 of 1 November 2013.

d) the unconstitutionality of an ordinance cannot be covered by being approved by Parliament.

The Constitutional Court has consistently ruled in its case-law that "*the unconstitutional flaws of an ordinance or of an emergency ordinance issued by the Government cannot be covered by the approval by Parliament of the ordinance in question. Consequently, the law which approves an unconstitutional emergency ordinance is itself unconstitutional*"[803]. Therefore, by the approval by Parliament of an emergency ordinance which is manifestly unconstitutional, its unconstitutional nature is transferred to the law that has approved it.

4.3.5 Conclusions

Constitutional and legal norms referred to above establish the dialogue between the Constitutional Court and the Government, such as to achieve a circumstantiation of the activity of the Government within the limits of the Basic Law, including in terms of the relationships with the other representative authorities of state powers.

The dialogue and the loyal cooperation between the state authorities are necessary because "*the rule of law cannot constitute a reality as long as the Constitution enshrines the absolutism of one of the state bodies, be it legislative or executive. Therefore, the rule of law means the existence of a political settlement based on the separation of state powers, namely a system of «impediments and balances» in order to prevent the public bodies to abuse the powers that were conferred upon them*"[804]. From this perspective and given the large number of the Government's assumptions of responsibility, the large number of emergency ordinances issued by the Government, to the detriment of lawmaking by the authority which has unlimited constitutional competence in this regard – Parliament –, as well as the challenges in specialised doctrine, the role of the Constitutional Court and the need for a dialogue between them, the Government and Parliament, seem to be essential.

Of course, in order to solve these issues, it would be required the establishment of a constitutional framework limiting in a clearer way the possibility of the Government to legislate by way of emergency ordinances and to assume its responsibility before Parliament, as well as the broadening of the possibilities to refer to the Constitutional Court regarding the unconstitutionality of the Government Ordinances.

---

803 Decision no. 421 of 9 May 2007; Decision no. 584 of 13 June 2007; Decision no. 1008 of 7 July 2009, published in the Official Gazette of Romania no. 507 of 23 July 2009; Decision no. 738 of 19 September 2012, published in the Official Gazette of Romania no. 690 of 8 October 2012.

804 T. Drăganu, *Comparative constitutional law*, Lumina Lex Publishing House, Bucharest, 2007, p. 62.

Likewise, a loyal behaviour of the public authorities is also necessary, in order to comply not only with the word, but also with the spirit of the Constitution, which assigns a restrictive meaning to the conditions in which emergency ordinances may be issued or the assumption of responsibility on a bill may be achieved. We note in this respect the Constitutional Court's observation which noted in a case that "*the solution chosen by the Government to issue, even on the day before the day when the Constitutional Court was to rule on the constitutionality of the law approving the Government Emergency Ordinance no. 37/2009, a new emergency ordinance repealing the emergency ordinance approved by Parliament under the law, but which fully takes its content, calls into question the constitutional legislative behaviour of the Executive in relation to Parliament, and, not least, in relation to the Constitutional Court*"[805]. Likewise, the Court found that "*the solution chosen by the Government to adopt, shortly before the constitutional court was to rule on the constitutionality of the Law amending Article 27 para. (1) of Law no. 47/1992, an emergency ordinance that fully takes the normative content of the impugned law, calls into question the unconstitutional and abusive behaviour of the Government in relation the Constitutional Court*"[806].

We consider that such circumstances constitute in themselves a plea for the need for an institutional dialogue, subsumed into the constitutional values and loyalty in relation to them.

5. The dialogue between the Constitutional Court and the courts of law and commercial arbitration

5.1 General aspects

The dialogue between the Constitutional Court and the courts of law or the court of commercial arbitration causes a complex issue which, in itself, would require a much broader treatment than the one covered by this paper.

In what follows, we will underline a few landmarks which we consider particularly relevant within this dialogue, aiming, in particular, at the notification of the Constitutional Court by the courts of law or by the courts of commercial arbitration and the association, from this perspective, of the courts of law or the courts of commercial arbitration with the constitutional review, as well as at a series of statuaries on the role of the courts of law, particularly in the light of the acceptance of the case-law of the Constitutional Court.

805 Decision no. 1257 of 7 October 2009, published in the Official Gazette of Romania no. 758 of 6 November 2009.

806 Decision no. 727 of 9 July 2012, published in the Official Gazette of Romania no. 477 of 12 July 2012.

5.2 The notification of the Constitutional Court by the courts of law or commercial arbitration

5.2.1 The constitutional and legal framework

Pursuant to Article 146 a) of the Constitution, the Constitutional Court "*adjudicates on the constitutionality of laws before promulgation, upon referral by (...) the High Court of Cassation and Justice (...)*".

Likewise, pursuant to Article 146 d) first sentence of the Constitution of Romania, the Constitutional Court "*rules upon objections as to the unconstitutionality of laws and ordinances which are raised before the courts of law or commercial arbitration*". The provisions of the Basic Law are developed by those contained in Law no. 47/1992, Articles 15–18 (for the *a priori* review, through objections of unconstitutionality) and Articles 29–31 (for the *a posteriori* review, through exceptions of unconstitutionality).

As concern the powers in pursuit of which the Constitutional Court enters into dialogue with the courts of law, proceeding to examine the dynamics of referrals brought before the Constitutional Court under the constitutional texts mentioned above, it is found that, even if within the *a priori* constitutional review – of laws before promulgation – we can talk about a relationship between the Constitutional Court and the courts of law, embodied in the possibility set forth in Article 146 a) of the Constitution concerning the High Court of Cassation and Justice to refer to the Constitutional Court, this relationship is most fully manifested within the *a posteriori* review – of laws and ordinances in force – by way of the exception of unconstitutionality, a power governed by Article 146 d) of the Constitution[807].

Thus, analysing the activity of the Constitutional Court from the establishment up to the present[808], one may note that 31.955 referrals were settled, among which:

- 266 referrals within the constitutional review of laws before promulgation;
- 7 examinations on the initiative for the revision of the Constitution, pursuant to Article 144 a) final sentence of the Constitution;
- 37 referrals within the constitutional review of the Standing Orders of Parliament;
- 31.178 exceptions of unconstitutionality, out of which 31.129 exceptions raised before courts of law [pursuant to Article 144 c) of the Constitution, respectively to Article 146 d) first sentence of the Constitution, republished], and 49 exceptions raised directly by the Advocate of the People [pursuant to Article146 d) second sentence of the Constitution, republished];

807 Developed, from procedural point of view, by the provisions of Articles 29–31 of Law no. 47/1992 on the Organisation and Operation of the Constitutional Court.

808 Reference date – 31 October 2014, *www.ccr.ro* – Publications and statistics.

- 28 requests for the settlement of legal disputes of a constitutional nature between public authorities, pursuant to Article 146 e) of the Constitution, republished;
- 386 challenges raised within the procedure for the election of the President of Romania [pursuant to Article 144 d) of the Constitution, respectively to Article 146 f) of the Constitution, republished], out of which 43 in 1992, 132 in 1996, 70 in 2000, 50 in 2004, 41 in 2009 and 50 in 2014;
- 2 requests for the ascertainment of any circumstance as may justify the interim in the exercise of office of President of Romania [pursuant to Article 146 g) of the Constitution, republished], out of which one in 2007 and one in 2012;
- 3 proposals for the suspension from office of the President of Romania [pursuant to Article 144 f) of the Constitution, respectively to Article 146 h) of the Constitution, republished], out of which one in 1994, one in 2007 and one in 2012;
- 13 challenges regarding the observance of the procedure for the organisation and holding of a referendum [pursuant to Article 144 g) of the Constitution, respectively to Article 146 i) of the Constitution, republished], out of which 2 in 2003, 4 in 2007, one in 2009 and 6 in 2012;
- 6 referrals to verify whether conditions are met for the citizens' exercise of their legislative initiative [pursuant to Article 144 h) of the Constitution, respectively to Article 146 j) of the Constitution, republished], out of which two in 1994, one in 1996, one in 2004, one in 2007 and one in 2009;
- 2 challenges regarding the constitutionality of a political party [pursuant to Article 144 i) of the Constitution, respectively to Article 146 k) of the Constitution, republished], out of which one in 1993, sent back to the Chamber of Deputies and the Senate to attach to it the necessary evidence and to be examined, and one in 2014;
- 27 challenges regarding other prerogatives as provided by the Court's organic law pursuant to Article 146 l) of the Constitution, republished, out of which 2 in 2010, 3 in 2011, 12 in 2012, 3 in 2013 and 7 in 2014.

These statistical data determines the obvious conclusion that the substance of the Constitutional Court's activity (in terms of volume) is given by the settlement of exceptions of unconstitutionality of laws and ordinances raised before courts of law or courts of commercial arbitration. But the settlement of the exceptions of unconstitutionality is a framework within which the dialogue between the constitutional court and the courts of law is fully manifested in order to achieve the purpose of free access to justice and to guarantee fundamental rights and freedoms. As it has been noted[809], "the exception of unconstitutionality creates a triangular relation between the party to the proceedings and whose rights or interests have been prejudiced by an unconstitutional norm, the court before which the exception is invoked and

809 I. Deleanu, *Institutions and constitutional procedures – in Romanian and comparative law*, C.H. Beck Publishing House, Bucharest, 2006, p. 854.

the court required to adjudicate upon it. Thus, it is settled within a relationship determined between the *a quo* judge and the *a quem* judge".

5.2.2 The settlement of the exceptions of unconstitutionality of laws and ordinances

5.2.2.1 Procedural phases

Corroborating the incident constitutional provisions with the provisions of Law no. 47/1992, it results that the settlement procedure of the exceptions of unconstitutionality involves two phases:

- judicial phase – preliminary phase which begins with raising the exception of unconstitutionality before the court of law or the court of commercial arbitration and it finalizes with referring to the Constitutional Court (if the court does not reject the exception as inadmissible, in the cases expressly and restrictively provided by Law no. 47/1992), and
- constitutional contentious phase, being conducted before the Constitutional Court, which begins with the interlocutory order of the Constitutional Court by the court of law or the court of commercial arbitration and it finalizes with the decision delivered by the Court.

5.2.2.2 The judicial phase for the settlement of exceptions of unconstitutionality

It has been shown[810] that the judicial phase is the one where the courts of law or the courts of commercial arbitration are particularly associated with the Constitutional Court in exercising the constitutional review of laws and ordinances, an association which can be performed in *three ways*, consisting of:

- the possibility of the court to reject a request for referral to the Constitutional Court with an exception of unconstitutionality brought before it, if it does not meet the requirements of admissibility laid down by Law no. 47/1992;
- their power to refer to the Constitutional Court with an exception of unconstitutionality raised in the cases that are referred to them;
- by allowing the court itself to refer to the Court with an exception of unconstitutionality raised ex officio.

When the court invokes ex officio an exception of unconstitutionality, it must motivate it, and as for the exceptions of unconstitutionality raised by the parties or by the Public Ministry, it must express its viewpoint on it in the content of the interlocutory order.

---

810 B. Selejean-Guţan, *Association of the courts of law to the constitutional review of laws within the procedure of invocation and settlement of an exception of unconstitutionality*, in RDP no. 1/2003, p. 47 et seq.

The obligation of the court of law to refer to the Constitutional Court

Pursuant to Article 29 of Law no. 47/1992: "*(1) The Constitutional Court shall decide upon the exceptions raised before the courts of law or courts of commercial arbitration referring to the unconstitutionality of laws and ordinances which are in force, or any provision thereof, where such is related to adjudication of the case, regardless in which stage of trial proceedings or subject-matter thereof. (2) The exception can be raised at the request of either party or ex officio, by the court of law or of commercial arbitration hearing the case. Likewise, the prosecutor is entitled to raise this exception before the court in cases where he attends trial proceedings. (3) Legal provisions whose unconstitutionality has been found by prior decision of the Constitutional Court cannot form the subject-matter of an exception. (4) The case shall be referred to the Constitutional Court by the court before which the exception of unconstitutionality was raised, through an interlocutory order which shall include the parties' for and against viewpoints, and the instance's opinion on the exception, together with the evidence provided by the parties. If the exception has been raised ex officio, the interlocutory order shall be motivated, including the parties' arguments, as well as the necessary evidence. Alongside with the interlocutory order, the referring court must also send to the Constitutional Court the full name of the litigant parties and other details comprising necessary data for the accomplishment of the summons proceedings in respect thereof. (5) If the exception is inadmissible, being contrary to provisions under paragraphs (1), (2) or (3) above, the adjudicating court shall, through a motivated interlocutory order, dismiss the request for referring the case to the Constitutional Court. The interlocutory judgment is subject only to an appeal lodged to the superior court, within forty-eight hours from the pronouncement. The appeal shall be heard within three days*".

In relation to the cited norms, it results that the court must refer to the Constitutional Court whenever an exception of unconstitutionality is raised before it. The court is a first legal filter as the Constitutional Court shall be notified only when the exception of unconstitutionality meets the requirements provided by law. However, the filter role of the court of law or the court of commercial arbitration occurs only in terms of the cases of inadmissibility provided by law; in other words, the refusal to refer to the Constitutional Court can be motivated only by the existence of a case of inadmissibility, and against the decision whereby the request for referral to the Court is rejected on this ground is open to appeal. In this respect, the law provides a short term (48 hours as from delivery), as well as its rapid judging (within 3 days).

The conclusion by which the court refers to the Constitutional Court for the settlement of the exception of unconstitutionality is not subject to appeal. It has been showed in this regard that the legislature considered that any error of the *a quo* judge to allow the application for referral to the constitutional court can be corrected by the *ad quem* judge when settling the exception of unconstitutionality[811].

---

811 M. Fodor, *Aspects regarding the invocation of an exception of unconstitutionality, the settlement of a referral to the Constitutional Court and the legal status of the decision delivered on this referral*, in RRDP no. 6/2007, pp. 47–64.

As concerns the cases of inadmissibility, we consider that their strict interpretation deemed necessary, in the sense that the court shall be limited only to those that are expressly and restrictively provided by law, without interfering with the activity of the Constitutional Court, such as, for example, the assessment of the competence of the constitutional contentious court to settle an exception of unconstitutionality in relation to the grounds of the author of the referral. Thus, for example, in violation of the constitutional and legal provisions of reference in a case settled by the Bucharest Court, Criminal Division, the request for referral to the Constitutional Court has been rejected on the ground that "*the allegations of the defender in motivating the exception of unconstitutionality relate to the merits of the case, and the assessment of the foreseeability of the norm, choosing the applicable sanction, the incrimination or not of a certain behaviour do not fall within the competence of the constitutional contentious court. The fact that in its case-law the Constitutional Court exceeded its powers and made assessments in certain decisions of this case on the foreseeability of certain norms or on the legality of certain evidence in a pending criminal trial may not result in choosing another solution, namely to allow the request for referral to the Constitutional Court. The fact that, following the amendments in 2010 the admission of the request for referral to the Constitutional Court no longer results in the suspension of criminal proceedings does not mean that the court before which the exceptions of unconstitutionality are raised must turn into a simple instrument to refer to the Constitutional Court, without filtering anymore the requests for referral for the reasons thereof*". We consider that this is a situation where the court violated the competence of the Constitutional Court, ruling practically on the merits of the exception of unconstitutionality, not on its admissibility. Moreover, an appeal was formulated against this decision, which was accepted, and the decision was cancelled. Being judged again, the court of appeal found that the conditions of admissibility of the exception of unconstitutionality were met[812].

In the same respect it is also the established case-law of the High Court of Cassation and Justice, which has held that, in the matter of referral to the constitutional contentious court, the court has limited powers to verify whether the admissibility requirements are fulfilled, without verifying the merits of the exception and without adding other admissibility requirements, such as, for example, the observance of the reasonable term of the judicial phase or the motivation of the merits of the exception of unconstitutionality[813].

Therefore, the judgment and the settlement of the request for referral to the Constitutional Court with the exception of unconstitutionality fall within the

---

812 F.C. Plopeanu, *The offence of market abuse. Referral to the Constitutional Court with an exception of unconstitutionality. The limits of the appreciation rights of the criminal court before which the exception of unconstitutionality was raised, with critical note*, in PR no. 1/2011, pp. 225–232.

813 *Ibidem*, with reference to the Decisions of the High Court of Cassation and Justice, Criminal Section, no. 3422/2008, no. 2287/2008 and no. 2497/2009.

competence of the court of law or the court of commercial arbitration before which it has been raised, and the settlement of the exception of unconstitutionality falls exclusively within the competence of the Constitutional Court. The dialogue between the *a quo* judge and the *a quem* judge is conducted within the limits and the observance of the competence of each of them, and only in this context the association of the courts of law within the exercise of the constitutional review may be achieved.

The obligation of the court of law to express its viewpoint on the exception of unconstitutionality raised

The text of law governing such obligation of the court of law, namely Article 29 para. (4) of Law no. 47/1992, formed, inter alia, the subject-matter of an exception of unconstitutionality raised by the Advocate of the People[814]. This exception has started from a non-unitary practice of both the courts of law and the Constitutional Court, which has revealed two distinct situations if the court of law has not expressed its viewpoint on the exception of unconstitutionality raised. In the first situation, the Constitutional Court, before settling the exception, returned the file to the court of law in order to express its viewpoint[815], and in the second situation, the Constitutional Court has kept the file and proceeded to the settlement of the exception of unconstitutionality, without the viewpoint of the court of law[816].

The author of the exception considered that, "in order to achieve a unitary case-law and to give efficiency to the provisions of Article 29 para. (4) of Law no. 47/1992", republished, which are mandatory, it is necessary "to examine the possible unconstitutionality of the provisions of Article 29 para. (4) of Law no. 47/1992, republished". Thus, the Advocate of the People argued that the obligation of the court of law to express its viewpoint on the exception of unconstitutionality raised may be interpreted "as a prejudice on the constitutionality of the legal provisions which are to be subject to the constitutional review exercised by the Constitutional Court", which, in his opinion, "is in conflict with the independence and impartiality of judges and contrary to the word and spirit of the provisions of Article 124 of the Constitution". According to the viewpoint of the Advocate of the People, it is unthinkable that the courts of law have a different practice regarding the legal obligation to express its viewpoints on the exception of unconstitutionality raised. As grounds for the exception of unconstitutionality, the author of the exception also considered that if the court of law did not prepare the referral of the Constitutional Court under the terms provided by law, any action taken by the Constitutional Court "would result in the ignorance of the constitutional provisions and of the provisions of the organic law

814 Decision no. 353 of 29 June 2005, published in the Official Gazette of Romania no. 693 of 2 August 2005.

815 For example: Decision no. 46 of 10 September 1993, published in the Official Gazette of Romania no. 283 of 7 December 1993; Decision no. 27 of 25 May 1993, published in the Official Gazette of Romania no. 163 of 15 July 1993.

816 For example, Decision no. 245 of 27 May 2004, published in the Official Gazette of Romania no. 716 of 9 August 1994.

(its organic law)". However, the Advocate of the People claimed that the impugned legal provisions are contrary to Article 1 para. (5) of the Constitution, because, in the absence of the viewpoint of the court of law, the Constitutional Court would be unable to accomplish its constitutional and legal mission, as guarantor for the supremacy of the Constitution, capacity conferred by Article 142 of the Basic Law. He also claimed that the impugned legal provisions "affect the parties' right to a fair trial, enshrined in Article 21 para. (3) of the Constitution and are contrary to the provisions of Article 24 of the Constitution", as, in the absence of the viewpoint of the court of law, the Constitutional Court "would be prevented from approaching the merits of the constitutional dispute and adjudicating upon the exception of unconstitutionality raised by the author, through its decision".

From a comparative examination of the impugned legal provisions and of the constitutional provisions which are invoked as grounds for the exception, the Court found that there is no incompatibility between the impugned legal text and the constitutional provisions invoked. On the contrary, the viewpoint of the court of law on the exception of unconstitutionality constitutes an expression of the relationship that should exist between the "a quo" judge and the "a quem" judge in the settlement procedure of the exception or, in other words, between the judge entrusted with the proceedings and the one of the constitutional contentious court who shall judge the exception of unconstitutionality raised before the first court.

The Court noted that, as it results from the provisions of Article 29 para. (1)-(3) and (6) of Law no. 47/1992, this relationship is more manifested since in the enforcement of the mentioned texts, the court of law, the "a quo" judge, has even a filter role of the exception of unconstitutionality raised by the parties, being obliged to reject as inadmissible the exceptions of unconstitutionality which do not comply with the requirements of the law.

Consequently, the Constitutional Court found that the obligation set forth in the impugned text, in the sense that the court of law shall express its viewpoint on the exception that it is judged by it, does not violate any constitutional provision or principle. The legal text has been established since 1992, for the purpose that alongside the presidents of the two Chambers of Parliament and the Government, who are involved in lawmaking, the court which shall enforce the law shall also express its viewpoint on the exception which challenges the law applicable in the settlement of the dispute by the court. The expression of the court's viewpoint on the exception of unconstitutionality cannot mean a prejudice forbidden by the provisions of the Code of Civil Procedure to the court, since such court is not competent to settle the exception, as this power to rule upon the exception of unconstitutionality belongs exclusively to the Constitutional Court, in accordance with the provisions of Article 146 d) of the Constitution.

The fact that certain courts of law, increasingly less lately, do not fulfil their legal duty to express their viewpoint on the exceptions of unconstitutionality cannot constitute a basis for the ascertainment of the unconstitutionality of that legal text. Accepting the viewpoint expressed by the Advocate of the People would mean to transfer to the impugned legal text the possible consequences of its infringement by some courts of law, which ignore a legal obligation regarding the content of the interlocutory order whereby the court of law refers to the Constitutional Court for the settlement of an exception of unconstitutionality.

Moreover, in its case-law, the Constitutional Court stated that "the absence of the viewpoint of the court of law in its interlocutory order cannot stop the Court to adjudicate upon the cases which were referred to it, because the violation by the court of law of the obligation to express its viewpoint cannot freeze the exercise of the right conferred by the Constitution upon the authors of the exception, to invoke it and, accordingly, to receive the solution resulting from the review of the law, exercised by the Constitutional Court "[817]. Likewise, in relation to the failure of the court to express its viewpoint on the exception of unconstitutionality, the Court held that "the lack of diligence of the public authority and its negligence in fulfilling the obligations arising from the law cannot be an impediment in order to fully use the right of defence in this case, for notifying the Constitutional Court to exercise the constitutional review of a legal text on which the settlement of the case depends"[818]. In relation to the above-mentioned aspects, the Constitutional Court found that the exception of unconstitutionality is unfounded[819].

The doctrine has also expressed the same opinion because "the constitutionality is a matter of public law, it does not impede the independence of the judge"[820].

Formal aspects of the referral to the Constitutional Court

In the enforcement of the constitutional texts and the legal texts of reference and in order to avoid a non-unitary practice as concerns the referral to the Constitutional Court by the courts of law and the courts of commercial arbitration, with the consequence of delaying the settlement of the cases and even the rejection of the referrals for failure to fulfil certain formal requirements, the Plenum of the Constitutional Court ruled, by a series of rulings, on the requirements provided for by the law in this regard. We consider that these rulings reveal a direct dialogue between the Constitutional Court and the courts of law, which have proved to be an effective way of solving the ascertained issues.

Thus, by **Ruling no. 26 on the referrals to the Constitutional Court**, pursuant to **Article 146 d) of the Constitution,** of 16 December 2010[821], taking into account the following provisions:

---

817 Decision no. 47 of 5 March 1997, published in the Official Gazette of Romania no. 146 of 10 April 1998.

818 By Decision no. 171 of 22 March 2005, published in the Official Gazette of Romania no. 388 of 9 May 2005.

819 Decision no. 353 of 29 June 2005, published in the Official Gazette of Romania no. 693 of 2 August 2005.

820 I. Muraru, *Advocate of the People and the constitutional review*, in RRDP no. 1/2010, pp. 121–142.

821 *www.ccr.ro.*

- Article 29 para. (4) of Law no. 47/1992, republished, according to which:

"*The case shall be referred to the Constitutional Court by the court before which the exception of unconstitutionality was raised, through an interlocutory order which shall include the parties' for and against viewpoints, and the court's opinion on the exception, together with the evidence provided by the parties. If the exception has been raised ex officio, the interlocutory order shall be motivated, including the parties' arguments, as well as the necessary evidence. Alongside with the interlocutory order, the referring court must also send to the Constitutional Court the full name of the litigant parties and other details comprising necessary data for the accomplishment of the summons proceedings in respect thereof*".

- Article 255 of the Code of Civil Procedure, according to which: "*The rulings whereby the merits of the case is settled by the first court are called «judgments», and the rulings whereby the request, the appeal and the appeal on points of law or for annulment are called «decisions».*

All the other rulings rendered by the court during the trial are called «resolutions»".

- Article 261 of the Code of Civil Procedure, according to which: "*The ruling shall be rendered in the name of the law and it shall include:*

1. *the name of the court which renders it and the name of the judges who took part in the proceedings;*
2. *the name, the address or the residence of the parties, the capacity in which they took part in the proceedings; the name of the agents or of the legal representatives and of the lawyers;*
3. *the subject matter of the application and the brief allegations of the parties, presenting the evidence;*
4. *the prosecutor's conclusions;*
5. *the grounds de facto and de jure which led to the conviction of the court, as well as for which the parties' claims have been rejected;*
6. *the operative part;*
7. *the remedy and the term within which it may be exercised;*
8. *the mention that the pronouncement was made in open court, as well as the signatures of the judges and the registrar*", as well as the fact that in the operative part all the parties' claims must be settled, as it must have a full content, contain clear elements on how to settle these claims, the extent of the rights recognized to the parties and their identification; noting that certain courts do not proceed to prepare a distinct interlocutory order to refer to the Constitutional Court with the exception of unconstitutionality, but they settle this procedural incident in the recitals of the interlocutory order (judgment, decision), the proceedings are continued, so that in the operative part of the interlocutory order (sentences, decisions) submitted to the Constitutional Court, there are mentioned the measures ordered for the next hearing or even the rendered solution, without making any mention regarding the notification of the Constitutional Court;

noting that this practice has arisen as a result of the repeal, through Article I section 3 of Law no. 177/2010 amending and supplementing Law no. 47/1992 on the Organization and Operation of the Constitutional Court, the Code of Civil Procedure and the Code of Criminal Procedure of Romania, published in the Official Gazette of Romania, Part I, no. 672 of 4 October 2010, of the provisions of Article 29 para. (5) of Law no. 47/1992 which provided the obligation to suspend the settlement of the case until the settlement of the exception of unconstitutionality; since there is no justification for this practice, as long as the provisions regarding the legal nature and the content of the notification of the Constitutional Court, set forth in Article 29 para. (4) of Law no. 47/1992, republished, have not been amended; given the need for the cooperation with the courts of law in order to ensure the parties' right to a fair trial and to settle cases within a reasonable period of time, materialized also in the proper enforcement of the provisions of Article 29 para. (4) of Law no. 47/1992, republished; in order to avoid the pronouncement of certain decisions rejecting the exceptions of unconstitutionality on formal grounds concerning the legality of the notification of the Constitutional Court, the Plenum of the Constitutional Court has decided that **the files of the Constitutional Courts** covering exceptions of unconstitutionality referred to the Court under Article 146 d) of the Constitution of Romania, republished, **shall be formed only on the basis of the notification act by a distinct interlocutory order, which shall contain the viewpoints of the parties and of the court on the exception. If the exception has been raised ex officio, the interlocutory order must be motivated, containing also the parties' allegations. The operative part of the interlocutory order shall refer to the solution of the court regarding the notification of the Constitutional Court.**

According to Article 2 of the above-mentioned Ruling, since the date of its entry into force, the referrals which do not comply with the legal provisions set forth in this Ruling shall be returned to the courts of law in order to fulfil the requirements provided by the law.

The Ruling was communicated to the Superior Council of Magistracy, to the High Court of Cassation and Justice and to the Presidents of Courts of Appeal, in the light of the provisions of Article 43 para. (2) of Law no. 304/2004 on judicial organization, republished, as subsequently amended and supplemented, according to which they exercise powers of coordination and administration control of the court where they operate, as well as of the district courts.

Basically, by its Ruling, the Court only retained the legal provisions in the matter of the referral with the exception of unconstitutionality by the courts of law or the courts of commercial arbitration, underlining the importance to comply with them in terms of ensuring their access to constitutional justice.

The Ruling of 9 February 2010 on the preparation and the content of the files covering the exceptions of unconstitutionality referred to the Constitutional Court under Article 146 d) of the Constitution[822] is the expression of the same dialogue.

Thus, pursuant to Article 29 para. (4) of Law no. 47/1992, noting the existence of different practices of the courts of law regarding the referral to the Constitutional Court with the settlement of the exceptions of unconstitutionality under Article 146 d) of the Constitution, in the sense that certain courts of law communicate to the Court, together with the interlocutory order, the entire file of the case, while other courts of law communicate only the interlocutory order, accompanied or not, as appropriate, by other documents deemed necessary in the settlement of the exceptions, being communicated either in original, in copy or certified copy; given that, if the court send the copy of the interlocutory order, this shall be returned, in order to notify the Court, in original, accompanied by the file of the case, and this additional communication, prior to the preparation of the files pending before the Constitutional Court, is susceptible to affect the celerity of settling the case; whereas the assessment on the need for the communication of the file of the case falls, according to Article 17 para. (2) of the Regulations on the organization and functioning of the Constitutional Court, within the competence of the Judge-Rapporteur or the Plenum of the Constitutional Court, so that the communication of files of the courts of law in the phase prior to the registration of the interlocutory order and the preparation of the file pending before the Court are not required; in order to avoid difficulties and costs resulting from the communication, handling, storage and return of the files that are not useful, in their entirety, for the settlement of the exceptions of unconstitutionality, the Plenum of the Constitutional Court adopted a ruling regarding the content of its files covering the exceptions of unconstitutionality.

According to Article 1 of the Ruling, these files should contain: "the interlocutory order of the Constitutional Court, in original or certified copy, accompanied by the requests of the author of the exceptions and, where appropriate, the evidence submitted by the parties in the file of the court as grounds for the exception of unconstitutionality; the motivated interlocutory order containing the allegations of the parties, accompanied by the necessary evidence, if the exception has been raised ex officio; the list prepared by the court of law containing the necessary data in order to accomplish the summons procedure of the parties". Pursuant to Article 2 of the same Ruling, "the documents communicated in copy by the court of law before which the exception has been raised shall be taken into account insofar as they are certified by the court of law, bearing the mention "true copy" on each page.

Since after compiling the file, upon its examination, it is possible to note the need for further clarifications, Article 3 of the Ruling provided that after compiling the file and the designation of Judge-Rapporteur, it shall decide whether, for the examination of the file, it is necessary to request the file from the court before which the exception was raised.

822 *www.ccr.ro* – Legal basis.

The adopted Ruling was communicated to the Ministry of Justice, to the High Court of Cassation and Justice and to the Presidents of Appeal Courts, in order to support the activity of the Constitutional Court by communicating the documents and data specified in Article 1, in all cases brought before the Constitutional Court regarding exceptions of unconstitutionality under Article 146 d) of the Constitution and Article 29 of Law no. 47/1992.

We should mention that nowadays the cases in which the referrals addressed to the Constitutional Court diverge from the legal provisions have significantly decreased, as they were specified in the two rulings adopted by the Plenum of the Constitutional Court, which demonstrates the positive effects of the dialogue by this way.

5.2.2.3 The constitutional contentious stage held before the Constitutional Court

Specific procedural aspects of this stage are provided by the organic law of the Constitutional Court (Articles 30–31) and developed in the Regulations on the organization and functioning of the Constitutional Court, approved by Resolution no. 6 of 7 March 2012[823]. Likewise, within this stage, the dialogue with the courts of law is particularly expressed on the exact establishment of the procedural framework for the settlement of exceptions of unconstitutionality.

Thus, on receiving the interlocutory order, the President of the Constitutional Court shall designate the Judge-Rapporteur and communicate it to the Presidents of the two Chambers of Parliament, to the Government and to the Advocate of the People, indicating the date by which they can submit their viewpoint.

The Judge designated as rapporteur shall be bound to take the necessary measures for evidence to be given by the date of judgment. If the Judge-Rapporteur or, at a later point, the Plenum so deems necessary, the referring court shall be requested to send the files of the original case in which the exception of unconstitutionality was raised, as well any other act, in certified copy, related to the case in which the exception of unconstitutionality was raised. The Judge-Rapporteur, having examined the draft report, the viewpoints and other information made available, or conclusions from Romanian and foreign case-law and/or literature, as well as other elements that appear to be necessary for the debate, shall prepare a written report on the case.

The date of trial shall be set by the President of the Court, subject to the law. Judgment shall take place at the date established, on the basis of the deeds of the case, with due summoning of the parties and of the Public Ministry. The parties may be represented by lawyers having the right to plead before the High Court of Cassation and Justice.

The Constitutional Court has established that, once legally notified, it shall examine the constitutionality of the normative act which has been brought before it, the provisions of the Code of Civil Procedure regarding the suspension, interruption

823 Published in the Official Gazette of Romania no. 198 of 27 March 2012.

or cessation of the trial shall not be applicable. The Court also held that it is not possible to withdraw the exception of unconstitutionality[824]. These solutions are based on the public law nature of the procedure brought before the Constitutional Court, which excludes the consequences that would arise from the application of the principle of availability, applicable in the private law.

At this stage, the Constitutional Court decides on the exception of unconstitutionality raised and motivated before the court of law, namely within the procedural framework, as it results from the interlocutory order. In this respect, in an established case-law, the Court held that the invocation as grounds for the exception of certain constitutional provisions directly before the Court, and not before the court of law, is contrary to Article 10 para. (2) and Article 29 para. (1)-(4) of Law no. 47/1992, since the specific procedural framework of the exception of unconstitutionality results from the interlocutory order and the written reasoning of the author, and the latter cannot be supplemented before the Constitutional Court with new elements that have not been debated by the parties before the court of law[825].

From this perspective, the preparation and the reasoning of the interlocutory order of the Constitutional Court are more important in the sense of an accurate mention of the impugned texts, both in the recitals and in the operative part, respectively in the recitals, of the reasoning of the author of the exception. It is also worth noting the doctrinal concerns, even for the purpose of developing a "small guide on the referral to the Constitutional Court"[826].

The extension of subject-matter of the exception of unconstitutionality can only be achieved under Article 31 para. (2) of Law no. 47/1992, according to which "*If the exception is upheld, the Court shall also pronounce upon the constitutionality of other provisions of the normative act being challenged, of which those mentioned in the case referral act cannot obviously and necessarily be dissociated*".

5.2.2.4 Inadmissibility of the exception of unconstitutionality

The cases of inadmissibility of the exceptions of unconstitutionality require a separate treatment as they represent an important part of the dialogue between the constitutional court and the courts of law. In terms of their classification, in the specialized literature two major categories of inadmissibility cases have been underlined:

824 Decision no. 786 of 7 November 2006, published in the Official Gazette of Romania no. 11 of 8 January 2007.

825 Decision no. 1313 of 4 October 2011, published in the Official Gazette of Romania no. 12 of 6 January 2012; Decision no. 169 of 20 March 2014, published in the Official Gazette of Romania no. 397 of 29 May 2014.

826 D.C. Dănişor, *Brief guide on the referral to the Constitutional Court*, in PR no. 1/2011, pp. 75–88.

- those relating to the legality of the referral (the subject-matter of the referral, the authors of the referral or its constitutional ground), specific to the procedural stage held before the court;
- those relating to the extent of review, specific to the settlement procedure of the exception brought before the Constitutional Court.

A. Inadmissibility regarding the lawfulness of the referral

1. The subject-matter of the referral

a) Only laws and Government ordinances or any provision thereof may be subject to constitutional review

The Constitutional Court rejected as **inadmissible** the exceptions of unconstitutionality relating to other normative acts or other types of legal acts than those expressly provided by the constituent legislature within its competence.

Inadmissibility of the exceptions of unconstitutionality covering ***Government Decisions***

Secondary regulatory acts shall not be subject to the constitutional review exercised by the Constitutional Court, but they can be verified, including in terms of their constitutionality, indirectly, by courts of administrative contentious. Thus, for example, the Constitutional Court rejected as inadmissible the exception of unconstitutionality of Article 22 w) of the Annex to the Government Decision no. 257/2011 approving the Rules for the application of Law no. 263/2010 on the public pension unitary system[827], holding that, "according to the provisions of Article 29 para. (1) of Law no. 47/1992, only laws or ordinances, or provisions thereof, may be subject to constitutional review by way of exceptions of unconstitutionality, so that the examinations of the constitutionality of the provisions of other normative acts, such as the decisions of the Government, do not fall within the competence of the constitutional court, being inadmissible".

We should mention the challenges formulated in the specialised literature on this case-law of the Constitutional Court, which is considered to excessively restrict the subject-matter of the constitutional review. Thus, it was noted that, as concerns the concept of "law", it "must be defined by reference to the duty exercised by regulation, and not only in relation to the issuing body. (...) Thus, if a document is issued in the exercise of its legislative duty, it shall be legislative, regardless of the authority which adopts it and the given name. A legislative act shall be any normative act which primarily regulates a field, amends such legislation or provides a generally binding interpretation. If we function under such a definition, then the case-law of the Constitutional Court, which states that no Government Decision will ever

827 Decision no. 474 of 23 September 2014, published in the Official Gazette of Romania no. 792 of 30 October 2014.

be reviewed from the point of view of its constitutionality, should emphasize: a Government decision may be unconstitutional if this name hides a legislative act"[828].

Inadmissibility of the exceptions of unconstitutionality covering ***methodological rules*** *for the application of a law*
Thus, for example, the Constitutional Court rejected as inadmissible the exceptions of unconstitutionality of the provisions of Article 27 and of Article 59 of the Methodological Rules for the application of Law no. 26/1990 regarding the trade registers and the records, issued by the Chamber of Commerce and Industry of Romania and by the Ministry of Justice, published in the Official Gazette of Romania, Part I, no. 176 of 11 May 1998, noting that the subject-matter of the constitutional review by way of exception shall be exercised only on laws and ordinances. The Court also held that the notion "law" referred to in Article 146 d) of the Constitution, republished (which specifies the powers of the Court) is not used in a broad sense, including all normative acts, but only in its strict sense, under the law, which means the legislative act adopted by Parliament and promulgated by the President, and the ordinance, which is the act adopted by the Government on the basis of a legislative delegation. The concept of law results from combining the formal criterion with the material one, since the content of the law is determined by the importance given by the legislature to the regulated matters. Thus, "it is obvious that the settlement of the exception of unconstitutionality regarding other normative acts does not fall within the competence of the Constitutional Court, as such acts shall be controlled, in terms of legality, by the courts of administrative contentious"[829].

Inadmissibility of the exceptions of unconstitutionality covering ***ministerial orders***
Thus, for example, the Court rejected as inadmissible the exception of unconstitutionality of the Order of the Minister of Health and Family and of the President of the National Health Insurance House no. 20/2003 approving the Methodological Rules for the application of the Framework Agreement on the conditions for granting medical assistance within the health insurance system in primary healthcare, published in the Official Gazette of Romania, Part I, no. 78 and no. 78 bis, both of 6 February 2003, noting that "the exception of unconstitutionality does not concern the provisions of a law or of an ordinance, but it concerns normative acts issued by the Minister of Health and Family and by the President of the National Health Insurance House. This exception is contrary to the provisions of Article 146 d) of the Constitution and of Article 29 para. (1) of Law no. 47/1992, and according to Article 29 para. (6) of Law no. 47/1992, the court of law itself should reject such exception, as inadmissible, by a motivated interlocutory order, without notifying the

828 D.C. Dănişor, *Excessive limitation of the object of the constitutional review by the case-law of the Constitutional Court*, in RRDJ no. 4/2009, pp. 32–36.
829 Decision no. 58 of 17 February 2004, published in the Official Gazette of Romania no. 222 of 15 March 2004.

Constitutional Court. Since the court of law failed to apply these legal provisions, the Court shall reject the exception as inadmissible"[830].

Inadmissibility of the exceptions of unconstitutionality covering ***judgments of the courts of law***

The Constitutional Court rejected as inadmissible the exceptions of unconstitutionality whose subject-matter was the decisions delivered by the High Court of Cassation and Justice, in United Sections, other judgments of the courts of law. Thus, for example, the Court rejected as inadmissible the exception of unconstitutionality covering Decision no. VI of 27 September 1999 of the United Sections of the Supreme Court, noting that "both the Constitution and the law on the organization and operation of the Constitutional Court established that the subject-matter of an exception of unconstitutionality may exclusively be the provisions of a law or of an ordinance. That being so, the referral regarding Decision no. VI/1999 of the United Sections of the Supreme Court, so on a judgment, cannot be the subject-matter of a constitutional review"[831].

However, exceptions of unconstitutionality covering legal provisions as interpreted by judgments on appeal on points of law are admissible. Thus, depending on the subject-matter of the challenge of unconstitutionality, there are two cases. The first case is the one in which the author of the exception challenges the decision itself rendered in an appeal on points of law; the exception has an inadmissible nature. The second case is where the exception of unconstitutionality refers to legal texts interpreted by the High Court of Cassation and Justice during the settlement of an appeal on points of law, when the exception is admissible; the Court has the competence to rule on its merits[832].

Referring and developing this distinction, the Court held that, "as concerns the challenge of the provisions of a judgment rendered in an appeal on points of law, it cannot be the subject-matter of an exception of unconstitutionality, being, in this light, inadmissible because the constitutional court, in accordance with the provisions of Article 146 of the Basic Law, has no power so as to censor the constitutionality of judgments, whether they are rendered for the interpretation of certain issues of common law or for the unitary interpretation and enforcement of the law. Therefore, the High Court of Cassation and Justice, in accordance with the constitutional provisions of Article 126 para. (3), has exclusive competence to decide on matters related to the unitary interpretation and enforcement of the law whenever the case-law requires. That being so, a decision rendered in such a

---

830 Decision no. 435 of 13 September 2005, published in the Official Gazette of Romania no. 924 of 17 October 2005.

831 Decision no. 409 of 4 November 2003, published in the Official Gazette of Romania no. 848 of 27 November 2003.

832 Decisions no. 202 of 18 April 2013 and no. 212 of 29 April 2013, published in the Official Gazette of Romania no. 365 of 19 June 2013 and, respectively, Official Gazette of Romania no. 371 of 21 June 2013.

procedure cannot constitute *eo ipso* the object of censorship of the constitutional court (...). However, the fact that by a decision rendered in an appeal on points of law a legal text may be given a certain interpretation is not likely to be converted into a plea of inadmissibility so as to oblige the Court, despite its role as guarantor for the supremacy of the Constitution, not to examine the text in question as interpreted by the supreme court (...). The Constitution shall be the framework and the extent to which the legislature and the other authorities can act; therefore, the interpretations which may be brought to the legal norm must also take account of this constitutional requirement contained in Article 1 para. (5) of the Basic Law, according to which the observance of the Constitution and of its supremacy shall be obligatory in Romania. With reference to the provisions of the Constitution, the Constitutional Court reviews the constitutionality of the applicable legal texts in the interpretation enshrined by appeals on points of law. The acceptance of a contrary sentence is contrary to the very existence of the Constitutional Court, which would deny its constitutional role if it accepts that a legal text is applied within limits which could infringe the Basic Law"[833].

Moreover, by Decision no. 536 of 28 April 2011 published in the Official Gazette of Romania, Part I, no. 482 of 7 July 2011, the Constitutional Court also established that "regardless of the interpretations that could be given to a text, when the Constitutional Court ruled that only one interpretation is consistent with the Constitution, thus maintaining the presumption of constitutionality of the text under this interpretation, both the courts of law and the administrative bodies must comply with the Court's decision and enforce it as such". In interpreting the law, the courts of law, including the High Court of Cassation and Justice, must comply with the constitutional framework, and the sanction for exceeding/breaching it belongs exclusively to the Constitutional Court.

b) Only laws and ordinances which are "in force", or any provision thereof may be subject to constitutional review. Jurisprudential upturn of the phrase "in force"

As concerns the meaning of the phrase "in force", the Constitutional Court has reconsidered its case-law, stating that it "is constitutional insofar as it is interpreted in the sense that laws or ordinances or any provision thereof which continue to produce legal effects also after they are no longer in force are also subject to the constitutional review"[834]. We have thoroughly examined this issue in the chapter on the development of the constitutional review, namely the strengthening of the Constitutional Court's role by its case-law.

Laws and Government ordinances, which are suspended on the date the Court delivers its decision, may also be subject to constitutional review. Since

833 Decision no. 854 of 23 June 2011, published in the Official Gazette of Romania no. 672 of 21 September 2011.

834 Decision no. 766 of 15 June 2011, published in the Official Gazette of Romania no. 549 of 3 August 2011.

the normative acts in question are in force, even if they cannot take legal effects, the Court has competence to rule upon their constitutionality. In this respect, the Constitutional Court ruled, in noting a case[835] that "by the sole article of the Government Emergency Ordinance no. 167/2005, published in the Official Gazette of Romania, Part I, no. 1100 of 6 December 2005, the application of the Government Emergency Ordinance no. 110/2005 has been suspended until 31 March 2006. Given that this suspension is limited and concerns the enforcement of the impugned ordinance that took effects, until the entry into force of the Government Emergency Ordinance no. 167/2005, the Court is to decide on the merits of its constitutionality".

The normative acts amended following the referral to the Constitutional Court, indicating the legislative solution enshrined in the impugned amended act, *may also be subject to constitutional review.* The Constitutional Court established that, if the new wording of the legal provision holds the legislative solution of principle before the amendment, the grounds of unconstitutionality being the same, the exception shall be admissible and a new referral shall not be necessary. In this respect we refer to the Plenum's Decision no. III of 31 October 1995 on the constitutionality of a legal provision amended subsequently to the invocation of the exception[836], whereby the Court held that "if, however, after the exception was raised before the courts of law, the legal text has been amended, thus holding in its new wording the legislative solution of principle, prior to the amendment, the grounds of unconstitutionality being the same, a new referral shall not be necessary for the settlement of the exception raised". This is because "the exception of unconstitutionality covers a legal provision, not particularly in a formal meaning, but rather in a material one, since, in this respect, the one who may raise it argues that the legal text is contrary to a constitutional provision".

c) Laws and ordinances, or any provision thereof, where such is related to adjudication of the case, regardless the stage of trial proceedings or subject-matter thereof, may be the subject-matter of exceptions of unconstitutionality

The importance of the exception of unconstitutionality underlined the relationships between the work of the judge *a quo* and that of a judge *a quem*. The Constitutional Court's decision must be likely to take a specific effect on the holding of a trial, as the relevance requirement shall be the expression of the usefulness which the settlement of the exception raised has in solving the dispute between the parties. In the absence of any relation to the case, the exception of unconstitutionality is inadmissible because the solution delivered by the Court is not useful in settling the dispute in which it has been raised.

According to the case-law of the Constitutional Court, "the relation to the settlement of the case" requires, within the meaning of Article 29 para. (1) of Law

835 Decision no. 238 of 9 March 2006, published in the Official Gazette of Romania no. 334 of 13 April 2006.

836 Published in the Official Gazette of Romania no. 259 of 9 November 1995.

no. 47/1992, republished, both the enforcement of the impugned text in the case brought before the court and the need for the invocation of the exception of unconstitutionality in order to re-establish the legal status, conditions which must be cumulatively met so as the requirements imposed by these legal provisions shall be fulfilled, regarding the relevance of the exception of unconstitutionality in carrying out the trial[837]. Consequently, the relevance of the exception of unconstitutionality, respectively the incidence of the impugned legal text within the settlement of the case brought before the court, should not be analyzed *in abstracto*, but first of all the procedural interest of raising the exception of unconstitutionality must be reviewed, especially in terms of effects of a possible ascertainment of unconstitutionality of the impugned legal text[838].

d) Inadmissibility of the exceptions of unconstitutionality when the subject-matter of the main case brought before the court of law is the ascertainment of the unconstitutionality of a Government ordinance or emergency ordinance, or any provision thereof

Thus, the Constitutional Court rejected as inadmissible the exceptions of unconstitutionality raised in cases covering the settlement of an action of administrative contentious by which the ascertainment of the unconstitutionality of an ordinance or of any provision thereof was directly requested, pursuant to Article 9 of Law no. 554/2004 on administrative contentious matters. The Court held on that occasion that the referral was unlawful, being contrary to the provisions of Article 146 d) of the Constitution and of Article 29 para. (1) and (6) of Law no. 47/1992[839].

Being notified with the very exception of unconstitutionality of the provisions of Article 9 of Law no. 554/2004 on administrative contentious matters, the Court rendered Decision no. 660 of 4 July 2007, published in the Official Gazette of Romania, Part I, no. 525 of 2 August 2007, by which it found that, "*as far as Article 9 shall be interpreted within the meaning that an aggrieved person, regarding his/her right or legitimate interest, by an ordinance or any provision thereof, may bring an action before the court of administrative contentious, whose main subject-matter is the direct notification of the Constitutional Court so as to declare the unconstitutionality of*

---

837 Decision no. 438 of 8 July 2014, published in the Official Gazette of Romania no. 600 of 12 August 2014.

838 See also Decision no. 465 of 23 September 2014, published in the Official Gazette of Romania no. 788 of 29 October 2014.

839 Decision no. 761 of 31 October 2006, published in the Official Gazette of Romania no. 980 of 7 December 2006; Decision no. 764 of 31 October 2006, published in the Official Gazette of Romania no. 8 of 5 January 2007; Decision no. 5 of 9 January 2007, published in the Official Gazette of Romania no. 74 of 31 January 2007; Decision no. 66 of 25 January 2007, published in the Official Gazette of Romania no. 114 of 15 February 2007; Decision no. 174 of 6 March 2007, published in the Official Gazette of Romania no. 257 of 17 April 2007; Decision no. 342 of 3 April 2007, published in the Official Gazette of Romania no. 308 of 9 May 2007.

those provisions, the text is unconstitutional(...).When the subject-matter of the main proceedings brought before the court of law is the ascertainment of the unconstitutionality of a simple ordinance or of Government emergency ordinance or of any provision thereof, the exception of unconstitutionality shall become a true direct action, thus losing its exceptional nature and being understood as an instrument of defence which does not refer to the merits of the claim brought before the court".

As grounds for this solution, the Court reiterated the reasons of the mentioned case-law, noting that "*the exception of unconstitutionality is one of the ways by which the Constitutional Court may be notified in order to exercise the* a posteriori *constitutional review of laws and ordinances*". The Court also held that "*within the judicial trial, the exception of unconstitutionality is enrolled among the procedural exceptions whereby the party who raises them, the court of law ex officio or the prosecutor, seek to prevent a judgment that would be based on an unconstitutional legal provision. In the same conceptual order, the exception of unconstitutionality is an interlocutory matter, namely a legal issue whose settlement must precede the resolution of the related dispute. (...) The exception of unconstitutionality cannot be the subject-matter of main proceedings, either before the court of law or of arbitration, as it is always an instrument of defence in a pending dispute, or before the Constitutional Court. (...) It results that the possibility of raising an exception of unconstitutionality involves the existence of a dispute before the court of law, and its settlement depends on the settlement by the Constitutional Court of an exception related to the case*".

Article 9 of Law no. 554/2004 was amended/supplemented by Law no. 262/2007 published in the Official Gazette of Romania, Part I, no. 510 of 30 July 2007 [paragraphs (3) and (4) of Article 9 were amended and a new paragraph, paragraph (5), was inserted] and by Law no. 100/2008 published in the Official Gazette of Romania, Part I, no. 375 of 16 May 2008 [paragraph (1) of the same article was amended], the norm of reference subject to review shall currently read as follows: "(1) A person whose right or legitimate interest has been harmed by an ordinance or any provision thereof may take legal action before the court of administrative contentious, accompanied by the exception of unconstitutionality, insofar as the main subject-matter shall not be the ascertainment of the unconstitutionality of an ordinance or of any provision thereof. (2) If the court of administrative contentious finds that the exception so raised meets the requirements of Article 29 para. (1) and (3) of Law no. 47/1992 on the Organization and Operation of the Constitutional Court, republished, the court of administrative contentious, through a motivated judgment, shall refer the case to the Constitutional Court and suspend the adjudication on the merits of the case. (3) After the Constitutional Court has delivered its decision, the court of administrative contentious shall reschedule the case and set a hearing date, with summons to the parties. If the challenged ordinance or any provision thereof was found unconstitutional, the court of administrative contentious shall settle the case on the merits; in the contrary case, the case shall be rejected as inadmissible. (4) When the decision of unconstitutionality is the effect of an exception raised in a different case, the action can be brought directly before the competent court of administrative contentious, within a maximum negative prescription deadline of one year, which starts counting as of the date the Constitutional Court's decision is published in the Official Gazette of Romania, Part I. (5) The action provided for in this Article can be a claim for compensation for damage caused through Government Ordinances, cancellation of administrative acts issued on the basis of such ordinances and, as the case may be, compelling a certain public authority to issue an administrative act or to exercise a specific administrative duty".

Following the amendment of Article 9 of Law no. 554/2004, the case-law of the Constitutional Court has taken the reasons of Decision no. 660/2007, cited above, as the Court rejected as inadmissible the exceptions of unconstitutionality raised in cases whose subject-matter of the main proceedings itself was the ascertainment of the unconstitutionality of an emergency ordinance. Thus, for example, Decision no. 169 of 26 February 2008, published in the Official Gazette of Romania, Part I, no. 204 of 17 March 2008: "*(...) in the present case, the subject-matter of the main proceedings, based on the provision of the Article 9 of Law no. 554/2004, (...) is the very challenge of the constitutionality of the Government Emergency Ordinance no. 56/2007 on the employment and deployment of foreigners in Romania. By amending Law no. 554/2004 on administrative contentious matters, by Law no. 262/2007, a new paragraph was inserted to Article 9, after paragraph (4), which states that a person who considers him/herself aggrieved in his/her right or legitimate interest by an ordinance or any provision thereof may take legal action before the court of administrative contentious, accompanied by the exception of unconstitutionality, insofar as the main subject-matter shall be «a claim for compensation for damage caused through Government Ordinances, cancellation of administrative acts issued on the basis of such ordinances and, as the case may be, compelling a certain public authority to issue an administrative act or to exercise a specific administrative duty» and not the cancellation itself on grounds of unconstitutionality of an ordinance or of any provisions thereof*". Similarly, by Decision no. 762 of 20 September 2012, published in the Official Gazette of Romania, Part I, no. 719 of 23 October 2012, the Court found that "*(...) when the subject-matter of the main proceedings brought before the court is the ascertainment of the unconstitutionality of a simple ordinance or a Government emergency ordinance or of any provision thereof, the exception of unconstitutionality shall become a true direct action, thus losing its exceptional nature and being understood as an instrument of defence which does not refer to the merits of the claim brought before the court. However, in this case, the subject-matter of the main proceedings brought before Bucharest Court of Appeal – Section VIII of the Administrative Contentious and Fiscal is the very challenge of the constitutionality of the Government Emergency Ordinance no. 101/2011 regarding the regulation of the conditions for the sale of properties, private property of the state, under the administration of the Autonomous Administration «Administration of State Protocol Patrimony», properties owned by the Autonomous Administration «Administration of State Protocol Patrimony», as well as the amendment of certain laws*".

Referring to this case-law and rejecting as inadmissible an exception of unconstitutionality where the main subject-matter of main proceedings brought before the court of administrative contentious was the exception of unconstitutionality of a Government Emergency Ordinance, the Court held[840] that "*it is unacceptable to be entrusted with the examination of the unconstitutionality of a normative act in a procedural framework specifically created for this purpose. In the same regard there are also the statuaries of the Court of Justice of the European Union in Judgment of 11 March 1980, delivered in Case Foglia v. Novello, where this court accepted that it has no jurisdiction if it would be obliged to deliver judgments on caused cases «which would jeopardize the entire system of remedies available to private individuals in order to enable them to defend themselves»*".

These considerations are also applicable *mutatis mutandis* where the subject-matter of the main proceedings brought before a court of law is the ascertainment of unconstitutionality of a law or a text of law.

e) Inadmissibility of exceptions regarding provisions which have already been found unconstitutional

The exceptions regarding legal provisions which have already been found unconstitutional by a decision of the Constitutional Court are inadmissible. This solution takes account of the effects that such a decision may produce, pursuant to the provisions of Article 147 para. (1) of the Constitution, according to which "*Any provisions of the laws and ordinances in force, as well as any of the regulations which are held as unconstitutional, shall cease their legal effects within 45 days from publication of the decision rendered by the Constitutional Court where Parliament or Government, as may be applicable, have failed, in the meantime, to bring these unconstitutional provisions into accord with those of the Constitution. For this limited length of time the provisions declared unconstitutional shall be suspended as of right*".

A particular situation is that of *interpretative decisions/reserve of interpretation*. The Court held in this regard that, in this case, "only the interpretation of the legal norm that has not been excluded from the constitutional framework can be subject to the constitutional review exercised by way of raising an exception of unconstitutionality, otherwise the exception shall be inadmissible"[841].

To avoid any misunderstanding regarding the effects which the decisions finding unconstitutionality shall take in other cases brought before the courts of law in which those norms are applicable, the Court has emphasized a practice in order to clarify such effects even in the content of the decisions rejecting the exceptions of unconstitutionality that became inadmissible.

Thus, with reference to the situation of a simple decision finding unconstitutionality, the Court held that, "since the Constitutional Court's decisions shall take effect only for the future, according to Article 147 para. (4) of the Constitution, the provisions in these decisions are to be applied as from the date of their publication in the Official Gazette of Romania, Part I; at the same time, the courts of law will

840 Decision no. 460 of 16 September 2014, published in the Official Gazette of Romania no. 738 of 9 October 2014.

841 See, for example, Decision no. 486 of 25 September 2014, published in the Official Gazette of Romania no. 794 of 31 October 2014.

apply the admission decision of the Constitutional Court only in cases *pending* at the time of publication thereof, cases where the provisions of Article 8 para. (2) of Law no. 61/1991 shall be applicable, as well as in the cases where the exception of unconstitutionality was raised until the aforementioned date, in the latter case, if the dispute has been irrevocably settled, the decisions of the Constitutional Court shall constitute the ground for review under Article 322 section 10 of the Civil Procedure Code of 1865 or Article 509 para. (1) section 11 of the new Civil Procedure Code, as the case may be"[842].

For emphasis, with reference to the situation of a decision that declared the unconstitutionality of a legal text in a particular interpretation, we will mention the situation by which an exception of unconstitutionality of the provisions of Article 40 para. (3) of Law no. 41/1994 on the organisation and functioning of the Romanian Broadcasting Corporation and the Romanian Television Corporation[843] has been rejected as it became inadmissible. The Court has held that, although it shall deliver a solution rejecting the exception as it became inadmissible, those ruled by the previous decision finding the unconstitutionality of the impugned norm in question, it is also "to be enforced, as from the moment of its publication in the Official Gazette of Romania, Part I, in the pending case in which the exception of unconstitutionality has been raised, since by that decision the constitutional interpretation of the text covering that exception was definitively and generally binding established. Incidentally, at the same time, the courts of law shall interpret and apply the provisions of Article 40 para. (3) of Law no. 41/1994, in accordance with this

842 Decision no. 61 of 21 February 2013, published in the Official Gazette of Romania no. 204 of 10 April 2013; Decision no. 319 of 29 March 2012, published in the Official Gazette of Romania no. 274 of 25 April 2012; Decision no. 223 of 13 March 2012, published in the Official Gazette of Romania no. 256 of 18 April 2012.

843 Previously, by Decision no. 448 of 29 October 2013, published in the Official Gazette of Romania no. 5 of 7 January 2014, the Court established that only the interpretation of Article 40 para. (3) of Law no. 41/1994, meaning that legal entities residing in Romania, including subsidiaries, branches, agencies and representative offices, as well as representative offices in Romania of foreign legal entities are obliged to pay a fee for broadcasting public service and a fee for television public service, *as actual beneficiaries of such services*, is the only interpretation that can eliminate the unconstitutional flaw of the legal text by the absence of any express mention in this regard. Since there is a way to interpret the text in compliance with the Constitution, resulting even from the case-law of the Constitutional Court, and given that the unconstitutionality is both an ultimate sanction applied by the constitutional court with repercussions on the normative existence of a law, and part of the normative legal order, by Decision no. 448 of 29 October 2013, the Court found that the provisions of Article 40 para. (3) of Law no. 41/1994 on the organisation and functioning of the Romanian Broadcasting Corporation and the Romanian Television Corporation are constitutional insofar the fee for public services of broadcasting and television is applied only to legal entities which benefit from such services.

decision, in all pending cases in which they are present, as well as in cases where the exception of unconstitutionality was raised until the aforementioned date; in the latter case, if the dispute has been settled, the decisions of the Constitutional Court shall constitute the ground for review under Article 322 section 10 of the Civil Procedure Code of 1865 or Article 509 para. (1) section 11 of the new Civil Procedure Code, as the case may be"[844].

It is worth mentioning in this context that, from the *per a contrario* interpretation of the provisions of Article 29 para. (3) of Law no. 47/1992 on the Organization and Operation of the Constitutional Court, according to which "*Legal provisions whose unconstitutionality has been found by prior decision of the Constitutional Court cannot form the subject-matter of an exception*", it results that the legal texts on which the Constitutional Court delivered solutions rejecting exceptions of unconstitutionality may still form the subject-matter of the exceptions of unconstitutionality, which calls into question issues of jurisprudential upturn.

Since the quoted legal text makes no distinction, it results that the same texts declared constitutional by the Court may form the subject-matter of a new exception of unconstitutionality, and the challenges may be formulated in relation to different constitutional grounds or to the same constitutional grounds as in the precedent. We consider that this clarification is necessary because, when the Constitutional Court allows an exception of unconstitutionality of legal provisions in relation to the constitutional grounds other than those which were raised in relation to other constitutional grounds than those invoked in the precedent which was settled by way of an exception of unconstitutionality, we are not in the presence of a genuine jurisprudential upturn. Such an upturn exists when the Court delivers an admission solution on the same constitutional grounds which substantiated the rejection solution of the same exception.

Approaching the issues of legal certainty in the light of legislative amendments, the Court held that "*as concerns the legislative stability, the Court finds that the obligation to comply with the laws, enshrined in Article 1 para. (5) of the Constitution, does not ensure, by its content, an inflexible legislative framework. The legislative intervention is necessary both in order to adapt normative acts to the economic, social and political life, and to ensure, as in the case of the law subject to constitutional review, a uniform legislative framework, which may contribute to a better enforcement of the law and to the elimination of any ambiguous situations or inequities in the enforcement of the law*"[845]. This reasoning subsists, *mutatis mutandis*, even in the jurisprudential upturns.

---

844 *Ibidem.*

845 Decision no. 1237 of 6 October 2010, published in the Official Gazette of Romania no. 785 of 24 November 2010.

f) The treaty of the international agreement whose unconstitutionality was found according to Article 146 b) of the Constitution cannot form the subject-matter of an exception of unconstitutionality

We refer to a case of inadmissibility resulting from the systematic interpretation of the constitutional provisions and which has not been applied so far in practice, as the hypothesis set forth in the constitutional texts of reference has not been accomplished in any of the Court's cases. Pursuant to Article 147 para. (3) of the Constitution, "*If a treaty or international agreement has been declared constitutional according to Article 146 b), such may no longer be demurred against via an exception of unconstitutionality*".

g) Res judicata authority of the Constitutional Court's decisions

This case of inadmissibility has been judicially established by the Constitutional Court, which has established that, as long as the subject-matter of an exception, the case and the author are the same in the event of certain successive exceptions, the res judicata authority of the decision which settled the first exception shall function[846]: "the party who has invoked the exception cannot reiterate it, since, being contrary to the res judicata authority, the exception shall be inadmissible"[847].

2. The authors of the exceptions of unconstitutionality/referrals to the Constitutional Court

a) Exceptions of unconstitutionality may be raised upon request by a party or, ex officio, by the court of law or the court of commercial arbitration. Likewise, the exception may also be raised by the prosecutor before the court of law, in the cases attended by him

Thus, the notification of the Constitutional Court with an exception of unconstitutionality does not suppose the active procedural capacity only of the subjects of law expressly and restrictively specified by the constitutional or legal text.

The exception of unconstitutionality may be also invoked by the legal or conventional representatives of the parties, on their behalf and in their interest. In this regard, the courts before which an exception has been raised shall distinguish,

846 Raising an exception of unconstitutionality with an identical subject-matter, by other parties and for other reasons then those which determined its prior rejection is inadmissible, this possibility is justified by the development of the "constitutionality status", by the development of the social- economic and political conditions of the society (I. Muraru, M. Constantinescu, S. Tănăsescu, M. Enache, Gh. Iancu, *Interpretation of the Constitution*, Lumina Lex Publishing House, Bucharest, 2002).

847 Decision no. 57 of 17 February 2004, published in the Official Gazette of Romania no. 214 of 11 March 2004; Decision no. 146 of 7 October 1999, published in the Official Gazette of Romania no. 628 of 23 December 1999; Decisions: no. 27 of 25 May 1993, published in the Official Gazette of Romania no. 163 of 15 July 1993; no. 36 of 5 July 1993, published in the Official Gazette of Romania no. 230 of 22 September 1993 and no. 31 of 12 April 1994, published in the Official Gazette of Romania no. 177 of 12 July 1994.

before referring to the Constitutional Court, whether the exception invoked by the defenders or the representatives of the parties has been raised on behalf and in the interest of the party they represent or on their own; in the latter case the exception shall be rejected as inadmissible[848].

The issue regarding the invocation of an exception of unconstitutionality by the representatives of the parties in criminal proceedings resulted in a jurisprudential upturn of the Constitutional Court. Following the rejection of several referrals, as inadmissible[849], covering the provisions of Article 174 para. (1) of the Criminal Procedure Code[850], the Court reconsidered its case-law in the sense of the admissibility of the exception of unconstitutionality raised by the defendant's lawyer absent from the trial before the first court[851]. By its decision[852], the Court held that "it is necessary to reconsider its earlier case-law in terms of admissibility of the exception of unconstitutionality raised upon the request of the defendant's lawyer, in his absence, in cases where, according to Article 174 para. (1) a) of the Code of Criminal Procedure, the representation shall not be possible. (...) the adoption, by the previous decisions, of the solution of inadmissibility on the exception of unconstitutionality of Article 174 para. (1) a) of the Criminal Procedure Code was based on a literal interpretation of Article 23 para. (2) of Law no. 47/1992, republished, resulting that, because the defendant cannot be represented, his defender, even legally employed, cannot require, on behalf of the absent party, the invocation of the exception of unconstitutionality. (...) From a teleological interpretation of Article 174 para. (1) a) of the Criminal Procedure Code, it results that the limitation of the exercise by the defender of the defendant's procedural rights refers only to the examination and judgment of the proceedings on the merits, and not to any incidents or claims which may be formulated regarding the procedural part of the criminal case. Although the exercise by the defender of the defendant's procedural rights will always assume his/her presence or the presence of

---

848 See, for example, Decision no. 81 of 25 May 1999, published in the Official Gazette of Romania no. 325 of 8 July 1999, on the exception of unconstitutionality raised by a legal adviser on his own.

849 Decision no. 484 of 2 December 1997, published in the Official Gazette of Romania no. 105 of 6 March 1998, as well as Decision no. 34 of 4 March 1999, published in the Official Gazette of Romania no. 317 of 2 July 1999.

850 According to which: "During the trial, the accused can be represented: a) in the proceedings of the case by the court of first instance court or at rehearing it after the cancellation of the judgment on appeal or after the cassation by the appeal court, only if the sanction provided for the offence subject to judgment is a fine or imprisonment of up to one year".

851 Subsequently, by Decision no. 145/2000, published in the Official Gazette of Romania no. 665 of 16 December 2000, the Court upheld the exception of unconstitutionality of the provisions of Article 174 para. (1) a) of the Code of Criminal Code, finding that the provision is unconstitutional," only if the sanction provided for the offence subject to judgment is a fine or imprisonment of up to one year".

852 Decision no. 16 of 27 January 2000, published in the Official Gazette of Romania no. 278 of 20 June 2000.

his/her representative, when the defendant is allowed to be represented [Article174 para. (1) of the Criminal Procedure Code], however, in the event of any requests (for example, delays, objections, displacements) or exceptions (lack of competence, non-accomplishment of the procedure) which do not compromise the merits, the defender may exercise such rights of the defendant, even in his absence. It is obvious that among the rights of the defendant, which his/her lawyer can exercise even in his absence, it is also mentioned the right to raise an exception of unconstitutionality, as this does not either compromise any merits and therefore it does not require the presence or representation of the defendant. This interpretation is consistent with the provisions of Article 24 of the Constitution concerning the parties' right to be assisted by a lawyer throughout the trial, and its activity, even limited, in cases where the representation is not possible, contributes to the fulfilment of the defendant's right of defence. The same conclusion, in the sense of the admissibility of an exception of unconstitutionality of Article 174 para. (1) a) of the Code of Civil Procedure, results from a systematic interpretation of the provisions regarding an exception of unconstitutionality. The great importance of an exception of unconstitutionality as a means to verify whether the legal provisions in force comply with the Constitution, and also as a means of exercising the any person's right to request, before a court, to verify this compliance, in order to ensure the supremacy of the Constitution, and therefore the general interest of society, justifies the reason for it to be accepted and examined as such, even when it has been raised upon the request of the defendant's defender, in his/her absence. The admission of the exception of unconstitutionality raised in this way corresponds both to the general interest of ensuring the supremacy of the Constitution and protecting the fundamental human rights and freedoms, and to the personal interest of the defendant to benefit from a qualified defence, in accordance with Article 24 of the Constitution. Likewise, the admission of an exception of unconstitutionality raised upon the request of the defendant's defender, in his/her absence, is not contrary to the purpose of Article174 para. (1) a) of the Code of Criminal Procedure, because an exception of unconstitutionality does not mean the judgment of the case before the first instance court, in the absence of the defendant".

In relation to these considerations and returning on its solutions rejecting as inadmissible the exception of unconstitutionality of Article 174 para. (1) a) of the Criminal Procedure Code, when the exception was raised upon the request of the defendant's lawyer who could not be represented in the proceedings before the first instance court, the Court found that such an exception is admissible and shall be considered as such.

b) Exceptions of unconstitutionality may be raised before courts of law and courts of commercial arbitration

The meaning of the phrase "court of law"

Initially, the case-law of the Constitutional Court gave a broad interpretation of the concept of "court of law"[853]. However, later, the Plenum of the Constitutional Court

853 "The judiciary, in a broad sense, includes all jurisdiction bodies, regardless of their nature" (Decision no. 3/1993, published in the Official Gazette of Romania

narrowly interpreted such concept; only the courts of law specified by the Law on judicial organization were recognized the right to refer to the Constitutional Court with the exceptions of unconstitutionality raised before them. Thus, by Decision no. II/1995 of the Plenum of the Constitutional Court regarding the meaning of "court of law" within the constitutional review by way of exception[854], the Court held that "in order to establish the courts of law, we shall primarily refer to the Constitution, which, in Article 125 para. (1) (text governed by the title «Courts of law»), provides that «Justice shall be meted out by the Supreme Court of Justice, and by the other courts set up under the law». Law no. 92/1992 on judicial organization provides for in Article 10 that «The courts of law shall be: a) the courts; b) the tribunals; c) the courts of appeal; d) the Supreme Court of Justice». In addition to these, military courts may be added, which are organized, pursuant to Article 11 of Law no. 92/1992, by Law no. 54/1993, in: military tribunals, territorial military tribunals, Military Court of Appeal. That being so, the notification of the Constitutional Court with an exception of unconstitutionality cannot be legally done only by one of the courts provided by law".

Consequently, the Court rejected as inadmissible the exceptions of unconstitutionality raised before the Court of Accounts[855] or before the Superior Council of Magistracy[856].

In terms of the cases of inadmissibility of the exception of unconstitutionality, the competence of that court to settle the case in which the exception has been raised is irrelevant. In this regard, the Constitutional Court held that "according to Article 29 para. (4) of Law no. 47/1992 on the Organization and Operation of the Constitutional Court, the conditions regarding the legality of a referral shall take account of the notification of a court. (...) In terms of the *a posteriori* constitutional review provided for by Article 146 d) first sentence of the Constitution, the Court's role is exclusively involved in the censorship regarding the compliance of the legal rules with the Basic Law and it cannot intervene in any way in the merits of the case. A particular court shall be or not competent to rule on the merits of the case and this fact does not legitimize the Constitutional Court to proceed to such an

---

no. 95 of 17 May 1993); "The referral to the Constitutional Court has been raised by an administrative court. Such a situation is not contrary to the provisions of Article 144 c) of the Constitution (A/N, prior to revision) which refer expressly to the exception of unconstitutionality raised before the courts of law. (...) If he/she (A/N, the administrative judge) could not refer to the Constitutional Court, it would mean that he/she could solve the dispute related to the denial of constitutional legitimacy of the challenged provision" (Decision no. 64/1994, published in the Official Gazette of Romania no. 177 of 12 July 1994).

854 Published in the Official Gazette of Romania no. 47 of 13 March 1995.

855 Decision no. 90 of 4 March 2003, published in the Official Gazette of Romania no. 220 of 2 April 2003.

856 Decision no. 514 of 29 May 2007, published in the Official Gazette of Romania no. 464 of 10 July 2007.

analysis. The only verification that the constitutional court is obliged to exercise is related to the legality of the referral, which (...) involves the analysis of the conditions of admissibility of an exception of unconstitutionality. (...) To the extent that the Constitutional Court would examine the matters related to the competence of the courts, it would turn it into a court which would reform the judgments, a situation which is forbidden by the Constitution"[857].

Courts of commercial arbitration
The possibility of the courts of commercial arbitration to notify the Constitutional Court with an exception of unconstitutionality was introduced within the revision of the Constitution in 2003, revealing the constituent legislature's will resulted from the broadening of the scope of the subjects which may refer to the Constitutional Court for the exercise of the constitutional review.

Analyzing the cases in which the Constitutional Court was notified by the courts of commercial arbitration in Romania, one may note that in the quasi-majority of those cases, the legal texts that formed the subject-matter of the constitutional review refers to the very regulation of commercial arbitration, being called into question the issues regarding the legal nature of arbitration and of the courts of commercial arbitration.

Thus, the main challenges brought before the Constitutional Court concerned the fact that the Code of Civil Procedure "allows arbitration tribunals to do justice, without being courts of law and without being established by law, but only by the agreement between the parties, whereas the arbitration judgment is not subject to judicial control on all aspects of the case". Thus, it was argued that legal provisions whose unconstitutionality is invoked represent "the establishment of parallel justice", and "the court of law shall not exercise a review of full jurisdiction on the cases settled by arbitration tribunals. In this way the free access to justice enshrined in Article 21 of the Constitution is prevented, an article which sanctions the establishment of any filters regarding the access to courts of law"[858]. Similarly, it was argued that "the impugned legal texts refer to an exceptional court, prohibited by the Constitution, which consists of persons who are not independent magistrates, who do not obey the law, but who judge disputes whose settlement falls within the exclusive jurisdiction of the courts of law, according to Law no. 304/2004 on judicial organization"[859].

Rejecting as unfounded the exceptions of unconstitutionality raised, the Court held that arbitration is an exception from the principle according to which justice

857 Decision no. 678 of 13 November 2014, published in the Official Gazette of Romania no. 886 of 5 December 2014, see also Decision no. 493 of 21 November 2013, published in the Official Gazette of Romania no. 49 of 21 January 2014.

858 Decision no. 533 of 31 May 2007, published in the Official Gazette of Romania no. 416 of 21 June 2007.

859 Decision no. 8 of 9 January 2007, published in the Official Gazette of Romania no. 73 of 31 January 2007.

shall be exercised through courts of law and represents "that legal effective mechanism, aimed at ensuring a fair trial, faster and less formal, confidential, accomplished by enforceable judgments". Distinguishing in this respect between courts of law and courts of commercial arbitration, the Court held that the latter are not courts of law within the meaning of Articles 126 and 73 para. (3) of the Constitution, but jurisdictions expressly mentioned in the Basic Law in Article 146 d), and their establishment is not conditional on the adoption of an organic law. The disputes settled by the courts of commercial arbitration are completed by judgments subject to judicial review under Article 364 of the Code of Civil Procedure.[860]. Arbitration shall be organized and held according to the arbitration agreement signed between the parties, while respecting the principle of their free will, subject to the observance of public order, morality, as well as the provisions of the law, as required by Article 341 of the Code of Civil Procedure. Therefore, the parties may establish, by an arbitration agreement or by an addendum subsequently signed, the rules on the establishment of an arbitration tribunal, the appointment, dismissal and replacement of the arbitration judges, the time and place of arbitration, the procedural rules that the arbitration tribunal must follow in the arbitration proceedings and, in general, any other rules on the good conduct of arbitration. If the parties have not agreed on such rules, the arbitration tribunal may regulate the procedure which is to be applied.

Regarding the alleged violation of the constitutional provisions that do not allow the exercise of justice than by the courts of law, the Court found that "the courts of commercial arbitration do not meet the characteristic features of the extraordinary courts, as the procedure followed by them does not either violate or restrict the procedural rights of the parties set out in the Civil Procedure Code and any other of their rights or freedoms"[861]. Likewise, the Court held that "the Constitution itself, in Article 146 d), recognizes the existence of courts of commercial arbitration, stating that the exceptions of unconstitutionality may be raised before those courts, in addition to the courts of law". Concerning the alleged infringement of Article 21 of the Constitution, regarding free access to justice, the Court found that "before the court of arbitration, the case brought before it shall be analyzed in all aspects invoked by the parties, free access to justice shall be in no way prevented since there is a possibility to cancel action, which is a way of judicial review (and therefore access to justice) required by law"[862].

---

860 Decision no. 1121 of 10 September 2009, published in the Official Gazette of Romania no. 727 of 27 October 2009.

861 In the same regard, see Decision of 10 January 2008 of the Constitutional Court of Ukraine, available on *www.venice.coe.int.* CODICES – identification UKR-2008-1-001.

862 Decision no. 533 of 31 May 2007, published in the Official Gazette of Romania no. 416 of 21 June 2007; Decision no. 181 of 6 March 2007, published in the Official Gazette of Romania no. 291 of 3 May 2007; Decision no. 1277 of 8 October 2009, published in the Official Gazette of Romania no. 775 of 12 November 2009;

Therefore, it is noted that, judicially, the Constitutional Court made a number of clarifications from the perspective of the constitutional texts of reference, regarding the nature and features of commercial arbitration and of courts of commercial arbitration.

The specialised literatures have expressed both positive views and challenges concerning the regulation of the possibility to raise an exception of unconstitutionality before the courts of commercial arbitration. It has been also invoked a waiver of the circumstantiation achieved currently by the constitutional text, which refers only to the courts of commercial arbitration, specifying that the possibility to raise an exception of unconstitutionality before an arbitration tribunal must be recognized, otherwise they would arrive at solutions which are "illogical, unlawful and aberrant: the settlement of the exception by the arbitration tribunal; the ignorance of the exception by the arbitration tribunal and the settlement of a dispute, deliberately, under unconstitutional conditions. Above all, it would lead to a fundamentally different legal treatment in similar legal situations, in breach of the right to equality before law and justice"[863]. However, it has been expressed the view that "the inclusion of the courts of commercial arbitration in the context of Article 146 d) was a hasty operation, hard to reach, especially in this carousel of regulations. Their association with the constitutional review shall have to be removed in a constitutional perspective"[864].

A particular situation of the case-law of the Constitutional Court in this matter consists of the referral by a foreign court of commercial arbitration, a context in which the Court had to rule upon the admissibility of such referrals. The Constitutional Court was notified by the International Court of Arbitration of the International Chamber of Commerce in Paris. The author of the exception and sole arbitrator found that it is a "*court of commercial arbitration*" under the laws of Romania, while the respondent claimed that this was not within the constitutional text of reference.

With respect to these claims, the Court found, firstly, that the logical interpretation of the provisions of Article 146 d) of the Constitution and Article 29 of Law no. 47/1992 on the Organisation and Operation of the Constitutional Court, texts governing the competence of the Constitutional Court of Romania to settle "exceptions of unconstitutionality of laws and ordinances raised before courts of law and courts of commercial arbitration", leads to the conclusion that the legislature did not make any distinction between commercial arbitration courts in relation to the place where they operate. According to the principle "*where the law does not distinguish,*

Decision no. 263 of 16 March 2010, published in the Official Gazette of Romania no. 295 of 6 May 2010; Decision no. 1027 of 14 September 2010, published in the Official Gazette of Romania no. 739 of 5 November 2010.

863 I. Deleanu, *Civil Procedure Treaty*, volume I, Wolters Kluwer Publishing House, Bucharest, 2010, pp. 756–757.

864 I. Muraru, A. Muraru, *cited paper*, pp. 171–186.

neither ought we to distinguish" (*ubi lex non distinguit nec nos distinguere debemus*), it results that such a distinction shall not be permitted and, therefore, the notification of the Constitutional Court of Romania is legal, even if it was raised by a court of commercial arbitration in France. This argument is supported by teleological and systematic interpretations of the legal provisions in question, noted in the recitals underlying the Constitutional Court's decision.

Furthermore, the systematic interpretation of the Constitution reveals that if in case of courts [covered by the same texts – Article 146 d) of the Constitution and Article 29 of Law no. 47/1992], the constituent legislature expressly referred to the national courts system, through the reference made in Article 126 of the Constitution to the High Court of Cassation and Justice and its role in the uniform interpretation and application of the law by the courts, in case of commercial arbitration court there is no such reference, clarification or explanation, the constituent legislature's approach being manifestly wider. This approach can be justified by the specificity of the commercial arbitration court against the ordinary court, given the contractual, jurisdictional and mixed legal nature of arbitration.

Addressing the same legal texts from a teleological perspective, the Court found that the objective pursued by the legislature by introducing the commercial arbitration courts within bodies before which the exception of unconstitutionality can be raised (upon the constitutional revision in 2003) was to ensure the widest possible access to constitutional justice. This view regarding the courts which may refer to the Court is in line with the interpretation given by the European Court of Human Rights in its case-law to the concept of "tribunal" provided by Article 6 of the Convention for the Protection of Human Rights and Fundamental Freedoms in the sense that it "*does not necessarily have to be understood as a court of a classic type, integrated into the structures of the ordinary courts in the country (...); it may also contain a body responsible for the examination of a small number of disputes, provided that it always ensures the appropriate safeguards*" (Judgment delivered in Case *Campbell and Fell v. Great Britain*, of 28 June 1984, para. 76, of Judgment delivered in Case *Lithgow and Others v. Great Britain*, of 8 July 1986, para. 201). However, to the extent that an exception of unconstitutionality may be raised before a court of commercial arbitration – regardless of its location – whose subject-matter is the Romanian law, according to the Constitution, a refusal of the Constitutional Court of Romania to judge this exception would be contrary to the legislature's will, in violation of the constitutional provisions of Article 21, "Free access to justice", of Article 142 para. (1) regarding the role of the Constitutional Court as guarantor for the supremacy of the Constitution and of Article 1 para. (5), according to which: "*Observance of the Constitution, of its supremacy, and the laws shall be obligatory in Romania*".

However, the Court noted that any interpretation in terms of limiting the scope of courts of commercial arbitration before which an exception of unconstitutionality can be raised, and their circumstantiation only to the courts of commercial arbitration within Romanian territory cannot be accredited as a procedural condition in order to exercise the right of access to constitutional justice. This is because the choice of the place of arbitration outside Romania cannot be interpreted as a waiver of the fundamental right of access to justice. Such an interpretation would be tantamount to a real sanction applied to the parties of the arbitration agreement for the option to submit the settlement of disputes (resulting from a contract signed in Romania and subject to Romanian law) to the jurisdiction of a court of arbitration in another country, given that even the Romanian law (Article 369^1 of the Civil Procedure Code, in force on the signing date of the Privatization Contract) expressly provides the possibility of such option, without restriction. On the other hand, in such a situation, the court of commercial arbitration would be compelled to apply a law presumed unconstitutional, without having any procedural possibility to review or to adjudicate upon the referrals of unconstitutionality, as the only court competent to ensure the constitutional review of the Romanian law in relation to the Constitution of Romania shall be the Constitutional Court of Romania.

Or, if, by principle, the requirement by law of certain requirements, such as the establishment of certain procedural conditions for use of the subjective right by the holder, although it represents restrictions on the free access to justice, has a solid and indisputable justification in terms of the objective pursued, consisting of the restriction of the possibilities to abusively exercise that right, the requirements thus established should be sufficiently reasonable so that they shall not entail an excessive restriction on the exercise of that right, which may call into question its very existence. Moreover, the interpretation of the requirements thus established must not lead to a limitation on the exercise of the right beyond the objective pursued by imposing them. Thus, adding, by way of interpretation, additional conditions, so as to restrict the scope of the bodies before which an exception of unconstitutionality can be raised (already circumstantiated by the constituent legislature before the courts of law and the courts of commercial arbitration), would result in an excessive restriction of access to justice. Both in terms of access to constitutional justice, and in terms of access to a court of commercial arbitration, whereas the free possibility of the parties to manifest an option regarding the location of arbitration, this fact would be restricted by the imposition of the restriction to raise exceptions of unconstitutionality before some of these courts.

For these reasons, the Court found that the condition of referral to the Constitutional Court by "a court or commercial arbitration" provided by Article 146 d) of the Constitution and Article 29 para. (1) of Law no. 47/1992 is fulfilled. In this way, the Constitutional Court held that it was legally notified and it has jurisdiction to rule on an exception of unconstitutionality regarding laws belonging to the Romanian system of law, challenged by Romanian legal entities, but before certain courts of arbitration which are not situated in Romania[865].

---

865 Decision no. 123 of 5 March 2013, published in the Official Gazette of Romania no. 214 of 16 April 2013.

Constitutional grounds/exceptions of unconstitutionality which do not comply with the written and motivated form

Pursuant to Article 10 para. (2) of Law no. 47/1992, "*referrals shall be made in writing and they shall be motivated*". In conjunction with Article 29 para. (4) second sentence of the law, providing that, "*If the exception has been raised ex officio, the interlocutory order shall be motivated, including the parties' arguments, as well as the necessary evidence*", it results that, where an exception of unconstitutionality is raised by the parties in the trial or by the prosecutor, they must motivate in writing or orally the exception of unconstitutionality. However, in this case, the court is not required to give reasons for its interlocutory order, but to indicate the reasons given by the author of the exception. In the absence of the motivation of the exception of unconstitutionality by its author, the solution shall be inadmissible. This does not mean a restriction of the citizens' access to constitutional justice, but it is the consequence of the fact that, in exercising the constitutional review, the Court cannot act ex officio (except for the initiatives for the revision of the Constitution), but only upon referral and within its limits. The acceptance of the possibility of a mere invocation of an exception of unconstitutionality, without indicating at least the constitutional texts considered to be violated by the impugned legal provisions, would mean a violation of the express provisions of the law that obliges to motivate the referral (without distinguishing between the abstract review, *a priori*, and the specific review, *a posteriori*) and at the same time, a defeat of the principle of review on the "referral", and not ex officio, whereas, therefore, the Constitutional Court would be placed in a position so as to determine itself the grounds of unconstitutionality of the law which form the subject-matter of the exception[866].

Thus, for example, the Court rejected as inadmissible the exception of unconstitutionality in which its author invoked the infringement of the "universally accepted principles underlying the rule of law", without specifying them[867]. On that occasion, the Court held that "referrals to the Court to be motivated, which involves, necessarily, invoking constitutional grounds for challenging the constitutional legitimacy of the provision that is the subject of referral". The Court also found that it "cannot substitute the author of the referral on invoking any specific reason of unconstitutionality", otherwise "within the settlement procedure of exceptions of

---

866 For example, see Decision no. 341/1997, published in the Official Gazette of Romania no. 38/1998, where the Court established that "(...) the failure of the author of the exception to indicate the constitutional norms in relation to which he considers that the impugned legal provisions are unconstitutional is also a reason for rejection as the raised exception does not constitution, within the constitutional meaning of the term, an exception of unconstitutionality. If the constitutional court would have jurisdiction to adjudicate on such an exception, it would substitute the party regarding the invocation of the reasons of unconstitutionality raised, thus exercising ex officio the constitutional review, which is inadmissible".

867 Decision no. 465 of 4 December 2003, published in the Official Gazette of Romania no. 55 of 22 January 2004.

unconstitutionality, the review of the Constitutional Court would not be exercised on the referral, but ex officio, being contrary to Article 144 c) of the Constitution [which became Article 146 d) after the revision and republication of the Constitution], which refers explicitly to «the exceptions raised before the courts»".

With similar reasoning, the Court rejected the exceptions of unconstitutionality in which the author of the exception only enumerated the constitutional texts considered to be violated without specifying the concrete reasons underlying the contrariety with the Basic Law[868]; "formal enumeration of certain constitutional provisions and international regulations, without, however, specifying their concrete and effective contrariety with the impugned legal texts, is, according to the settled case-law of the Constitutional Court, a reason of inadmissibility of the exception of unconstitutionality"[869].

B. Cases of inadmissibility in relation to the extent of constitutional review

We mentioned that this second category of inadmissibility of the exception of unconstitutionality is specific to the second stage regarding the settlement of the exception, that of constitutional dispute. These have been developed by the Constitutional Court, by way of case-law.

a) The Constitutional Court shall adjudicate only on the constitutionality of the acts in regard of which it has been appraised, and shall not be competent to modify or to supplement the provisions under review

In relation to this ground, the Court rejected, as inadmissible, exceptions of unconstitutionality in which their authors challenged certain gaps of the laws. Thus, for example, rejecting the exception of unconstitutionality of Article 8 of Chapter I in Annex no. 5 of Law no. 63/2011 on employment and wages in 2011 regarding the teachers and auxiliary staff in education system, the Court held that the bonus for the PhD scientific title has been removed since 1 January 2010, according to the Framework Law no. 330/2009 regarding the unitary remuneration of personnel paid from public funds, published in the Official Gazette of Romania, Part I, no. 762 of 9 November 2009. However, the fact that the amount of money related to the bonus for a PhD scientific title was still maintained as a transitional compensatory amount for the persons who earned it until 31 December 2009 does not concern the existence or the lack of the bonus, but a transitional measure until the entry into force, as a whole, of the Framework Law no. 284/2010 regarding the unitary remuneration of personnel paid from public funds, published in the Official Gazette of Romania, Part I, no. 877 of 28 December 2010, law which does not contain this bonus. Consequently, the Court found that it is for the legislature to eliminate or, conversely, to grant additional salary rights, without having any constitutional relevance. That

868 Decision no. 627 of 29 May 2008, published in the Official Gazette of Romania no. 555 of 23 July 2008.

869 Decision no. 415 of 3 July 2014, published in the Official Gazette of Romania no. 577 of 1 August 2014.

being so, the Court found that the admission of the exception would be tantamount to its subrogation to the jurisdiction of the legislature, in the sense of granting the bonus, thus infringing Article 2 para. (3) of Law no. 47/1992 on the Organization and Operation of the Constitutional Court, according to which the constitutional court shall adjudicate only on the constitutionality of acts which have been brought before it, without being able to amend or supplement the provisions subject to review[870].

But where the legal gap has constitutional relevance, namely it generates a flaw of unconstitutionality of the regulation, the Court shall correct it, considering the exception of unconstitutionality as admissible and vesting itself accordingly with its settlement.

Thus, for example, allowing the exception of unconstitutionality of Article 10 para. (1) of the Government Emergency Ordinance no. 24/2008 concerning access to personal files and desconspiracy of Securitate, because, "as they are written, they determine difficulties in terms of interpretation and application of law and create, without any objective or rational reasoning, an impediment to the effective exercise of the right to address to court in order to defend its rights and legitimate interests", the Court held that "even if in current hypothesis a legislative omission is discussed, the Court, in its role as guarantor for the supremacy of the Constitution, cannot ignore the existing unconstitutional flaw, because the very failure and imprecision of laws are those which create a violation of the fundamental right of free access to justice for the persons that receive the certificate, according to Article 10 para. (1) of the Emergency Government Ordinance no. 24/2008"[871].

Based on similar reasons, the Court ascertained the unconstitutionality of Article 48 para. (17) of Law no. 35/2008 on the elections for the Chamber of Deputies and the Senate, as well as amending and supplementing Law no. 67/2004 on the election of local public authorities, Law no. 215/2001 on local public administration and Law no. 393/2004 on the Status of local elected officials[872]. On that occasion, the Court held that "indeed, the impugned legal text does not expressly provide, directly, the elimination of independent candidates from the partial parliamentary elections, but this results precisely from the formula «only the parties and the organizations (...)», a restrictive and imperative wording, which logically excludes any other interpretation. Although it appears as a legislative omission, the referred flaw of unconstitutionality cannot be ignored, because such omission is the one that generates, *eo ipso*, the violation of the constitutional right to be elected. However, pursuant to Article 142 of the Basic Law, the Constitutional Court is the guarantor for the supremacy of the Constitution, which requires, among other things,

---

870 Decision no. 89 of 27 February 2014, published in the Official Gazette of Romania no. 349 of 13 May 2014.

871 Decision no. 107 of 27 February 2014, published in the Official Gazette of Romania no. 318 of 30 April 2014.

872 Decision no. 503 of 20 April 2010, published in the Official Gazette of Romania no. 353 of 28 May 2010.

the compliance of the entire legislation with the Constitution, the constitutional review of laws. Therefore, the electoral law may specify the conditions under which a person may run as an independent candidate (to establish a financial deposit, to have a certain number of supporters), but it cannot, in any way, eliminate from the electoral procedure the candidature as independent of a person, in case of partial elections, without consequently infringing the fundamental constitutional right enshrined in Article 37 – «Right to be elected»".

In the same respect there are also opinions expressed in the specialised literature, which state that "when the Constitution imposes the legislature a positive obligation of regulation, then the failure to regulate, after a reasonable time has passed since the date of adoption of the Constitution during which the legislature could have done it, constitutes a violation of the Constitution that could affect the fundamental rights and freedoms. Likewise, although there is a law governing a range of social relations, when the failure to regulate some of their aspects affects by itself a fundamental right or freedom, even if there is no positive obligation of regulation, the legislature violates the constitutional provisions"[873].

b) The Constitutional Court cannot adjudicate on the interpretation and enforcement of the law, but only on its unconstitutionality

The Law on the Organization and Operation of the Constitutional Court does not contain anymore any express text which may establish such a rule[874], but any exception of unconstitutionality which does not aim at a law or an ordinance or any provision thereof, but only at their interpretation or application, will be rejected as inadmissible, according to Article 126 of the Constitution; they fall within the competence of the courts of law.

This plea of inadmissibility must be distinguished from situations where the Constitutional Court sanctions a certain interpretation of legal texts, contrary to the Constitution, ruling by way of an interpretative decision, or from those situations ruling on the law as interpreted by decisions of the High Court of Cassation and Justice, delivered on appeals on points of law.

c) The Constitutional Court shall neither compare legal provisions nor relate the conclusion that would result from it to the provisions and principles of the Constitution nor analyze the correlation of the normative acts

In exercising constitutional review, the Constitutional Court has jurisdiction to rule on the constitutionality of laws and ordinances challenged by reference to the provisions and principles enshrined in the Basic Law and not to corroborate or correlate the various normative acts that are part of national law. Legislative coordination

873 D.C. Dănişor, *Limitation..., cited paper*, pp. 32–36.

874 Prior to the amendment to Law no. 47/1992 by Law no. 232/2004, Article 2 para. (3) last sentence of the Law expressly stipulated, "The Constitutional Court shall not adjudicate on the interpretation and enforcement of the law, but only on its meaning contrary to the Constitution".

falls within the competence of the legislative power and its technical aspects are part of the powers of the Legislative Council.

Thus, for example, the Court held that "pursuant to Article 2 para. (2) of Law no. 47/1992 on the Organization and Operation of the Constitutional Court, the constitutional court performs a constitutional review in terms of laws and other normative acts, while the issues on the legislative coordination belong to the legislative authority, and those relating to law enforcement belong to the court of law"[875].

Likewise, the Court held that "the constitutional review of a legal text takes into account the compliance of the text with the constitutional provisions allegedly violated, and not the comparison of the provisions of several laws between them and reporting the conclusion that would result from this comparison to the provisions or principles of the Constitution. Proceeding as such, it would inevitably reach the conclusion that although each of the laws is constitutional, only their coexistence would call into question the constitutionality of one of them. Therefore, it results that we are not in the presence of an issue on constitutionality, but of a simple annoyance between legal norms in the same field, as the coordination of the laws in force falls within the competence of the legislative power"[876].

5.3 The role of the courts of law and the courts of commercial arbitration within the acceptance and the enforcement of the Constitutional Court's decisions

5.3.1 The binding nature of the Constitutional Court's decisions in the relationships with the courts of law

5.3.1.1 General aspects

The provisions of Article 124 of the Constitution also regulate, along with the guarantee of the judges' independence, their obligation to obey the law only. The notion of "law" set forth in Article 124 para. (3) of the Constitution "*is used in its broadest sense, which includes the Constitution, as Basic Law, but also all other normative acts, legally equivalent to laws or of lower force, which constitute the normative assembly on which the act of justice should be based upon*"[877]. The principles governing the administration of justice should be interpreted in conjunction with the constitutional provisions which enshrine the role and the competence of other powers, in compliance with the principles of the rule of law, as stated by Article 1 of the Basic Law. A legislative framework that would allow the ignorance, circumvent or censorship

875 Decision no. 249 of 10 May 2005, published in the Official Gazette of Romania no. 536 of 23 June 2005.

876 Decision no. 81 of 25 May 1999, published in the Official Gazette of Romania no. 325 of 8 July 1999.

877 Decision no. 799 of 17 June 2011, published in the Official Gazette of Romania no. 440 of 23 June 2011.

by the courts of law of the decisions delivered by the High Court of Cassation and Justice or by the Constitutional Court in the exercise of their constitutional powers is not compatible with these principles[878].

The Constitutional Court has expressed on various occasions certain considerations of principle on the role and relationships between the Constitutional Court and the courts of law, in particular with the High Court of Cassation and Justice, on its jurisdiction for resolving the appeals on points of law, clearly specifying the limits which ensure the exercise of their powers, so as they do not come into collision, and the acts of the two courts can be both respected and applied[879].

Over time, there have been violations of the Constitutional Court's competence, which resulted in the legislature's actions[880], or – as in this case – in the actions of the courts. However, the Constitutional Court of Romania does not have separate legal instruments to ensure the compliance with its decisions; the only framework in which it may act is the powers expressly and restrictively provided by the Constitution and the law governing its organization and operation. Or, those powers shall

---

878 Decision no. 2 of 11 January 2012, published in the Official Gazette of Romania no. 131 of 23 February 2012.

879 Decision no. 838 of 27 May 2009, published in the Official Gazette of Romania no. 461 of 3 July 2009; Decision no. 2 of 12 January 2012 published in the Official Gazette of Romania no. 131 of 23 February 2012.

880 Thus, as concerns the actions of the legislature on non-compliance with the acts of the court of administrative contentious, we mention that by Decision no. 1018 of 19 July 2010, published in the Official Gazette of Romania no. 511 of 22 July 2010, the Court ascertained the unconstitutionality of the provisions of Law on the integrity in the exercise of public functions and public dignities, amending and supplementing Law no. 144/2007 on the establishment, organisation and functioning of the National Integrity Agency, as well as amending and supplementing other normative acts, an act which resumed provisions found unconstitutional. On that occasion, the Court held that "the adoption by the legislature of certain norms contrary to those decided by a decision of the Constitutional Court, aiming at maintaining the legislative solution affected by flaws of unconstitutionality, violates the Basic Law. However, in a rule of law, as Romania is proclaimed under Article 1 para. (3) of the Constitution, the public authorities do not enjoy any autonomy in relation to law, as the Constitution establishes in Article 16 para. (2) that no one shall be above the law, and in Article 1 para. (5) that the observance of the Constitution, its supremacy and the law shall be obligatory". Similarly, the Court emphasized that the solution adopted by the Government, to adopt, right before the court of administrative contentious shall adjudicate on the constitutionality of the Law amending Article 27 para. (1) of Law no. 47/1992, an emergency ordinance which fully resumes the normative content of the impugned law, calls into question the unconstitutional and abusive behaviour of the Government in relation to the Constitutional Court [Decision no. 727/2012 on the referral of unconstitutionality of Law amending Article 27 para. (1) of Law no. 47/1992 on the Organisation and Operation of the Constitutional Court, published in the Official Gazette of Romania no. 477 of 12 July 2012].

not be exercised ex officio, except for the constitutional review of the initiatives for the revision of the Constitution [Article 146 a) second sentence of the Constitution] and the constitutional review of the law amending the Constitution adopted by Parliament [Article 146 l) of the Constitution, with reference to Article 23 of Law no. 47/1992 on the Organization and Operation of the Constitutional Court]. As a result, the sanction of the acts which infringed Article 147 para. (4) of the Constitution was applied only as a result of certain referrals of unconstitutionality.

5.3.1.2 Ensuring the compliance with the binding nature of the Constitutional Court's decisions – jurisprudential landmarks

One of the most active interventions of the Constitutional Court **during the period prior to the revision of the Constitution**[881] was made in a case regarding an exception of unconstitutionality, on which an interpretative decision had already been pronounced[882]. Noting that another court of law before which the same exception of unconstitutionality was raised, expressing its opinion, has considered that the text – Article 278 of the Criminal Procedure Code – violates Article 21 of the Constitution, but, however, it did not comply with the Constitutional Court's decision, notifying again the Constitutional Court so as to settle the exception of unconstitutionality of the same text, the Court held a number of considerations that we consider likely to support the importance of the dialogue existing between the two authorities[883].

The Court held that[884], "acting so, the court of law:

I. did not directly apply the provisions of Article 21 of the Constitution concerning the free access to justice; it is therefore necessary to examine the issue regarding the obligation of the courts of law to directly apply the provisions of the Constitution when there is no statutory regulation or when it has been ascertained the unconstitutionality of the existing legal regulation;

---

881 This is the reason for which throughout the invoked decision there is reference to the numbering of the constitutional texts prior to the revisions and, likewise, to concepts which are currently amended, for example, that of suspension of the case until the settlement of the exception of unconstitutionality.

882 Decision no. 486 of 2 December 1997, published in the Official Gazette of Romania no. 105 of 6 March 1998; on that occasions, the Court upheld the exception of unconstitutionality and found that Article 278 (6) of the Code of Criminal Procedure is unconstitutional insofar as the person unsatisfied with the settlement of the application against the measures and the acts accomplished by the prosecutor or taken based on the provisions given by him/her and which are not raised before the courts shall not be prevented from presenting before the court under Article 21 of the Constitution, which is to be directly enforced.

883 Decision no. 186 of 18 November 1999, published in the Official Gazette of Romania no. 213 of 16 May 2000.

884 As we refer to the decision delivered before the revision of the Constitution, the numbering of the constitutional and legal texts invoked corresponds to that period.

II. did not comply either with the provisions of Article 145 para. (2) first sentence of the Constitution, according to which «The Constitutional Court's decisions shall be binding (...)»,or with the provisions of Article 23 para. (3) of Law no. 47/1992 on the Organization and Operation of the Constitutional Court, republished, under which «legal provisions whose unconstitutionality has been found according to Article 145 para. (1) of the Constitution or legal provisions whose unconstitutionality has been found by prior decision of the Constitutional Court cannot form the subject-matter of an exception»; it is therefore necessary to examine the effects of the decisions delivered by the Constitutional Court, according to Article 144 c) of the Constitution, in order to settle the exceptions of unconstitutionality raised before the courts of law;
III. did not comply with the provisions of Article 23 para. (6) of Law no. 47/1992, republished, according to which «if the exception is inadmissible, being contrary to the provisions under paragraph (...) (3), the court of law shall reject it through a motivated interlocutory order, without referring the case to the Constitutional Court»; therefore it is necessary to examine the way in which the courts of law should proceed when, regarding the legal provisions on which the settlement of the case depends, the Constitutional Court ruled previously a decision finding the unconstitutionality".

Detailing and properly solving each of the issues identified, the Court held as follows:

"I. In connection with the issue regarding the obligation of the courts of law to directly apply the provisions of the Constitution when there is no statutory regulation or when it has been ascertained the unconstitutionality of the existing legal regulation:

By Decision no. 486/1997, the Constitutional Court found that Article 278 of the Code of Criminal Procedure is unconstitutional insofar as the person unsatisfied with the settlement of the application against the measures or the acts accomplished by the prosecutor or taken based on the provisions given by him/her and which are not raised before the courts of law is prevented from presenting before the court under Article 21 of the Constitution, according to which: «(1) Everyone shall have access to the courts in order to defend his rights, freedoms and legitimate interests.

(2) No law shall allow restrictions on the exercise of that right».

On the contrary, in this case, by a simple ascertainment in the sense that the prosecutor's decision not to prosecute «(...) should be checked, investigated and censured by the court of law (...)», the court before which the exception of unconstitutionality was raised, being the subject-matter of this decision, joined – implicitly – the ways in which, in similar cases, the other courts of law proceeded, which have considered – explicitly – that the direct application by the judiciaries of Article 21 of the Constitution is inadmissible in the absence of existence, at legal level, of a regulation on the procedure to be followed by the unsatisfied person to address to the court of law and also on the procedure to be conducted by the court of law in order to solve the request of the unsatisfied person. Consequently, these courts of law, without directly denying the binding nature of the Constitutional Court's decisions, according to Article 145 para. (2) first sentence of the Constitution, did not comply with Decision no. 486/1997, waiting for Parliament to implement this decision by the regulation, under the Code of Criminal Procedure, of the concrete procedure enabling the control by the courts of law of the measures referred to in Article 278 of this Code. In order to reach the conclusion of inadmissibility of direct application of constitutional provisions by courts of law, the following two categories of allegations were essentially used:

1. Claims related to the peculiarity of justice activity, peculiarity established by special constitutional texts applicable to it, such as:
- pursuant to Article 123 para. (1) of the Constitution: «(1) Justice shall be rendered in the name of the law», and under paragraph (2) of the same constitutional law, «(2) Judges shall be independent and subject only to the law»;
- pursuant to Article 125 para. (3) of the Constitution: «The jurisdiction of the courts of law and the judging procedure shall only be stipulated by law».

Starting with the wording contained in these constitutional texts, it is considered that, consequently, the constitutional provisions do not address directly to the justice which shall apply laws in force, but only through legislative bodies, which must comply with the Constitution and properly amend the legislation.

2. Allegations according to which, similarly to the conclusion reached by the aforementioned statements (under point 1), the decisions of the Constitutional Court would represent, in reality, a request addressed to the legislature, which, proceeding to analyze this request, must properly amend the legislation in force "challenged" by the Constitutional Court's decisions; accordingly, the courts of law would not directly invoke the decisions of the Constitutional Court, but only by the incorporation of such solutions in the positive legislation by the legislature. In relation to the latter claim, the Court notes that, in essence, it actually concerns the effects of the Constitutional Court's decisions, particularly in relation to the judicial authority. Therefore, the examination of these claims will be made later in the recitals contained in point II of this decision, on the issue of the effects of the decisions delivered by the Constitutional Court, according to Article 144 c) of the Constitution, in order to settle the exceptions of unconstitutionality raised before the courts of law.

Analyzing the first category of claims, the Constitutional Court finds that they are unfounded and the conclusion reached based on them represents the direct violation of Article 51 of the Constitution («Observance of the Constitution, of its supremacy, and the laws shall be obligatory»), as well as the infringement by way of circuitous route of Article 145 para. (2) first sentence of the Constitution [«The Constitutional Court's decisions shall be binding (...)»], as it will result from what follows.

Thus, firstly, regarding the assembly of the first category of claims, whose content is summarized in point 1 above, the Constitutional Court notes that the refusal to directly apply the provisions of Article 21 of the Constitution is based, in a contradictory way, just on the direct invocation and application of other constitutional texts, namely on the direct application of Article 123 para. (1) and (2) and Article 125 para. (1) of the Basic Law. This is tantamount to the allegation that the Constitution itself prohibits the direct application of the Constitution or to the allegation that the direct application of the Constitution means the violation of the Constitution. We reach in this way such logical inconsistencies.

Secondly, the Constitutional Court observes that the meaning given by the court to the term «law» used in Article 123 para. (1) and (2) and Article 125 para. (3) of the Constitution is incorrect, leading to the exclusion, from this meaning, of the Basic Law, therefore of the Constitution. In fact, under the marginal title «Classes of laws», Article 72 of the Constitution (placed in a section called «Legislation») governs the existence of three classes of «laws»: constitutional laws, organic laws and ordinary laws, and the courts of law, in their work, cannot select from such laws only the organic laws and ordinary laws, setting aside the implementation of the constitutional laws.

Thirdly, it is clear that the purpose of Article 123 para. (1) and (2) and of Article 125 para. (3) of the Constitution is not the exclusion of the Basic Law from the activity of the court of law to apply the law, but the prohibition of the application by them over the «law», of the normative acts that have a power lower than the «law». In other words, the real purpose of these constitutional texts is, as appropriate: to prohibit justice on behalf of certain normative acts which, having a power lower than the «law», are contrary to it – Article 123 para. (1); to prohibit «duplication» of Judges in relation such normative acts – Article 123 para. (2); to prohibit the establishment by such normative acts of «jurisdiction and judging procedure» – Article 125 para. (3).

That being so, it is clear that the constitutional provisions can and should be applied directly by the courts of law when the legislature has not enacted laws to proceed with the details of the constitutional regulation. The adoption by the legislature of such laws is usually necessary, but their absence cannot prevent the immediate implementation of the will of the constituent legislature. In addition, there are situations when it is obvious that for the application of constitutional regulations the adoption of laws shall not be required. It is, for example, Article 51 of the Constitution («Observance of the Constitution, of its supremacy, and the laws shall be obligatory»), that of Article 72 (which governs «classes of laws») etc.

For the same reasons, constitutional provisions can and should be applied directly by the courts and if, the decision of the Constitutional Court has declared the unconstitutionality of the existing legal provisions and the legislature has not yet amended or repealed, where appropriate, those legal provisions.

II. In relation to the issue of the effects of decisions delivered by the Constitutional Court, according to Article 144 c) of the Constitution, in order to settle the exceptions of unconstitutionality raised before the courts of law:

It is known that such review is exercised on «(...) laws and ordinances which are in force, or any provision thereof, on which the settlement of the case depends» – Article 23 para. (1) of Law no. 47/1992, republished.

The nature of the effects of these decisions of the Constitutional Court have already been examined by it.

Thus, by Decision no. 169 of 2 November 1999, published in the Official Gazette of Romania, Part I, no. 151 of 12 April 2000, it has been shown that, in terms examined, a fundamental text is that of Article 145 para. (2) first sentence of the Constitution, under which «The Constitutional Court's decisions shall be binding (...)». Likewise, it was noted that this text should be read in conjunction with the other constitutional provisions and constitutional principles, which together shape the content of Article 23 para. (3) second sentence and para. (6) of Law no. 47/1992 on the Organization and Operation of the Constitutional Court, republished. According to Article 23 para. (3), «legal provisions whose unconstitutionality has been found according to Article 145 para. (1) of the Constitution or legal provisions whose unconstitutionality has been found by prior decision of the Constitutional Court cannot form the subject-matter of an exception», and paragraph (6) of Article 23 rules that: «if the exception is inadmissible, being contrary to the provisions under paragraph (...) (3), the court of law shall reject it through a motivated interlocutory order, without referring the case to the Constitutional Court». It results that the court of law before which an exception of unconstitutionality regarding a law or ordinance (or to one or more provisions of a law or ordinance), whose unconstitutionality had been confirmed by the Constitutional Court in a decision published before the invocation of the exception of unconstitutionality, shall apply the earlier decision of the Constitutional Court – including where that decision was rendered under Article 144 c) of the Constitution. Accordingly, the decisions delivered within the settlement of the exceptions of unconstitutionality do not produce only relative effects (*inter partes*), in the case where the exception of unconstitutionality was raised, but they produce absolute effects (*erga omnes*).

(...)

As a consequence of the *erga omnes* binding nature of the Constitutional Court's decisions, delivered under Article 144 c) of the Constitution, whereby the unconstitutionality of a law or ordinance is found, the legal provision whose unconstitutionality has been found cannot be applied by any subject of law (even less by the public authorities and bodies), ceasing its legal effects for the future, namely as from the date of publication in the Official Gazette of Romania of the decision of the Constitutional Court, according to the second sentence of the first phrase of Article 145 (1) of the Constitution. No doubt that, following the ascertainment of the unconstitutionality of a law or ordinance by a decision delivered by the Constitutional Court, Parliament or, where appropriate, the Government, shall intervene in order to amend or repeal the normative act declared unconstitutional. But – as mentioned by Decision no. 169/1999 – this does not mean that, where such an action would not occur or delay, the decision of the Constitutional Court would cease its effects. On the contrary, those effects still occur, being opposable *erga omnes*, in order to guarantee the supremacy of the Constitution, under Article 51 thereof.

Finally, according to Decision no. 169/1999, the *erga omnes* binding nature of the Constitutional Court's decisions, whereby the unconstitutionality of a law or ordinance is found, involves the existence of a legal liability for the non-observance of these decisions. In this respect, there is equivalence with the situation where a law passed by Parliament or an ordinance issued by the Government is not complied with. Or, in more general terms, we refer to the issue on identifying the legal liability when one of the State authorities refuses to implement the measures established by another State authority, within the jurisdiction conferred by the Constitution. In such a situation the identification of legal liability arises from the mandatory nature of the provisions of Article 1(3) of the Constitution, according to which «Romania is governed by the rule of law (...) ». Otherwise it would lead to the removal of this fundamental constitutional principle by one of the powers of the state, which is unacceptable. Also, in light of the provisions of Articles 11 and 20 of the Constitution, the legal responsibility for the non-observance of a decision of the Constitutional Court may consist in a judgment pronounced by the European Court of Human Rights against Romania, insofar as the conditions laid down in the Convention for the Protection of Human Rights and Fundamental Freedoms are complied with.

All these reasons contained in the Constitutional Court's Decision no. 169/1999 are also fully applicable to this case.

III. As to the issue relating to the way in which the courts of law should proceed when, regarding the legal provisions on which the settlement of the case depends, the Constitutional Court ruled previously a decision finding the unconstitutionality:

The courts have the power – under the law – to establish, through a reasoned interlocutory order, that an exception of unconstitutionality is «admissible» or «inadmissible» or, more precisely, that it the application of a party or of the prosecutor to raise an exception of unconstitutionality is «admissible» or «inadmissible», with the consequence to suspend the case and to refer to the Constitutional Court in order to setlle the exception. In the event that a court of law wrongly allows such a request, rather than to reject it – under the law – as inadmissible, the Constitutional Court has the power to determine that the notification has been made illegal and, consequently, to reject it itself, by decision, the exception of unconstitutionality, as « inadmissible». On the other hand, when the notification of the Constitutional Court was made correctly, since – according to law – the exception of unconstitutionality was «admissible» [in which case the court has the obligation under Article 23 para. (4) of Law no. 47/1992, republished, to express its «viewpoint on the exception»], only the Constitutional Court is competent to «allow» or to «reject» the exception of unconstitutionality, therefore, to settle the exception «on the merits», i.e. to ascertain that the legal provisions which form the subject-matter of the exception are, as the case may be, unconstitutional («admission of the exception») or constitutional («rejection of the exception»).

Thus, as it results from the provisions of Article 23 para. (3) and (6) of Law no. 47/1992, republished, one of the «inadmissibility» cases for raising an exception of unconstitutionality is the one where the subject-matter of the exception is «(...) the provisions whose unconstitutionality has been found by a prior decision of the Constitutional Court ». This means, firstly, that it is inadmissible for the court itself to raise its own motion, such exception. Secondly, it also means that, if such an exception is raised by the parties or by the prosecutor, the court of law is obliged to reject as inadmissible the application by which the exception has been raised, without notifying the Constitutional Court and without suspending the proceedings [as required by Article 23 para. (5), in the event of raising an exception of unconstitutionality by an admissible application]. Finally, thirdly, it also means that by rejecting the application by which the exception of unconstitutionality is raised, the court, continuing the settlement of the case, has the obligation to respect the decision of the Constitutional Court, therefore, as appropriate, it must:

- not apply in that case the legal provisions whose unconstitutionality was established by a decision of the Constitutional Court;
- apply the legal provisions on which the settlement of the case depends and which relate to the decision of the Constitutional Court, but never in that sense that, as found by that decision, is contrary to the Constitution.

In either of the two situations above and to the extent that it is necessary, the court of law shall apply directly the provisions of the Constitution, on which the settlement of the case depends, in the absence of certain legal regulations that replace or supplement the provisions on which the Constitutional Court's decision was rendered.

From all the foregoing considerations it results that in this case the court of law was obliged, as to the existence of the Constitutional Court's Decision no. 486/1997 on the provisions of Article 278 of the Criminal Procedure Code, to comply with the *erga omnes* obligatory effects thereof and therefore to reject the application to raise the exception of unconstitutionality, as inadmissible, without notifying the Constitutional Court, following that, in view of solving the case pending before it, to directly apply the provisions of Article 21 of the Constitution on the guarantee of free access to justice. Not proceeding in this way requires that, by this decision of the Constitutional Court, the exception of unconstitutionality be rejected as inadmissible under Article 23 para. (3) and (6) of Law no. 47/1992, republished".

One of the most energetic interventions of the Court after the revision of the Constitution concerns the situation of an appeal on points of law, respectively a decision of the High Court of Cassation and Justice in contradiction with the decision of the Constitutional Court.

Thus, by way of an exception of unconstitutionality covering the provisions of Article 414^5 para. (4) of the Code of Criminal Procedure, which establishes the binding nature of the interpretations on matters of law by the High Court of Cassation and Justice through the appeal on points of law, a legal situation was brought before the constitutional court, consisting of exceeding the limits of jurisdiction of the High Court of Cassation and Justice, determined by an unconstitutional interpretation of the provisions governing the appeal on points of law. Although, according to Article

126 para. (3) of the Constitution, the High Court of Cassation and Justice ensures the uniform interpretation and application of the law by the other courts of law, and not the decisions of the Constitutional Court, by Decision no. 8/2010, it has invested itself and ruled on the "*consequences of the Constitutional Court's Decision no. 62 of 18 January 2007 on the exception of unconstitutionality of Article I section 56 of Law no. 278/2006 amending the Criminal Code, as well as amending and supplementing other laws regarding the function of the provisions of Articles 205, 206 and 207 of the Criminal Code*". In other words, the High Court of Cassation and Justice proceeded to the interpretation of a decision of the Constitutional Court, and not of the law, ruling on the effects of this decision which have already been established by the Constitutional Court, even within the decision in question. Moreover, it stated to the contrary to those noted by the Constitutional Court, confirming a practice of the courts of law which is contrary to the Constitutional Court's decision.

The settlement of an exception of unconstitutionality of the provisions of the Code of Criminal Procedure on appeal on points of law required the Constitutional Court to respond to this violation of the constitutional provisions. A solution rejecting as inadmissible the exception of unconstitutionality in this situation would have meant the assumption by the Constitutional Court of a purely formal role of clear acceptance of the non-compliance with the Basic Law. Such a position, similar to denial of justice, is incompatible with the role of the Constitutional Court in a rule of law. Thus, even if the problem itself, namely the non-compliance with the decisions of the Constitutional Court by the High Court of Cassation and Justice was exceeded for a long time, whereas the latter considered again its own, the solution of the Constitutional Court in the case brought before it could only be therefore the sanctioning of the violation of the Constitution by "*sanctioning any interpretation of the provisions of Article 414^{5} para. (4) of the Code of Criminal Procedure, which establishes the binding nature of the interpretations on matter of law by the High Court of Cassation and Justice through the appeal in the interest of the law, in the sense that it would allow this court, on the grounds of an infraconstitutional rule, to give binding interpretations that are contrary to the Constitution and to the decisions of the Constitutional Court*". It is a solution required by principle, irrespective of the regulations to which the decisions of the two courts have referred, as also demonstrated by Decision no. 206/2013 delivered by the Constitutional Court, unanimously, even though in terms of the regulations in question (on the criminalization of insult and libel) there was another point of view of one of the judges of the Constitutional Court, expressed in a concurring opinion.

However, the operative part of the decision delivered by the Constitutional Court on that occasion[885] is not limited to the removal of the "*flaw of unconstitutionality*", namely to that interpretation of the impugned legal text, contrary to the Constitution, as the Court has proceeded several times in the past, but it refers exactly to the

885 Decision no. 206 of 29 April 2013, published in the Official Gazette of Romania no. 350 of 13 June 2013.

"*interpretation on points of law*" by Decision no. 8/2010 of the High Court of Cassation and Justice – United Sections, finding its unconstitutionality. Trying to enrol the solution delivered in a typology, we may characterize it as a delimiting decision, as the constitutional court circumstantiates the applicability of the impugned legal text by clarifying both the existing legal framework within the reviewed field, and the effects of the decision which is to be delivered in relation to the actual situation that caused it. We believe that an extreme decision – meaning the simple admission of the exception of unconstitutionality – or a decision strictly interpreting the provisions of Article 414^5 para. (4) of the Code of Criminal Procedure, without reference to the solution delivered by the High Court of Cassation and Justice, would deprive the access to constitutional justice of effectiveness, meaning that it would not respond to the interest which caused the raise of the exception. However, the solution given to the exception of unconstitutionality must be useful firstly to the person who raises the exception[886] and uses it as a defence in the particular case brought before the court. The rigors of the specific constitutional review require the existence of a relationship between the exceptions of unconstitutionality, including in terms of the delivered solution, which should be an advantage for the case. As one may note by reading the practice of the Constitutional Court's decision, the reason which resulted in raising the exception of unconstitutionality was the substantiation of the solution of non-indictment, challenged in the case of Decision no. 8/2010 of the High Court of Cassation and Justice, a decision resulting from an unconstitutional interpretation of the provisions on an appeal on points of law. The ascertainment of the unconstitutionality of "*the interpretation on points of law*" by Decision no. 8/2010 of the High Court of Cassation and Justice, United Sections, determined – as the Constitutional Court has held even in the recitals of its decision – the re-establishment, for the future, of the generally binding effect of Decision no. 62/2007 of the Constitutional Court in the sense that the rules of criminality relating to insult and libel shall apply as from the date of publication of this decision, and the authors of the exception shall benefit from their application in the case in which they raised the exception of unconstitutionality. Without the Constitutional Court's direct reference to the decision of the High Court of Cassation and Justice it would not have been possible to remove the state of unconstitutionality, in the sense

886 See, in this respect, Decision no. 766 of 15 June 2011, published in the Official Gazette of Romania no. 549 of 3 August 2011, which marked an upturn of the case-law of the Constitutional Court, in line with trends under this aspect in other European countries, to abandon the purely formal criteria in order to ensure effective access to constitutional justice (Constitutional Court has noted as examples Germany, Italy, Hungary, the Czech Republic, Poland or France, where, based on regulatory provisions or jurisprudential guidelines jurisprudence, the constitutional courts have considered more important to analyze the substance of the impugned provisions criticized in order to eliminate those which do not meet the constitutional imperatives than setting a purely formal procedural criterion, which would result in the termination of the process).

of re-establishing the effects of Decision no. 62/2007 of the Constitutional Court, the exception of unconstitutionality being thus limited to a sterile theoretical exercise.

5.3.2 *Taking over the case-law of the European courts*[887] *by the courts of law as a consequence of the fact that the constitutional court has taken it into consideration in its own decisions*

The provisions of Articles 20 and 148 of the Constitution confer upon national courts the power to apply with priority the provisions of the international treaties ("*the covenants and treaties on fundamental human rights to which Romania is a party*", respectively "*the founding Treaties of the European Union, as well as other binding regulations under community law*") if the internal laws contain contrary provisions [with the exception provided for in Article 20 (2) final sentence of the Constitution, for ensuring a high protection of the fundamental rights and freedoms].

However, unlike court decisions, producing effects *inter partes litigantes*, the decisions of the Constitutional Court are binding *erga omnes*, according to Article 147 para. (4) of the Constitution. By judicial decisions, the Constitutional Court of Romania established that the compliance with the general binding effect of its decisions does not mean only giving efficiency to their operative part, but also, equally, to the recitals, respectively the interpretation given by the Constitutional Court to the texts of the Constitution, therefore inclusively by reference to the rules of international law and the case-law of European courts, based on the provisions of Articles 20 and 148 of the Constitution.

The influence exercised by the Constitutional Court, from the analyzed perspective, upon national courts has been especially remarked with regard to the case-law of the European Court of Human Rights. It was shown that[888], "*in the decisions of the Constitutional Court for the first time the European Convention on human rights and the ECHR practice were perceived. It is an undeniable reality, that all legal courts should take into account, especially that they are also concerned with the application of the European Convention and the ECHR case-law*". The Romanian constitutional judge assumed his role and authority to ensure the acceptance of the Convention and European court's practice, with effects in the regulation of the issue of fundamental rights and freedoms, as well as in the application of these regulations by national courts. In the practice of the contentious constitutional court there can be identified decisions which, in the interpretation of the constitutional texts on human rights,

---

887 We take account of the European Court of Human Rights and the Court of Justice of the European Union.

888 N. Popa, *The impact of the jurisprudence of the European Court of Human Rights and Constitutional Court of Romania in the practice of legal courts, paper presented at the national Conference on the Jurisprudence of the Constitutional Court of Romania and the European Convention on Human Rights*, Sinaia, 15–16 June 2005, volume of the Conference, pp. 38–44.

give priority to the provisions of the Convention, when they are more favourable, as well as decisions which are based, in the determination of the content of the constitutional concepts, on the provisions of the Convention and the interpretation given to them by the European Court of Human Rights. And if – as it was pointed out – "*the constitutional court states that the European Court's interpretation of the Convention rules, as results from its case-law, is also imposed (...) towards this one,* a fortiori *the case-law of the European court is imposed to the other Romanian public authorities, inclusively to legal courts, from those adjudicating on the substance until the level of the High Court of Cassation and Justice (...)*"[889].

We have mentioned in the previous chapters the reasons indicated in an established case-law, whereby the Court ruled on the obligations undertaken by the courts of law in relation to the provisions of Article 148 of the Constitution. Thus, the Court found[890] that "*such power, namely to establish whether there is a contrariety between national law and the EC Treaty, belongs to the court of law, which, in order to reach a fair and lawful conclusion, ex officio or upon request of the party, may submit a preliminary question in the meaning of Article 234 of the Treaty establishing the European Community before the Court of Justice of the European Communities*". Similarly, the Court also held that [891] "*the attribution of priority application of the binding Community rules binding in relation to the provisions of the national legislation belongs to the court of law. It is a matter of the enforcement of law, not of constitutionality*"[892], and that "*within the relations between the Community and the national law (except the Constitution), we can only refer to priority application of the former in relation to the latter and such matter falls within the competence of the courts of law*".

Having developed the above-mentioned reasons in a series of decisions by which the constitutional review was exercised on a certain regulation on which the ECJ had already formulated an answer to a preliminary question raised by a Romanian court, the Court ruled on the relations of power among the ECJ, national courts and the Constitutional Court, referring to the mechanism of preliminary questions[893].

---

889 C. Bîrsan, *European Convention on Human Eights. Comments on articles, Vol. I Rights and Freedoms,* All Beck Publishing House, Bucharest, 2005, p. 104.

890 Decision no. 1596/2009, published in the Official Gazette of Romania no. 37 of 18 January 2010, or Decision no. 1289/2011, published in the Official Gazette of Romania no. 830 of 23 November 2011.

891 Decision no. 137/2010, published in the Official Gazette of Romania no. 182 of 22 March 2010.

892 In the same regard, for example, the Constitutional Court of Austria; see, for developments, G. Kucsko-Stadlmayer, *Constitutional review in Austria – Traditions and new developments,* communication prepared for the International Conference dedicated to the 20th anniversary of the Constitutional Court of Romania, available on the website of the Constitutional Court of Romania– *www.ccr.ro.*

893 Decision no. 668/2011, published in the Official Gazette of Romania no. 487 of 8 July 2011; Decision no. 1088/2011, published in the Official Gazette of Romania no. 668 of 20 September 2011; Decision no. 921/2011, published in the Official

The preliminary question is seen and promoted as a form of judicial dialogue in order to seek "technical" justification for the settlements delivered by the national judge, without affecting its competence or independence. "The dialogue between judges", at the initiative of the national judge, constitutes, according to the view expressed in the specialized literature, "an indispensable tool" for the European legal system, whose observance is also ensured by the courts of law, pursuant to Article 148 para. (4) of the Constitution[894], and, at the same time, an indispensable tool for the national judge to achieve its duties entrusted to him/her from this perspective[895].

This is all the more as compliance with the obligations set forth in Article 148 of the Constitution by the courts of law also involves the responsibility of the national judge, an aspect which is noted by the Constitutional Court when it had to examine regulations regarding the sanctioning of disciplinary offences of judges and prosecutors[896]. Invoking a series of decisions of the ECJ, the Court held in this respect, that "*Member States cannot defend themselves from liability for infringement of EU law, alleging that the infringement is determined by the way in which the national courts interpret the law, consider the facts or evidence, and this liability cannot remain without effect regarding national judge's responsibility. (...) the constitutional principle on judge's independence involves, necessarily, another principle, that of responsibility. The judge's independence shall not constitute or be construed as a discretionary power thereof or a hindrance to its responsibility under the law, whether this responsibility may be criminal, civil or disciplinary. It is the legislature the one who shall achieve the necessary balance between independence and responsibility of judges, in compliance with the constitutional provisions in the matter and with the obligations undertaken by Romania by the treaties to which it is a party*".

5.4 Conclusions

The dialogue between the Constitutional Court and the courts of law reveals complex situations; those presented above are likely to emphasize some of them. In principle, the different competences and different systems to which the Constitutional Court and the courts of law belong should be a guarantee in itself of the coexistence and achievement of this dialog, so as to ensure the observance of citizens' rights and freedoms, namely the observance of the principle of the rule of law, and only the exceeding of the limits of jurisdiction laid down by the constituent legislature shall determine a "collision" as shown above.

Gazette of Romania no. 673 of 21 September 2011; Decision no. 903 of 30 June 2011, published in the Official Gazette of Romania no. 673 of 21 September 2011.

894 See I. Deleanu, *cited paper*, p. 38.

895 For an analysis of the role of national judge in the process of integration, see I. Maher, *National Courts as European Community Courts*, HeinOnline, 14 Legal Stud. 226, 1994.

896 Decision no. 2/2012, published in the Official Gazette of Romania no. 131 of 23 February 2012.

Presenting, finally, an overview on the relationships and the dialogue between the Constitutional Court and the national courts of law, respectively the European courts, deemed obviously necessary, given the framework in which these relationships are held and developed at the same time with the accession of Romania to the European Union, we can conclude that we are witnessing certain reconsiderations on the dialogue between the Constitutional Court and the public authorities, and in particular with the courts of law.

The cases presented in our paper reveal the Constitutional Court of Romania as a judge which shall apply the fundamental law, EU law and the Convention for the Protection of Human Rights and Fundamental Freedoms. In this triple role, it has the power to ensure a harmonious enforcement and, if possible, conciliatory of at least three legal systems based on common values and benchmarks, but different in their normative content. This is the context in which a general conception to promote mutual respect shall be developed, based on understanding the phenomenon of multiple existing constitutional systems in the European Union, and any conflicts of competence in this context, respectively of the Court of Justice of the European Union, shall be avoided.

6. The dialogue between the Constitutional Court and the Advocate of the People

6.1 General aspects

The relationships of the Advocate of the People with the constitutional court were re-established by the revision of the Constitution in 2003. In the light of this dialogue[897], the involvement of the Advocate of the People in the constitutional review concerns the constitutional review of normative acts, but not the category of powers of the Constitutional Court included in the verification of certain activities, behaviours, attitudes.

6.2 The Advocate of the People in the relationship with the constitutional court

6.2.1 Statistical data

A direct way of the Advocate of the People to access to the constitutional justice is the possibility to challenge it under the circumstances expressly and restrictively provided for by law, as follows:

a) to adjudicate upon the constitutionality of laws, before their promulgation [Article 146 a) first sentence of the Constitution];

897 I. Muraru, *The Advocate..., cited paper*, pp. 121–142.

b) to decide on the exceptions of unconstitutionality of laws and ordinances, where the referral may be raised directly by the Advocate of the People [Article 146 d) second sentence of the Constitution].

This possibility was regulated during the revision of the Constitution of Romania, in 2003, thus granting the Advocate of the People an effective instrument in order to achieve its constitutional role[898]. The constitutional framework is supplemented by the rules of the organic law governing the organization and operation of the Constitutional Court, which contain a number of procedural provisions.

Of course, the effectiveness of this instrument depends also on how it is used, respectively on the activism of the Advocate of the People in relation to the constitutional court. In this respect, one may note that, by the time of writing this study, a number of 51 referrals raised by the Advocate of the People were brought before the Constitutional Court, 20 of them were upheld or partially upheld, as appropriate[899]. If the number of referrals brought before the Constitutional Court is not very significant, given that it has been more than 10 years since this possibility of the Advocate of the People was established, the number of those upheld, reaching half of the referrals, is considerable, given the structure and the overall dynamics of the activity of the Constitutional Court.

One may also find that only three of the raised referrals concern the constitutional review of laws before promulgation, the rest of them being exceptions of unconstitutionality which were directly raised.

Among the raised referrals, a number of 21 aim at the exceptions of unconstitutionality covering Government Ordinances / Government Emergency Ordinances.

6.2.2 The possibility to refer to the Constitutional Court in order to exercise the constitutional review of laws before promulgation

Pre-submission procedure for promulgation of law is regulated by Law no. 47/1992 on the organization and functioning of the Constitutional Court, which shall, by the provisions of Article 15 para. (2) and (3), the following: "*(2) In order to exercise the right to submit a case to the Constitutional Court, the law shall be remitted to the Government, to the High Court of Cassation and Justice, as well as to the Advocate of the People, and it shall be handed in to the Secretary General of the Chamber of Deputies and of the Senate, five days before it is presented for promulgation. If the law has been passed under an emergency procedure, the time limit shall be two days. (3) The date on which the law has been handed in to the Secretaries General of the*

---

898 For the same purpose, Article 514 of the new Code of Civil Procedure has recognised the active procedural capacity of the Advocate of the People to refer to the High Court of Cassation and Justice in order to adjudicate on the legal issues which have been settled differently by the courts of law – see V.M. Ciobanu, *The Advocate of the People, the Superior Council of Magistracy, the Ministry of Justice and the new Code of Civil Procedure,* in RRDP no. 6/2013, pp. 50–64.

899 *www.ccr.ro.*

two Chambers shall be brought to the notice of the plenary of each Chamber within twenty-four hours from its registration. The handing in and the notification shall be made only on the days in which the Chambers of Parliament sit in plenum".

In the same regard, the provisions of Article 133 para. (3)-(5) of the Regulations of the Chamber of Deputies establish that: "*(3) A law adopted by the Chamber of Deputies on which the Senate has pronounced as a first notified Chamber or, as the case may be, as a decisional Chamber for some of the provisions, signed by the President of the Chamber of Deputies and the President of the Senate, shall be communicated to the Government, the High Court of Cassation and Justice, the Advocate of the People, as well as to the Secretary General of the Chamber of Deputies and the Secretary General of the Senate, 5 days before being sent for promulgation, with a view to ensuring exercise of the right to notify the Constitutional Court. If the law is adopted under an emergency procedure, the deadline shall be two days. (4) The date on which the adopted law was handed in to the Secretary General of the Chamber of Deputies shall be passed on to the Deputies, within 24 hours of its submission. (5) After reaching the deadlines stipulated under paragraph (3), the law shall be sent, under the signature of the President of the Chamber of Deputies, to the President of Romania, in view of promulgation*".

With respect to these provisions, an issue raised in the case-law of the Constitutional Court and which concerns the effectiveness of access to constitutional justice of the subjects of the referral who are not directly involved in the drafting/adoption of the law is the limits provided by law and the calculation thereof. It is also the reasons for which we approach it in this context, as the Advocate of the People is such a subject-matter of the referral which is not directly involved in the drafting/adoption of the law.

With respect to the calculation of the time limits on days provided by the cited legal texts, the Constitutional Court ruled upon it, noting that they "*are terms concerning the constitutional relationships between public authorities and, therefore, insofar as it is not otherwise expressly provided, such terms shall not be calculated on days off*"[900]. The Court held that the rule for calculating the terms on days off, covered by the provisions of the civil procedure, is not applicable to public law, "*subject to the rule under which the terms in this field shall be calculated on calendar days, in the sense that such term also includes the day when it starts to run and the day it is met*".

As far as we are concerned, we appreciate[901] that it would be necessary to reconsider the calculation regarding the terms for referring to the Constitutional Court, so that, in order to exercise the right to refer to the Constitutional Court, the terms shall be calculated on days off, in the sense that the term shall not include either the

900 Decision no. 233 of 10 December 1999, published in the Official Gazette of Romania no. 638 of 28 December 1999; Decision no. 89 of 26 January 2010, published in the Official Gazette of Romania no. 115 of 19 February 2010.

901 See the dissenting opinion to Decision no. 89 of 26 January 2010, published in the Official Gazette of Romania no. 115 of 19 February 2010.

day when it starts to run or the day it is met. We take into account the nature of the term, the distinctions between the terms regarding measures limiting the rights and those provided for the use and the exercise of a right, the effectiveness of the right, and the importance of the constitutional relationships between public authorities. The provisions of Article 15 para. (2) of Law no. 47/1992 on the Organization and Operation of the Constitutional Court establish that those terms are provided in order to exercise the right to refer to the Constitutional Court, in the sense that the law shall be handed in to the Secretary General of the Chamber of Deputies and the Senate within 5/2 days before being sent for promulgation. However, the interpretation that they are calculated on full day determines that, at least for the subjects of the referral who are not parliamentary or government ones, meaning that they are not directly involved in the development /adoption of the law, the period of time that they actually have to be too short for the use of this instrument which even the Constitution made it available for them.

6.2.3 The possibility to raise directly the exceptions of unconstitutionality in relation to laws and ordinances

Beyond the obvious imperfection of the constitutional text which uses in an inappropriate way the expression "exception", although an exception is formulated within a process and not directly, we note that the reference constitutional norm confers upon the Advocate of the People a so-called privileged position. We particularly take account of the Emergency Ordinances, a category of normative acts on which only the Advocate of the People may have the possibility to challenge them directly to the Constitutional Court.

The procedural aspects are developed by the provisions of Article 32 and 33 of Law No. 47/1992, which properly relate to the provisions of Articles 29–31 of the same law, texts governing the notification of the Constitutional Court by the courts of law or by the court of commercial arbitration.

Thus, the exception is not raised before the court of law, but directly by the Advocate of the People. Its subject-matter may be a law or ordinance in force / any provision thereof. The referral addressed to the Constitutional Court must be motivated. On receiving the referral, the President of the Constitutional Court shall designate the Judge-Rapporteur and also notify the Presidents of the two Chambers of Parliament, the Government and the Advocate of the People, of the interlocutory order by which the Constitutional Court was apprised, indicating the date by which they can submit their viewpoint. The Judge designated as rapporteur, according to Article 30 para. (1), shall be bound to take the necessary measures for evidence to be given by the date of judgment. Judgment shall take place at the date established, on the basis of the deeds of the case, with due summoning of the parties and of the Public Ministry. The prosecutor's attendance to the proceedings is mandatory.

6.2.4 *The possibility to express viewpoints in the cases brought before the Constitutional Court*

Both within the constitutional review of laws before promulgation, and within the settlement of the exceptions of unconstitutionality of laws and ordinances, the Constitutional Court must require the viewpoint of the Advocate of the People [Article 16 para. (2) and (3), respectively Article 30 para. (1) of Law no. 47/1992].

It is worth noting that the intervention of the Advocate of the People, in this respect, within the constitutional review, was legally enshrined prior the revision of the Constitution, namely in 2002, when its law of organization and functioning was amended by inserting the obligation of the Constitutional Court to require the viewpoint of the Advocate of the People "*in case of referrals regarding the exception of unconstitutionality of laws and ordinances concerning human rights and freedoms*". Currently, the law does not distinguish anymore, so that the obligation of the Constitutional Court subsists regardless of the subject-matter of the exception of unconstitutionality. We consider that even a waiver of the above-mentioned distinction constitutes an expression of strengthening the role of the Advocate of the People, positioned in this regard with the authorities which have direct competence in the development/adoption of normative acts.

6.2.5 *Communication of the decisions delivered by the Constitutional Court, under the conditions provided for by law*

The decisions whereby the Constitutional Court adjudicates upon the referrals raised by the Advocate of the People shall be communicated to the author of the referral. Article 58 para. (2) and (3) of the Regulations on the organization and functioning of the Constitutional Court establishes in this respect that: "*(2) In case of unconstitutionality ascertained pursuant to Article 31 of Law no. 47/1992, republished, the decision of the Court shall be communicated to the two Chambers of Parliament, to the Government, as well as to the concerned public authorities. (3) Decisions rendered in constitutional review proceedings provided by Article 146 d) of the Constitution, republished, shall be communicated to the referring court or to the Advocate of the People, as the case may be*".

6.3 The relationship between the Constitutional Court and the Advocate of the People

6.3.1 *The constitutional review of the Parliament's resolutions in relation to the appointment of the Advocate of the People or for the purpose of ensuring the interim office*

The legal requirements on the appointment of the Advocate of the People, respectively to ensure the interim office, were discussed within the constitutional review of the Resolution no. 75/2013 by which Parliament took note of the resolution of the permanent joint Bureaux of the Chambers of Deputies and Senate on the ascertainment of the resignation of the person who held at that moment the office of the Advocate of the People and ordered, by Article 2 of the same resolution, that one of the deputies of the Advocate of the People accomplish the powers of the Advocate of the People, until the appointment of a new Advocate of the People. The authors challenged the constitutionality of the Parliament's Resolution no. 75/2013 on the grounds of two main reasons: on the one hand, Parliament did not have the competence to transfer the powers of the Advocate of People to another person and this action could have been taken solely by the Advocate of People itself, for a determined period of time and, on the other hand, the person appointed by Parliament to exercise the powers of the Advocate of People, until a new Advocate of People would be appointed, does not meet the appointment requirements imposed by Article 6 para. (2) of Law no. 35/1997, in conjunction with Article 143 of the Constitution.

As concerns the first challenge, the Court found that, under Article 65 para. (2) i) of the Constitution and Article 6 para. (1) of Law no. 35/1997, the Advocate of People shall be appointed by Parliament, in the joint session of the Chamber of Deputies and Senators. In case of temporary impossibility to exercise the position of Advocate of People, his powers will be accomplished by his deputies, according to Articles 10 para. (3) and 12^1 e) of Law no. 35/1997, in the order laid down by him. The hypothesis of permanent impossibility to exercise the position is not regulated by any constitutional or legal rule. In relation to the allegations of the authors of the referral in the sense that, in order to meet the requirements of Article 1 para. (3) and (5) of the Constitution, on the rule of law and binding nature to comply with the law, Parliament should have firstly supplemented Law no. 35/1997 with a text which could have also allowed it to cover the situation occurred in this case, the noted that this option would have been possible and desirable at the same time, "but the adoption of a supplementing law for Law no. 35/1997, which requires the binding reading of a certain legislative procedure, including the drafting of a bill, its debate and adoption by the two Chambers of Parliament, would have supposed a significant period of time in which the legal operation of the institution of Advocate of People would have been affected". By the challenged Resolution, Parliament ordered that the powers of the Advocated of People be temporarily exercised by another person, until the appointment of a new Advocate of People, a solution designated to maintain the institution of the Advocate of People as operative, "*institution which is absolutely necessary for the constitutional democracy, having a significant role for the guarantee of the fundamental rights and freedoms of individuals*". The Court stated that it is "*a logical consequence of the constitutional provisions since the Basic Law has allowed it the competence to appoint the Advocate of People, as it implicitly may regulate the interim of the position, by the implementation of the interpreting rule qui potest plus, potest minus. Therefore, if it has the competence and the obligation at the same time to appoint a person as Advocate of People, it may be claimed even more that Parliament is fully entitled to appoint a person to accomplish, for a definite period of time, the power of that position, until the appointment of a new holder, in terms of Article 65 para. (2) i) of the Constitution*".

In this respect, the Court noted the lacks of the infra-constitutional normative framework on the assurance of the continuity of the institution of the Advocate of People if the term of office of the person appointed by Parliament to accomplish this position terminates until the due time according to Article 9 para. (1) of Law no. 35/1997.

As for the second challenge of unconstitutionality, which directly brought into question the appointment, namely the assurance of the interim office of the Advocate of the People, the Court held that, according to Article 11 para. (1^6) of Law no. 35/1997, graduates of faculties of legal field, as well as of other fields, may be appointed as deputy of the Advocate of People. Likewise, Article 7 of the Regulations on the organization and functioning of the institution of Advocate of People, approved by the Resolution no. 5/2002 of the Standing Bureau of Senate, republished in the Official Gazette of Romania, Part I, no. 758 of 27 October 2011, as subsequently amended, provides the conditions for the appointment of deputy of the Advocate of People. Thus, as concerns the studies, he must have a degree in a faculty of legal sciences, administrative sciences, political sciences or economic sciences and at least eight-years of experience in the graduated specialization. Considering that for the appointment as deputy of the Advocate of People there are not provided the same conditions with those laid down for the appointment as Advocate of People, the Court argued that "*Parliament had not had any constitutional or legal obligation to exclusively appoint a person to meet these conditions. All the more so as in an objective way, it is possible that none of the deputies of the Advocate of People may meet them, and, if the reasoning of the authors of the referral was followed, it would be impossible to ensure the interim of the position and the activity of an institution provided by the Basic Law would be obstructed in this way*". The Court also noted that, according to Article 10 para (3) of Law no. 35/1997, in case of temporary impossibility of exercising the position, the Advocate of People establishes the order in which the deputies will accomplish his powers; "*since the law allows the hypothesis that the Advocate of People, himself/herself, transfers the exercise of the powers to a deputy who has not graduated the Law School, consequently, Parliament cannot be denied such a right*". Thus, the deputies of the Advocate of People are appointed, according to Article 11(1) first sentence of the same law, by the Standing Bureaus of the Chamber of Deputies and Senate, at the Advocate of People's proposal, having the opinion of the legal committees of the two Chambers of Parliament.

Even if the recitals contained in the Constitutional Court's decision did not lead to a solution finding the unconstitutionality of the impugned resolution of Parliament, they constitute an invitation to the legislature, within their dialogue, to reconsider the legal framework of the Advocate of the People, as an institution, in terms of supplementing the lacks of the challenged regulations.

6.3.2 *The constitutional review of the Parliament's resolutions in relation to the revocation of the Advocate of the People from office*

This issue was examined by the Constitutional Court when settling the referral of unconstitutionality raised in relation to Parliament Resolution no. 32 of 3 July 2012 for the revocation from office of the Advocate of the People. As grounds for the referral, it was essentially argued that, according to Article 58 para. (1) of the Constitution, the Advocate of the People is appointed for a five-year constitutional term of office which cannot be interrupted except for the existence of certain concrete violations of the Constitution and the law, violations that have not been proven in the case, and therefore, the revocation is unconstitutional.

Having rejected as inadmissible the referral, the Court held that the Advocate of the People is responsible before Parliament and its activity is subject to parliamentary control. Consequently, Parliament is the sole authority capable to decide whether the activity conducted by the Advocate of the People, in his capacity as head of the institution, was performed within the limits set forth by the Constitution and law or, on the contrary, in breach of them and, accordingly, through an objective assessment within the exclusively parliamentary methods and procedures, he may order the legal measures. To decide otherwise would mean to recognize the Constitutional Court's possibility to replace Parliament, to invalidate the assessments made by it and to replace them with the Court's own assessments, which would obviously exceed the powers of the constitutional court[902].

However, we believe that, as far as the revocation resolution of Parliament violates the principle of legality enshrined in Article 1 para. (5) of the Constitution (in terms of the developments in the case-law of the Constitutional Court delivered within the constitutional review of those resolutions), the Constitutional Court may ascertain its unconstitutionality, without noting any substitution for the purposes indicated above. Thus, to the extent that the challenge of unconstitutionality is not formal, by reference to the provisions of Article 1 para. (5) of the Constitution concerning the obligation to comply with the laws, but it is clearly substantiated by reference to a law governing an objective requirement, the case of inadmissibility identified by the Constitutional Court in the precedent does not subsist. "Accepting this contrary thesis, with the consequence of exclusion from the exercise of constitutional review of the Resolution of the Romanian Parliament delivered in breach of the express provisions of the law would result in placing the supreme representative body of the Romanian people – Parliament – above the law, and accepting the idea that the very authority which is legally constitutional to adopt laws can violate them without being sanctioned in any way. Or, in a rule of law, no

902 Decision no. 732 of 10 July 2012, published in the Official Gazette of Romania no. 480 of 12 July 2012.

one is above the law"[903]. Of course that an issue in this respect would be the lack or the insufficient regulation of such objective requirements that would determine Parliament to exercise on a discretionary basis its appreciation on the revocation of the Advocate of the People.

We note in this respect that in 2014, on the occasion of the revision of the Constitution, point 44 of the Sole Article of the legislative proposal for the revision of the Constitution inserts a new paragraph under Article 58, paragraph (1^1), which reads as follows: "*The Advocate of the People shall be appointed for a term of office of 5 years. The deputies of the Advocate of the People are specialized per fields of activity. The term of office of the Advocate of the People shall cease before its expiry in case of resignation, incompatibility with other public or private offices, impossibility to exercise his powers for more than 90 days or in case of death*".

The Court noted that[904] the proposed revision brings to constitutional level the regulation of cases of early termination of the mandate of the Advocate of the People, currently enshrined in Article 9 (1) of Law no. 35/1997 on the organisation and functioning of the institution of Advocate of the People (resignation, removal from office, incompatibility with other public/private functions, the inability to perform duties for more than 90 days, established by medical examination, and death). The Court noted that the proposed constitutional amendments rules out the possibility of revocation from office of the Advocate of the People, maintaining all other situations. Although the proposed text is without prejudice to the limits of the constitutional revision, the Court considers that the cases of early termination of the mandate of the Advocate of the People should be listed in the organic law on the organisation and functioning of the institution, not in the Basic Law. At the same time, the Court also held that revocation should be amongst the cases of early termination of the mandate of the Advocate of the People; "*at least in theory, it cannot be ruled out that the person appointed as Advocate of the People can abuse of the powers which are conferred on him by the Constitution and the law, or divert them from their legal purpose or fail to fulfil them properly, infringing thus the constitutional values and principles*". The abolition of the possibility of Parliament to remove from office the person who, in the performance of his duties as Advocate of the People, is found to have acted in breach of the Constitution and of the law, "*would be unacceptable and incompatible with the fundamental values of the Romanian State laid down in Article 1 para. (3) of the Basic Law*". Of course, the situation in which the revocation may occur must be individualised precisely in the law and the procedure to be followed in that case should also be established by rules lacking any ambiguity so as to avoid the risk of an arbitrary revocation. Consequently, the Constitutional Court recommended regulating the cases of early termination of the mandate of

903 Decision no. 251 of 30 April 2014, published in the Official Gazette of Romania no. 376 of 21 May 2014.

904 Decision no. 80 of 16 February 2014, published in the Official Gazette of Romania no. 246 of 7 April 2014.

the Advocate of the People by the law on the organisation and functioning of the institution, including among them also the case of revocation.

We believe that, in accordance with the Constitutional Court's decision mentioned above, the remedy against any possible discretionary behaviour of Parliament in its relationships with the Advocate of the People is not the elimination of the possibility to revoke the latter, but the rigorous regulation regarding the revocation cases, i.e. the existence of certain guarantees which are susceptible to protect the institutional stability and, ultimately, even its independence.

6.3.3 *Statuaries of the Constitutional Court on the role and statute of the Advocate of the People*

The proposal for the revision of the constitutional framework of reference

Point 43 of the Sole Article of the legislative proposal for the revision of the Constitution amended Article 58 para. (1), as follows: "*The Advocate of the People is an independent institution whose purpose is to promote and protect the rights and freedoms of citizens in their relations with public authorities*".

The Court found that the proposed wording of Article 58 para. (1) is unconstitutional in limiting the powers of the Advocate of People to the protection of "*the rights and freedoms of citizens in their relations with public authorities*".

Underlining the fundamental role exercised by the Advocate of the People on the protection of the human rights and freedoms, the Court also invoked the Venice Commission's Opinion no. 685 of 17 December 2012 on the compatibility with constitutional principles and the rule of law of actions taken by the Government of Romania and the Parliament of Romania in respect of other State institutions and on the Government Emergency Ordinance amending Law no. 47/1992 on the Organisation and Operation of the Constitutional Court and on the Government Emergency Ordinance amending and supplementing Law no. 3/2000 on the organisation and holding of a referendum in Romania, adopted at its 93rd Plenary Session, Venice, 14-15 December 2012, which states that "the Advocate of the People performs an essential role for the protection of human rights" (para. 80).

Noting that the scope of subjects of law who can benefit from the protection offered by the Advocate of the People is envisaged, in the above-mentioned document, in a much broader perspective than in the exhaustive formula referring exclusively to "*citizens*", proposed by the authors of the legislative proposal for the revision of the Constitution, the Court held that "*the proposed wording represents a step backwards with respect to the current constitutional rules regarding the protection of the rights and freedoms through the Advocate of the People, which should cover all natural persons who are on Romanian territory, in the spirit of the Universal Declaration of Human Rights and other international covenants and treaties that put the safety of the individual at the centre of attention and consider it essential that human rights should be guaranteed, but also protected by effective legal and institutional mechanisms*".

In this respect, moreover, the Court noted that Article 18 para. (1) of the Constitution provides that aliens and stateless persons who are resident in Romania shall enjoy general protection of person and wealth as guaranteed by the Constitution and other laws. However, the proposed revision excludes aliens and stateless persons from the scope of action of the Advocate of the People, as an institution designed to ensure effective protection of human rights and fundamental freedoms. Even if the proposed text would be interpreted under the *principle ubi lex non distinguit, nec nos distinguere debemus* in the sense that it refers not only to Romanian citizens but also to foreign ones, a category of individuals would still remain outside the protective action of the Advocate of the People where there is nothing to justify a discriminatory treatment, namely the stateless persons.

As a result of this limitation of the scope of powers of the Advocate of the People, its competence is reduced and its role within a democratic and social State governed by the rule of law can no longer be carried out fully. For these reasons, the Court found the unconstitutionality of replacing the term "individual" with the term "citizens" in Article 58 para. (1) of the Constitution as it violates the revision limits set forth in Article 152 para. (2) of the Constitution.

Furthermore, the Court held that, currently, one of the ways in which the Basic Law gives the Advocate of the People the possibility to fulfil the role enshrined at constitutional level is contained in Article 146 (d) second sentence and consists of its competence to raise directly exceptions of unconstitutionality. The entry which is proposed to be introduced in Article 58 para. (1) of the Constitution, on promoting and protecting "citizens" rights and freedoms only "*in their relations with public authorities*", is capable of calling into question the possibility of effective and efficient exercise by the Advocate of the People of that right, since there are also laws and simple or emergency Government Ordinances that do not concern citizens' relations with public authorities. A possible restriction of the right of the Advocate of the People to challenge the constitutionality of such legislation by means of the exception of unconstitutionality would be antinomy to Article 146 (d) of the Constitution, which states that the Advocate of the People has the specific power to refer to the Constitutional Court on laws and Government Ordinances, without making any distinction according to whether or not their regulatory object contain provisions that relate to the protection of human rights. In order to strengthen these reasons, that continues the case-law by which it stated the lack of a restriction of the Advocate of the People as regards the exceptions of unconstitutionality raised directly, the Court also invoked the Venice Commission Opinion cited above, according to which

"*If the Advocate of the People were not able to appeal to the Constitutional Court against government emergency ordinances in all cases – not only in human rights cases –, a serious gap in the necessary control of such ordinances would occur. No other state body than the Advocate of the People can directly appeal against such ordinances to the Constitutional Court and, consequently, all emergency ordinances, which do not relate to human rights, could not be controlled at all" (paragraph 55).* Furthermore, referring to the hypothesis that the Advocate of the People would be deprived of the possibility to challenge the constitutionality of government emergency ordinances directly, independently of the existence of court proceedings, the Venice Commission found that "*Such a serious lacuna in the system of democratic checks and balances cannot be justified by the purported urgency of the measures adopted*" (paragraph 55).

The Court also extended this reasoning to laws, noting that "*It is true that they can be subject to constitutional review before promulgation thereof, pursuant to Article 146 (a) first sentence of the Constitution, upon notification from certain subjects of law, expressly set out in the text of the Constitution, including the Advocate of the People. But, once in force, laws and ordinances can be subject to constitutional review only during their application in a trial before a court of law or of commercial arbitration, upon request of the parties, the public prosecutor or the court of its own motion. However, it is possible that none of those listed take the initiative to raise an exception of unconstitutionality, and therefore unconstitutional legislation would continue to be enforceable, which would be in contradiction with the principle of the rule of law as a fundamental feature of the Romanian State and as a precondition for enshrining, guaranteeing, maintaining and protecting fundamental rights and freedoms*".

For these reasons, the Court held that restriction of the scope of action of the Advocate of the People exclusively to citizens' relations with public authorities affect its role in the protection of human rights against any infringements which may originate from any type of entity. Such a restriction represents, in some cases, a lack of one of the guarantees of fundamental rights and freedoms, contrary to Article 152 para. (2) of the Constitution. For these reasons, by majority vote, the Court finds unconstitutional the supplementation of Article 58 para. (1) of the Constitution with the phrase "in their relations with public authorities" as it violates the revision limits set forth in Article 152 para. (2) of the Constitution[905].

The subject-matter *of the exceptions of unconstitutionality raised directly by the Advocate of the People*

Required to adjudicate upon the claim according to which "from the systematic interpretation of the legal texts governing the role and powers of the Advocate of the People, as well as of the constitutional provisions governing the scope of the subject of law who may refer to the Constitutional Court an exception of unconstitutionality, it results that the Advocate of the People has the power to determine the constitutional review by referring to the Constitutional Court only in terms of the protection of the individuals' rights and freedoms"[906], the Court held that "Article 146 of the Constitution does not condition, in the way indicated by the Government, the cases in which the Advocate of the People is entitled to bring before the Constitutional Court referrals, respectively exceptions of unconstitutionality". Moreover, in this respect, this is an established case-law[907].

---

905 Decision no. 80 of 16 February 2014, published in the Official Gazette of Romania no. 246 of 7 April 2014.

906 By Decision no. 1133 of 27 November 2007, published in the Official Gazette of Romania no. 851 of 12 December 2007.

907 See: Decision no. 544 of 28 June 2006, published in the Official Gazette of Romania no. 568 of 30 June 2006; Decision no. 567 of 11 July 2006, published in the Official

Being notified again with the same issue, by way of an exception of unconstitutionality raised directly by the Advocate of the People, regarding the provisions Article 13 para. (1) f) of Law no. 35/1997 on the organization and functioning of the Advocate of the People, as an institution[908], challenged on the ground that they violate Article 58 of the Constitution "*to the extent that they are interpreted in the sense that the Advocate of the People may notify the Constitutional Court with objections or exceptions of unconstitutionality in cases other than those relating to the individuals' rights and freedoms*", the Court rejected as inadmissible the exception of unconstitutionality[909].

On this occasion, the Court has distinguished between the possibility provided by the constitutional text and the appreciation achieved by the Advocate of the People when notifying the Constitutional Court. The Court held that Article 146 d) second sentence of the Constitution has been interpreted in its case-law, in the sense that the Advocate of the People is not restricted to notify the Constitutional Court by way of the exception of unconstitutionality only on aspects regarding the fundamental rights and freedoms; consequently, since the constitutional text has not been reviewed, such an interpretation of the Constitutional Court cannot be called into question. Any jurisprudential upturn requires the existence of certain new elements likely to cause the amendment of the case-law of the constitutional court. However, in the present case, the Advocate of the People has not brought such elements. As a result, according to the established case-law of the Constitutional Court, the Advocate of the People may cause the constitutional review by way of the exception of unconstitutionality regardless of the matters covered by it, but "*the direct raise of the exception of unconstitutional is and remains at the sole discretion of the Advocate of the People, as he cannot be obliged or prevented by any public authority to raise such an exception*". Accordingly, the Court found that "the Advocate of the People has exclusivity in deciding whether it raises an exception of unconstitutionality, being a part of its institutional and functional independence,

---

Gazette of Romania no. 613 of 14 July 2006; Decision no. 392 of 17 April 2007, published in the Official Gazette of Romania no. 325 of 15 May 2007; Decision no. 742 of 24 June 2008, published in the Official Gazette of Romania no. 570 of 29 July 2008; Decision no. 365 of 17 March 2009, published in the Official Gazette of Romania no. 237 of 9 April 2009; Decision no. 1555 of 17 November 2009, published in the Official Gazette of Romania no. 916 of 28 December 2009; Decision no. 1105 of 21 September 2010, published in the Official Gazette of Romania no. 684 of 8 October 2010.

908 Article 13 para. (1) f) of Law no. 35/1997 on the organisation and functioning of the Advocate of the People, as an institution, republished in the Official Gazette of Romania no. 844 of 15 September 2004, shall read as follows: "*(1) The Advocate of the People shall have the following duties: (...) f) may directly refer to the Constitutional Court, except for the exceptions of unconstitutionality of laws and ordinances*".

909 Decision no. 336 of 24 September 2013, published in the Official Gazette of Romania no. 684 of 7 November 2013.

so that the Advocate of the People has no interest in raising such exceptions of unconstitutionality, since, by its very way of action, it can comply with the meaning provided by the constitutional text"[910].

The possibility to refer to the court of administrative contentious by the Advocate of the People

The Court ruled on this competence covered by the provisions of Law no. 554/2004 on administrative contentious, challenged by way of the objection of unconstitutionality raised even by the Advocate of the People. Among other challenged provisions, there were also challenged those of Article 1 para. (3) of the Law on Administrative Contentious, as follows: "*The Advocate of the People, following the control exercised by it, according to its organic law, based on an individual's referral, if it considers that the illegality of the act or the excess of power of the administrative authority can be removed only through justice, can notify the competent court of administrative contentious falling within the applicant's residence. The applicant acquires by law the capacity of plaintiff and he/she is to be summoned as such*". According to the viewpoint of the author of the referral, this provision is contrary to Article 21 para. (1) of the Constitution, which enshrines the principle of free access to justice, in that the Advocate of the People is included among the subjects who may refer to the court of administrative contentious with a case formulated in the name of an individual. However, in the same opinion, free access to justice means the right, and not the obligation, of any person whose rights, freedoms and legitimate interests have been violated to go to court in an administrative case.

Having examined these challenges, the Court held that the Advocate of the People has the possibility to refer to the court of administrative contentious, according to circumstances, when, following the control of the referral formulated by an individual, it considers that the illegality of the act or the excess of power of the

910 The doctrine expressed the opinion according to which, although a) and d) of Article 146 make no difference, the Advocate of the People cannot determine the constitutionality review of laws or ordinances on any ground as the constitutional texts should be interpreted systematically. Therefore, those provisions concerning the quality of the Advocate of the People as the person entitled to refer to the constitutional justice must be read and interpreted according to the principle of specialization, the constitutional role of the Advocate of the People, set forth in Article 58 para. (1), namely the protection and freedoms of individuals. The Advocate of the People has the constitutional legitimacy to determine the constitutional review only if it is for the protection of the rights and freedoms of individuals, so if the law or ordinance impugned as unconstitutional infringes the rights and freedoms of individuals. A referral to the Advocate of the People, which is not motivated by the protection of the rights and freedoms of individuals, exceeds its jurisdiction, so it is inadmissible and must be rejected as such – C.-L. Popescu, *The Advocate of the People as the persons entitled to refer to the Constitutional Court according to the revised Constitution*, in Dreptul no. 6/2004, pp. 54–68; In the same regard, see V.M. Ciobanu, The Advocate of the People..., *cited paper*, pp. 50–64.

administrative authority can be removed only by justice. In terms of the provisions of Article 2 para. (1)[911] b) of the Law on Administrative Contentious, the notion "*public authority*" means "*any State body or any body of the administrative-territorial units which act, as a public power, to accomplish the public interest; under this law, the private legal persons are treated as public authorities which, according to the law, have obtained the status of public utility or are authorized to provide a public service*", and according to letter m) of the same Article, "*the excess of power*" *means* "*the exercise of the discretion power belonging to public administrative authorities, in violation of the citizens' fundamental rights and freedoms provided by the Constitution or by law*". The public interest which is to be accomplished by the public authority, according to Article 2 para. (1) l) of the Law, represents "*the interest aiming at the rule of law and the constitutional democracy, the guarantee of the citizens' fundamental rights, freedoms and duties, the accomplishment of the community needs, the accomplishment of the competence of public authorities*". Therefore, establishing the power of the Advocate of the People regarding the possibility to refer to the court of administrative contentious under the terms set forth in Article 1 para. (3) of the law subject to constitutional review provides both the protection of the public interest and the observance of private interest of the individual whose rights, freedoms and legitimate interests have been prejudiced, without infringing Article 21 para. (1) of the Constitution. This is because granting such power to the Advocate of the People, as well as to other authorities – prefect, the Public Ministry, the National Agency of Civil Servants – set forth in Article 1 para. (4) and (8) of the Law, to which, however, this objection of unconstitutionality does not refer, does not either exclude or limit the right of a prejudiced person to his right or to his legitimate interest by a public authority to go to court. Furthermore, according to Article 1 of the Law, entitled "Litigation Cases", the first litigation case provided by paragraph (1) is the person. Thus, according to this Article of the Law: "*Any person that deems him/herself aggrieved in a legitimate right or interest by a public authority, through administrative action, or as a consequence of such authority's failure to resolve such person's application within the timeframe provided by law may address to the competent court of administrative contentious with a request for the rescinding of the alleged action, or the recognition of the claimed right or of the legitimate interest, and for the reparation of the damage sustained as a consequence thereof. The legitimate interest may be both private and public*"[912]. That being so, the Court cannot note that the impugned legal provision violates the free access to justice set forth in Article 21 of the Constitution.

Similarly, in relation to the claim contained in the objection of unconstitutionality according to which the Advocate of the People replaces the aggrieved individual in his own right, by exercising its power to refer to the court of administrative contentious, the Court found that it cannot be accepted. Exercising the power

911 Article 2 para. (1) was amended by Article I section 3 of Law no. 262/2007.

912 Currently, this text has received another name, respectively "Subjects of referral of the court".

provided by the impugned legal text, the Advocate of the People does not replace the procedural rights of a citizen, but it supports him/her, including by referring to the court of administrative contentious, as it is the only one who decides whether to continue or not the proceedings against the abusive administrative authority. Thus, the applicant who, under the law, has acquired the capacity of plaintiff may state, under the rules of common law, before the court, at the first hearing, to what extent he/she endorses the action brought by the Advocate of the People, as he/she may waive the application or leave it inactive, during the trial. This procedure has its counterpart in the principle of availability and, consequently, it is in line with the principle enshrined in Article 21 para. (1) of the Constitution regarding the free access to justice.

The author of the referral has also claimed that the provisions of Article 1 para. (3) of the Law, which confers upon the Advocate of the People the possibility to refer to the court of administrative contentious, "are tantamount to an extension of the right of petition in the scope of free access to justice". Having examined this claim, the Court finds that exercising the right of petition provided by Article 51 of the Constitution is an effective method to settle certain personal issues and it can be achieved either individually by a citizen or by a group of citizens or by legally established organizations. Under this constitutional right, the aggrieved persons may address to the Advocate of the People, as an institution, with applications regarding the infringement of the citizens' rights or freedoms by public authorities. Pursuant to Article 59 of the Constitution, exercising its powers under Law no. 35/1997 on the organization and functioning of the Advocate of the People, it seeks the legal settlement of the applications received and it requests the authorities or the civil servants of the public authority concerned not to violate anymore the citizens' rights and freedoms, to reinstate the applicant and to repair the damage, according to the possibilities laid down by the same law. Therefore, the citizen addresses to the Advocate of the People by virtue of his right of petition, whereas the latter is conferred by the Law on Administrative Contentious the possibility to support citizens also by way of action before the court, according to circumstances, under the law, without thereby the impugned provisions to be tantamount "to an extension of the right of petition in the scope of the free access to justice".

As concerns the allegation that the individual's possibility to go to court turns into an obligation which means a violation of its freedom to choose the legal way of using its right, infringing the provisions of Article 52 of the Constitution regarding "Right of a person aggrieved by a public authority", the Court found that the establishment of such powers for a public authority constitutes a guarantee for the protection of the public interest and ensures its observance, under the limits and the terms provided by law.

As for the allegation according to which "*The Advocate of the People should be vested with an excessive power and, moreover, an inconsistent one, namely to bring a case before the court of administrative contentious, on behalf of a person deemed him/herself aggrieved in his rights or legitimate interests*", as well as for certain considerations regarding the appropriateness or relevance of the legal texts in question, the Court found that these issues fall within the exclusive competence of Parliament[913].

As in the previous case, we note that the Advocate of the People tends to have a restrictive approach in relation to its competence and solution, respectively the recitals contained in the Constitutional Court's decision to approach this competence in a plenary manner, interpreted under the constitutional texts of reference. This is in consideration of the role set up by the constituent legislature for the Advocate of the People, as an institution, to which the Court has extensively referred during the initiative for the revision of the Constitution in 2014, as shown below.

6.4 Conclusions

Beyond the constitutional and legal framework that maintain the dialogue between the Constitutional Court and the Advocate of the People, the involvement of the Advocate of the People within the constitutional review is obvious, as it is the role of the Constitutional Court in strengthening the role of this authority and the position that it actually should have among the authorities of the rule of law, as a protector of human rights and freedoms.

Meanwhile, both the Constitutional Court and the international bodies, such as the Venice Commission, support the active involvement of the Advocate of the People in this dialogue, being underlined the key role conferred by the constituent legislature through regulating the possibility of direct referral to the Constitutional Court, particularly regarding the Government Emergency Ordinances.

7. The dialogue of the Constitutional Court with/by the mass media

7.1 General considerations

The Constitution of Romania governs, in accordance with the international legal instruments in the field, any person's right to have access to any piece of information of public interest, as well as the correlative obligation of public authorities, according to their competence, to ensure correct information to citizens on public affairs and matters of personal interest[914]. Developing these constitutional provisions, Law no. 544/2001 **regarding the free access to information of public interest**[915] defines the concept of information of public interest as "*any piece of information that*

---

913 Decision no. 507 of 17 November 2004 on the referral of unconstitutionality of the provisions of Article 1 para. (3), Article 7 para. (5), Article 11 para. (3), Article 13 para. (2) and Article 28 para. (2) of Law on administrative contentious, published in the Official Gazette of Romania no. 1154 of 7 December 2004.

914 Article 31 of the Constitution – *Right to information.*

915 Published in the Official Gazette of Romania no. 663 of 23 October 2001.

regards the activities or results from the activities of the public authority or institution, no matter the prop or form or the way of expressing the information".

The constitutional text of reference also provides the obligation of media to ensure correct information to public opinion.

Therefore, it can be claimed that the relations and the dialogue between the Constitutional Court and mass-media are governed by the constitutional obligation to provide for all citizens access to information of public interest which are related to the activity of the Constitutional Court, taking into account, on the one hand, the importance of its activity, and, on the other hand, the position and the role held by media[916] in a democratic society.

Thus, the activity of the Constitutional Court, as authority which ensures the supremacy of the Constitution, is deemed to be known by all public authorities, as by any citizen. Equally, it is necessary to know its powers, the manner in which the access to the constitutional jurisdiction is achieved, as well as the decisions of the Constitutional Court. Given that such decisions are published in the Official Gazette of Romania and are generally binding[917], they affect the entire normative system.

By specific means of transmitting information, media ensures faster knowledge and by a wide range of people of the mentioned issues, thus serving the public interest, respectively the Constitutional Court's activity as a whole.

From this perspective, the correct, objective, impartial information to the public on the activity of the Constitutional Court is essential, therefore, the compliance by the mass media with the constitutional and legal obligations. A clear, accurate and on time information to the public can constitute an element in order to strengthen the constitutional justice and the rule of law. In this way, misinterpretations, various unsubstantiated speculations regarding the Court and even educating the public, for the purposes of a correct understanding of the role and the position of constitutional justice in the rule of law can be avoided. On the contrary, incorrect and biased information, promoting views that are contrary to the values of democracy, can represent a real risk, being excluded by definition from the instruments aiming at developing and maintaining freedom of opinion in a rule of law[918].

In what follows, we will make a short presentation of the communication development of the Constitutional Court of Romania, especially through the media, in order to underline the achievements in this field during the lifetime of the Court, the issues encountered, the aspects that have been or remained susceptible to be improved, all giving shape to what we called the dialogue of the Constitutional Court within and by the media.

---

916 All means of mass communication (radio, television, press).

917 See the provisions of Article 147 of the Constitution of Romania.

918 For development, see also A. Koltay, *Hungary's new media regulations and the Constitutional Court*, electronically available on *http://ssrn.com/abstract.*

7.2 Organisation of the Constitutional Court of Romania in matters of communication with/by the mass-media

7.2.1 Communication ways

7.2.1.1 Website

The development of the media in institutions must take account of the general developments in the society and technology field. The position held at the moment by the Internet as a means of communication also leaves its mark on communication through mass media. Even if the print media did not quite give in to the electronic one, the latter dominates as a source of information[919].

Adapting to this reality, a website of the Constitutional Court – *www.ccr.ro*[920]– has been created since 1999. In 2002, a database was added, having a search engine for the acts delivered in the case of the Constitutional Court – decisions, rulings, advisory opinions. During 2013, the website acquired a new interface, more dynamic and filled with new entries in order to ensure access to a wider range of information.

Thus, on the website of the Constitutional Court, one can access information relating to legislation governing the organization and functioning of the Court, its composition and structure, the hearings (the lists of public session), decisions, rulings, advisory opinions delivered by the Court, publications and statistics, external relations, the list of public information, press statements. Information that is not of public interest remains exclusively internal, as well as the other aspects regarding the procedures of the Constitutional Court, such as, for example, the assignment of cases, the Judge-Rapporteur appointed to cases.

We shall mention the *FAQs*, where one can find a number of answers to questions concerning the activity of the Court and access information on the acts upon which it shall rule.

On the website of the Court, the decisions/rulings of the Constitutional Court are posted as soon as they are drafted, by which the Court upheld referrals of unconstitutionality, as well as those giving rise to a particular public interest.

It was implemented a program that provides parties, through the website, access to the files registered with the Constitutional Court. Even if this aspect does not relate to communication by media, it is worth mentioning as a way that facilitates parties their access to files, reducing costs related to any travel at the headquarters of the Court in order to study the files or photocopy them.

---

919 For considerations, including the aspects referring to regulations, see E. Barendt, *Freedom of expression*, in The Oxford Handbook of Comparative Constitutional Law, Oxford University Press, 2012, pp. 891–907.

920 In Romanian, English and French.

7.2.1.2 Audiovisual recording and television broadcasting of the Constitutional Court's sessions

Within the project "Transparency of constitutional justice", the Constitutional Court has implemented a system of audiovisual recording of the sessions and television broadcasting.

This system allows media access, as well as watching/listening the sessions of the Constitutional Court by all those interested.

7.2.1.3 Press statements

The Constitutional Court broadcasts press statements on various events or situations regarding its activity, as well as on the admission solutions of the referrals of unconstitutionality or other cases of a higher public interest. Since 2000 press statements have been posted on the website of the Constitutional Court – www.ccr.ro.

The applicable provisions are set forth in the Regulations on the Organisation and functioning of the Constitutional Court, approved by Resolution no. 6/2012 of the Plenum of the Constitutional Court.

The information posted on the website or communicated through news feeds are taken from mass media and the intensity level of its broadcasting and the resulted comments depend mainly on the interest raised by the issue which formed the subject of the press statement.

For a clear communication and in order to avoid misinterpretations, the current statements of the Constitutional Court have a higher level of complexity in the sense that they provide the essential considerations which substantiated the solutions delivered by the Court. This approach has had a positive effect as concerns the communication of the Constitutional Court by media as the considerations given in the wording of press statements are taken and provided as such. Previously, even the assumptions provided in the media regarding the reasons that substantiated certain solutions delivered by the Court, especially amid a lack of knowledge on the institution and on the specifics of the constitutional review and in the context of political tensions, have sometimes resulted in the public's misinformation, with negative effects on the image of the Constitutional Court, which required the identification of remedies.

7.2.1.4 Press conferences and statements

The Constitutional Court holds press conferences on the occasion of certain events such as international congresses and conferences. There is no regularity for the organization of press conferences, as they are means of communication reserved to special events within the activity of the Constitutional Court.

The press conferences are attended by the President and the Judges of the Constitutional Court.

Of course, information communicated on such occasions is subject to the general obligations imposed on the constitutional judges by the organic law of the Court.

Thus, according to **Article 64 of Law no. 47/1992 on the Organisation and Operation of the Constitutional Court:** "*The Judges of the Constitutional Court shall be under an obligation:*

a) to perform their function unbiasedly and in abidance by the Constitution;
b) to keep the secret of the deliberations and of the votes, and not to take a public stand, or to give legal opinion in matters within the competence of the Constitutional Court;
c) to express their affirmative or negative vote in adopting the acts of the Constitutional Court, abstention from voting not being permitted;
d) to impart to the President of the Constitutional Court any activity which might entail incompatibility with the mandate exercised;
e) to preclude the use of the office performed for purposes of trade publicity or propaganda of any kind whatsoever;
f) to abstain from any activity or manifestation contrary to the independence or dignity of their office".

Therefore, the approached issues cannot engage aspects that could involve the infringement of the legal obligations of the Constitutional Court's Judges. Even if media representatives ask questions in this regard, the Judges of the Court have a backup obligation.

7.2.1.5 Other ways to make public the activity of the Constitutional Court

The Constitutional Court holds anniversary[921] or commemorative[922] celebrations; it hosts book launches[923], it publishes volumes of studies on the occasion of its hosted conferences[924], as well as brochures concerning its composition and activity.

Thus, a review of the Court was elaborated, entitled The Constitutional Court Bulletin, which is published in Romanian, English and French, posted on its website in order to ensure the widest possible access to the information contained therein: specialized studies prepared usually by judges and assistant-magistrates of the Constitutional Court of Romania or of other Constitutional Courts, summaries

---

921 For examples, those which mark annually the celebration of the "Constitution Day" (8 December).

922 For example, the scientific session with the topic "*Vasile Gionea: Life and work*", an event intended as a celebration of 100 years since the birth of the first President of the Constitutional Court (20 February 2014).

923 For example, the organization of a conference, in collaboration with the Rule of law Program South East Europe of the Foundation Konrad Adenauer, on the occasion of the launch of the publication *"Selection of Decisions of the Federal Constitutional Court of Germany"*.

924 See, for example, *Constitutional justice – functions and relationships with the other public authorities– Comparative constitutional law*, representing the works of the XVth Congress of the Conference of European Constitutional Courts, 23–25 May 2011, Universul Juridic Publishing House, Bucharest, 2012.

of relevant case-law of the Court during the reference period for that issue of the Bulletin, the external relations of the Court during the same period. The Bulletin is sent to a large number of universities, libraries, other constitutional courts, public authorities, as it represents a genuine "business card" for the Constitutional Court of Romania. Furthermore, the landmark decisions of the Constitutional Court are selected and published *in extenso* in volumes, including their translation into English.

The Constitutional Court holds study visits relating mainly to the collaboration between the courts of law and various universities, the visits of the magistrates in other countries within the collaboration with the Higher Institute of Magistracy and the Ministry of Justice, as well as the visits of the students at the National School of Clerks. There are various ways to open the collaboration between the Constitutional Court and academia and other public institutions and authorities. Such visits are not publicised as they are considered inherent in the regular activity of the Court – but we believe that they should be made public for a more complete image on the activity conducted by the Court.

7.3 Responsibilities related to the communication of the Constitutional Court by the mass-media. Internal regulations

7.3.1 Organisation of the Constitutional Court

If we look broadly at this activity, one can note that both the Judges of the Constitutional Court and its personnel, in part, are responsible for the communication with and by media. Narrowly, within the Court, the activities mentioned in the previous section shall be assigned to the Compartments of the Court and the persons in charge, according to their object of activity, but the most involved compartments are the External Relations, Press Relations and Protocol Compartment, Research, Documentation and Library Compartment (under the direction of the First Assistant-Magistrate), Statistics and It Office (under the direction of the Secretary General).

Of these, the External Relations, Press Relations and Protocol Compartment of the Constitutional Court has specific tasks within the communication with the media, as evidenced by its name. Under this name and the current organisational structure, the above-mentioned Compartment is governed by the provisions of the Regulations on the Organisation and functioning of the Constitutional Court, approved by the Resolution no. no. 6 of 7 March 2012 of the Plenum of the Constitutional Court[925].

According to Article 14 para. (2) of the Regulations on the Organisation and Functioning of the Constitutional Court, "*The personnel employed in the External Relations, Press Relations and Protocol Compartment consists of specialized legal staff assimilated to Assistant-Magistrates and administrative personnel, whose duties are*

925 Published in the Official Gazette of Romania no. 198 of 27 March 2012.

detailed under their individual job description" and according to Article 14 para. (1) section B of the same Regulations, has the following duties concerning press relations: "*a) to provide journalists with information of public interest concerning the Constitutional Court's jurisdictional activity;*

b) to ensure, on a regular basis or whenever there is an immediate public interest in the Constitutional Court's activity, press releases, press briefings, the organisation of press conferences or interviews;
c) to prepare and distribute press reviews about the Constitutional Court's activity to the Judges' individual offices;
d) to provide periodic information about the principal scientific and cultural events taking place in the country".

The personnel employed in the External Relations, Press Relations and Protocol Compartment has legal or philological studies, or both.

7.3.2 The rights and the obligations of the mass-media representatives

The Regulation on Accreditation of mass media representatives at the Constitutional Court of Romania, annex to the Resolution no. 3 of 27 February 2012 of the Plenum of the Constitutional Court[926], provides in Article 1 para. (1), (2) and (3) that "representatives of national and local media institutions – hereinafter journalists – dailies, periodicals, news agencies, Romanian and foreign radio stations and televisions, as well as freelance journalists can be accredited in order to attend the activities, public sessions and press conferences held by the Constitutional Court of Romania".

Pursuant to Article 11 l) of the Regulation, "accreditation shall be granted by the Assistant-Magistrate-in-Chief, Director of the Office of the President of the Constitutional Court, coordinator of the External Relations, Press Relations and Protocol Compartment, upon the request of the media institution where the journalist is employed or upon the request of a freelance journalist who meets the requirements of this Regulation, based on the proposal made by the Adviser in charge with press relations. Accreditation does not entail the Constitutional Court's control over the materials published by the accredited journalist or over the news broadcast by the mass media". Accreditation at the Constitutional Court may be permanent or temporary. Permanent accreditation shall be renewed annually and temporary accreditation shall be granted only on the occasion of special events taking place at the Constitutional Court.

As concerns the obligations of media representatives under Article 8 of the Regulation: "(1) The accredited journalists, photographers and TV operators shall comply with the dignity and privacy of all persons in the building. (2) Filming and photography are strictly forbidden within: a) the perimeter of control equipments ensuring access into building; b) the offices and halls designated for the activities

926 Published on the website of the Constitutional Court of Romania –*www.ccr.ro.*

held by the members of the Constitutional Court and the personnel of the institution. (3) The accredited photographers and TV operators using mobile television camera shall have access to the courtroom only with the consent of the President of the Constitutional Court, for a maximum period of 10 minutes after the opening of the session. (4) The accredited journalists, photographers and TV operators shall have access to the spaced designated for press and for the installation of cameras. (5) The accredited journalists shall not intervene under any circumstances in the activities of the Constitutional Court which they attend. (6) The use of hidden audio and video recording equipments is forbidden. (7) Failure to comply with these rules leads to the withdrawal of the press accreditation".

7.4 The mass-media's interest in the activity of the Constitutional Court and the issues related to the freedom of expression

7.4.1 The powers of the Constitutional Court reflected in the mass-media

There is a growing interest in the activity of the Constitutional Court. Its intensity is determined by the punctual issue of constitutionality settled by the Court or by the nature of its activities carried out at a certain moment.

Thus, if we proceed to an analysis in the light of the powers of the Constitutional Court, the highest interest is raised by the settlement of legal disputes of a constitutional nature, in consideration of the subjects that can be parties of such conflicts (public authorities nominated by Title III of the Constitution), as well as the object of the conflict. The most frequent conflicts are those of competence between authorities, such as the President of Romania, Parliament, the High Court of Cassation and Justice, the Government, i.e. authorities whose activity itself represents a high public interest.

The activity of the Constitutional Court during the procedure for the election of the President of Romania represents a high level of media coverage, given its power to supervise the observance of the procedure for the election of the President and to confirm the results of the suffrage[927], as well as during the referendum, given its power to supervise the procedure for the organization and carrying out of a referendum and to confirm its results[928].

Likewise, certain decisions delivered by the Constitutional Court within the exercise of its powers regarding the constitutional review of laws before[929] or after promulgation[930], attracted media attention, especially when they aimed at broad

927 Article 146 f) of the Constitution of Romania.
928 Article 146 i) of the Constitution of Romania.
929 Article 146 a) sentence I of the Constitution.
930 Article 146 d) of the Constitution.

social impact measures (for example, the cutting of pensions and wages, administrative decentralization).

Finally, the power of the Constitutional Court to rule upon the constitutionality of the initiatives for the revision of the Constitution, given its specific nature, attracts the attention of the media and the general public.

It is worth mentioning that the interest of the mass media is not attracted only by the solutions delivered by the Court in the various cases brought before it, but also by the separate opinions formulated by the judges of the Court in those cases.

7.4.2 Problems of communication with/by the mass-media. Limits of the freedom of expression

The lack of journalists specialized in constitutional field, the influences of the political context on such journalists, the lack of a careful verification of the information obtained from various sources, other than the official ones of the Constitutional Court, the desire to create news with an impact on public cause issues in terms of the communication of the Constitutional Court by media.

Problems may arise when there is a lack of communication with the media, an insufficient or incorrect understanding of certain acts, facts or when, for various reasons, such acts or facts may suffer distortions, with the consequence of misinformation about the activity of the Constitutional Court.

As concerns the lack of communication, over time there were provided measures to ensure the transparency of the activity of the Constitutional Court. But the correction of certain misinterpretations of the acts of the Constitutional Court, respectively the considerations underlying them, proves to be more difficult.

Thus, referring to an example that was considered by some of the media as an "attack" against freedom of the press, we mention Decision no. 62/2007[931] of the Constitutional Court of Romania, by which it was ascertained the unconstitutionality of the provisions of Article I section 56 of Law no. 278/2006 amending and supplementing the Criminal Code, as well as amending and supplementing other laws, the part referring to the repeal of Articles 205, 206 and 207 of Criminal Code, texts that criminalize insult and libel. A part of the media considered that, by the ascertainment of the unconstitutionality of the repealing rules and consequently the re-entry into force of the criminalization of insult and libel, freedom of expression through press is violated.

However, the Court has stated in its decision that it takes into considerations the provisions on freedom of expression set forth in Article 30 of the Constitution, Article 10 para. 2 of the Convention for the Protection of Human Rights and Fundamental Freedoms and Article 19 para. 3 of the International Covenant on Civil and Political Rights. According to Article 30 para. (1) of the Constitution of Romania, "*freedom of expression of thoughts, opinions, or beliefs, and freedom of any*

931 Published in the Official Gazette of Romania no. 104 of 12 February 2007.

creation, whether by spoken words, in writing, in pictures, by sounds or any other means of communication in public, is inviolable". However, the same article of the Constitution provides for in paragraph (6) that "*freedom of expression shall not be prejudicial to dignity, honour, privacy of person, nor to one's right for his own image*". The Court noted in this regard that "*the limits of freedom of expression provided for in Article 30 para. (6) of the Constitution of Romania, are fully in compliance with the concept of freedom, which shall not and would not be understood as an absolute right (...) a person's freedom shall end where another person's freedom shall begin. In this respect, Article 57 of the Constitution expressly stipulates the obligation of all Romanian citizens, aliens and stateless persons to exercise their constitutional rights in good faith, without encroaching on the rights and freedoms of others*". In the same regard, the Court also noted that an identical limitation is also provided for in Article 10 para. 2 of the Convention for the Protection of Human Rights and Fundamental Freedoms, according to which "*The exercise of these freedoms, since it carries with it duties and responsibilities, may be subject to such formalities, conditions, restrictions or penalties as are prescribed by law and are necessary in a democratic society (...)* for the protection of the reputation or rights of others *(...)*", as well as in Article 19 para. 3 of the International Covenant on Civil and Political Rights, which establishes that the exercise of freedom of expression carries with it special duties and responsibilities and may therefore be subject to certain restrictions, but these shall only be such as are provided by law, taking into account the rights or reputation of others. As concerns the acts of insult and defamation through the press, the Court held that the provisions of Article 30 para. (8) of the Constitution stipulate that "indictable offences of the press shall be established by law". In the absence of any distinction, that indictable offences of the press can be established by a special law – for example, through a law on press or through the common criminal law, that is, in this case, the Criminal Code. Thus, "the constitutional dimension of indictable offences of the press requires not to be removed from the legislation, but, as indicated, to be subject to a sanction regime to the free choice of the legislature".

For the correct understanding of the Constitutional Court's decision and of the considerations that substantiated it, it is necessary to understand both the rights and the obligations of those who provide information through the media, as well as the fact that freedom of expression, including by press, is not an absolute right. Furthermore, the Court also underlined in other occasions the role and the importance of the media, as well as its great responsibility, reminding[932] also the case-law of the European Court of Human Rights, which held as an important element the indispensable role of "watchdog" played by the press in a democratic society (for example, Judgment of 27 March 1996 delivered in Case Goodwin v. The United Kingdom, paragraph 39). However, the press must not exceed certain limits, especially in relation to the reputation and the rights of others. Nonetheless, it shall

932 Decision no. 206 of 29 April 2013, published in the Official Gazette of Romania no. 350 of 13 June 2013.

communicate, in the fulfilment of its duties and responsibilities, information and ideas on political issues, as well as on other matters of general interest (see, among many others, Judgment of 24 February 1997, delivered in Case De Haes and Gijsels v. Belgium, para. 37; Judgment of 25 June 2002, delivered in Case Colombani and others v. France, para. 55; Judgment of 17 December 2004, delivered in Case Cumpănă and *Mazăre* v. Romania, para. 93).

7.5 Conclusions

The experiences of the Constitutional Court of Romania in dealing with the media and the issues that have emerged over time have led to changes in its communication strategy, as well as to the regulation of this communication.

Information on the activity of the Constitutional Court and its members is made public, in particular on its website and in press statement. This is the essence of communication with and by the media or the press, the latter, in order to fully exercise its role, need information from all public authorities regarding their activity[933].

For a greater transparency and in order to avoid misinterpretations, press statements are more elaborated, stating specifically and explicitly the reasons which substantiated the decisions/rulings/ advisory opinions delivered by the Constitutional Court. When the mass media promoted misinterpretations of the acts of the Court, it intervened in order to provide the necessary clarifications. Thus, for example, in the situation that have arisen due to "the comments published in the media regarding the interpretation and application of the provisions of Law no. 35/2008 for elections to the Chamber of Deputies and the Senate and amending and supplementing Law no. 67/2004 for the election of local public administration authorities, the Law no. 215/2001 on local public administration and Law no. 393/2004 on the Statute of the local officials" in relation to the Constitutional Court's Decision no. 682 of 27 June 2012, the Constitutional Court provided a press statement which indicated essentially the reasons that substantiated the delivered decision (www.ccr.ro – Press Statements, 13 December 2012).

The Court also regulated adequately the obligations of the mass media. Thus, according to Article 1 para. (5) of the Regulation on Accreditation of mass media representatives at the Constitutional Court of Romania, annex to the Resolution no. 3 of 27 February 2012 of the Plenum of the Constitutional Court (www.cccr.ro): "The Constitutional Court recommends that all journalists and mass media take into account and apply the ethical principles contained in the Resolutions no. 1003 (1993) and no. 1215 (1993) of the Parliamentary Assembly of the Council of Europe, given the social and legal responsibility they bear for the correct information to the public opinion and the observance of the moral values and civil rights."

Of course, the dialogue of the Constitutional Court with and by the mass media is susceptible to improvement. Such improvements refer to the concrete actions of

---

933 For developments, see E. Barendt, *cited work*, pp. 891–907.

the Constitutional Court (such as, for example, the development of certain information of the type of newsletter, containing more details about the Court's activities than those which are currently posted on the website, as well as a regularity of press conferences, in order to provide the opportunity to respond directly to questions regarding the activities of the Constitutional Court). Likewise, the quality of this communication depends on the professionalism and responsibility of the mass media representatives and their compliance with the rules of professional conduct.

www.ingramcontent.com/pod-product-compliance
Ingram Content Group UK Ltd.
Pitfield, Milton Keynes, MK11 3LW, UK
UKHW021830100926
8556IPUK00004B/265

9 783631 678909